MANAGEMENT

4th Edition

MANAGEMENT

4th Edition

RICKY W. GRIFFIN
Texas A&M University

HOUGHTON MIFFLIN COMPANY
Boston   Toronto
Dallas   Geneva, Illinois   Palo Alto   Princeton, New Jersey

Sponsoring Editor: Diane L. McOscar
Development Editor: Julie Hogenboom
Project Editor: Liza Martina
Design/Production Coordinator: Karen Meyer Rappaport
Manufacturing Coordinator: Sharon Pearson

Cover Photograph: Peter Aaron/ESTO

Part Opening Photo Credits: 1, Michael Freeman, London; 2, Nicholas De Vore III/ Photographers Aspen; 3, Michael Freeman, London; 4, Don Klumpp/The Image Bank; 5, Pete Saloutos/The Stock Market; 6, Hiko Miyao/Photonica; 7, Michael Freeman, London.

Photo Credits: Chapter 1: p. 7, Courtesy MTV Networks; p. 10, Courtesy British Information Services; p. 11, Reprinted from *Financial World,* 1328 Broadway, New York, N.Y. 10001 © copyrighted 1992 by Financial World Partners. All rights reserved; (*Continued on p. 674*)

Printed in the U.S.A.
Library of Congress Catalog Card Number: 92-72375
Student book ISBN: 0-395-63007-X
Instructor's Annotated Edition ISBN: 0-395-63704-X

123456789-DW-96 95 94 93 92

For Glenda . . .
Who is always full of joy and who
willingly shares it with others

Part Opening Photographs

Part I: Corinthian columns of the Temple of Olympian Zeus, dedicated by the Roman Emperor Hadrian in 132 A.D. The Temple is in central Athens, Greece.

Part II: Detail of the Pompidou Museum in Paris, France.

Part III: Detail of the Orthodox church, Shipka, near the town of Kazanluk, Bulgaria.

Part IV: Detail of the Central market in Kuala Lumpur, Malaysia.

Part V: High-rise building in Los Angeles, California, 1991.

Part VI: Detail from the 1989–90 Expo in Yokohama, Japan.

Part VII: Detail of the Temple roof at Kyongbok-gung Palace (Palace of Shining Happiness), built in 1394, in Seoul, Korea.

Brief Contents

PART I   **An Introduction to Management**   1

Chapter 1   Managing and the Manager's Job   2
Chapter 2   The Evolution of Management   28

PART II   **The Environmental Context of Management**   59

Chapter 3   The Organizational Environment and Effectiveness   60
Chapter 4   The Ethical and Social Context of Management   88
Chapter 5   The Global Context of Management   114

PART III   **Planning and Decision Making**   145

Chapter 6   Managing Organizational Goals and Planning   146
Chapter 7   Managing Strategy and Strategic Planning   174
Chapter 8   Managerial Decision Making   200
Chapter 9   Management Tools for Planning and Decision Making   224

PART IV   **The Organizing Process**   255

Chapter 10   Components of Organization Structure   256
Chapter 11   Managing Organization Design   282
Chapter 12   Managing Organization Change   308
Chapter 13   Managing Human Resources   332

PART V   **The Leading Process**   363

Chapter 14   Motivating Employee Performance   364
Chapter 15   Leadership and Influence Processes   390
Chapter 16   Managing Interpersonal and Group Processes   416
Chapter 17   Managing Communication in Organizations   442

PART VI   **The Controlling Process**   471

Chapter 18   The Nature of Control   472
Chapter 19   Managing Quality, Productivity, and Operations   498
Chapter 20   Managing Technology and Innovation   522
Chapter 21   Managing Information Systems   546

PART VII   **Special Challenges of Management**   573

Chapter 22   Managing Cultural Diversity   574
Chapter 23   Entrepreneurship and New Venture Formation   596
Appendix 1   Managerial Careers   622
Appendix 2   Tools for Budgetary and Financial Control   630

Contents

Preface   xxvii
Acknowledgments   xxxiii

PART I AN INTRODUCTION TO MANAGEMENT   1

Chapter 1 Managing and the Manager's Job   2

The Nature of Management   4

The Management Process   7
Planning and Decision Making: Determining Courses of Action   8
Organizing: Coordinating Activities and Resources   8
• *Management in Practice: J.B. Hunt Rolls Along*   9
Leading: Managing People   10
Controlling: Monitoring and Evaluating Activities   10

Kind of Managers   11
Differentiation by Levels of Management   11
Differentiation by Areas of Management   13
Becoming a Manager   14

Critical Roles and Skills   16
Managerial Roles   16
• *The Global View: Skills for the Global Manager*   17
Managerial Skills   19
The Nature of Managerial Work   21

The Scope of Management   21
Management in Profit-Seeking Organizations   22
Management in Not-for-Profit Organizations   23
• *Case 1.1 Bumper Crops for State Farm*   26
• *International Case 1.2 Doing Business with the Former Soviet Republics*   27

Chapter 2 The Evolution of Management   28

The Role of Theory and History in Management   30
The Importance of Theory and History   30
The Historical Context of Management   32

- *Management in Practice: Contributions From Outside the Discipline* 33
  Precursors to Management Theory 33
- *The Global View: The Origins of Far Eastern Management* 35

The Classical Perspective 36
Scientific Management 36
Administrative Management 38
Contributions and Limitations of the Classical Perspective 38

The Behavioral Perspective 40
The Hawthorne Studies 41
The Human Relations Movement 42
The Emergence of Organizational Behavior 43
Contributions and Limitations of the Behavioral Perspective 44

The Quantitative Perspective 45
Management Science 45
Operations Management 45
Contributions and Limitations of the Quantitative Perspective 46

Integrating Perspectives 47
The Systems Perspective 47
The Contingency Perspective 48
An Integrating Framework 49

Contemporary Management Thought 51
Popular Management Theory 51
Contemporary Management Challenges 52
- *Case 2.1 UPS: The Giant that Keeps Competing* 56
- *International Case 2.2 Lloyd's Keeps Evolving* 57

PART II THE ENVIRONMENTAL CONTEXT OF MANAGEMENT 59

Chapter 3 The Organizational Environment and Effectiveness 60

The Nature of the Organizational Environment 62

The External Environment 63
The General Environment 64
The Task Environment 67
- *Management in Practice: During the Computer Slump, Dell Scores* 69

The Internal Environment 72
Board of Directors 72

Employees   72
Culture   73

Organization-Environment Relationships   74
How Environments Affect Organizations   74
How Organizations Respond to Their Environments   79

Organizational Effectiveness   81
● *The Global View: Trying to Bring Back the Shine*   83
● *Case 3.1 Bringing Coleman Up to Speed*   86
● *International Case 3.2 Can Everyone Win From Nintendo's Price Fixing Settlement?*   87

Chapter 4 The Ethical and Social Context of Management   88

Individual Ethics in Organizations   90
The Formation of Individual Ethics   90
Managerial Ethics   92
Ethics in an Organizational Context   93
Managing Ethical Behavior   94
● *Management in Practice: Dow Corning's Implant Nightmare*   95

Social Responsibility and Organizations   97
Historical Views of Social Responsibility   97
Areas of Social Responsibility   98
Arguments For and Against Social Responsibility   101
Organizational Approaches to Social Responsibility   102

The Government and Social Responsibility   104
● *The Global View: International Corporate Philanthropy*   105
How Government Influences Organizations   105
How Organizations Influence Government   106

Managing Social Responsibility   107
Formal Organizational Dimensions   108
Informal Organizational Dimensions   108
Evaluating Social Responsibility   109
● *Case 4.1 Herman Miller: Building Furniture and the Future*   112
● *International Case 4.2 Realigning Priorities at The Body Shop*   113

Chapter 5 The Global Context of Management   114

The Nature of International Business   116
The Meaning of International Business   116
Trends in International Business   117
Managing the Process of Internationalization   119

Managing in an International Market   122
● *The Global View: Furnishing the World*   123

The Structure of the Global Economy   123

Mature Market Economies and Systems   124
Developing Economies   126
Other Economies   127

Environmental Challenges of International Management   128

The Economic Environment   128
The Political/Legal Environment   130
The Cultural Environment   132

Competing in a Global Economy   133

Globalization and Organization Size   133
Management Challenges in a Global Economy   134
● *Management in Practice: Talking the Language of Success*   135
● *Case 5.1 Whirlpool and the Appliance Industry Head Overseas*   140
● *International Case 5.2 Building Global Airplanes*   141
● *Video Exercise 1 The New Powerful Global Customer*   142

PART III PLANNING AND DECISION MAKING   145

Chapter 6 Managing Organizational Goals and Planning   146

The Planning Process   148

Organizational Goals   149

Purposes of Goals   149
Kinds of Goals   150
Responsibilities for Setting Goals   153
Managing Multiple Goals   153

Organizational Planning   153

Kinds of Organizational Plans   154
Time Frames for Planning   154
● *The Global View: The World's Most Powerful Business Alliances*   155
Responsibilities for Planning   156
Contingency Planning   157

Tactical Planning   158

Developing Tactical Plans   159
Executing Tactical Plans   160

Operational Planning   160

Single-Use Plans   160
Standing Plans   161
● *Management in Practice: Reebok Heads Outside—and Up*   163

Managing Goal-Setting and Planning Processes   164

Barriers to Goal Setting and Planning   164
Overcoming the Barriers   166
Using Management by Objective to Implement Plans   167
● *Case 6.1 ConAgra's Menu Keeps Growing*   172
● *International Case 6.2 Sony's Long-Term Gamble*   173

Chapter 7 Managing Strategy and Strategic Planning   174

The Nature of Strategic Management   176

Components of Strategy   176
Levels of Strategy   177
Strategy Formulation and Implementation   178

Strategy Formulation   179

Strategic Goals   179
Environmental Analysis   179
Organizational Analysis   179
Matching Organizations and Environments   180

Corporate-Level Strategy   181

Grand Strategy   181
The Business Portfolio   182
● *The Global View: The Emperor of Luxury*   183

Business-Level Strategy   184

Adaptation Model   185
● *Management in Practice: Wrigley Sticks to Its Chewing*   187
Porter's Competitive Strategies   187
Product Life Cycle   188

Functional Strategies   190

Marketing Strategy   190
Financial Strategy   191
Production Strategy   192
Human Resources Strategy   192
Research and Development Strategy   193

Strategy Implementation   193

Implementation Through Structure   193
Implementation Through Leadership   194

Implementation Through Information and Control Systems 194
Implementation Through Human Resources 195
Implementation Through Technology 195
- *Case 7.1 Rewarming Campbell Soup* 198
- *International Case 7.2 Honda Goes Local* 199

Chapter 8 Managerial Decision Making 200

The Nature of Decision Making 202
Decision Making Defined 202
Types of Decisions 203
Decision-Making Conditions 204

Rational Perspectives on Decision Making 205
The Classical Model of Decision Making 206
Steps in Rational Decision Making 206
- *The Global View: Britain's Best Retailer* 207

Behavioral Aspects of Decision Making 211
The Administrative Model 212
Political Forces in Decision Making 213
Intuition and Escalation of Commitment 213
- *Management in Practice: The Maturing of the Turner Empire* 215
Risk Propensity and Decision Making 215
Ethics and Decision Making 216

Group Decision Making in Organizations 216
Forms of Group Decision Making 216
Advantages of Group Decision Making 217
Disadvantages of Group Decision Making 218
Managing Group Decision-Making Processes 219
- *Case 8.1 The Technology Company Goes to Market* 222
- *International Case 8.2 Selling Toys to Japan* 223

Chapter 9 Management Tools for Planning and Decision Making 224

Forecasting 226
Sales and Revenue Forecasting 226
Technological Forecasting 227
Other Types of Forecasting 228
Forecasting Techniques 228
- *The Global View: Developing Just-in-Time at Toyota* 229

Other Planning Techniques 232
Linear Programming 232
Breakeven Analysis 235

Simulation 238
PERT 239

Decision-Making Tools 241

Payoff Matrix 241
Decision Tree 243
Other Decision-Making Tools 244

Strengths and Weaknesses of Planning Tools 246

Weaknesses and Problems 246
Strengths and Advantages 246
● *Management in Practice: Telemarketing Decisions at L.L. Bean* 247
● *Case 9.1 Scheduling Airline Flight Crews* 250
● *International Case 9.2 Planning the Future of New Zealand's Forests* 251
● *Video Exercise 2 Quality as an Organizational Goal* 252

PART IV THE ORGANIZING PROCESS 255

Chapter 10 Components of Organization Structure 256

Building Blocks of Organizations 258

Designing Jobs 258

Job Specialization 259
Benefits and Limitations of Specialization 259
Alternatives to Specialization 260

Grouping Jobs: Departmentalization 263

Rationale for Departmentalization 263
Common Bases for Departmentalization 263

Establishing Reporting Relationships 266

The Chain of Command 266
● *Management in Practice: Improving Accountability at Ryder* 267
Narrow Versus Wide Spans 267
Tall Versus Flat Organizations 268
Determining the Appropriate Span 269
● *The Global View: Avoiding the "Large Man" Syndrome at Toyota* 271

Distributing Authority 271

The Delegation Process 272
Decentralization and Centralization 273

Coordinating Activities 275

The Need for Coordination 275
Structural Coordination Techniques 275

Differentiating Between Positions 277

Differentiation Between Line and Staff   277
Administrative Intensity   278
● *Case 10.1 Reorganizing for Profit in a Slow-Growth Industry*   280
● *International Case 10.2 Creating a Global Structure at ICI*   281

Chapter 11 Managing Organization Design   282

The Nature of Organization Design   284

Universal Perspectives on Organization Design   284

Bureaucratic Model   285
Behavioral Model   286

Situational Influences on Organization Design   288

Core Technology   288
Environment   289
Organizational Size   291
Organizational Life Cycle   291

Strategy and Organization Design   292

Corporate Strategy   292
● *Management in Practice: Big Is Beautiful at Bordon*   293
Business Strategy   293
Functional Strategy   294

Basic Forms of Organization Design   294

Functional (U-Form) Design   294
Conglomerate (H-Form) Design   295
Divisional (M-Form) Design   296
● *The Global View: Which Way for Pearson?*   297
Matrix Design   298
Hybrid Designs   300

Emerging Issues in Organization Design   300

Managing Information   301
Global Organizations   302
Adapting Organizations   302
● *Case 11.1 Xerox's Adaptive Organization*   306
● *International Case 11.2 Learning to Think Small at Bechtel*   307

Chapter 12 Managing Organization Change   308

The Nature of Organization Change   310

Forces for Change   310
Planned Versus Reactive Change   311

Managing Change in Organizations   312

Steps in the Change Process   312
Reasons for Resistance to Change   314
Overcoming Resistance to Change   315

Areas of Organization Change   317

Changing Strategy   318
Changing Structure and Design   318
Changing Technology and Operations   318
● *Management in Practice: Changes at Chemical Banking*   319
Changing People   320

Organization Development   321

OD Assumptions   321
OD Techniques   321
The Effectiveness of OD   325

Organization Revitalization   325

The Need for Revitalization   325
Approaches to Revitalization   326
● *The Global View: Changing Adidas on Two Continents*   327
● *Case 12.1 Navistar Pulls Back From the Brink*   330
● *International Case 12.2 Preparing for the European Community*   331

Chapter 13 Managing Human Resources   332

The Environmental Context of Human Resources Management   334

The Strategic Importance of HRM   334
The Legal Environment of HRM   335
Social Change and HRM   338

Attracting Human Resources   338

● *Management in Practice: Sexual Harassment in the Workplace*   339
Human Resources Planning   339
Recruiting Human Resources   341
Common Selection Methods   342
● *The Global View: Desperately Seeking Japanese Managers*   343

Developing Human Resources   345

Training and Development   345
Performance Appraisal   348
Performance Feedback   350

Maintaining Human Resources   351

Determining Compensation   351
Determining Benefits   352
Career Planning   353

Managing Labor Relations   353

How Employees Form Unions   354

Collective Bargaining   355

● *Case 13.1 What's Fair in Union-Management Battles?*   358

● *International Case 13.2 Can Japanese and Americans Mix in Michigan?*   359

● *Video Exercise 3 Designing an Organization Dedicated to Quality*   360

PART V THE LEADING PROCESS   363

Chapter 14 Motivating Employee Performance   364

The Nature of Motivation   365

Importance of Employee Motivation in the Workplace   366

Historical Perspectives on Motivation   367

Content Perspectives on Motivation   368

Need Hierarchy Approach   368

● *The Global View: Russian Workers Get a Second Chance*   369

Two-Factor Theory   371

Individual Human Needs   373

Process Perspectives on Motivation   374

Expectancy Theory   374

Equity Theory   378

Reinforcement Perspectives on Motivation   379

Kinds of Reinforcement in Organizations   379

Providing Reinforcement in Organizations   380

Emerging Perspectives on Motivation   381

Goal-Setting Theory   381

Japanese Approach   381

Popular Motivational Strategies   382

● *Management in Practice: Motivating the Work Force of the Future*   383

Using Reward Systems to Motivate Performance   383

Effects of Organizational Rewards   384

Designing Effective Reward Systems   384

New Approaches to Rewarding Employees   385

● *Case 14.1 Waking Up BankAmerica*   388

● *International Case 14.2 Listening and Caring at Hitachi*   389

Chapter 15 Leadership and Influence Processes   390

The Nature of Leadership   392
The Meaning of Leadership   392
Leadership Versus Management   392
Power and Leadership   393
● *The Global View: Leaning SAS into the Big Leagues*   395

The Search for Leadership Traits   396

Leadership Behaviors   397
Michigan Studies   397
Ohio State Studies   398
Leadership Grid   399

Situational Approaches to Leadership   399
The LPC Theory   400
The Path-Goal Theory   403
The Vroom-Yetton-Jago Model   404
● *Management in Practice: A Nation's Retail Leader*   405
Other Situational Approaches   407

New Perspective on Leadership   408
Substitutes for Leadership   408
Transformational Leadership   409

Political Behavior in Organizations   410
Common Political Behaviors   410
Managing Political Behavior   411
● *Case 15.1 A Leader on the Move*   414
● *International Case 15.2 Chairman Kim Reasserts Control*   415

Chapter 16 Managing Interpersonal and Group Processes   416

The Interpersonal Nature of Organizations   418
Interpersonal Dynamics   419
Outcomes of Interpersonal Behaviors   420

Groups in Organizations   420
Types of Groups   420
● *The Global View: ODS—An Experiment in Group Processes*   421
Why People Join Groups   423
Stages of Group Development   424

Characteristics of Mature Groups   426

Role Structures   426
Behavioral Norms   428
Cohesiveness   430
Informal Leadership   432

Using Teams in Organizations   433

Creating Work Teams   433
Managing Work Teams   433

Interpersonal and Intergroups Conflict   434

- *Management in Practice: Teaming Up to Save a Product*   435
Causes of Conflict   435
Managing Conflict   437
- *Case 16.1 Chrysler Learns from Its Viper Team*   440
- *International Case 16.2 Ford and Mazda Team Up*   421

Chapter 17 Managing Communication in Organizations   442

Communication and the Manager's Job   444

A Definition of Communication   444
The Role of Communication in Management   445
The Communication Process   445

Forms of Interpersonal Communication   447

Oral Communication   447
Written Communication   448
Choosing the Right Form   449

Forms of Group and Organizational Communication   449

Vertical Communication   449
Horizontal Communication   451
Communication Networks   451
The Grapevine   452
Other Forms of Communication   453

Behavioral Elements of Communication   454

Perception   454
- *Management in Practice: Mattel Talks—And Listens*   455
Nonverbal Communication   456

Improving Communication Effectiveness   457

Barriers to Communication   458
Overcoming Barriers to Communication   459

Managing Organizational Communication   461

Formal Information Systems   461
Electronic Communication   462
- *The Global View: Robert Horton Talks British Petroleum Back to Life*   463
- *Case 17.1 A Devastating Rumor*   466
- *International Case 17.2 BASF's Ambassador*   467
- *Video Exercise 4 Achieving Quality Through Worker Empowerment*   468

PART VI THE CONTROLLING PROCESS   471

Chapter 18 The Nature of Control   472

Control in Organizations   474

Purpose of Control   474
Areas of Control   474
Importance of Control   475
Responsibilities for Control   476
The Planning-Control Link   477

Steps in the Control Process   477

Establishing Standards   478
Measuring Performance   479
Comparing Performance Against Standards   480
Evaluation and Action   480

Forms of Operations Control   481

Preliminary Control   482
Screening Control   482
Postaction Control   483
Multiple Control Systems   483

Forms of Organizational Control   483

Bureaucratic Control   483
Clan Control   484
- *Management in Practice: Making It Big in the Computer Bargain Business*   485

Strategic Control   485
- *The Global View: No Longer Just Italy's Oil Company*   487

Managing the Control Process   487

Developing Effective Control Systems   488
Understanding Resistance to Control   489
Overcoming Resistance to Control   490

Choosing a Style of Control   491

- *Case 18.1 The McDonald's of Video Rental?*   496
- *International Case 18.2 Benetton Stays in Control*   497

Chapter 19 Managing Operations, Productivity, and Quality   498

Managing Quality   500

The Meaning of Quality   500
The Importance of Quality   500
- *Management in Practice: The Quality Revolution*   502
Total Quality Management   503

Managing Productivity   504

The Meaning of Productivity   505
The Importance of Productivity   506
Productivity Trends   506
Improving Productivity   507

Managing Quality and Productivity Through Operations Management   508

The Importance of Operations   509
Manufacturing and Production   509
Service Operations   510
The Role of Operations in Organizational Strategy   510

Designing Operations Systems   511

Products–Service Mix   511
Capacity   512
Facilities   512
- *The Global View: A Not-So-Sweet Business for a Foreigner*   513

Using Operations Systems   514

Operations Management as Control   514
Purchasing Management   515
Inventory Management   516
Operations Control Techniques   517
- *Case 19.1 General Motors Keeps Searching for the Secret*   520
- *International Case 19.2 Quality Through Amoebas*   521

Chapter 20 Managing Technology and Innovation   522

Technology and the Organization   524

Manufacturing Technology   524
Service Technology   528

Creativity and Innovation   528

The Creative Individual   529
The Creative Process   530

Organizational Innovation   532

● *Management in Practice: Infiniti's Creative Designers*   533
The Innovation Process   533
Forms of Innovation   536
Failure to Innovate   538

Promoting Innovation in Organizations   539

Reward System   539
Intrapreneurship   539
● *The Global View: Tapping Into Japanese R&D*   541
Organizational Culture   542
● *Case 20.1 Patience Pays*   544
● *International Case 20.2 A Bike Built Just for You*   545

Chapter 21 Managing Information Systems   546

Information and the Manager   548

The Role of Information in the Manager's Job   548
Characteristics of Useful Information   549
Information Management as Control   550

Building Blocks of Information Systems   551

Determinants of Information Systems Needs   552

Organizational Determinants   552
Managerial Determinants   553

Basic Kinds of Information Systems   555

Transaction-Processing Systems   555
Management Information Systems   555
Decision Support Systems   556
● *Management in Practice: The Chipmaker Turns to Its Scanners*   557
Executive Information Systems   557

Managing Information Systems   558

Establishing Information Systems   558
Integrating Information Systems   560
Using Information Systems   560
● *The Global View: Merrill Lynch Trades Around the World*   561

The Impact of Information Systems on Organizations   562

Performance Effects   562
Organizational Effects   563

Behavioral Effects   563
Information Systems Limitations   563

Recent Advances in Information Management   564
Telecommunications   564
Networks and Expert Systems   564
● *Case 21.1 Building Retailing's Next Superstar*   568
● *International Case 21.2 Information Systems Key to Package Delivery Competition*   569
● *Video Exercise 5 Updating the Old "Quality Control"*   570

PART VII SPECIAL CHALLENGES OF MANAGEMENT   573

Chapter 22 Managing Cultural Diversity   574

The Nature of Cultural Diversity   576
The Meaning of Cultural Diversity   576
Reasons for Increasing Diversity   576

Dimensions of Diversity   578
Age Distributions   578
Gender   579
Ethnicity   580
Other Dimensions of Diversity   580

The Impact of Diversity on Organizations   581
Diversity in Other Countries   581
● *The Global View: Encouraging Diversity in Europe*   583
Diversity as a Force for Social Change   583
Diversity as Competitive Advantage   584
Diversity as a Source of Conflict   585

Managing Diversity in Organization   586
Individual Strategies for Dealing with Diversity   586
Organizational Approaches to Managing Diversity   587

Toward the Multicultural Organization   590
● *Management in Practice: Confronting Differences at Digital*   591
● *Case 22.1 Learning to Value Monsanto's Diversity*   594
● *International Case 22.2 The Slow Rise of Japan's Salarywoman*   595

Chapter 23 Entrepreneurship and New Venture Formation   596

The Nature of Entrepreneurship   598

The Importance of Small Business   599

The Impact of Small Business   599
Major Areas of Small Business   601
Small Business and the Global Economy   602

Small Business Successes and Failures   602

Common Causes of Success   602
● *The Global View: You Don't Have to Be Big to Go Overseas*   603
Common Causes of Failure   604

Business Plan   605

Issues of Ownership   607

Approaches to Starting A Business   607
Forms of Ownership   608
Sources of Financing   608

Managing the Small Business   609

Planning in the Small Business   609
Organizing in the Small Business   611
Leading in the Small Business   613
Controlling in the Small Business   616
● *Management in Practice: New Life for an Old Park*   617
●

Entrepreneurship in Large Businesses   617
● *Case 23.1 Blue Bell Blossoms*   620
● *International Case 23.2 Sogeti and the Future of Software*   620

Appendix 1 Managerial Careers   622

The Nature of Managerial Careers   623

Career Management   625

Individual Career Planning   625
Organizational Career Planning   626

Special Issues in Careers   627

Women and Minorities   627
Dual Career Couples   628
Career Transitions   628

Appendix 2 Tools for Budgetary and Financial Control   630

Budgetary Control   631

Types of Budgets   631
Fixed and Variable Costs in Budgets   633
Developing Budgets   634
Zero-Base Budgets   636
Strengths and Weaknesses of Budgets   636

Other Tools of Financial Control   637

Financial Statements   637
Ratio Analysis   637
Financial Audits   640
Using Financial Control Techniques Effectively   641

Notes   642

Name Index   676

Organization and Product Index   685

Subject Index   695

Preface

Since its publication in 1984, over a third of a million students have used *Management* in preparation for their careers in business. And *Management* continues to be used in hundreds of universities, graduate programs, community colleges, and management development programs throughout the world.

In this edition I tried to retain all the elements that have contributed to the book's success in the past while also taking a clear look toward the future—the future of business, of management, and of textbooks. Writing a survey book poses a number of challenges. First, because it is a survey, it has to be comprehensive. Second, it has to be accurate and objective. Third, because management is a real activity, the book has to be relevant. Fourth, it has to be timely and up-to-date. And fifth, it needs to be as interesting and as engaging as possible.

Feedback on my previous editions has always suggested that I have done an effective job of meeting these goals. In this edition, I think these goals have been met even more effectively. I believe that previous users of the book will be pleased with how we retained the essential ingredients while adding a variety of new elements and perspectives. I also believe people new to this edition will be drawn to the solid foundation of management theory and practice balanced with new and exciting material.

IMPROVEMENTS IN THE FOURTH EDITION

The fourth edition of *Management* is a significant revision of the earlier work. Rather than simply addressing the "hot topics" of the moment, I have revised this book with the long-term view in mind. New chapters on technology and cultural diversity, increased emphasis on quality, ethics, and global management, and a more modern organization of chapters reflect what I believe and reviewers have confirmed students will need to know as they enter a brand new world of management.

Improved Chapter Organization

- Chapters on ethics, social responsibility (Chapter 4), and the global context of management (Chapter 5) have been moved to the front of the book, where they are organized under a new Part II, "The Environmental Context of Management." This chapter reorganization more fully recognizes ethics and the global economy as critical aspects of the managerial environment. As Chapters 4 and 5 make clear, managers can no longer afford to treat these issues as marginal. Virtually every business decision today is made in a global and ethical context.

- In Part III, "Planning and Decision Making," the chapter on managerial decision making now follows the planning and strategy chapters, reflecting a more logical and straightforward view of the planning process.
- Chapter 19, "Managing Quality, Productivity, and Operations" has been revised to highlight up-to-date thinking on total quality management. The "Management in Practice" box for Chapter 19 features early leaders of the quality movement and their philosophies, and explains how quality theories first traveled to Japan and now have returned to be embraced in the United States.
- Chapter 16 has been significantly revised to include more material on work teams. This new approach to assigning and completing work projects give workers more autonomy and promotes flexibility in the organization. Work teams are catching on at many different organizations, including Texas Instruments, General Mills, Inc., 3M, Procter & Gamble, and Digital Equipment Corp. Case 16.1 tells of Chrysler's exciting experiment with work teams used to develop the hot-selling Dodge Viper.

New Material for a Brand New World of Management

- A new Chapter 20, "Managing Technology and Innovation," anticipates the need for companies to be technologically savvy about their in-house operations systems, as well as the products and services they offer. New manufacturing and service technologies are discussed, as well as the challenge to develop an organizational culture conducive to creativity and innovation. Creativity and the creative process are also analyzed. Case 20.1 describes how Pfizer Inc., a company once scorned by drug industry analysts for a slow performance and too much invested in R&D, is being taken more seriously today, now that its R&D investment is paying off.
- A new Chapter 22, "Managing Cultural Diversity," was written to address issues managers already face and will continue to face as the workforce becomes more varied across ethnic groups, age groups, and gender. Diversity as a competitive advantage is discussed, as are approaches to promoting harmony and understanding in the new heterogeneous organization. The fact that women still have not been able to penetrate the top echelons of management in the United States is explained by the concept of the *glass ceiling*. International Case 22.2 talks about the slow progress Japanese women have made in their native Japanese organizations where strict adherence to tradition has greatly limited their opportunities in the business world.
- We are delighted to be able to offer a series of five integrated end-of-part video exercises for the first time in *Management*. The five video segments explore the total quality phenomenon in depth, including such management issues as competing on a global scale, meeting the needs of today's powerful customer, employee involvement in devising total quality programs, and Japan's successful employment of total quality methods. Companies such as Siemens AG, Motorola, Federal Express, Xerox, and Milliken are featured. Accompanying exercises in the text challenge students to think critically about the issues raised in the videos, and provide

numerous points of departure for lively class discussions or homework assignments.

Streamlining for a More Effective Presentation

With each edition of *Management,* the array of topics has expanded, and so has the length of this book. We made length a special priority for this edition. With help from my editor, reviewers, and a fresh, new, more efficient design, we were able to reduce the book by approximately 150 pages.

- Chapters on tactical/operational planning and organizational goals have been combined, forming Chapter 6, "Managing Organizational Goals and Planning."
- Of the ten enhancement modules appearing in the previous edition, four were retained and either merged with chapters, or recast as appendices.
- The third edition chapter on control techniques and methods was pared down and made part of Appendix 2.

FEATURES OF THE BOOK

Basic Themes

Several key themes are prominent in this edition of *Management.* One, as noted already, is the global character of the field of management. Examples and cases throughout the book reinforce this. Another timely theme is quality. While we cover quality and quality-related material in detail in Chapter 19, quality is also woven into the discussion of several related topics throughout the book and in the video exercises. Still another theme is the balance of theory and practice. Managers need to have a sound basis for their decisions, but theories that provide that basis must be grounded in reality. Throughout the book I explain the theoretical frameworks that guide managerial activities, and then I provide illustrations and examples of how and when those theories do and do not work. A fourth theme is that management is a generic activity not confined to large businesses. I use examples and discuss management in both small and large businesses as well as in not-for-profit organizations.

A Pedagogical System that Works

The pedagogical elements built into *Management,* Fourth Edition continue to be effective learning and teaching aids for students and instructors. This edition also features some noted improvements.

- Learning objectives and a chapter outline serve to preview key themes at the start of every chapter as in the previous edition. When a key term is defined in the chapter which satisfies one of the learning objectives, the term definition is preceded by a red bullet (●) in the margin.
- Three kinds of questions are found at the end of every chapter, designed to test different levels of student understanding. Questions for Review

ask students to recall specific information; Questions for Analysis ask students to integrate and synthesize material; and Questions for Application ask students to apply what they've learned to their own experiences.

Applications that Keep Students Engaged

To fully appreciate the role and scope of management in contemporary society, it is important to see examples and illustrations of how concepts apply in the real world. I rely heavily on fully researched examples to illustrate real-world applications. They vary in length, and all were carefully reviewed for currency. To give the broadest view possible, I vary examples of traditional management roles with non-traditional roles; profit-seeking businesses with non-profits; large corporations with small businesses; and international examples with U.S. examples. Other applications include:

- *Opening Incidents* at the beginning of every chapter. These brief vignettes draw the student into the chapter with a real-world scenario which introduces a particular management theme. Most opening incidents were revised for this edition.

- *"The Global View"* and *"Management in Practice."* These two boxed inserts are found in every chapter, and are intended to briefly depart from the the flow of the chapter with extensions of points made in the text. As always, special care was taken in this edition to rewrite or update every piece. Forty-three out of forty-six boxes are entirely new, three are updates of pieces that appeared in the third edition.

- Two end-of-chapter cases. The first case focuses on a problem or challenge faced by a U.S. company, and the second is based on either a foreign company or a U.S. company doing business in another country. Forty-two of forty-six cases were replaced with new cases, featuring entirely new companies.

- Ethics questions. In order to keep students thinking about ethics and social responsibility beyond Chapter 4, ethics questions were written to accompany most cases. Identified by an **E** symbol, these questions make use of companies and situations portrayed in the cases to illustrate the kinds of difficult decisions managers in organizations face every day. Some questions pose ethical dilemmas, others simply ask students to fully consider who might be affected by the activities of a particular organization. The questions are designed to teach students to view every business decision with the array of possible organizational constituents in mind (as illustrated in Figure 4.3).

An Effective Teaching and Learning Package

- *Instructor's Annotated Edition.* The IAE version of the text provides the instructor with a complete teaching tool. A series of six kinds of marginal annotations appearing in every chapter arm the instructor with valuable cross-referencing information accessing other pieces of the *Management* package, timely anecdotes from business literature to supplement text material, and teaching tips for on-the-spot discussion starters.

- *Production/Operations Management Supplement.* Written by Frederik P. Williams of the University of North Texas, *Production/Operations Management* is designed for instructors who would like to provide students with a more comprehensive coverage of production and operations management. Your Houghton Mifflin sales representative can give you the details on providing your students with this free supplement.

- *Exercises In Management.* This student manual, by Gene E. Burton of California State University—Fresno, provides experiential exercises for every chapter in *Management.* The overall purpose of each exercise is stated, along with the time required for each step, the materials needed, the procedure to be followed, and questions for discussion.

- *Instructor's Resource Manual.* Michele Kacmar of Florida State University restructured the *Instructor's Resource Manual* to make it even more useful and integral to teaching the course. Chapter outlines are thorough, and include film ideas, references to experiential exercises, and ideas for assigned student reading, positioned at appropriate points in the chapter. Boxed inserts are summarized, as are end of chapter cases, and all end of chapter questions and case questions are answered fully. Instructor's Guidelines to all experiential exercises included in Exercises in Management appear in a separate section of the IRM. Transparency masters reproducing art and tables from the book are found in the back of the IRM.

- *Computerized Lecture Outlines.* The *Computerized Lecture Outlines* consist of the comprehensive lecture outlines from the *Instructor's Resource Manual* on disk, available for use on IBM-compatible machines.

- *Test Bank.* Careful revision of the *Test Bank* by Michele Kacmar of Florida State University has resulted in an up-to-date test item pool suited to instructor's needs. The *Test Bank* includes true/false, multiple choice, completion, matching, and essay questions. The questions are labeled according to whether they test knowledge, understanding, or an application, and a level of difficulty has been assigned to each question.

- *Computerized Test Bank.* The *Computerized Test Bank* allows instructors to edit or add questions, and to select questions or generate randomly selected tests. This product is available for Macintosh and IBM-compatible machines.

- *Study Guide.* Written by Joe G. Thomas of Middle Tennessee State University, the *Study Guide* is designed to assist students in learning the definitions, concepts, and relationships presented in *Management.* Each chapter contains a pretest and a posttest, learning objectives, a chapter outline, key terms, multiple choice, true/false, matching, and completion questions, and ends by providing annotated answers.

- *Computerized Study Guide.* The *Computerized Study Guide* allows students to work through questions of various types and tells students why incorrect answers are wrong. The *Computerized Study Guide* also allows students to print out reports of their progress and to keep and print out notes. This product is available for IBM and IBM compatibles.

- *Color Transparencies.* 130 full-color transparencies illustrate every major topic in the text. The transparencies consist of the entire art program from the text, and many tables.

- *Five-Part Video Series.* As mentioned earlier, a video program has been integrated with the book for this edition. Five video segments explore the total quality phenomenon in depth, including such management issues as competing on a global scale, meeting the needs of today's powerful customer, employee involvement in devising total quality programs, and Japan's successful employment of total quality methods. Companies such as Siemens AG, Motorola, Federal Express, Xerox, and Milliken are featured.

Acknowledgments

I am frequently asked by my colleagues why I write textbooks, and my answer is always "because I enjoy it." I've never enjoyed writing a book more than this one. For me, writing a textbook is a challenging and stimulating activity that brings with it a variety of rewards. My greatest reward continues to be the feedback I get from students and instructors about how much they like this book.

I owe an enormous debt to many different people for helping me create *Management.* My colleagues at Texas A&M have helped create a wonderful academic climate. The rich and varied culture at Texas A&M makes it a pleasure to go to the office every day. My secretary, Phyllis Washburn, deserves special recognition for putting up with me and making me look good.

The fine team of profesionals at Houghton Mifflin has also been instrumental in the success of this book. Bill Setton, Jeff Sund, Pat Menard, Chere Bemelmans, Bernice Colt, Nancy Doherty-Schmitt, Mary Mars, Don Golini, David Barton, Nancy Seglin, Mary Jo Conrad, Liz Hacking, and Nader Darehshori have all had a significant impact on the quality of this book. Julie Hogenboom, Liza Martina, Diane McOscar, and Greg Tobin deserve special recognition for their many contributions to the fourth edition. Patrick Boles, my good friend and former sponsoring editor, worked with me to elevate the quality of each edition.

Many reviewers have played a critical role in the evolution of this project. They reviewed my work with a critical eye and in detail. I would like to tip my hat to the following reviewers, whose imprint can be found throughout this text:

Ramon J. Aldag
University of Wisconsin

Dr. Raymond E. Alie
Western Michigan University

William P. Anthony
Florida State University

Jay B. Barney
Texas A&M University

John D. Bigelow
Boise State University

Allen Bluedorn
University of Missouri

Gunther S. Boroschek
University of Massachusetts—Harbor Campus

George R. Carnahan
Northern Michigan University

Thomas G. Christoph
Clemson University

Joan Dahl
California State University, Northridge

Charles W. Cole
University of Oregon

Carol Danehower
Memphis State University

Gregory G. Dess
University of Texas—Arlington

Gary N. Dicer
University of Tennessee

Thomas J. Dougherty
University of Missouri

Shad Dowlatshahi
University of Wisconsin—
Platteville

John Drexler, Jr.
Oregon State University

Stan Elsea
Kansas State University

Douglas A. Elvers
University of South Carolina

Dan Farrell
Western Michigan University

Ari Ginsberg
New York University,
Graduate School of Business

Carl Gooding
Georgia Southern College

George J. Gore
University of Cincinnati

Stanley D. Guzell, Jr.
Youngstown State University

Mark A. Hammer
Washington State University

Paul Harmon
University of Utah

John Hughes
Texas Tech University

J. G. Hunt
Texas Tech University

John H. Jackson
University of Wyoming

Neil W. Jacobs
University of Denver

Arthur G. Jago
University of Houston

Gopol Joshi
Central Missouri State University

Norman F. Kallaus
University of Iowa

Ben L. Kedia
Memphis State University

Thomas L. Keon
Florida Atlantic University

Charles C. Kitzmiller
Indian River Community College

William R. LaFollete
Ball State University

Clayton G. Lifto
Kirkwood Community College

Patricia M. Manninen
North Shore Community College

Myrna P. Mandell, Ph.D.
California State University,
Northridge

Thomas Martin
University of Nebraska—Omaha

Barbara J. Marting
University of Southern Indiana

Wayne A. Meinhart
Oklahoma State University

Melvin McKnight
Northern Arizona University

Linda L. Neider
University of Miami

Mary Lippitt Nichols
University of Minnesota

Winston Oberg
Michigan State University

E. Leroy Plumlee
Western Washington University

Paul Preston
University of Texas—
San Antonio

John M. Purcell
State University of New York—
Farmingdale

James C. Quick
University of Texas—Arlington

Ralph Roberts
University of West Florida

Nick Sarantakas
Austin Community College

Gene Schneider
Austin Community College

H. Schollhammer
University of California—
Los Angeles

Nicholas Siropolis
Cuyahoga Community College

Michael J. Stahl
University of Tennessee

Charlotte D. Sutton
Auburn University

Robert L. Taylor
University of Louisville

Mary Thibodeaux
North Texas State University

Robert D. Van Auken
University of Oklahoma

Fred Williams
North Texas State University

Carl P. Zeithaml
University of North Carolina

I would also like to make a few personal acknowledgements. The fine work of Andrew Lloyd Webber, R.E.M., Lyle Lovett, Elton John, Phil Collins, Johnny Rivers, and the Nylons helped me make it through many late evenings and early mornings of work on the manuscript that became the book you hold in your hands. And Stephen King, Tom Clancy, John Sandford, Peter Straub, and Carl Barks provided me with a respite from my writings with their own.

Finally, there is the most important acknowledgement of all—my feelings for and gratitude to my family. My wife, Glenda, and our children, Dustin and Ashley, are the foundation of my professional and personal life. They help me keep work and play in perspective and give meaning to everything I do. It is with all my love that I dedicate this book to them.

R.W.G.

AN
INTRODUCTION
TO MANAGEMENT

1 *Managing and the
Manager's Job*

2 *The Evolution
of Management*

Managing and the Manager's Job

OBJECTIVES

After studying this chapter, you should be able to:

● Describe the nature of managment, define management and managers, and characterize their importance to organizations.

● Identify and briefly explain the four basic management functions in organizations.

● Describe different kinds of managers from the standpoints of level and area of the organization and discuss how people become managers.

● Identify the primary roles and skills of managers in organizations and characterize the nature of managerial work.

● Summarize the scope of management in organizations.

OUTLINE

The Nature of Management
The Management Process
  Planning and Decision Making:
    Determining Courses of Action
  Organizing: Coordinating Activities and
    Resources
  Leading: Managing People
  Controlling: Monitoring and Evaluating
    Activities
Kinds of Managers
  Differentiation by Levels of
    Management
  Differentiation by Areas of Management
  Becoming a Manager
Critical Roles and Skills
  Managerial Roles
  Managerial Skills
  The Nature of Managerial Work
The Scope of Management
  Management in Profit-Seeking
    Organizations
  Management in Not-for-Profit
    Organizations

SOUTHWEST AIRLINES CO. flies no international routes, serves no meals on any of its flights, has no first-class or assigned seats, subscribes to no computerized reservation systems, and refuses to transfer passenger baggage to other airlines. Southwest is also one of the most financially secure airlines in the industry. Its annual revenues exceed $1 billion, it has little debt, and its profits continue to grow. Southwest has 120 aircraft (all Boeing 737s) serving thirty-two cities in fourteen states.

Under the leadership of CEO Herbert Kelleher, Southwest has remained profitable by providing high-frequency, short-distance flights between American cities. There are eighty-three Southwest flights between Dallas and Houston every day, for example, with some fares as low as $29. No Southwest flight is longer than two hours, and many are less than one hour.

In an industry long plagued by labor problems, Kelleher is affectionately known by his employees as "Uncle Herbie." One of Kelleher's policies is that no employee will be laid off, even when times get tough. His concern and commitment to them have been repaid many times over. For example, as jet fuel prices increased during the 1990–1991 Persian Gulf crisis, more than one-third of Southwest's 8,600 employees took voluntary pay cuts to buy more fuel for the airline.

One of Kelleher's real challenges at Southwest is to keep costs down. Because of its low fares, Southwest cannot afford to let its planes sit idle nor to spend money on frills. Many airlines take an hour to clean and reboard between flights—Southwest can generally do it in fifteen minutes. The firm's operating expenses are also considerably lower than those of other airlines. All things considered, then, it looks like Southwest Airlines will be in the air for a long time to come.[1] ●

Herb Kelleher is clearly a manager. So, too, are James Kinnear (CEO of Texaco, Inc.), Shinroku Morohashi (president of Mitsubishi Corp.), Sir David Wilson (director of the British Museum), Debbie Fields (president of Mrs. Fields Inc. cookie stores), Red Auerbach (president of the Boston Celtics), George Bush (president of the United States), John Paul II (pope of the Roman Catholic Church), and Mark Ferguson (owner of Contemporary Landscape in Bryan, Texas). As diverse as they and their organizations are, all of these managers are confronted by many of the same challenges, they strive to achieve many of the same goals, and they apply many of the same concepts of effective management in their work.

For better or worse, our society is strongly influenced by managers and their organizations.[2] Most Americans are born in a hospital (an organization), educated by public schools (all organizations), and buy virtually all of their consumable products and services from businesses (organizations). And much of our behavior is influenced by various government agencies (also organizations). We will define an **organization** as a group of people working together in a structured and coordinated fashion to achieve a set of goals. The goals may include such things as profit (Southwest Airlines), the discovery of knowledge (Florida State University), national defense (the U.S. Army), the coordination of various local charities (United Way of America), or social satisfaction (a sorority). Because they play such a major role in our lives, it is important to understand how organizations operate and how they are managed.

This book is about managers and the work they do. In Chapter 1, we examine the general nature of management, its dimensions, and its challenges. We explain the concepts of management and managers, discuss the management process and present an overview of the book, and identify various kinds of managers. We describe the different roles and skills of managers and examine the scope of management in contemporary organizations. In Chapter 2 we describe how both the practice and theory of management have evolved. As a unit, then, these first two chapters provide an introduction to the field by introducing both contemporary and historical perspectives on management.

organization

A group of people working together in a structured and coordinated fashion to achieve a set of goals

THE NATURE OF MANAGEMENT

There are probably as many definitions of management as there are books on the subject. Many of the definitions are relatively concise and simplistic. For example, one early writer defined management as "Knowing exactly what you want [people] to do, and then seeing that they do it in the best and cheapest way."[3] Management, however, is a complex process—much more complex than this simple definition leads us to believe.[4] Thus we need to develop a definition of management that better captures the nature of its complexities and challenges.

Management is perhaps best understood from the viewpoint of systems theory. Systems theory, described more completely in Chapter 2, suggests that all organizations use four basic kinds of inputs, or resources, from

TABLE 1.1   Examples of Resources Used by Organizations

Organization	Human Resources	Financial Resources	Physical Resources	Information Resources
Mobil Corp.	Drilling platform workers Corporate executives	Profits Stockholder investments	Refineries Office buildings	Sales forecasts OPEC proclamations
Penn State University	Faculty Secretarial staff	Alumni contributions Government grants	Computers Campus facilities	Research reports Government publications
New York City	Police officers Municipal employees	Tax revenue Government grants	Sanitation equipment Municipal buildings	Economic forecasts Crime statistics
Joe's Corner Grocery Store	Grocery clerks Bookkeeper	Profits Owner investment	Building Display shelving	Price lists from suppliers Newspaper ads for competitors

their environment: human, financial, physical, and information. Human resources include managerial talent and labor. Monetary resources are the financial capital used by the organization to finance both ongoing and long-term operations. Physical resources include raw materials, office and production facilities, and equipment. Information resources are usable data needed to make effective decisions. Examples of resources used in four very different kinds of organizations are given in Table 1.1.

Managers are responsible for combining and coordinating these various resources to achieve the organization's goals. A manager at Mobil Corporation, for example, uses the talents of executives and drilling platform workers, profits earmarked for reinvestment, existing refineries and office facilities, and sales forecasts to make decisions regarding the amount of oil to be refined and distributed during the next quarter. Similarly, the mayor (manager) of New York City might use current police officers, a government grant (perhaps supplemented with surplus tax revenues), existing police stations, and detailed crime statistics to launch a major crime prevention program in the city.

How do these and other managers go about combining and coordinating the various kinds of resources? They do so by carrying out four basic managerial functions or activities: planning and decision making, organizing, leading, and controlling. Management, then, as illustrated in Figure 1.1, can be defined as follows:

Management is a set of activities (including planning and decision making, organizing, leading, and controlling) directed at an organization's resources

All organizations, regardless of whether they are large or small, profit-seeking or not-for-profit, use some combination of human, financial, physical, and information resources to achieve their goals. These resources, or inputs, are generally obtained from the organization's environment.

● **management**
A set of activities (including planning and decision making, organizing, leading, and controlling) directed at an organization's resources (human, financial, physical, and information), with the aim of achieving organizational goals in an efficient and effective manner

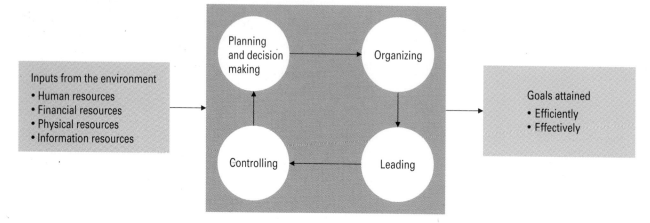

Basic managerial activities include planning and decision making, organizing, leading, and controlling. Managers engage in these activities to combine human, financial, physical, and information resources efficiently and effectively and work toward attainment of the goals of the organization.

efficient
Using resources wisely and without unnecessary waste

effective
Doing things successfully

● **manager**
Someone whose primary responsibility is to carry out the management process

(human, financial, physical, and information) with the aim of achieving organizational goals in an efficient and effective manner.

The last phrase in our definition is especially important because it highlights the basic purpose of management—to ensure that an organization's goals are achieved in an efficient and effective manner. By **efficient**, we mean using resources wisely and without unnecessary waste. For example, a firm like Toyota Motor Corp. that produces high-quality products at relatively low costs is efficient. By **effective**, we mean doing things successfully. Toyota also makes cars with the styling and craftsmanship that inspire consumer confidence. A firm could produce black-and-white console televisions very efficiently but still not succeed because black-and-white televisions are no longer popular. In general, successful organizations are both efficient and effective.[5]

With this basic understanding of management, defining the term *manager* becomes relatively simple:

> A **manager** is someone whose primary responsibility is to carry out the management process. In particular, a manager is someone who plans and makes decisions, organizes, leads, and controls human, financial, physical, and information resources.

Today's managers face a variety of interesting and challenging situations. The average executive works sixty hours a week, has enormous demands placed on his or her time, and faces increased complexities posed by globalization, domestic competition, government regulation, and shareholder pressure.[6] The task is further complicated by rapid change, unexpected disruptions, and both minor and major crises. The manager's job is unpredictable and fraught with challenges, but it is also filled with opportunities to make a difference.

Many of the characteristics that contribute to the complexity and uncertainty of management stem from the environment in which organizations function. For example, as shown in Figure 1.1, the resources used by organizations to create products and services all come from the environment. Thus it is critical that managers understand this environment. Part 2 of the text discusses the environmental context of management in detail. Chapter 3 provides a general discussion of the organizational environment and effectiveness, while Chapters 4 and 5 address two specific aspects of the environment more fully. In particular, Chapter 4 discusses the ethical and social context of management, and Chapter 5 explores the global context of management. After reading those chapters, you will be better prepared to study the essential activities that comprise the management process.

THE MANAGEMENT PROCESS

We noted earlier that management involves the four basic functions of planning and decision making, organizing, leading, and controlling. Because these functions represent the framework around which this book is organized, we introduce them here and note where they are discussed more fully. Their basic definitions and interrelationships are shown in Figure 1.2. (Note that Figure 1.2 is an expanded version of the central part of Figure 1.1 with additional detail.)

Recall the example of Herb Kelleher discussed earlier. Kelleher has created a clear set of goals that articulate what he wants Southwest to be. He has set up an effective organization to help make that vision a reality. Kelleher also pays close attention to the people who work for Southwest. And he keeps a close eye on how well the airline is performing. Each of these activities represents one of the four basic managerial functions illustrated in

You can grab it, but you can't shake it.

Management is important to any organization. One of the biggest challenges facing managers at MTV is keeping the music video network ahead of its competition while staying abreast of current tastes in music, fashion, and design.

FIGURE 1.2 The Management Process

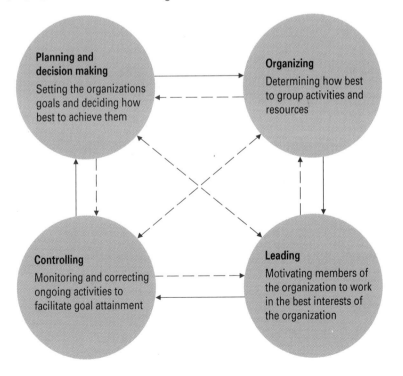

Planning and decision making
Setting the organizations goals and deciding how best to achieve them

Organizing
Determining how best to group activities and resources

Controlling
Monitoring and correcting ongoing activities to facilitate goal attainment

Leading
Motivating members of the organization to work in the best interests of the organization

Management involves four basic activities—planning and decision making, organizing, leading, and controlling. Most managers engage in more than one activity at the same time.

the figure. Setting goals is part of planning, setting up the organization is part of organizing, managing people is part of leading, and monitoring performance is part of control. "Management in Practice" describes how another manager, J. B. Hunt, performed these same activities in the trucking industry.

It is important to note, however, that the functions of management do not usually occur in a tidy, step-by-step fashion. Managers do not plan on Monday, make decisions on Tuesday, organize on Wednesday, lead on Thursday, and control on Friday. At any given time, a manager is likely to be engaged in several different activities simultaneously. Indeed, there are as many differences as similarities in managerial work from one setting to another. The similarities that pervade most settings are the phases in the management process. Key differences include the emphasis, sequencing, and implications of each phase.[7] Thus the solid lines in Figure 1.2 indicate how, in theory, the functions of management are performed. The dotted lines, however, represent the true reality of management. In the sections that follow, we explore each of these activities.

Planning and Decision Making: Determining Courses of Action

● **planning**
Setting an organization's goals and deciding how best to achieve them

● **decision making**
Part of the planning process that involves selecting a course of action from a set of alternatives

In its simplest form, **planning** means setting an organization's goals and deciding how best to achieve them. **Decision making**, a part of the planning process, involves selecting a course of action from a set of alternatives. Planning and decision making help maintain managerial effectiveness by serving as guides for future activities. For example, General Electric Co. owns a number of businesses in different industries. Jack Welch, the firm's CEO, has established a goal that every business owned by GE will be either number 1 or number 2 in its industry.[8] This goal provides clear guidelines for managerial action. If a particular business is nowhere near the top of its industry and shows little potential for improvement, GE managers will most likely sell it. On the other hand, a business that is number 3 and gaining on its rivals may receive an extra infusion of resources to gain the number-2 spot. Thus the organization's goals and plans help managers know how to allocate their time and resources.

Four chapters making up Part 3 of this text are devoted to planning and decision making. Chapter 6 examines organizational goals and the planning process itself in more detail. Chapter 7 focuses on strategy and strategic planning. Chapter 8 explores managerial decision in detail. Finally, Chapter 9 summarizes several useful tools that managers use in planning and decision making.

Organizing: Coordinating Activities and Resources

Once a manager has developed a workable plan, the next phase of management is to organize people and other resources necessary to carry out the plan. To illustrate how managers organize, consider the following scenario. You have a $90,000 budget and three subordinates to execute a plan. One approach is to give each subordinate a $30,000 budget and have each one report back to you. A different method might be to establish one subordinate as a supervisor of the other two, who would have budgets of $45,000

J.B. HUNT ROLLS ALONG

J.B. Hunt is not a typical manager or entrepreneur. He doesn't have an MBA—in fact, he dropped out of school at age 12, drove trucks for twenty-one years, and got his big break when he hit on the idea of using rotting rice hulls as poultry litter. Yet as the head of the nation's fastest-growing trucking business, J.B. Hunt Transport Services, Inc., Hunt does possess all the fundamental management skills that most people acquire only through years of education and experience.

Hunt's head is always full of ideas, many of them crazy, as he is quick to admit. Admiring his new four-story headquarters, he already envisions skyscrapers. His fresh ideas about the trucking industry—using uniformed, nonunion drivers and arranging routes and loads so that trucks are almost always full—made him very rich very quickly. But other ideas—like making oil out of used tires—have been shot down by Hunt executives.

Hunt says his lack of education may be an asset, because he has always known that he couldn't run the show himself and had to hire good people and delegate responsibility to them. According to Hunt CEO Kirk Thompson, even the ideas that got the company rolling were company ideas, not Hunt's alone. Still, Hunt's sense of style and desire to drive a bargain allow him to lead, delegate, and set an example for his employees. He put $15 million into the lavishly decorated company headquarters because he believes the artificial palm trees and Italian tile will attract the right customers. On the other hand, always trying to pinch pennies, Hunt buys all his tires from one source in an effort to save half a cent per mile.

Perhaps Hunt's most surprising managerial quality, given his background, is his ability to run a tight operation based on precise timing and careful planning. These attributes are critical to Hunt's latest venture, Quantum, a door-to-door rail-and-truck service developed with Santa Fe Pacific Corporation (railroad). In 1990, when Hunt's customary 20 percent profit margins were dwindling and labor costs, industry overcapacity, and stagnant rates were threatening to shrink them further, Hunt began working with, rather than against, truckers' biggest competitor—the railroad. Hunt picks up freight and delivers it to one of Santa Fe's hubs throughout California and in Chicago, Kansas City, or Fort Worth. The trailer is loaded onto a Santa Fe railroad car, moved to another hub, loaded onto another Hunt truck, and driven to its destination. The concept was greeted with skepticism throughout the transportation industry, but soon other companies were hurrying to set up their own "intermodal" services, a sure sign that J.B. Hunt was once again doing something right.

References: Daniel Machalaba, "J.B. Hunt Reinvented Trucking, But Now Has Load of Problems," *The Wall Street Journal*, May 9, 1991, pp. A1, A5; Ira Rosenfeld, "Hunt, Santa Fe Restructure Quantum As Intermodal Service Fights for Business," *Traffic World*, March 11, 1991, pp. 59–60; Gus Welty, "Quantum's Pace Quickens," *Railway Age*, May 1991, pp. 43–47.

each. At GE, Welch has decided that each division head within the company should have a great deal of freedom to run his or her operation as though it were a separate business. The heads of each of the twenty major businesses that constitute GE therefore have considerable autonomy. Welch has also changed many of the firm's bureaucratic rules and procedures. Determining how activities and resources are to be grouped is the **organizing** process. Organizing is the subject of Part 4.

Chapter 10 introduces basic components of organizing such as job design, departmentalization, authority relationships, span of control, and line and staff roles. Chapter 11 explains how managers fit these elements and concepts together to form an overall organization design. Organization change

● **organizing**
Grouping activities and resources in a logical fashion

One of the biggest engineering feats in history is nearing completion. A tunnel under the English Channel (the source of its nickname, "The Chunnel") will soon make regular train service between England and France possible. Building the 23 mile tunnel posed enormous organizing challenges for managers of the project. With a cost of $14.7 billion and a work force of thousands of engineers, technicians, and laborers, the project required careful coordination of people, equipment, and money.

is the focus of Chapter 12. Processes associated with hiring and assigning people to carry out organizational roles are described in Chapter 13.

Leading: Managing People

The third basic managerial function is leading. Some people consider leading to be both the most important and the most challenging of all managerial activities. **Leading** is the set of processes used to get people to work together to advance the interests of the organization. For example, at GE, Jack Welch works hard to inspire confidence and trust in other managers, and he expects them to do the same for their subordinates.

Leading involves a number of different processes and activities. Part 5 discusses these activities. Motivating employees is discussed in Chapter 14, and leadership itself and the leader's efforts to influence others are covered in Chapter 15. Managing interpersonal and group processes is the subject of Chapter 16. Finally, communication, another important part of leading, is addressed in Chapter 17.

Controlling: Monitoring and Evaluating Activities

The final phase of the management process is **controlling**, or monitoring the organization's progress toward its goals. As the organization moves toward its goals, management must monitor its progress. It must make sure that the organization is performing in such a way as to arrive at its "destination" at the appointed time. A good analogy is that of a space mission to Mars. NASA does not simply shoot a rocket in the general

● **leading**
The set of processes used to get members of the organization to work together to advance the interests of the organization

● **controlling**
Monitoring organizational progress toward goal attainment

direction of the planet and then look again in four months to see whether the rocket hit its mark. NASA monitors the spacecraft almost continuously and makes whatever course corrections are needed to keep it on track. Controlling helps ensure the effectiveness and efficiency needed for successful management.

The control function is explored in Part 6. First, Chapter 18 explores the general nature of the control process, including the increasing importance of strategic control. Other important areas of management control—operations management, productivity, and quality—are explored in depth in Chapter 19. Managing technology and innovation, also an important element of control, is described in Chapter 20. Finally, Chapter 21 addresses the management of information, still another critical area of organizational control.

Organizations require many different kinds of managers in order to function. And this holds true for both business and non-business organizations. Steve Barlett, mayor, and Jan Hart, city manager, are responsible for managing the city of Dallas. Recently selected by *Financial World* as the best city for business in the United States, Dallas is also one of the largest cities to use a council/manager form of government.

These then, are the four primary functions of management: planning and decision making, organizing, leading, and controlling. Beyond these functions, however, are a variety of special challenges that are of increasing concern and significance to all managers. Two particularly important challenges are discussed in Part 7. Chapter 22 is devoted to the increasingly important area of managing cultural diversity. The nation's changing demographic picture has brought considerable changes to the workplace, to which managers must be sensitive and responsive. Chapter 22 is devoted to the issues a culturally varied workplace poses for managers. Chapter 23 discusses the nature of entrepreneurship and small-business management.

KINDS OF MANAGERS

Earlier in this chapter we identify as managers people from a variety of organizations. Clearly, there are many kinds of managers. One point of differentiation is among organizations, as those earlier examples imply. Another occurs within an organization. Figure 1.3 indicates how managers within an organization can be differentiated by level and area.

Differentiation by Levels of Management

● **levels of management**
Managers can be differentiated according to their level in the organization: top, middle, or first-line

Managers can be differentiated according to their level in the organization. Although large organizations typically have a number of levels of management, the most common view considers three basic levels: top, middle, and first-line managers.

Top Managers Top managers make up the relatively small group of executives who control the organization. Titles found in this group include president, vice president, and chief executive officer (CEO). Herb Kelleher is a top manager. An organization's top managers establish its goals, overall strategy, and operating policies. They also officially represent the organization to the external environment by meeting with government officials, executives of other organizations, and so forth. The job of a top manager is likely to be complex and varied. Top managers make decisions about such activities as acquiring other companies, investing in research and devel-

Managers differ within organizations according to their level, and the area of the organization in which they work. As CEO, Herb Kelleher is a top manager at Southwest Airlines. A person in charge of flight services at Southwest Airlines is an example of a first-line manager.

FIGURE 1.3 Kinds of Managers by Level and Area

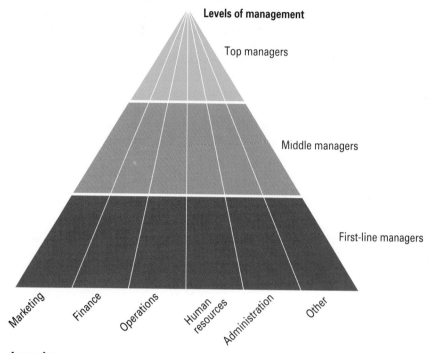

Levels of management

Top managers

Middle managers

First-line managers

Marketing Finance Operations Human resources Administration Other

Areas of management

opment, entering or abandoning various markets, and building new plants and office facilities.[9] They often work long hours and spend much of their time in meetings or on the telephone.[10]

Middle Managers Middle management is probably the largest group of managers in most organizations. Common middle-management titles include plant manager, operations manager, and division head. Southwest Airlines' route control manager in Dallas is a middle manager. Middle managers are primarily responsible for implementing the policies and plans developed by top management and for supervising and coordinating the activities of lower-level managers.[11] Plant managers, for example, handle inventory management, quality control, equipment failures, and minor union problems. They also coordinate the work of supervisors within the plant. In recent years, many organizations have thinned the ranks of middle managers to lower costs and rid themselves of excess bureaucracy. For example, Mobil has eliminated 17 percent of its middle managers since 1982, and E.I. du Pont de Nemours & Co. has made cuts of 15 percent.[12] Still, middle managers are necessary to bridge the upper and lower levels of the organization and to implement the strategies developed at the top. While many organizations have found that they can indeed survive with fewer middle managers, those who remain play an even more important role in determining how successful the organization will be.[13]

First-line Managers First-line managers supervise and coordinate the activities of operating employees. Common titles for first-line managers are foreman, supervisor, and office manager. A flight services manager on a Southwest Airlines' flight is a first-line manager. These are often the first positions held by employees who enter management from the ranks of operating personnel. In contrast to top and middle managers, first-line managers typically spend a large proportion of their time supervising the work of subordinates.[14]

Differentiation by Areas of Management

Regardless of their level, managers may work in various areas within an organization. In any given firm, for example, there may be marketing, financial, operations, human resource, administrative, and other kinds of managers at all three levels.

Marketing Managers Marketing managers work in areas related to the marketing function—getting consumers and clients to buy the organization's products or services (be they Ford automobiles, *Newsweek* magazines, Associated Press news reports, or flights on Southwest Airlines). These areas include new product development, promotion, and distribution. Given the importance of marketing for virtually all organizations, developing good managers in this area can be critical. John Akers, CEO of IBM (International Business Machines Corp.), and William P. Stiritz, CEO of Ralston Purina Co., started their careers as marketing managers.[15]

Financial Managers Financial managers deal primarily with an organization's financial resources. They are responsible for activities such as accounting, cash management, and investments. In some businesses, such as banking and insurance, financial managers are found in especially large numbers. Duane L. Burnham, CEO of Abbott Laboratories, and James C. Cotting, CEO of Navistar International Corp., spent much of their careers as financial managers.[16]

Operations Managers Operations managers are concerned with creating and managing the systems that create an organization's products and services. Typical responsibilities of operations managers include production control, inventory control, quality control, plant layout, and site selection. Robert E. Allen, CEO of American Telephone & Telegraph Co. (AT&T), and James Near, CEO of Wendy's International Inc., started their careers as operations managers.[17]

Human Resource Managers Human resource managers are responsible for hiring and developing employees. They are typically involved in human resource planning, employee recruitment and selection, training and development, designing compensation and benefit systems, formulating performance appraisal systems, and discharging low-performing and problem employees. William J. Alley, CEO of American Brands, Inc., and John W. Teets, CEO of Greyhound Dial, each worked in human resources management earlier in their careers.[18]

Administrative Managers Administrative, or general, managers are not associated with any particular management specialty. Probably the best ex-

● **areas of management**
Managers can be differentiated into marketing, financial, operations, human resource, administration, and other areas

ample of an administrative management position is that of a hospital or clinic administrator. Administrative managers tend to be generalists; they have some basic familiarity with all functional areas of management rather than specialized training in any one area. Katharine Graham, CEO of the Washington Post Co., and James Houghton, CEO of Corning Incorporated, spent much of their careers as administrative managers.[19]

Other Kinds of Managers   Many organizations have specialized management positions in addition to those already described. Public relations managers, for example, deal with the public and media for firms like Philip Morris Companies, Inc. and The Dow Chemical Co. to protect and enhance the image of the organization. Research and development (R&D) managers coordinate the activities of scientists and engineers working on scientific projects in organizations such as Monsanto Company, NASA, and Merck & Co. Internal consultants are used in organizations such as The Prudential Insurance Co. of America to provide specialized expert advice to operating managers. Many areas of international management are coordinated by specialized managers in organizations like Eli Lilly and Rockwell International Corp. The number, nature, and importance of these specialized managers vary tremendously from one organization to another. As contemporary organizations continue to grow in complexity and size, the number and importance of such managers are also likely to increase.

becoming a manager
Most people become managers by combining education and experience

Becoming a Manager

How does one acquire the skills necessary to become a successful manager? The most common path, although there are as many variations as there are managers, involves a combination of education and experience. Figure 1.4 illustrates how this generally happens.

The Role of Education   Many of you reading this book right now are doing so because you are enrolled in a management course at a college or university. You are acquiring management skills in an educational setting. When you complete the course (and this book), you will have a foundation for developing your management skills in more advanced courses.

Most managers acquire their skills as a result of education and experience. Though some CEOs today do not hold college degrees, most students preparing for management careers complete college degrees and may go on to enroll in MBA programs.

F I G U R E   1 . 4 Sources of Management Skills

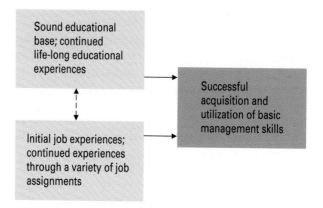

Sound educational base; continued life-long educational experiences

Initial job experiences; continued experiences through a variety of job assignments

Successful acquisition and utilization of basic management skills

Enrollments in business schools and colleges have mushroomed in recent years as more and more students seek undergraduate degrees in business and management.[20] Indeed, a college degree has become almost a requirement for career advancement in business. Of the CEOs of the 1000 largest U.S. companies, 916 have a college degree.[21] MBA programs (conferring master's degrees in business administration) have also experienced rapid growth, and they often attract students whose undergraduate majors were in other fields. More and more foreign universities, especially in Europe, are also beginning to offer academic programs in management.

Even after obtaining a degree, most prospective managers have not seen the end of their management education. Many middle and top managers periodically return to campus to participate in executive or management development programs (MDPs) ranging in duration from a few days to several weeks. First-line managers also take advantage of extension and continuing education programs offered by institutions of higher education. A recent innovation in extended management education is the Executive MBA program offered by many top business schools. Under this system, middle and top managers with several years of experience complete an accelerated program of study on weekends. Finally, many large companies have in-house training programs for furthering the education of managers.

The primary advantage of education as a source of management skills is that a student can follow a well-developed program of study, becoming familiar with current research and thinking on management. And many college students can devote full-time energy and attention to learning. On the negative side, management education may have to be very general to meet the needs of a wide variety of students, and specific know-how may be hard to obtain. Further, many aspects of the manager's job can be discussed in a book but cannot really be appreciated and understood until they are experienced.

The Role of Experience   This book will help provide you with a solid foundation for enhancing your management skills. Even if you were to memorize every word in every management book ever written, however, you could not then step into a top-management position and be effective. The reason? Management skills must also be learned through experience. Most managers advanced to their present position from other jobs. By experiencing the day-to-day pressures a manager faces and by meeting a variety of managerial challenges, the individual develops insights that cannot be learned from a book.

For this reason most large companies, and many smaller ones as well, have developed management training programs for their prospective managers. People are hired from college campuses, from other organizations, or from the ranks of the organization's first-line managers and operating employees. These people are systematically assigned to a variety of jobs. Over time, the individual is exposed to most, if not all, of the major aspects of the organization. In this way the manager learns by experience.

The training programs at some companies, such as the Procter & Gamble Co., General Foods Corporation, and General Mills, Inc., are so good that other companies try to hire people who have gone through their training. Even without formal training programs, it is possible for managers to achieve success as they profit from varied experiences. For example, Herb

Kelleher was a practicing attorney before he took over at Southwest. Of course, natural ability, drive, and self-motivation also play roles in acquiring experience and developing management skills.

Most effective managers learn their skills through a combination of education and experience. Some type of college degree, even if it is not in business administration, usually provides a foundation. The individual then participates in an initial job experience and subsequently progresses through a variety of management situations. During the manager's rise in the organization, occasional education "updates," such as management development programs, may supplement on-the-job experience. And increasingly, managers need to acquire international expertise as part of their personal development. As with general managerial skills, international expertise can also be acquired through a combination of education and experience. "The Global View" provides additional information about becoming a global manager.

CRITICAL ROLES AND SKILLS

Exactly what skills are managers developing as they are educated and acquire experience? Management skills are the talents necessary for effective performance. Certain roles are also required of all managers, no matter what their specialty or level. The concept of a role, in this sense, is similar to the role an actor plays in a theatrical production. A person does certain things, meets certain needs in the organization, and has certain responsibilities. In the sections that follow we first highlight the basic roles managers play and then discuss the skills they need to be effective.

Managerial Roles

Henry Mintzberg offers a number of interesting insights into the nature of managerial roles.[22] He closely observed the day-to-day activities of a group of CEOs by literally following them around and taking notes on what they did. From his observations, Mintzberg concluded that managers play ten different roles and that these roles fall into three basic categories: interpersonal, informational, and decisional. Table 1.2 summarizes these roles.

● **interpersonal roles**
The managerial roles of figurehead, leader, and liaison that involve interacting with other people

Interpersonal Roles There are three **interpersonal roles** inherent in the manager's job. First, the manager is often asked to serve as a *figurehead*—taking visitors to dinner, attending ribbon-cutting ceremonies, and the like. These activities are typically more ceremonial and symbolic than substantive. The manager is also asked to serve as a *leader*—hiring, training, and motivating employees. A manager who formally or informally shows subordinates how to do things and how to perform under pressure is leading. Finally, managers can have a *liaison* role. This role often involves serving as a coordinator or link between people, between groups, or between organizations. For example, IBM and Apple Computer recently agreed to cooperate on developing new technology. Representatives from each firm meet regularly to coordinate this new venture. Thus they are serving as liaisons for their respective companies.

SKILLS FOR THE GLOBAL MANAGER

Most U.S. businesses have by now accepted that they must think globally and be ready to find resources or markets anywhere in the world. Surprisingly, however, a majority of U.S. corporations still don't provide cross-cultural training for the people they're about to send overseas. U.S. expatriate managers must have many of the same managerial strengths as their stay-at-home counterparts, but most will do well only with additional specialized training or expertise.

Many U.S. companies have learned the hard way that what works in Peoria won't necessarily work in Prague. So first on the list of a global manager's prerequisites is an appreciation of how cultural differences can affect the functioning of organizations. Having accepted the general premise that doing business in Rome may mean learning the Roman way of business, managers must develop a knowledge of the specific country they're headed for. Because English is the language of business worldwide, managers don't *have* to learn a new language, but it certainly helps. And they should also become attuned to nonverbal communication in the host country and learn such things as how the particular culture deals with stress.

With this basic background in the foreign culture, managers can go on to study the culture's particular business practices. In the new culture, is it appropriate to "get right down to business," as Americans do, or would that approach appear rude, as it does to the Japanese? What are the priorities, expectations, and assumptions of the new clients? Managers must engage in significant self-study, trying to understand how their own cultural background is likely to influence their perceptions and interpretations of people in the new culture. Managers may need to learn new ways of gathering customer information in a different culture. Such information is crucial to a marketing strategy like IBM's, which relies on building the same basic product worldwide but modifying that product to suit local needs.

Overseas assignments often involve more responsibility and autonomy than a manager is used to, and such shifts in the scope of an individual's job may be difficult to cope with both when the manager is taking the new position and when he or she is returning to narrower duties back in the states. Companies can help individual managers by designating host-country experts to train or mentor newly arrived managers.

Foreign assignments were once seen as the surest way to slow down a career. Today many companies, particularly large corporations, see a foreign assignment as a necessary part of a top executive's experience. So learning the skills necessary for global management becomes more important every year.

References: Madelyn R. Callahan, "Preparing the New Global Manager," *Training and Development Journal*, March 1989, pp. 29–32; Edward Dunbar and Allan Katcher, "Preparing Managers for Foreign Assignments," *Training and Development Journal*, September 1990, pp. 45–47; "The Global Executive," *The Journal of Business Strategy*, July/August 1990, p. 62; Andrew Kupfer, "How To Be A Global Manager," *Fortune*, March 14, 1988, pp. 52–58.

Informational Roles   The three **informational roles** identified by Mintzberg flow naturally from the interpersonal roles just discussed. The process of carrying out these roles place the manager at a strategic point to gather and disseminate information. The first informational role is that of *monitor*, one who actively seeks information that may be of value. The manager questions subordinates, is receptive to unsolicited information, and attempts to be as well informed as possible. The manager is also a *disseminator* of information, transmitting relevant information back to others in the workplace. When the roles of monitor and disseminator are viewed together, the manager emerges as a vital link in the organization's chain of communication. The third informational role focuses on external communication. The

● **informational roles**
The managerial roles of monitor, disseminator, and spokesperson that involve processing information

Research by Henry Mintzberg suggests that managers play ten basic managerial roles.

TABLE 1.2   Ten Basic Managerial Roles

Category	Role	Sample Activities
Interpersonal	Figurehead	Attending ribbon-cutting ceremony for new plant
	Leader	Encouraging employees to improve productivity
	Liaison	Coordinating activities of two project groups
Informational	Monitor	Scanning industry reports to stay abreast of developments
	Disseminator	Sending memos outlining new organizational initiatives
	Spokesperson	Making a speech to discuss growth plans
Decisional	Entrepreneur	Developing new ideas for innovation
	Disturbance handler	Resolving conflict between two subordinates
	Resource allocator	Reviewing and revising budget requests
	Negotiator	Reaching agreement with a key supplier or labor union

Managers today must play a variety of different roles, and Keenan Ivory Wayans, creator of the Fox Television series "In Living Color," is no exception. As the series' creator, he had to "sell" his idea to the network (entrepreneur). As the series' producer, he kept crew members motivated (leader), coordinated production activities (liaison), and ensured that people were informed about future activities (disseminator). Wayans has also written scripts and acted in the series.

spokesperson formally relays information to people outside the unit or outside the organization. For example, a plant manager at Union Carbide may transmit information to top-level managers so that they will be better informed about the plant's activities. The manager may also represent the organization before a chamber of commerce or consumer group. Although the roles of spokesperson and figurehead are similar, there is one basic difference between them. When a manager acts as a figurehead, the manager's presence as a symbol of the organization is what is of interest. In the spokesperson role, however, the manager carries information and communicates it to others in a formal sense.

Decisional Roles The manager's informational roles typically lead to the **decisional roles**. The information acquired by the manager as a result of performing the informational roles has a significant bearing on important decisions that he makes. Mintzberg identified four decisional roles. First, the manager has the role of *entrepreneur,* the voluntary initiator of change. A manager at 3M Company developed the idea for the Post-it Note Pad but had to "sell" it to other skeptical managers inside the company. A second decisional role is initiated not by the manager but by some other individual or group. The manager responds to her role as *disturbance handler* by handling such problems as strikes, copyright infringements, and energy shortages.

> ● **decisional roles**
> The managerial roles of entrepreneur, disturbance handler, resource allocator, and negotiator that primarily relate to decisions that must be made

The third decisional role is that of *resource allocator*. As resource allocator, the manager decides how resources are distributed, and with whom he or she will work most closely. For example, a manager typically allocates the funds in the unit's operating budget among the unit's members and projects. A fourth decisional role is that of *negotiator*. In this role the manager enters into negotiations with other groups or organizations as a representative of the company. For example, managers may negotiate a union contract, an agreement with a consultant, or a long-term relationship with a supplier. Negotiations may also be internal to the organization. The manager may, for instance, mediate a dispute between two subordinates or negotiate with another department for additional support.

Managerial Skills

In addition to fulfilling numerous roles, managers also need a number of specific skills if they are to succeed. One classic study of managers identified three important types of managerial skills: technical, interpersonal, and conceptual.[23] Diagnostic and analytic skills are also prerequisites to managerial success.

Technical Skills **Technical skills** are the skills necessary to accomplish or understand the specific kind of work being done in an organization. For example, David Packard and Bill Hewlett understand the inner workings of their company, Hewlett-Packard Co., because they were trained as engineers. Project engineers, physicians, and accountants all have the technical skills necessary for their respective professions. They each develop basic technical skills by completing recognized programs of study at colleges and universities. Then they gain experience in actual work situations, honing their skills before actually becoming R&D manager, chief of surgery, or

> ● **technical skills**
> Skills necessary to accomplish or understand tasks relevant to the organization

partner in a certified public accounting firm. Similarly, the top marketing executive of any large firm probably started as a sales representative or sales manager, whereas the operations vice president was probably a plant manager at one time. Technical skills are especially important for first-line managers. These managers spend much of their time training subordinates and answering questions about work-related problems. They must know how to perform the tasks assigned to those they supervise if they are to be effective managers.

● interpersonal skills

The ability to communicate with, understand, and motivate both individuals and groups

Interpersonal Skills Managers spend considerable time interacting with people both inside and outside the organization. For obvious reasons, then, the manager also needs **interpersonal skills**—the ability to communicate with, understand, and motivate individuals and groups. As a manager climbs the organizational ladder, she must be able to get along with subordinates, peers, and those at higher levels of the organization. Because of the multitude of roles managers must fulfill, she must also be able to work with suppliers, customers, investors, and others outside of the organization. One reason for Sam Walton's success with Wal-Mart Stores was his ability to motivate his employees and to inspire their loyalty and devotion to his vision for the firm. These skills were underscored when hundreds of Wal-Mart employees cried at the recent news of Walton's death. Although some managers have succeeded with poor interpersonal skills, a manager who has good interpersonal skills is likely to be more successful.

● conceptual skills

Skills that depend on ability to think in the abstract

Conceptual Skills **Conceptual skills** depend on the manager's ability to think in the abstract. Managers need the mental capacity to understand the overall workings of the organization and its environment, to grasp how all the parts of the organization fit together, and to view the organization in a holistic manner. This allows them to think strategically, to see the "big picture," and to make broad-based decisions that serve the overall organization. A few years ago, The Boeing Co. was on the verge of discontinuing its 737 aircraft line because of sliding domestic sales. Then suddenly one manager, Bob Norton, realized that the company needed to take a more global view of the aircraft market. By focusing on the same things that had made the 737 an earlier success in the United States, Boeing was able to reintroduce the aircraft in developing nations. Increased sales there have offset declines at home, and the end result is that the company has been able to maintain a highly profitable product line beyond its normal life expectancy. The conceptual skills of a single manager helped pave the way.[24]

● diagnostic and analytic skills

Skills that enable a manager to visualize the most appropriate response to a situation

Diagnostic and Analytic Skills Successful managers also possess **diagnostic and analytic skills,** or skills that enable a manager to visualize the most appropriate response to a situation. A physician diagnoses a patient's illness by analyzing symptoms and determining their probable cause. Similarly, a manager can diagnose and analyze a problem in the organization by studying its symptoms and then developing a solution. For example, a manager at a Texas Instruments plant recently noted that one particular department was suffering from high employee turnover. He analyzed the situation and decided that the turnover was caused by one of three things: dissatisfaction with pay, boring work, or a supervisor with poor interpersonal skills. After interviewing several employees, he concluded that the problem was the supervisor. He reassigned the supervisor to a position that required less interaction with people, and the turnover problem soon disappeared. The ability to diagnose and analyze enabled him to define his problem, recognize its possible causes, focus on the most direct problem, and then solve it. Diagnostic and analytic skills are also useful in favorable situations. The company may find that its sales are increasing at a much higher rate than anticipated. Possible causes might include low price, greater demand than predicted, and high prices charged by a competitor. The manager uses diagnostic skills to determine what is causing the sales explosion and how best to take advantage of it.

The Nature of Managerial Work

We noted earlier that managerial work does not follow an orderly, systematic progression through the workweek. Indeed, the manager's job is fraught with uncertainty, change, interruption, and fragmented activities. One study, for example, found that in a typical day CEOs are likely to spend 59 percent of their time in scheduled meetings, 22 percent doing "desk work," 10 percent in unscheduled meetings, 6 percent on the telephone, and the remaining 3 percent on tours of company facilities. (These proportions, of course, are different for managers at lower levels.)[25]

In addition, managers also perform a wide variety of tasks. In the course of a single day, for example, a manager might have to make a decision about the design of a new product, settle a complaint between two subordinates, hire a new secretary, write a report for his boss, coordinate a joint venture with an overseas colleague, form a task force to investigate a problem, and deal with a labor grievance. At each juncture, the manager has to assess the ethical implications of his decisions and actions. Moreover, the pace of the manager's job can be relentless. She may feel bombarded by mail, telephone calls, and people waiting to see her. Decisions may have to be made quickly and plans formulated with little time for reflection.

In many ways, however, these characteristics of managerial work also contribute to its richness and meaningfulness. Making critical decisions under intense pressure, and making them well, can be a major source of intrinsic satisfaction. And managers are generally well paid for the pressures they bear.

THE SCOPE OF MANAGEMENT

When most people think of managers and management, they think of profit-seeking organizations. Throughout this chapter, we used people like Herb Kelleher of Southwest Airlines and Jack Welch of GE as examples of managers. But we also mentioned examples from sports, religion, and other fields in which management is essential. Indeed, any group of two or more people working together to achieve a goal and having human, material, financial, or informational resources at its disposal requires the practice of management.

Management in Profit-Seeking Organizations

Large Businesses Most of what we know about management comes from large profit-seeking organizations, because their survival has long depended on efficiency and effectiveness. Examples of large businesses include industrial firms (Tenneco Inc., British Petroleum Co. p.l.c., Toyota, Xerox Corp., Unilever, Levi Strauss), commercial banks (Citicorp; The Fuji Bank, Ltd.; Wells Fargo & Company; The Chase Manhattan Bank, N.A.), insurance companies (The Prudential Insurance Co. of America, State Farm, Metropolitan Life Insurance Co.), retailers (Sears, Roebuck and Co.; Safeway Stores, Inc.; Kmart Corp.), transportation companies (Delta Air Lines, Inc.; Consolidated Freightways, Inc.; Sohio Pipe Line Co.), utilities (Pacific Gas & Electric Co., Consolidated Edison Co. of New York), communication companies (CBS, The New York Times Company), and service organizations (Kelly Services, Inc.; Kinder-Care, Inc.; and Century 21 Real Estate Corporation).

Small and Start-Up Businesses Although many people associate management primarily with large businesses, effective management is also essential for small businesses, which play an important role in the country's economy. In fact, most of this nation's businesses are small. In some respects, effective management is more important in a small business than in a large one. A large firm such as Exxon Corporation or Monsanto can easily recover from losing several thousand dollars on an incorrect decision, whereas a small business may ill afford even a much smaller loss. Of course, it is also true that some small businesses become big ones. Compaq Computer Corporation, for example, was started by three men in 1982. By 1991 it had become the 157th largest business in the United States, with sales in excess of almost $3 billion.

International Management In recent years, the importance of international management has increased dramatically. The list of U.S. firms doing business in other countries is staggering. Exxon, for example, derives almost 75 percent of its revenues from foreign markets, and Ford Motor Co. derives more than one-third of its sales from foreign markets.[26] Other major U.S. exporters include General Motors Corp., General Electric, Boeing, and Caterpillar Inc. And even numbers like Ford's are deceptive. For example, the auto maker has large subsidiaries based in many European countries whose sales are not included as foreign revenue. Moreover, a number of major firms that do business in the United States have their headquarters in other countries. Firms in this category include the Royal Dutch/Shell Group (the Netherlands), Fiat S.p.A. (Italy), Nestlé SA (Switzerland), and Massey-Ferguson Inc. (Canada). International management is not, however, confined to profit-seeking organizations. There are several international sports federations (such as Little League Baseball); the federal government has branches (embassies) in most countries; and the Roman Catholic Church is established in most countries too. In some respects, the military was one of the first multinational organizations. International management is covered in depth in Chapter 4.

Management in Not-for-Profit Organizations

Intangible goals such as education, social services, public protection, and recreation are often the primary aim of not-for-profit organizations. Examples include the United Way, the U.S. Postal Service, Girl Scouts of the United States of America, the International Olympic Committee, art galleries, museums, and the Public Broadcasting System. Although these and similar organizations may not have to be profitable to attract investors, they must still employ sound management practices if they are to survive and work toward their goals.[27] And they must handle money in an efficient and effective way. If the United Way were to begin to spend large portions of its contributions on administration, contributors would lose confidence in the organization and make their charitable donations elsewhere.

Government Organizations   The management of government organizations and agencies is often regarded as a separate specialty: public administration. Government organizations include the Federal Trade Commission, the Environmental Protection Agency, the National Science Foundation, all branches of the military, state highway departments, federal and state prison systems, and other government units familiar to all of us. Tax dollars support government organizations, so politicians and citizens' groups are acutely sensitive to the need for efficiency and effectiveness.

Educational Organizations   Public and private schools, colleges, and universities all stand to benefit from the efficient use of resources. Taxpayer "revolts" in states such as California and Massachusetts have drastically cut back the tax money available for education, forcing administrators to make tough decisions about allocating remaining resources.

As chancellor of the New York City school system, Joe Fernandez faces a number of decisions daily. The wide variety of major problems—including a budget crisis, bureaucratic governing structure, and poverty-ridden student body—means that Fernandez must often make critical decisions under intense pressure. To cope with the situation, he is working twelve-hour days and overseeing many activities previously delegated to others.

Healthcare Facilities Managing healthcare facilities such as clinics, hospitals, and HMOs (health maintenance organizations) is now considered a separate field of management. Here, as in other organizations, scarce resources dictate an efficient and effective approach. In recent years many universities have established healthcare administration programs to train managers as specialists in this field.

Management in Nontraditional Settings Good management is also required in nontraditional settings to meet established goals. To one extent or another, management is practiced in religious organizations, terrorist groups, fraternities and sororities, organized crime, street gangs, neighborhood associations, and households. In short, as we note at the beginning of this chapter, management and managers have a profound influence on all of us.

SUMMARY OF KEY POINTS

Management is a set of activities (including planning and decision making, organizing, leading, and controlling) directed at an organization's resources (human, financial, physical, and information) with the aim of achieving organizational goals in an efficient and effective manner. A manager is someone whose primary responsibility is to carry out the management process within an organization.

The basic activities that comprise the management process are planning and decision making (determining courses of action), organizing (coordinating activities and resources), leading (managing people), and controlling (monitoring and evaluating activities). These activities are not performed on a systematic and predictable schedule.

Managers can be differentiated by level and by area. By level, we can identify top, middle, and first-line managers. Kinds of managers by area include marketing, financial, operations, human resource, administrative, and specialized managers. Most managers attain their skills and positions through a combination of education and experience.

Managers have ten basic roles to play: three interpersonal roles (figurehead, leader, and liaison), three informational roles (monitor, disseminator, and spokesperson), and four decisional roles (entrepreneur, disturbance handler, resource allocator, and negotiator). Effective managers also tend to have technical, interpersonal, conceptual, diagnostic, and analytic skills. Managers do many different activities, often at a relentless pace. They also receive a variety of intrinsic and extrinsic rewards.

Management processes are applicable in a wide variety of settings, including profit-seeking organizations (large, small, and start-up businesses and international businesses) and not-for-profit organizations (government organizations, educational organizations, healthcare facilities, and nontraditional organizations).

WELLS FARGO & COMPANY is a business with a strong sense of history. The company was established in San Francisco in 1852 to provide banking and express services. Wells Fargo ran the western leg of the Pony Express and also had an extensive stagecoach route system throughout the western United States. Indeed, the Wells Fargo wagon plays a familiar role in a number of Western movies and is even the title of a popular song from *The Music Man.*

The express services branch of the company was moved to New York in 1905 and nationalized by the U.S. government during World War I. After the war, Wells Fargo decided to concentrate solely on the banking business. Several mergers and acquisitions transformed the firm into a major banking operation. Today it is one of the largest banking-services companies in the United States. Wells Fargo generated more than $300 million in revenues in 1991.

Even though Wells Fargo is a modern and successful banking firm today, it has not forgotten its historic past. For example, the company maintains an extensive archival library of its old banking documents and records and even has a full-time corporate historian. New managers at the bank also take courses to learn about its past. This interest in history helps Wells Fargo maintain its culture and preserve its heritage. It has also had some bottom-line impact as well. For example, the bank was recently sued for $480 million for allegedly stealing an idea from a competitor about credit-card operations. Historical records, however, demonstrated conclusively that Wells Fargo managers had in fact developed the idea first.[1] ●

anagers at Wells Fargo clearly recognize the value of history. Like Wells Fargo, many other companies also appreciate the value of remembering their pasts.[2] For example, Polaroid Corp., Consolidated Edison Co. of New York, AT&T, and Navistar International Corp. have each sought to preserve information about their past and their heritage.[3] In addition, Lloyds of London, Honda Motor Co., Ltd., Nestlé SA, and Unilever also pay frequent homage to their historical roots.

This chapter provides an overview of the history and evolution of management thought so that you, too, can better appreciate the importance of history in today's business world. We set the stage by establishing the historical context of management. We then discuss the three traditional management perspectives—classical, behavioral, and quantitative. Next we describe the systems and contingency approaches to management theory as approaches that help integrate the three traditional perspectives. Finally, we discuss popular management theory and several contemporary management challenges.

THE ROLE OF THEORY AND HISTORY IN MANAGEMENT

This section demonstrates that knowledge of both theory and history is useful to the practicing manager. It goes on to establish the historical context of management and then identifies important precursors to management theory.

The Importance of Theory and History

Some people question the value of history and theory. Their arguments are usually based on the assumptions that history has no relevance to contemporary society and that theory is abstract and of no practical use. In reality, however, both theory and history are important to all managers today.

Why Theory?   A theory is simply a conceptual framework for organizing knowledge and providing a blueprint for action. Management theories, used to build organizations and guide them toward their goals, are grounded in reality.[4] Practically any organization that uses assembly lines (such as Emerson Electric Co., Black & Decker Corp., and Fiat S.p.A.) is drawing on what we describe later in this chapter as scientific management. Many organizations, including Kimberly-Clark Corporation, Borden, Inc., and Seiko use the behavioral perspective (also introduced later) to improve employee satisfaction and motivation. And it would be difficult to name a large company that does not use one or more techniques from the quantitative management perspective. For example, retailers like Safeway Stores, Inc., and Kmart Corp. routinely use management science formulas to determine how many check-out stands they need to have. In addition, most managers develop and refine their own theories of how they should run their organiza-

Management has been practiced for hundreds of years. For example, the historic sanctuary of Machu Picchu was built in Peru by Inca laborers in the 1400s. The large rectangular stones mesh together so tightly that even a knife blade cannot fit between them. Such a project would be an enormous undertaking today. It could have been completed by the Incas only after careful planning and with precise coordination.

tions and manage the behavior of their employees. For example, Andrew Grove, CEO of Intel Corp., has developed his own operating theory of organizations. The basis of his theory is that organizations need to become more agile and responsive to their environment. Grove is implementing his theory at Intel and transforming it into just such a company.[5] "Management in Practice" explains a new approach to developing management theory that some organizations are using.

Why History? As noted in the chapter introduction, awareness and understanding of important historical developments are also important to contemporary managers.[6] Understanding the historical context of management provides a sense of heritage and can help managers avoid the mistakes of others. Most courses in U.S. history devote time to business and economic developments in this country, including the Industrial Revolution, the early labor movement, and the Great Depression, and to such captains of U.S. industry as Cornelius Vanderbilt (railroads), John D. Rockefeller (oil), and Andrew Carnegie (steel). The contributions of those and other industrialists left a profound imprint on contemporary culture.[7] Many managers are also realizing that they can benefit from a greater understanding of history in general. For example, Ian M. Ross of AT&T Bell Laboratories cites *The Second World War* by Winston Churchill as a major influence on his approach to leadership. Other books often mentioned by managers for their relevance to today's business problems include such classics as Plato's *Republic,* Homer's *Iliad,* and Machiavelli's *The Prince.*[8]

The Historical Context of Management

Management thought has been shaped over a period of centuries by three major sets of forces. These social, economic, and political forces continue to affect management theory today.

social forces
The norms and values that characterize a culture

Understanding Social Forces **Social forces** are the norms and values that characterize a culture. In the early days of U.S. enterprise, owners generally managed their own companies. As businesses grew, however, professional managers were called in to run them, and organized labor took root. Workers in the larger organizations were often treated with disdain, and bitter strikes polarized management and labor. Vanderbilt proclaimed, "The public? The public be damned!" Such arrogance would hardly be tolerated today, but years ago it reflected the power and attitude of business in our society. The social contract between workers and the businesses they work for has changed dramatically over the years. At first, workers were paid only token wages and worked purely at the whim of their employer. Today's workers, however, have made great strides. Ideas of liberty and justice in the workplace are becoming increasingly common, workers are protected by a variety of federal laws, and organizations themselves are becoming increasingly sensitive to the needs and values of workers.[9] Changes in these and other social forces have played a major role in shaping management theories in such areas as motivation, leadership, and human resource management.

economic forces
Forces associated with economic systems and general economic conditions and trends

Understanding Economic Forces In similar fashion, **economic forces,** or forces associated with economic systems and general economic conditions and trends, have also shaped management theory. The United States has a market economy based on the principles of private ownership of property, economic freedom, competitive markets, and a limited role for government. Most major industrial countries use similar systems. In such systems the availability of resources, the ease of acquiring those resources, and the kinds of goods and services wanted by consumers all play a role in dictating what management can do. General economic trends and the nature of the competition also greatly affect organizations. Increased global competition in recent years has also played a role. Within contemporary management theory, economic forces have affected thinking in a variety of areas, including environment analysis, strategic planning, and organization design.[10]

political forces
Governing institutions and general governmental policies and attitudes toward business

Understanding Political Forces **Political forces** are governing institutions and general governmental policies and attitudes toward business. They influence management theory in both general and specific ways. General government policies toward the regulation of business play an important role in how organizations choose to manage themselves. Management theory regarding companies in highly regulated industries like utilities, for example, varies considerably from parallel theories regarding companies like Sears, Roebuck and Co. in less regulated industries such as retailing. In a more specific case, legal judgments like those handed down against Exxon Corporation (for the *Valdez* oil spill) and Texaco Inc. (for interfering in a previously announced merger between Getty Petroleum Corp. and

CONTRIBUTIONS FROM OUTSIDE THE DISCIPLINE

 There are theorists who devote their lives to the study of management and organizational behavior, and the scholarly journals in the field are full of fresh ideas and theories about how best to work with and manage people in organizations. Yet frequently the most radical changes within the field of management result from the contributions of people from outside the discipline. Free of the traditions and assumptions that underlie much of managerial theory, outsiders can sometimes challenge those assumptions and champion valuable new approaches to management.

Anthropologists, for instance, are often stereotyped as feeling more at home studying exotic cultures than in a U.S. business, yet they are taking jobs in the private sector in record numbers. According to the director of Xerox Corp.'s Palo Alto Research Center, they can provide "dramatic improvements in productivity."* Anthropologists can learn things about a corporation's culture that people who have been working in that culture for decades may overlook. Anthropologist Julian Orr, for instance, set out to discover how Xerox could improve its long and expensive training program for service technicians. After taking the training himself and going out on service calls, Orr found that service technicians spend much of their time not repairing machines but teaching confused customers how to use them. That insight should allow Xerox to improve its training and help service technicians more often fill their customers' needs.

Philosophers, too, have proven that their discipline can contribute to corporations' financial health. One philosophy Ph.D. who works for an economic consulting firm uses his background in logic for such practical purposes as convincing a bankruptcy court that a company had misrepresented the causes of its bankruptcy.

On a larger scale, the very basis of most U.S. businesses—the pursuit of profit—has been challenged by thinkers from disciplines as diverse as quantum physics, cybernetics, and religion. Although their approaches vary widely, those calling for a "new paradigm" of U.S. organizations—a radical shift in why and how they operate—generally agree that organizations of the future must focus on people and take a systems view, acknowledging the interconnectedness of all aspects of the environment. With business markets and environments changing so rapidly, no one can afford to ignore a serious visionary from any discipline who has a prescription for how to better manage change and the organization of the future.

*John Seely Brown, quoted in Christina Elnora Garza, "Studying the Natives on the Shop Floor," *Business Week,* September 30, 1991, p. 74.

References: Christina Elnora Garza, "Studying the Natives on the Shop Floor," *Business Week,* September 30, 1991, pp. 74–78; John Huey, "Nothing's Impossible," *Fortune,* September 23, 1991, pp. 134–140; Dana Milbank, "Some Manage; Some Muse; Some Do Both," *The Wall Street Journal,* April 4, 1991, pp. B1, B6; Frank Rose, "A New Age for Business?" *Fortune,* October 8, 1990, pp. 156–164.

Pennzoil) have major implications for the management of other organizations. Both general and specific political forces affect management theory in areas like environmental analysis, planning, organization design, employee rights, and control.

Precursors to Management Theory

Even though large businesses have been around for only a few hundred years, management has been practiced for thousands of years. In this section, we describe management in antiquity and identify important early management pioneers.

F I G U R E   2 . 1 Management in Antiquity

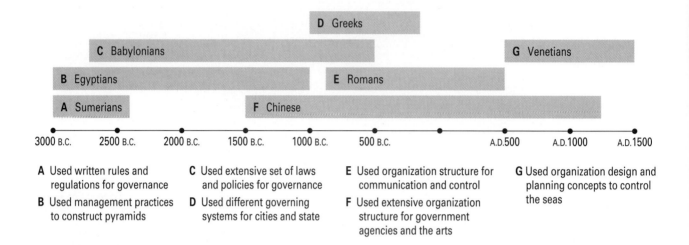

A Used written rules and regulations for governance	**C** Used extensive set of laws and policies for governance	**E** Used organization structure for communication and control
B Used management practices to construct pyramids	**D** Used different governing systems for cities and state	**F** Used extensive organization structure for government agencies and the arts

G Used organization design and planning concepts to control the seas

---

Management has been practiced for thousands of years. For example, the ancient Babylonians used management in governing their empire and the ancient Romans used management to facilitate communication and control throughout their far-flung territories. The Egyptians used planning and controlling techniques in the construction of their pyramids.

Management in Antiquity   The practice of management can be traced back thousands of years. The Egyptians applied the management functions of planning, organizing, and controlling when they constructed the great pyramids. Alexander the Great employed a staff organization to coordinate activities during his military campaigns. The Roman Empire developed a well-defined organizational structure that greatly facilitated communication and control. Management practices and concepts were discussed by Socrates in 400 B.C.; Plato described job specialization in 350 B.C.; and Alfarabi listed several leadership traits in A.D. 900.[11] Figure 2.1 is a simple time line showing these and other important management breakthroughs and practices. The Global View provides some additional insights into historical approaches to management in Japan.

In spite of this history, however, management was not given serious attention for several centuries. One reason for this was that the first discipline devoted to commerce was economics. Economists generally assumed that managerial practice was efficient and therefore focused their attention on national economic policies and other nonmanagerial aspects of business. Another reason is that there were very few large organizations until the late 1800s. When family businesses first emerged, their goal was not growth or expansion but survival. If a family could produce and sell enough to sustain itself, nothing else was needed. Finally, even though management was practiced during earliest recorded history, the focus even then was not on efficiency. These early organizations were governmental, with unlimited powers of taxation and little accountability for waste.

Early Management Pioneers   The serious study of management did not begin to develop until the nineteenth century. Robert Owen (1771–1858), a British industrialist and reformer, was one of the first managers to recognize the importance of an organization's human resources. Until his era, factory workers were generally viewed in much the same way that machin-

THE ORIGINS OF FAR EASTERN MANAGEMENT

 During the 1980s, Korea, Taiwan, Hong Kong, and Singapore joined Japan as major sources for both products and managerial ideas imported into the United States. Businesspeople in the West have watched in amazement as these "Five Dragons" have come to dominate industry after industry. At first, some Western companies tried to match their Far Eastern rivals' successes by importing such elements of Asian management as quality circles or managerial training camps. But slowly Western managers have been learning that the secret of the success of the Five Dragons lies not in a particular technique but in an entire philosophy with both ancient and modern roots.

Some aspects of Far Eastern management can be traced back to Confucius [Kong Fu Ze], a Chinese civil servant who lived around 500 B.C. Confucius's wisdom won him many disciples who recorded and studied his teachings, keeping them alive. Confucianism has four basic teachings: (1) unequal relationships between people are normal and required for a stable society; (2) the family is the model for all organizations; (3) people should treat others as they would like to be treated; and (4) people should educate themselves, work hard, and not spend more than necessary.

Ironically, some of the more modern elements of Far Eastern management originated in the United States. One key individual who traveled to Japan after World War II to help rebuild the Japanese economy was U.S. statistician, Dr. W. Edwards Deming. Deming preached a new approach to management based on the statistical insights of another U.S. citizen, Walter Shewhart. Deming convinced the Japanese businesspeople to focus on continuously improving their operations by identifying and eliminating waste in every aspect of their work. Although Western companies have only recently begun to heed Deming's work, his ideas have been so influential in the Far East that the highest honor a Japanese company can earn is the Deming Prize, named in his honor.

Western businesses have learned that they cannot get ahead by simply copying techniques that seem to work for the Five Dragons. But perhaps by learning how Far Eastern managers have combined old and new teachings, Western managers can start catching up.

References: William E. Conway, *The Quality Secret: The Right Way to Manage* (Nashua, N.H.: Conway Quality Inc., 1991); David D. Van Fleet and Ricky W. Griffin, "Quality Circles: A Review and Suggested Further Directions," in Cary L. Cooper and Ivan Robertson, eds., *1989 International Review of Industrial & Organizational Psychology* (London: Wiley, 1989), pp. 213–233; Geert Hofstede and Michael Harris Bond, "The Confucius Connection: From Cultural Roots to Economic Growth," *Organizational Dynamics*, Summer 1988, pp. 5–21.

ery and equipment were. A factory owner himself, Owen believed that workers deserved respect and dignity. He implemented better working conditions, a higher minimum working age for children, meals for employees, and reduced work hours. He assumed that giving more attention to workers would pay off in increased output. Although no one followed his lead at the time, his ideas were later developed in the behavioral management perspective.

Whereas Owen was primarily interested in employee welfare, Charles Babbage (1792–1871), an English mathematician, focused his attention on efficiencies of production. His primary contribution was his book, *On the Economy of Machinery and Manufactures.*[12] Babbage placed great faith in division of labor and advocated the application of mathematics to such problems as the efficient use of facilities and materials. In a sense, his work was a forerunner to both the classical and quantitative management perspectives.

Frederick W. Taylor was a pioneer in the field of labor efficiency. He introduced numerous innovations in how jobs were designed and how workers were trained to perform them. These innovations resulted in higher quality products and improved employee morale. Taylor also formulated the basic ideas of scientific management.

● **classical perspective**
Consists of two distinct branches—scientific management and administrative management

● **scientific management**
An approach to management concerned with improving the performance of individual workers

soldiering
Employees deliberately working at a pace slower than their capabilities

Nor did he overlook the human element. He understood that a harmonious relationship between management and labor could serve to benefit both, and he favored such devices as profit-sharing plans. In many ways, Babbage was an originator of modern management theory and practice.

In addition to these visionaries, a few other early pioneers deserve mention. Andrew Ure was one of the world's first professors to teach management principles, in the early seventeenth century at Anderson's College in Glasgow. Charles Dupin soon followed suit in France. Daniel McCallum developed several basic principles of management and published one of the first organization charts. In the late nineteenth century, Henry Poor wrote extensively about management inefficiencies in the railroad industry.[13]

THE CLASSICAL PERSPECTIVE

The **classical perspective** on management emerged during the early years of this century. These ideas represent the first well-developed framework of management. Their emergence was a natural outgrowth of both the pioneering earlier works just noted and the evolution of large-scale business and management practices. The classical management perspective includes two different approaches to management: scientific management and administrative management.

Scientific Management

Productivity emerged as a serious business problem during the first few years of this century. Business was expanding and capital was readily available, but labor was in short supply. Hence, managers began to search for ways to use existing labor more efficiently. In response to this need, experts began to focus on ways to improve the performance of individual workers. Their work led to the development of **scientific management.** Some of the earliest advocates of scientific management included Frederick W. Taylor (1856–1915), Frank Gilbreth (1868–1924), Lillian Gilbreth (1878–1972), Henry Gantt (1861–1919), and Harrington Emerson (1853–1931).[14] Taylor played the dominant role.

One of Taylor's first jobs was as a foreman at the Midvale Steel Company in Philadelphia. At Midvale he observed what he called **soldiering**— employees deliberately working at a pace slower than their capabilities. Taylor studied and timed each element of the steelworkers' jobs. He determined what each worker should be producing, and then he designed the most efficient way of doing each part of the overall task. Next he implemented a piecework pay system. Rather than paying all employees the same wage, he began increasing the pay of each worker who met and exceeded the target level of output set for his or her job.

After Taylor left Midvale, he worked as a consultant for several companies, including Simonds Rolling Machine Company and Bethlehem Steel. At Simonds he studied and redesigned jobs, introduced rest periods to reduce fatigue, and implemented a piecework pay system. The results were higher quality and quantity of output and improved morale. At Bethlehem Steel, Taylor studied efficient ways of loading and unloading rail cars and

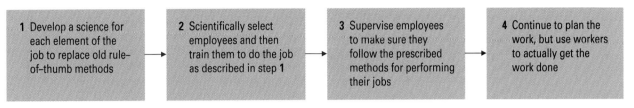

| **1** Develop a science for each element of the job to replace old rule-of-thumb methods | → | **2** Scientifically select employees and then train them to do the job as described in step **1** | → | **3** Supervise employees to make sure they follow the prescribed methods for performing their jobs | → | **4** Continue to plan the work, but use workers to actually get the work done |

applied his conclusions with equally impressive results. During these experiences, he formulated the basic ideas that he called scientific management. Figure 2.2 illustrates the basic steps Taylor suggested. He believed that managers who followed his guidelines would improve the efficiency of their workers.[15]

Taylor's work had a major impact on U.S. industry. By applying his principles, many organizations achieved major gains in efficiency. He was not without his detractors, however. Labor argued that scientific management was just a device to get more work from each employee and to reduce the total number of workers needed by a firm. There was a congressional investigation into Taylor's ideas, and evidence suggests that he falsified some of his findings.[16] Nevertheless, Taylor left a lasting imprint on society.[17]

Frank and Lillian Gilbreth, contemporaries of Taylor, were a husband-and-wife team of industrial engineers. One of Frank Gilbreth's most interesting contributions was to the craft of bricklaying. After studying bricklayers at work, he developed several procedures for doing the job more efficiently. For example, he specified standard materials and techniques, including the positioning of the bricklayer, the bricks, and the mortar at different levels. The results of these changes were a reduction from eighteen separate physical movements to five and an increase in output of about 200 percent. Lillian Gilbreth made equally important contributions to several different areas of work, helped shape the field of industrial psychology, and made substantive contributions to the field of personnel management. Working individually and together, the Gilbreths developed numerous techniques and strategies for eliminating inefficiency. They applied many of their ideas to their family. Their experiences in raising twelve children are documented in a book and movie called *Cheaper by the Dozen*.

Henry Gantt, another contributor to scientific management, was an associate of Taylor at Midvale, Simonds, and Bethlehem Steel. Later, working alone, he developed other techniques for improving worker output. One, called the Gantt chart, is still used today. A Gantt chart is essentially a means of scheduling work and can be generated for each worker or for a complex project as a whole. Gantt also refined Taylor's ideas about piecework pay systems.

Like Taylor, the Gilbreths, and Gantt, Harrington Emerson was also a management consultant. He made quite a stir in 1910 when he appeared before the Interstate Commerce Commission to testify about a rate increase requested by the railroads. As an expert witness, Emerson asserted that the railroads could save $1 million a day by using scientific management. He was also a strong advocate of specialized management roles in organizations.

Frederick Taylor developed this system of scientific management which he believed would lead to a more efficient and productive work force. Bethlehem Steel was among the first organizations to profit from scientific management and still practices some parts of it today.

Administrative Management

administrative management
An approach to management that focuses on managing the total organization

Whereas scientific management deals with the jobs of individual employees, **administrative management** focuses on managing the total organization. The primary contributors to administrative management were Henri Fayol (1841–1925), Lyndall Urwick (1891–1983), Max Weber (1864–1920), and Chester Barnard (1886–1961).

Henri Fayol was administrative management's most articulate spokesperson. A French industrialist, Fayol was unknown to American managers and scholars until his most important work, *General and Industrial Management,* was translated into English in 1930.[18] Drawing on his own managerial experience, he attempted to systematize the practice of management to provide guidance and direction to other managers. Part of his thinking was expressed in fourteen principles for effective management. These principles are listed in Table 2.1. Fayol also was the first to identify the specific managerial functions of planning, organizing, leading, and controlling. He believed that these functions accurately reflect the core of the management process. Most contemporary management books (including this one) still use this framework, and most practicing managers are familiar with this description of their jobs.

After a career as a British army officer, Lyndall Urwick became a noted management theorist and consultant. He integrated scientific management with the work of Fayol and other administrative management theorists. He also advanced modern thinking about the functions of planning, organizing, and controlling. Like Fayol, he developed a list of guidelines for improving managerial effectiveness. Urwick is noted not so much for his own contributions as for his synthesis and integration of the work of others.

Although Max Weber lived and worked at the same time as Fayol and Taylor, his contributions were not recognized until some years had passed. Weber was a German sociologist, and his most important work was not translated into English until 1947.[19] Weber's work on bureaucracy laid the foundation for contemporary organization theory, discussed in detail in Chapter 11. The concept of bureaucracy, as we discuss later, is based on a rational set of guidelines for structuring organizations in the most efficient manner.

Chester Barnard, former president of New Jersey Bell Telephone Co., made notable contributions to management in his book *The Functions of the Executive.*[20] The book proposes a major theory about the acceptance of authority. The theory holds that subordinates weigh the legitimacy of a supervisor's directives and then decide whether to accept them. An order is accepted if the subordinate understands it, is able to comply with it, and views it as appropriate. The importance of Barnard's work is enhanced by his experience as a top manager.

Contributions and Limitations of the Classical Perspective

The contributions and limitations of the classical management perspective are summarized in Table 2.2. The classical perspective is the framework from which later theories evolved, and many of its insights still hold true today. Also, these theorists were the first to focus attention on management

T A B L E 2 . 1	Fayol's Principles of Effective Management Practice
Division of labor	A high degree of specialization should result in efficiency. Both managerial and technical work are amenable to specialization.
Authority	Authority is needed to carry out managerial responsibilities: the formal authority to command and personal authority deriving from intelligence and experience.
Discipline	People in the organization must respect the rules that govern the organization.
Unity of command	Each subordinate should report to one and only one superior.
Unity of direction	Similar activities in an organization should be grouped together under one manager.
Subordination of individuals to the common good	Interests of individuals should not be placed before the goals of the overall organization.
Remuneration	Compensation should be fair both to employees and to the organization.
Centralization	Power and authority should be concentrated at the upper levels of the organization as much as possible.
Scalar chain	A chain of authority should extend from the top to the bottom of the organization and should be followed at all times.
Order	Human and material resources should be coordinated so that they are in the required place at the required time.
Equity	Managers should be kind and fair when dealing with subordinates.
Stability	High turnover of employees should be avoided.
Initiative	Subordinates should have the freedom to take initiative.
Esprit de corps	Teamwork, team spirit, and a sense of unity and togetherness should be fostered and maintained.

Henri Fayol, a French industrialist, summarized the practice of management with fourteen principles.

Source: From Henri Fayol, *General and Industrial Management*, Revised Edition. Copyright © 1984 by Lake Publishing Company.

TABLE 2.2   The Classical Perspective

General Summary	The classical perspective had two primary thrusts. Scientific management focused on employees within organizations and on ways to improve their productivity. Noted pioneers of scientific management were Frederick Taylor, Frank and Lillian Gilbreth, Henry Gantt, and Harrington Emerson. Administrative management focused on the total organization and on ways to make it more efficient and effective. Prominent administrative management theorists were Henri Fayol, Lyndall Urwick, Max Weber, and Chester Barnard.
Period of Greatest Interest	1895 to mid-1930s; renewed interest in recent years as a means of cutting costs and increasing productivity.
Contributions	Laid the foundation for later developments in management theory. Identified key management processes, functions, and skills that are still recognized as such today. Focused attention on management as a valid subject of scientific inquiry.
Limitations	More appropriate for stable and simple organizations than for today's dynamic and complex organizations. Often prescribed universal procedures that are not appropriate in some settings. Even though some writers (such as Lillian Gilbreth and Chester Barnard) were concerned with the human element, many viewed employees as tools rather than resources.

as a meaningful field of study. Several aspects of the classical perspective are important to our later discussions of planning, organizing, and controlling.

The limitations of the classical perspective, however, should not be overlooked. The theory dealt with stable, simple organizations; many organizations today, in contrast, are changing and complex. It proposed universal guidelines that do not fit every organization. A third limitation of classical management theory is that it slighted the role of the individual in organizations. This role was much more fully developed by the behavioral perspective.

THE BEHAVIORAL PERSPECTIVE

Early advocates of the classical perspective essentially viewed organizations and jobs from a mechanistic point of view: that is, they characterized organizations as machines and workers as cogs within those machines. Even though most classical theorists recognized the role of individuals, they focused on controlling and standardizing the behavior of those individuals. In contrast, the **behavioral perspective** placed much more emphasis on individual attitudes and behaviors and on group processes and recognized the importance of behavioral processes in the workplace.

The behavioral perspective was stimulated by a number of writers and theoretical movements. One of those movements was industrial psychology, the practice of applying psychological concepts to industrial settings. Hugo Munsterberg (1863–1916), a noted German psychologist, is recognized as the father of industrial psychology. He established a psychological laboratory at Harvard in 1892, and his pioneering book *Psychology and Industrial Efficiency* was translated into English in 1913.[21] Munsterberg suggested that psychologists could make valuable contributions to managers in the areas of employee selection and motivation. Industrial psychology is still a major course of study at many colleges and universities.

Another early advocate of the behavioral approach to management was Mary Parker Follett.[22] Follett worked during the scientific management era, but she also anticipated the behavioral perspective and appreciated the need to understand the role of behavior in organizations. Her specific interests were in adult education and vocational guidance. She believed that organizations should become more democratic in accommodating employees and managers.

The Hawthorne Studies

Munsterberg and Follett made major contributions to the development of the behavioral approach to management, but its primary catalyst was a series of studies conducted near Chicago at Western Electric's Hawthorne plant between 1927 and 1932. The research, originally sponsored by General Electric Co., was conducted by Elton Mayo and his associates.[23] Mayo was a faculty member and consultant at Harvard. The first study involved manipulating illumination for one group of workers and comparing their subsequent productivity with the productivity of another group whose illumination was not changed. Surprisingly, when illumination was increased for the experimental group, productivity went up in both groups. Productivity continued to increase in both groups, even when the lighting for the experimental group was decreased. Not until the lighting was reduced to the level of moonlight did productivity begin to decline (and General Electric withdrew its sponsorship).

Another experiment established a piecework incentive pay plan for a group of nine men assembling terminal banks for telephone exchanges. According to earlier theories, each man would try to maximize his pay by producing as many units as possible. Mayo and his associates, however, found that the group itself informally established an acceptable level of output for its members. Workers who overproduced were branded ''rate busters,'' and underproducers were labeled ''chiselers.'' To be accepted by the group, workers produced at the accepted level. As they approached this level, workers slacked off to avoid overproducing.

Other studies, including an interview program involving several thousand workers, led Mayo and his associates to conclude that human behavior

The Hawthorne studies were a series of early experiments that focused on behavior in the workplace. In one experiment involving this group of workers, for example, researchers monitored how productivity changed as result of changes in working conditions. The Hawthorne studies and subsequent experiments led scientists to the conclusion that the human element is very important in the workplace.

was much more important in the workplace than had been previously believed. In the lighting experiment, for example, the results were attributed to the fact that both groups received special attention and sympathetic supervision for perhaps the first time. The incentive pay plans did not work because wage incentives were less important than social acceptance in determining output. In short, individual and social processes played a major role in shaping worker attitudes and behavior.[24]

The Human Relations Movement

human relations movement
An approach to management that argued that workers respond primarily to the social context of the workplace

The **human relations movement,** which grew from the Hawthorne studies and was a popular approach to management for many years, proposed that workers respond primarily to the social context of the workplace, including social conditioning, group norms, and interpersonal dynamics. A basic assumption of the human relations movement was that the manager's concern for workers would lead to increased satisfaction, which would, in turn, result in improved performance.[25] Two writers who helped advance the human relations movement were Abraham Maslow and Douglas McGregor.

In 1943, Maslow advanced a theory suggesting that people are motivated by a hierarchy of needs, including monetary incentives and social acceptance.[26] Maslow's hierarchy, perhaps the best known human relations theory, is described in detail in Chapter 14. Meanwhile, Douglas McGregor's Theory X and Theory Y model best represents the essence of the human relations movement (see Table 2.3).[27] According to McGregor, Theory X and Theory Y reflect two extreme belief sets that different managers have about their workers. **Theory X** is a relatively negative view of workers and is consistent with the views of scientific management. **Theory Y** is more positive and represents the assumptions that human relations advocates make. In McGregor's view, Theory Y was a more appropriate philosophy for managers to adhere to. Both Maslow and McGregor notably influenced the thinking of many practicing managers.

Theory X
A pessimistic and negative view of workers that is consistent with the views of scientific management

Theory Y
A positive view of workers that represents the assumptions that human relations advocates make

TABLE 2.3	Theory X and Theory Y	
Theory X Assumptions	1. People do not like work and try to avoid it. 2. People do not like work, so managers have to control, direct, coerce, and threaten employees to get them to work toward organizational goals. 3. People prefer to be directed, to avoid responsibility, to want security; they have little ambition.	Douglas McGregor developed Theory X and Theory Y. He argued that Theory X best represented the views of scientific management, while Theory Y represented the human relations approach. He believed Theory Y was the best philosophy for all managers.
Theory Y Assumptions	1. People do not naturally dislike work; work is a natural part of their lives. 2. People are internally motivated to reach objectives to which they are committed. 3. People are committed to goals to the degree that they receive personal rewards when they reach their objectives. 4. People will both seek and accept responsibility under favorable conditions. 5. People have the capacity to be innovative in solving organizational problems. 6. People are bright, but under most organizational conditions their potentials are underutilized.	

Source: Douglas McGregor, *The Human Side of Enterprise* (New York: McGraw-Hill, 1960), pp. 33–34, 47–48. Used with permission of the publisher.

The Emergence of Organizational Behavior

Munsterberg, Mayo, Maslow, McGregor, and others have made valuable contributions to management. Contemporary theorists, however, have noted that many assertions of the human relationists were simplistic and inadequate descriptions of work behavior. For example, the assumption that worker satisfaction leads to improved performance has been shown to have little, if any, validity.[28] If anything, satisfaction follows good performance rather than precedes it. (These issues are addressed in Chapter 14.)

Current behavioral perspectives on management, known as **organizational behavior,** acknowledge that behavior is much more complex than the human relationists realized. The field of organizational behavior draws from a broad, interdisciplinary base of psychology, sociology, anthropology, economics, and medicine. Organizational behavior takes a holistic view of behavior and addresses individual, group, and organization processes.[29] These processes are significant elements in contemporary management theory. Important topics in this field include job satisfaction, stress, motivation, leadership, group dynamics, organizational politics, interpersonal conflict, and the structure and design of organizations.[30] A contingency orientation also characterizes the field (discussed later in this chapter). Our discussions of organizing (Chapters 10–13) and leading (Chapters 14–17) are heavily influenced by organizational behavior.

organizational behavior
A contemporary behavioral perspective on management that takes a holistic view of behavior by addressing individual, group, and organization processes

TABLE 2.4   The Behavioral Perspective

General Summary	The behavioral perspective focuses on employee behavior in an organizational context. Stimulated by the birth of industrial psychology, the human relations movement supplanted scientific management as the dominant approach to management in the 1930s and 1940s. Prominent contributors to this movement were Elton Mayo, Abraham Maslow, and Douglas McGregor. Organizational behavior, the contemporary outgrowth of the behavioral perspective, draws from an interdisciplinary base and recognizes the complexities of human behavior in organizational settings.
Period of Greatest Interest	Human relations enjoyed its peak of acceptance from 1931 to the late 1940s. Organizational behavior emerged in the late 1950s and is presently of great interest to researchers and managers.
Contributions	Provided important insights into motivation, group dynamics, and other interpersonal processes in organizations. Focused managerial attention on these same processes. Challenged the view that employees are tools and furthered the belief that employees are valuable resources.
Limitations	The complexity of individual behavior makes prediction of that behavior difficult. Many behavioral concepts have not yet been put to use because some managers are reluctant to adopt them. Contemporary research findings by behavioral scientists are often not communicated to practicing managers in an understandable form.

Contributions and Limitations of the Behavioral Perspective

Table 2.4 summarizes the behavioral perspective and lists its contributions and limitations. The primary contributions relate to ways in which this approach has changed managerial thinking. Managers are now more likely to recognize the importance of behavioral processes and to view employees as valuable resources rather than as mere tools. On the other hand, organizational behavior is still very imprecise in its ability to predict behavior. It is not always accepted or understood by practicing managers. Hence, the contributions of the behavioral school have yet to be fully realized.

THE QUANTITATIVE PERSPECTIVE

Of the three major schools of management thought, the quantitative perspective is the newest. The classical approach was born in the early years of this century, and the behavioral approach began to emerge in the 1920s and 1930s. The **quantitative perspective** was not fully developed until World War II. During the war, managers, government officials, and scientists were brought together in England and the United States to help the military deploy its resources more efficiently and effectively. Led by experts like Professor P.M.S. Blackett, these groups took some of the mathematical approaches to management developed decades earlier by Taylor and Gantt and applied them to logistical problems during the war.[31] Decisions regarding troop, equipment, and submarine deployment were all solvable through mathematical analysis.

After the war, consulting firms like Arthur D. Little, Inc., and industrial firms such as E.I. du Pont de Nemours & Co. and General Electric began to use the same techniques for deploying employees, choosing plant locations, and planning warehouses. Basically, then, this perspective is concerned with applying quantitative techniques to management. More specifically, quantitative management focuses on decision making, economic effectiveness, mathematical models, and the use of computers. There are two branches of the quantitative approach: management science and operations management.

● **quantitative perspective**
An approach to management in which quantitative techniques are applied to management

Management Science

Unfortunately, the term *management science* sounds very much like *scientific management,* the approach developed by Taylor and others early in this century. But the two have little in common and should not be confused. **Management science** focuses specifically on the development of mathematical models. A mathematical model is a simplified representation of a system, process, or relationship.

In its early years, management science focused specifically on models, equations, and similar representations of reality. For example, managers at Detroit Edison used mathematical models to determine how best to route repair crews during blackouts. The Bank of New England Corp. used other models to figure out how many tellers needed to be on duty at each location at various times throughout the day. In recent years, paralleling the advent of the personal computer, management science techniques have become more sophisticated. For example, automobile manufacturers like Daimler-Benz AG and Chrysler Corp. are able to use realistic computer simulations to study collision damage to cars. This gives them more precise information and avoids the costs of "crashing" so many real test cars.[32]

management science
An approach to management that focuses specifically on the development of mathematical models

Operations Management

Operations management is somewhat less mathematical and statistically sophisticated than management science and can be applied more directly to managerial situations. Indeed, we can think of **operations management** as a form of applied management science. Operations management techniques are generally concerned with helping the organization produce its

operations management
Techniques that are concerned with helping the organization more efficiently produce its products or services

products or services more efficiently and can be applied to a wide range of problems.[33]

For example, Rubbermaid Incorporated and The Home Depot, Inc., use operations management techniques to manage their inventories. (Inventory management is concerned with specific inventory problems such as balancing carrying costs and ordering costs and determining the optimal order quantity.) Linear programming (which involves computing simultaneous solutions to a set of linear equations) helps United Air Lines, Inc., plan its flight schedules, Consolidated Freightways, Inc., develop its shipping routes, and General Instrument Corp. plan what instruments to produce at various times. Other operations management techniques include queuing theory, breakeven analysis, and simulation. All of these techniques and procedures apply directly to operations, but they are also helpful in such areas as finance, marketing, and human resource management. We discuss their uses more fully in Chapter 19.

Contributions and Limitations of the Quantitative Perspective

Like the other management perspectives, the quantitative perspective has made important contributions and has certain limitations. Both are summarized in Table 2.5. It has provided managers with an abundance of decision-

TABLE 2.5	The Quantitative Perspective
General Summary	The quantitative perspective focuses on applying mathematical models and processes to management situations. Management science specifically deals with the development of mathematical models to aid in decision making and problem solving. Operations management focuses more directly on the application of management science to organizations. Management information systems are systems developed to provide information to managers.
Period of Greatest Interest	1940s to present.
Contributions	Developed sophisticated quantitative techniques to assist in decision making. Application of models has increased our awareness and understanding of complex organizational processes and situations. Has been very useful in the planning and controlling processes.
Limitations	Cannot fully explain or predict the behavior of people in organizations. Mathematical sophistication may come at the expense of other important skills. Models may require unrealistic or unfounded assumptions.

making tools and techniques and has increased understanding of overall organizational processes. It has been particularly useful in the areas of planning and controlling. On the other hand, mathematical models cannot fully account for individual behaviors and attitudes. Some believe that the time needed to develop competence in quantitative techniques retards the development of other managerial skills. Finally, mathematical models typically require a set of assumptions that may not be realistic.

INTEGRATING PERSPECTIVES

It is important to recognize that the classical, behavioral, and quantitative approaches to management are not necessarily contradictory or mutually exclusive. Even though very different assumptions and predictions are made by each of the three perspectives, each also complements the other. Indeed, a complete understanding of management requires an appreciation of all three perspectives. The systems and contingency perspectives can help us integrate the earlier approaches and can enlarge our understanding of all three.

The Systems Perspective

We briefly introduced the systems perspective in Chapter 1 in our definition of management. A **system** is an interrelated set of elements functioning as a whole.[34] As shown in Figure 2.3, by viewing an organization as a system, we can identify four basic elements: inputs, transformation processes, outputs, and feedback. First, inputs are the material, human, financial, and information resources the organization gets from its environment. Next, through technological and managerial processes, these are transformed into outputs. Outputs include products, services, or both (tangible and intangible); profits, losses, or both (even not-for-profit organizations must operate within their budgets); employee behaviors; and information. Finally, the environment reacts to these outputs and provides feedback to the system.

Thinking of organizations as systems provides us with a variety of important viewpoints on organizations. These include the concepts of open sys-

● **system**
An interrelated set of elements functioning as a whole

FIGURE 2.3 The Systems Perspective of Organizations

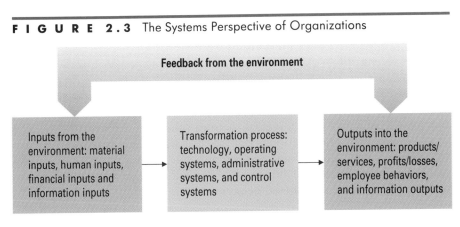

Feedback from the environment

Inputs from the environment: material inputs, human inputs, financial inputs and information inputs

Transformation process: technology, operating systems, administrative systems, and control systems

Outputs into the environment: products/services, profits/losses, employee behaviors, and information outputs

By viewing organizations as systems, managers can better understand the importance of their environment and the level of interdependence among subsystems within the organization. They must also understand how their decisions affect and are affected by other subsystems within the organization.

open systems
Systems that interact with their environment

tems, subsystems, synergy, and entropy. **Open systems** are systems that interact with their environment. All organizations are open systems but sometimes make the mistake of ignoring their environment. The big U.S. auto companies made this mistake when they essentially ignored their Japanese competitors for several years. By the time General Motors Corp., Ford Motor Co., and Chrysler recognized that consumers would indeed buy high-mileage, high-quality cars even if the nameplate said Nissan or Toyota, it was almost too late to take effective action in response to their foreign competitors.

subsystems
Systems within a broader system

The systems perspective also stresses the importance of **subsystems**—systems within a broader system. For example, the marketing, production, and finance functions within Mattel Inc. are systems in their own right but are also subsystems within the overall organization. Because they are interdependent, a change in one subsystem can affect other subsystems as well. If the production department at Mattel lowers the quality of the toys being made (by buying lower-quality materials, for example), the effects are felt in finance (improved cash flow in the short run owing to lower costs) and marketing (decreased sales in the long run because of customer dissatisfaction). Managers must therefore remember that although organizational subsystems can be managed with some degree of autonomy, their interdependence should not be overlooked.

synergy
Two subsystems working together produce more than the total of what they might produce if working alone

Synergy suggests that organizational units (or subsystems) may often be more successful working together than working alone. American Express Company, for example, has been quite successful at cross-selling among its life-insurance, credit-card, stock-brokerage, and financial-planning divisions.[35] In Europe today, banks and insurance companies are linking up in an effort to market a wide array of financial products that each would have trouble selling on its own.[36] Synergy is an important concept for managers because it emphasizes the importance of working together in a cooperative and coordinated fashion.

entropy
A normal process leading to system decline

Finally, **entropy** is a normal process that leads to system decline. When an organization does not monitor feedback from its environment and make appropriate adjustments, it may fail. For example, witness the problems of Studebaker, W. T. Grant, and Penn Central Railroad. Each of these organizations went bankrupt because it failed to revitalize itself and keep pace with changes in its environment. A primary objective of management, from a systems perspective, is to continually re-energize the organization to avoid entropy.

The Contingency Perspective

universal perspective
An attempt to identify the one best way to manage organizations

● **contingency perspective**
An approach to management that suggests that appropriate managerial behavior in a given situation depends on, or is contingent on, a wide variety of elements

Another recent noteworthy addition to management thinking is the contingency perspective. The classical, behavioral, and quantitative approaches are considered **universal perspectives** because they tried to identify the "one best way" to manage organizations. The **contingency perspective,** in contrast, suggests that universal theories cannot be applied to organizations because each organization is unique. Instead, the contingency perspective suggests that appropriate managerial behavior in a given situation depends on, or is contingent on, unique elements in that situation.[37] Stated differently, effective managerial behavior in one situation cannot always be generalized to other situations. Recall, for example, that Frederick Taylor assumed that all workers would generate the highest possible level of output to maximize their own personal economic gain. We can imagine some people being motivated primarily by money—but we can just as easily imagine other people being motivated by the desire for leisure time, status, social acceptance, or any combination of these (as Mayo found at the Hawthorne plant).

Continental Airlines, Inc., recently hired Hollis Harris, a respected and successful executive at Delta Air Lines, Inc., to become its CEO. At the time, Delta was very profitable and had its costs under control. Continental, however, was losing money and its costs were not being controlled. Harris tried to manage at Continental just as he had at Delta, with relatively little concern for costs. As a result, he failed to rescue the airline from bankruptcy and was forced to resign. He made the mistake of not recognizing that he needed to manage Continental differently because it was in a different situation.[38]

An Integrating Framework

We noted earlier that the classical, behavioral, and quantitative perspectives can be complementary and that the systems and contingency perspectives can help integrate them. Our framework for integrating the various approaches to management is shown in Figure 2.4. The initial premise of the framework is that before attempting to apply any concepts or ideas from the three major perspectives, managers must recognize the interdependence of units within the organization, the effect of environmental influences, and the need to respond to the unique characteristics of each situation. The ideas

MANNY MOE & JACK

Synergy results when two or more units of an organization are able to accomplish together more than each would have been able to do independently. While its logo featuring Manny, Moe, and Jack may seem like a throwback to the 1930s, Pep Boys Automotive Supercenters are capitalizing on synergy to fuel rapid expansion plans in the 1990s. For example, Pep Boys retail stores actively promote such services as installation and repair work in addition to selling products, while parts and accessories can be purchased at Pep Boys service centers.

FIGURE 2.4 An Integrative Framework of Management Perspectives

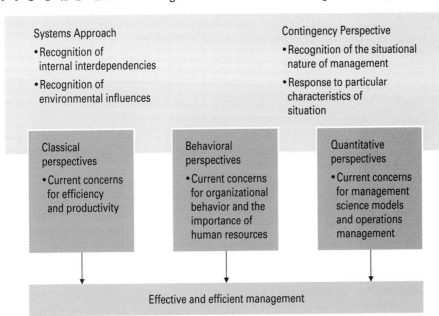

Each of the major perspectives on management can be useful to modern managers. Before using any of them, however, the manager should recognize the situational context within which they operate. The systems and contingency perspectives serve to integrate the classical, behavioral, and quantitative perspectives.

of subsystem interdependencies and environmental influences are given to us by systems theory, and the situational view of management is derived from a contingency perspective.

With these ideas as basic assumptions, the manager may use valid tools, techniques, concepts, and theories of the classical, behavioral, and quantitative perspectives. For example, managers can still use many of the basic techniques from scientific management. In many contemporary settings, the scientific study of jobs and production techniques can enhance productivity. But managers should not rely solely on these techniques, nor should they ignore the human element. The behavioral perspective is also of use to modern managers. By drawing on contemporary ideas of organizational behavior, the manager can better appreciate the role of employee needs and behaviors in the workplace. Motivation, leadership, communication, and group processes are especially important. The quantitative perspective provides the manager with a set of useful tools and techniques. The development and use of management science models and the application of operations management methods can help managers increase their efficiency and effectiveness.

Consider the new distribution manager of a large wholesale firm whose job is to manage one hundred truck drivers and to coordinate standard truck routes in the most efficient fashion. This new manager, with little relevant experience, might attempt to increase productivity by employing strict work specialization and close supervision (as suggested by scientific management). But doing so may decrease employee satisfaction and morale and increase turnover (as predicted by organizational behavior). The manager might also develop a statistical formula to use route driver time more efficiently (from management science). But this new system could disrupt existing work groups and social patterns (from organizational behavior). The manager may create even more problems by trying to impose programs and practices derived from her previous job. An incentive program welcomed by retail clerks, for example, might not work for truck drivers.

The manager should soon realize that a broader perspective is needed. Systems and contingency perspectives help provide broader solutions. Also, as the integrative framework in Figure 2.4 illustrates, applying techniques from several schools works better than trying to make one approach solve all problems. To solve a problem of declining productivity, the manager might look to scientific management (perhaps jobs are inefficiently designed or workers improperly trained), organizational behavior (worker motivation may be low or group norms may be limiting output), or operations management (facilities may be improperly laid out or material shortages may be resulting from poor inventory management). And before implementing any plans for improvement, the manager should try to assess their effect on other areas of the organization.

Now suppose that the same manager is involved in planning a new warehouse. She will probably consider what type of management structure to create (classical perspective), what kinds of leaders and work-group arrangements to develop (behavioral perspective), and how to develop a network model for designing and operating the facility itself (quantitative perspective). As a final example, if employee turnover is too high, the manager might consider an incentive system (classical perspective), plan a motivational enhancement program (behavioral perspective), or use a mathematical model (quantitative perspective) to discover that turnover costs may actually be lower than the cost of making any changes at all.

CONTEMPORARY MANAGEMENT THOUGHT

In recent years, interest in management theory and practice has increased. This interest is reflected in the increased sales of business books in the mass market and the appeal of charismatic executives like Lee Iacocca. This section summarizes some of these popular theories and then identifies contemporary management challenges.

Popular Management Theory

Several writers have attempted to develop new and imaginative management models and theories. Although it is still too early to assess the validity of their ideas, the work of William Ouchi, Thomas Peters, and Robert Waterman has caught the attention of many managers.

popular management theory
New and imaginative approaches to management that include the Type Z model and concerns for excellence

The Type Z Model   The **Type Z model,** as argued by William Ouchi in 1981, is an attempt to integrate common business practices in the United States and Japan into a single middle-ground framework.[39] Ouchi suggests that there are many traditional U.S. firms (which he calls Type A companies) and a similar set of traditional Japanese companies (Type J). He argues that these firms are different along seven important dimensions: (1) length of employment, (2) mode of decision making, (3) location of responsibility, (4) speed of evaluation and promotion, (5) mechanisms of control, (6) specialization of career path, and (7) nature of concern for the employee. For example, some Japanese firms are characterized by lifetime employment opportunities and collective decision making, whereas their U.S. counterparts offer short-term employment and rely on individual decision making.

Type Z model
An attempt to integrate common business practices in the United States and Japan into one middle-ground framework

Ouchi also observes that a few particularly successful U.S. firms (such as IBM, Hewlett-Packard Co., Eastman Kodak Company, and The Procter & Gamble Co.) do not follow the typical Type A model. Instead, they use a hybrid, or Type Z, approach that has one characteristic from Type A (individual responsibility), three characteristics from Type J (collective decision making, slow evaluation and promotion, and holistic concern), and modified characteristics corresponding to the other three dimensions (for instance, they postulate long-term employment as opposed to short-term employment in Type A and lifetime employment in Type J).

Ouchi's ideas have been well received by practicing managers. His book was on most best-seller lists for several weeks following its publication in 1981, and many organizations are trying to implement his suggestions. However, controversy has arisen about whether some of Ouchi's research was conducted as scientifically as it should have been.[40] Like many scientific breakthroughs, the Type Z model will quite likely be supplanted by more refined and valid models as we learn more about the international domain of management. Still, it deserves special recognition because it gave early momentum to theory development in the global arena.

The Concern for Excellence Another popular management theory is the so-called excellence movement. Originally presented by Thomas J. Peters and Robert H. Waterman, Jr.,[41] this approach suggests that certain "excellent" companies, or those with a long-term history of success, do things in a systematic fashion that sets them apart from other firms. The basic set of characteristics that presumably lead to excellence include (1) getting things done on time, (2) staying close to the customer, (3) promoting autonomy and entrepreneurship, (4) maximizing productivity through people, (5) using a hands-on approach to managing, (6) doing what the company knows best, (7) maintaining a simple, lean organizational structure, and (8) promoting both centralization and decentralization simultaneously. Well-known firms presumed to have these characteristics include Digital Equipment Corp., Hewlett-Packard, IBM, Eastman Kodak, Procter & Gamble, Delta Air Lines, Intel Corp., Avon Products, Inc., Maytag Corporation, The Walt Disney Company, The Dow Chemical Co., and du Pont. The excellence movement has also been an important catalyst for other theorists and management scholars, although it too has been subjected to criticism.[42]

Contemporary Management Challenges

One thing that makes the manager's job exciting is the array of new challenges that continue to arise. This concluding section identifies and briefly discusses a number of contemporary challenges that confront all managers today.

● **contemporary management challenges**
Include the globalization of business, quality and productivity, downsizing and cutbacks, ownership issues, ethics and social responsibility, and work-force diversity

Managers and organizations today must contend with a wide array of challenges as they pursue their missions. Globalization, quality, productivity, and workforce diversity have all emerged as important factors in today's business environment. Grau Limited, a European equipment manufacturer with offices in England and Germany, is working hard to protect its domestic market share from increased foreign competition by raising the quality of its trucks and related equipment. In an effort to enhance product quality the firm is recruiting workers from more diverse cultures and placing them together in workgroups.

Globalization of Business   We noted in Chapter 1 that international business has become increasingly important. No longer can any organization—regardless of its size, vitality, or industry—ignore the globalization of business. Ford competes with Nissan Motor Co. Ltd. and Volkswagen AG, Timex Group Ltd. with Seiko, and Exxon with British Petroleum Co. p.l.c. Small retailers carry merchandise from around the globe. And businesses from just about any country can borrow funds from lenders in New York, Tokyo, or London. We explore the international challenges of managers in Chapter 5.

Quality and Productivity   Another area of interest to emerge in recent years has been quality and productivity. As they attempt to understand why Japanese and West German firms have been so successful, U.S. companies have discovered that their foreign counterparts have an edge in quality. As a result, U.S. firms have developed renewed interest in how they can enhance the quality of their products and services. As a part of this discovery process, U.S. managers have also learned that many of their foreign competitors are producing higher-quality products with fewer resources. Hence, managers have become more and more interested in how to increase the productivity of U.S. workers.[43] We address these issues in several chapters, especially Chapter 19.

Downsizing and Cutbacks   In an effort to increase their competitiveness, many organizations have also sought ways to eliminate unnecessary operations and cut costs. Many firms, for example, have sold unprofitable businesses, laid off workers, and taken similar measures to become more efficient. We discuss downsizing and cutbacks in Chapter 12.

Ownership   Ownership of business has also become a controversial subject for managers in recent years. Large institutional investors (such as pension funds and mutual funds) control major blocks of stock in many companies today. This has led to some managers feeling great pressure to produce short-term results and, consequently, not always making decisions that have only a longer-term payoff. More and more foreign firms have also taken ownership stakes in U.S. industry. This trend also concerns many observers. We discuss these issues in Chapters 3 and 7.

Ethics and Social Responsibility   Although ethical scandals in business are not really new, media attention focused on them in recent years has increased public sensitivity about them. Many organizations today are taking steps to enhance the ethical standards of their managers and to avoid legal or public sentiment problems. These issues are discussed in Chapter 4. Environmentalism, a related set of issues, is also addressed in that same chapter.

Work-Force Diversity   A final set of issues that managers today must confront involves work-force diversity. A wide variety of factors—globalization, an aging population, an influx of workers into new career and occupational tracks—have created work forces that are much more heterogeneous than at any time in history. Managers in every organization are finding that they must learn to be more sensitive to the needs, perceptions, and aspirations of many different kinds of workers. We discuss work-force diversity in more detail in Chapter 22.

SUMMARY OF KEY POINTS

Theories are important as organizers of knowledge and as road maps for action. Understanding the historical context and precursors of management and organizations provides a sense of heritage and can also help managers avoid repeating the mistakes of others. Evidence suggests that interest in management dates back thousands of years, but a scientific approach to management has emerged only in the last hundred years. During the first few decades of this century, three primary perspectives on management emerged. These are called the classical perspective, the behavioral perspective, and the quantitative perspective.

The classical perspective had two major branches: scientific management and administrative management. Scientific management was concerned with improving efficiency and work methods for individual workers. Administrative management was more concerned with how organizations themselves should be structured and arranged for efficient operations. Both branches paid little attention to the role of the worker.

The behavioral perspective, characterized by a concern for individual and group behavior, emerged primarily as a result of the Hawthorne studies. The human relations movement recognized the importance and potential of behavioral processes in organizations but made many overly simplistic assumptions about those processes. Organizational behavior, a more realistic outgrowth of the behavioral perspective, is of interest to many contemporary managers.

The quantitative perspective and its two components, management science and operations management, attempt to apply quantitative techniques to decision making and problem solving. These areas are also of considerable importance to contemporary managers. Their contributions have been facilitated by the tremendous increase in the use of personal computers.

The three major perspectives should be viewed in a complementary, not a contradictory, light. Each has something of value to offer. The key is understanding how to use them effectively. Two relatively recent additions to management theory, the systems and contingency perspectives, appear to have great potential both as approaches to management and as frameworks for integrating the other perspectives.

Two recent popular contributions to management theory include the Type Z approach to management and the concern for excellence. Challenges facing managers today include the globalization of business, the importance of quality and productivity, downsizing and cutbacks, ownership issues, ethics and social responsibility, and work-force diversity.

DISCUSSION QUESTIONS

Questions for Review

1. Briefly summarize the classical, behavioral, and quantitative perspectives on management and identify the most important contributors to each.

2. Briefly summarize the Hawthorne studies. What are the primary conclusions that were reached following their completion?

3. Describe the contingency perspective and outline its usefulness to the study and practice of management.

4. What are some contemporary challenges that managers must confront?

Questions for Analysis

5. What social, political, and economic conditions might have influenced the development of each of the major perspectives on management? Why?

6. What are the major strengths and limitations or shortcomings of each of the major perspectives on management? Why?

7. What recently published popular business books have been especially successful? Who are the prominent business leaders today whose ideas are widely accepted?

Questions for Application

8. Go to the library and locate material on Confucius. Outline his major ideas. Which seem to be applicable to management in the United States today?

9. Identify a local firm that has been in existence for a long time. Interview the current owner about the history of the firm and see if you can gain a better understanding of its current practices by knowing about its past.

10. Read a history of a company in which you are interested. Prepare for the class a brief report that stresses the impact of the firm's history on its current practices.

UPS: THE GIANT THAT KEEPS COMPETING

United Parcel Service Inc.'s 62,000 drivers seem as ubiquitous as mail carriers. They make daily stops at more than 1.1 million U.S. accounts. But UPS is not content to be the most profitable and respected package delivery company in the United States. It continues to expand its services and customer base and to find new ways of using technology to improve its efficiency.

Until recently, UPS was known as an old, conservative company that changed with all the speed and abruptness of a glacier. Founded in 1907, UPS has always operated "by the watch," changing only when its engineers found new ways to make the delivery process more efficient (like beveling the fronts of the drivers' seats so they can slide out of them faster). It has always been owned by its managers, most of whom are veteran employees, so it hasn't had to change to satisfy the whims of Wall Street investors.

But in the early 1980s, UPS began to change more rapidly than in the past, as Big Brown realized that Federal Express Corp.'s overnight delivery posed a major threat. UPS made a belated entry into overnight delivery in 1982, and although it still trails Federal Express in that area, it has established a healthy edge over all other competitors.

To catch up to Fed Ex and to help it expand overseas, UPS is turning to technology that it hopes will top Fed Ex's. UPS's $1.4 billion computerization budget has produced its own version of the bar code, called a dense code. In less than a square inch, the fingerprint-like swirls of dense code can hold twice as much information as a normal bar code. A scanner on a conveyor or in a delivery truck can therefore read a package's origin, destination, contents, and price.

UPS continues to test even more advanced tracking devices, and with the purchase of a number of foreign companies in the late 1980s, it has markedly increased its share of the overseas package delivery business. Not content with the array of domestic services it already offers, in 1991 it began testing a second-day letter delivery service that some observers believe might compete with the U.S. Post Office's mail monopoly.

Traditionally, everyone who rose into managerial positions had long ago accepted the company's unusual policies, such as its prohibitions against beards and coffee at work desks. Now the challenge for UPS management is to find a way to enable such a solid, steady company to cope with rapid changes in its environment and its competition.

Discussion Questions

1. Why is UPS expanding around the world and into other services rather than sticking to the business that it has long dominated?

2. What changes in management thinking since the time of scientific management might force UPS to change its attitude toward its workers?

E 3. Speed is extremely important at UPS, and drivers and sorters in particular are expected to complete their tasks within sharply defined time frames. Would you consider such rigid time requirements to be unethical treatment of employees by UPS management? Why or why not?

References: Resa W. King, "UPS Isn't About to Be Left Holding the Parcel," *Business Week*, February 13, 1989, p. 69; Kenneth Labich, "Big Changes at Big Brown," *Fortune*, January 18, 1988, pp. 56–64; Daniel Pearl, "UPS Plans Test of Second-Day Delivery of Letters," *The Wall Street Journal*, May 16, 1991, pp. B1, B6; Daniel Pearl, "UPS Takes On Air-Express Competition," *The Wall Street Journal*, December 20, 1990, p. A4; Todd Vogel, "Can UPS Deliver the Goods in a New World?" *Business Week*, June 4, 1990, pp. 80–82.

*L*loyd's of London insures unusual things, like a comedian's moustache or the nose of a whiskey sniffer. But contrary to popular assumption, Lloyd's is not an insurance company—it has no shareholders and is not liable as a corporation for risks insured through its services. It has broken a lot of territory for insurance companies; it was responsible for the first aviation insurance, burglary insurance, and worker's compensation insurance. It takes pride in its four centuries of history, but that history is giving Lloyd's trouble in a world very far removed from Edward Lloyd's seventeenth-century coffee house.

Because there were no marine insurance companies in the seventeenth century, insurance brokers would take a policy around to rich merchants, persuading each to cover part of a ship's total liability, until the ship's entire value was insured. A place where merchants and shipowners went to relax, such as Lloyd's coffee house, was therefore an ideal setting for brokers and for the potential underwriters.

In many ways, Lloyd's today is a direct descendant of the coffee shop that opened in 1688. Lloyd's provides services beyond the coffee and news that Edward Lloyd could offer his patrons, but it still doesn't underwrite insurance itself. It brings together rich people willing to underwrite a venture and the agents or brokers of those looking for insurance.

The underwriters at Lloyd's—known as "members" or "names"—have long grouped themselves into syndicates. Currently about 27,000 members are divided into about 400 syndicates. Members make a profit if their syndicate takes in more money in premiums than it disburses to claims. But if a member's syndicate gets hit with a very large claim, members are liable for the entire amount, down to the last cent of their personal wealth. This possibility that a disaster somewhere in the world could lead to members' bankruptcy is one of the holdovers from former times that is now causing Lloyd's problems. In good years, mem-

bers can earn a good deal more than they could through other investments. But few other investments carry such risks. One of Lloyd's biggest worries is the number of members who quit each year.

Other Lloyd's traditions make it relatively easy for more modern, efficient insurance companies or exchanges to win business away from Lloyd's. Most business at Lloyd's is still conducted face to face, which means that brokers spend much of their time waiting in line to see underwriters.

Lloyd's is still the exchange of choice for people wanting to insure unusual things, and its history and unique mode of operation make it an institution without parallel in the insurance world. Lloyd's has played a prominent role in the business world and in the development of organizations for more than 300 years, but it will need radical changes if it hopes to celebrate its four hundredth birthday.

Discussion Questions

1. Could an organization with Lloyd's structure be founded today?

2. Why would history and tradition be a powerful asset for an institution in the insurance business?

3. What about the history or structure of Lloyd's has led it to be responsible for so many insurance innovations?

References: Nicholas Bray, "Losses Leave Lloyd's Investors Exposed," *The Wall Street Journal,* June 20, 1991, p. A10; Craig Forman, "Lloyd's of London, An Insurance Bulwark, Is a Firm Under Siege," *The Wall Street Journal,* October 24, 1989, pp. A1, A18; "Lloyd's of London: A Sketch History," *Lloyd's of London brochure;* Richard A. Melcher, "The New Broom at Lloyd's of London," *Business Week,* January 14, 1991, p. 54.

PART

II

THE ENVIRONMENTAL CONTEXT OF MANAGEMENT

3 The Organizational Environment and Effectiveness

4 The Ethical and Social Context of Management

5 The Global Context of Management

The Organizational Environment and Effectiveness

OBJECTIVES

After studying this chapter, you should be able to:

● *Discuss the nature of the organizational environment and identify the three environments of interest to most organizations.*

● *Describe the external environment of organizations, identify the components of the general and task environments, and discuss their impact on organizations.*

● *Identify the components of the internal environment and discuss their impact on organizations.*

● *Identify and describe how the environment affects organizations and how organizations respond to their environment.*

● *Discuss the basic models of organizational effectiveness and describe how they can be used together.*

OUTLINE

The Nature of the Organizational Environment

The External Environment
  The General Environment
  The Task Environment

The Internal Environment
  Board of Directors
  Employees
  Culture

Organization–Environment Relationships
  How Environments Affect Organizations
  How Organizations Respond to Their Environments

Organizational Effectiveness

THE TOURISM INDUSTRY took a beating in 1991. Two major factors were the Persian Gulf war and the recession, which combined to keep many vacationers close to home. The cruise-ship industry was especially hard-hit. In addition to these problems, the sinking of a Greek cruise ship in August caused even more people to delay or postpone their cruises. To get customers to come back, most cruise lines began to offer dramatic discounts. These discounts helped fill empty cabins, but they also sliced profit margins.

One firm that sailed through these troubled waters with hardly a ripple, however, was Carnival Cruise Lines, Inc. For years most cruise lines targeted their marketing efforts at older and more affluent customers. Carnival, meanwhile, had been building a strong market niche for itself among younger customers. And these younger customers continued to travel.

Carnival focused most of its attention on customers between the ages of twenty-five and thirty-nine years old. For example, its advertising stresses fun—as opposed to relaxation—and uses popular entertainers like Kathie Lee Gifford as spokespersons. Its commercials are shot in its ships' casinos and on their sun decks. And by offering short cruises priced at only a few hundred dollars, Carnival attracted many customers who would not otherwise be interested in or able to go on a cruise.

Carnival controls more than 26 percent of the market and is planning an aggressive expansion strategy aimed at gaining an even larger share. Because it costs around $30 million to build a modern cruise ship today, the most economical approach to expansion may be acquiring an existing cruise line. Toward this end Carnival recently tried to buy Premier Cruise Lines, Ltd., but the deal fell through when the two sides could not agree on price. Consequently, the firm is looking closely at other possible acquisitions that could make it an even more formidable competitor on the open seas.[1] ●

*T*he cruise line industry has been buffeted by economic forces and international upheavals. But Carnival Cruise Lines has remained effective because of its clear understanding of its customers and astute management of its image. And during a time when other cruise lines are cutting back, Carnival wants to expand. Economic and international forces, customers, and competitors are just a few of the many elements of the environment that affect not only Carnival but every organization in the world today.

As we noted in Chapter 1, managers must have a deep understanding and appreciation of the environment in which they and their organizations function. Without this understanding they would be like one of Carnival's ships without its rudder—adrift with no way of maneuvering or changing course. This chapter is the first of three devoted to the environmental context of management. After introducing the nature of the organizational environment, we describe the external and internal environments of organizations. Next, we address organization-environment relationships. Because how these relationships are managed largely determines the effectiveness of the organization, we conclude by discussing models of effectiveness.

THE NATURE OF THE ORGANIZATIONAL ENVIRONMENT

To illustrate the importance of the environment to an organization, consider the analogy of a swimmer crossing a wide stream. The swimmer must assess the current, obstacles, and distance before setting out. If these elements are properly evaluated, the swimmer will arrive at the expected point on the far bank of the stream. But if they are not properly understood, the swimmer might end up too far upstream or downstream. The organization is like a swimmer, and the environment is like the stream. The organization must understand the basic elements of its environment to properly maneuver among them.

external environment
Everything outside an organization that might affect it

The **external environment** is everything outside an organization that might affect it. Of course, the boundary that separates the organization from its external environment is not always clear and precise. In one sense, for example, stockholders are part of the organization, but in another sense they are part of its environment. As shown in Figure 3.1, the external environment is composed of two layers: the general environment and the task environment.

● internal environment
The conditions and forces within an organization

An organization's **internal environment** consists of conditions and forces within the organization. Its major components include the board of directors, employees, and the organization's culture. Of course, not all aspects of the environment are equally important for all organizations. A small, nonunion firm may not need to concern itself too much with unions, for example. A private university with a large endowment (like Harvard) may be less concerned about general economic conditions than might a state university (like the University of Oregon) that is dependent on state funding from tax revenues. Still, organizations need to fully understand which envi-

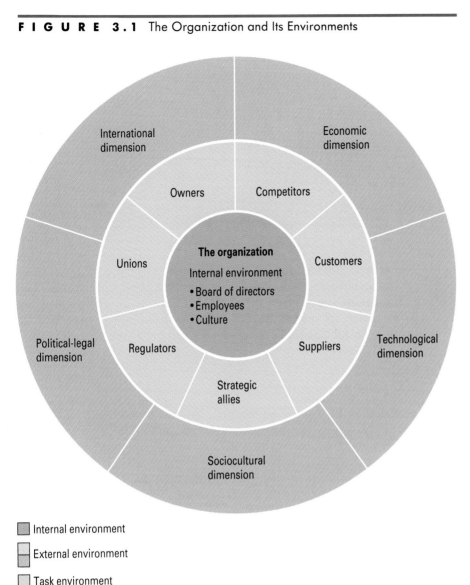

Organizations have both an external and an internal environment. The external environment consists of two layers, one called the general environment and the other called the task environment.

☐ Internal environment

☐ External environment

☐ Task environment

☐ General environment

ronmental forces are important and how the importance of other forces might increase.

THE EXTERNAL ENVIRONMENT

As we just noted, an organization's external environment consists of two layers. The **general environment** of an organization is the nonspecific dimensions and forces in its surroundings that might affect its activities. These elements are not necessarily associated with other specific organiza-

● **general environment**
Those nonspecific dimensions and forces in an organization's surroundings that might affect its activities

The environment of business is growing increasingly complex and uncertain. Meanwhile, managers must do an effective job of managing within that changing environment. General Motors' Saturn division and Ryder are collaborating in ways that help each cope with its environment. Ryder provides the transportation system for both delivering parts to Saturn and transporting finished automobiles away, and in return gets a dependable customer and source of revenues.

tions. The general environment of most organizations has economic, technological, sociocultural, political-legal, and international dimensions. The **task environment** consists of specific organizations or groups that are likely to influence an organization. The task environment may include competitors, customers, suppliers, regulators, unions, owners, and strategic allies.

● **task environment**
Specific organizations or groups that are likely to affect the organization

The General Environment

Each dimension of the general environment embodies conditions and events that have the potential to influence the organization in important ways. The general environment of Ford Motor Co. is shown in Figure 3.2.

The Economic Dimension   The **economic dimension** of an organization's general environment is the overall health of the economic system in which the organization operates.[2] Particularly important economic factors are inflation, interest rates, unemployment, and demand. During times of inflation, for example, a company pays more for resources and must raise its prices to cover the higher costs. When interest rates are high, consumers are less willing to borrow money and the company itself must pay more when it borrows. When unemployment is high, the company is able to be very selective about whom it hires, but consumer buying may decline. As shown in Figure 3.2, Ford has benefited from low inflation and interest rates, but also faces more competition and lower consumer demand. The economic dimension is also of importance to nonbusiness organizations. For example, poor economic conditions affect funding for state universities. Charitable organizations like the Salvation Army are asked to provide greater assistance during bad times, while their incoming contributions dwindle. Hospitals are affected by the availability of government grants and the number of charitable cases they must treat for free.

economic dimension
The overall health of the economic system in which the organization operates

The Technological Dimension   The **technological dimension** of the general environment refers to the methods available for converting resources into products or services. Although technology is applied within the organization, the forms and availability of that technology come from

technological dimension
The methods available for converting resources into products or services

FIGURE 3.2 Ford's General Environment

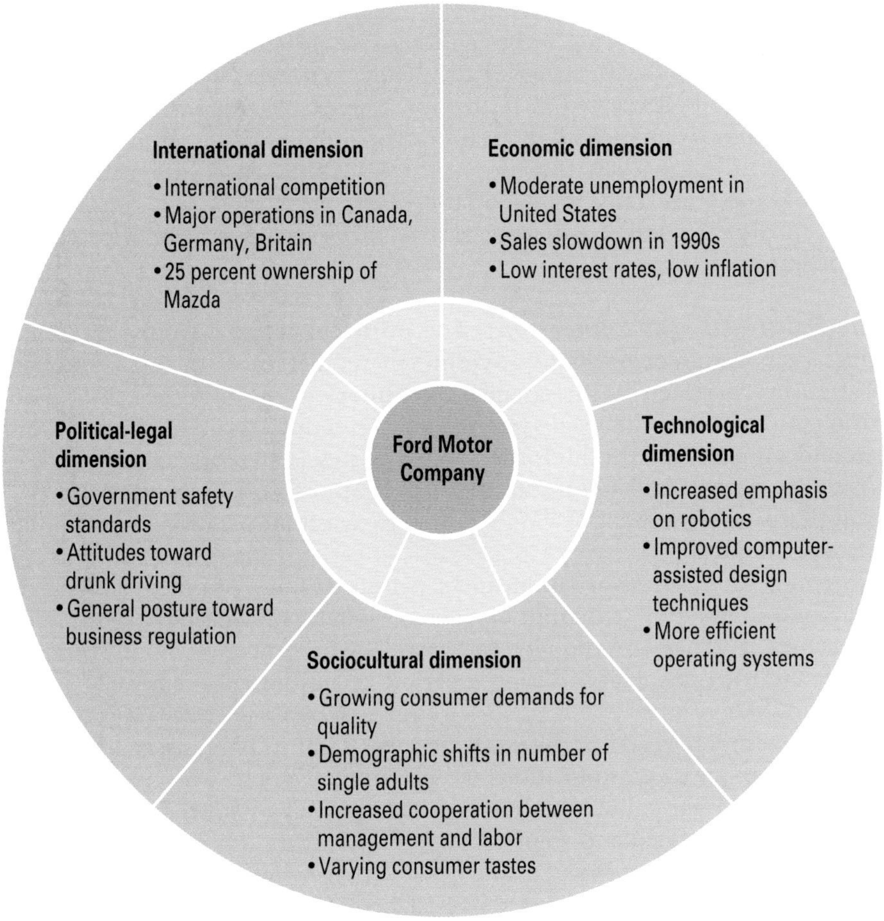

International dimension
- International competition
- Major operations in Canada, Germany, Britain
- 25 percent ownership of Mazda

Economic dimension
- Moderate unemployment in United States
- Sales slowdown in 1990s
- Low interest rates, low inflation

Political-legal dimension
- Government safety standards
- Attitudes toward drunk driving
- General posture toward business regulation

Ford Motor Company

Technological dimension
- Increased emphasis on robotics
- Improved computer-assisted design techniques
- More efficient operating systems

Sociocultural dimension
- Growing consumer demands for quality
- Demographic shifts in number of single adults
- Increased cooperation between management and labor
- Varying consumer tastes

the general environment. Computer-assisted manufacturing and design techniques, for example, allow McDonnell Douglas Corp. to simulate the three miles of hydraulic tubing that run through a DC-10. The results include decreased warehouse needs, higher-quality tube fittings, fewer employees, and major time savings.[3] New innovations in robotics and other manufacturing techniques also have implications for managers. Ford is affected by all of these innovations.

The Sociocultural Dimension   The **sociocultural dimension** of the general environment includes the customs, mores, values, and demographic characteristics of the society in which the organization functions. Sociocultural processes are important because they determine the products, services, and standards of conduct that the society is likely to value. In some countries, for example, consumers are willing to pay premium prices for designer clothes. But the same clothes have virtually no market in other countries. Consumer tastes also change over time. Drinking hard liquor and smoking cigarettes are far less acceptable today than they were just a few

sociocultural dimension
The customs, mores, values, and demographic characteristics of the society in which the organization functions

years go. And sociocultural factors influence how workers in a society feel about their jobs and organizations.

Appropriate standards of business conduct also vary across cultures. In the United States accepting bribes and bestowing political favors in return are considered unethical. In other countries, however, payments to local politicians may be expected in return for a favorable response to common business transactions such as applications for zoning and operating permits. The shape of the market, the ethics of political influence, and attitudes in the work force are only a few of the many ways in which culture can affect an organization. Figure 3.2 shows that Ford is clearly affected by sociocultural factors.

political-legal dimension
The government regulation of business and the general relationship between business and government

The Political-Legal Dimension   The **political-legal dimension** of the general environment refers to government regulation of business and the relationship between business and government. It is important for three basic reasons. First, the legal system partially defines what an organization can and cannot do. Although the United States is basically a free market economy, there is still significant regulation of business activity.[4] Ford, for example, is subject to a growing concern in Washington about automobile safety standards.

Second, probusiness or antibusiness sentiment in government influences business activity. For example, during periods of probusiness sentiment, firms find it easier to compete and have fewer concerns about antitrust issues. On the other hand, during a period of antibusiness sentiment firms may find their competitive strategies more restricted and have fewer opportunities for mergers and acquisitions because of antitrust concerns. Finally, political stability has ramifications for planning. No company wants to set up shop in another country unless trade relationships with that country are relatively well defined and stable. Hence, U.S. firms are more likely to do business with England, Mexico, and Canada than with Iran and El Salvador. Similar issues are also relevant to assessments of local and state governments. A change in the mayor's or the governor's position can affect many organizations, especially small firms that do business in only one location and are susceptible to deed and zoning restrictions, property and school taxes, and the like.

international dimension
The extent to which an organization is involved in or affected by business in other countries

The International Dimension   Yet another component of the general environment for many organizations is the **international dimension,** or the extent to which it is affected by or involved in businesses in other countries.[5] As we discuss in Chapter 5, multinational firms such as The Boeing Co., IBM, Monsanto Company, and Exxon Corporation clearly affect and are affected by international conditions and markets. Specific examples relevant to Ford are noted in Figure 3.2. Ford employs less than 50 percent of its total work force on U.S. soil. Even firms that do business in only one country may face foreign competition at home, and they may use materials or production equipment imported from abroad. The international dimension also has implications for not-for-profit organizations. For example, the Peace Corps sends representatives to underdeveloped countries. Medical breakthroughs achieved in one country spread rapidly to others, and cultural exchanges of all kinds take place between countries. As a result of advances in transportation and communication technology in the past century, almost no part of the world is cut off from the rest. Virtually every organization is affected by the international dimension.[6]

The Task Environment

Because the impact of the general environment is often vague and long-term, most organizations focus more on the task environment. While it is also quite complex, the task environment provides useful information more readily than does the general environment because the manager can identify environmental factors of specific interest to the organization rather than having to deal with the more abstract dimensions of the general environment. Figure 3.3 depicts the task environment of Ford Motor Company. As noted earlier, this environment consists of seven dimensions. In Ford's case, competitors include General Motors Corp. and Toyota Motor Corp.; some customers are Ford dealers, The Hertz Corp. (rental-car company) and individual consumers; suppliers include The Goodyear Tire & Rubber Company, USX Corporation, Eaton, Trinova Corporation, and Johnson Controls Inc.; and strategic allies include Volkswagen AG and Mazda Mo-

FIGURE 3.3 Ford's Task Environment

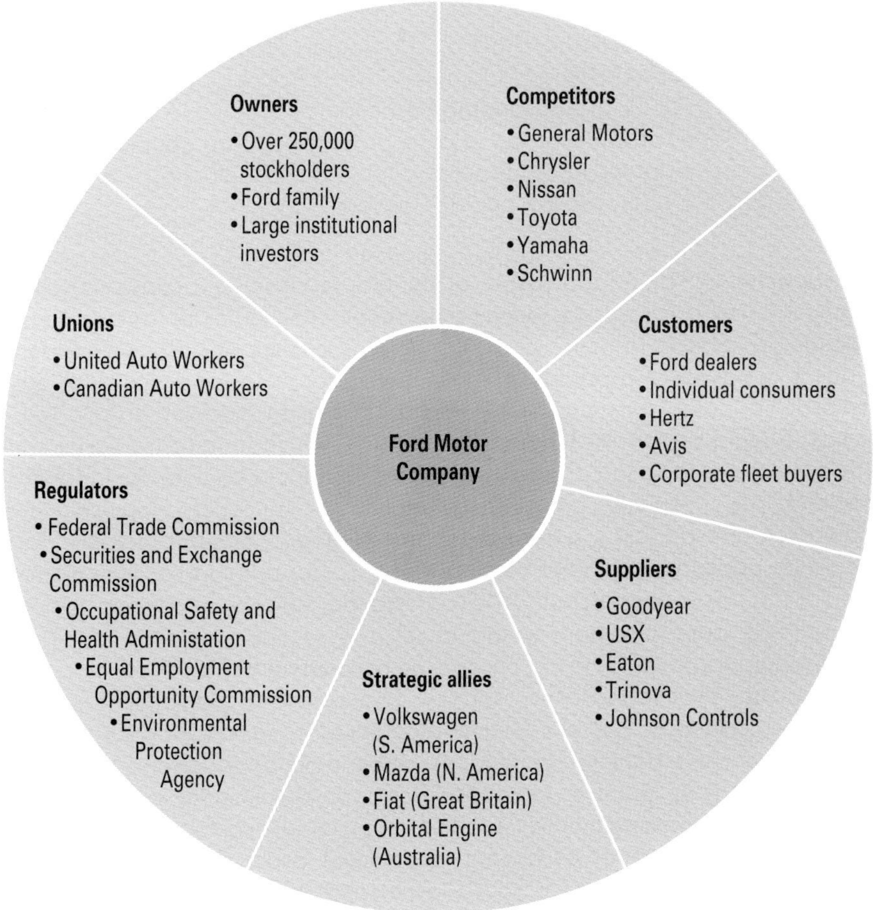

Owners
• Over 250,000 stockholders
• Ford family
• Large institutional investors

Competitors
• General Motors
• Chrysler
• Nissan
• Toyota
• Yamaha
• Schwinn

Unions
• United Auto Workers
• Canadian Auto Workers

Customers
• Ford dealers
• Individual consumers
• Hertz
• Avis
• Corporate fleet buyers

Ford Motor Company

Regulators
• Federal Trade Commission
• Securities and Exchange Commission
• Occupational Safety and Health Administration
• Equal Employment Opportunity Commission
• Environmental Protection Agency

Suppliers
• Goodyear
• USX
• Eaton
• Trinova
• Johnson Controls

Strategic allies
• Volkswagen (S. America)
• Mazda (N. America)
• Fiat (Great Britain)
• Orbital Engine (Australia)

tor Corporation. Key regulators of Ford are the Federal Trade Commission and the Environmental Protection Agency; important labor unions include the United Auto Workers; and major owners include the Ford family. "Management in Practice" describes how Dell Computer Corp. achieved success by exploiting its task environment.

competitors
Organizations that compete for resources

Competitors An organization's **competitors** are other organizations that compete with it for resources. The most obvious resources that competitors vie for are customer dollars. Reebok International Ltd., Adidas, and Nike, Inc. are competitors, as are A&P, Safeway Stores, Inc., and The Kroger Co. Competition also occurs between substitute products. Thus Chrysler competes with Yamaha (motorcycles) and Schwinn Bicycle Co. (bicycles) for your transportation dollars, and The Walt Disney Company, Club Med, Inc., and Carnival Cruise Lines compete for your vacation dollars. Nor is competition limited to business firms. Universities compete with trade schools, the military, other universities, and the job market to attract good students. Art galleries compete with each other to attract the best exhibits.

Organizations may also compete for different kinds of resources besides consumer dollars. Two totally unrelated organizations may compete to acquire a loan from a bank that has only limited funds to lend. In a large city, the police and fire departments may compete for the same tax dollars. Firms compete for quality labor, technological breakthroughs and patents, and scarce raw materials.

Information about competitors is often quite easily obtained. Kmart Corp. can monitor J.C. Penney Company, Inc.'s prices by reading its newspaper advertisements or by sending someone to a store to inspect price tags. Other kinds of information may be more difficult to obtain. Research activities, new product developments, and future advertising campaigns, for example, are often closely guarded secrets.[7]

customers
Whomever pays money to acquire an organization's products or services

Understanding its customers is an important factor in the success of any business. The Gap, led by President Mickey Drexler, has become a major player in the retailing industry by keeping in touch with what its customers want. New ventures such as GapKids and BabyGap, for example, have succeeded because adult customers had indicated that they liked The Gap's merchandise, its pricing, and its store policies and that they would be attracted to similar features in stores that sold clothing for their children.

Customers A second dimension of the task environment consists of customers. **Customers** are whomever pays money to acquire an organization's product or service. In many cases, however, the chain of customer transactions is deceivingly complex. As consumers, for example, we do not buy a bottle of Coke from Coca-Cola. We buy it from Safeway Stores, Inc., which bought it from an independent bottler, which bought the syrup and the right to use the name from Coca-Cola. Customers need not be individuals. Schools, hospitals, government agencies, wholesalers, retailers, and manufacturers are just a few of the many kinds of organizations that may be major customers of other organizations. Common sources of information about customers include market research, surveys, consumer panels, and reports from sales representatives.

Dealing with customers has become increasingly complex in recent years. Many firms have found it necessary to focus their advertising on specific consumer groups or regions. General Foods Corporation, for example, has found it necessary to promote its Maxwell House coffee differently in different regions of the country, even though doing so costs two or three times what a single national advertising campaign would cost.[8] Pressures from consumer groups about packaging and related issues also complicate the lives of managers.

DURING THE COMPUTER SLUMP, DELL SCORES

The recession took its toll on computer makers at the beginning of the decade. IBM scrambled to reduce its overhead, Compaq Computer Corporation's profits fell dramatically, and Apple Computer, Inc., laid off 10 percent of its work force. But at the same time, in Austin Texas, Dell Computer's earnings were doubling.

Dell Computer, the mail-order cut-rate clone-maker that Michael Dell started when he was a 19-year-old student at the University of Texas, is doing just fine. Its success says a lot about how to make it in what is at best a difficult environment.

Like thousands of other young hackers, Dell became fascinated by computers in high school, but unlike most, he also quickly developed a keen sense of marketing. While still in high school, he sold subscriptions for the *Houston Post.* He realized that newly married couples were his best prospects, collected newlyweds' names from the county courthouse, and began setting sales records. His computer business started with similar common-sense moves—selling hard-drive upgrades for IBM PCs, and then buying excess PCs and selling them through newspaper ads. Eventually, he was telemarketing his own PC clones.

By the time he was twenty-one, Dell was doing $34 million of mail-order business, and he was smart enough to get help from more experienced business people. He worked with a venture capitalist, took his company public, and finally learned how to sell to big corporations. He made mistakes that caused earnings to drop in 1990, but he says, "I'm not guilty of . . . making the same mistake twice."*

One mistake Dell hasn't made is believing all the advice given him by others in the computer business. They said that customers wouldn't buy computers over the phone, but when cutting out retailers meant that Dell could undersell his bigger competitors by 25 percent or more, he found plenty of customers. He makes sure that customers stay happy, too. Dell's 150 technicians handle customer problems, earning the company a number-one ranking in J.D. Power & Associates first PC customer satisfaction survey. Dell was also advised that foreign customers wouldn't buy through the mail, but 40 percent of Dell's business is now from overseas, where the company employs 2,100 persons.

And when the recession hit and other PC-makers were cutting prices and employees, Dell attracted buyers looking to stretch their dollars. Michael Dell hasn't produced a new product or marketing method, but by intelligently molding product to buyer, he has become a multimillionaire while still in his mid-twenties.

*Quoted in Claire Poole, "The Kid Who Turned Computers Into Commodities," *Forbes*, October 21, 1991, p. 322.

References: Barbara Buell and Deidre A. Depke, "How Much More Can PC Makers Toss Overboard?" *Business Week*, June 10, 1991, p. 78; Stephanie Anderson Forest, "PC Slump? What PC Slump?" *Business Week*, July 1, 1991, pp. 66–67; Claire Poole, "The Kid Who Turned Computers Into Commodities," *Forbes*, October 21, 1991, pp. 318–322.

Suppliers **Suppliers** are organizations that provide resources for other organizations. Disney World buys soft-drink syrup from Coca-Cola, monorails from Dae-Woo, food from Sara Lee Corp. and J.M. Smucker Co., and paper products from The Mead Corporation. Suppliers for manufacturers like Corning Inc. include the suppliers of raw materials as well as firms that sell machinery and other equipment. Another kind of supplier provides the capital needed to operate the organization. Banks and federal lending agencies are both suppliers of capital for businesses. Other suppliers provide human resources for the organization. Examples include public and private employment agencies like Kelly Services, Inc., and college placement offices.

suppliers
Organizations that provide resources for other organizations

Still other suppliers furnish the organization with the information it needs to carry out its mission. Many companies subscribe to periodicals such as *The Wall Street Journal, Fortune,* and *Business Week* to help their managers keep abreast of news. Market research firms are used by some companies. And some firms specialize in developing economic forecasts and in keeping managers informed about pending legislation. Most organizations try to avoid depending exclusively on particular suppliers. A firm that buys all of a certain resource from one supplier may be crippled if the supplier goes out of business or is faced with a strike. Most organizations try to develop and maintain relationships with a variety of suppliers.[9]

regulators
Units that have the potential to control, regulate, or otherwise influence the organization's policies and practices

regulatory agencies
Created by the government to protect the public from certain business practices or to protect organizations from one another

Regulators **Regulators** are units in the task environment that have the potential to control, regulate, or influence an organization's policies and practices. There are two important kinds of regulators. The first, **regulatory agencies,** are created by the government to protect the public from certain business practices or to protect organizations from one another. Powerful federal regulatory agencies include the Environmental Protection Agency (EPA), the Occupational Safety and Health Administration (OSHA), the Securities and Exchange Commission (SEC), the Food and Drug Administration (FDA), and the Equal Employment Opportunity Commission (EEOC).

Many of these agencies play important roles in protecting the rights of individuals. The FDA, for example, helps ensure that the food we eat is free from contaminants. The costs a firm incurs in complying with government regulations may be substantial, but these costs are usually passed on to the customer. Even so, many organizations complain that there is too much regulation at the present time. One study found that forty-eight major companies spent $2.6 billion in one year—over and above normal environmental protection, employee safety, and similar costs—because of stringent government regulations. On the basis of these findings, the extra costs of government regulations for all businesses have been estimated at more than $100 billion per year.[10] Obviously, the impact of regulatory agencies on organizations is considerable.

Although federal regulators get a lot of publicity, the effect of state and local agencies is also important. California has more stringent automobile emission requirements than those established by the EPA. Not-for-profit organizations must also deal with regulatory agencies. Most states, for example, have coordinating boards that regulate the operation of colleges and universities.

interest groups
Formed by their own individual members to attempt to influence business

The other basic form of regulator is the **interest group.** An interest group is organized by its members to attempt to influence organizations. Prominent interest groups include the National Organization for Women (NOW), Mothers Against Drunk Drivers (MADD), the National Rifle Association (NRA), the League of Women Voters, the Sierra Club, Ralph Nader's Center for the Study of Responsive Law, Consumers Union, and industry self-regulation groups like the Council of Better Business Bureaus. Interest groups lack the official power of government agencies. They can, however, exert considerable influence by using the media to call attention to their positions. MADD, for example, puts considerable pressure on alcoholic-beverage producers (to put warning labels on their products), automobile companies (to make it more difficult for intoxicated people to start their cars), local governments (to stiffen drinking ordinances), and bars and restaurants (to refuse to sell alcohol to people who are drinking too much).

Labor Organizations must also concern themselves with **labor,** especially when it is organized into unions. The National Labor Relations Act of 1935 requires organizations to recognize and bargain with a union if that union has been legally established by the organization's employees. Presently, around 23 percent of the American labor force is represented by unions. Some large firms such as Ford, Exxon, and General Motors have to deal with a great many unions. Even when an organization's labor force is not unionized, its managers do not ignore unions. For example, Kmart, J.P. Stevens, Honda of America Motor Co., Ltd., and Delta Air Lines, Inc., all actively seek to avoid unionization. And even though people think primarily of blue-collar workers as union members, many government employees, teachers, and other white-collar workers are also represented by unions.

labor
Employees, particularly those organized into unions

Owners **Owners** are also becoming a major concern of managers in many businesses.[11] Until recently, stockholders of major corporations were generally happy to sit on the sidelines and let top management run their organizations. Lately, however, more and more of them are taking active roles in influencing the management of companies they hold stock in. This is especially true of owners who hold large blocks of stock. For example, in 1991 Time Warner Inc. announced that it was going to issue new stock to reduce its debt. Current stockholders were to be given first option on buying the stock, but its price was not going to be known at the time options had to be exercised. Several large stockholders complained and some threatened lawsuits. Time Warner eventually backed down and cancelled its plans.[12]

owners
Whoever owns the organization

Another group increasingly exerting influence is the managers of large corporate pension funds. These enormous funds control 50 percent of the shares traded on the New York Stock Exchange and 65 percent of *Standard & Poor's 500* stocks. AT&T's pension fund, for example, exceeds $35 billion. Because pension funds are growing at twice the rate of the U.S. gross national product (GNP), it follows that their managers will have even more power in the future.[13] And given the increased power wielded by owners (and willingness to use that power), some fear that managers are sacrificing long-term corporate effectiveness for the sake of short-term results. For example, managers at Carnation Company were afraid to increase advertising costs too much for fear of attracting the attention of institutional investors. As a result, sales declined. After Nestlé SA took over and loosened the purse strings, sales took off again.[14] Thus managers are finding today that they are having to be considerably more concerned about owners now than in the past.

Strategic Allies A final dimension of the task environment is **strategic allies**—two or more companies that work together in joint ventures. As shown in Figure 3.3, Ford has a number of strategic allies, including Volkswagen (to make cars in South America) and Nissan Motor Co. Ltd. (to make vans in the United States). Ford and Mazda Motor Corporation also jointly make the Probe automobile. Alliances such as these have been around for a long time, but they became popular in the 1980s and are now

strategic allies
Two or more organizations working together in a joint venture or similar arrangement

increasing at a rate of around 22 percent per year.[15] IBM used to shun strategic alliances but now has forty active partnerships around the globe.[16]

Strategic alliances help companies get from other companies the expertise they may lack. They also help spread risk. Managers must be careful, however, not to give away sensitive competitive information. For example, when Unisys Corp. entered into a strategic alliance with Hitachi, Ltd., a Japanese computer maker, it found that it had to divulge valuable trade secrets to make the partnership work. Strategic alliances need not always involve business. Texas A&M University and the University of Texas, for example, often work together to secure government grants. And some churches sponsor joint missionary projects.

THE INTERNAL ENVIRONMENT

As shown earlier in Figure 3.1, organizations also have an internal environment comprising their board of directors, employees, and organizational culture.

Board of Directors

The board of directors is an integral component of the internal environment of many organizations. Farmland Industries, Inc. is a cooperative that provides its members with information, advice, discounts on materials, and assistance in marketing. Jim Allen, along with his three sons, manages a herd of 300 cattle on their 6,500 acre ranch in Oklahoma. Mr. Allen has also served on the board of directors of his local Farmland Co-Op for two years.

Not every organization has a board of directors. Corporations, of course, are required to have them but nonincorporated businesses and many non-business organizations are not. Most universities, however, do have a board of regents, and most other large organizations, including hospitals and charities, have a board of trustees that serves essentially the same purpose. A corporate board of directors is elected by the stockholders and is charged with overseeing the general management of the firm to ensure that it is being run in a way that best serves the stockholders' interests.[17] Some directors, called inside directors, are also full-time employees of the firm holding top-management jobs. Outside directors, in contrast, are elected to the board for a specific purpose—to assist with financial management, legal issues, and so forth. They are not full-time employees of the organization, however. The board plays a major role in helping set corporate strategy and seeing that it is implemented properly. The board also reviews all important decisions made by top management and determines compensation for top managers.

Employees

External labor-force issues, including those associated with unions, are part of the external task environment. Once employees become members of the organization, however, they also become part of its internal environment. When managers and employees embrace the same values and have the same goals, everyone wins. When managers and employees work toward different ends, however, or when conflict and hostility pervade the organization, everyone suffers.[18] Many of the issues that we discuss in Part 4, The Organizing Process, are aimed at enhancing interpersonal relationships in the organization. Of particular interest to managers today is the changing nature of U.S. workers. The work force of tomorrow will have more women,

Hispanics, blacks, and older people than the work force of today. The worker of tomorrow is also expected to want more job ownership—either partial ownership in the company or at least more say in how the job is performed.

Culture

The **culture** of an organization is the set of values that helps its members understand what the organization stands for, how it does things, and what it considers important. Culture is an amorphous concept that defies objective measurement or observation. Nevertheless, because it is the foundation of the organization's internal environment, it plays a major role in shaping managerial behavior.[19]

● **culture**
The set of values that helps an organization's members understand what it stands for, how it does things, and what it considers important

The Importance of Culture   Several years ago, executives at Levi Strauss & Co. felt that the company had outgrown its sixty-eight-year-old building. Even though everyone enjoyed its casual and relaxed atmosphere, more space was needed. So Levi Strauss moved into a modern office building in downtown San Francisco, where its new headquarters spread over twelve floors in a skyscraper. It quickly became apparent that the change was affecting the corporate culture—and that people did not like it. Executives felt isolated, and other managers missed the informal chance meetings in the halls. Within just a few years, Strauss moved out of the skyscraper and back into a building that fosters informality. For example, there is an adjacent park area where employees converge for lunchtime conversation. Clearly, Levi Strauss has a culture that is important to everyone who works there.[20]

Culture determines the "feel" of the organization. The stereotypic image of the IBM executive is someone wearing a white shirt and dark suit. In contrast, Texas Instruments Incorporated likes to talk about its "shirt-sleeve" culture, in which ties are avoided and few managers ever wear jackets. Of course, the same culture is not necessarily found throughout an entire organization. For example, the sales and marketing department may have a culture quite different from that of the operations and manufacturing department. Regardless of its nature, however, culture is a powerful force in organizations, one that can shape the firm's overall effectiveness and long-term success. Companies that can develop and maintain a strong culture, such as Hewlett-Packard Co. and Procter & Gamble Co., tend to be more effective than companies that have trouble developing and maintaining a strong culture.[21]

Determinants of Culture   Where does a culture come from? Typically it develops and blossoms over a long period of time. Its starting point is often the organization's founder. For example, James Cash Penney believed in treating employees and customers with respect and dignity. Employees at J.C. Penney are still called associates rather than employees (to reflect partnership), and customer satisfaction is of paramount importance. As an organization grows, its culture is modified, shaped, and refined by symbols, stories, heroes, slogans, and ceremonies. For example, a key value at Hewlett-Packard is the avoidance of bank debt. A popular story still told at the company involves a new project being considered for several years.

All objective criteria indicated that HP should incur bank debt to finance it, yet Bill Hewlett and David Packard rejected it out of hand simply because "HP avoids bank debt." This story, involving two corporate heroes and based on a slogan, dictates corporate culture today.[22]

Corporate success and shared experiences also shape culture. For example, Hallmark Cards Inc. has a strong culture derived from its years of success in the greeting cards industry. Employees speak of the Hallmark family and care deeply about the company; many of them have worked at the company for years. At Atari Corp., in contrast, the culture is quite weak, the management team changes rapidly, and few people sense any direction or purpose in the company. The differences in culture at Hallmark and Atari are in part attributable to past successes and shared experiences.

Managing Organizational Culture How can managers deal with culture, given its clear importance but intangible nature? The key is for the manager to understand the current culture and then decide if it should be maintained or changed. By understanding the organization's current culture, managers can take appropriate actions. At Hewlett-Packard, the values represented by "the HP way" still exist. Moreover, they guide and direct most important activities undertaken by the firm. Culture can also be maintained by rewarding and promoting people whose behaviors are consistent with the existing culture and by articulating the culture through slogans, ceremonies, and so forth.

To change culture, managers must have a clear idea of what it is they want to create. Many organizations today are attempting to create a culture like that espoused by Ouchi (Theory Z) or Peters and Waterman (excellence framework).[23] As described in Chapter 2, each of those approaches represents a form of organizational culture. Another way to shape culture is by bringing outsiders into important managerial positions. The choice of a new CEO from outside the organization is often a clear signal that things will be changing. Adopting new slogans, telling new stories, staging new ceremonies, and breaking with tradition can also alter culture. Culture can also be changed by methods discussed in Chapter 12.

ORGANIZATION-ENVIRONMENT RELATIONSHIPS

The preceding discussion identifies and describes the various dimensions of organizational environments. Because organizations are open systems, they interact with these various dimensions in many different ways. We now turn our attention to these interactions. We first discuss how environments affect organizations and then note a number of ways in which organizations respond to their environments.

How Environments Affect Organizations

Three basic frameworks can be used to describe how environments affect organizations: environmental change and complexity, competitive forces, and environmental turbulence.

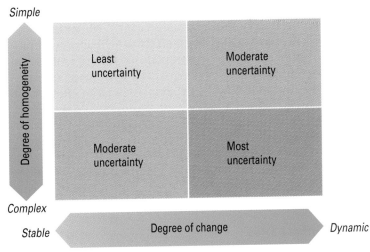

FIGURE 3.4 Environmental Change, Complexity, and Uncertainty

Simple

Degree of homogeneity

| Least uncertainty | Moderate uncertainty |
| Moderate uncertainty | Most uncertainty |

Complex

Stable ◁ Degree of change ▷ *Dynamic*

The degree of homogeneity and the degree of change combine to create uncertainty for organizations. For example, a simple and stable environment creates the least uncertainty, and a complex and dynamic environment create the most uncertainty.

Source: Adapted from J.D. Thompson, *Organizations in Action* (New York: McGraw-Hill, 1967), p. 72. Used with permission of the publisher.

Environmental Change and Complexity   James D. Thompson was one of the first people to recognize the importance of organizational environments.[24] Thompson suggests that an organization's environment can be described along two dimensions: its degree of change and its degree of homogeneity. The degree of change is the extent to which the environment is relatively stable or relatively dynamic. The degree of homogeneity is the extent to which the environment is relatively simple (few elements, little segmentation) or relatively complex (many elements, much segmentation). These two dimensions interact to determine the level of **uncertainty** faced by the organization. Uncertainty, in turn, is a driving force that influences many organizational decisions. Figure 3.4 illustrates a simple view of the four levels of uncertainty defined by different levels of homogeneity and change.

The least environmental uncertainty is faced by organizations with stable and simple environments. Although no environment is totally without uncertainty, many franchised food operations (such as Subway and Taco Bell) and many container manufacturers (like Ball and Federal Paper Board Co., Inc.) have relatively low levels of uncertainty to contend with. Subway, for example, focuses on a certain segment of the consumer market, produces a limited product line, has a constant source of suppliers, and faces relatively consistent competition.

Organizations with dynamic but simple environments generally face a moderate degree of uncertainty. Examples of organizations functioning in such environments include clothing manufacturers (targeting a certain kind of clothing buyer but sensitive to fashion-induced changes) and compact disc (CD) producers (catering to certain kinds of record buyers but alert to changing tastes in music). Levi Strauss faces few competitors (Wrangler and Lee), has few suppliers and few regulators, and uses limited distribution channels. This relatively simple task environment, however, also changes

uncertainty
A major force caused by change and complexity that affects many organizational activities

quite rapidly as competitors adjust prices and styles, consumer tastes change, and new fabrics become available.

Another combination of factors is one of stability and complexity. Again, a moderate amount of uncertainty results. General Motors faces these basic conditions. Overall, the organization must deal with a myriad of suppliers, regulators, consumer groups, and competitors. Change, however, occurs quite slowly in the automobile industry. Despite many stylistic changes, cars of today still have four wheels, a steering wheel, an internal combustion engine, and so forth.

Finally, very dynamic and complex environmental conditions yield a high degree of uncertainty. The environment has a large number of elements, and the nature of those elements is constantly changing. Intel Corp., IBM, and other firms in the electronics field face these conditions because of the rapid rate of technological innovation and change in consumer markets that characterize their industry, their suppliers, and their competitors.

Five Competitive Forces Although Thompson's general classifications are useful and provide some basic insights into organization-environment interactions, in many ways they lack the precision and specificity needed by managers who must deal with their environments on a day-to-day basis. Michael E. Porter, a Harvard professor and expert in strategic management, recently proposed a more refined way to assess environments. In particular, he suggests that organizations view their environments in terms of **five competitive forces**.[25]

The *threat of new entrants* is the extent to which new competitors can easily enter a market or market segment. It takes a relatively small amount of capital to open a dry-cleaning service or a pizza parlor, but it takes a tremendous investment in plant, equipment, and distribution systems to enter the automobile business. Thus the threat of new entrants is fairly high for a local hamburger restaurant but fairly low for General Motors and Toyota.

Jockeying among contestants is the nature of the competitive relationship between dominant firms in the industry. In the soft-drink industry, Coca-Cola and PepsiCo, Inc. often engage in intense price wars, comparative advertising, and new-product introductions. And U.S. auto companies continually try to outmaneuver each other with warranty improvements and rebates. Local car-washing establishments, in contrast, seldom engage in such practices.

The *threat of substitute products* is the extent to which alternative products or services may supplant or diminish the need for existing products or services. The electronic calculator eliminated the need for slide rules. The advent of microcomputers, in turn, has reduced the demand for calculators as well as for typewriters and large mainframe computers. And Nutra-Sweet is a viable substitute product threatening the sugar industry.

The *power of buyers* is the extent to which buyers of the products or services in an industry have the ability to influence the suppliers. For example, a Boeing 747 has relatively few potential buyers. Only companies such as American Airlines, Inc., United Air Lines, Inc., and KLM can purchase them; hence, they have considerable influence over the price they are willing to pay, the delivery date for the order, and so forth. On the other hand, Japanese car makers charged premium prices for their cars in the United

States during the late 1970s energy crisis because if the first customer wouldn't pay the price, there were two more customers waiting in line who would.

The *power of suppliers* is the extent to which suppliers have the ability to influence potential buyers. The local electric company is the only source of electricity in your community. Subject to local or state regulation (or both), it can therefore charge what it wants to for its product, provide service at its convenience, and so forth. Likewise, even though Boeing has few potential customers, those same customers have few suppliers that can sell them a 300-passenger jet. So Boeing too has power. On the other hand, a small vegetable wholesaler has little power in selling to restaurants because if they don't like the produce, they can easily find an alternative supplier.

Environmental Turbulence Although always subject to unexpected changes and upheavals, the five competitive forces can be studied and assessed systematically, and a plan can be developed for dealing with them. At the same time, though, organizations also face the possibility of environmental change or turbulence, occasionally with no warning at all. The most common form of organizational turbulence is a crisis of some sort. Table 3.1 lists a number of crises that different organizations have had to confront in recent years.

The effects of crises like those can be devastating to an organization, especially if managers are unprepared to deal with them. At NASA, for example, the shuttle disaster essentially paralyzed the U.S. space program for almost three years. The cost to Johnson & Johnson of the Tylenol poisonings has been estimated at $750 million in product recalls and changes in packaging and product design.[26] Exxon's legal problems arising from the Alaskan oil spill will not be settled for years. And Dow Corning Corporation faces long-term problems associated with its silicone gel breast implants.

Environmental turbulence is difficult to predict but of profound importance for many firms. PepsiCo has had entrenched business operations in the former Soviet Union for years. During the attempted coup in 1991, PepsiCo managers there were relatively unaffected because they understood how the system worked and what they needed to do to keep their operation going.

Environmental turbulence can often force an organization to respond to catastrophic events with little or no warning. Although organizations could have developed contingency plans for some of these crises, many of them are events that would have been hard to anticipate.

TABLE 3.1 Recent Organizational Crises

Date	Organization	Nature of Crisis
1979	Metropolitan Edison	Near meltdown at Three Mile Island nuclear power plant
1982	Johnson & Johnson	Cyanide poisoning of Tylenol capsules results in 8 deaths
1984	Union Carbide	Poison gas leak at plant in Bhopal, India, kills 3,000 and injures another 300,000
1985	Jalisco	Bacteria in cheese kills 84
1986	NASA	Space shuttle Challenger explodes after takeoff, killing 7 crew members
1989	Exxon	The supertanker *Valdez* hits a rocky reef off the coast of Alaska and spills more than 10 million gallons of oil
1989	Pacific Gas & Electric	San Francisco earthquake leaves dozens of gas leaks and millions of homes without electricity
1992	Dow Corning	After hundreds of women file lawsuits complaining of adverse affects from the company's silicone breast implants, the Food and Drug Administration conducts an investigation resulting in a ban on the implants. Dow Corning is criticized for its handling of the disaster and announces its withdrawal from the implant-making business a month later.*

*Not included in original article.

Source: Suggested by Ian Mitroff, Paul Shrivastava, and Firdaus E. Udwadia, "Effective Crisis Management," *The Academy of Management Executive*, August 1987, pp. 283–292.

Such crises affect organizations in different ways, and many organizations are developing crisis plans and teams. When a Delta Air Lines plane crashed in 1988 at the Dallas–Fort Worth airport, for example, fire-fighting equipment was at the scene in minutes. Only a few flights were delayed, and none had to be canceled. In 1987, a grocery store in Boston received a threat that someone had poisoned cans of its Campbell's tomato juice. Within six hours, a crisis team from Campbell Soup Company removed two truckloads of juice from all eighty-four stores in the grocery chain. Still, fewer than half of the major companies in the United States have a plan for dealing with major crises.[27]

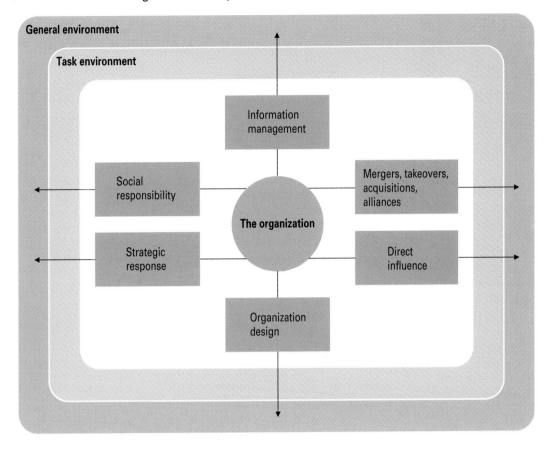

How Organizations Respond to Their Environments

Given the myriad issues, problems, and opportunities in an organization's environments, how should the organization respond? Obviously, each organization must assess its own unique situation and then react according to the wisdom of its senior management.[28] Figure 3.5 illustrates the six basic ways in which organizations react to their environment. One reaction, social responsibility, is discussed in Chapter 4.

Information Management   One way organizations respond to the environment is through information management. Information management is especially important when forming an initial understanding of the environment and when monitoring the environment for signs of change. Organizations use several techniques for managing information. One is defining boundary spanners. A *boundary spanner* is someone like a sales representative or a purchasing agent who spends much of her time in contact with others outside the organization. Such people are in a good position to learn what other organizations are doing. All effective managers engage in *environmental scanning,* the process of actively monitoring the environment through activities such as observation and reading. Within the organization, Merrill

Organizations attempt to influence their environments. The most common methods for this are through information management, strategic response, mergers, takeovers, acquisitions, alliances, organization design, and direct influence.

techniques for information management
Boundary spanners, environmental scanning, and information systems

Organizations sometimes attempt to influence their environment through a strategic response. Birkenstock Footprint Sandals, Inc., was born from just such a response. While traveling in Europe in the late 1960s Margot Fraser discovered a style of sandals that were wider and more comfortable than conventional shoes. She convinced the German manufacturer to let her import them into the United States. At first the shoes appealed only to counterculture "hippie" types. But Fraser has worked to strategically alter the Birkenstock image and now carries more than 125 varieties of shoes aimed at several different market segments.

Lynch & Co., Inc., Federal Express Corp., Ford Motor Company, and many other firms have also established elaborate *information systems* to gather and organize relevant information for managers and to assist in summarizing that information in the form most pertinent to each manager's needs (information systems are covered more fully in Chapter 21).

Strategic Response   Another way that an organization responds to its environment is through a strategic response. The response may involve doing nothing (for example, if its management believes that it is doing very well with its current approach), altering its strategy a bit, or adopting an entirely new strategy. If the market that a company currently serves is growing rapidly, the firm might decide to invest even more heavily in products and services for that market. Likewise, if a market is shrinking or does not provide reasonable possibilities for growth, the company may decide to cut back. For example, when Tenneco Inc.'s managers recently decided that oil and gas prices were likely to remain depressed for some time to come, they decided to sell the company's oil and gas business and invest the proceeds in its healthier businesses like Tenneco Automotive.[29]

Mergers, Takeovers, Acquisitions, and Alliances   A merger occurs when two or more firms combine to form a new firm. For example, Time and Warner recently merged to create Time-Warner. A takeover occurs when one firm buys another, sometimes against its will (a hostile takeover). Usually, the firm that is taken over ceases to exist and becomes part of the other company. For example, when AT&T took over NCR Corp., it folded that company into an existing operations. After an acquisition, the acquired firm often continues to operate as a subsidiary of the acquiring company. And as already discussed, in an alliance the firm undertakes a new venture with another firm. A company engages in these kinds of strategies for a variety of reasons, such as easing entry into new markets or expanding its presence in a current market.

Organization Design   An organization may also respond to environmental conditions through its structural design. For example, a firm that operates in an environment with relatively low levels of uncertainty might choose to use a design with many basic rules, regulations, and standard operating procedures. Alternatively, a firm that faces a great deal of uncertainty might choose a design with relatively few standard operating procedures, instead allowing managers considerable discretion over how they do things. The former type, called a mechanistic organization design, is characterized by formal and rigid rules and relationships. The latter, called an organic design, is considerably more flexible and permits the organization to respond more quickly to environmental change.[30] We learn much more about these and related issues in Chapter 11.

Direct Influence of the Environment   Organizations are not necessarily helpless in the face of their environments.[31] Indeed, many organizations are able to directly influence their environment in many different ways. For example, firms may influence their suppliers by signing long-term contracts with fixed prices as a hedge against inflation. Or a firm may become its own supplier. Sears, for example, owns some of the firms that produce the goods it sells. E.I. du Pont de Nemours & Co. bought Conoco Inc. a few years ago partially to ensure a reliable source of petroleum for its chemical operations.

Almost any major activity a firm engages in affects its competitors. When JVC lowers the prices of its CD players, Sony Corp. may be forced to follow suit. When The Prudential Insurance Co. of America lowers its life-insurance rates, New York Life Insurance Co. is likely to do the same.[32] Organizations may also influence their customers. One method involves creating new uses for a product, finding entirely new customers, and taking customers away from competitors. Developing new kinds of software, for example, expands the customer base of computer firms. Organizations also influence their customers by convincing them that they need something new. Automobile manufacturers use this strategy in their advertising to convince people that they need a new car every two or three years.

Organizations influence their regulators through lobbying and bargaining. Lobbying involves sending a company or industry representative to Washington in an effort to influence relevant agencies, groups, and committees. For example, the U.S. Chamber of Commerce lobby, the nation's largest business lobby, has an annual budget of more than $100 million. The automobile companies have been successful on several occasions in bargaining with the EPA to extend deadlines for compliance with pollution control and mileage standards.[33] Mobil Corporation tries to influence public opinion and government action through an ongoing series of advertisements about the virtues of free enterprise.

Most bargaining sessions between management and unions are also attempts at mutual influence. Management tries to get the union to accept its contract proposals, and unions try to get management to sweeten its offer. When unions are not represented in an organization, management usually attempts to keep them out. When Honda opened its first plant in the United States, it helped establish a plant union to head off efforts by the United Auto Workers to set up a branch of its own union in the plant. Corporations influence their owners with information contained in annual reports, by meeting with large investors, and by pure persuasion. And strategic alliance agreements are almost always negotiated through contracts. Each party tries to get the best deal it can from the other as the final agreement is hammered out.

ORGANIZATIONAL EFFECTIVENESS

We noted in Chapter 1 the distinction between organizational effectiveness and efficiency. Efficiency involves using resources wisely and without waste, and effectiveness is doing the right things. Given the interactions between organizations and their environments, it follows that effectiveness is related to how well an organization understands, reacts to, and influences its environment.[34] Carnival Cruise Lines does an effective job of understanding its customer base and controlling its costs. In contrast, "The Global View" describes a firm that has been less effective.

Unfortunately, there is no consensus about what constitutes effectiveness. For example, an organization can make itself look extremely effective

● **models of organizational effectiveness**
Systems resource approach, goal approach, internal processes approach, and strategic constituencies approach

in the short-term by ignoring R&D, buying cheap materials, ignoring quality control, and skimping on wages. Over time, though, the firm will no doubt falter. On the other hand, taking a longer view and making appropriate investments in R&D and so forth may displease investors who have a short-term outlook. Little wonder, then, that there are many different models of effectiveness.

The *systems resource approach* to organizational effectiveness focuses on the extent to which the organization can acquire the resources it needs.[35] A manufacturer that can get raw materials during a shortage, a college of engineering that can hire qualified faculty despite competition from industry, and a firm that can borrow at low interest rates are all effective from this perspective. They are acquiring the material, human, financial, and information resources they need to compete successfully in the marketplace.

The *goal approach* to effectiveness focuses on the degree to which an organization obtains its goals.[36] When a firm establishes a goal of increasing sales by 10 percent and then achieves that increase, the goal approach maintains that the organization is effective. How successful General Electric Co. is at its goal of being either number 1 or number 2 in every industry it enters is used by CEO Jack Welch as an indicator of effectiveness.

The *internal processes approach* to organizational effectiveness deals with the internal mechanisms of the organization. It focuses on minimizing strain, integrating individuals and the organization, and conducting smooth and efficient operations.[37] An organization that focuses primarily on maintaining employee satisfaction and morale and being efficient subscribes to this view. A well-managed firm like IBM is clearly effective from this point of view.

Finally, the *strategic constituencies approach* to organizational effectiveness focuses on the groups that have a stake in the organization.[38] The strategic constituencies of Ralston Purina Co., for example, include its suppliers (food producers and container manufacturers), lenders (stockholders and banks), participants (employees and managers), customers, and others who are influenced by the company. In this view, effectiveness is the extent to which the organization satisfies the demands and expectations of all these groups.

Although these four basic models of effectiveness are not necessarily contradictory, they do focus on different things. The systems resource approach focuses on inputs, the goal approach focuses on outputs, the internal processes approach focuses on transformation processes, and the strategic constituencies approach focuses on feedback. Thus, rather than adopting a single approach, organizational effectiveness can best be understood by an integrated perspective such as the one illustrated in Figure 3.6. At the core of this unifying model is the organizational system, with its inputs, transformations, outputs, and feedback. Surrounding this core are the four basic approaches to effectiveness as well as a combined approach, which incorporates each of the other four. The basic argument is that an organization must essentially satisfy the requirements imposed on it by each of the effectiveness perspectives.

Achieving organizational effectiveness is not an easy task. The key to doing so is understanding the environment in which the organization functions. With this understanding as a foundation, managers can then chart the "correct" path for the organization as it positions itself in that environment.

TRYING TO BRING BACK THE SHINE

 The name Mikimoto used to be better known than Honda or Sony, and women around the world proudly used to display its products—pearls. Mikimoto pearls have filled jewelry cases from Shanghai to Paris ever since Kokichi Mikimoto developed a new method for culturing pearls in the 1890s.

That Mikimoto is no longer a familiar name is testimony to what can happen to a company that doesn't respond to changes in its environment. Because of Japan's severe problems with water pollution, growing pearls in Japan has become a risky business. And pearls in general have lost some of their luster in the jewelry market, now accounting for only about 10 percent of Japanese jewelry sales. If Mikimoto had noticed these trends and responded to them, it could have used its name recognition to branch out successfully into non-pearl jewelry. But the Mikimoto heirs that ran the company until the 1980s were true to the founder's product, if not his innovativeness, and not until a former banker took the helm in 1984 did the company begin seriously broadening its product line and responding to changing tastes.

Mikimoto might learn something from one of its main rivals, Tiffany & Co., which has also been trying to recover from managerial misdirection. Tiffany's image was seriously tarnished during the early 1980s, when it was owned by Avon Products, Inc. Avon pushed Tiffany into the lower end of the jewelry market at a time when many wealthy Americans had plenty to spend on luxuries. Avon sold off Tiffany's large inventory of unmounted diamonds, neglected Tiffany's advertising, and filled showcases with affordable—not glamorous—pieces.

After Avon sold Tiffany in 1984, the company rebounded by taking as its model Cartier, Inc., the high-class Parisian jeweler. It has been expanding rapidly in Japan, where it sells through a Japanese department store. Mikimoto executives might point to Tiffany's problems under Avon as proof of what happens when a company tries to appeal to mass-market tastes. But the real lesson is that companies must be responsive to changes in their environment, even if those changes are inconsistent from one country to the next. Even now, Mikimoto pins much of its future on the hope that Japanese women will emulate Princess Kiko's love of pearls. Meanwhile it watches a rejuvenated Tiffany getting rich from selling to Japan's young people.

References: Hiroko Katayama, "Faded Luster," *Forbes*, September 16, 1991, p. 88; Faye Rice, "Tiffany Tries the Cartier Formula," *Fortune*, November 20, 1989, pp. 141–148.

If managers can identify where they want the organization to be relative to other parts of their environment, and how to best get there, they stand a good chance of achieving effectiveness. On the other hand, if they pick the wrong target to aim for, or if they go about achieving their goals in the wrong way, they are likely to be less effective.

SUMMARY OF KEY POINTS

Environmental factors play a major role in determining an organization's success or failure. All organizations have both external and internal environments.

The external environment is composed of general and task environment layers. The general environment is composed of the nonspecific elements of the organization's surroundings that might affect its activities. It consists

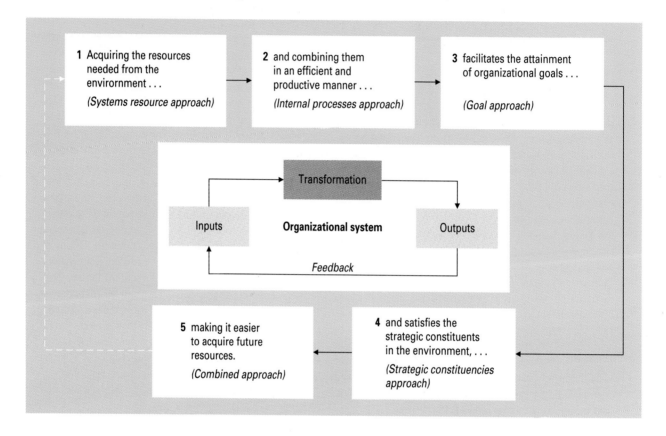

1 Acquiring the resources needed from the environment . . .

(Systems resource approach)

2 and combining them in an efficient and productive manner . . .

(Internal processes approach)

3 facilitates the attainment of organizational goals . . .

(Goal approach)

Transformation

Inputs **Organizational system** Outputs

Feedback

5 making it easier to acquire future resources.

(Combined approach)

4 and satisfies the strategic constituents in the environment, . . .

(Strategic constituencies approach)

The systems resource, internal processes, goal, and strategic constituencies approaches to organizational effectiveness each take a different focus on what constitutes effectiveness. Thus they can be combined to create an overall integrative perspective on effectiveness.

of five dimensions: economic, technological, sociocultural, political-legal, and international. The effects of these dimensions on the organization are broad and gradual.

The task environment consists of specific dimensions of the organization's surroundings that are very likely to influence the organization. It consists of seven elements: competitors, customers, suppliers, regulators, labor, owners, and strategic allies. Because these dimensions are associated with specific organizations in the environment, their effects are likely to be direct.

The internal environment consists of the organization's board of directors, employees, and culture. Culture is especially important. Managers must understand not only its importance but also how it is determined and how it can be managed.

Organizations and their environments affect each other in several ways. Environmental influences on the organization can occur through uncertainty, competitive forces, and turbulence. Organizations, in turn, use information management; strategic response; mergers, takeovers, acquisitions, and alliances; organization design; direct influence; and social responsibility to influence their task environments, and they occasionally try to influence broader elements of their general environment as well.

A key indicator of how well an organization deals with its environment is its level of effectiveness. Organizational effectiveness requires that the organization do a good job of procuring resources, managing them properly, achieving its goals, and satisfying its constituencies. Adequate planning is a key determinant of effectiveness.

DISCUSSION QUESTIONS

Questions for Review

1. What is an organization's general environment? Identify and discuss each of the major dimensions of the general environment.

2. What is an organization's task environment? What are the major dimensions of that environment?

3. What are the major forces that affect organization-environment relationships? Describe those forces.

4. What is organizational effectiveness? How is it studied and assessed?

Questions for Analysis

5. Can you think of dimensions of the task environment that are not discussed in the text? Indicate their linkage to those that are discussed.

6. Some organizations come to be part-owners of other firms through mergers and acquisitions. How does the nature of partial ownership complicate the organization-environment relationship?

7. How would each dimension of an organization's task environment and internal environment assess the organization's effectiveness? Can an organization be equally effective to each of these different groups? Why or why not?

Questions for Application

8. Go to the library and research a company. Characterize its level of effectiveness according to each of the four basic models. Share your results with the class.

9. Interview a manager from a local organization about his or her organization's environments—general, task, and internal. In the course of the interview, are all of the major dimensions identified? Why or why not?

10. Outline the several environments of your college or university. Be detailed about the dimensions and provide specific examples to illustrate how each dimension impacts on your institution.

BRINGING COLEMAN UP TO SPEED

Coleman's name is so well known, it's almost generic. Founder W.C. Coleman began selling lanterns to storekeepers in 1900, and Coleman Co., Inc., lanterns dominate lighting in America's campgrounds. Coleman's pocket stove was one of the GI's best friends in World War II.

With a company image so strong on tradition, it's perhaps not surprising that Coleman found itself suffering in the 1980s from what might be called "the slows." The company took as long as two months to get a shipment off to big retailers like Wal-Mart Stores, Inc., and Kmart, and above the floor of its huge 350,000-square-foot factory hung ceiling racks filled with parts. The huge inventory tended to cover up problems in the assembly process.

In 1989 the company's new owners brought in consultants to speed things up. One thing that the consultants did *not* try to do was pressure the workers to work faster, an approach almost sure to provoke resistance and increase errors. Instead, the consultants targeted waste, starting with the company's huge inventory. All those parts gathering dust in the racks represented a huge amount of idle cash, and one of the company's first tasks was to put that capital to work. It began adopting just-in-time manufacturing techniques, drastically cutting down on inventory.

As the sea of inventory receded, problems that it had long covered became more obvious. Now when a machine breaks, the assembly process stops, and the company fixes the problem as soon as possible. Instead of ordering the needed part from its tool and die shop twelve miles away, as it used to do, Coleman moved the shop into the factory, and the repair people are only a few minutes away.

At the same time, changes were occurring throughout the company. At the top level, management sold off unrelated businesses that Coleman had acquired over the years, including Hobie Cat sailboats, Dixon riding mowers, and O'Brien windsurfers and skis. The

Coleman reputation is an asset to camping-related products, but not necessarily to riding mowers. Coleman's management also realized that it had to change its old piecework system, which even paid workers for making defective parts. And it linked its computers to those of its biggest customers so orders could go directly from cash register to factory, cutting the time needed to fill customers' orders.

The changes at Coleman have been dramatic. While raising productivity 35 percent, Coleman has reduced scrap by 60 percent and trimmed inventory costs by $10 million. A new order can be made and shipped in a week rather than two months. And such progress in efficiency has not come at the expense of Coleman's products; it now offers 140 models of ice coolers in twelve colors instead of the 20 models in three colors of two years ago. Coleman is now truly up to speed.

Discussion Questions

1. Why did Coleman need the help of outside consultants to drastically change?

2. Lowering its inventory meant that Coleman had to put up with lots of stops and starts in its manufacturing process as it uncovered problems. Why was the company *glad* to confront such problems?

E 3. Changing from a piecework system to an hourly wage meant a drop in pay for some of Coleman's most productive workers. Is it possible for Coleman to motivate these workers to continue working at their current pace for less money?

References: Brian Dumaine, "Earning More by Moving Faster," *Fortune*, October 7, 1991, pp. 89–94; Michael Selz, "Coleman's Familiar Name Is Both Help and Hindrance," *The Wall Street Journal*, May 17, 1990, p. B2.

CAN EVERYONE WIN FROM NINTENDO'S PRICE-FIXING SETTLEMENT?

Nintendo was one of the great success stories of the 1980s. At a time when most toymakers thought video games were dead, Nintendo developed a system that became so popular that 30 million American homes now own at least one. Americans spend close to $4 billion a year on Nintendo's consoles and game cartridges, giving the Japanese company better than an 80 percent share of the home video game market.

Such dominance of its market recently led Nintendo into a legal and ethical gray area and eventually brought down the wrath of the Federal Trade Commission and prosecutors in New York and Maryland. According to the prosecutors, Nintendo took the concept of "manufacturer's suggested retail price" too far. From June 1988 to December 1990, Nintendo insisted that retailers sell its Nintendo Entertainment System consoles for $99.95. Prosecutors said that stores that tried to undercut the official price were threatened with slow shipments or perhaps a total cut-off of Nintendo products. This alleged price-fixing made healthy profits for retailers but restricted consumers' ability to shop for the best price.

Nintendo and the various prosecutors agreed to an unusual settlement. While continuing to assert that it was innocent of violating antitrust laws, Nintendo agreed to settle to avoid drawn-out court proceedings. It must pay $4.75 million to the states in damages and legal costs. And to reimburse those consumers who may have been hurt by the price-fixing, the settlement requires Nintendo to send $25 million worth of coupons for its products to its customers.

Nintendo's price-fixing problems weren't the only charges brought against the company. Nintendo's in-house designers come up with only about one-tenth of its games—its software—and it contracts with independent software designers for the rest. The company's relations with its creativity contractors rankle many people in the business. Nintendo keeps control of the software but forces the contractors to shoulder the risk of developing and marketing new games. Until 1990, Nintendo insisted on manufacturing—for a fee, of course—all games that could be played on its machines, even those that another company designed and sold. Even after it relaxed its grip on making the games, it kept control over the content of the games and their packaging.

Perhaps in response to the lawsuits, Nintendo is not trying to keep such exclusive control over the games played on its new 16-bit Super NES system, introduced in 1991. So in the future, more companies may profit from the Nintendo success story.

Discussion Questions

1. Why should it be illegal for a company to control the price of its products?

E 2. What particular issues are likely to be faced by companies that dominate their industries? What can management do to make sure it handles such issues well?

3. Nintendo's settlement forced customers to purchase another Nintendo product to get their refund. Previous settlements required customers to apply for a refund, which very few took the time to do. Can you think of a better way in which Nintendo could have been required to reimburse its customers?

References: Paul M. Barrett, "Nintendo's Latest Novelty Is a Price-Fixing Settlement," *The Wall Street Journal*, April 11, 1991, pp. B1, B2; Susan Moffat, "Can Nintendo Keep Winning?" *Fortune*, November 5, 1990, pp. 131–136; Joseph Pereira, "Nintendo Is Counting On New Super Game to Rescue Its Sales," *The Wall Street Journal*, May 10, 1991, pp. A1, A4.

The Ethical and Social Context of Management

OBJECTIVES

After studying this chapter, you should be able to:

● *Discuss the formation of individual ethics and describe three areas of special ethical concern for managers.*

● *Trace the development of the concept of social responsibility and specify to whom or what an organization might be considered responsible.*

● *Identify and describe four types of organizational approaches to social responsibility.*

● *Explain the relationship between the government and organizations regarding social responsibility.*

● *Describe some of the activities organizations may engage in to manage social responsibility.*

OUTLINE

Individual Ethics in Organizations
    The Formation of Individual Ethics
    Managerial Ethics
    Ethics in an Organizational Context
    Managing Ethical Behavior

Social Responsibility and Organizations
    Historical Views of Social Responsibility
    Areas of Social Responsibility
    Arguments For and Against Social
      Responsibility
    Organizational Approaches to Social
      Responsibility

The Government and Social
Responsibility
    How Government Influences
      Organizations
    How Organizations Influence
      Government

Managing Social Responsibility
    Formal Organizational Dimensions
    Informal Organizational Dimensions
    Evaluating Social Responsibility

SPURRED ON BY a rising tide of environmentalism and social consciousness during the last several years, many businesses have begun to realize that being good to the environment can be good for business. By trying to position their products as being good for the environment (or at least not as bad for the environment as alternative products), dozens of businesses have achieved important gains in both market share and profits.

One notable example of this trend is found in the trash business itself—more specifically, in the business of making plastic trash bags. Mobil Corporation started the practice when it began to advertise its line of Hefty trash bags as being biodegradable. Almost as soon as Mobil unveiled this new advertising campaign and started putting biodegradable claims on its packages, sales of its trash bags increased notably.

Unfortunately, so too did criticisms of the firm and its claims. As it turns out, Mobil's trash bags are indeed biodegradable—but only as long as they are left in direct sunlight. Because most trash bags end up in landfills covered with other trash, few of Mobil's bags will actually break down into compost as the term "biodegradable" actually implies.

Several states and the Federal Trade Commission are trying to force not only Mobil but all firms that take an enviromental slant on their advertising to be more truthful. Texas, for example, filed a lawsuit against Mobil on the basis of its exaggerated claims. Although Mobil did not admit guilt, it did provide a cash settlement and agreed to back off on its claims.[1] ●

obil Corporation has confronted one of the most challenging and controversial areas that organizations must face today—its relationship with the social environment in which it functions. Every society proscribes certain types of behaviors that organizations can and cannot pursue. Organizations that violate these social expectations may face consequences including public humiliation, loss of business, and legal sanctions. The ingredients that determine how an organization will respond to its social environment are the ethics of individuals within the organization and the social responsibility of the organization itself.

This chapter explores basic issues of ethics and social responsibility in detail. We first look at individual ethics and their organizational context and then expand our discussion to the somewhat contentious topic of social responsibility. After we explore some of the ways government attempts to persuade organizations to adopt socially responsible practices, we examine how organizations might more effectively manage these activities themselves.

INDIVIDUAL ETHICS IN ORGANIZATIONS

● **ethics**
An individual's personal beliefs regarding right and wrong behavior

We define **ethics** as an individual's personal beliefs regarding right and wrong behavior.[2] Although this definition communicates the essence of this concept, three implications of it warrant additional discussion. First, note that ethics are defined in the context of the individual—people have ethics, organizations do not. Second, what constitutes ethical behavior can vary from one person to another. For example, one person who finds a twenty-dollar-bill on the floor may believe that it is okay to stick it in his pocket whereas another will feel compelled to turn it in to the lost-and-found department. Third, ethics are relative, not absolute: although **ethical behavior** is in the eye of the beholder, it usually refers to behavior that conforms to generally accepted social norms. **Unethical behavior**, then, is behavior that does not conform to generally accepted social norms. In the sections that follow, we discuss the factors that influence the formation of individual ethics and consider ethical behavior in an organizational context. (Throughout our discussion we make references to higher and lower ethical standards or behavior that is more or less ethical; keep in mind that these distinctions are relative, as just discussed, as opposed to absolute.)

● **ethical behavior**
Behavior that conforms to generally accepted social norms

● **unethical behavior**
Behavior that does not conform to generally accepted social norms

The Formation of Individual Ethics

As Figure 4.1 shows, an individual's ethics are determined by a combination of family influences, peer influences, life experiences, personal values and morals, and situational factors.

Family Influences Individuals start to form ethical standards as children in response to their perceptions of the behavior of their parents and the behaviors their parents allow them to choose. Children are more likely to adopt high ethical standards if they see that other family members adhere

FIGURE 4.1 Determinants of Individual Ethics

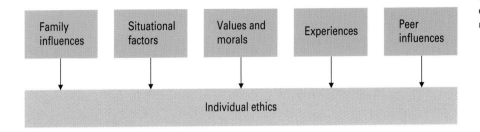

Individual ethics are determined by family and peer influences, experiences, values and morals, and situational factors.

to these high standards and if they receive rewards for conforming, and punishment for not conforming, to them. On the other hand, if family members engage in unethical behaviors and allow children to do the same, those children are likely to develop low ethical standards.

Peer Influences As children grow and enter school, they are also influenced by peers with whom they interact every day. For example, if a child's friends engage in shoplifting, vandalism, or drug abuse, he may decide to engage in these same activities. But if the child's peers have high ethical standards and reject such behaviors as drug abuse or theft, the child is more likely to adopt these standards.

Life Experiences Dozens of important individual events shape people's lives and contribute to their ethical beliefs and behavior. These events are a normal and routine part of growing up and maturing. Both positive and negative kinds of events will shape an individual's ethics. For example, if a person steals something and does not get caught, she may feel no remorse and continue to steal. But if she is caught stealing she may feel guilty enough to revise her ethical standards and not steal in the future.

Personal Values and Morals A person's values and morals also contribute to his or her ethical standards. A person who places financial gain and personal advancement at the top of his list of priorities, for example, will adopt a personal code of ethics that promotes the pursuit of wealth. Thus he may be ruthless in efforts to gain these rewards, regardless of the costs to others. In contrast, if a person's family is his top priority, he will adopt different ethical standards. One manager strongly influenced by his values is Kazuo Wada, a Japanese entrepreneur who is expanding his chain of grocery-and-department stores around the world. Each employee in his company must take lessons in the ancient religion of Seicho No Ie, and Wada uses its doctrines to guide every decision he makes.[3]

Situational Factors A final determinant of an individual's ethics is situational factors that arise. Sometimes people find themselves in unexpected situations that cause them to act against their better judgment. For example, many people who steal money from their employers do so because of personal financial difficulties. Although this does not justify their theft, it does provide some context for understanding how people may behave unethically if they believe that they have no other choice in the situation.[4]

There are three basic areas of concern for managerial ethics. These are the relationships of the firm to the employee, the employee to the firm, and the firm to other economic agents. Managers need to approach each set of relationships from an ethical and moral perspective.

TABLE 4.1   Special Areas of Concern for Managerial Ethics

Area of Concern	Sample Issues
Relationship of the firm to the employee	Hiring and firing Wages and working conditions Privacy
Relationship of the employee to the firm	Conflicts of interest Secrecy Honesty and expense accounts
Relationship of the firm to other economic agents	Customers Competitors Stockholders Suppliers Dealers Unions

Source: Adapted from Thomas M. Garrett and Richard J. Klonoski, *Business Ethics,* 2nd ed. (Englewood Cliffs, N.J.: Prentice-Hall, 1986). Adapted by permission.

Managerial Ethics

● **managerial ethics**
Standards of behavior that guide individual managers in their work

Managerial ethics are the standards of behavior that guide individual managers in their work. Although ethics can affect managerial work in any number of ways, three areas of special concern for managers are summarized in Table 4.1.

Relationship of the Firm to Its Employees   The behavior of managers defines the ethical standards according to which the firm treats its employees. This includes such areas as hiring and firing, wages and working conditions, and employee privacy. For example, many people consider it unethical for a manager to hire a family member or other close relative or to fire someone because of her religion (this latter action is also illegal in the United States). A manager's spreading a rumor that an employee has AIDS or is having an illicit affair is also generally seen as an unethical breach of privacy.

Relationship of Employees to the Firm   Numerous ethical issues also surround the relationship of employees to the firm, especially in regard to conflicts of interest, secrecy, and honesty in keeping expense accounts. A conflict of interest occurs when a decision potentially benefits the individual to the possible detriment of the organization. For example, if a manager in charge of selecting a new supplier accepts gifts from one supplier trying to land the account he may award the contract to that supplier even though another one might have offered the firm a better deal. To avoid such conflicts of interest, Wal-Mart Stores, Inc., does not allow its merchandise buyers to accept meals or gifts from sales representatives.[5] Divulging company secrets to a competing organization is also unethical, as is padding an expense account. Even so, some managers routinely add false meals, service charges, and car mileage to their expense account reports to unethically pad their income.

Relationship of the Firm to Other Economic Agents Managerial ethics also come into play in the relationship between the firm and other economic agents. Normal business ethics in customer relations suggest that products be safe; be accompanied by information about product features, uses, and limitations; and be reasonably priced.[6] The behavior of managers toward competitors is also dictated by ethical standards—unfair business practices (for example, pricing products low to drive a competitor out of business) and denigration of competitors (such as making false claims in advertising about a competitor's products) are examples of unethical treatment of competitors. Similarly, ethical standards also dictate that managers be truthful with stockholders. The CEO of Regina Co., Inc., was recently charged with violating regulations of the Securities and Exchange Commission. He allegedly altered financial records to make it seem as though the firm had more cash reserves than it actually did, and he told investors that the firm was making high profits when it was really operating at a loss.[7] Managers should also be fair and honest with suppliers, dealers, and unions. Convincing a supplier that a price break is needed or convincing a union that wage concessions are needed because of impending losses is unethical if the firm actually expects to make a profit. "Management in Practice" discusses some ethical issues regarding Dow Corning's dealings with its customers.

Ethics in an Organizational Context

It is vital to note that ethical or unethical actions by particular managers do not occur in a vacuum.[8] Indeed, they most often occur in an organizational context that is conducive to them. Actions of peer managers and top managers, as well as the organization's culture, all contribute to the ethical context of the organization. A recent Wall Street scandal at Salomon Brothers Inc. involved illegal transactions in the bond market. It occurred in an organizational context that stressed making money and controlling information.[9]

The starting point in understanding the ethical context of management is the individual's own ethical standards. Some people, for example, are willing to risk personal embarrassment or lose their job before they would do something unethical. Other people are much more easily swayed by the unethical behavior they see around them and other situational factors, and they may be willing to commit major crimes to further their own careers or for financial gain. Organizational practices may strongly influence the ethical standards of employees. Some organizations openly permit unethical business practices as long as they are in the best interests of the firm.

If a manager becomes aware of an unethical practice then allows it to continue, he has contributed to the organizational culture that says such activity is permitted. For example, when the CEO of Beech-Nut discovered that his firm was using additives in its apple juice advertised as 100-percent pure, he decided to try to cover up the deception until the remaining juice could be disposed of. Many employees participated in his plan. When the cover-up was finally discovered, the company suffered grave damages to its reputation and had to pay several million dollars in fines. In addition, the CEO was sentenced to a jail term.[10]

Anheuser-Busch educates the public on alcohol awareness by providing videos and trained speakers to schools and financial support for alcohol-abuse programs. Their "Susie Collins" ad dramatically shows the difficulty retailers face in guessing whether someone is of legal drinking age. With this ad Anheuser-Busch is demonstrating its commitment to the safe and legal consumption of alcohol to employees, as well as to those in its external environment, such as stockholders, parents, retailers and other companies.

The organization's environment also contributes to the context for ethical behavior. In a highly competitive or regulated industry, for example, a manager may feel more pressure to achieve high performance. In Japan managerial success is often determined by the kinds of connections the manager is able to establish with important people. One Japanese manager, Hiromasa Ezoe, CEO of the Recruit Company conglomerate, was recently found guilty of giving lucrative stock options to a variety of well-placed governmental officials to facilitate this process of networking.[11]

Managing Ethical Behavior

Spurred partially by the recent spate of ethical scandals and partially from a sense of enhanced corporate consciousness about the importance of ethical and unethical behaviors, many organizations have reemphasized ethical behavior on the part of employees.[12] This emphasis takes many forms, but any effort to enhance ethical behavior must begin with top management. It is this group that establishes the organization's culture and defines what will and will not be acceptable behavior. Some companies have also started offering employees training in how to cope with ethical dilemmas. At The Boeing Co., for example, line managers lead training sessions for other employees, and the company also has an ethics committee that reports directly to the board of directors. The training sessions involve discussions of different ethical dilemmas that employees might face and how managers might handle those dilemmas. Chemical Bank, Xerox Corp., and McDon-

DOW CORNING'S IMPLANT NIGHTMARE

 From 1962 until 1992, Dow Corning, a joint venture of The Dow Chemical Co. and Corning Incorporated, was the country's largest maker of silicone gel breast implants, although the product accounted for less than 1 percent of the company's $1.84 billion in annual sales. An estimated one million U.S. women have had silicone breast implants, most of them without any complications. About twenty precent of the women who wear them receive the implants after breast cancer surgery; most other implants are used to increase breast size.

Although more than 100,000 women were receiving implants each year, the Federal Food and Drug Administration (FDA) was slow to investigate the safety of the implants and did not demand safety data from the manufacturers until 1988. Finally, in 1992, an FDA panel recommended that use of implants be sharply curtailed. The panel found that some implants ruptured and others leaked without rupturing, and a number of women blamed the implants for causing tumors and immune disorders. Most damaging to Dow Corning's credibility were internal memos, some of them dating from twenty years ago, that showed that some company scientists had been concerned about the implants' safety for years. Other documents revealed that Dow Corning had kept test studies and other reports showing problems with the implants from the public.

Dow Corning has already lost some million-dollar lawsuits stemming from the implants. Critics liken the company's attitude and apparent cover up to Exxon Corporation's unpopular and inadequate response to the *Valdez* oil spill. The company's defenders, among them plastic surgeons who profit much more from the implants than implant makers do, pointed out that if the lawsuits and media attention drive implants off the market, the victims will be those women who want and can't get implants, particularly cancer patients.

Parent company Dow Chemical has received much criticism for making napalm and Agent Orange during the Vietnam war, but Dow Corning's corporate ethics had not been seriously challenged until the implant scandal. In fact, the company was widely praised for agreeing in 1985 to continue making silicone contact lenses, despite slim profits, when it learned that the lenses were used to treat infant blindness. And some of Dow Corning's recent problems may have stemmed from well-intentioned employees who were trying to help. When the company set up a hot line for women with questions about implants, for instance, many of the operators gave unrealistic information about the implants. Were they being unethical, or just trying to calm unwarranted fears? Such questions will be argued in the press and the courts for years.

References: Barnaby J. Feder, "P.R. Mistakes Seen In Breast-Implant Case," *The New York Times*, January 29, 1992, pp. D1, D2; Philip J. Hilts, "Biggest Maker of Breast Implants Is Said to Be Abandoning Market," *The New York Times*, March 19, 1992, pp. A1, B11.

nell Douglas Corp. have also established ethics training programs for their managers.[13]

Organizations are also going to greater lengths to formalize their ethical standards. Some, such as General Mills, Inc., and Johnson & Johnson, have prepared guidelines that detail how employees are to treat suppliers, customers, competitors, and other constituents. Others, such as Whirlpool Corporation and Hewlett-Packard Co., have developed formal **codes of ethics**—written statements of the values and ethical standards that guide the firms' actions. The Whirlpool code of ethical conduct is reproduced in Figure 4.2.

Of course, no code, guideline, or training program can truly make up for the quality of an individual's personal judgment about what is right

● **codes of ethics**
Formal, written statements of the values and ethical standards that guide a firm's actions

ETHICS AS A PRACTICAL MATTER

A message from David R. Whitwam Chairman of the Board

The question of ethics in business conduct has become one of the most serious challenges to the business community in modern times.

At Whirlpool, we share with millions of other Americans a deep concern over recent revelations of unethical and often illegal conduct on the part of some of this nation's most prominent business people and corporations.

The purpose of this message is not to pass judgement on any of these occurrences; each must and will be judged on its own merits by those charged with that responsibility.

Rather this message is intended to place firmly on record the position of Whirlpool Corporataion regarding business ethics and the conduct of every Whirlpool employee. It represents an irrevocable commitment to our customers and stockholders that our actions will be governed by the highest personal and professional standards in all activities relating to the operation of this business.

Over the years, circumstances have prompted us to develop a number of specific policies dealing with such critical elements of ethical business practice as **conflicts of interest, gifts, political activities, entertainment, and substantiation of claims.**

We also have a basic statement of ethics which places the ultimate responsibility for ethical behavior precisely where it belongs in any organization . . . on the shoulders of the person in charge:

"No employee of this company will ever be called upon to do anything in the line of duty that is morally, ethically or legally wrong.

Furthermore, if in the operation of this complex enterprise, an employee should come upon circumstances of which he or she cannot be personally proud, it should be that person's duty to bring it to the attention of top management if unable to correct the matter in any other way."

Every Whirlpool manager carries the dual responsibility implicit in this policy statement, including the chairman of the board.

In the final analysis, "ethical behavior" must be an integral part of the organization, a way of life that is deeply ingrained in the collective corporate body.

I belive this condition exits at Whirlpool, and that is consititutes our greatest single assurance that this company's employees will conduct the affairs of this business in a manner consistent with the highest standards of ethical behavior.

At Whirlpool we have certain ways of doing things. They are commonly accepted practices, enforced not by edict, but rather by a mutual conviction that they will, in the long term, work in the best interest of our customers, our stockholders, the company and all its employees.

In any business enterprise, ethical behavior must be a tradition, a way of conducting one's affairs that is passed on from generation to generation of employees at all levels of the organization. It is the responsibility of management, starting at the very top, to both set the example by personal conduct and create an environment that not only encourages and rewards ethical behavior, but which also makes anything less total unacceptable.

Sincerely,

David Whitwam

David R. Whitwam

David R. Whitwam, chairman of the board for Whirlpool Corporation, recently made this statement of ethics on behalf of the organization. Many other firms, including Hewlett-Packard, Levi Strauss, Philip Morris, and Texaco also have written codes of ethical conduct.

| TABLE 4.2 | Arguments For and Against Social Responsibility |

Arguments For Social Responsibility	Arguments Against Social Responsibility
1. Business creates problems and should therefore help solve them.	1. The purpose of business in American society is to generate profit for owners.
2. Corporations are citizens in our society.	2. Involvement in social programs gives business too much power.
3. Business often has the resources necessary to solve problems.	3. There is potential for conflicts of interest.
4. Business is a partner in our society, along with the government and the general population.	4. Business lacks the expertise to manage social programs.

Arguments For and Against Social Responsibility

On the surface, there would seem to be little disagreement about the need for organizations to be socially responsible. In truth, though, there are several convincing arguments used by those who oppose these wider interpretations of social responsibility.[26] Some of the more salient arguments on both sides of this contemporary debate are summarized in Table 4.2 and further explained in the following sections.

Arguments Against Some people, including the famous economist Milton Friedman, argue that widening the interpretation of social responsibility will undermine the U.S. economy by detracting from the basic mission of business: to earn profits for owners. For example, money that Chevron Corporation or General Electric Co. contributes to social causes or charities is money that could otherwise be distributed to owners as a dividend. Another objection to deepening the social responsibility of businesses points out that corporations already wield enormous power and that pushing them to be more active in social programs gives them even more power.

Other arguments against social responsibility focus on the potential for conflict of interest. Suppose, for example, that one manager is in charge of deciding which local social program or charity will receive a large grant from her business. The local civic opera company (a not-for-profit organization that relies on contributions for its existence) might offer her front-row tickets for the upcoming season in exchange for her support. If opera is her favorite form of music, she might be tempted to direct the money toward the local company, when it might actually be needed more in other areas.

Finally, critics argue that organizations lack the expertise to understand how to assess and make decisions about worthy social programs. Beyond the conflict of interest example just noted, how can a company truly know which cause or program is most deserving of its support? People who ask these questions also see an alarming trend on the part of organizations to

tie products to social causes. This practice began in 1983 when American Express Company pledged to donate one cent to the Statue of Liberty restoration project each time one of its credit cards was used. More recently MCI Communications Corp. has begun to contribute a share of its long-distance telephone profits to a reforestation program, and several other firms have employed similar promotional activities. Critics of this practice fear that it will enable companies to exert too much influence over the charitable causes with which they become associated and that charities will begin to function merely as marketing agents to help the firms sell their products.[27]

Arguments For People who argue in favor of social responsibility claim that because organizations create many of the problems that need to be addressed, such as air and water pollution and resource depletion, they should play a major role in solving them. They also argue that because corporations are legally defined entities with most of the same privileges as private citizens, businesses should not try to avoid their obligations as citizens. Advocates of social responsibility point out that while governmental organizations have stretched their budgets to the limit, many large businesses often have surplus revenues that could potentially be used to help solve social problems. For example, IBM routinely donates surplus computers to schools.

While each of the arguments just summarized are distinct justifications for socially responsible behaviors on the part of organizations, another basic reason for social responsibility is profit itself. For example, organizations that make clear and visible contributions to society can achieve enhanced reputations and garner greater market share for their products. While claims such as those made by Mobil (as described in the beginning of this chapter) can haunt a company if they are exaggerated or untrue, they can also work to the benefit of both the organization and society if the advertised benefits are true and accurate. For example, during MCI's advertising campaign for its contributions to reforestation, the firm's spokesperson acknowledged that the firm was doing it to get more business. But she went on to argue that that was okay because everybody could win: the consumer would get a good product for a competitive price, the firm would increase its profits, and the natural environment would get more trees.

Organizational Approaches to Social Responsibility

As we have seen, some people advocate a larger social role for organizations, and others argue that the role is already too large. Not surprisingly, organizations themselves adopt a wide range of positions on social responsibility. As Figure 4.4 illustrates, the four stances that an organization can take concerning their obligations to society fall along a continuum ranging from the lowest to the highest degree of socially responsible practices.

● **social obstruction**
An approach to social responsibility in which firms do as little as possible to solve social or environmental problems

Social Obstruction The few organizations that take what might be called a **social obstruction** approach to social responsibility usually do as little as possible to solve social or environmental problems. When they cross the ethical or legal line that separates acceptable from unacceptable practices, their typical response is to deny or cover up their actions. We noted earlier

Degree of social responsibility

Social obstruction	Social obligation	Social response	Social contribution

Lowest   *Highest*

Organizations can adopt a variety of approaches to social responsibility. For example, a firm that never considers the consequences of its decisions and tries to hide its transgressions is taking a social opposition stance. At the other extreme, a firm that actively seeks to identify areas where it can help society is pursuing a social contribution approach.

Beech-Nut's attempt to hide the truth about its apple juice additives. Ashland Oil also has an unfortunate history of alleged social wrongdoing followed by less-than-model responses. For example, Ashland was found guilty of rigging bids with other contractors to charge higher prices for highway work in Tennessee and North Carolina. It was also recently charged with wrongfully firing two employees because they refused to cover up illegal payments that the company made.[28]

Social Obligation   One step removed from social obstruction is **social obligation**, whereby the organization will do everything that is required of it legally but nothing more. This approach is most consistent with the arguments used against social responsibility just described. Managers in organizations that take a social obligation approach insist that their job is to generate profits. For example, such a firm would install pollution control equipment dictated by law, but would not install higher-quality equipment even though it might limit pollution further. Tobacco companies such as Philip Morris Incorporated take this position regarding their international marketing efforts. In the United States, they are legally required to include warnings to smokers on their products and to limit their advertising to prescribed media. Domestically they follow these rules to the letter of the law but use stronger marketing methods in countries that have no such rules. In many African countries, for example, cigarettes are heavily promoted, contain higher levels of tar and nicotine than those sold in the United States, and carry few or no health warning labels.

● **social obligation**
A social responsibility stance in which an organization will do everything that is required of it legally but nothing more

Social Response   A firm that adopts the **social response** approach meets its legal and ethical requirements but will also go beyond these requirements in selected cases. Such firms voluntarily agree to participate in social programs, but solicitors have to convince the organization that they are worthy of their support. Both Exxon and IBM, for example, will match contributions made by their employees to selected charitable causes. And many organizations will respond to requests for donations to Little League, Girl Scouts of the United States of America, and so forth. The point, though, is that someone has to knock on the door and ask—the organizations do not proactively seek such avenues for contributing.

● **social response**
A social responsibility stance in which an organization meets its basic legal and ethical obligations and also goes beyond social obligation in selected cases

Social Contribution   The highest degree of social responsibility that a firm can exhibit is the **social contribution** approach. Firms that adopt this approach take to heart the arguments in favor of social responsibility. They view themselves as citizens in a society and proactively seek opportunities to contribute. An excellent example of a social contribution is the Ronald McDonald House program undertaken by McDonald's Corp. These

● **social contribution**
A social responsibility stance in which an organization views itself as a citizen in a society and proactively seeks opportunities to contribute to that society

A firm that adopts the social contribution approach to social responsibility proactively seeks opportunities to contribute to society. Du Pont, for example, actively recruits women, minorities, and persons with disabilities in the United States and abroad. At the Du Pont plant in Buenos Aires, Du Pont manager Nelson Culler works with Ruben Kunz, the local fire chief, and Mabel de Slingo of the community's environmental association on community outreach programs.

houses, located close to major medical centers, can be used by families for minimal cost while their sick children are receiving medical treatment nearby. Sears, Roebuck and Co. offers fellowships that support promising young performers while they continue to develop their talents. These and related activities and programs exceed the social response approach—they indicate a sincere and potent commitment to improving the general social welfare in this country. "The Global View" summarizes how many international businesses are also adopting a social contribution approach.

Remember that these categories are not discrete but merely define stages along a continuum of approach. Organizations do not always fit neatly into one category. The Ronald McDonald House program has been widely applauded, for example, but McDonald's also came under fire a few years ago for allegedly misleading consumers about the nutritional value of its food products.[29] And even though Beech-Nut and Ashland Oil took a social obstruction approach in the cases we cited, many individual employees and managers at both firms have no doubt made substantial contributions to society in a number of different ways.

THE GOVERNMENT AND SOCIAL RESPONSIBILITY

We saw earlier in our historical overview the government's increasing part in shaping the role of organizations in contemporary society. The relationship between organizations and government is two-way, however. As Figure 4.5 shows, organizations and the government use several methods in their attempts to influence each other.

INTERNATIONAL CORPORATE PHILANTHROPY

 Many American communities take for granted the charity of their local corporations. Educational institutions, not-for-profit community groups, and local chapters of national organizations such as the United Way of America often look to local corporate sponsors for money and other forms of support. But now that so many organizations do business around the globe, philanthropy, too, is becoming global. And the money flows to many sources.

In 1990 Alcoa gave $112,000 to a small city in southern Brazil to build a sewage treatment plant, improving the water quality for 15,000 people, some of them Alcoa employees. Du Pont sent 1.4 million water-jug filters to eight African nations to help remove parasitic worms from the drinking water. IBM donated computers and expertise to Costa Rica's National Parks Foundation, which is working to save rain forests.

When contrasted to the $1.8 billion in total donations that the country's 333 largest corporations made in 1989, these philanthropic gestures may seem small. In fact, only about six percent of that $1.8 billion goes overseas. But many American corporations are increasing their overseas contributions, reasoning that if charity makes sense at home, it makes sense wherever they do business.

More rapid has been the increase in the rate at which Japanese companies have funded American charities. In 1991 they contributed some $500 million to U.S. not-for-profit organizations, sixteen times as much as in 1986. And while traditionally Japanese companies had seemed interested only in such elite recipients as top universities or high-brow cultural events, now they are spreading their money around to organizations with more varied needs. Some corporations are specifically targeting minorities; Hitachi, Ltd., for instance, has earmarked about half of its contributions over the past five years for minority organizations.

Whether the money is flowing east or west, corporate motivations tend to be the same. Companies want to improve their images, help their communities, create good will, and increase their profile and name recognition. The rapid rise in Japanese contributions to U.S. not-for-profit organizations is clearly linked to the desire among Japanese corporations to improve their image among the American public and reduce Japan-bashing and the hesitancy among some Americans to buy Japanese products. The Japanese government has encouraged such moves by giving Japanese companies a tax break twice as large for foreign contributions as for domestic. Some economists consider all corporate donations to be self-serving, ultimately aimed at increasing sales and profits. But even if the corporations' motives are mixed, few recipients of the increased aid are complaining.

References: Suzanne Alexander, "Japanese Firms Embark on a Program of Lavish Giving to American Charities," *The Wall Street Journal*, May 23, 1991, pp. B1, B5; Michael Schroeder, "Charity Doesn't Begin At Home Anymore," *Business Week*, February 25, 1991, p. 91.

How Government Influences Organizations

Direct Regulation   The government most often influences organizations through **regulation**, the establishment of laws and rules that dictate what organizations can and cannot do. To implement legislation, the government creates special agencies to monitor and control certain aspects of business activity. For example, the Environmental Protection Agency handles environmental issues; the Federal Trade Commission and the Food and Drug Administration focus on consumer-related concerns; the Equal Employee Opportunity Commission, the National Labor Relations Board, and the Occupational Safety and Health Administration help protect employees;

regulation
Government's attempts to influence business by establishing laws and rules that dictate what businesses can and cannot do in prescribed areas

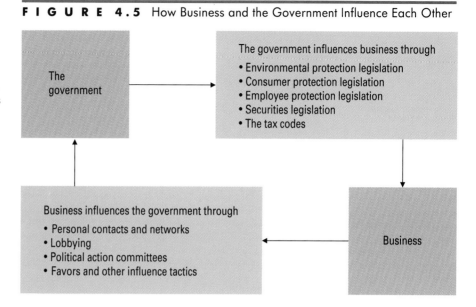

FIGURE 4.5 How Business and the Government Influence Each Other

The government

The government influences business through

• Environmental protection legislation
• Consumer protection legislation
• Employee protection legislation
• Securities legislation
• The tax codes

Business influences the government through

• Personal contacts and networks
• Lobbying
• Political action committees
• Favors and other influence tactics

Business

and the Securities and Exchange Commission handles investor-related issues. These agencies have the power to levy fines or bring charges against organizations that violate regulations.[30] Although these are the major governmental regulating agencies, there are many other more specialized agencies at both federal and state levels.

Indirect Regulation   Other forms of regulation are indirect. For example, the government can indirectly influence the social responsibility of organizations through its tax codes. In effect, the government can influence how organizations spend their social responsibility dollars by providing greater or lesser tax incentives. For instance, suppose the government wanted organizations to spend more on training the hard-core unemployed. Congress could then pass laws that provided tax incentives to companies that opened new training facilities. As a result, more businesses would probably do so. Of course, some critics argue that regulation is already excessive. They maintain that a free market system would eventually accomplish the same goals as regulation, but with lower costs to both organizations and the government.

How Organizations Influence Government

As we mentioned in Chapter 3 organizations can influence their environment in many different ways. They have four main methods of addressing governmental pressures for more social responsibility.

Personal Contacts   Because many corporate executives and political leaders travel in the same social circles, personal contacts and networks offer one method of influence. A business executive may be able to contact a politician directly and present his or her case regarding a piece of legislation being considered.

Lobbying   **Lobbying**, or the use of persons or groups to formally represent an organization or group of organizations before political bodies, is also an effective way to influence the government. For example, a few years ago Congress was close to passing the Family and Medical Leave Act, which would require organizations to give unpaid leave to parents of newborns. More than 150 businesses and trade associations joined forces and sent lobbyists to Washington to argue against the proposed law. As a result, passage of the bill was blocked.[31]

Political Action Committees   Companies themselves cannot legally make direct donations to political campaigns, so they influence the government through political action committees. **Political action committees (PACs)** are special organizations created to solicit money and then distribute it to political candidates. Employees of a firm may be encouraged to make donations to particular PACs, because managers know that it will support candidates with political views similar to their own. PACs, in turn, make the contributions themselves, usually to a broad slate of state and national candidates. For example, Federal Express Corp.'s PAC is called Fepac. It makes most of its donations to Democrats because that party currently has control of both the House and the Senate.[32]

Favors   Finally, organizations sometimes rely on favors and other influence tactics to gain support. A few years back, for example, two key members of a House committee attending a fund-raising function in Miami were needed in Washington to finish work on a piece of legislation that Federal Express wanted passed. The law being drafted would allow the company and its competitors to give their employees standby seats on airlines as a tax-free benefit. As a favor, Federal Express provided one of its corporate jets to fly the committee members back to Washington.[33] The company was eventually reimbursed for its expenses, so its assistance was not illegal, but some people might argue that such actions are dangerous because they can easily lead to practices that are illegal. Bribes, blackmail, and other tactics have been part of the arsenal businesses call on to make their wishes known in Washington. To combat illegal practices, numerous regulations have been passed in recent years stipulating what kinds of services organizations can and cannot provide for government officials.

MANAGING SOCIAL RESPONSIBILITY

The demands for social responsibility placed on contemporary organizations by an increasingly sophisticated and educated public are probably stronger than ever. As we have seen, there are pitfalls for managers who fail to adhere to high ethical standards and for companies that try to circumvent their legal obligations. Organizations therefore need to fashion an approach to social responsibility the way they develop any other business strategy. That is, they should view social responsibility as a major challenge that requires careful planning, decision making, consideration, and evaluation. They may accomplish this through both formal and informal dimensions of managing social responsibility.[34]

Formal Organizational Dimensions

Some dimensions of managing social responsibility are a formal and planned activity on the part of the organization. Formal organizational dimensions that can help manage social responsibility are legal compliance, ethical compliance, and philanthropic giving.[35]

legal compliance
The extent to which an organization complies with local, state, federal, and international laws

ethical compliance
The extent to which an organization and its members follow basic ethical standards of behavior

philanthropic giving
Awarding funds or other gifts to charities or worthy causes

Legal Compliance **Legal compliance** is the extent to which the organization conforms to local, state, federal, and international laws. The task of managing legal compliance is generally assigned to the appropriate functional managers. For example, the organization's top human resource executive is generally responsible for ensuring compliance with regulations concerning recruiting, selection, pay, and so forth. Likewise, the top finance executive generally oversees compliance with securities and banking regulations. The organization's legal department is also likely to contribute to this effort by providing general oversight and answering queries from managers about the appropriate interpretation of laws and regulations.

Ethical Compliance **Ethical compliance** is the extent to which the members of the organization follow basic ethical (and legal) standards of behavior. We noted earlier that organizations have started doing more in this area—providing training in ethics and developing guidelines and codes of conduct, for example. These activities serve as vehicles for enhancing ethical compliance. Many organizations also establish formal ethics committees, which may be asked to review proposals for new projects, help evaluate new hiring strategies, or assess a new environmental protection plan. They might also serve as a peer review panel to evaluate alleged ethical misconduct by an employee.

Philanthropic Giving Finally, **philanthropic giving** is the awarding of funds or other gifts to charities or other social programs. Dayton-Hudson Corp. routinely gives 5 percent of its taxable income to charity and social programs. Unfortunately, in this age of cutbacks, many corporations have had to limit their charitable gifts over the past several years as they continue to trim their own budgets. For example, Atlantic Richfield Co.'s corporate giving decreased from $37 million in 1983 to $11.4 million in 1987.[36] Firms that do engage in philanthropic giving usually have a committee of top executives who review requests for grants and decide how much and to whom money will be allocated.

Ethical compliance—or the extent to which an organization's employees follow basic ethical and legal standards of behavior—is on the increase. An example of a firm that is behaving ethically toward the environment is Wendy's International. In February 1991, Wendy's began packaging its Kids' Meals in recyclable paper bags. Making the switch is eliminating an estimated 2.6 million pounds of waste.

Informal Organizational Dimensions

In addition to these formal dimensions for managing social responsibility, there are also informal ones. Two of the more effective ways to clarify the organization's approach are to provide appropriate leadership and culture and to allow for whistle blowing.

Organization Leadership and Culture Leadership practices and organization culture can go a long way toward defining the social responsibility stance an organization and its members will adopt. For example, Johnson &

Johnson executives for years provided a consistent message to employees that customers, employees, communities where the company did business, and shareholders were all important—and primarily in that order. Thus when packages of poisoned Tylenol showed up on store shelves in the 1980s, Johnson & Johnson employees didn't need to wait for orders from headquarters to know what to do: they immediately pulled all the packages from shelves before any other customers could buy them.[37] By contrast, the message sent to Beech-Nut employees by the actions of their top managers communicates much less regard for social responsibility.

Whistle Blowing **Whistle blowing** is the disclosure by an employee of illegal or unethical conduct on the part of others within the organization. How an organization responds to this practice often indicates its stance toward social responsibility. Whistle blowers may have to proceed through a number of channels to be heard and may even get fired for their efforts. Many organizations, however, welcome their contributions. A person who observes questionable behavior typically reports the incident to his or her boss at first. If nothing is done, the whistle blower may then inform higher-level managers or an ethics committee if one exists. Eventually, the person may have to go to a regulatory agency or even the media to be heard.[38] For example, the apple juice scandal at Beech-Nut started with a whistle blower. A manager in the firm's R&D department began to suspect that its apple juice was not "100% pure." His boss, however, was unsympathetic, and when the manager went to the president of the company, he too turned a deaf ear. Finally, the manager took his message to the media, which publicized the incident, eventually leading to a criminal investigation.

whistle blowing
The disclosing by an employee of illegal or unethical conduct on the part of others within the organization

Rosemary Jefferson, Accounting Assistant at PSE&G, works with AIDS-infected babies at St. Clare's Home in Jersey City. PSE&G's support and encouragement of its employees' efforts in this and other community service areas communicates the organization's high regard for social responsibility.

Evaluating Social Responsibility

Any organization that is serious about social responsibility must ensure that its efforts are producing the desired benefits. Essentially this requires applying the concept of control to social responsibility. Many organizations now require current and new employees to read their guidelines or code of ethics and then sign a statement agreeing to abide by it. An organization should also evaluate how it responds to instances of questionable legal or ethical conduct. Does it follow up immediately? Does it punish those involved? Or does it use delay and cover-up tactics? Answers to these questions can help an organization form a picture of its approach to social responsibility.

Additionally, some organizations occasionally conduct corporate social audits. A **corporate social audit** is a formal and thorough analysis of the effectiveness of the firm's social performance. The audit is usually conducted by a task force of key managers from within the firm. It requires that the organization clearly define all its social goals, analyze the resources devoted to each goal, determine how well the various goals are being achieved, and make recommendations about which areas need additional attention. Unfortunately, such audits are not conducted very often because they are expensive and time consuming. Indeed, most organizations probably could do much more to evaluate the extent of their social responsibility than they do.

corporate social audit
A formal and thorough analysis of the effectiveness of a firm's social performance

SUMMARY OF KEY POINTS

Ethics are an individual's personal beliefs about what constitutes right and wrong behavior. Ethics are formed by family and peer influences, life experiences, personal values and morals, and situational factors. Important areas of ethical concern for managers are the relationship of the firm to employees, the relationship of employees to the firm, and the relationship of the firm to other economic agents. The ethical context of organizations consists of each manager's individual ethics and messages sent by organizational practices. Organizations use leadership, culture, training, codes, and guidelines to help them manage ethical behavior.

Social responsibility is the set of obligations an organization has to protect and enhance the society in which it functions. Views of social responsibility have developed from the entrepreneurial era, through the Depression era and the social era, up to the present time. Organizations may be considered responsible to their constituents, to the natural environment, and to the general social welfare. Even so, organizations present strong arguments both for and against social responsibility. The approach an organization adopts toward social responsibility falls along a continuum of lesser to greater commitment: social obstruction, social obligation, social response, and social contribution.

Government influences organizations through regulation, which is the establishment of laws and rules that dictate what businesses can and cannot do in prescribed areas. Organizations, in turn, rely on personal contacts, lobbying, political action committees, and favors to influence the government.

Organizations use three types of activities to formally manage social responsibility: legal compliance, ethical compliance, and philanthropic giving. Leadership, culture, and allowing for whistle blowing are informal means for managing social responsibility. Organizations should evaluate the effectiveness of their socially responsible practices as they would any other strategy.

DISCUSSION QUESTIONS

Questions for Review

1. What are ethics? How are an individual's ethics formed?
2. Summarize the basic historical views of social responsibility.
3. What are the arguments for and against social responsibility?
4. How does the government influence organizations? How do organizations influence the government?

Questions for Analysis

5. What is the relationship between the law and ethical behavior? Is it possible for illegal behavior to be ethical?

6. How are the ethics of an organization's CEO related to social responsibility?

7. How do you feel about whistle-blowing activity? If you were aware of a criminal activity taking place in your organization, and if reporting it might cost you your job, what would you do?

Questions for Application

8. Refresh your memory about the Exxon *Valdez* oil spill. Evaluate the social responsibility dilemmas facing the company. For example, if Exxon had pledged unlimited resources to the cleanup, would this have been fair to the company's stockholders?

9. Research the social responsibility activities of ten large companies. What is your personal assessment of each?

10. Review the arguments for and against social responsibility. On a scale of 1 to 10, rate the validity and importance of each point. Use these ratings to develop a position regarding how socially responsible an organization should be. Now compare your ratings and position with those of two of your classmates. Discuss your respective positions, focusing primarily on disagreements.

HERMAN MILLER: BUILDING FURNITURE AND THE FUTURE

Herman Miller, Inc., proves that financial success and a constant striving to be a better corporate citizen are complementary, not contradictory, goals. The company has long been as well known for its participative management system as for its innovative office furniture designs. Anyone from any level is free to talk to anyone else at Miller; the company even videotapes officers' and directors' meetings and shows them to employees at work-team meetings. Miller's growth has been tremendous, from $50 million in sales in 1976 to more than $850 million today.

Herman Miller is now leading the way in another area: it is doing everything it can to lessen its adverse effect on the environment. It recycles leather, vinyl, foam, office paper, telephone books, lubricating oil, and even old office furniture, which it reconditions and re-sells. When it found that recycling 800,000 Styrofoam cups every year wasn't practical, it banned the cups and handed out 5,000 mugs. Instead of dumping into landfills the 4,000 tons of scrap fabric that it produces each year, it now ships them to a North Carolina firm that shreds them and turns them into insulation for car-roof linings and dashboards.

Since 1982, much of the trash that can't be recycled has fueled Miller's waste-to-energy plant, which saves $750,000 a year in fuel and landfill costs and paid for itself in ten years, a decade ahead of schedule. Miller also recently spent $800,000 for two high-tech incinerators to burn the toxic solvents that escape during staining and varnishing, even though it hopes to make the incinerators obsolete by switching to water-based and powder-based finishes.

Miller's environmental consciousness extends beyond local and national boundaries. One of the company's best-known products, the $2,277 Eames chair, was always finished with rosewood until the company's research manager realized that Herman Miller was contributing to the destruction of tropical rain for-ests. He consequently banned the use of rose-wood and Honduran mahogany.

Another test of Herman Miller's humane attitude came when some of its employees contracted the AIDS virus. When an AIDS victim in the company's Georgia plant decided to let the rest of the workers know about his condition, his supervisor took charge, acting as what Herman Miller Chairman Max DePree calls a "roving leader." The supervisor told two managers, and then the three of them quickly told everyone in the plant, ensuring that rumors didn't get started. On the next work day after the announcement, the company's director of health and wellness flew down from Michigan to show a video on AIDS and answer questions. With a history of such sensitivity to its environment and its workers, it's no surprise that Herman Miller tops lists of best-managed and most-admired companies.

Discussion Questions

1. How could a Herman Miller manager convince a stockholder interested only in profit that treating an AIDS patient well was good for the company?

2. What approach to social responsibility do you think Miller takes? Do you agree with this strategy? Why or why not?

E 3. What do you think are the underlying forces at work or the causes for Miller's approach to social responsibility?

References: "Designs to Live By," *Architectural Record*, June 1989, pp. 106–107; Joani Nelson-Horchler, "The Magic of Herman Miller," *Industry Week*, February 18, 1991, pp. 11–17; David Woodruff, "Herman Miller: How Green Is My Factory," *Business Week*, September 16, 1991, pp. 54–56.

REALIGNING PRIORITIES AT THE BODY SHOP

*A*nita Roddick and her husband Gordon own more than $120 million worth of stock in their company, Body Shop International, but say they don't care about the money. Most companies in Body Shop's business—selling body lotions and shampoos—rely heavily on marketing, yet Body Shop never spends a cent on advertising. In an industry that thrives on "secret formulas" and sells products by displaying beautiful models with perfect skin, Body Shop sees education as one of its major goals and covers its shop walls with posters of rain forests, not sexy models.

Anita Roddick is the company's magic. It's not just that she has a charismatic personality and the kind of energy that could turn a $6000 investment into a multimillion dollar fortune in a little more than a decade. Anita Roddick is passionately committed to what her company does, and she has been able to infect both her employees and her customers with her fervor.

Roddick does things because she believes they are right. There is no gap between the policies that her company pursues and her personal beliefs in such principles as feminism, environmentalism, and the rights of native peoples. Because of her belief in education, The Body Shop outlets offer endless cards, pamphlets, and videos about products and ingredients. To avoid hard-sell hype, the shops are basically self-serve. Each shop, however, does have salespeople trained at the company's London training center, where they learn about what goes into their products and what those products do, not how to sell them.

Roddick's dedication to animals and to the environment leads her to go well beyond other companies' commitments to avoid animal ingredients and to stop testing products on animals. Acting on her belief in helping developing communities in Third World countries and impoverished communities in the industrialized world, Roddick built a soap factory in a high-unemployment section of Glasgow, Scotland, and sent people to Nepal to teach the Nepalese how to make paper from the water hyacinths that were clogging their waterways.

Although Roddick is quick to admit that she knew nothing about the Brazilian rain forests or ozone depletion until a few years ago, her crusades are based on knowledge and experience, not on a sense of what is trendy or politically expedient. Her company's policy of selling its products in refillable bottles might seem like a response to recent pressures to recycle, but in fact it started because in the beginning the company couldn't afford to buy all the new bottles it needed.

Unlike many environmentalists, Roddick sees no fundamental conflict between business and environmental concerns. In fact, she believes that businesses should be leading the way in solving the world's problems. Such a belief is unusual—perhaps even unique—among the world's multimillionaires, but Roddick already has thousands of customers and employees who believe in her vision.

Discussion Questions

E 1. Some people in the business world remain skeptical about Roddick's motives and priorities. Why do you think some businesspeople have trouble believing that a successful person *really* cares about improving the world?

2. In what ways do The Body Shop's unusual features and Roddick's well-publicized beliefs help the business succeed?

E 3. Have you noticed other firms making attempts to be socially responsible?

References: Bo Burlingham, "This Woman Has Changed Business Forever," *INC.*, June 1990, pp. 34–46; Laura Zinn, "Whales, Human Rights, Rain Forests—And The Heady Smell of Profits," *Business Week*, July 15, 1991, pp. 114–115.

The Global Context of Management

OBJECTIVES

After studying this chapter, you should be able to:

● *Describe the nature of international business, including its meaning, recent trends, managing internationalization, and managing in an international market.*

● *Discuss the structure of the global economy and how it affects international management.*

● *Identify and discuss the environmental challenges inherent in international management.*

● *Describe the basic issues involved in competing in a global economy, including organization size and the management challenges in a global economy.*

OUTLINE

The Nature of International Business
    The Meaning of International Business
    Trends in International Business
    Managing the Process of
      Internationalization
    Managing in an International Market

The Structure of the Global Economy
    Mature Market Economies and Systems
    Developing Economies
    Other Economies

Environmental Challenges of
International Management
    The Economic Environment
    The Political/Legal Environment
    The Cultural Environment

Competing in a Global Economy
    Globalization and Organization Size
    Management Challenges in a Global
      Economy

A MAJOR BATTLE is brewing in Europe today. But this battle is not between countries or armies. It's between cereal manufacturers. Europeans did not eat much cereal until just a few decades ago. Kellogg Co. began marketing cereal in Great Britain in the 1920s and introduced its popular brands like Corn Flakes and Rice Krispies to the rest of Europe in the 1950s. In effect, Kellogg created the European cereal market. All told, the firm sells its cereal in more than 130 countries, controls more than one-half of the European market, and earns 35 percent of its profits outside of the United States.

In 1989 another U.S. cereal maker, General Mills, Inc. (maker of such brands as Cheerios and Golden Grahams), decided it wanted to enter the European market. But the firm was afraid that Kellogg was so firmly entrenched there that it would be difficult to succeed. So General Mills approached Nestlé S.A., a Swiss-based food producer, about a joint venture. Nestlé agreed, and soon the two firms had created Cereal Partners Worldwide, or CPW. General Mills agreed to provide the technology, its proven brand names, and its marketing prowess. Nestlé agreed to contribute its widely recognized name, access to European retailers, and extra production capacity. Each firm also kicked in $80 million to get started.

The two cereal giants are now facing off in a battle of monumental importance to each. Kellogg is digging in to protect its hard-won market share and dominance in Europe. Meanwhile, CPW is aggressively plotting strategies to take away part of Kellogg's market share. Its goals are to become profitable by 1995 and to have 20 percent of the European market by the end of this decade.

Moreover, as it looks further down the road, CPW figures that if it can succeed in Europe, the rest of the world will be its for the taking. Nestlé has such strong name recognition in Latin America, Asia, and Africa, for example, that when CPW introduces its cereals in those markets success is virtually guaranteed.[1] ●

he economic battle between Kellogg and CPW's partners is not unique. Firms from around the world are entering new markets, taking on new challengers, and forming alliances with other firms. And all for the same reason—to compete more effectively in the global business environment. To be successful today, managers have to understand the global context within which they function. This holds true regardless of whether the manager runs a *Fortune* 500 firm or a small independent manufacturing concern.

This chapter explores the global context of management. We start by describing the nature of international business. We then discuss the structure of the global market in terms of different economies and economic systems. The basic environmental challenges of management are introduced and discussed next. We then focus on issues of competition in a global economy. Finally, we conclude by characterizing the managerial functions of planning, organizing, leading, and controlling as management challenges in a global economy.

THE NATURE OF INTERNATIONAL BUSINESS

As you prepared breakfast this morning, you may have plugged in a coffee pot manufactured in Asia and perhaps ironed a shirt or blouse made in Taiwan with an iron made in Mexico. The coffee you drank was probably made from beans grown in South America. To get to school, you may have driven a Japanese car. Even if you drive a Ford or Chevrolet, some of its parts were manufactured abroad. Perhaps you didn't drive a car to school but rather rode a bus (manufactured by Daimler-Benz, a German company, or by Volvo AB, a Swedish company) or a motorcycle (manufactured by Honda Motor Co., Ltd., Kawasaki Heavy Industries, Suzuki, or Yamaha Motor Co., Ltd.—all Japanese firms).

Our daily lives are strongly influenced by businesses from around the world. But we aren't unique in this respect. People living in other countries have much the same experience. They drive Fords in Germany, use IBM computers in Japan, eat McDonald's hamburgers in France, and snack on Mars candy bars in England. They drink Pepsi and wear Levi Strauss jeans in China. The Japanese buy Kodak film and use American Express credit cards. People around the world fly on United Air Lines or American Airlines in planes made by The Boeing Company. Their buildings are constructed with Caterpillar and Deere & Company machinery, and they buy Mobil oil.

In truth, we have become part of a global village and have a global economy where no organization is insulated from the effects of foreign markets and competition. More and more firms are viewing themselves as international businesses or multinational businesses.[2] What do these terms mean, and why has this pattern developed? These and related questions are addressed first.

The Meaning of International Business

There are many different forms and levels of international business. While the lines that distinguish one from another are perhaps arbitrary, we identify

FIGURE 5.1 Levels of International Business Activity

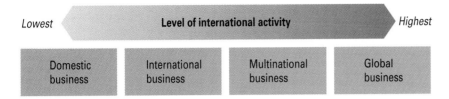

four forms of international business.[3] These are illustrated in Figure 5.1. A **domestic business** acquires essentially all of its resources and sells all of its products or services within a single country. Many (but not all) small businesses are essentially domestic. However, there are few, if any, large domestic businesses left in the world today.

Indeed, most large firms today are either international or multinational operations. An **international business** is primarily based in a single country but acquires some meaningful share of its resources or revenues from other countries. Wal-Mart Stores, Inc., might fit this description. Virtually all of its stores are in the United States, but many of the products it sells are manufactured abroad. A **multinational business** has a worldwide marketplace from which it buys raw materials, borrows money, and manufactures its products and to which it subsequently sells its products. Ford Motor Co. is an excellent example of a multinational company. It has design and production facilities around the world. For example, the Mercury Tracer is designed and engineered in Japan, manufactured in Mexico, and sold in the United States. Ford makes and sells cars in Europe that are never seen in the United States. Ford cars are designed, produced, and sold for individual markets, wherever they are and without regard for national boundaries.[4] Multinational businesses are often called *multinational enterprises* or *MNEs*.

The final form of international business is the global business. A **global business** transcends national boundaries and is not committed to a single home country. Although no business has truly achieved this level of international involvement, Nestlé SA comes close. Nestlé is based in Vevey, Switzerland, but has a German CEO. The firm gets more than 98 percent of its revenues and has more than 95 percent of its assets outside of Switzerland. The firm has ten general managers, only five of which are Swiss. About the only things that make Nestle a Swiss firm are that its headquarters are in Switzerland and Swiss investors still own more than one-half of the firm's stock.[5]

Trends in International Business

To understand why these different levels of international business have emerged, we must briefly look to the past. Forty years ago, when anyone in the world wanted to buy automobiles, electronic equipment, or machine tools, there was fundamentally only one place to shop—the United States. After World War II, the United States was by far the dominant economic force in the world. Virtually all of the countries in Europe had been devastated during the war. Most Asian countries had fared no better. There were few passable roads, few standing bridges, and even fewer factories dedicated

domestic business
A business that acquires all of its resources and sells all of its products or services within a single country

● **international business**
A business that is primarily based in a single country but acquires some meaningful share of its resources or revenues (or both) from other countries

● **multinational business**
One that has a worldwide marketplace from which it buys raw materials, borrows money, and manufactures its products and to which it subsequently sells its products

global business
A business that transcends national boundaries and is not committed to a single home country

Increasingly U.S. firms are finding markets for their products around the world. Political forces such as Germany's unification and improving economic conditions in areas like Latin America are creating enormous possibilities for growth. Holger U. Birkigt (vice president Kellogg Company, director, continental European operations), Thomas A. Knowlton (executive vice president, Kellogg Company, area director, Europe), and Arnold G. Langbo (chairman of the board and CEO, Kellogg Company) continuously review political and economic environments and develop strategies to take advantage of opportunities around the world.

to the manufacture of peacetime products. Places not destroyed in the war—Canada, South and Central America, and Africa—had not yet developed the economic muscle to threaten the economic pre-eminence of the United States.

Businesses in war-torn countries like Germany and Japan had no choice but to rebuild from scratch. They were in the unfortunate but eventually advantageous position of having to rethink every facet of their operations, including technology, production, finance, and marketing. Although it took many years for these countries to recover, they eventually did so and their economic systems were poised for growth. During the same era, U.S. companies grew complacent. Their customer base was growing rapidly. Increased population spurred by the baby boom and increased affluence resulting from the postwar economic boom greatly raised the average person's standard of living and expectations. The U.S. public continually wanted new and better products and services. U.S. companies profited greatly from this pattern but were perhaps guilty of taking it for granted.

United States firms are no longer isolated from global competition or the global market.[6] A few simple numbers help tell the full story of international trade and industry. First of all, the volume of international trade increased more than 2,000 percent from 1960 to 1990. Foreign investment in the United States by foreign firms was more than $37 billion in 1990 alone, and U.S. firms invested more than $33 billion in foreign markets. In 1960, seventy of the world's one hundred largest firms were American. This figure dropped to sixty-four in 1970, to forty-five in 1985, and to thirty in 1991.[7] Clearly, U.S. dominance of the global economy is a thing of the past.

United States firms are also finding that international operations are an increasingly important element of their sales and profits. For example, in 1990 Exxon Corporation realized 74.9 percent of its revenues and 83.5 percent of its profits abroad. For Citicorp, these percentages were 54.9

percent and 56 percent, respectively.[8] From any perspective, then, it is clear that we live in a truly global economy. The days when U.S. firms could safely ignore the rest of the world and concentrate only on the U.S. market are gone forever. Now these firms must be concerned with the competitive situations they face in lands far from home and with how companies from distant lands are competing in the United States.

Managing the Process of Internationalization

Managers should also recognize that their global context dictates two related but distinct sets of challenges. One set of challenges must be confronted when an organization chooses to change its level of international involvement. For example, a firm that wants to move from being an international to a multinational business has to manage that transition. The other set of challenges occurs when the organization has achieved its desired level of international involvement and must then function effectively within that environment. This section highlights the first set of challenges, and the next section introduces the second set of challenges. When an organization makes the decision to increase its level of international activity, there are several alternative strategies that can be adopted.[9] The most basic ones are shown in Figure 5.2.

Importing and Exporting Importing or exporting (or both) is usually the first type of international business in which a firm gets involved. **Exporting**, or making the product in the firm's domestic marketplace and selling it in another country, can involve both merchandise and services.

exporting
Making a product in the firm's domestic marketplace and selling it in another country

The process of internationalization can be managed with different strategies. These include importing and exporting, licensing, joint ventures/strategic alliances, and direct investment

FIGURE 5.2 The Process of Internationalization

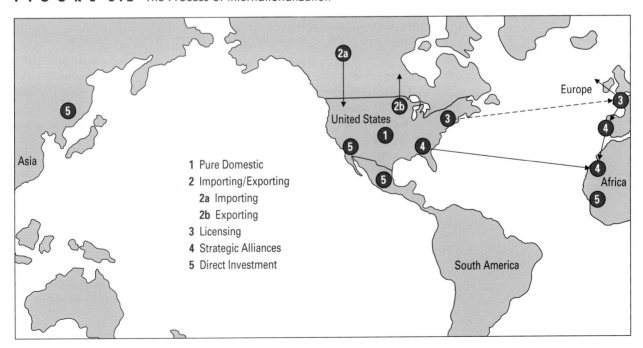

1 Pure Domestic
2 Importing/Exporting
  2a Importing
  2b Exporting
3 Licensing
4 Strategic Alliances
5 Direct Investment

importing
Bringing a good, service, or capital into the home country from abroad

When a firm exports, it produces its product or service in its domestic marketplace and sells it in another country. Exporting is often a firm's first link with the global market. Commonwealth Metals Company depends on its international trading relationships, developed over many years, to export its raw materials and products to markets around the world.

licensing
An arrangement whereby one company allows another to use its brand name, trademark, technology, patent, copyright, or other assets in exchange for a royalty based on sales

joint venture/strategic alliance
Two or more firms sharing in the ownership of an operation on an equity basis

Importing is bringing a good, service, or capital into the home country from abroad. For example, automobiles (Mazda Motor Corporation, Volkswagen AG, Mercedes-Benz, Ferrari), stereo equipment (Sony Corp., Bang and Olufsen, Sanyo), and wine (Riunite, Dom Perignon, Swartzkatz) are imported into the United States. And firms in the United States routinely export grain to the former Soviet Union, gas turbines to Saudi Arabia, locomotives to Indonesia, blue jeans to Great Britain, and diapers to Italy.

An import/export operation has many advantages. For example, it is the easiest way of entering a market with a small outlay of capital. Because the products are sold "as is," there is no need to adapt the product to the local conditions, and little risk is involved. Nevertheless, there are also disadvantages. For example, imports and exports are subject to taxes, tariffs, and higher transportation expenses. Furthermore, because the products are not adapted to local conditions, they may miss the needs of a large segment of the market. Finally, some products may be restricted and thus can be neither imported nor exported.

Licensing   A company may prefer to arrange for a foreign company to manufacture or market its products under a licensing agreement. Factors that may lead to this decision include excessive transportation costs, government regulations, and home production costs. **Licensing** is an arrangement whereby a firm allows another company to use its brand name, trademark, technology, patent, copyright, or other assets. In return, the licensee pays a royalty, usually based on sales. For example, General Instrument Corp. recently signed a licensing agreement with Hyundai Electronics Industries Company in South Korea. Under terms of the agreement, Hyundai will manufacture some of General Instrument's integrated circuit products. General Instrument initiated the arrangement because it felt that the demand for its products would exceed the capacity of its plant in Chandler, Arizona.

Two advantages of licensing are increased profitability and extended profitability. This strategy is frequently used for entry into less developed countries where older technology is still acceptable and, in fact, may be state of the art. A primary disadvantage of licensing is inflexibility. A firm can tie up control of its product or expertise for a long period of time. And if the licensee does not develop the market effectively, the licensing firm can lose profits. A second disadvantage is that licensees can take the knowledge and skill that they have been given access to for a foreign market and exploit them in the licensing firm's home market. When this happens, what used to be a business partner becomes a business competitor.

Joint Ventures/Strategic Alliances   In a **joint venture** or **strategic alliance**, two or more firms share in the ownership of an operation on an equity basis. (*Joint venture* is the traditional term used for such arrangements; however, more and more firms today are choosing to call them *strategic alliances*.)[10] This is the type of activity undertaken by General Mills and Nestlé in their formation of Cereal Partners Worldwide. Strategic alliances have enjoyed a tremendous upsurge in the past few years. In most cases each party provides a portion of the equity or the equivalent in physical plant, raw materials, cash, or other assets. The proportion of the investment then determines the percentage of ownership in the venture.

Strategic alliances have both advantages and disadvantages. For example, they can allow quick entry into a market by taking advantage of the existing strengths of participants. Japanese automobile manufacturers employed this strategy to their advantage to enter the U.S. market by using the already established distribution systems of U.S. automobile manufacturers. Strategic alliances are also an effective way of gaining access to technology or raw materials. And they allow the firms to share the risk and cost of the new venture. The major disadvantage of this strategy lies with the shared ownership of the operation. Although it reduces the risk for each participant, it also limits the control and the return that each firm can enjoy.

Direct Investment   Another level of commitment to internationalization is direct investment. **Direct investment** occurs when a firm headquartered in one country builds or purchases operating facilities or subsidiaries in a foreign country. The foreign operations then become wholly owned subsidiaries of the firm. Kodak recently made a direct investment when it built a new research laboratory in Japan.

direct investment
When a firm headquartered in one country builds or purchases operating facilities or subsidiaries in a foreign country

Like the other approaches for increasing a firm's level of internationalization, direct investment carries with it a number of benefits and liabilities. Managerial control is more complete, and profits do not have to be shared as they do in strategic alliances. Purchasing an existing organization provides additional benefits in that the human resources, plant, and organizational infrastructure are already in place. Acquisition is also a way to purchase the brand-name identification of a product. This could be particularly important if the cost of introducing a new brand is high. When Nestle bought the U.S. firm Carnation Company a few years ago, it retained the firm's brand names for all of its products sold in the United States. Notwithstanding these advantages, the company is now operating a part of itself entirely within the borders of a foreign country. The additional complexity in the decision making, the economic and political risks, and so forth may outweigh the advantages that can be obtained by international expansion.

One special form of direct investment is called outsourcing. **Outsourcing**, sometimes referred to as global sourcing, involves transferring production to locations where labor is cheap. Japanese businesses have moved much of their production to Thailand because labor costs are much lower there than in Japan. Many U.S. firms are using maquiladoras for the same purpose. **Maquiladoras** are light assembly plants built in northern Mexico close to the U.S. border. The plants are given special tax breaks by the Mexican government, and the area is populated with workers willing to work for very low wages. More than one thousand plants in the region employ 300,000 workers, and more are planned. The plants are owned by major corporations, primarily from the United States, Japan, South Korea, and major European industrial countries. This concentrated form of direct investment benefits the country of Mexico, the companies themselves, and workers who might otherwise be without jobs. Some critics argue, however, that the low wages paid by the maquiladoras amount to little more than slave labor.[11]

outsourcing
Transferring production to locations where labor is cheap

maquiladoras
Light assembly plants built in northern Mexico close to the U.S. border that are given special tax breaks by the Mexican government

Of course, we should also note that these approaches to internationalization are not mutually exclusive. Indeed, most large firms use all of them simultaneously. MNEs and global businesses have a global orientation and

When organizations decide to increase their level of internationalization, there are several strategies they can adopt. Each strategy is a matter of degree, as opposed to being a discrete and mutually exclusive category. And each has unique advantages and disadvantages that must be considered.

TABLE 5.1 Advantages and Disadvantages of Different Approaches to Internationalization

Approach to Internationalization	Advantages	Disadvantages
Importing or exporting	1. Small cash outlay 2. Little risk 3. No adaptation necessary	1. Tariffs and taxes 2. High transportation costs 3. Government restrictions
Licensing	1. Increased profitability 2. Extended profitability	1. Inflexibility 2. Helps competitors
Joint ventures/ Strategic alliance	1. Quick market entry 2. Access to materials and technology	1. Shared ownership (limits control and profits)
Direct investment	1. Enhances control 2. Existing infrastructure	1. Complexity 2. Greater economic and political risk 3. Greater uncertainty

worldwide approach to foreign markets and production. They search for opportunities all over the world and select the best strategy to serve each market. In some settings, they may use direct investment, in others licensing, in others strategic alliances; in still others they might limit their involvement to exporting and importing. The advantages and disadvantages of each approach are summarized in Table 5.1.

Managing in an International Market

Even when a firm is not actively seeking to increase its desired level of internationalization, its managers are still responsible for seeing that it functions effectively within whatever level of international involvement the organization has achieved. In one sense, the job of a manager in an international business may not be that much different from the job of a manager in a domestic business. Each may be responsible for acquiring resources and materials, making products, providing services, developing human resources, advertising, or monitoring cash flow.

In another sense, however, the complexity associated with each of these activities may be much greater for managers in international firms. Rather than buying raw materials from sources in California, Texas, and Missouri, an international purchasing manager may buy materials from sources in Peru, India, and Spain. Rather than train managers for new plants in Michigan, Florida, and Oregon, the international human resources executive may be training new plant managers for facilities in China, Mexico, and Scotland. And instead of developing a single marketing campaign for the United States, an advertising director may be working on promotional efforts in France, Brazil, and Japan.

The key question that must be addressed by any manager trying to be

FURNISHING THE WORLD

You may not have heard of IKEA yet, but chances are if you live on the East or West Coast and will furnish a new house or apartment in the next few years, you will become an IKEA customer. Once a small company based in Älmhult, Sweden, IKEA now has more than ninety-five stores in twenty-three countries, with sales approaching $4 billion. With a strategy the reverse of that usually pursued by U.S. companies, IKEA first conquered the world, then came to Philadelphia. And it continues to expand, basing its growth not on targeting a particular group of buyers or promoting a narrowly defined style but by offering something that has universal appeal: value.

Walking into a friend's house furnished at IKEA, you wouldn't necessarily know you were in an IKEA room, but a trip through an IKEA store is a unique experience that some shoppers compare to Disneyland for adults. The blue-and-yellow buildings are huge—six times the size of the average supermarket. Customers are greeted not by salespeople but by information in the form of catalogues that give prices and specifications. Each piece of furniture displayed is graded for construction and durability on a scale from A to C, and curious consumers can easily find out what the piece is made of and how it was constructed.

Serious shoppers can leave their children in the free playroom, change the infant in the changing room, or retire to the restaurant and snack bar to debate purchases. Couples who can't agree on the right bookcase can move to the lower level to be tempted by stacks of household items like glassware and rugs. Most of the goods are stylish and, though made of inexpensive materials, are attractive. But the big draw is price—20 to 40 percent lower than comparable items in other stores.

IKEA works hard to offer such prices. For one thing, it buys on a global scale, in huge quantities. And it will go anywhere in the world to find the lowest-cost supplier, which means that it now uses some 1,800 suppliers in forty-five countries. It ships items using the smallest possible amount of packaging material, saving up to 30 percent of an item's total cost. And when customers have made a decision, they drive to the loading dock, pick up the boxes that contain their item, and put them together at home. Other furniture sellers didn't think Americans would be tempted by furniture-in-a-box, but five million Americans each year are buying from IKEA and proving them wrong.

References: Diane Harris, "*Money*'s Store of the Year," *Money*, December 1990, pp. 144–153; Bill Saporito, "Ikea's Got 'Em Lining Up," *Fortune*, March 11, 1991, p. 72; Barbara Solomon, "A Swedish Company Corners the Business: Worldwide," *Management Review*, April 1991, pp. 10–13; Jeffrey A. Trachtenberg, "IKEA Furniture Chain Pleases With Its Prices, Not With Its Service," *The Wall Street Journal*, September 17, 1991, pp. A1, A5.

effective in an international market is whether to focus on globalization or regionalism.[12] A global thrust requires that activities be managed from an overall global perspective as part of an integrated system. Regionalism, on the other hand, involves managing within each region with less regard for the overall organization. In reality, most larger MNEs manage some activities globally (for example, finance and manufacturing) and others locally (such as human resources management and advertising). We explore these approaches more fully later.

THE STRUCTURE OF THE GLOBAL ECONOMY

One thing that can be helpful to managers seeking to operate in a global environment is to better understand the structure of the global economy. Although each country, and indeed many regions within any given country,

Source: J. D. Daniels/Lee H. Radebaugh, *International Business,* © 1992, by Addison-Wesley Publishing Company, Inc. Reprinted with permission of the publisher.

are unique, we can still note some basic similarities and differences. We describe three different elements of the global economy: mature market economies and systems, developing economies, and other economies.

Mature Market Economies and Systems

market economy
An economy based on the private ownership of business and allows market factors such as supply and demand to determine business strategy

A **market economy** is based on the private ownership of business and allows market factors such as supply and demand to determine business strategy. Mature market economies include the United States, Japan, the United Kingdom, France, Germany, and Sweden. These countries have

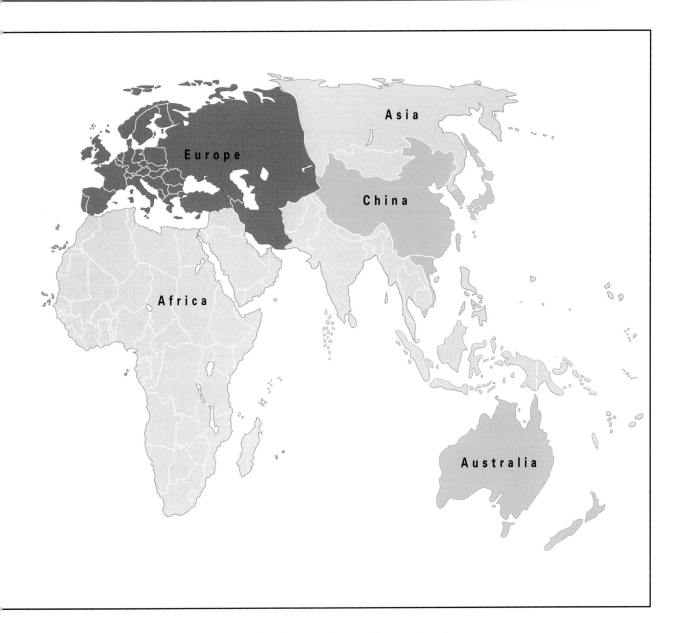

several things in common. For example, they tend to employ market forces in the allocation of resources. They also tend to be characterized by private ownership of property, although there is some variance along this dimension. France, for example, has a relatively high level of government ownership among the market economies. "The Global View" discusses how a Swedish firm, IKEA, is expanding into other market economies.

U.S. managers have relatively few problems operating in market economies. Many of the business "rules of the game" that apply in the United States, for example, also apply in Germany or England. And consumers there often tend to buy the same kinds of products. For these reasons it is not unusual for U.S. firms seeking to expand geographically to begin operations in some other market economy. Although the task of managing an international business in an industrial market country is somewhat less complicated than operating in some other type of economy, it still poses some challenges. Perhaps foremost among them is that the markets in these economies are typically quite mature. Many industries, for example, are already dominated by large and successful companies. Thus competing in these economies poses a major challenge.[13]

The map in Figure 5.3 highlights three relatively mature market systems. **Market systems** are clusters of countries that engage in high levels of trade with each other. One mature market system is North America. The United States, Canada, and Mexico are major trading partners with one another: more than 70 percent of Mexico's exports go to the United States, and more than 65 percent of what Mexico imports comes from the United States. During the last several years these countries have negotiated a variety of agreements to make trade even easier.

Another mature market system is Europe. Until recently, Europe was two distinct economic areas. The eastern region consisted of communist countries such as Poland, Czechoslovakia, and Rumania. These countries relied on government ownership of business and greatly restricted trade. In contrast, western European countries with traditional market economies have been working together to promote international trade for decades. In particular, the **European Community** (or **EC** as it is often called) has long been a formidable market system. The formal members of the EC are Denmark, the United Kingdom, Portugal, the Netherlands, Belgium, Spain, Ireland, Luxembourg, France, Germany, Italy, and Greece. For years these countries followed a basic plan that led to the elimination of most trade barriers in 1992. The European situation has recently grown more complex, however. Communism has collapsed in most eastern countries, and they are trying to develop market economies. They also want greater participation in trade with the western European countries. In some ways the emergence of the east has slowed and complicated business activities in the west. Long-term, however, the new markets in the east are likely to make Europe an even more important part of the world economy.

Yet another mature market system is the so-called **Pacific Rim**. As shown in Figure 5.3, the Pacific Rim includes Japan, China, Thailand, Malaysia, Singapore, Indonesia, South Korea, Taiwan, Hong Kong, the Philippines, and Australia. Whereas Japan has been a powerhouse for years, Taiwan, Hong Kong, Singapore, and South Korea have recently become major economic forces themselves. Trade among these nations is on the rise, and talk has started about an Asian economic community much like the EC.[14]

Developing Economies

In contrast to the highly developed and mature market economies just described, other countries have what is termed *developing economies*. These economies are relatively underdeveloped and immature. They are generally characterized by weak industry, weak currency, and relatively poor consumers. The government in these countries, however, is actively working to strengthen its economy by opening its doors to foreign investment and by promoting international trade. Some of these countries have only recently adopted market economies, while others still use a command econ-

---

market systems
Clusters of countries that engage in high levels of trade with each other

European Community (EC)
The first and most important international market system

Pacific Rim
A market system located in Southeast Asia

---

omy. Even though it is technically part of the Pacific Rim, The People's Republic of China is largely underdeveloped. Many of the countries in South America and Africa are only now developing in an economic sense. And the various republics that previously made up the Soviet Union are also viewed as developing economies.

The primary challenges presented by the developing economies to those interested in conducting international business there are the lack of wealth on the part of potential consumers and the underdeveloped infrastructure. Developing economies have enormous economic potential, but much of it remains untapped. Thus international firms entering these markets often have to invest heavily in distribution systems, in training consumers how to use their products, and in providing living facilities for their workers.

Other Economies

There are some economic systems around the world that defy classification as either mature markets or developing economies. One major area that falls outside of these categories is the oil-exporting region generally called the Middle East. The oil-exporting countries present mixed models of resource allocation, property ownership, and the development of infrastructure. These countries all have access to major amounts of crude oil, however, and thus are important players in the global economy.

These countries include Iran, Iraq, Kuwait, Saudi Arabia, Libya, Syria, and the United Arab Emirates. High oil prices in the 1970s and 1980s created enormous wealth in these countries. Many of them invested heavily in their infrastructures. Whole new cities were built, airports were constructed, and the population was educated. As oil prices have fallen, many of the oil-producing countries have been forced to cut back on these activities. Nevertheless, they are still quite wealthy. The per capita incomes of the United Arab Emirates and Qatar, for example, are among the highest in the world. Although there is great wealth in the oil-producing nations, they

Because of its market leadership position in Europe, Chiquita Bananas is in an ideal position to take advantage of the rapidly developing markets of Eastern Europe—Poland, Hungary, Czechoslovakia, Yugoslavia, the former Soviet Union, and others. With the collapse of Communism, these countries are trying to develop market economies, and the growth potential for many products—including bananas— is great.

Managers functioning in a global context must be aware of several environmental challenges. Three of the most important include economic, political/legal, and cultural challenges.

FIGURE 5.4 Environmental Challenges of International Management

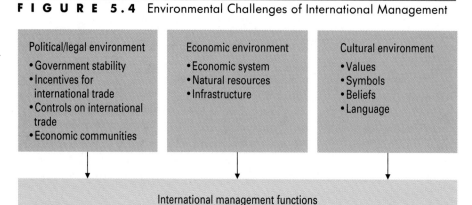

Political/legal environment	Economic environment	Cultural environment
• Government stability • Incentives for international trade • Controls on international trade • Economic communities	• Economic system • Natural resources • Infrastructure	• Values • Symbols • Beliefs • Language

International management functions

provide great challenges to managers. Political instability (as evidenced by the Persian Gulf war in 1991) and tremendous cultural differences, for example, combine to make doing business in the Middle East both very risky and very difficult.

Other countries pose risks to business of a different sort. Politically and ethnically motivated violence, for example, still characterizes some countries. Foremost among these are Peru, El Salvador, India, Turkey, Colombia, and Northern Ireland.[15] Cuba presents special challenges because it is so insulated from the outside world. With the fall of Communism, some experts believe that Cuba will eventually join the ranks of the market economies. If so, its strategic location will quickly make it an important business center.

ENVIRONMENTAL CHALLENGES OF INTERNATIONAL MANAGEMENT

We noted earlier that managing in a global context both poses and creates additional challenges for the manager. As illustrated in Figure 5.4, three environmental challenges in particular warrant additional exploration at this point—the economic environment, the political/legal environment, and the cultural environment of international management.[16]

The Economic Environment

Every country is unique and creates a unique set of challenges for managers trying to do business there. However, there are three aspects of the economic environment that in particular can help managers anticipate the kinds of economic challenges they are likely to face in working abroad.

Economic System   The first of these is the economic system used in the country. As we described earlier, most countries today are moving toward market economies. In a mature market economy, the key element for managers is freedom of choice. Consumers are free to make decisions about

A manager deciding whether to do business in a foreign country must take many things into account. Each country is unique and has its own set of challenges and opportunities. A company deciding to do business in Portugal, for example, must be aware of its high interest rates, stable currency, and government liberalization of capital markets—factors that are attracting large amounts of foreign investment.

which products they prefer to purchase, and firms are free to decide what products and services to provide. As long as both the consumer and the firm are free to decide to be in the market, then supply and demand determine which firms and which products will be available.

A related characteristic of market economies that is relevant to managers concerns the nature of property ownership. There are two pure types—complete private ownership and complete public ownership. In systems with private ownership, individuals and organizations—not the government—own and operate the companies that conduct business. In systems with public ownership, the government directly owns the companies that manufacture and sell products. Few countries have pure systems of private ownership or pure systems of public ownership. Most countries tend toward one extreme or the other, but usually a mix of public and private ownership exists.

Natural Resources Another important aspect of the economic environment in different countries is the availability of natural resources. A very broad range of resources is available in different countries. Some countries, like Japan, have virtually no natural resources of their own. Japan is thus forced to import all of the oil, iron ore, and other natural resources it needs to manufacture products for its domestic and overseas markets. The United States, in contrast, has enormous natural resources and is a major producer of oil, natural gas, coal, iron ore, copper, uranium, and other metals that are vital to the development of a modern economy. One natural resource that is particularly important in the modern global economy is oil. As we noted earlier, a small set of countries in the Middle East, including Saudi Arabia, Iraq, Iran, and Kuwait, controls a very large percentage of the world's total known reserves of crude oil. Access to this single natural resource has given these oil-producing countries enormous clout in the international economy.

Infrastructure   Yet another important aspect of the economic environment of relevance to international management is infrastructure. A country's **infrastructure** comprises its schools, hospitals, power plants, railroads, highways, ports, communication systems, air fields, commercial distribution systems, and so forth. The United States has a highly developed infrastructure. For example, its educational system is modern, roads and bridges are well developed, and most people have access to medical care. Overall, the United States has a relatively complete infrastructure sufficient to support most forms of economic development and activity.

Many countries, on the other hand, lack a well-developed infrastructure. Some countries do not have enough electrical generating capacity to meet demand. Such countries often schedule periods of time during which power is turned off. These planned power failures reduce power demands but can be an enormous inconvenience to business. In the extreme, when a country's infrastructure is greatly underdeveloped, firms interested in beginning business may have to build an entire township, including housing, schools, hospitals, and perhaps even recreation facilities, to attract a sufficient overseas work force.

The Political/Legal Environment

A second environmental challenge facing the international manager is the political/legal environment in which he or she will do business. Four important aspects of the political/legal environment of international management are government stability, incentives for multinational trade, controls on international trade, and the influence of economic communities on international trade.

Government Stability   Stability can be viewed in two ways—as the ability of a given government to stay in power against other opposing factions in the country and as the permanence of government policies toward business. A country that is stable in both respects is preferable because managers have a higher probability of successfully predicting how government will affect their business. Civil war in countries such as Lebanon has made it virtually impossible for international managers to predict what government policies are likely to be and whether the government will be able to guarantee the safety of international workers. Consequently, international firms have been very reluctant to invest in Lebanon.

In many countries—the United States, Great Britain, and Japan, for example—changes in government occur with very little disruption. In other countries—India, Argentina, and Greece, for example—changes are likely to be chaotic. Even if a country's government remains stable, the risk remains that the policies adopted by that government might change. In some countries foreign businesses may be **nationalized** (taken over by the government) with little or no warning. For example, the government of Peru recently nationalized Perulac, a domestic milk producer owned by Nestle, because of a local milk shortage.

Incentives for International Trade   Another facet of the political environment is incentives to attract foreign business. For example, municipal governments in Texas have offered foreign companies like Fujitsu, Ltd., huge tax breaks and other incentives to build facilities there.[17] In like fashion, the French government sold land to The Walt Disney Company far below its market value and agreed to build a connecting freeway in exchange for the company's agreeing to build a theme park outside of Paris. Incentives can take a variety of forms, including reduced interest rates on loans, construction subsidies, and tax incentives. Less-developed countries tend to offer different packages of incentives. In addition to lucrative tax breaks, for example, they can also attract investors with duty-free entry of raw materials and equipment, market protection through limitations on other importers, and the right to take profits out of the country.

Controls on International Trade A third element of the political environment that managers need to consider is the extent to which there are controls on international trade. In some instances, the government of a country may decide that foreign competition is hurting domestic trade. To protect domestic business, such governments may enact barriers to international trade. These barriers include tariffs, quotas, export restraint agreements, and "buy national" laws.

A **tariff** is a tax collected on goods shipped across national boundaries. Tariffs can be collected by the exporting country, countries through which goods pass, and the importing country. Import tariffs, which are the most common, can be levied to protect domestic companies by increasing the cost of foreign goods. Japan charges U.S. tobacco producers a tariff on cigarettes imported into Japan as a way to keep their prices higher than the prices charged by domestic firms. Tariffs can also be levied, usually by less-developed countries, to raise money for the government.

Quotas are the most common form of trade restriction. A quota is a limit on the number or value of goods that can be traded. The quota amount is typically designed to ensure that domestic competitors will be able to maintain a certain market share. Honda Motor Co., Ltd., is allowed to import 425,000 autos each year into the United States. This quota is one reason Honda opened manufacturing facilities here. The quota applies to cars imported into the United States, but the company can produce as many other cars within our borders as it wants, as they are not considered imports. **Export restraint agreements** are designed to convince other governments to voluntarily limit the volume or value of goods exported to a particular country. They are, in effect, export quotas. Japanese steel producers voluntarily limit the amount of steel they send to the United States each year.

"Buy national" legislation gives preference to domestic producers through content or price restrictions. Several countries have this type of legislation. Brazil requires that Brazilian companies purchase only Brazilian-made computers. The United States requires that the Department of Defense purchase only military uniforms manufactured in the United States, even though the price of foreign uniforms would be half as much. Mexico requires that 50 percent of the parts of cars sold in Mexico be manufactured in Mexico.

Economic Communities Just as government policies can either increase or decrease the political risk facing international managers, trade relations between countries can either help or hinder international business. Relations dictated by quotas, tariffs, and so forth can hurt international trade. There is currently a strong movement around the world to reduce many of these barriers. This movement takes its most obvious form in international economic communities.

tariff
A tax collected on goods shipped across national boundaries

quota
A limit on the number or value of goods that can be traded

● **export restraint agreements**
Accords reached by governments in which countries voluntarily limit the volume or value of goods they export and import from one another

An international **economic community** is a set of countries that agree to markedly reduce or eliminate trade barriers among its member nations. The first, and in many ways still the most important, of these economic communities is the European Community (EC), discussed earlier. Other important economic communities include the Latin American Integration Association (Bolivia, Brazil, Colombia, Chile, Argentina, and other South American countries) and the Caribbean Common Market (the Bahamas, Belize, Jamaica, Antigua, Barbados, and twelve other countries).

The Cultural Environment

Another environmental challenge for the international manager is the cultural environment and how it affects business. A country's culture includes all the values, symbols, beliefs, and language that guide behavior.

Values, Symbols, and Beliefs Cultural values and beliefs are often unspoken; they may even be taken for granted by those who live in a particular country. Cultural factors do not necessarily cause problems for managers when the cultures of two countries are similar. Difficulties can arise, however, when there is little overlap between the home culture of a manager and the culture of the country in which business is to be conducted. For example, most U.S. managers find the culture and traditions of England familiar. The people of both countries speak the same language and share strong historical roots, and there is a history of strong commerce between the two countries. When U.S. managers begin operations in Japan or the People's Republic of China, however, most of those commonalities disappear.[18]

Even when the cultures of two countries are similar, there is still substantial room for misunderstanding and embarrassment. For example, when someone from the United Kingdom tells you that he is going to "knock you up," "take a lift," and "put the telly in the boot," he has told you that he will (1) wake you up in the morning, (2) take an elevator, and (3) put a television set in the trunk of your car.

Things become even more complicated when the cultures are truly different. In Japanese, for example, the word "hai" (pronounced "hi") means "yes." In conversation, however, this word is used much like people in the U.S. use "uh-huh": it moves a conversation along or shows the person you are talking to that you are paying attention. So when does "hai" mean "yes" and when does it mean "uh-huh"? This turns out to be a relatively difficult question to answer. If an American manager asks a Japanese manager if he agrees to some trade arrangement, the Japanese manager is likely to say "hai"—which may mean "yes, I agree," or "yes, I understand," or "yes, I am listening." Many U.S. managers become very frustrated in negotiations with the Japanese because they believe that the Japanese continue to raise issues that have already been settled (the Japanese managers said "yes"). What many of these managers fail to recognize is that "yes" does not always mean "yes" in Japan.

Cultural differences between countries can have a direct impact on business practice. For example, the religion of Islam teaches that people should not make a living by exploiting the misfortune of others and that making interest payments is immoral. This means that in Saudi Arabia there are no businesses that provide auto-wrecking services to tow stalled cars to the garage (because that would be capitalizing on misfortune), and in the Sudan banks cannot pay or charge interest. Given these cultural and religious constraints, those two businesses—automobile towing and banking—don't seem to hold great promise for international managers in those particular countries.

Some cultural differences between countries can be even more subtle and yet have a major impact on business activities. For example, in the United States most managers clearly agree about the value of time. Most U.S. managers schedule their activities very tightly and then adhere to their schedules. Other cultures don't put such a premium on time. In the Middle East, managers do not like to set appointments, and they rarely keep appointments set too far in advance. U.S. managers interacting with managers from the Middle East might misinterpret the late arrival of a potential business partner as a negotiation ploy or an insult, when it is rather a simple reflection of different views of time and its value.

Language Language itself can be an important factor. Beyond the obvious and clear barriers posed by people who speak different languages, subtle differences in meaning can also play a major role. For example, Esso S.A.F. realized it was in trouble when it learned that its name meant "stalled car" in Japanese. The Chevrolet Nova was not selling well in Latin America and General Motors executives couldn't understand why until it was brought to their attention that, in Spanish, *no va* means "it doesn't go." The color green is used extensively in Moslem countries, but it signifies death in some other countries. The color associated with femininity in the United States is pink, but in many other countries yellow is the most feminine color. "Management in Practice" explains how one firm is capitalizing on language differences to fuel its own growth.

COMPETING IN A GLOBAL ECONOMY

Competing in a global economy is both a major challenge and opportunity for businesses today. The nature of these challenges depends on a variety of factors, including the size of the organization. In addition, international management also has implications for the basic functions of planning, organizing, leading, and controlling.

Globalization and Organization Size

Although organizations of any size may compete in international markets, there are some basic differences in the challenges and opportunities faced by MNEs, medium-size organizations, and small organizations.

Multinational Organizations The large MNEs have long since made the choice to compete in a global marketplace. In general, these firms take a global perspective. They transfer capital, technology, human resources, inventory, and information from one market to another. They actively seek new expansion opportunities wherever feasible. MNEs tend to allow local managers a great deal of discretion in addressing local and regional issues. At the same time, each operation is ultimately accountable to a central authority. Managers at this central authority (headquarters, a central office, etc.) are responsible for setting the overall strategic direction for the firm, making major policy decisions, and so forth. MNEs need senior managers who understand the global economy and who are comfortable dealing with executives and government officials from a variety of cultures. Table 5.2 lists several of the world's largest MNEs in different industries.

Medium-Size Organizations   Many medium-size businesses remain primarily domestic organizations. But they still may buy and sell products made abroad and compete with businesses from other countries in their own domestic market. Increasingly, however, medium-size organizations are expanding into foreign markets as well. For example, Molex Incorporated is a medium-size firm based in Chicago. Its recent annual sales have been in the range of $300 to 400 million. Molex manufactures electronic connectors. The firm operates several plants in Japan and derives more than one-half of its sales from the Pacific Rim.[19] In contrast to MNEs, medium-size organizations doing business abroad are much more selective about the markets they enter. They also depend more on a few international specialists to help them manage their foreign operations.

Small Organizations   More and more small organizations are also finding that they can benefit from the global economy. Some, for example, serve as local suppliers for MNEs. A dairy farmer who sells milk to Carnation Company, for example, is actually transacting business with Nestle. Local parts suppliers also have been successfully selling products to the Toyota and Honda plants in the United States. Beyond serving as local suppliers, some small businesses also buy and sell products and services abroad. For example, the Collin Street Bakery, based in Corsicana, Texas, ships fruitcakes around the world. In 1990, the firm shipped 145,000 pounds of fruitcake to Japan.[20] Most small businesses rely on simple importing or exporting operations (or both) for their international sales. Thus only a few specialized management positions are needed. Collin Street Bakery, for example, has one local manager who handles international activities. Mail-order activities within each country are subcontracted to local firms in each market.

Management Challenges in a Global Economy

The management functions that constitute the framework for this book—planning, organizing, leading, and controlling—are just as relevant to international managers as to domestic managers. International managers need to have a clear view of where they want their firm to be in the future; they have to organize to implement their plans; they have to motivate those who work for them; and they have to develop appropriate control mechanisms.

Planning in a Global Economy   To effectively plan in a global economy, managers must have a broad-based understanding of both environmental issues and competitive issues. They need to understand local market conditions and technological factors that will affect their operations. At the corporate level, executives need a great deal of information to function effectively. What markets are growing? What markets are shrinking? What are our

TALKING THE LANGUAGE OF SUCCESS

If you needed to learn a foreign language quickly, to whom would you turn? People around the world answer "Berlitz," and that name recognition combined with the rapid moves toward a global economy have helped Berlitz International's revenues grow 41 percent in three years.

The company is currently run by Elio Boccitto, who was born in Italy and started teaching Italian part-time for Berlitz thirty years ago. But Boccitto rose to the top not because of his knowledge of romance languages, but because he helped the company's Japanese division keep pace with the explosive growth of interest in Japan during the past two decades.

As multinational and global companies have expanded to Japan and elsewhere, more and more have accepted Boccitto's belief that "knowledge of a language . . . means money to someone's career."* In fact, while many people may associate Berlitz classes and books with people wanting to learn enough Spanish to find the bathrooms in Barcelona during their summer vacation, 60 percent of Berlitz's business comes from corporate accounts. The company has 284 centers around the world, and because English continues to be the closest thing to a universal language, three-fifths of the 5 million Berlitz lessons given each year are in English. (German, French, Spanish, and Japanese round out the company's top five.) People take such courses not just to keep up with world trends but to deal with the more radical changes of the past few years. In the six months after the Berlin Wall fell, Berlitz's German licensee sold 45,000 English self-teaching packages in what used to be East Germany.

But Berlitz doesn't just rely on the expansion of the global economy to keep its profits flowing. It sells 4.5 million travel guides each year, translates corporate business documents, and has given its name to a hand-held electronic translator.

Running Berlitz does pose some unusual problems. Fluctuations among different currencies can make the company's balance sheet look unrealistically good or bad. And when Robert Maxwell, who had bought Berlitz's parent company, Macmillan, decided to sell nearly half of Berlitz to the public in 1989, some financial analysts grumbled that Berlitz was too reliant on the strength of its name. They pointed out that the number of lessons has not risen as quickly as the company's revenues. Still, it's hard to imagine that Berlitz will do anything but grow as around the world people strive to overcome language barriers as national boundaries fall.

*Quoted in Seth Lubove, "Ovo je Line Extension," *Forbes*, July 22, 1991, p. 64.

References: Thomas N. Cochran, "In Any Language," *Barron's*, November 13, 1989, p. 16; Seth Lubove, "Ovo je Line Extension," *Forbes*, July 22, 1991, pp. 64–65.

---

domestic and foreign competitors doing in each market? They must also make a variety of strategic decisions about their organization. For example, if a firm wishes to enter the market in France, should it buy a local firm there, build a plant, or seek a strategic alliance? Critical issues include understanding environmental circumstances, the role of goals and planning in a global organization, and how decision making affects the global organization. We note special implications for global managers as we discuss planning in Chapters 6 through 9.

Organizing in a Global Economy   Managers in international businesses must also attend to a variety of organizing issues. For example, General Electric Co. has operations scattered around the globe. The firm has made the decision to give local managers a great deal of responsibility for how they run their business. In contrast, many Japanese firms give managers of

At one time the United States dominated the list of the world's largest organizations. As these lists show, however, U.S. dominance is a thing of the past.

TABLE 5.2 The World's Largest MNEs

Industrial Corporations

Rank Corporation	Country	Annual Sales (in $ millions)
1. General Motors	United States	123,780
2. Royal Dutch/Shell Group	Britain/Netherlands	103,835
3. Exxon	United States	103,242
4. Ford	United States	88,963
5. Toyota	Japan	78,061
6. IBM	United States	65,394
7. IRI	Italy	64,096
8. General Electric	United States	60,236
9. British Petroleum	Britain	58,355
10. Daimler-Benz	Germany	57,321
11. Mobil	United States	56,910
12. Hitachi	Japan	56,053
13. Matsushita Electric Industrial	Japan	48,595
14. Philip Morris	United States	48,109
15. Fiat	Italy	46,812

Commercial Banks

Rank Bank	Country	Deposits (in $ millions)
1. Dai-Ichi Kangyo Bank	Japan	435,718
2. The Sumitomo Bank, Ltd.	Japan	407,105
3. The Fuji Bank	Japan	403,725
4. Mitsubishi Trust & Banking	Japan	392,208
5. Sanwa Bank Limited	Japan	387,452
20. Citicorp	United States	216,986

Insurance Companies

Rank Company	Country	Assets (in $ millions)
1. Nippon Life	Japan	157,657
2. Prudential of America	United States	133,157
3. Dai-Ichi Mutual Life	Japan	110,004
4. Metropolitan Life	United States	103,228
5. Sumitomo Life	Japan	94,168

Retailing Companies

Rank Company	Country	Annual Sales (in $ millions)
1. Sears, Roebuck	United States	55,971
2. Wal-Mart	United States	32,601
3. K mart	United States	32,080
4. Tengelmann	Germany	23,762
5. American Stores	United States	22,155

their foreign operations relatively little responsibility. As a result, those managers must frequently travel back to Japan to present problems or get decisions approved. Managers in an international business must address the basic issues of organization structure and design, managing change, and dealing with human resources. We address the special issues of organizing the international organization in Chapters 10 through 13.

Leading in a Global Economy We noted earlier some of the cultural factors that affect international organizations. Individual managers must be prepared to deal with these and other factors as they interact with people from different cultural backgrounds. Supervising a group of five managers, each of whom is from a different state in the United States, is likely to be much simpler than supervising a group of five managers, each of whom is from a different culture. Managers must understand how cultural factors

To effectively plan in a global economy, managers must understand each country's environmental and competitive issues and local market conditions. When Toys "Я" Us expanded into Japan, it faced hurdles such as a law that enabled local shop owners to stall large retailers for as many as ten years, and exclusive relationships existing among retailers, wholesalers, and manufacturers that shut out newcomers. But thorough planning paid off: the first outlet opened in December, 1991, and each new Japanese Toys "Я" Us outlet is expected to ring up sales of at least $15 million during its first year.

affect individuals, how motivational processes vary across cultures, the role of leadership in different cultures, how communication varies across cultures, and the nature of interpersonal and group processes in different cultures. In Chapters 14 through 17 we note special implications for international managers that relate to leading and interacting with others.

Controlling in a Global Economy Finally, managers in international organizations must also be concerned with control. Distances, time zone differences, and cultural factors all play a role in control. For example, in some cultures close supervision is seen as being appropriate, and in other cultures it is not. Likewise, executives in the United States and Japan may find it difficult to communicate vital information to one another because of the time zone differences. Basic control issues for the international manager revolve around operations management, productivity, quality, technology, and information systems. These issues are integrated throughout our discussion of control in Chapters 18 through 21.

SUMMARY OF KEY POINTS

International business has grown to be one of the most important features of the world's economy. Learning to operate in a global economy is an important challenge facing many managers today. Businesses can be primarily domestic, international, multinational, or global in scope. Managers need to understand both the process of internationalization as well as how to manage within a given level of international activity.

To compete in the global economy, managers must understand its structure. Mature market economies and systems dominate the global economy today. North America, Europe, and the Pacific Rim are especially important. Developing economies in eastern Europe, South America, and Africa may play bigger roles in the future. The oil-exporting economies in the Middle East are also important.

Many of the challenges of management in a global context are unique issues associated with the international environmental context. These challenges reflect the economic, political/legal, and cultural environments of international management.

Basic issues of competing in a global economy vary according to whether the organization is a MNE, a medium-size organization, or a small organization. In addition, the basic managerial functions of planning, organizing, leading, and controlling must all be addressed in international organizations.

DISCUSSION QUESTIONS

Questions for Review

1. Describe the four basic levels of international business activity. Do you think any organization will achieve the fourth level? Why or why not?

2. Summarize the basic structure of the global economy. What are the major changes occurring today within that structure?

3. Briefly note some of the basic environmental challenges of international management.

4. What are some of the competitive differences for MNEs, medium-size organizations, and small organizations?

Questions for Analysis

5. An organization seeking to expand its international operations must monitor several different environments. Which aspect of each environment is likely to have the greatest impact on decisions involved in such a strategic move? Why?

6. What industries do you think will have the greatest impact on international business? Are there any industries that might not be affected by the trend toward international business? If so, which ones? If there are none, why are there none?

7. You are the CEO of an up-and-coming toy company and have plans to go international soon. What steps would you take to carry out that strategy? What areas would you stress in your decision-making process? How would you organize your company?

Questions for Application

8. Identify a local company that does business abroad. Interview an executive in that company. Why did the company go international? What major obstacles did it face? How successful has that decision been? Share your findings with the class.

9. Go to the library and find some information about the European Community's move toward a relaxation of trade barriers. What will be the effect of that relaxation? What will be some of the difficulties? Do you think that it is a good idea? Why or why not?

10. Many organizations fail to allow for cultural and language differences when they do business with other countries. For example, Pepsi was introduced into Asia with the slogan "Come alive with Pepsi." The slogan, however, was translated as "Bring your ancestors back from the dead with Pepsi." Go to the library and locate mistakes made by other companies entering foreign markets. What did they do wrong? How could they have prevented their mistakes?

WHIRLPOOL AND THE APPLIANCE INDUSTRY HEAD OVERSEAS

The four companies that dominate the American appliance industry—Whirlpool Corporation, General Electric Co., Electrolux (AB), and Maytag Corporation—have done virtually everything they can to improve their competitive position, cutting costs and improving efficiency. Since 1945, the big four have squeezed out 245 other appliance makers, including giants like Westinghouse and General Motors. They are so good at what they do that 98 percent of the "white goods" sold in the United States are still made here. But they don't act like a conspiratorial oligopoly. Prices on major appliances rose just 1 percent between 1986 and 1990, while overall consumer prices went up more than 14 percent. The trouble is, the American market for appliances is not growing, and in fact fell after a peak in 1987. So what happens when a big, successful maker of a high-quality, low-price product can't make money?

Led by Whirlpool, American appliance makers are expanding overseas. In the long run, Whirlpool knows that it must sell appliances in the Third World and Asia, and it is already selling variations of a new model nicknamed the World Washer. Built and sold in Brazil and Mexico, the machines are about half the size of the standard American washer. Whirlpool hopes to sell the same machines with slight variations around the world.

In the shorter term, however, Whirlpool and its American rivals are looking for profits in Europe. Fewer than 20 percent of European households own a dishwasher or clothes dryer. All eyes are on Eastern Europe, which could become a valuable new market once Eastern Europeans find some way to pay for new purchases. Overall, the European appliance market is expected to grow 4 percent per year during the 1990s, more than twice the rate expected in the United States.

Taking advantage of this new market will not be easy. Aware that its American brand names mean nothing to Europeans, Whirlpool bought 53 percent of the appliance business of Holland's Philips Industries in 1989. Although it will be able to keep the Philips name on appliances for only ten years, Whirlpool is making the transition to its own brand by selling products under the Philips Whirlpool label and spending heavily on advertising.

Whirlpool also must deal with decidedly different tastes in different countries. In most of Europe, 90 percent of washing machines are front-loading, but the French prefer top-loaders. Until the World Washers catch on and Third World families find the money to afford them, however, Whirlpool and its competitors must overcome such barriers if they are to continue to grow.

Discussion Questions

1. Whirlpool and the other white goods manufacturers are facing a limited U.S. demand for their products. What other industries in the U.S. are facing the same type of situation?

2. How has Whirlpool responded to the challenge of international competition? Do you think that its response has been effective? Why or why not?

E 3. Although many American households view a washing machine as a necessity, it is a luxury for most people in less industrialized nations. How can Whirlpool expand its sales to poorer nations without being vulnerable to the charge that it is convincing people to buy something they don't need?

References: Thomas A. Stewart, "A Heartland Industry Takes On the World," *Fortune*, March 12, 1990, pp. 110–112; David Woodruff, "Whirlpool Goes Off On A World Tour," *Business Week*, June 3, 1991, pp. 98–100; David Woodruff, "A Little Washing Machine That Won't Shred a Sari," *Business Week*, June 3, 1991, p. 100.

BUILDING GLOBAL AIRPLANES

The Boeing Company, the world's largest airplane manufacturer, doesn't seem to have much to worry about. It has a $97 billion backlog of business, which will keep its factories busy until close to the year 2000. Its 747 is so popular that companies from around the world wait five years to get one. It doesn't look as though Boeing *has* to change, but in fact it is taking new approaches to building planes, breaking traditional barriers in the process.

Boeing's next new plane is the 777, a widebody smaller than the 747. It isn't scheduled to take off until 1994, but already hundreds of designers and engineers are working on it. That alone is news. Traditionally, designers had free reign on a plane's design, and after months or years of work they would hand the design over to engineers who figured out how to build it. If the design proved too expensive or difficult to build, the engineers would ask for a redesign. Considering that each 777 has more than 132,000 engineered parts, you can see why Boeing wanted a more efficient process.

So Boeing has gathered together eight of IBM's largest mainframe computers and created 238 design-build teams. Engineers work with designers, trying out new ideas on videoscreens, virtually eliminating the blueprints and plaster duplicates that have long been crucial parts of airplane manufacturing. The teams get input from customers and have already modified a 777 wing flap as a result of a suggestion from United Air Lines, Inc.

A crucial part of the design team are the suppliers, and for the 777, that means companies from Italy, Australia, Korea, Canada, France, Great Britain, and especially Japan. Three of Japan's industrial giants—Fuji, Mitsubishi Corp., and Kawasaki—are building about 20 percent of the 777 and funding an equal amount of the plane's development. In the past, high-tech companies like those in airplane manufacturing shied away from alliances with overseas companies.

But increased costs and complexity make the task of building a new airplane so colossal that even huge companies like Boeing have to look for partners. Developing the 777 is expected to cost at least $4 billion; $1.5 billion was spent on research and development in 1991 alone.

Even while it is sinking so much money into the 777, Boeing must face a new challenge from Airbus, which is discussing plans to build a superjumbo jet bigger than Boeing's 747. Having owned the jumbo jet market for years, Boeing is not about to give it up and is starting to talk about developing its own superjumbo. To do so, Boeing would almost certainly have to bring its Japanese partners on board again. The engineers and designers on the two sides of the Pacific may not talk the same language, but the development of the 777 proves that they can successfully hook up to the same computer.

Discussion Questions

1. Boeing's use of computers and design teams seems to be an efficient way to design and develop a plane. What other industries could benefit from these techniques?

2. What are the advantages and disadvantages to the partners of the kind of joint venture that is building the 777?

E 3. Should Boeing limit access to its design innovations because other companies might steal its secrets?

References: Jeremy Main, "Making Global Alliances Work," *Fortune*, December 17, 1991, pp. 121–126; Dori Jones Yang, "Boeing Knocks Down the Wall Between the Dreamers and the Doers," *Business Week*, October 28, 1991, pp. 120–121; Dori Jones Yang, "Will Boeing Build a Behemoth To Defend Its Turf?" *Business Week*, August 19, 1991, pp. 28–29.

Meeting the Global Challenge

The purpose of this exercise is to illustrate how improved quality is directly related to the challenge today's multinational companies face in trying to please ever more demanding customers.

Learning Objectives

When you have completed this exercise you should have a better understanding of

1. How quality is defined and the changes total quality management requires of American business.

2. How quality is related to the challenges and pressures facing multinational companies today.

3. How Procter & Gamble has maintained a competitive position in the global economy.

Preview

Procter & Gamble

Based in Cincinnati, Ohio, Procter & Gamble is a multinational producer of laundry and cleaning products, food and beverages, and personal care products. P&G is a leader in many product areas in the United States as well as in world markets. P&G's Ultra Pampers are now the number-one disposable diapers around the world. The company employs 79,000 people worldwide and operates in 47 countries. P&G attributes 40 percent of its 1990 revenues to international sales and expects this figure to increase to 50 percent by 1995.

A World Standard of Quality

Artzt says, "A very exciting development for us has been the realization that we don't need to alter the quality or the technology in our products from place to place in order to be successful. Consumers have very much the same value system around the world. . . . just as the world is shrinking in a lot of ways, the evaluation of quality worldwide is coming together. . . . people everywhere have the same demand, the same grading system for evaluating quality. We tend to think in terms of electronic devices, or appliances, or automobiles, or high tech equipment, but it applies to a diaper, or a bar of soap, or a sanitary napkin, or a shampoo just as well, and that is now driving our business. . . . If the toughest market in the world in terms of judging the quality and performance of a disposable diaper is Japan, develop a product that is superior and more successful in the Japanese market and sell it all over the world."

In the old economy, a producer could please the customers in one country or even one region and be successful. For a major manufacturer, customers are now everywhere, with different backgrounds, different tastes, different demands, and the product has to please them all. That makes doing business in the global marketplace a lot tougher.*

Background Assignment

Go to the library and find articles on Procter & Gamble during the period from 1983 to 1988. If possible, locate annual reports from this period and identify what is said about the corporation's commitment to quality. Characterize the world markets Procter & Gamble was operating in at the time, including major competitors, threats, and challenges.

The Video

Though the quality movement is discussed in detail in Chapter 19, this video exercise will serve as an introduction to this important area of management thinking.

As the video you are about to watch illustrates, American companies are facing an increasingly competitive global economy and must make changes in order to survive.

Questions for Discussion

1. How and where did the total quality approach to management get its start?

2. Based on what you have seen in this video, how would you define quality?

3. What kinds of challenges does the global market pose for American companies such as Procter & Gamble?

4. How is quality related to a nation's standard of living?

5. Do you agree that the nationality of a company no longer matters? Should we as Americans be concerned with the success of American companies, or is such loyalty no longer relevant in today's global economy?

Follow-Up Assignment

Return to the library and find more recent articles that discuss the performance of Procter & Gamble since 1988. Also review annual reports from the last few years and note any discussion of quality or quality systems you find there. Can you make any links between company performance and the implementation of quality systems at Procter & Gamble?

*Source: Lloyd Dobyns and Clare Crawford-Mason *Quality or Else*. (Boston: Houghton-Mifflin Company, 1991) pp. 236–237. Copyright © Houghton Mifflin Company. Used with permission.

PLANNING AND DECISION MAKING

6 *Managing Organizational Goals and Planning*

7 *Managing Strategy and Strategic Planning*

8 *Managerial Decision Making*

9 *Management Tools for Planning and Decision Making*

Managing Organizational Goals and Planning

OBJECTIVES

After studying this chapter, you should be able to:

● *Summarize the planning process.*

● *Discuss the purposes of organizational goals, identify different kinds of goals, discuss who sets goals, and describe how to manage multiple goals.*

● *Identify different kinds of organizational plans, note the time frames for planning, discuss who plans, and describe contingency planning.*

● *Discuss how tactical plans are developed and executed.*

● *Describe the basic types of operational plans used by organizations.*

● *Identify the major barriers to goal setting and planning, how organizations overcome those barriers, and how to use MBO to implement plans.*

OUTLINE

The Planning Process

Organizational Goals
    Purposes of Goals
    Kinds of Goals
    Responsibilities for Setting Goals
    Managing Multiple Goals

Organizational Planning
    Kinds of Organizational Plans
    Time Frames for Planning
    Responsibilities for Planning
    Contingency Planning

Tactical Planning
    Developing Tactical Plans
    Executing Tactical Plans

Operational Planning
    Single-Use Plans
    Standing Plans

Managing Goal-Setting and Planning Processes
    Barriers to Goal Setting and Planning
    Overcoming the Barriers
    Using Management by Objective to
      Implement Plans

CONSIDER THE DIFFERENT experiences of Hewlett-Packard Co. and one of its competitors. A few years ago top management at HP set a goal of reducing the firm's overall warranty expenses by 90 percent within five years. A written statement summarizing this goal and describing how it was to be achieved was sent to every employee throughout the organization.

Specific managers in every division of the firm were given the responsibility of monitoring progress toward achieving the goal. And all employees were told that the firm would pay a profit-sharing bonus if the goal was attained. HP achieved its goal in less than five years. Soon thereafter, top management announced another goal of reducing software defects by 90 percent. It set about achieving it in the same way. And so far, Hewlett-Packard is making great strides toward achieving this new goal.

At about the same time HP announced its warranty reduction goal, a top manager at one of its major competitors made a more sweeping announcement. He proclaimed that his firm was going to make major improvements throughout its operations and become a world leader in quality. This goal was not communicated to employees, however, and no guidelines were presented as to how it was going to be achieved. Moreover, the manager gave no indication of how long it would take nor how the organization would know when it had achieved its goal.

Over the next few years, company literature made references to its commitment to improve quality, but little was ever said about what the firm was actually doing to reach its goal. Customers of the firm continued to report that the quality of its products was not getting any better, and some even complained that quality was deteriorating. At about the same time HP achieved its first goal, its competitor announced a major drop in revenue and a massive layoff of employees.[1] ●

lthough Hewlett-Packard and its competitor are similar in some respects, they are quite different in many others. For example, they differ markedly in how they go about planning. They also differ in how they set and accomplish goals. HP sets clear and precise goals, decides how to best achieve them, involves its employees, and is usually effective. Its competitor, however, sets vague and imprecise goals, pays little attention to how to accomplish them, does not involve its employees, and is much less effective.

As we noted in Chapter 1, planning is the first managerial function that organizations must address. This chapter is the first of four that explores planning in more detail. We begin by introducing the basic planning process that most organizations follow. We then discuss the nature of organizational goals and introduce the basic concepts of planning. We then discuss tactical and operational planning more fully. Finally, we conclude with a discussion of how to manage goal setting and planning process.

THE PLANNING PROCESS

Planning is a generic activity. All organizations do it, but no two organizations do it in exactly the same fashion. Figure 6.1 is a general representation of the planning process that many organizations attempt to follow.[2] But although most firms follow this general framework, each also has its own nuances and variations.

As Figure 6.1 shows, all planning occurs within an environmental context. If managers do not understand this context, they will be unable to develop effective plans. Thus understanding the environment is essentially

The planning process takes place within an environmental context. Managers must develop a complete and thorough understanding of this context to determine the organization's mission and develop its strategic, tactical, and operational goals and plans.

FIGURE 6.1 The Planning Process

the first step in planning. The three previous chapters cover many of the basic environmental issues that affect organizations and how they plan. With this understanding as a foundation, managers must then establish the organization's mission. The mission outlines the organization's purpose, premises, values, and directions. Flowing from the mission are parallel streams of goals and plans. Directly following the mission are strategic goals. These goals and the mission help determine strategic plans. Strategic goals and plans are primary inputs for developing tactical goals. Tactical goals and the original strategic plans help shape tactical plans. Tactical plans, in turn, combine with the tactical goals to shape operational goals. These goals and the appropriate tactical plans determine operational plans. Finally, goals and plans at each level can also be used as input for future activities at all levels. This chapter discusses goals and tactical and operational plans. Chapter 7 covers strategic plans.

ORGANIZATIONAL GOALS

Goals are critical to organizational effectiveness and they serve a number of purposes. Organizations can also have several different kinds of goals, all of which must be appropriately managed. And a number of different kinds of managers must be involved in setting goals.

Purposes of Goals

Goals serve four important purposes.[3] First, they provide guidance and a unified direction for people in the organization. Goals can help everyone understand where the organization is going and why getting there is important. General Electric Co.'s goal of being either number 1 or number 2 in every industry it enters helps set the tone for each decision made by GE managers. And HP's goal regarding warranty reductions let everyone know that the firm was committed to quality and cost reduction.

Second, goal-setting practices affect planning. Effective goal setting promotes good planning, and good planning facilitates future goal setting. The success of Hewlett-Packard demonstrates how setting goals and developing plans to reach them are complementary activities. Without goals, plans to enhance quality would have had little meaning. Moreover, the successful implementation of those plans has made future goal setting easier.

Third, goals can serve as a source of motivation to employees of the organization.[4] Goals that are specific and moderately difficult can motivate people to work harder, especially if attaining the goal is likely to result in rewards. When Stanley Gault became CEO of Rubbermaid, he set a goal of increasing sales 15 percent annually. He also promised to give employees more say in how the company was run and bigger rewards for success. Workers in the company were galvanized into actions aimed at meeting the goal and have succeeded for each of the last eight years.[5]

Finally, goals provide an effective mechanism for evaluation and control. This means that performance can be assessed in the future in terms of how successfully today's goals are accomplished. For example, suppose officials of the United Way of America set a goal of collecting $250,000 from a particular community. If midway through the campaign they have raised only $50,000, this will suggest that they need to change or intensify their efforts. If they end up only raising $100,000 by the end of their drive, they will need to carefully study why they did not reach their goal and what they need to do differently next year. On the other hand, if they succeed in raising $265,000, evaluations of their efforts will take on an entirely different character.

Kinds of Goals

Organizations establish many different kinds of goals. In general, these goals vary by level, by area, and by time frame. Figure 6.2 provides examples of each type of goal for a hypothetical fast-food chain.

Level Goals are set for and by different levels within an organization. As noted earlier, the four basic levels of goals are the mission and strategic, tactical, and operational goals. An organization's **mission** is a statement of its "fundamental, unique purpose that sets a business apart from other firms of its type and identifies the scope of the business's operations in product and market terms."[6] Table 6.1 identifies the basic components of a typical corporate mission statement and provides an example of each component taken from actual mission statements.

Strategic goals are goals set by and for top management of the organization. They focus on broad, general issues. For example, Sony Corp. recently set a strategic goal of reducing its reliance on the consumer-electronics market. Managers believed that the volatile nature of the market made continued reliance on it too risky.[7] **Tactical goals** are set by and for middle managers. Their focus is on how to operationalize actions necessary to achieve the strategic goals. One tactical goal at Sony was to acquire a firm in the entertainment industry; the goal was realized when Sony bought Columbia Pictures Entertainment Inc. **Operational goals** are set by and for lower-level managers. Their concern is with shorter-term issues associated with the tactical goals. An operational goal for Sony might be target level of market share for a new electronics device. (Some people use the words *objectives* and *goals* interchangeably. When they are differentiated, however, the term *objectives* is usually used instead of *operational goals*.)

Area Organizations also set goals for different areas. The restaurant chain represented in Figure 6.2 has goals for operations, marketing, and finance. HP sets production goals for quality, productivity, and so forth. Human resource goals might be set for employee turnover and absenteeism. 3M and Rubbermaid set goals for product innovation.

Time Frame Organizations set goals across different time frames. In Figure 6.2, three goals are listed at the strategic, tactical, and operational levels. The first is a long-term goal, the second an intermediate-term goal, and the third a short-term goal. Some goals have an explicit time frame (i.e., open 150 new restaurants during the next ten years) and others have an open-ended time horizon (i.e., maintain 10-percent annual growth). Finally, we should also note that the meaning of different time frames varies by level. For example, at the strategic level, long-term often means ten years or

mission
A statement of an organization's fundamental purpose

● **strategic goals**
Goals set by and for top management of the organization

● **tactical goals**
Goals set by and for middle managers of the organization

● **operational goals**
Goals set by and for lower-level managers of the organization

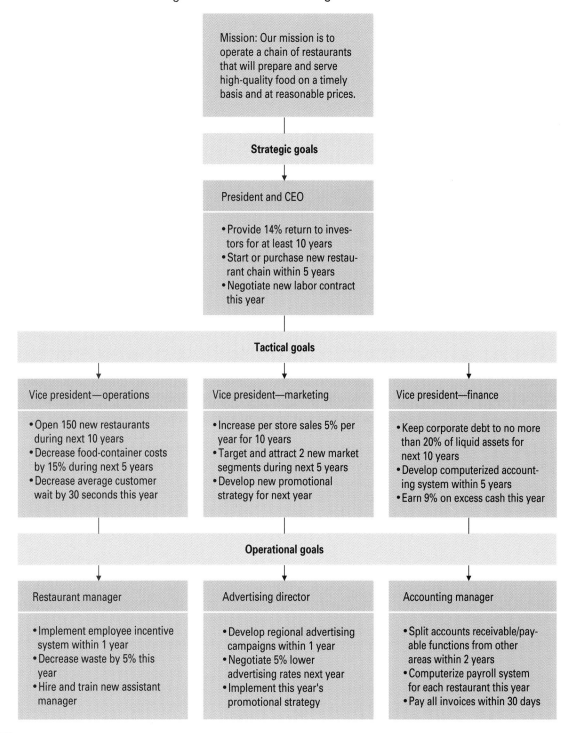

Mission: Our mission is to operate a chain of restaurants that will prepare and serve high-quality food on a timely basis and at reasonable prices.

Strategic goals

President and CEO

- Provide 14% return to investors for at least 10 years
- Start or purchase new restaurant chain within 5 years
- Negotiate new labor contract this year

Tactical goals

Vice president—operations

- Open 150 new restaurants during next 10 years
- Decrease food-container costs by 15% during next 5 years
- Decrease average customer wait by 30 seconds this year

Vice president—marketing

- Increase per store sales 5% per year for 10 years
- Target and attract 2 new market segments during next 5 years
- Develop new promotional strategy for next year

Vice president—finance

- Keep corporate debt to no more than 20% of liquid assets for next 10 years
- Develop computerized accounting system within 5 years
- Earn 9% on excess cash this year

Operational goals

Restaurant manager

- Implement employee incentive system within 1 year
- Decrease waste by 5% this year
- Hire and train new assistant manager

Advertising director

- Develop regional advertising campaigns within 1 year
- Negotiate 5% lower advertising rates next year
- Implement this year's promotional strategy

Accounting manager

- Split accounts receivable/payable functions from other areas within 2 years
- Computerize payroll system for each restaurant this year
- Pay all invoices within 30 days

Organizations develop many different types of goals. A regional fast-food chain, for example, might develop goals at several different levels and for several different areas.

An organization's mission statement can have a variety of components. Basic components include target customers and markets, principal products or services, geographic domain, core technologies, concern for survival, growth and profitability, company philosophy, company self-concept, and desired public image.

TABLE 6.1   Components of Corporate Mission Statements

Component	Example
Target customers and markets	"We believe our first responsibility is to the doctors, nurses, and patients, to mothers and all others who use our products." (Johnson & Johnson)
Principal products or services	"AMAX's principal products are molybdenum, coal, iron ore, copper, lead, zinc, petroleum and natural gas, potash, phosphates, nickel, tungsten, silver, gold, and magnesium."
Geographic domain	"We are dedicated to the total success of Corning Glass Works as a worldwide competitor."
Core technologies	"Control Data is in the business of applying microelectronics and computer technology in two general areas: computer-related hardware; and computing-enhancing services, which include computation, information, education, and finance."
Concern for survival, growth, and profitability	"In this respect, the company will conduct its operations prudently, and will provide the profits and growth which will assure Hoover's ultimate success." (Hoover Universal, Inc.)
Company philosophy	"It's all part of the Mary Kay philosophy—a philosophy based on the golden rule. A spirit of sharing and caring where people give cheerfully of their time, knowledge, and experience." (Mary Kay Cosmetics)
Company self-concept	"Hoover Universal is a diversified, multi-industry corporation with strong manufacturing capabilities, entrepreneurial policies, and individual business unit autonomy."
Desired public image	"To share the world's obligation for the protection of the environment." (Dow Chemical)

Source: John A. Pearce II and Fred David, "Corporate Mission Statements: The Bottom Line," *The Academy of Management Executive*, May 1987, pp. 109–115. Reprinted with permission.

longer, intermediate term around five years or so, and short-term around one year. But two or three years may be long-term at the operational level, and short-term may mean a matter of weeks or even days.

Responsibilities for Setting Goals

Who sets goals? The answer is actually quite simple: all managers should be involved in the goal-setting process. Each manager, however, generally has responsibilities for setting goals that correspond to his or her level in the organization. The mission and strategic goals are generally determined by the board of directors and top managers. Top and middle managers then work together to establish tactical goals. Finally, middle and lower-level managers are jointly responsible for operational goals. Many managers also set individual goals for themselves. These goals may involve career paths, informal work-related goals outside the normal array of official goals, or just about anything of interest or concern to the manager.

Managing Multiple Goals

Organizations set many different kinds of goals and sometimes experience conflicts or contradictions among goals. Nike, Inc., had problems with inconsistent goals a few years ago. The firm was producing high-quality shoes (a manufacturing goal) but they were not particularly stylish (a marketing goal). As a result, the company lost substantial market share when Reebok International Ltd. started making shoes that were both high quality and fashionable. When the inconsistencies were recognized and corrected, Nike regained its industry standing.[8]

To deal with such problems, managers must understand the concept of optimizing. **Optimizing** involves balancing and reconciling possible conflicts between goals. Because goals may conflict with one another, the manager must look for inconsistencies and decide whether to pursue one goal to the exclusion of another or to find a midrange target between the extremes. American Express Company, for example, has long had a goal of maintaining good relations with the banks that sell its travelers checks. However, the company recently began offering its own customers products and services previously available only from banks. An example is the Optima credit card, with terms and uses similar to Visa's and MasterCard's but a lower interest rate. Not surprisingly, this has changed American Express's relationship with banks. A few have stopped carrying American Express travelers checks. Officials at American Express hope that the extra profits earned by Optima will offset the lost business from the banks that begin to push competitors' travelers checks.[9]

Strategic goals focus on broad, general issues for an organization and are set by top management. A company whose product or service affects the environment might set a strategic goal of preserving natural resources as much as possible. By identifying wetlands and overseeing their reestablishment, Clayton Environmental Consultants helps its clients make conservation-oriented goals operational.

● **optimizing**
Balancing and reconciling possible conflicts among goals

ORGANIZATIONAL PLANNING

Given the clear link between organizational goals and plans, we now turn our attention to various concepts and issues associated with planning itself. In particular, this section identifies kinds of plans, time frames for planning, who is responsible for planning, and contingency planning. "The Global

View" also presents additional insights into setting goals and making plans in Japan.

Kinds of Organizational Plans

Organizations establish many different kinds of plans. At a general level, these include strategic, tactical, and operational plans.

Strategic Plans   Strategic plans are the plans developed to achieve strategic goals. More precisely, a **strategic plan** is a general plan outlining decisions of resource allocation, priorities, and action steps necessary to reach strategic goals.[10] These plans are set by the board of directors and top management, generally have an extended time horizon, and address questions of scope, resource deployment, competitive advantage, and synergy. We discuss strategic planning further in Chapter 7.

● **strategic plan**
A general plan outlining decisions of resource allocation, priorities, and action steps necessary to reach strategic goals

Tactical Plans   A **tactical plan,** aimed at achieving tactical goals, is developed to implement specific parts of a strategic plan. Tactical plans typically involve upper and middle management, have a somewhat shorter time horizon than strategic plans, and have a more specific and concrete focus. Thus tactical plans are concerned more with actually getting things done than with deciding what to do. Tactical planning is covered in detail in a later section.

● **tactical plan**
A plan aimed at achieving tactical goals and is developed to implement parts of a strategic plan

Operational Plans   An **operational plan** focuses on carrying out tactical plans to achieve operational goals. Developed by middle and lower-level managers, operational plans have a short-term focus and are relatively narrow in scope. Each one deals with a fairly small set of activities. We also cover operational planning in more detail later.

● **operational plan**
Focuses on carrying out tactical plans to achieve operational goals

Time Frames for Planning

As we previously noted, strategic plans tend to have a long-term focus, tactical plans an intermediate-term focus, and operational plans a short-term focus. The sections that follow address these time frames in more detail.

Long-Range Plans   A **long-range plan** covers many years, perhaps even decades. Large firms like General Motors Corp. and Exxon Corporation routinely develop plans for ten- to twenty-year intervals. The time span for long-range planning varies from one organization to another. For our purposes, we regard any plan that extends beyond five years as long-range. Managers of organizations in complex, volatile environments face a special dilemma. These organizations probably need a longer time horizon than do organizations in less dynamic environments, yet the complexity of their environment makes long-range planning difficult. Managers at these companies therefore develop long-range plans but also must constantly monitor their environment for possible changes.[11]

● **long-range plan**
A plan that covers many years, perhaps even decades; common long-range plans are for five years or more

Intermediate Plans   An **intermediate plan** is somewhat less tentative and subject to change than is a long-range plan. Intermediate plans usually cover periods from one to five years and are especially important for middle and first-line managers. Thus they generally parallel tactical plans. For many

intermediate plan
A plan that generally covers from one to five years

THE WORLD'S MOST POWERFUL BUSINESS ALLIANCES

 If they existed in the United States, they would be torn apart by antitrust suits brought by government agencies and competitors. Yet in Japan, the business alliances known as *keiretsu* are not only tolerated, they are seen as necessary to keep Japan stable and one step ahead of competitors around the world.

The ties between *keiretsu* members are both horizontal and vertical. Toyota is part of a *keiretsu* that includes 175 of its primary suppliers and 4,000 secondary suppliers. The Mitsubishi *keiretsu* includes 190 companies that produce everything from motors to beer to paper and collectively do more than $300 billion of business each year.

Members of the *keiretsu* are connected in a variety of ways. Many Japanese innovations, like just-in-time manufacturing, almost require *keiretsu*-style relationships, because they call for companies to work closely with suppliers they trust. As Japanese auto makers have built plants in the United States, suppliers from their *keiretsu* have moved with them. Toyota's Michigan plant is surrounded by more than twenty-five members of Toyota's *keiretsu*. Executives from one member of a *keiretsu* often sit on the boards of directors of other members, and member companies commonly own large chunks of each other's stock.

The much-criticized difficulty in selling to the Japa-nese is due in part to the *keiretsu*. Tenneco Automotive sells parts to the Toyota *keiretsu* around the world and used to supply shock absorbers to Mazda as well. But when a member of Mazda's *keiretsu* began making shocks, Mazda suddenly had no more use for Tenneco. *Keiretsu* members also protect each other. Corporate raider T. Boone Pickens wanted to take control of Japanese auto parts maker Koito in 1989 and spent $1.2 billion to get 26 percent of the company, more than any other stockholder. But Koito is in Toyota's *keiretsu;* Toyota holds 19 percent of Koito's stock and buys half of its output. And it made sure that Pickens never even got a seat on Koito's board of directors.

A few American companies are beginning to emulate rather than complain about the *keiretsu*. Eastman Kodak Company, for instance, has bought some of its distributors and owns shares in fifty of its suppliers and customers. And in Great Britain, Marks & Spencer has used a *keiretsu*-style supplier network for years, giving suppliers a sure market in return for flexibility and responsiveness. *Keiretsu* may be unAmerican, but they seem to work very well.

References: John Marcom, Jr., "Blue Blazers and Guacamole," *Forbes*, November 25, 1991, pp. 64–68; Carla Rapoport, "Why Japan Keeps On Winning," *Fortune*, July 15, 1991, pp. 76–85.

organizations intermediate planning has become the central focus of planning activities.[12] Philip Morris Incorporated developed a long-range plan for diversifying away from the tobacco industry. The firm bought General Foods Corporation after two years of planning, and its recent purchase of Kraft General Foods grew from an intermediate plan developed about a year earlier. Thus, although long-range planning guided Philip Morris's actions, intermediate plans actually defined those actions.[13]

Short-Range Plans A manager also develops a **short-range plan,** which deals with a time frame of one year or less. Short-range plans greatly affect the manager's day-to-day activities. There are two basic kinds of short-range plans. An **action plan** serves to operationalize any other kind of plan. For example, when the CEO of Philip Morris made the actual decision to buy Kraft, lawyers and top managers worked through the weekend on the proposal so that it could be delivered to Kraft's CEO the following Monday.[14] Their actions and accomplishments were action plans that flowed logically from a decision made by their CEO. A **reaction plan,** in turn, is

short-range plan
A plan that generally covers a span of one year or less

action plan
A plan used to operationalize any other kind of plan

reaction plan
A plan developed to react to an unforeseen circumstance

a plan designed to allow the company to react to an unforeseen circumstance. When Kraft received the takeover bid from Philip Morris, its managers had to decide whether to accept the terms, fight the offer, or some other alternative. Any of these constitutes a reaction plan—the firm reacting to a condition created by its environment. In fact, reacting to any form of environmental turbulence, as described in Chapter 3, is a form of reaction planning.

Responsibilities for Planning

We earlier noted briefly who is responsible for setting goals. We can now expand that initial perspective a bit and examine more fully how different parts of the organization participate in the overall planning process. All managers engage in planning to some degree. Marketing sales managers develop plans for target markets, market penetration, and sales increases. Operations managers plan cost-cutting programs and better inventory control methods. As a general rule, however, the larger an organization becomes, the more the primary planning activities become associated with groups of managers rather than with individual managers.[15]

The Planning Staff Some large organizations develop a professional planning staff. Tenneco Corporation, General Motors Corp., General Electric Co., Caterpillar Inc., Raytheon Co., NCR Corp., Ford Motor Co., and The Boeing Co. all have planning staffs.[16] And although the planning staff was pioneered in the United States, foreign firms like Nippon Telegraph & Telephone have also started using them.[17] Organizations might use a planning staff for a variety of reasons. In particular, a planning staff can reduce the workload of individual managers, help coordinate the planning activities of individual managers, bring to a particular problem many different tools and techniques, take a broader view than individual managers, and go beyond pet projects and particular departments.

Planning Task Force Organizations sometimes use a planning task force to help develop plans. Such a task force often comprises line managers with a special interest in the relevant area of planning. The task force may also have members from the planning staff if the organization has one. A planning task force is most often created when the organization wants to address a special circumstance. For example, when Electronic Data Systems Inc. decided to expand its services to Europe, managers knew that the firm's normal planning approach would not suffice, and top management created a special planning task force. The task force had representatives from each of the major units within the company, the corporate planning staff, and the management team that would run the European operation. Once the plan for entering the European market was formulated and implemented, the task force was eliminated.[18]

Board of Directors Among its other responsibilities, the board of directors establishes the corporate mission and strategy. In some companies the board takes an active role in the planning process. At CBS, for example, the board of directors has traditionally played a major role in planning. In other companies the board selects a competent chief executive and delegates planning to that individual.

To strengthen its leadership in the North American lighting market, General Electric made the decision to focus on customer service and develop and introduce energy-efficient lighting products—its Energy Choice line. Strengthening its leadership was GE's strategic goal; emphasizing customer service and introducing Energy Choice were its tactical plans, or the plans it developed to implement specific parts of its strategic goals.

The Chief Executive Officer The chief executive officer (CEO) is usually the president or the chairman of the board of directors. The CEO is probably the single most important individual in any organization's planning process. The CEO plays a major role in the complete planning process and is responsible for implementing the strategy. The board and CEO, then, assume direct roles in planning. The other organizational components involved in the planning process have more of an advisory or consulting role.

The Executive Committee The executive committee is usually composed of the top executives in the organization working together as a group. Committee members usually meet on a regular basis to provide input to the CEO on the proposals that affect their own units and to review the various strategic plans that develop from this input. Members of the executive committee are frequently assigned to various staff committees, subcommittees, and task forces to concentrate on specific projects or problems that might confront the entire organization at some time in the future.

Line Management The final component of most organizations' planning activities is line management. Line managers are those persons with formal authority and responsibility for the management of the organization. They play an important role in an organization's planning process for two reasons. First, they are a valuable source of inside information for other managers as plans are formulated and implemented. Second, it is usually the line managers at the middle and lower levels of the organization who must execute the plans developed by top management. Line management identifies, analyzes, and recommends program alternatives, develops budgets and submits them for approval, and finally sets the plans in motion.

Contingency Planning

Another important type of planning is the development of contingency plans. **Contingency planning** is the determination of alternative courses of action to be taken if an intended plan of action is unexpectedly disrupted or rendered inappropriate.[19] Suppose that a rapidly expanding franchised food company has made plans to build 100 new stores during each of the next four years. Its top managers realize, however, that a shift in the economy might call for a different rate of expansion. Therefore, the firm develops two contingency plans based on extreme positive or negative economic shifts. First, the company decides that if the economy begins to expand beyond some specific level (contingency event), then (contingency plan) the rate of the company's growth will increase from 100 to 150 new stores per year. Second, the company also decides that if inflation increases substantially, the expansion rate will drop from 100 to 75 new stores per year. The organization has now specified two crucial contingencies (expansion or inflation in the economy outside the tolerable range) and two alternative plans (increased or decreased growth).

The mechanics of contingency planning are shown in Figure 6.3. In relation to an organization's other plans, contingency planning comes into play at four action points. At action point 1, the basic plans of the organization are developed. These may include strategic, tactical, and operational plans. As part of this development process, managers usually consider various contingency events. Some management groups even assign someone

contingency planning
The determination of alternative courses of action to be taken if an intended plan is unexpectedly disrupted or rendered inappropriate

F I G U R E 6.3 Contingency Planning

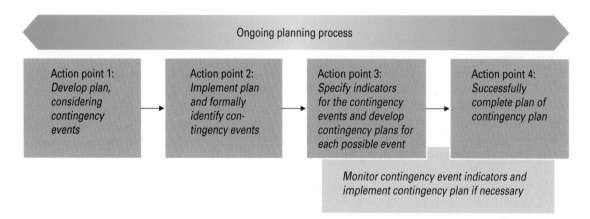

Ongoing planning process

Action point 1:
*Develop plan,
considering
contingency
events*

Action point 2:
*Implement plan
and formally
identify con-
tingency events*

Action point 3:
*Specify indicators
for the contingency
events and develop
contingency plans for
each possible event*

Action point 4:
*Successfully
complete plan of
contingency plan*

*Monitor contingency event indicators and
implement contingency plan if necessary*

Most organizations develop contingency plans. These plans specify alternative courses of action to be taken if an intended plan is unexpectedly disrupted or rendered inappropriate.

the role of devil's advocate to ask "But what if . . ." about each course of action. A variety of contingencies are usually considered.

At action point 2, the plan that has been chosen is put into effect. The most important contingency events are also defined. Only the events that are likely to occur and whose effects would have a substantial impact on the organization are used in the contingency-planning process. Next, at action point 3, the company specifies certain indicators or signs that might suggest that a contingency event is about to take place. A bank might decide that a 2-percent drop in interest rates should be considered a contingency event. An indicator might be two consecutive months with a drop of .5 percent in each. As indicators of contingency events are being defined, the contingency plans themselves should also be developed. Possible contingency plans for various situations might include delaying plant construction, developing a new manufacturing process, and cutting prices.

After this stage, the managers of the organization monitor the indicators identified at action point 3. If the situation dictates, a contingency plan may be implemented. Otherwise the primary plan of action continues in force. Finally, action point 4 marks the successful completion of either the original or a contingency plan.

Contingency planning is becoming increasingly important for most organizations and especially for those operating in particularly complex or dynamic environments. Few managers have such an accurate view of the future that they can anticipate and plan for everything. Contingency planning is a useful technique for helping managers cope with uncertainty and change.[20]

TACTICAL PLANNING

As we noted earlier, tactical plans are developed to implement specific parts of a strategic plan. You have probably heard the saying about "winning the battle but losing the war." Tactical plans are to battles what strategy is to a war: an organized sequence of steps designed to execute strategic plans.

Strategy focuses on resources, environment, and mission, whereas tactics deal primarily with people and action.[21] Figure 6.4 identifies the major elements in developing and executing tactical plans.

Developing Tactical Plans

Although effective tactical planning depends on many factors that vary from one situation to another, some basic guidelines can be identified. First, the manager needs to recognize that tactical planning must address a number of tactical goals derived from a broader strategic goal.[22] An occasional situation may call for a stand-alone tactical plan, but most of the time tactical plans flow from and must be consistent with a strategic plan.

For example, when Roberto Goizueta became CEO of Coca-Cola, he developed a strategic plan for carrying the firm into the twenty-first century. As part of developing the plan, Goizueta identified a critical environmental threat—considerable unrest and uncertainty among the independent bottlers who packaged and distributed Coca-Cola's products. To simultaneously counter this threat and strengthen the company's position, Coca-Cola bought several large independent bottlers and combined them into one new organization called Coca-Cola Enterprises, Inc. Selling half of the new company's stock reaped millions in profits while still effectively keeping control of the enterprise in Coca-Cola's hands. Thus the creation of the new business was a tactical plan developed to contribute to the achievement of an overarching strategic goal.[23]

Second, although strategies are often stated in general terms, tactics must deal more with specific resource and time issues. A strategy can call for being number 1 in a particular market or industry, but a tactical plan must specify precisely what activities will be undertaken to achieve that goal.[24] Consider the Coca-Cola example again. Another element of its strategic plan involves increased worldwide market share. To facilitate additional sales in Europe, managers developed tactical plans for building a new plant in the south of France to make soft-drink concentrate and for building another canning plant in Dunkirk. Building these plants represents a concrete action involving measurable resources (i.e., funds to build the plants) and a clear time horizon (i.e., a target date for completion).

Finally, tactical planning requires the use of human resources. Managers involved in tactical planning spend a great deal of time working with other

F I G U R E 6 . 4 Developing and Executing Tactical Plans

Tactical plans are used to accomplish specific parts of a strategic plan. Each strategic plan is generally implemented through several tactical plans. Effective tactical planning involves both development and execution.

Developing tactical plans
- Recognize and understand overarching strategic plans and tactical goals
- Specify relevant resource and time issues
- Recognize and identify human resource commitments

Executing tactical plans
- Evaluate each course of action in light of its goal
- Obtain and distribute information and resources
- Monitor horizontal and vertical communication and integration of activities
- Monitor ongoing activities for goal achievement

people. They must be in a position to receive information from others in and outside the organization, process that information in the most effective way, and then pass it on to others who might make use of it. Coca-Cola executives have been intensively involved in planning the new plants, setting up the new bottling venture noted earlier, and exploring a joint venture with Cadbury Schweppes in the United Kingdom. Each activity has required considerable time and effort from dozens of managers. One manager, for example, crossed the Atlantic twelve times while negotiating the Cadbury deal.

Executing Tactical Plans

Regardless of how well a tactical plan may be formulated, its ultimate success depends on the way it is carried out. Successful implementation, in turn, depends on the astute use of resources, effective decision making, and insightful steps to ensure that the right things are done at the right time and in the right ways. A manager can have an absolutely brilliant idea, but it can fail if not properly executed.

Proper execution depends on a number of important factors. First the manager needs to evaluate every possible course of action in light of the goal it is intended to reach. Next he or she needs to make sure each decision maker has the information and resources necessary to get the job done. Vertical and horizontal communication and integration of activities must be present to minimize conflict or inconsistent activities. And finally, the manager must monitor ongoing activities derived from the plan to make sure that they are achieving the desired results. This monitoring typically takes place within the context of the organization's ongoing control systems.

For example, managers at the Walt Disney Company recently developed a new strategic plan aimed at spurring growth and profits. One tactical plan developed to stimulate growth was to build one or more new theme parks in California. One possible park, called Westcot Center, would be built adjacent to Disneyland in Anaheim and patterned after Disney World's Epcot Center in Florida. Although building this park will be a big undertaking, it is still a tactical plan within the overall strategic plan focusing on growth.

OPERATIONAL PLANNING

Another critical element in effective organizational planning is the development and implementation of operational plans. Operational plans are derived from tactical plans and are aimed at achieving operational goals. Thus operational plans tend to be narrowly focused, have relatively short time horizons, and involve lower-level managers. The two most basic forms of operational plans, and specific types of each, are summarized in Table 6.2.

● **single-use plan**
Developed to carry out a course of action that is not likely to be repeated in the future

Single-Use Plans

A **single-use plan** is developed to carry out a course of action that is not likely to be repeated in the future. As Disney proceeds with its expansion

TABLE 6.2 Types of Operational Plans

Plan	Description
Single-use plan	Developed to carry out a course of action not likely to be carried out in the future
Program	Single-use plan for a large set of activities
Project	Single-use plan of less scope and complexity than a program
Standing plan	Developed for activities that recur regularly over a period of time
Policy	Standing plan specifying the organization's general response to a designated problem or situation
Standard operating procedure	Standing plan outlining steps to be followed in particular circumstances
Rules and regulations	Standing plans describing exactly how specific activities are to be carried out

Organizations develop various operational plans to help achieve operational goals. In general, there are two types of single-use plans and three types of standing plans.

plans on the West Coast, it will develop numerous single-use plans for individual rides, attractions, hotels, and so forth. The two most common forms of single-use plans are programs and projects.

Programs A **program** is a single-use plan for a large set of activities. It might consist of identifying procedures for introducing a new product line, opening a new facility, or changing the organization's mission. A few years ago Black & Decker Corp. bought General Electric's small-appliance business. The deal involved the largest brand-name switch in history, with a total of 150 products being converted from GE to the Black & Decker label. Each product was carefully studied, redesigned, and reintroduced with an extended warranty. A total of 140 steps were used for each product. It took three years to convert all 150 products over to Black & Decker. The total conversion of the product line was a program.[25]

● **program**
A single-use plan for a large set of activities

Projects A **project** is similar to a program but is generally of less scope and complexity. A project may be a part of a broader program, or it may be a self-contained single-use plan. For Black & Decker, the conversion of each of the 150 products was a separate project in its own right. Each product had its own manager, its own schedule, and so forth. Projects are also used to introduce a new product within an existing product line or to add a new benefit option to an existing salary package. "Management in Practice" discusses one of Reebok's more successful projects, the Blacktop.

● **project**
A single-use plan of less scope and complexity than a program

Standing Plans

Whereas single-use plans are used for nonrecurring situations, a **standing plan** is used for activities that recur regularly over a period of time. Standing

standing plan
Developed for activities that recur regularly over a period of time

plans can greatly enhance efficiency by routinizing decision making. Policies, standard operating procedures, and rules and regulations are three kinds of standing plans.[26]

Policies   As a general guide for action, a policy is the most general form of standing plan. A **policy** specifies the organization's general response to a designated problem or situation. For example, McDonald's has a policy that it will not grant a franchise to an individual who already owns another fast-food restaurant. Likewise, a university admissions office might establish a policy that admission will be granted only to applicants with a minimum SAT score of 1,000 and a ranking in the top quarter of their high-school classes. Admissions officers may routinely deny admission to applicants who fail to reach these minimums. A policy is also likely to describe how exceptions are to be handled. The university's policy statement, for example, might create an admissions appeals committee to evaluate applicants who do not meet minimum requirements but may warrant special consideration.

Standard Operating Procedures   Another type of standing plan is the **standard operating procedure,** or **SOP.** A SOP is more specific than a policy in that it outlines the steps to be followed in particular circumstances. The admissions clerk at the university, for example, might be told that when an application is received, he or she should (1) set up a file for the applicant; (2) add test-score records, transcripts, and letters of reference to the file as they are received; and (3) give the file to the appropriate admissions director when it is complete. Gallo Vineyards in California has a 300-page manual of standard operating procedures. This planning manual is credited for making Gallo one of the most efficient wine operations in the United States.[27] McDonald's has SOPs explaining exactly how Big Macs are to be cooked, how long they can stay in the warming rack, and so forth.

policy

A standing plan that specifies the organization's general response to a designated problem or situation

standard operating procedure (SOP)

A standing plan that outlines the steps to be followed in a particular circumstance

Standard operating procedures outline the steps employees take in specific situations, and at Union Pacific's Laredo, Texas yard, SOPs direct the loading and unloading of trailers and containers with goods coming from and going to Mexico. Laredo is the main border crossing point for shipments to and from Mexico.

REEBOK HEADS OUTSIDE—AND UP

 The sneaker wars between Nike and Reebok have generated almost as much consumer interest as the cola wars between Coke and Pepsi. Every year or so, each company comes up with a new line of shoes, a new gimmick, or a new ad campaign that catches the public's interest. Often their relative fortunes change again.

Nike is the old-timer in this battle, and Reebok is the upstart. Though Reebok can trace its lineage back to a spiked running shoe invented in 1894, it didn't appear in the United States until the early 1980s. Unable to compete with established giants like Nike and Adidas in the running shoe market, Reebok instead studied other sports and saw that the millions of people joining aerobics classes needed a special shoe. It filled that need with Freestyle, which became the most popular shoe in history. And the sneaker wars were on.

Reebok's biggest salvo in the latest round is the Pump, a new high-tech gimmick that allows wearers to pump up certain parts of the shoe to the desired fit. The Pump basketball shoe sells for $170, and in 1991 the entire line earned Reebok $250 million. But the real hero for Reebok that year was a more moderately priced sneaker called the Blacktop.

The Blacktop seems to perform two different and important functions. The shoe is built specifically to fill a need that no other manufacturer has addressed, and its black-and-white design makes a distinctive style statement. Because 80 percent of athletic shoes are bought simply for their looks, this latter quality is important. But the Blacktop's purpose is what took other makers by surprise. As its ads make clear, the Blacktop is intended not for the parquet floors where the likes of Michael Jordan make their millions, but for the hard concrete and asphalt where most people play basketball—outside. The soles are made of rubber similar to that used on race car tires, and the leather uppers are heavier than on most sneakers. The Blacktop weighs a couple of ounces more than its competitors, but that doesn't seem to matter to the more than two million people who had bought the shoe by the end of 1991.

It may well be that most Blacktop wearers never attempt a jump shot, much less a slam dunk. But in any case, they have helped Reebok jump back into the sneaker wars with a vengeance.

References: Keith H. Hammonds, "The 'Blacktop' Is Paving Reebok's Road to Recovery," *Business Week*, August 12, 1991, p. 27; Gary Hoover, Alta Campbell, and Patrick J. Spain (eds.), *Hoover's Handbook 1991—Profiles of Over 500 Major Corporations* (Austin, Tex.: The Reference Press, 1990), p. 456.

Rules and Regulations The narrowest of the standing plans, **rules and regulations** describe exactly how specific activities are to be carried out. Rather than guiding decision making, rules and regulations actually take the place of decision making in various situations. Each McDonald's restaurant has a rule prohibiting customers from using its telephones, for example. The university admissions office might have a rule stipulating that if an applicant's file is not complete two months prior to the beginning of a semester, the student cannot be admitted until the next semester. Of course, in most organizations a manager at a higher level can suspend or bend the rules. If the high-school transcript of the daughter of a prominent university alumnus and donor arrives a few days late, the director of admissions would probably waive the two-month rule. Rules and regulations can become a problem if they become excessive or if they are enforced too rigidly.

Rules and regulations and SOPs are similar in many ways. They are both relatively narrow in scope, and each can serve as a substitute for decision

rules and regulations
Describe exactly how specific activities are to be carried out

making. A SOP typically describes a sequence of activities, however, whereas rules and regulations focus on one activity. Recall our examples: the admissions-desk SOP consisted of three activities, whereas the two-month rule related to one activity only. In an industrial setting, the SOP for orienting a new employee could involve enrolling the person in various benefit options, introducing him or her to coworkers and supervisors, and providing a tour of the facilities. A pertinent rule for the new employee might involve when to come to work each day.

MANAGING GOAL-SETTING AND PLANNING PROCESSES

Obviously, all of the elements of goal setting and planning discussed to this point involve managing these processes in some way or another. In addition, however, it is also helpful to understand that major barriers sometimes impede effective goal setting and planning. Likewise, it is important to know how to overcome some of the barriers.

Barriers to Goal Setting and Planning

Several circumstances can serve as barriers to effective goal setting and planning. Some of the more common ones are listed in Table 6.3.

Inappropriate Goals Inappropriate goals come in many forms. Paying a large dividend to stockholders may be inappropriate if it comes at the expense of research and development. Goals may also be inappropriate if they are unattainable. If Chrysler Corp. were to set a goal of selling more cars than General Motors next year, people at the company would probably be embarrassed because achieving such a goal would be impossible. Goals may also be inappropriate if they place too much emphasis on either quantitative or qualitative measures of success. Some goals, especially those relating to financial areas, are quantifiable, objective, and verifiable. Other goals, such

As part of managing the goal-setting and planning process, it is important to understand the barriers that can disrupt them. It is also just as important to know how to overcome the barriers.

TABLE 6.3	Barriers to Goal Setting and Planning
Major barriers	Inappropriate goals Improper reward system Dynamic and complex environment Reluctance to establish goals Resistance to change Constraints
Overcoming the barriers	Understanding the purposes of goals and planning Communication and participation Consistency, revision, and updating Effective reward systems

as employee satisfaction and development, are difficult if not impossible to quantify. Organizations are asking for trouble if they put too much emphasis on one type of goal to the exclusion of the other.

Improper Reward System In some settings, an improper reward system acts as a barrier to goal setting and planning. For example, people may inadvertently be rewarded for poor goal-setting behavior or go unrewarded or even be punished for proper goal-setting behavior. Suppose a manager sets a goal of decreasing turnover next year. If turnover is decreased by even a fraction, the manager can claim success and perhaps be rewarded for the accomplishment. In contrast, a manager who attempts to decrease turnover by 5 percent but actually achieves a decrease of only 4 percent may receive a smaller reward because of her or his failure to reach the established goal. And if an organization places too much emphasis on short-term performance and results, managers may ignore longer-term issues as they set goals and formulate plans to achieve higher profits in the short-term.

Dynamic and Complex Environment The nature of an organization's environment is also a barrier to effective goal setting and planning. Rapid change, technological innovation, and intense competition can each make it difficult for an organization to accurately assess future opportunities and threats. For example, when an electronics firm like IBM develops a long-range plan, it tries to take into account how much technological innovation is likely to occur during that interval. But forecasting such events is extremely difficult. During the early boom years of personal computers, data were stored primarily on floppy disks. Because these disks had a limited storage capacity, hard disks were developed. Whereas the typical floppy disk can hold hundreds of pages of information, a hard disk can store thousands of pages. Today computers are increasingly relying on optical disks to store information. The manager attempting to set goals and plan in this rapidly changing environment faces a truly formidable task.

Reluctance to Establish Goals Another barrier to effective planning is the reluctance of some managers to establish goals for themselves and their units of responsibility. The reason for this reluctance may be lack of confidence or fear of failure. If a manager sets a goal that is specific, concise, and time related, then whether he or she attains it is obvious. Managers who consciously or unconsciously try to avoid this degree of accountability are likely to hinder the organization's planning efforts. Pfizer Inc., a large pharmaceutical company, recently ran into problems because its managers did not set goals for research and development. Consequently, the organization fell farther and farther behind because the managers had no way of knowing how effective their R&D efforts actually were.[28]

Resistance to Change Another barrier to goal setting and planning is resistance to change. Planning essentially involves changing something about the organization. As we see in Chapter 12, people tend to resist change. Avon Products almost drove itself into bankruptcy because it insisted on continuing a policy of large dividend payments to its stockholders. When profits started to fall, managers resisted cutting the dividends and started borrowing to pay them. The company's debt grew from $3 million to $1.1 billion in eight years. Eventually, managers were forced to confront the problem and decided to cut dividends.[29]

Constraints   Constraints that limit what an organizaton can do are another major obstacle. Common constraints include a lack of resources, government restrictions, and strong competition. For example, Owens-Corning Fiberglass Corp. recently took on an enormous debt burden as part of its fight to avoid being taken over by Wickes Companies, Inc. The company now has such a large debt to service that it has been forced to cut back on capital expenditures and research and development. And those cutbacks have greatly constrained what the firm can plan for the future.[30] Time constraints are also a factor. It's easy to say, "I'm too busy to plan today; I'll do it tomorrow." Effective planning takes time, energy, and an unwavering belief in its importance.

Overcoming the Barriers

Fortunately, there are several guidelines for making goal setting and planning effective. Some of the guidelines are also listed in Table 6.3.

Understand the Purposes of Goals and Plans   One of the best ways to facilitate goal-setting and planning processes is to recognize their basic purposes. The organization should also recognize that there are limits to the effectiveness of setting goals and making plans. Planning is not a panacea that will solve all of an organization's problems, nor is it an iron-clad set of procedures to be followed at any cost. And effective goals and planning do not necessarily ensure success; adjustments and exceptions are to be expected as time passes. For example, Coca-Cola followed a logical and rational approach to setting goals and planning when it introduced its new formula to combat inroads being made by PepsiCo, Inc. But all the plans proved to be wrong as consumers rejected the new version of Coca-Cola. Managers quickly reversed the decision and reintroduced the old formula as Coca-Cola Classic. And it has a larger market share today than before. Thus even though careful planning resulted in a big mistake, the company came out ahead in the long run.[31]

Harold A. Wagner, president and chief operating officer of Air Products, meets with employees to discuss the company's strategies and plans, and hear their opinions on company-related issues. By keeping lines of communication open between the levels of management, he is helping ensure employees' commitment to the company's goals and strategies.

Communication and Participation Although goals and plans may be initiated at high levels in the organization, they must also be communicated to others in the organization. Everyone involved in the planning process should know what the overriding organizational strategy is, what the various functional strategies are, and how they are all to be integrated and coordinated. It is also important that people responsible for achieving goals and implementing plans have a voice in developing them from the outset. These individuals almost always have valuable information to contribute, and because they will be implementing the plans, their involvement is critical: people are usually more committed to plans that they have helped to shape. Even when an organization is somewhat centralized or uses a planning staff, managers from a variety of levels in the organization should be involved in the planning process. Ford Motor Co. has demonstrated leadership in this area. Managers from all levels of the organization, and even operating employees, are given a large voice in how things are done.

Consistency, Revision, and Updating Goals should be consistent both horizontally and vertically. Horizontal consistency means that goals should be consistent across the organization. Vertical consistency means that goals should be consistent up and down the organization—strategic, tactical, and operational goals must agree with one another. Because goal setting and planning are dynamic processes, they must also be revised and updated regularly. Many organizations are seeing the need to revise and update on an increasingly frequent basis. Citicorp, for example, used to use a three-year planning horizon for developing and providing new financial services. That cycle has been cut to two years, and the bank hopes to reduce it to one year very soon.

Effective Reward Systems In general, people should be rewarded both for establishing effective goals and plans and for successfully achieving them. Because failure sometimes results from factors outside the manager's control, however, people should also be assured that failure to reach a goal will not necessarily bring punitive consequences. Frederick Smith, founder and CEO of Federal Express Corp., has a stated goal of encouraging risk. Thus when Federal Express lost $233 million on an unsuccessful new service called ZapMail, no one was punished. Smith believed that the original idea had been a good one but was unsuccessful for reasons beyond the company's control.

Using Management by Objectives to Implement Plans

A widely used method for managing the goal-setting and planning processes concurrently to make sure that both are done effectively is **management by objectives,** or **MBO.**

The Nature and Purpose of MBO The purpose of MBO is to give subordinates a voice in the goal-setting and planning processes and to clarify for them exactly what they are expected to accomplish in a given time span. MBO is concerned with goal setting and planning for individual managers and their units or work groups.[32]

● **management by objectives (MBO)**
The process of collaborative goal setting by a manager and subordinate; the extent to which goals are accomplished is a major factor in evaluating and rewarding the subordinate's performance

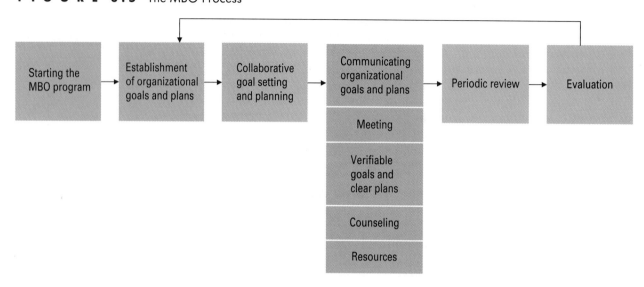

Management by objectives, or MBO, is an effective technique for integrating goal setting and planning. This figure portrays the general steps that most organizations use when they adopt MBO. Of course, most organizations adapt this general process to fit their own unique needs and circumstances.

The MBO Process   The basic mechanics of the MBO process are shown in Figure 6.5. The MBO process is described here from an ideal perspective. In any given organization the steps of the process are likely to vary in importance and may even take a different sequence. As a starting point, however, most managers believe that if an MBO program is to be successful, it must start at the top of the organization. Top managers must communicate why they have adopted MBO, what they think it will do, and that they have accepted and are committed to MBO. Employees must also be educated about what MBO is and what their role in it will be. Having committed to MBO, managers must implement it in a way that is consistent with overall organizational goals and plans. The idea is that goals set at the top will cascade down throughout the organization in a systematic way.

Although establishing the organization's basic goals and plans is extremely important, collaborative goal setting and planning are the essence of MBO. The collaboration involves a series of distinct steps. First, managers tell their subordinates what organizational and unit goals and plans have been established. Then managers meet with their subordinates on a one-to-one basis to arrive at a set of goals and plans for each subordinate that both the subordinate and the manager have helped develop and to which both are committed. Next, the goals are refined to be as verifiable (quantitative) as possible and to specify a time frame for their accomplishment. They should also be written. Further, the plans developed to achieve the goals need to be as clearly stated as possible and relate to each goal in a direct way. Managers must play the role of counselors in the goal-setting and planning meeting. For example, they must ensure that the subordinates' goals and plans are attainable and workable and that they will facilitate both the unit's and the organization's goals and plans. Finally, the meeting should spell out the resources that the subordinate will need to implement his or her plans and work effectively toward goal attainment.

4. What are the barriers to goal setting and planning? How can they be overcome? Can you think of any ways to overcome the barriers other than the ways identified in the text?

Questions for Analysis

5. Almost by definition, organizations cannot accomplish all of their goals. Why?

6. Which kind of plan—tactical or operational—should an organization develop first? Why? Does the order of development really make a difference as long as plans of both types are made?

7. Think of examples of each type of operational plan you have used at work, in your school work, or even in your personal life.

Questions for Application

8. Interview the head of the department in which you are majoring. What kinds of goals exist for the department and for the members of the department? Share your findings with the rest of the class.

9. Interview a local small-business manager about the time frames for planning that he or she uses. How do your results compare with what you might have expected from the presentation in the textbook?

10. Interview a college or university official to determine the use of single-use and standing plans at your institution. How were these plans developed?

ConAgra's Menu Keeps Growing

Some companies grow by "sticking to their knitting," or doing what they know best and avoiding risky ventures into new areas. Others thrive by purchasing floundering companies and finding new ways to make them profitable. ConAgra is one of the rare companies that has managed to do both.

ConAgra's business is food, and though it swallowed more than fifty other companies during the 1980s, some of them huge, it has not lost its focus. Profits are not always easy to come by in the food business. Consumers are losing their loyalties to particular brands, which means manufacturers have more difficulty charging premium prices and sometimes must even pay for shelf space in supermarkets. Yet the growth of ConAgra's net income would make a CEO in any industry happy.

ConAgra's secret is its CEO, Charles Harper, who has run the company since 1974. There's nothing particularly magical about Harper's approach, but his overall accomplishments are astonishing. When he took over the company it was on the edge of bankruptcy; now it does more than $19 billion in sales yearly. Admiring fellow executives say that Harper has no equal as a dealmaker. He knows what to buy and when. For example, in 1980 RCA was trying to sell off Banquet frozen food company, which hadn't put out a new product in a decade. RCA wanted $250 million; but when no other buyers appeared, Harper got the company for about one-fourth of that figure. To run the company, Harper recruited a frozen-foods expert from Campbell Soup Company, who soon had Banquet producing new products in more attractive packaging. In less than three years, operating profits tripled.

The Banquet acquisition demonstrates one of Harper's strengths—he makes the deals, but he doesn't try to control the particular decisions that make a ConAgra unit profitable. While its major rival, Kraft, has been consolidating its brands into seven major units, Con-Agra consists of seventy operating units, each with its own president and corporate staff, each under strict orders to find its own ways to produce a 20-percent return on equity.

This decentralization does not keep ConAgra from profiting from traditional economies of scale. Harper's typical approach is to avoid overpaying for an acquisition, which keeps its operating costs low. Then he finds ways of cutting inefficiencies and increases volume.

Even Harper's personal problems have turned into profits for his company. After a heart attack in 1985, he turned to a low-fat, low-sodium diet, but couldn't find any prepared foods on the market that met the criteria for his diet and his palate. His wife, Josie, came to the rescue, and her own concoctions were so successful that they inspired Harper to launch Healthy Choice frozen dinners, the food industry's most successful new product in years.

Discussion Questions

1. What are the advantages and disadvantages of keeping so many different units operating under the ConAgra name?

2. How has ConAgra managed to avoid the problems that have plagued many companies that grew through extensive acquisitions?

E 3. Do you think ConAgra should endeavor to make all of its prepared foods healthier, or should it continue to offer a range of foods with different levels of "unhealthy" ingredients?

References: Mark Ivey, "How ConAgra Grew Big—and Now, Beefy," *Business Week*, May 18, 1987, pp. 87–88; Lois Therrien, "ConAgra Turns Up the Heat in the Kitchen," *Business Week*, September 2, 1991, pp. 58–60.

How long can a company wait for its investment to pay off? Critics of American business practices—including many Japanese executives—believe that American businesses too often base decisions on how their balance sheet will look at the end of the quarter or the end of the year. Such short-sightedness, critics charge, encourages gambling on get-rich-quick schemes while it discourages the kind of investment in research and development that can lead to real long-term growth.

Stung by such criticisms, many American businesspeople are watching the fate of Columbia Pictures Entertainment Inc. with particular interest. For Sony, one of Japan's most respected companies, has invested $6.5 billion in Columbia, and has yet to see any tangible return. Has Sony taken long-range planning to an irrational extreme?

Sony based its 1989 purchase of Hollywood's biggest-grossing moviemaker on the belief that entertainment software drives the market for entertainment hardware. In other words, the people most likely to buy VCRs are those who want to watch movies at home. While this logic makes some sense, at least one economist, Benjamin Stein, compares it to the idea that someone who owns a restaurant should also own a huge ranch.

Sony has certainly done fine up to now by making just hardware. It produced the first Japanese tape recorder in 1950 and followed that with a long string of technological breakthroughs. Sony's move into software may be a result of its one major hardware failure, the Betamax VCR. Although Sony's entry into the VCR market was in some ways superior to the rival technology, VHS, VHS became the industry standard, in part because Hollywood began releasing movies in the VHS format.

So now Sony can control an entertainment product from start to finish, from studio to living room. Sony's new Play Station demonstrates the kind of integration of hardware and software that the company is betting will become standard in the future. Instead of Nintendo-style video game cartridges, the Play Station takes compact discs. The games combine film, graphics, music, and special effects. Sony hopes that many Nintendo lovers will switch to its more sophisticated offerings.

To make the game discs, Sony will call on its expensive subsidiaries, CBS Records and Columbia Pictures. Sony can create scenes and shoot film with both the movie and the game in mind. During the filming of the movie *Hook,* for instance, the head of Sony's electronic publishing business kept visiting the set to determine what music and scenery to borrow from the film for use in the video game.

This kind of synergy between elements of Sony's entertainment empire won't make Sony's investment in Columbia pay off any time soon. But for now, Sony is willing to bide its time and upgrade its facilities, confident that it will be in the best position to profit from the next revolution in movies or home entertainment.

Discussion Questions

1. Why is Sony not afraid to take the long-range view that its purchase of Columbia Pictures represents?

2. What pressures make it difficult for many U.S. managers to focus on the long term?

E 3. By pouring money into an enterprise that is not currently returning notable profit, is Sony being unfair to its shareholders?

References: Gary Hoover, Alta Campbell, Alan Chai, and Patrick J. Spain (eds.), *Hoover's Handbook of World Business 1992* (Austin, Tex.: The Reference Press, 1991), p. 287; Nancy J. Perry, "Will Sony Make It in Hollywood?" *Fortune,* September 9, 1991, pp. 158–166.

Managing Strategy and Strategic Planning

OBJECTIVES

After studying this chapter, you should be able to:

- *Describe the nature of strategic management.*

- *Describe how strategy is formulated.*

- *Discuss the meaning of and major approaches to corporate-level strategy.*

- *Discuss the meaning of and major approaches to business-level strategy.*

- *Identify and discuss the major functional strategies.*

- *Describe the major ways strategy is implemented.*

OUTLINE

The Nature of Strategic Management
   Components of Strategy
   Levels of Strategy
   Strategy Formulation and
     Implementation

Strategy Formulation
   Strategic Goals
   Environmental Analysis
   Organizational Analysis
   Matching Organizations and
     Environments

Corporate-Level Strategy
   Grand Strategy
   The Business Portfolio

Business-Level Strategy
   Adaptation Model
   Porter's Competitive Strategies
   Product Life Cycle

Functional Strategies
   Marketing Strategy
   Financial Strategy
   Production Strategy
   Human Resources Strategy
   Research and Development Strategy

Strategy Implementation
   Implementation Through Structure
   Implementation Through Leadership
   Implementation Through Information
     and Control Systems
   Implementation Through Human
     Resources
   Implementation Through Technology

IN THE 1960s, one of the world's most successful food-processing firms—H. J. Heinz Company—made a decision to expand into new markets and attempt to become a major player in its industry. For almost one hundred years the Heinz family had been content to maintain steady growth and profits while protecting its existing market share and product lines—primarily ketchup, pickles, horseradish, and other condiments.

The firm bought Star-Kist Foods, Inc. (1963), Ore-Ida Food Co., Inc. (1965), Tuffy's Pet Food (1971), and Weight Watchers International Inc. (1978). Adding these acquisitions to its existing business gave Heinz large market shares in a number of different markets. For example, Weight Watchers frozen entrees, 9-Lives canned cat food, Heinz ketchup, and Heinz relish each control more than 50 percent of their respective markets. In addition, Ore-Ida has more than 48 percent of the frozen potato market and Star-Kist in excess of 37 percent of the canned tuna market.

In 1979 the firm hired Anthony F. J. O'Reilly as its CEO. O'Reilly immediately set goals of even faster growth. To fuel this growth, he cut back on less-successful product lines and shifted advertising dollars away from entrenched products (like ketchup) toward products that face stronger competition (like cat food). He is also pushing aggressively into foreign markets. Today more than 40 percent of sales come from overseas: Heinz manufactures more than 3,000 products and markets them in more than 200 different countries. The firm also operates seventy food-processing plants in seventeen countries, including Kuwait, Thailand, and England.

To date, O'Reilly's efforts seem to be paying off: annual sales have increased from around $100 million in 1980 to more than $500 million in 1990. And profits have increased at the same pace.[1] ●

everal years ago managers at Heinz recognized that slow, steady growth was not an effective way to manage in their increasingly competitive and dynamic market. Thus they elected to pursue a path based on aggressive expansion and growth. Not all firms can achieve the level of growth that Heinz has attained, nor do all firms need this level of growth. Given the circumstances that Heinz faced at the time, however, its new approach seems to have been the right one. In short, Heinz engaged in effective strategic management.

This chapter explores strategic management in depth. We examine the general nature of strategic management. We then discuss how strategy is formulated. Next we describe the three basic levels of strategic management—corporate, business, and functional strategy. Finally, we conclude with a discussion of how strategy is actually implemented.

THE NATURE OF STRATEGIC MANAGEMENT

In Chapter 6 we described a strategic plan as a general plan outlining decisions of resource allocation, priorities, and action steps necessary to reach strategic goals. Strategic management, however, is much more than this. It is a way of thinking about management—and a way of approaching business opportunities and challenges. **Strategic management** is a comprehensive and ongoing management process aimed at formulating and implementing effective strategies that promote a superior alignment between the organization and its environment and the achievement of strategic goals.[2] To fully understand how strategic management is practiced, it is first necessary to understand the components of strategy, the different levels of strategy, and the distinction between strategy formulation and strategy implementation.

Components of Strategy

What exactly does a strategy address? What questions does it try to answer? In general, a well-conceived **strategy** deals with four basic areas: scope, resource deployment, distinctive competence, and synergy.[3]

Scope   The **scope** of a strategy specifies the range of markets in which the organization will compete. Heinz has essentially defined its scope as the food-processing industry. Some firms with a limited scope compete in only a few markets, whereas others with a broad scope compete in many different markets. For example, Pearson PLC, a British firm, has interests in publishing, fine china, investment banking, oil services, and entertainment. Because their potential range of markets is especially great, international firms pay particularly close attention to scope in their strategies.

Resource Deployment   A strategy should include an outline of the organization's projected **resource deployment**—how it plans to distribute its resources across various areas. For example, when O'Reilly took over Heinz

---

● **strategic management**
A management process aimed at formulating and implementing strategies that promote a superior alignment between the organization and its environment and the achievement of strategic goals

● **strategy**
A well-conceived strategy consists of four basic areas—scope, resource deployment, distinctive competence, and synergy

scope
Specifies the range of markets in which the organization will compete

resource deployment
How the organization will distribute its resources across various areas

he immediately cut back its line of pickles arguing that the firm was devoting too many resources to one product line. More recently he has decided to reduce the advertising budget for Heinz ketchup and use the funds to support advertising for other products. Resource deployment in different countries is again, very important for international firms.

Distinctive Competence   A strategy should specify the distinctive competence the organization has relative to its competitors. A **distinctive competence** is what the organization does exceptionally well. Heinz believes that processing food is its distinctive competence. The Limited, Inc., a large clothing chain, stresses the distinctive competence of speed. It tracks consumer preferences daily with point-of-sale computers, uses facsimile machines to transmit orders to suppliers in Hong Kong, charters 747s to fly products to the United States, and has products in stores forty-eight hours later. Other retailers take weeks or sometimes months to accomplish the same things. Thus The Limited uses its distinctive competence to stay ahead of the competition.[4]

Synergy   **Synergy** refers to how different areas of the business complement or enhance other areas, and a strategy should specify the synergy expected to result from decisions about scope, resource deployment, and distinctive competence. The Walt Disney Company uses synergy among all of its businesses. Its movies make money at the box office and then spur sales of videotapes; it operates hotels, theme parks, and restaurants at the same location; vacations at the parks lead to purchases of licensed souvenirs and greater interest in movies; and the Disney Channel cable network helps promote the whole empire.[5] Some international organizations achieve synergy from operations in different parts of the world. For example, Ford Motor Co.'s resurgence in the 1980s was partially brought about by new approaches to automotive design pioneered in its European division.

Levels of Strategy

A business may formulate strategies at the corporate, business, and functional levels.

Corporate Strategy   **Corporate strategy** is the course charted for the total organization. It is primarily concerned with scope and resource deployment, and it answers the question "In what markets will we compete?" Mars, Inc., has chosen to compete in four basic areas: candy, food, pet food, and electronics. Mars could have chosen to compete in a single business (like its biggest competitor, Hershey Foods Corp., which makes only confectioneries), or in dozens of other businesses. Instead, its managers chose those four areas.[6]

Business Strategy   **Business strategy** is focused less on scope and resource deployment than on competitive advantage and synergy. It attempts to answer the question "How should we compete in each of the markets we have chosen to enter?" Thus Mars has separate business strategies for each of its four businesses.

distinctive competence
What the organization does especially well

synergy
How different areas of the business complement or enhance one another

Tandy Corporation relies on synergy—using different areas of its business to complement each other—in a variety of ways. For example, because both education and small business markets use the similar approach of bundled hardware-software solutions systems, Tandy is supplementing its Radio Shack education sales force with a sales force of account executives and system engineers to focus on the small business market.

● **corporate strategy**
The course charted for the total organization that specifies in what markets the organization will compete

● **business strategy**
A strategy that focuses on how the organization will compete in each of its chosen areas

In a well-managed firm, strategy formulation and implementation across corporate, business, and functional levels systematically follow from one another and are logically integrated. All managers must therefore be aware of the firm's strategy because it affects managerial decisions and plans at all levels of the organization.

FIGURE 7.1 Strategy Formulation and Implementation Across Three Levels

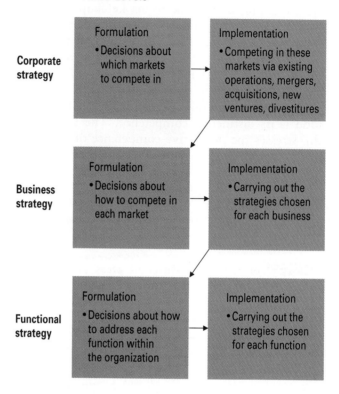

● functional strategy
A strategy developed for a single functional area

strategy formulation
The processes of creating or determining the strategies of the organization

● strategy implementation
The methods by which strategies are operationalized or executed within the organization

Functional Strategy   Organizations also establish **functional strategies** for each of the major areas they engage in. The most common functions are marketing, finance, production, human resources, and research and development. For example, Mars' candy business has a marketing strategy of expanding sales of existing products rather than developing new ones. And it has a production strategy centered on high-quality, state-of-the-art manufacturing.

Strategy Formulation and Implementation

It is also instructive to distinguish between strategy formulation and strategy implementation.[7] Simply, **strategy formulation** is the process of creating or determining the strategies of the organization, and **strategy implementation** is the methods by which strategies are carried out within the organization. Formulation therefore determines what the strategy is, and implementation focuses on how the strategy will be achieved.

Figure 7.1 illustrates the relationship between formulation and implementation across the three levels of strategy. At a general level, the formulation-implementation cycle starts at the corporate level, then follows systematically across the business and functional levels. Of course, the process is considerably more complex and dynamic than this simple example, but the example does represent the general nature of the strategic-planning process.

STRATEGY FORMULATION

Although every organization has its own unique approach to formulating strategy, most use a general framework consisting of four steps: setting strategic goals, analyzing the environment, analyzing the organization, and attempting to match the organization with the environment.

Strategic Goals

Establishing strategic goals is the starting point in formulating strategy. The processes and issues associated with strategic goal setting were explored in Chapter 6. In particular, recall that strategic goals are set by top management; focus on broad, general issues; and have a long-range time horizon.

A firm that does not monitor its environment carefully will miss both opportunities and threats. Harold Martin, through environmental analysis, found a new way to capitalize on an old idea. Recognizing that college students spend billions on clothing in their school colors, he decided to sell them athletic shoes to match. Martin's idea has proven a success so far as twenty-two schools have let him use their school colors in exchange for royalty payments. The result: $400,000 in revenues.

Environmental Analysis

After establishing strategic goals, the organization conducts an environmental analysis. This analysis involves looking carefully at the environment to determine the primary opportunities and threats confronting the organization.[8] Organizations can gather the information they need for this analysis in many ways. One source is published articles in magazines and newspapers like *Business Week, The Wall Street Journal,* and *Fortune.* Personal contacts with managers in other firms are also a valuable source of information. Government reports, bankers, lawyers, suppliers, customers, consultants, and professional associations can also be useful.

Organizations can also learn valuable insights from their competitors. Managers at Heniz can sample the tastes of competing food products simply by purchasing them at a grocery store. In preparation for launching Fairfield Inn, an economy motel chain, Marriott Corporation sent managers around the country to stay in competing motels. The managers asked questions and recorded information about the kinds of soap provided, the number of towels in the rooms, and general cleanliness, and then Marriott used this information in setting up their new business, which has been a big success.[9]

Environmental opportunities and threats are especially important for international firms. Because they compete in such diverse markets, they must be constantly vigilant for opportunities and threats such as new markets and new competitors. For example, the newly opening European market poses both important challenges and lucrative opportunities for many organizations.[10]

Organizational Analysis

The organizational analysis phase of strategy formulation involves diagnosing thoroughly and in detail the strengths and weaknesses of the organization.[11] It generally includes, but is not limited to, the organization's human, physical, financial, and information resources; its market position; and its current research and development efforts. Some of this information is readily available from normal information systems within the organization; other information must be obtained specifically for the strategy formulation process. In general, however, the efforts needed to gather the necessary data are a good investment.

Matching Organizations and Environments

Once the strategic goals have been established and environmental and organizational analyses completed, an organization must match its strengths and weaknesses to the corresponding opportunities and threats in the environment.[12] In general, this process is intended to align the organization with its environment in such a way as to take advantage of opportunities in the environment and avoid threats through the recognition of internal strengths and weaknesses. Marriott used this approach recently to formulate a new strategy.[13] A simplified version of this analysis is shown in Figure 7.2. At the time, in addition to its successful hotel and food services businesses, Marriott owned cruise ship, travel agency, and theme park businesses. Because these three businesses were performing poorly, however, they represented a weakness. So, too, did a poor cash position. The environmental analysis identified low growth in the market for upscale lodging of the type currently offered by Marriott. Managers also saw an interesting opportunity, though—high growth in the market for low-cost lodging. And they realized that their distinctive competence was in hotels and food services, not in the other businesses currently being operated. So Marriott sold its low-performing businesses and used the cash to launch Fairfield Inns.

The framework suggests several specific relationships. First, organizational strengths and weaknesses and environmental opportunities and threats are usually interrelated. For example, a firm might have a surplus of cash (a strength) because it has not spent much on research and development (a weakness). Similarly, a growing market for a firm's products (an opportunity) has the potential to attract new entrants (a threat). Second, organizational strengths should generally be targeted toward environmental opportunities. For example, Eastman Kodak Company's dominance in the

Marriott was able to formulate a new strategy based on the results of extensive environmental and organizational analysis. To arrive at this strategy, managers at Marriott systematically matched environmental opportunities and threats with organizational strengths and weaknesses.

FIGURE 7.2 Strategy Formulation at Marriott

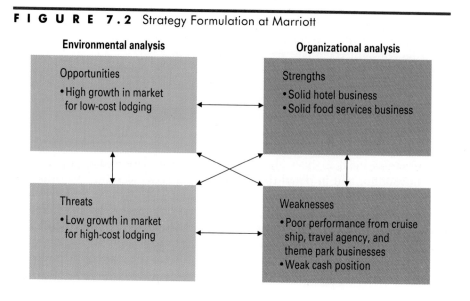

photography industry (a strength) made entry into the growing market for videotape products (an opportunity) a logical decision.

Third, the organization should recognize that its weaknesses are particularly vulnerable to environmental threats. For example, if the organization is dependent on a single supplier (organizational weakness), then the power of that supplier relative to the organization is extremely strong (environmental threat). Finally, to the extent possible, the firm might consider using its strengths to offset environmental threats. For example, E.I. du Pont de Nemours & Co. was dependent on petroleum companies for oil needed in its chemical business. But Du Pont became concerned that high oil prices might disrupt its operations (environmental threat). So the firm used surplus cash (organizational strength) to buy Conoco Inc. (environmental opportunity) and assure itself of a dependable source of petroleum.

CORPORATE-LEVEL STRATEGY

As we noted earlier, strategy formulation activities occur at three basic levels: corporate, business, and functional. This section focuses on the two dominant approaches to corporate strategy—grand strategy and the business portfolio.

Grand Strategy

Grand strategy is an overall framework for action developed at the corporate level. It is most commonly used when a corporation competes in a single market or in a few highly related markets.[14] Hershey Foods, for example, competes only in the confectionery market. There are three basic grand strategies that corporations choose to pursue: growth, stability, and retrenchment.

As the term implies, a **growth strategy** calls for overall corporate growth. Growth can be generated internally by introducing new products, opening new outlets, and increasing market share. It can be induced externally through acquisitions of other businesses, mergers, and joint ventures. Such growth is called **related diversification** when it is in the same or related businesses. Heinz's purchase of Weight Watchers was related diversification. Growth into areas unrelated to current operations is called **unrelated diversification.** The Dial Corporation, makers of such personal care products as Breck shampoo, Dial and Tone soaps, recently bought Premier Cruise Lines in a move toward unrelated diversification. Growth is most often appropriate when the corporation has ample resources to support it and when there is reasonable likelihood that growth is possible. For example, Wal-Mart Stores, Inc., has been growing rapidly by expanding into parts of the country not currently served. Many firms today see much of their potential growth as coming from foreign markets.[15]

A **retrenchment strategy** (also called a turnaround strategy) calls for shrinking current operations, cutting back in a variety of areas, or eliminating unprofitable operations altogether. Such downsizing has been quite popular in recent years. A firm is most likely to downsize when it is unprofitable, has excessive operating costs, has excess capacity, or has diversified

grand strategy
An overall framework for action developed at the corporate level

growth strategy
A strategy that calls for overall corporate growth in one or more dimensions

related diversification
Growing by expanding in the same or related markets in which the organization currently operates

unrelated diversification
Growing by expanding into areas unrelated to current operations

retrenchment strategy
Involves shrinking current operations, cutting back in a variety of areas, or eliminating unprofitable operations altogether

into markets it should never have entered.[16] It may also be necessary after a bitter price war with a competitor or when the firm takes extreme measures to protect itself. For example, in an effort to remain independent and avoid being taken over, Avon incurred substantial new debt and reduced its contributions to retained earnings by increasing its dividend payout. As a result, the firm also reduced its work force and implemented several cost-cutting measures.[17]

stability strategy
A strategy that calls for maintaining the status quo

A **stability strategy** calls for maintaining the status quo. A company adopting such a strategy plans to stay in the businesses it's currently in, manage them as they've been managed, and try to protect itself from environmental threats. This approach is most often adopted by companies that lack the resources to grow or are in markets where little growth is feasible or whose managers simply aren't interested in growth. Stability is also a useful strategy to adopt after a period of rapid growth or retrenchment. A few years ago, Mattel went through a period of retrenchment. The firm closed plants, laid off workers, and reduced its product line drastically. Many observers wrote the firm off. But by adopting a strategy of stability, Mattel was able to gradually recover from its retrenchment trauma and has now started to grow again.[18]

The Business Portfolio

An overall grand strategy is useful when the corporation has only a few related businesses. When it has many different businesses (that is, when it is diversified), and especially when those businesses are unrelated, the firm needs a different approach. A common tool used to manage multiple businesses is the business portfolio. The business portfolio involves viewing the corporation as a collection of businesses, each of which can have its own competitive business strategy.[19]

strategic business unit (SBU)
A separate division within the company that has its own mission, its own competitors, and its own unique strategy

Strategic Business Units The starting point in using the portfolio approach is to identify within the corporation each **strategic business unit (SBU).** Each SBU is usually a separate division within the company. It has its own mission, its own competitors, and its own unique strategy apart from that of other SBUs in the organization.[20] Managers at General Electric developed the concept of strategic business units when they realized that they needed a framework for evaluating their very large and diverse organization. They decided to conceptualize the firm as a portfolio of business units. For example, one business unit was defined as the set of all food preparation appliance producers (for example, toaster ovens and ranges). A total of forty-three SBUs were identified within the company. Soon several other firms, including Union Carbide and General Foods, also began to characterize themselves as a collection of SBUs. "The Global View" describes how a European firm has structured itself in terms of SBUs.

After a corporation's SBUs have been appropriately defined, the next step is to classify them. The most frequently used method of categorization is the BCG matrix.

BCG matrix
Classifies SBUs into four categories defined by market growth rate and market share

The BCG Matrix The **BCG matrix** classifies each SBU in terms of the growth rate of its market (high or low) and its relative share (high or low) of that market. It was the framework originally developed for General

WRIGLEY STICKS TO ITS CHEWING

Perhaps the stigma attached to chewing gum in public has to do with the conduct of young William Wrigley, Jr., founder of the nation's leading gum-maker. Wrigley got his start in sales when he was expelled from school at age 13. At first he didn't sell gum; he gave it away as a bonus to customers who bought his soap and baking powder. Soon customers demanded more gum, so Wrigley gave up on soap and took a big gamble, replacing spruce gum and wax with Central American chicle as the gum base. By 1893 he was selling Spearmint and Juicy Fruit, and by 1910 Spearmint was the country's leading gum.

Not much has changed since then. Sure, Doublemint has replaced Spearmint as U.S. gum chewers' favorite, but gum still accounts for more than 90 percent of the company's revenues. The Wm. Wrigley Jr. Company controls almost half of the $2.4 billion retail U.S. gum market, the Wrigley family still owns more than one-third of the company, and the company's current CEO is William Wrigley, the founder's grandson.

Wrigley's clinging to a successful product does not mean, however, that the company is stuck in the nineteenth century. Since the founder mailed a stick of gum to everyone listed in a U.S. telephone book in 1915, the company's marketing approach has become more conservative, and competitors laugh at the Doublemint twins and the 1950s aura of Wrigley's ads. But the ads work. Wrigley's distribution network can ship more than a million pounds of gum per day, and Wrigley feels that some of its high-tech manufacturing techniques are so valuable that it won't patent them for fear a competitor might copy the designs. Wrigley no longer relies on natural ingredients, having replaced chicle with such things as butadiene-styrene rubber, polyvinyl acetate, and petroleum wax.

Wrigley's one major failing resulted from its tardiness in realizing that U.S. consumers' gum-chewing tastes would not always remain the same as they'd been in 1900. Its market share dropped 35 percent in the late 1970s when competitors introduced sugar-free gums. Wrigley finally came out with sugar-free Extra in 1984, and by 1989 it was the leading sugar-free gum, thanks to the company's largest-ever advertising campaign. Adding sugarless gum to its products might not seem a radical move, but as one company director puts it, "The only thing [Wrigley] would consider as a new venture is something else in the gum business."*

*Brett Pulley, "Wrigley Is Thriving, Despite the Recession, In a Resilient Business," *The Wall Street Journal*, May 29, 1991, p. A1.

References: Gary Hoover, Alta Campbell, and Patrick J. Spain (eds.), *Hoover's Handbook 1991—Profiles of Over 500 Major Corporations* (Austin, Tex.: The Reference Press, 1990), p. 591; Brett Pulley, "Wrigley Is Thriving, Despite the Recession, In a Resilient Business," *The Wall Street Journal*, May 29, 1991, pp. A1, A8.

ditions. An excellent illustration of an organization employing the reactor strategy was W.T. Grant, one of the largest retailers in the United States before its bankruptcy in 1976. In response to the success of K mart Corp. in the discounting area, Grant adopted the ill-conceived strategy of expanding rapidly without the necessary resources. Further, the company had inadequate training programs for its managers and too few controls over day-to-day operations. The company simply tried to do too many things too fast, and then it refused to step back and retrench.[26]

Porter's Competitive Strategies

Michael Porter describes three competitive strategies presumed to be appropriate for a wide variety of organizations across diverse industries.[27] Porter suggests that a business should thoroughly analyze its industry and then define a competitive niche by adopting one of three generic strategies: differentiation, cost leadership, or focus. The goal is to develop a competitive advantage that can best serve the business.[28]

Differentiation   A company adopting a **differentiation strategy** attempts to develop an image of its product or service such that customers perceive it as being different. The product or service might be differentiated by attributes such as quality, design, and service. The rationale behind differentiation is that the organization can charge higher prices (and therefore make more profit per unit) for a unique product. Rolex Co. and BMW (on the basis of high quality) and Ralph Lauren Womenswear, Inc. (on the basis of image) have all been successful at differentiation.

Cost Leadership   Businesses that adopt the **cost leadership strategy** attempt to maximize sales by minimizing cost (and hence price) per unit. The business tries to increase its total sales volume by charging low prices, or exercising cost leadership. Low costs may be achieved through efficiencies in production, product design, distribution channels, and similar means. Volume retailers like Target make a low profit per unit but compensate by selling more units. Examples of other businesses that have successfully used this approach include Timex Group Ltd., Bic, and Motel 6.

Focus   In the **focus strategy** an organization targets products or services at a specific area such as a geographic location or customer group. Campbell Soup Company has recently started focusing on specific consumer groups like students. Another very successful company adopting this strategy is Fiesta Mart Inc., a Houston-based grocery chain. Its managers noted that the Houston population has large segments of immigrants, especially Hispanics, so the stores sell Mexican soft drinks, corn husks for wrapping tamales, and thousands of other products in demand by the various nationalities represented in the city.[29]

A business can also adopt more than one competitive strategy. Fort Howard Corp. (paper manufacturer) simultaneously stresses cost leadership by using recycled pulp products while also focusing on commercial customers like hotels and restaurants for sales of its tissue products. The key message underlying Porter's framework is that a business needs some form of competitive advantage. It might be one of the three Porter describes, some combination of the three, or perhaps something else altogether. Without some advantage, though, a business is likely to take on characteristics of a reactor from the adaptation model and drift toward eventual failure.[30]

Product Life Cycle

The **product life cycle** itself is not a true strategy, but it is a useful framework for managers to use as they plot strategy over time. The basic idea underlying the product life cycle is illustrated in Figure 7.5.

When a new product is introduced, some time generally passes before it becomes accepted. It may then go through a period of rapid growth. Eventually, however, demand slows and the market for the product matures.

---

differentiation strategy
A strategy that involves developing an image of the business's products or services that customers perceive as being different from others

cost leadership strategy
An attempt to maximize sales by minimizing costs (and hence price) per unit

focus strategy
A strategy that involves targeting products or services at a specific area such as a geographic location or customer group

product life cycle
A useful framework managers can use to better understand how demand for a product changes over time

FIGURE 7.5 The Product Life Cycle

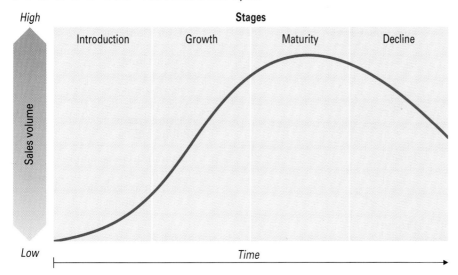

Stages

| Introduction | Growth | Maturity | Decline |

High

Low

Sales volume

Time

Managers can use the framework of the product life cycle—introduction, growth, maturity, and decline—to plot strategy. For example, management may decide on a differentiation strategy for a product in the introduction stage and a prospector approach for a product in the growth stage. By understanding this cycle and where a particular product falls within it, managers can develop more effective strategies for extending product life.

Finally, the product may enter into a decline stage. Consider the pocket calculator. After its initial introduction, prices started to drop and demand increased dramatically. Now the market for pocket calculators is mature, and decline may eventually set in. Just as the calculator replaced the slide rule, forcing it into decline, new innovations may someday do the same to the calculator. The duration of the life cycle varies dramatically for different kinds of products. Fad items like fashion accessories may go through the entire cycle in a matter of months or even weeks. Products like automobiles have been around for decades and are still in the maturity stage.

The life-cycle stages can also be viewed in a context similar to that of the other approaches we've discussed. During the introduction stage, a product may be viewed as a question mark. If its market share grows, it becomes a star. When it reaches maturity, it serves as a cash cow. When market share declines, it may become a dog. Similarly, different adaptation or competitive strategies may be appropriate at different stages of the cycle. During the introduction stage, the business may want to differentiate its product from others. And it may adopt an analyzer stance to avoid becoming too dependent on an unknown new product. As growth takes off, the business may choose a prospector approach as it seeks to find new opportunities for the product while simultaneously continuing to stress differentiation. When the product reaches maturity, the business may decide to shift to a defender position to hold on to its market share. A cost leadership or focus strategy might be useful as a means to increase profits and sales even more. Finally, as market share declines, the business might revert to an analyzer position to cautiously search for new opportunities, or it might go through a period of retrenchment.

Many international firms find that they can extend the life of a product by recognizing that different life cycles exist in different markets. Boeing, for example, sells many of its older-model planes in developing nations. The life cycles of computer equipment and clothing can also be extended by

Nabisco is using an analyzer strategy as it finds new opportunities for its Chips Ahoy. Realizing that a generation of U.S. consumers is eating on the run, it has introduced a variety of bite-size cookies and crackers. Mini Chips Ahoy is now marketed as a snack food as well as a dessert food to cater to this new trend in eating.

Most organizations develop strategies for different functional areas. The most common functions for which strategies are developed include marketing, finance, production, research and development, and human resources.

TABLE 7.1 Functional Strategies and Their Major Concerns

Functional Area	Major Concerns
Marketing	Product mix Market position Distribution channels Sales promotions Pricing issues Public policy
Finance	Capitalization structure Debt policies Assets management Dividend policies
Production	Quality Productivity improvement Production planning Government regulations Plant location Technology
Human resources	Human resources policies Labor relations Government regulation Executive development
Research and development	Product development Technological forecasting Patents and licenses

introducing them in developing countries as they are declining in primary markets.

FUNCTIONAL STRATEGIES

functional strategies
Commonly developed for marketing, financial, production, human resource, and research and development

Yet another basic level of strategic planning involves the development of functional strategies. These **functional strategies** focus on how the organization will approach its basic functional activities. Many organizations develop marketing, financial, production, research and development, and human resources strategies. Issues that these strategies typically address are summarized in Table 7.1.

Marketing Strategy

marketing strategy
A strategy that addresses issues such as promotion techniques to be used, pricing, product mix, and overall image

For many organizations, the **marketing strategy** is the most important functional strategy.[31] Some companies (like McDonald's Corp. and The Coca-Cola Company) promote their products heavily. Their goal is to es-

3M's marketing strategy for its Scotchcast Plus brand casting tape consists of attracting injured persons who want to continue to lead active lifestyles. The casting material is strong but lightweight, and it comes in seventeen colors. Many organizations are coming to see their marketing strategies as their most important functional strategy.

tablish customer loyalty and make sure customers always remember their products. Toys 'Я' Us has achieved phenomenal success by promoting itself as a warehouse where you can find any toy a child wants for a reasonable price. And Kellogg Co. has increased its sales in a stable cereal market by promoting the health benefits of some of its cereals. A company needs a marketing strategy whether it wants one or not. Managers at Coors Brothers, for example, would prefer to not advertise—they think that they make the best beer in the market and people should buy it for that reason. However, heavy marketing has been necessary for it to grow into a national brewing company.[32]

The marketing strategy deals with a number of major issues confronting the organization. One of these is the product mix. For General Motors Corp.'s Chevrolet Division, the product mix includes the various lines (Camero, Corsica, and Beretta) and different versions of each model. Other major issues in marketing strategy include the desired market position (Kmart and Wal-Mart Stores, Inc., compete for first place in retailing), distribution channels (a major reason for Timex's initial success was its decision to sell watches in drugstores), sales promotion (such as advertising budget and the size of the sales force), pricing issues (such as an initially high price to skim off the "cream" followed by planned price cuts), and public policy (dealing with legal, cultural, and regulatory constraints). International firms often find that they must tailor marketing strategies to each individual country where they do business.

Financial Strategy

Developing the right **financial strategy** is essential to an organization.[33] An important part of this strategy is deciding on the most appropriate

financial strategy
A strategy that specifies the capital structure of the organization, debt policy, assets management procedures, and dividend policy

capital structure: what combination of common stock, preferred stock, and long-term debt (such as bonds) will provide the firm with the capital it needs at the lowest possible costs? Another element in financial strategy is debt policy: how much borrowing is allowed and in what forms? Assets management focuses on the handling of current and long-term assets: how should the firm invest a cash surplus to optimize both return and availability? Dividend policy determines what proportion of earnings is distributed to stockholders and what proportion is retained for growth and development. Disney has adopted a financial strategy of low debt. It pays for most of its theme park additions from operating funds. The new European Disneyland outside Paris was paid for almost entirely by issuing special classes of stock rather than by borrowing money. In contrast, Continental Airlines, Inc., borrowed so much money to finance its growth in the 1980s that today it is barely able to cover its interest expenses. International firms usually manage their financial strategy from a centralized corporate perspective.

Production Strategy

production strategy
A strategy that is concerned with issues of quality, productivity, and technology

In some ways, an organization's **production strategy** stems from its marketing strategy.[34] If the marketing strategy calls for promoting high-quality, high-priced products, production should naturally focus on quality, with cost only a secondary consideration. Several major issues still remain, however. For example, methods for improving productivity need to be developed. Production planning (when to produce, how much to produce, and how to produce) is especially important for manufacturers. Finally, production strategy must take into account the regulations of government bodies such as the Environmental Protection Agency (EPA) and the Occupational Safety and Health Administration (OSHA). Areas of major importance for the production strategies of many companies are automation, robotics, and flexible manufacturing systems. Some companies (such as General Electric, Nissan Motor Co. Ltd., and Toyota Motor Corp.) are investing large sums of money in automated technology; other manufacturers (such as Du Pont and Exxon Corporation) are proceeding more slowly. Nevertheless, continuing breakthroughs in production technologies will ensure that these issues remain a major concern for managers. International firms often profit by locating production facilities in countries where labor or raw materials (or both) are inexpensive.

Human Resources Strategy

human resources strategy
A strategy that addresses issues such as compensation, selection, performance appraisal, and other aspects of the organization's human resources

Organizations find it useful to develop a **human resources strategy** for a number of reasons.[35] Human resources policies are required on such matters as compensation, selection, and performance appraisal. Another aspect of human resources strategy is labor relations, especially negotiations with organized labor. Government regulations, such as the Civil Rights Act of 1964, also need to be taken into account. And executive development usually warrants strategic attention. For example, if an organization anticipates opening eight new plants within the next six years, it must start now to locate and develop potential managers for those plants. We mentioned in

Chapter 1 that some companies have developed training programs that are so good that they are thought of by some recruiters as second MBAs. Strong emphasis on management development, then, is also an element of some firms' human resources strategy. Training managers for international assignments and adjusting to local labor market conditions are important issues for international firms to address in their human resources strategy.

Research and Development Strategy

Most large organizations, and many smaller ones as well, find it important to have a **research and development strategy**.[36] A primary area of concern here is making decisions about product development. Should the firm concentrate on new products or on the modification of existing products? What use should be made of technological forecasting—predictions of technical trends, new discoveries and breakthroughs, and so on? Some organizations' R&D strategies also include a policy on patents and licenses. If a firm develops a new product or procedure and patents it, other firms cannot use it. It may be profitable, however, to license the use of the patent—that is, to sacrifice some degree of competitive advantage in return for fees gained by allowing other firms to use the product or procedure. Merck & Co., Inc., is one of the United States' most-admired companies. One reason for its success has been a long history of new-product breakthroughs and technological innovation. This innovation is brought about by a strong and consistent commitment to research and development.[37] International firms must make important decisions regarding where they locate research and development facilities. Kodak, for instance, recently opened a major R&D center in Japan.

research and development strategy
A strategy that focuses on issues regarding product development, licensing, and the organization's commitment to innovation

STRATEGY IMPLEMENTATION

After strategy is formulated, it must be implemented. Although it is not possible to draw a precise line of demarcation between formulation and implementation, they are nevertheless conceptually distinct parts of strategic management.[38] Figure 7.6 provides a general framework of what is involved in implementing strategy.

Implementation Through Structure

Structure both affects and is affected by strategy.[39] For example, in a highly decentralized firm, lower-level managers will have a much greater impact on strategic management than they would have in a centralized firm. Adopting certain kinds of strategies will, in turn, dictate appropriate levels of future decentralization. The Franklin Mint recently developed a new strategy aimed at increasing its sales and profits. As part of the implementation process, the organization cut the number of levels of management from six to four and doubled the number of people reporting directly to the CEO.[40] These and related issues are explored again in Chapter 10.

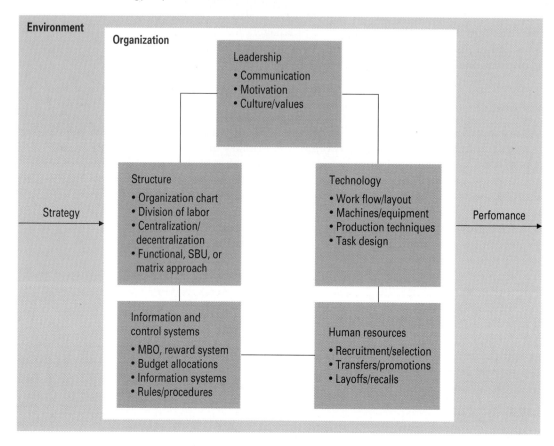

Source: Reprinted by permission from page 115 of *Strategy Implementation: Structure, Systems and Process, Second Edition* by Jay R. Galbraith and Robert K. Kazanjian; Copyright © 1986 by West Publishing Company. All rights reserved.

A manager must be aware of organizational strategy, as it determines the way the organization is structured, the type of leadership provided, the information and control systems, how human resources are developed, and the firm's approach to technology. Policies the manager implements will have their roots in corporate strategy.

Implementation Through Leadership

Effective leadership is necessary to successfully implement strategy.[41] The leader must promote communication and motivation and help establish the culture necessary to get things done. When John Sculley joined Apple Computer, Inc., he was mistrusted because he knew little about computers. He learned the business from the bottom up, however, and became a personal computer expert. When Sculley clashed with founder Steven Jobs, the board of directors had to choose which one to support. They supported Sculley and he has had little trouble selling his strategic ideas to the company ever since. (Leadership is discussed more fully in Chapter 15.)

Implementation Through Information and Control Systems

Managers formulating strategy need access to information.[42] Information systems are also necessary to communicate strategic goals and decisions to others in the organization. And control is important in monitoring ongoing efforts to reach those goals. Suppose that as part of a company's strategic plans management decides to open a new manufacturing facility. A key ingredient in implementing the decision is establishing a budget for constructing and operating the facility. Adherence to the budget will provide feedback to management about how well the strategy is being implemented. Information and control systems issues are explored in several chapters, especially 18 and 21.

Implementation Through Human Resources

Appropriate human resources are needed to implement strategies. The organization needs to have the right kinds of people trained in the right ways to carry out strategic plans. For example, S. C. Johnson & Son, Inc. recently adopted a new strategic plan calling for increased market share for its insect control products. For several years, Beth Pritchard had been groomed by the company to take over the division. After she was given her assignment, she changed product formulas, had packaging redesigned, and developed regional products for different areas of the country. Her employees responded with enthusiasm and dedication. Pritchard maintains, "My philosophy is that you can't do anything yourself. Your people have to do it."[43] We cover how organizations manage human resources in Chapter 13.

Implementation Through Technology

An organization must ensure that it has the proper technology to implement its strategies effectively. Proper technology includes plant and equipment and work-flow design. A major strategic issue facing managers today is speed—getting new products from the design stage to the customer as soon as possible. Thus Deere & Company recently generated a new product in two years; it used to take five to seven years to get a product to market. As rapidly as technology is changing today, its role in strategy implementation is likely to become even more important in the future. We cover technology in depth in Chapter 20.

SUMMARY OF KEY POINTS

Strategic management is a comprehensive and ongoing management process aimed at formulating and implementing effective strategies that promote a superior alignment between the organization and its environment and the achievement of strategic goals. Its components include scope, resource deployment, distinctive competence, and synergy. Strategy is implemented at the corporate, business, and functional levels. Strategies must first be formulated and then implemented.

Strategy formulation consists of four general steps. First, strategic goals are developed. Next, an analysis of the environment is conducted. Similarly, an analysis of the organization itself is needed. Finally, environmental opportunities and threats are matched with organizational strengths and weaknesses to develop a strategy.

Corporate strategy addresses the question of what businesses to be in. Grand strategies include growth, retrenchment, and stability. Portfolio management involves defining strategic business units (SBUs) and then classifying them using the BCG matrix or the GE business screen.

Business-level strategy is concerned with how to compete in a particular business. The adaptation model suggests aligning strategy with environmental conditions via defender, prospector, or analyzer strategies. Porter's competitive strategies are differentiation, overall cost leadership, and focus. The product life-cycle perspective can help managers plot business strategy for different situations.

The five basic functional strategies are marketing, financial, production, human resources, and research and development. These are usually developed for each business within a corporation.

Successful strategy implementation is dependent on the organization's structure, leadership, information and control systems, human resources, and technology.

DISCUSSION QUESTIONS

Questions for Review

1. Discuss the nature of strategic management. Be certain to include both the components and levels of strategy in your discussion.

2. What is meant by strategy formulation? Describe strategy implementation. Differentiate strategy formulation from strategy implementation.

3. Differentiate corporate, business, and functional strategies. Does an organization need all three? Why or why not?

4. Briefly describe each of the following: the business portfolio, the adaptation model, Porter's competitive strategies, product life cycles, and any two functional strategies.

Questions for Analysis

5. How would an organization ensure that high-quality strategic planning is taking place? Would an organization want to engage in strategic planning in all circumstances? Why or why not?

6. How would an organization ensure that all strategies developed at different levels within the organization are consistent with one another?

7. What impact would an organization's strategy have on the structure of that organization? Why? What impact would an organization's strategy have on the type of leadership exercised by the executives of that organization? Why?

Questions for Application

8. Read a history of a major corporation and determine what strategies seem to have been used by that corporation. Did the strategies affect the structure, leadership, or other aspects of the firm?

9. Interview the manager of a local small business to determine how (or if) he or she formulates strategy. How does what you found compare with what you expected after having read this chapter? Share your findings with the class.

10. Interview an executive of a business firm large enough to have multiple functions about how strategy is formulated in that organization. How does what you found compare with what you expected after having read this chapter? Share your findings with the class.

REWARMING CAMPBELL SOUP

You'd think that managing Campbell Soup Company would be an easy job. Campbell is the country's leading soupmaker, with a reputation that's more than 120 years old and a package so American that it helped make artist Andy Warhol famous. Campbell has been leaving rivals in the dust since chemist John Dorrance figured out how to condense soup in 1897, and although it is known as a conservative company with less than riveting advertising, its Campbell Kids have been familiar to U.S. households since 1904.

Yet in the late 1980s, Campbell shareholders, led by the Dorrance family, which still owns 58 percent of the stock, grumbled that the company wasn't making good use of that famous name. One branch of the family wanted to sell out. Instead, Campbell hired David Johnson away from Gerber Products, and Johnson set 20 percent goals for the company: 20 percent growth in earnings, 20 percent return on equity, and 20 percent return on invested cash.

Johnson believes in acting fast to do the painful work, and at Campbell that meant breaking with some traditions as well as handing out a lot of pink slips. Within the first eighteen months, Johnson had cut 364 jobs at headquarters and closed twenty plants, including the original soup factory in Camden, New Jersey.

One barrier to Campbell's growth had been rivalries and lack of communication between various geographical units. To eliminate old barriers and reflect his belief that trading ties between the United States, Canada, and Mexico will continue to strengthen, Johnson created a North American Division. Now, as the CEO of Campbell Canada puts it, the company's North American strategy is very simple: "You market locally, manufacture regionally, and resource globally—with common technology, knowledge, and supplies." To emphasize that there were to be no more turf wars at Campbell, Johnson tied managers' bonuses to the company's overall performance instead of linking them just with their unit's performance.

Johnson's approach mixed old and new. Because of high Canadian labor rates, Campbell's Toronto plant was more expensive to operate than plants in the United States, and workers worried it would be closed. Instead, Campbell decided to see what those expensive workers could do. Training programs and quality circles were initiated, and then much of the plant's direction was turned over to them. The workers made remarkable gains in efficiency. Johnson also left intact much of the company's top hierarchy instead of bringing in his own team, believing that there was no substitute for their expertise. Johnson has proven that you don't need new ingredients; you may just need to stir up the old ones.

Discussion Questions

1. In what ways can a strong company heritage be a hindrance as well as an asset?

2. From a consumer's perspective, what are the important parts of the Campbell tradition that a CEO wouldn't want to change?

E 3. The closing of Campbell's Camden plant dealt a serious blow to a city already facing a major unemployment problem. Should Campbell have lowered its goals slightly to keep the Camden plant open?

References: Gary Hoover, Alta Campbell, and Patrick J. Spain (eds.), *Hoover's Handbook 1991—Profiles of Over 500 Major Corporations* (Austin, Tex.: The Reference Press, 1990), p. 149; David Johnson, "Johnson's Turnaround Tips," *Fortune*, September 9, 1991, p. 146; Bill Saporito, "Campbell Soup Gets Piping Hot," *Fortune*, September 9, 1991, pp. 142–148.

*I*t may take years before there is any agreement about how the global corporation should structure itself and behave. Should it be centralized and produce a standard line of products that can be modified to suit local tastes, or should it be a loose confederation of autonomous local entities? Honda Motor Co., Ltd., is already well on its way to developing its answer to these questions, and it calls its strategy "localization."

Long before the first oil crisis, Honda found some consumers eager for an economical mode of transportation. And in 1959, American Honda Motor was formed in Los Angeles, in what might be viewed as the first step in Honda's localization.

Since then, a number of factors have added to Honda's desire to localize, including fluctuations in international currencies and especially the import restrictions and Japan-bashing promoted by nervous U.S. automakers. But Honda insists that localization is simply a good business strategy.

Currently Honda derives more than 60 percent of its total sales from outside of Japan and manufactures in seventy-seven plants in forty countries. The first part of its localization strategy is therefore localization of product. When buying motorcycles, for instance, U.S. cyclists tend to look for speed and horsepower, Southeast Asians generally want a low-maintenance, economical mode of transportation, and Australian shepherds are most interested in low-speed traction. To meet these divergent needs, Honda puts 5 percent of its yearly gross into research and development.

Honda also localizes profits because it believes that "a company investing abroad must regard itself as a local company and endeavor to prosper together with the host country."* Honda reinvests American Honda's profits in the United States, and has poured $1.7 billion into plants in Ohio. This same philosophy underlies localization of production, which helps both the company and the host country grow. Honda achieves this goal by increasing the amount of value that local workers add to the products and by using local suppliers and parts.

Honda built its first auto-production plant in the United States in 1982; ten years later, it was shipping cars built in Ohio back to Japan for sale. Its 1991 Accord wagon was designed and built in the U.S., which Honda trumpeted in its advertising. Honda is leading the way in global localization, and once it has worked out the bugs in the U.S. system, it plans to do the same thing in Europe.

*Hideo Sugiura, "How Honda Localizes Its Global Strategy," *Sloan Management Review*, Fall 1990, p. 78.

Discussion Questions

1. What risks does Honda face with its localization strategy that it could avoid by simply importing Japanese-built cars into the United States?

2. If you were a strategic planner for Honda, would you try to initiate all four localizations (product, profits, production, and management) at once, or would you begin with a particular one?

E 3. Does it make good business sense for Honda to localize profits and in general help the host country, or do you believe that this part of localization is simply a public relations effort to reduce objections to Honda's growing presence in the United States?

References: Jacqueline Mitchell, "Honda and Nissan Push American Roots of Some Models in a Major Tactical Shift," *The Wall Street Journal*, February 26, 1991, pp. B1, B5; Hideo Sugiura, "How Honda Localizes Its Global Strategy," *Sloan Management Review*, Fall 1990, pp. 77–82; Alex Taylor, III, "Japan's New U.S. Car Strategy," *Fortune*, September 10, 1990, pp. 65–80.

Managerial Decision Making

OBJECTIVES

After studying this chapter, you should be able to:

● *Define decision making and discuss types of decisions and decision-making conditions.*

● *Discuss rational perspectives on decision making, including the steps in decision making.*

● *Describe the behavioral nature of decision making.*

● *Discuss group decision making, including the advantages and disadvantages of group decision making and how it can be more effectively managed.*

OUTLINE

The Nature of Decision Making
  Decision Making Defined
  Types of Decisions
  Decision-Making Conditions

Rational Perspectives on Decision Making
  The Classical Model of Decision Making
  Steps in Rational Decision Making

Behavioral Aspects of Decision Making
  The Administrative Model
  Political Forces in Decision Making
  Intuition and Escalation of Commitment
  Risk Propensity and Decision Making
  Ethics and Decision Making

Group Decision Making in Organizations
  Forms of Group Decision Making
  Advantages of Group Decision Making
  Disadvantages of Group Decision Making
  Managing Group Decision-Making Processes

SUN MICROSYSTEMS INC. was founded in California's famed Silicon Valley in 1982 by four young engineers. Sun was a pioneer in the development of workstations (powerful, high-speed computers with high-resolution color graphics). Sun has been successful almost from the beginning: the firm grew to become a *Fortune* 500 company in only six years and now posts annual sales exceeding $1 billion.

One ingredient in Sun's phenomenal success has been its founders' original decision to create so-called open systems. An open computer system allows computers and software from different makers to interface with one another. By not aligning itself with IBM or Apple or with Microsoft or Lotus, Sun has been able to grow unfettered by the fortunes of other firms in the industry.

Another factor contributing to Sun's success is its unconventional approach to management. CEO Scott McNealy, one of the firm's original founders, believes that most businesses today are too bureaucratic. He also believes that most managers try to be too rational and logical.

To fend off both creeping bureaucracy and creeping rationality, McNealy works hard to maintain an atmosphere of unpredictability and emotion. Sun regularly schedules dress-down days and monthly beer parties. Few CEOs would come to work wearing a gorilla suit (as McNealy once did). And McNealy himself is sometimes the target of pranks. One night a group of his engineers broke into his office, moved all the furniture out, brought in a load of dirt, and created a one-hole golf course.

At meetings, McNealy presides over group discussions that seem chaotic but which are actually well-orchestrated exercises in decision making. Some participants are assigned to argue for each side of every issue and to make as strong a case as possible for their side. At the same time, everyone in the firm is committed to accepting and fully supporting a decision after it has been made.[1] ●

executives at Sun Microsystems exemplify one extreme view of how managers make decisions—spontaneously and with emotion. Despite Scott McNealy's disdain for rationality, many managers would argue that decisions must be made rationally and logically. Some experts believe that decision making is the most basic and fundamental of all managerial activities. Thus we discuss it here in the context of the first management function, planning. Keep in mind, however, that although decision making is perhaps most closely linked to the planning function, it is also part of organizing, leading, and controlling.

We begin our discussion by exploring the nature of decision making. We then describe rational perspectives on decision making. Behavioral aspects of decision making are then introduced and described. We conclude with a discussion of group decision making.

THE NATURE OF DECISION MAKING

Managers at Toyota Motor Corp. recently made the decision to build a new manufacturing plant in the United States at a cost of almost $200 million. At about the same time, the manager at the Toyota dealership in Bryan, Texas, made a decision to sponsor a local youth soccer team for $150. Each of these examples includes a decision, but the decisions differ in many ways. Thus as a starting point in understanding decision making, we must first explore its meaning as well as the types of decisions and conditions under which decisions are made.

Decision Making Defined

● **decision making**
The act of choosing one alternative from among a set of alternatives

decision-making process
Recognizing and defining the nature of a decision situation, identifying alternatives, choosing the "best" alternative, and putting it into practice

Decision making can refer either to a specific act or to a general process. **Decision making** is the act of choosing one alternative from among a set of alternatives. The decision-making process, however, is much more than this. One step of the process, for example, is that the person making the decision must recognize that a decision is necessary and identify the set of feasible alternatives before selecting one. Hence, the **decision-making process** includes recognizing and defining the nature of a decision situation, identifying alternatives, choosing the "best" alternative, and putting it into practice.[2]

The word "best" implies effectiveness. Effective decision making requires that the decision maker understand the situation driving the decision. Most people would consider an effective decision to be one that optimizes some set of factors such as profits, sales, employee welfare, and market share. In some situations, though, an effective decision may be one that minimizes loss, expenses, or employee turnover. It may even mean selecting the best method for going out of business, laying off employees, or terminating a contract.

Of course, it may take a long time before a manager can know if the right decision was made. For example, Jack Welch, CEO of General Electric Co., took an enormous gamble by trading his company's consumer-electronics business to Thomson SA, a French company, for its medical-equipment business. At the time of the exchange, GE held 23 percent of the U.S. color-television market and 17 percent of the U.S. VCR market. Moreover, it was the only serious consumer-electronics business left in the United States and was generating enormous profits. Welch, however, believed the medical-equipment business held even more promise for growth and profits. Analysts believe that the "winner" of the exchange will not be known until at least the turn of the century.[3]

Types of Decisions

Managers must make many different types of decisions. In general, however, most decisions fall into one of two categories: programmed and non-programmed.[4] A **programmed decision** is one that is fairly structured or recurs with some frequency (or both). For example, suppose a manager of a distribution center knows from experience that she needs to keep a thirty-day supply of a particular item on hand. She can then establish a system whereby the appropriate quantity is automatically reordered whenever the inventory drops below the thirty-day requirement. Likewise, the Bryan Toyota dealer made a decision that he will sponsor a youth soccer team each year. Thus when the soccer club president calls, the dealer already knows what he will do. Many decisions regarding basic operating systems and procedures and standard organizational transactions are of this variety and can therefore be programmed.

Nonprogrammed decisions, on the other hand, are relatively unstructured and occur much less often. Consider GE's decision to exchange businesses with Thomson and Toyota's decision to build a new plant: no business makes decisions like those on a regular basis. Managers faced with

programmed decision
A decision that is fairly structured or recurs with some frequency (or both)

nonprogrammed decision
A decision that is relatively unstructured; occurs much less often than a programmed decision

Deciding on the best long-term investments to improve operations is a nonprogrammed decision—that is, it is a decision that is unstructured and occurs relatively infrequently. When Tribune Company task force members Cynthia Ritter, Mike McLain, and Guy Baxter had to decide how to improve operations at the Newport News, Virginia, *Daily Press,* they invested a large amount of time, energy, and resources exploring all options.

FIGURE 8.1 Decision-Making Conditions

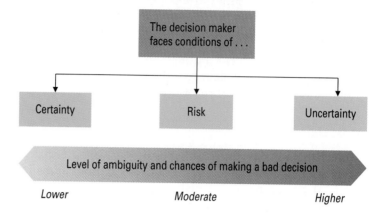

such decisions must treat each one as unique, investing enormous amounts of time, energy, and resources into exploring the situation from all perspectives. Intuition and experience are major factors in nonprogrammed decisions. Most of the decisions made by top managers involving strategy (including mergers, acquisitions, and takeovers) and organization design are nonprogrammed. So are decisions about new facilities, new products, labor contracts, and legal issues.

Decision-Making Conditions

Just as there are different kinds of decisions, there are also different conditions in which decisions must be made. Jack Welch at GE has no guarantees that the new medical-equipment business will be successful, whereas he had a pretty clear picture of how the electronics business was doing. Managers sometimes have an almost perfect understanding of conditions surrounding a decision, but at other times they have few clues about those conditions. In general, the circumstances that exist for the decision maker are conditions of certainty, risk, or uncertainty.[5] These conditions are represented in Figure 8.1.

Decision Making Under Certainty   When the decision maker knows with reasonable certainty what the alternatives are and what conditions are associated with each alternative, a **state of certainty** exists. Suppose, for example, that Singapore Airlines needs to buy five new jumbo jets. The decision is from whom to buy them. Singapore has only three choices: The Boeing Co., McDonnell Douglas Corp., and Airbus. Each has a proven product and will specify prices and delivery dates. The airline thus knows the alternative conditions associated with each. There is little ambiguity and relatively low chance of making a bad decision.

Few organizational decisions are made under conditions of true certainty.[6] The complexity and turbulence of the contemporary business world make such situations rare. Even the airplane purchase decision we just considered has less certainty than it appears. The aircraft companies may not be able to guarantee delivery dates so they may write cost-increase or inflation clauses into contracts. Thus the airline may not be truly certain of the conditions surrounding each alternative.

Decision Making Under Risk   A more common decision-making condition is a state of risk. Under a **state of risk,** the availability of each alternative and its potential payoffs and costs are all associated with probability estimates.[7] Suppose, for example, that a labor contract negotiator for a company receives a "final" offer from the union right before a strike deadline. The negotiator has two alternatives: to accept or to reject the offer. The risk centers on whether the union representatives are bluffing. If the company negotiator accepts the offer, she avoids a strike but commits to a costly labor contract. If she rejects the contract, she may get a more favorable contract if the union is bluffing; she may provoke a strike if it is not.

On the basis of past experiences, relevant information, the advice of others, and her own intuition, she may believe that there is a 75-percent chance that the union is bluffing and a 25-percent chance that they'll back up their threats. Thus she can base a calculated decision on the two alternatives (accept or reject the contract demands) and the probable consequences of each. When making decisions under a state of risk, managers must accurately determine the probabilities associated with each alternative. For example, if the union negotiators are committed to a strike if their demands are not met, and the company negotiator rejects their demands because she guesses they will not strike, her miscalculation will prove costly. As indicated in Figure 8.1, decision making under conditions of risk is accompanied by moderate ambiguity and chances of a bad decision.

state of risk
When the availability of each alternative and its potential payoffs and costs are all associated with probability estimates

Decision Making Under Uncertainty   Most of the major decision making in contemporary organizations is done under a **state of uncertainty.** The decision maker does not know all the alternatives, the risks associated with each, or the likely consequences of each alternative.[8] This uncertainty stems from the complexity and dynamism of contemporary organizations and their environments. Consider, for example, the decision Sun's founders made regarding open systems. If they had chosen to use IBM equipment and Microsoft operating systems, they could have had a stable and predictable customer base. By electing to pursue the open system option, however, Sun faced considerably greater uncertainty regarding factors such as new technology and customer acceptance.

state of uncertainty
When the decision maker does not know all the alternatives, the risks associated with each, or the consequences each alternative is likely to have

Indeed, many of the decisions already discussed—Toyota's decision to build a new plant and GE's decision to get out of consumer electronics—were made under conditions of uncertainty. To make effective decisions in these circumstances, managers must acquire as much relevant information as possible and approach the situation from a logical and rational perspective. Intuition, judgment, and experience always play major roles in the decision-making process under conditions of uncertainty. Even so, uncertainty is the most ambiguous condition for managers and the one most prone to error.

RATIONAL PERSPECTIVES ON DECISION MAKING

Most managers like to think of themselves as rational decision makers. And indeed, many experts argue that managers should try to be as rational as possible in making decisions.[9] "The Global View" describes how Marks &

F I G U R E 8.2 The Classical Model of Decision Making

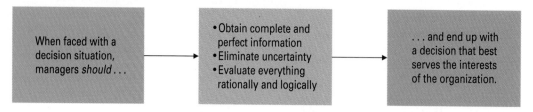

| When faced with a decision situation, managers *should* . . . | • Obtain complete and perfect information
• Eliminate uncertainty
• Evaluate everything rationally and logically | . . . and end up with a decision that best serves the interests of the organization. |

The classical model of decision making assumes that managers are rational and logical. It attempts to prescribe how managers should approach decision situations.

● **classical decision model**
A prescriptive approach to decision making that tells managers how they should make decisions. It assumes managers are logical and rational and that their decisions will be in the best interests of the organization

● **steps in rational decision making**
Recognize and define the decision situation; identify appropriate alternatives; evaluate each alternative in terms of its feasibility, satisfactoriness, and consequences; select the best alternative; implement the chosen alternative; follow-up and evaluate the results of the chosen alternative

Spencer, a British retailer, makes decisions logically and rationally. In this section we first describe the classical model of decision making and then discuss each of the steps in rational decision making.

The Classical Model of Decision Making

The **classical decision model** is a prescriptive approach that tells managers how they should make decisions. It assumes that managers are logical and rational and that they always make decisions that are in the best interests of the organization. Figure 8.2 shows how this view presumes decisions are made: (1) Decision makers have complete information about the decision situation and possible alternatives. (2) They can effectively eliminate uncertainty to achieve a decision condition of certainty. (3) They evaluate all aspects of the decision situation logically and rationally. As we will see later, these conditions rarely, if ever, actually exist.

Steps in Rational Decision Making

A manager who really wants to approach a decision rationally and logically should try to follow the steps listed in Table 8.1. These **steps in rational decision making** help keep the decision maker focused on facts and logic and help guard against inappropriate assumptions and pitfalls.

Recognizing and Defining the Decision Situation   The first step in rational decision making is recognizing that a decision is necessary—that is, there must be some stimulus or spark to initiate the process.[10] For many decisions, the stimulus may occur without any prior warning. When equipment malfunctions, the manager must decide whether to repair or replace it. Or when a major crisis erupts, as described in Chapter 3, the manager must quickly decide how to deal with it. The stimulus for a decision may be either positive or negative. A manager who must decide how to invest surplus funds, for example, faces a positive decision situation. A negative financial stimulus could involve having to trim budgets because of cost overruns.[11]

Inherent in problem recognition is the need to define precisely what the problem is. The manager must develop a complete understanding of the problem, its causes, and its relationship to other factors. This understanding comes from careful analysis and thoughtful consideration of the situation. Consider the recent situation faced by Rorer Group, Inc., makers of Maalox and other pharmaceuticals. Its CEO, Robert Cawthorn, recognized that

BRITAIN'S BEST RETAILER

In 1884, Michael Marks, a traveling peddler and Polish immigrant, laid out his wares at a small stall in a town market. Worried about his weak English, he hung out a sign reading "Don't Ask the Price, It's a Penny." Thus began one of Great Britain's most successful and most respected retail establishments.

A century later, Marks & Spencer does $10 billion worth of business each year, with one foot in the British past and the other in the rapidly expanding global economy of the future. To a shopper used to U.S. retailers, a Marks & Spencer clothing store might have a limited range of merchandise and few amenities. Shoppers can't charge purchases unless they have a Marks & Spencer card, and there are no dressing rooms. Everything carries the store's St. Michael brand.

Yet if you dream of owning an Armani jacket but can't afford one, you can probably find a good quality St. Michael copy for a fraction of the cost of the original. Marks & Spencer recently bought Brooks Brothers, the traditional U.S. clothier, and analyzed some of its top-selling items. It duplicated the fabric, tailoring, and stitching of a $300 Brooks Brothers ladies' blazer and sells it for less than half that price in Europe. Even during the recession, Marks & Spencer has netted five cents per dollar retail, outperforming America's Wal-Mart Stores, Inc.

Marks & Spencer succeeds in part because of its long-standing relationships with suppliers that resemble the Japanese *keiretsu* system. Supplier and retailer work closely together to assess and satisfy customers' tastes. M&S tests about 600 new items a year, shipping small batches to its busiest stores, watching sales for a week or two, then dropping or stocking the item based on this quick test.

M&S food stores offer more variety than its clothing stores but rely on the same supplier relationships and responsiveness to customers. M&S recently discovered through its testing program that many of its customers like guacamole, so now one of its suppliers flies fresh avocados from Mexico and makes them into guacamole in a plant 160 miles north of London; the guacamole is trucked to M&S stores. M&S has managed to stay a step ahead of changing British lifestyles, offering more prepared foods for busy two-career households. One M&S executive estimates the store carries chicken breasts prepared in 120 ways and does almost as much with broccoli.

M&S has yet to tackle North America, but that may change. It's well aware that its approach to selling prepared foods can succeed only in areas with a high density of affluent people, and the East Coast of the United States beckons.

References: Gary Hoover, Alta Campbell, Alan Chai, and Patrick J. Spain (eds.), *Hoover's Handbook of World Business 1992* (Austin, Tex.: The Reference Press, 1991), p. 232; John Marcom, Jr., "Blue Blazers and Guacamole," *Forbes*, November 25, 1991, pp. 64–68; John Marcom, Jr., "Your Broccoli, Sir," *Forbes*, November 25, 1991, p. 68.

other firms in the industry were dramatically increasing their product lines and, consequently, their market shares. Cawthorn reasoned that if Rorer was to keep pace, it, too, needed to expand its product lines. He further reasoned that the best route for expansion was to buy an existing firm.[12] Thus the stimulus that prompted the decision was rapid expansion by competitors, and the problem was subsequently defined as the need to buy another pharmaceutical company.

Identifying Alternatives Once the decision situation has been recognized and defined, the second step is to identify alternative courses of action that might be effective. It is generally useful to develop both obvious, standard alternatives and creative, innovative alternatives.[13] In general, the more im-

Step	Detail	Example
1. Recognizing and defining the situation	Some stimulus indicates that a decision must be made. The stimulus may be positive or negative.	A plant manager sees that employee turnover has increased by 5 percent.
2. Identifying alternatives	Both obvious and creative alternatives are desired. In general, the more important the decision, the more alternatives should be generated.	The plant manager can increase wages, increase benefits, or change hiring standards.
3. Evaluating alternatives	Each alternative is evaluated to determine its feasibility, its satisfactoriness, and its consequences.	Increasing benefits may not be feasible. Increasing wages and changing hiring standards may satisfy all conditions.
4. Selecting the best alternative	Consider all situational factors, and choose the alternative that best fits the manager's situation.	Changing hiring standards will take an extended period of time to cut turnover, so increase wages.
5. Implementing the chosen alternative	The chosen alternative is implemented into the organizational system.	The plant manager may need permission of corporate headquarters. The human resources department establishes a new wage structure.
6. Follow-up and evaluation	At some time in the future, the manager should ascertain the extent to which the alternative chosen in step 4 and implemented in step 5 has worked.	The plant manager notes that, six months later, turnover has dropped to its previous level.

Although the presumptions of the classical decision model rarely exist, managers can approach decision making with rationality. By following the steps of rational decision making, managers ensure that they are learning as much as possible about the decision situation and its alternatives.

portant the decision, the more attention is directed to developing alternatives. If the decision involves a multimillion-dollar relocation, a great deal of time and expertise will be devoted to identifying the best locations—J.C. Penney Company spent two years searching before selecting the Dallas–Fort Worth area for its new corporate headquarters. If the problem is to choose a color for the company softball-team uniforms, less time and expertise will be brought to bear.

Although managers should seek creative solutions, they must also recognize that various constraints often limit their alternatives. Common constraints include legal restrictions, moral and ethical norms, authority constraints, or constraints imposed by the power and authority of the manager, available technology, economic considerations, and unofficial social norms. After Robert Cawthorn of Rorer decided to acquire a new pharmaceutical company, he identified four possible candidates. He might have identified more, but he chose to limit his search to U.S. firms that might be obtained for a reasonable price.

Bill Brecht, owner of a California BMW dealership, followed a rational decision-making process when he was faced with losing two employees at the same time after their babies were born. He identified two alternatives: opening an on-site day-care center, or letting the employees care for their infants at work. After evaluating each alternative, he chose the second, which appears to be a success.

Evaluating Alternatives The third step in the decision-making process is evaluating each of the alternatives.[14] Figure 8.3 suggests a decision tree that can be used to judge different alternatives. The figure suggests that each alternative be evaluated in terms of its feasibility, its satisfactoriness, and its consequences. The first question to ask is whether an alternative is feasible. Is it within the realm of probability and practicality? For a small, struggling firm, an alternative requiring a huge financial outlay is probably out of the question. Other alternatives may not be feasible because of legal barriers. And limited human, material, and information resources may make other alternatives impractical.

When an alternative has passed the test of feasibility, it must next be examined to see how well it will satisfy the conditions of the decision situation. For example, a manager searching for ways to double production capacity might consider purchasing an existing plant from another company. If closer examination reveals that the new plant would increase production capacity by only 35 percent, this alternative may not be satisfactory. Finally, when an alternative has proven both feasible and satisfactory, its

Managers must thoroughly evaluate all of the alternatives, which increases the chances that the alternative finally chosen will be successful. Failure to evaluate an alternative's feasibility, satisfactoriness, and consequences can lead to a wrong decision.

FIGURE 8.3 Evaluating Alternatives in the Decision-Making Process

Is the alternative feasible?	→Yes→	Is the alternative satisfactory?	→Yes→	Are the alternative's consequences affordable?	→Yes→	Retain for further consideration
↓No		↓No		↓No		
Eliminate from consideration		Eliminate from consideration		Eliminate from consideration		

probable consequences must still be assessed. To what extent will a particular alternative influence other parts of the organization? What financial and nonfinancial costs will be associated with such influences? For example, a plan to boost sales by cutting prices may disrupt cash flows, need a new advertising program, and alter the behavior of sales representatives because it requires a different commission structure. The manager, then, must put "price tags" on the consequences of each alternative. Even an alternative that is both feasible and satisfactory must be eliminated if its consequences are too expensive for the total system. Managers at Rorer eliminated one acquisition target because it would cost too much (not feasible) and another because it competed too directly with existing Rorer products (consequences not affordable). This left them with two remaining targets for acquisition.

Selecting an Alternative   Even though many alternatives fail to pass the triple tests of feasibility, satisfactoriness, and affordable consequences, two or more alternatives may remain. Choosing the best of these is the real crux of decision making. One approach is to choose the alternative with the highest combined level of feasibility, satisfactoriness, and affordable consequences. Even though most situations do not lend themselves to objective, mathematical analysis, the manager can often develop subjective estimates and weights for choosing an alternative.

Optimization is also a frequent goal. Because a decision is likely to affect several individuals or subunits, any feasible alternative will probably not maximize all relevant goals. Suppose the manager of the Kansas City Royals needs to select a starting center fielder for the next baseball season. Bill might hit .350 but not be able to catch a fly ball; Joe might hit only .175 but be outstanding in the field; and Sam might hit .290 and be a solid but not outstanding fielder. The manager would probably select Sam because of the optimal balance of hitting and fielding. Decision makers should remember that it may be possible to find multiple acceptable alternatives—it may not be necessary to select just one alternative and reject all the others. For example, the Royals' manager might decide that Sam will start each game, Bill will be retained as a pinch hitter, and Joe will be retained as a defensive substitute. In many hiring decisions, the candidates remaining after evaluation are ranked. If the top candidate rejects the offer, it may be automatically extended to the number-2 candidate, and, if necessary, to the remaining candidates in order. Rorer managers chose to go after A.H. Robins Co., Inc. Robins makes numerous well-known products such as Chap Stick and Robitussin.

Implementing the Chosen Alternative   After an alternative has been selected, the manager must put it into effect. In some decision situations, implementation may be fairly easy; in others, it will be more difficult. In the case of an acquisition, for example, managers must decide how to integrate all the activities of the new business, including purchasing, human resource practices, and distribution, into an ongoing organizational framework. When American Telephone & Telegraph Co. (AT&T) acquired NCR Corp., it took months to consolidate NCR's operations into existing systems. Operational plans, discussed in Chapter 6, are useful in implementing alternatives.

Managers must also consider people's resistance to change when implementing decisions. The reasons for such resistance include insecurity, inconvenience, and fear of the unknown. When Penney's decided to move from New York to Texas, many employees resigned rather than relocate. Managers should anticipate potential resistance at various stages of the implementation process. (Resistance to change is covered in Chapter 12.) Managers should also recognize that, even when all alternatives have been evaluated as precisely as possible and the consequences of each alternative weighed, unanticipated consequences are still likely. Any number of situations such as unexpected cost increases, a less-than-perfect fit with existing organizational subsystems, or unpredicted effects on cash flow or operating expenses could develop after the implementation process has begun. When Rorer announced its intentions to buy A.H. Robins, other companies took note. Several decided that Robins would indeed be an attractive acquisition and also made offers. The bidding reached fever pitch, and Rorer eventually lost out to American Home Products Corp.

Following Up and Evaluating the Results   The final step in the decision-making process requires that managers evaluate the effectiveness of their decision—that is, they should make sure that the chosen alternative has served its original purpose. If an implemented alternative appears not to be working, the manager can respond in several ways. Another previously identified alternative (the second or third choice) could be adopted. Or the manager might recognize that the situation was not correctly defined to start with and begin the process all over again. Finally, the manager might decide that the original alternative is in fact appropriate but has not yet had time to work or should be implemented in a different way.

Failure to evaluate decision effectiveness may have serious consequences. The Pentagon spent $1.8 billion and eight years developing the Sergeant York anti-aircraft gun. From the beginning, tests revealed major problems with the weapon system, but not until it was in its final stages, when it was demonstrated to be completely ineffective, was the project scrapped.[15] In a classic case of poor decision making, managers at Coca-Cola decided to change the formula for the soft drink. Consumer response was extremely negative. In contrast to the Pentagon, however, Coca-Cola immediately reacted: it reintroduced the old formula within three months as Coca-Cola Classic. Had managers stubbornly stuck with their decision and failed to evaluate its effectiveness, the results would have been disastrous. And when Rorer lost its bid for A.H. Robins, Cawthorn decided to step back and explore other opportunities for expansion.

BEHAVIORAL ASPECTS OF DECISION MAKING

If all decision situations were approached as logically as described in the previous section, more decisions would prove to be successful. Yet, decisions are often made with little consideration for logic and rationality. Kepner-Tregoe, a Princeton-based consulting firm, estimates that American companies use rational decision-making techniques less than 20 percent of the time.[16] And even when organizations try to be logical, they sometimes

FIGURE 8.4 The Administrative Model of Decision Making

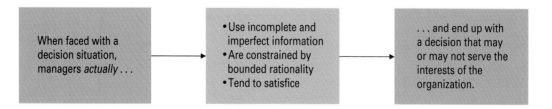

When faced with a decision situation, managers *actually* . . .

→

- Use incomplete and imperfect information
- Are constrained by bounded rationality
- Tend to satisfice

→

. . . and end up with a decision that may or may not serve the interests of the organization.

The administrative model is based on behavioral processes that affect how managers make decisions. Rather than prescribing how decisions should be made, it focuses more on describing how they are made.

● **administrative model**
A decision-making model that argues that decision makers (1) have incomplete and imperfect information, (2) are constrained by bounded rationality, and (3) tend to satisfice when making decisions

bounded rationality
Suggests that decision makers are limited by their values and unconscious reflexes, skills, and habits

satisficing
The tendency to search for alternatives only until one is found that meets some minimum standard of sufficiency

fail. For example, managers at Coca-Cola decided to change Coke's formula after four years of extensive marketing research, taste tests, and rational deliberation—but the decision was still wrong. On the other hand, sometimes when a decision is made with little regard for logic, it can still turn out to be correct. A key ingredient in how these forces work is the behavioral aspect of decision making.[17] The administrative model better reflects these subjective considerations. Other behavioral aspects include political forces, intuition and escalation of commitment, risk propensity, and ethics.

The Administrative Model

Herbert A. Simon was one of the first people to recognize that decisions are not always made with rationality and logic.[18] Simon was subsequently awarded the Nobel Prize in economics. Rather than prescribing how decisions should be made, his view of decision making, now called the **administrative model,** describes how decisions often actually are made. As illustrated in Figure 8.4, the model holds that managers (1) have incomplete and imperfect information, (2) are constrained by bounded rationality, and (3) tend to satisfice when making decisions.

Bounded rationality suggests that decision makers are limited by their values and unconscious reflexes, skills, and habits. They are also limited by less than complete information and knowledge. Bounded rationality partially explains how U.S. auto executives allowed Japanese car makers to become so strong in the United States. For years, executives at GM, Ford Motor Co., and Chrysler Corp. compared their companies' performance only to one another and ignored foreign imports. The foreign "threat" wasn't acknowledged until the domestic auto market had been changed forever. If managers had seen things more clearly from the beginning, they might have been better able to thwart foreign competitors. Essentially, then, the concept of bounded rationality suggests that although people try to be rational decision makers, their rationality has limits.

Another important part of the administrative model is **satisficing.** This concept suggests that rather than conducting an exhaustive search for the best possible alternative, decision makers tend to search only until they identify an alternative that meets some minimum standard of sufficiency. A manager looking for a site for a new plant, for example, may select the first site she finds that meets basic requirements for transportation, utilities, and price, even though further search might yield a better location. People satisfice for a variety of reasons. Managers may simply be unwilling to ignore their own motives (such as reluctance to spend time making a decision) and therefore not be able to continue searching after a minimally acceptable alternative is identified. The decision maker may be unable to weigh and evaluate large numbers of alternatives and criteria. Also, subjective and personal considerations often intervene in decision situations.

Because of the inherent imperfection of information, bounded rationality, and satisficing, the decisions made by a manager may or may not actually be in the best interests of the organization. A manager may choose a particular location for the new plant because it offers the lowest price and best availability of utilities and transportation. Or she may choose the location because it's in a community in which she wants to live.

In summary, then, the classical and administrative models paint quite different pictures of decision making. Which is more correct? Actually, each can be used to better understand how managers make decisions. The classical model is prescriptive: it explains how managers can at least attempt to be more rational and logical in their approach to decisions. The administrative model can be used by managers to develop a better understanding of their inherent biases and limitations. In the following sections, we describe more fully other behavioral forces that can influence decisions.

Political Forces in Decision Making

Political forces are another major element that contribute to the behavioral nature of decision making. Organizational politics is covered in Chapter 15, but one major element of politics, coalitions, is especially relevant to decision making. A **coalition** is an informal alliance of individuals or groups formed to achieve a common goal. This common goal is often a preferred decision alternative. For example, coalitions of stockholders frequently band together to force a board of directors to make a certain decision.

Coalitions led to the formation of Unisys Corporation, a large computer firm. Sperry was once one of America's computer giants, but a series of poor decisions put the company on the edge of bankruptcy. Two key executives waged battle for three years over what to do. One wanted to get out of the computer business altogether, and the other wanted to stay in. Finally, the manager who wanted to remain in the computer business, Joseph Kroger, garnered enough support to earn promotion to the corporation's presidency. The other manager, Vincent McLean, took early retirement. Shortly thereafter, Sperry agreed to be acquired by Burroughs Wellcome Co. The resulting combined company is called Unisys.[19]

coalition
An informal alliance of individuals or groups formed to achieve a common goal

The impact of coalitions can be either positive or negative. They can help astute managers get the organization on a path toward effectiveness and profitability, or they can strangle well-conceived strategies and decisions. Managers must recognize when to use coalitions, how to assess whether coalitions are acting in the best interests of the organization, and how to constrain their dysfunctional effects.

Intuition and Escalation of Commitment

Two other important decision processes that go beyond logic and rationality are intuition and escalation of commitment to a chosen course of action.

intuition
An innate belief about something without conscious consideration

Intuition   **Intuition** is an innate belief about something without conscious consideration. Managers sometimes decide to do something because it "feels right" or they have a hunch. This feeling is usually not arbitrary, however. Rather, it is based on years of experience and practice in making decisions in similar situations. An inner sense may help managers make an occasional decision without going through a full-blown rational sequence of steps. Liz Claiborne and three partners founded Liz Claiborne, Inc., to design and sell clothes for working women. Conventional wisdom at the time suggested that they needed to build plants to make the clothing and develop a traveling sales force to market it. Pure intuition, however, told them not to follow this "wisdom." They subcontracted production to other makers instead of building plants, and they sold their clothes only to large department and specialty store buyers willing to travel to New York. The result? Very low overhead and annual sales of more than $1 billion.[20] Of course, all managers, but most especially inexperienced ones, should be careful not to rely on intuition too heavily. If rationality and logic are continually flaunted for what "feels right," the odds are that disaster will strike one day.

escalation of commitment
A decision maker's staying with a decision even when it appears to be wrong

Escalation of Commitment   Another important behavioral process that influences decision making is **escalation of commitment** to a chosen course of action. In particular, decision makers sometimes make decisions and then become so committed to the course of action suggested by that decision that they stay with it even when it appears to have been wrong.[21] For example, when people buy stock in a company, they sometimes refuse to sell it even after repeated drops in price. They chose a course of action—buying the stock in anticipation of making a profit—and then stay with it even in the face of increasing losses.

In 1984 ABC television broadcast a miniseries called *The Winds of War.* It was a ratings success and made a reasonable profit for the network. A few years later the network was offered the sequel, *War and Remembrance,* for development as a new miniseries. Because of higher production costs and more time needed to tell the story on television, managers saw almost immediately that the project would lose money. But because they wanted the prestige of airing the feature, they went ahead anyway. At several different points in production, network officials considered dropping the project. At each juncture, however, they decided to go ahead, largely because they had already invested so much money. When the miniseries was finally aired in 1988 it earned only mediocre ratings; ABC lost at least $20 million. In retrospect, virtually every manager involved agreed that they should have cancelled the project.[22]

When Data General cut the project they were developing, employees Herb Osher and Joe Forgione were willing to assume the risk of developing it on their own, but they had to raise funds of between $3 and $5 million dollars within two months. Their risk paid off when a Japanese software company agreed to back them, and HyperDesk, Corp. was launched. Now HyperDesk anticipates sales of $20 million to $50 million within three to five years.

Thus decision makers must walk a fine line. On the one hand, they must guard against sticking with an incorrect decision too long. To do so can bring about financial decline. On the other hand, they should not bail out of a seemingly incorrect decision too soon, as did Adidas. Adidas once dominated the market for professional athletic shoes. It subsequently entered the market for amateur sports shoes and did well there also. But managers interpreted a sales slowdown as a sign that the boom in athletic shoes was over. They thought that they had made the wrong decision and ordered drastic cutbacks. The market took off again with Reebok International Ltd. and Nike, Inc., at the head of the pack, and Adidas never recovered.[23]

The trade barriers that make it difficult to sell foreign-made products to Japan have received considerable publicity, but few Americans are aware of the particular barriers that face any company trying to set up a large retail outlet in Japan. Toys "Я" Us is the largest children's specialty retail chain in the world, already controlling nearly one-quarter of the toy market in the United States. It has been selling outside the United States since 1984, starting with four stores in Canada and expanding into sixty-nine other outlets in Europe and the Far East. Japan is the logical next stop, especially because its $6 billion yearly appetite for toys is second only to the U.S.

But like many other Japanese goods, toys have long been sold in Japan by small shopkeepers, and in Japan small business owners have considerable political clout. That clout is responsible for the Large-Store Law, which gives the Ministry of International Trade and Industry (MITI) and local communities the ability to slow or stop the building of large stores that threaten to take business away from smaller ones.

Toys "Я" Us finally succeeded in opening its first Japanese store in 1991 with two major sources of help. One was the Structural Impediments Initiative, part of a number of agreements made in the late-1980s between the Japanese and U.S. governments with the aim of allowing more imports into Japan and easing Japan's trade imbalance. The Commerce Department hopes Toys "Я" Us's success will be the first in a long series.

Perhaps more important was Toys "Я" Us's link with Den Fujita, president of McDonald's Corp. (Japan). Fujita is bicultural, an entrepreneur in a business that appeals to families and children, an expert in Japanese real estate, and well aware of the barriers that his parent company had to overcome before it could start selling cheeseburgers in Tokyo. He also saw in the plans of Toys "Я" Us a golden opportunity for expansion—he could build new McDonald's restaurants near the Toys "Я" Us stores and feed the hungry toy-buyers. He agreed to work with Toys "Я" Us, and McDonald's Japan bought a 20 percent share in Toys "Я" Us Japan.

Soon after Toys "Я" Us and McDonald's agreed to work together, MITI began relaxing its stance on large stores and Toys "Я" Us began lobbying governments on both sides of the Pacific for help. MITI eventually agreed to reduce the length of the application process.

As it opened its first store, Toys "Я" Us was looking for Japanese suppliers, but among major Japanese toymakers, only Nintendo had agreed to sell directly to Toys "Я" Us. That may be good news for American toymakers; if all goes according to plan, by the end of the decade Toys "Я" Us will be selling $1.5 billion worth of toys yearly to the Japanese, and it expects to be importing half of its inventory.

1. What seems to be the key decision in the long process Toys "Я" Us went through to build its first store in Japan?

2. Do any of the lessons that Toys "Я" Us learned from its experience in Japan apply to companies trying to expand domestically?

E 3. Do you think laws that protect small shopkeepers against competition from huge chains are a good idea?

References: Gary Hoover, Alta Campbell, and Patrick J. Spain (eds.), *Hoover's Handbook 1991—Profiles of Over 500 Major Corporations* (Austin, Tex.: The Reference Press, 1990), p. 538; Robert Neff, "Guess Who's Selling Barbies In Japan Now?" *Business Week*, December 9, 1991, pp. 72–76.

Management Tools for Planning and Decision Making

OBJECTIVES

After studying this chapter, you should be able to:

● *Describe the basic types of forecasting done by most organizations.*

● *Identify and discuss planning techniques that managers use.*

● *Identify and describe common decision-making tools that are used in organizations.*

● *Discuss the strengths and weaknesses of quantitative tools for planning and decision making.*

OUTLINE

Forecasting
    Sales and Revenue Forecasting
    Technological Forecasting
    Other Types of Forecasting
    Forecasting Techniques

Other Planning Techniques
    Linear Programming
    Breakeven Analysis
    Simulation
    PERT

Decision-Making Tools
    Payoff Matrix
    Decision Tree
    Other Decision-Making Tools

Strengths and Weaknesses of Planning Tools
    Weaknesses and Problems
    Strengths and Advantages

DAYTON-HUDSON CORP. is one of the United States' largest retailers. And one of Dayton-Hudson's most profitable divisions is Target, a chain of discount stores. Whereas Wal-Mart, one of Target's main competitors, is growing rapidly, Target is expanding slowly and methodically. Whenever Target executives contemplate a new store, they go through a systematic series of steps to maximize its chances for success.

First, they carefully analyze the size of the potential market, taking into account factors such as the number of consumers and their median age and income. They also carefully assess the competition. Using sophisticated forecasting models, managers can then make projections about sales and profits that the new store might be expected to achieve.

Assuming the numbers "check out," Target managers then use another set of procedures to assess different sites in the potential market, factoring in such variables as distance from major thoroughfares, utility rates, and tax rates. After a site is located, managers use still other mathematical models to determine the optimal size of the new store.

After making a decision about the size of the store, managers then determine how many checkout lanes the store will need, how many products it will carry, how many people it will employ, and how large its stockroom will be. Each of these factors is calculated using various statistical procedures that balance organizational costs against customer demand and similar considerations.[1] ●

anagers at Dayton-Hudson and its Target subsidiary must make a number of decisions whenever they open a new store. These decisions are similar to others made by managers at Safeway Stores, Inc., Ford Motor Co., or Eastman Kodak Company whenever they undertake a capital expansion, change their operations, or simply make a change in work procedures. Regardless of the content of the decision, managers use a variety of different tools and techniques for making plans or decisions. For example, beyond those noted in the opening incident, literally hundreds of others are used whenever a new department store is opened.

This chapter discusses a number of the basic tools and techniques that managers can use to enhance the efficiency and effectiveness of planning and decision making. We first describe forecasting, an extremely important tool, and then discuss several other planning techniques. Next we discuss other tools that relate more to decision making. We conclude by assessing the strengths and weaknesses of the various tools and techniques.

FORECASTING

forecasting
The process of developing assumptions or premises about the future that managers can use in planning or decision making

To plan, managers must make assumptions about future events. But unlike wizards of old, planners cannot simply look into a crystal ball. Instead, they must develop forecasts of probable future circumstances. **Forecasting** is the process of developing assumptions or premises about the future that managers can use in planning or decision making.[2]

Sales and Revenue Forecasting

● **sales forecasting**
The prediction of future sales

As the term implies, **sales forecasting** is concerned with predicting future sales. Because monetary resources (derived mainly from sales) are necessary to finance both current and future operations, knowledge of future sales is of vital importance. Every business, from Exxon Corporation to a neighborhood pizza parlor, must forecast sales. Consider, for example, the following questions that a manager might need to answer:

1. How much of each of our products should we produce next week, next month, and next year?

2. How much money will we have available to spend on research and development and on new-product test marketing?

3. When and to what degree will we need to expand our existing production facilities?

4. How should we respond to union demands for a 15-percent pay increase?

5. If we borrow money for expansion, can we pay it back?

None of these questions can be adequately answered without some notion of what future revenues are likely to be. Thus sales forecasting is generally one of the first steps in planning.

Unfortunately, the term *sales forecasting* suggests that this form of forecasting is appropriate only for organizations that have something to sell. But other kinds of organizations also depend on financial resources, and so they also must forecast. The University of South Carolina, for example, must forecast future state aid before planning course offerings and staff size. Hospitals must forecast their future income from patient fees, insurance payments, and other sources to assess their ability to expand. Although we continue to use the term *sales forecasting,* keep in mind that what is really at issue is **revenue forecasting,** or forecasting that is concerned with predicting future revenue from all sources.

● **revenue forecasting**
The prediction of future revenues from all sources

Managers use several sources of information to develop a sales forecast. Previous sales figures and any obvious trends, such as the company's growth or stability, usually serve as the base. General economic indicators, technological improvements, new marketing strategies, and the competition's behavior all may be added together to ensure an accurate forecast. Once projected, the sales (or revenues) forecast becomes a guiding framework for a variety of other activities. Raw-material expenditures, advertising budgets, sales-commission structures, and similar operating costs are all based on projected sales figures.

Chapter 6 explained how firms integrate short-range, intermediate, and long-range planning horizons by means of systematic updating and refining. In similar fashion, organizations often forecast sales across several time horizons. The longer-term forecasts are updated and refined as various shorter-term cycles are completed. For obvious reasons, a forecast should be as accurate as possible, and the accuracy of sales forecasting tends to increase as organizations learn from their previous forecasting experience.[3] But the more uncertain and complex future conditions are likely to be, the more difficult it is to develop accurate forecasts. To partially offset these problems, forecasts are more useful to managers if they are expressed as a range rather than as an absolute index or number. If projected sales increases are expected to be in the range of 10 to 12 percent, a manager can consider all the implications for the entire range. A 10-percent increase could dictate one set of activities; a 12-percent increase could call for a different set of activities.

Technological Forecasting

Technological forecasting focuses on predicting what future technologies are likely to emerge and when they are likely to be economically feasible.[4] In an era when technological breakthrough and innovation have become the rule rather than the exception, managers must be able to anticipate new developments. If a manager invests heavily in existing technology (such as production processes, equipment, and computer systems) and the technology becomes obsolete in the near future, the company has wasted its resources. Gulf & Western, Inc., made this mistake several years ago. Gulf developed a strategy to become the number-two company in the low-density polyethylene film market over a five-year period. An explicit assumption made in building a new plant was that no new technological breakthroughs were likely. Unfortunately for Gulf, however, Union Carbide Corp. unexpectedly developed a new process that cut production costs

● **technological forecasting**
The prediction of what future technologies are likely to emerge and when they are likely to be economically feasible

Working with the Hungarian Telecommunications Company, U.S. West recently introduced the first cellular telephone system in Eastern Europe. U.S. West depended on technological forecasting to predict when Hungary's infrastructure would be able to handle the innovation. Budapest citizens had waited for up to fifteen years for traditional telephone service.

by 20 percent. As a result, Gulf's plant was obsolete before it was even finished.

The most striking technological innovations in recent years have been in electronics, especially semiconductors. Home computers, electronic games, and sophisticated communications equipment are all evidence of the electronics explosion. In contrast to Gulf, Steven Jobs did an excellent job of technological forecasting during the development of the NeXT computer. At three different stages, he committed to future actions based on technologies that did not exist at the time. In each instance, he gambled that breakthroughs would be achieved before he needed them—and he was right in each instance.[5] Given the increasing importance of technology and the rapid pace of technological innovation, managers will grow increasingly concerned with technological forecasting in the years to come.

Other Types of Forecasting

Other types of forecasting are also important to many organizations. Resource forecasting projects the organization's future needs for and the availability of human resources, raw materials, and other resources. Economic forecasts project general economic conditions. Some organizations undertake population or market-size forecasting, and others attempt to forecast future government fiscal policy and various government regulations that might be put into practice. Indeed, virtually any component in an organization's environment may be an appropriate area for forecasting. "The Global View" describes how Toyota developed a just-in-time technique to facilitate forecasting manufacturing schedules and priorities.

Forecasting Techniques

To carry out the various kinds of forecasting we have identified, managers use several different techniques. Time-series analysis and causal modeling are two common quantitative techniques.

● **time-series analysis**
A forecasting technique that extends past information into the future through the calculation of a best-fit line

Time-Series Analysis The underlying assumption of **time-series analysis** is that the past is a good predictor of the future. This technique is most useful when the manager has a lot of historical data available and when stable trends and patterns are apparent. In a time-series analysis, the variable

DEVELOPING JUST-IN-TIME AT TOYOTA

 Although U.S. companies have only recently discovered the benefits of just-in-time manufacturing, the technique is actually more than half a century old. It is the brainchild of Toyota Motor Corp.'s founder, Kiichiro Toyoda.

In the mid-1930s, Toyoda was developing plans for a new plant that was to be part of the automobile division of what was then Toyoda Automatic Loom Works. He recognized that the new plant would require a substantial investment in new machinery, and he wanted to get the best and most sophisticated machines available. He also saw that the machines had different productivity rates and therefore needed to be organized and operated according to some plan that would make the most efficient use of them. "Excess amounts to waste,"* he declared, and he ordered that no more than a day's supply of parts and materials be kept near the production lines. He hung a banner on the wall with the words "Just in Time" on it.

The just-in-time concept became the heart of the new Koromo plant. Buildings were laid out to achieve the smoothest possible production flow from one to the next and to radically reduce the need for warehouse space. Machine tools, too, were set up according to a process sequence rather than being grouped with similar tools. The completion of the new just-in-time plant was so important to the growth of Toyota that the day operations began in Koromo—

November 3, 1938—is the day designated as the official founding of Toyota Motor Corp.

The just-in-time system was disrupted during World War II, when the plant was put under military control, but refinements of the system continued after the war. Toyota trained employees to handle three machines instead of just one, and eventually they learned to be involved in a number of processes at the same time, ensuring that their efforts contributed to getting each assembly on to the next step as quickly as possible rather than to making excess parts.

In 1950, Toyota introduced an "andon" board, which displays code numbers and letters indicating how various operations are proceeding. Cords were installed that workers could pull to stop the production line. As the system continued to develop, it became evident that just-in-time required new pay plans, different labor-management relations, and new ways of planning and making decisions in the factory. It was, in fact, a whole new way of thinking about the manufacturing process.

---

* Quoted in Toyota Motor Corporation, *Toyota: A History of the First 50 Years* (Toyota City, Japan: Toyota Motor Corporation, 1988), p. 69.

References: Arthur M. Spinella, "Toyota City," *WARD'S Auto World,* June 1983, pp. 31–33; Toyota Motor Corporation, *Toyota: A History of the First 50 Years* (Toyota City, Japan: Toyota Motor Corporation, 1988).

---

under consideration (such as sales or enrollment) is plotted across time, and a "best-fit" line is identified.[6] Figure 9.1 shows how a time–series analysis might look. The dots represent the number of units sold for each year from 1985 through 1993. The best-fit line has also been drawn in. This is the line around which the dots cluster with the least variability. A manager who wants to know what sales to expect in 1994 simply extends the line. In this case, the projection would be around 8,200 units.

Real time-series analysis involves much more than simply plotting sales data and then using a ruler and a pencil to draw and extend the line. Sophisticated mathematical procedures, among other things, are necessary to account for seasonal and cyclical fluctuations and to identify the true best-fit line. In real situations, data seldom follow the neat pattern found in Figure

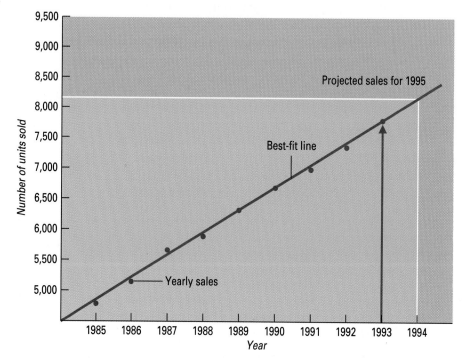

FIGURE 9.1 An Example of Time-Series Analysis

9.1. Indeed, the data points may be so widely dispersed that they mask meaningful trends from all but painstaking, computer-assisted inspection.

Causal Modeling The term **causal modeling** represents a group of several different techniques that determine causal relationships between different variables.[7] Table 9.1 summarizes three of the most useful approaches. A **regression model** is an equation that uses one set of variables (such as price and advertising) to predict another variable (such as sales volume). The variable being predicted is called the dependent variable; the variables used to make the prediction are called independent variables. A typical regression equation used by a small business might take this form:

● **causal modeling**
A group of different techniques that determine causal relationships between different variables

● **regression model**
An equation that uses one set of variables to predict another variable

$$y = ax_1 + bx_2 + cx_3 + d$$

where

$$y = \text{dependent variable (sales, in this case)}$$

$$x_1, x_2, \text{ and } x_3 = \text{independent variables (advertising budget, price, and commissions)}$$

$$a, b, \text{ and } c = \text{weights for the independent variables calculated during development of the regression model}$$

$$d = \text{a constant}$$

Regression models	Used to predict one variable (called the dependent variable) on the basis of known or assumed other variables (called independent variables). For example, we might predict future sales based on the values of price, advertising, and economic levels.
Econometric models	Make use of several multiple-regression equations to consider the impact of major economic shifts. For example, we might want to predict what impact the migration toward the Sun Belt might have on our organization.
Economic indicators	Various population statistics, indexes, or parameters that predict organizationally relevant variables such as discretionary income. Examples include cost-of-living index, inflation rate, and level of unemployment.

There are several different types of causal models managers use in planning and decision making. Three popular models are regression models, econometric models, and economic indicators.

To use the model, a manager can insert various alternatives for advertising budget, price, and commissions into the equation and then compute y. The calculated value of y represents the forecasted level of sales, given various levels of advertising, price, and commissions.[8]

Econometric models employ regression techniques at a much more complex level. An **econometric model** attempts to predict major economic shifts and their potential impact on the organization. It might be used to predict various age, ethnic, and economic groups that will characterize different regions of the United States in the year 2000 and to further predict the kinds of products and services these groups may want. A complete econometric model may consist of hundreds or even thousands of equations. Computers are almost always necessary to apply them. Given the complexities involved in developing econometric models, many firms that decide to use them rely on outside consultants specializing in this approach.

An **economic indicator,** another form of causal model, is a population statistic or index that reflects the economic well-being of a population. Examples of widely used economic indicators include the current rates of national productivity, inflation, and unemployment. In using such indicators, the manager draws on past experiences that have revealed a relationship between a certain indicator and some facet of the company's operations. Pitney Bowes's Data Documents Division, for example, can predict future sales of its business forms largely on the basis of current gross national product (GNP) estimates and other economic growth indexes.

Qualitative Forecasting Techniques Organizations also use several qualitative techniques to develop forecasts. A **qualitative forecasting tech-**

● **econometric model**
A causal model that predicts major economic shifts and their impact on the organization

● **economic indicators**
A key population statistic or index that reflects the economic well-being of a population

● **qualitative forecasting techniques**
Any of several techniques that rely on individual or group judgment rather than on mathematical analysis

nique relies more on individual or group judgment or opinion than on sophisticated mathematical analyses. The Delphi procedure, described in Chapter 8 as a mechanism for managing group decision-making activities, can also be used to develop forecasts. A variation of it—the *jury-of-expert-opinion* approach—involves using the basic Delphi process with members of top management serving as the collection of experts. They are asked to make a prediction about something—competitive behavior, trends in product demand, and so forth. Either a pure Delphi or a jury-of-expert-opinion approach might be useful in technological forecasting.

The *sales-force-composition* method of sales forecasting is a pooling of the predictions and opinions of experienced salespeople. Because of their experience, these individuals are often able to forecast quite accurately what various customers will do. Management combines and interprets the data from these forecasts to create plans. Textbook publishers use this procedure to project how many copies of a new title they might sell. The *customer evaluation* technique goes beyond an organization's sales force and collects data from the organization's customers. The customers provide estimates of their own future needs for the goods and services that the organization supplies. Managers must combine, interpret, and act on this information. This approach has two major limitations. Customers may be less interested in taking time to develop accurate predictions than are members of the organization itself, and the method makes no provision for including any new customers that the organization may acquire. Wal-Mart helps its suppliers use this approach by providing them with detailed projections regarding what it intends to buy several months in advance.

Selecting an appropriate forecasting technique can be as important as applying it correctly. Some techniques are appropriate only for specific circumstances. For example, the sales-force-composition technique is good only for sales forecasting. Other techniques, like the Delphi method, are useful in a variety of situations (but limited by time and money constraints). Some techniques, like the econometric models, require extensive use of computers, whereas others, like customer evaluation models, can be used with little mathematical expertise. For the most part, selection of a particular technique depends on the nature of the problem, the experience and preferences of the manager, and available resources.[9]

OTHER PLANNING TECHNIQUES

Of course, planning involves more than just forecasting. Other tools and techniques that are of help for a variety of planning purposes include linear programming, breakeven analysis, and simulations.

Linear Programming

● **linear programming**
A planning technique that determines the optimal combination of resources and activities

Linear programming is one of the most widely used quantitative tools for planning.[10] **Linear programming** is a procedure for calculating the optimal combination of resources and activities.[11] It is appropriate when an objective must be met (such as a sales quota or a certain production level)

TABLE 9.2 Production Data for Tuners and Receivers

| Department | Number of Hours Required per Unit | | Production Capacity for Day (in Hours) |
	Tuners (*T*)	Receivers (*R*)	
Production (PR)	10	6	150
Inspection and testing (IT)	4	4	80
Profit margin	$30	$20	

Linear programming can be used to determine the optimal number of tuners and receivers an organization might make. Key information needed to perform this analysis includes the number of hours each product needs in each department, the production capacity for each department, and the profit margin for each product.

within a set of constraints (such as a limited advertising budget or limited production capabilities).

To illustrate how linear programming can be used, assume that a small electronics company produces two basic products—a high-quality cable television tuner and a high-quality receiver for picking up television audio and playing it through a stereo amplifier. Both products go through the same two departments, first production and then inspection and testing. Each product has a known profit margin and a high level of demand. The production manager's job is to produce the optimal combination of tuners (*T*) and receivers (*R*) to maximize profits and use the time in production (PR) and in inspection and testing (IT) most efficiently. Table 9.2 gives the information needed for the use of linear programming to solve this problem.

The *objective function* is an equation that represents what we want to achieve. In technical terms, it is a mathematical representation of the desirability of the consequences of a particular decision. In our example, the objective function can be represented as follows:

$$\text{Maximize profit} = \$30X_T + \$20X_R$$

where

$$R = \text{the number of receivers to be produced}$$

$$T = \text{the number of tuners to be produced}$$

The $30 and $20 figures are the respective profit margins of the tuner and receiver, as noted in Table 9.2. The objective, then, is to maximize profits.

However, this objective must be accomplished within a specific set of constraints. In our example, the constraints are the time required to produce each product in each department and the total amount of time available. These data are also found in Table 9.2, and can be used to construct the relevant constraint equations:

$$10T + 6R \leq 150$$

$$4T + 4R \leq 80$$

We cannot use more capacity than is available, and, of course,

$$T \geq 0$$

$$R \geq 0$$

The set of equations consisting of the objective function and constraints can be solved graphically. To start, we first assume that production of each product is maximized when production of the other is at zero. The resultant solutions are then plotted on a coordinate axis. In the PR department, if $T = 0$, then:

$$10T + 6R \leq 150$$

$$10(0) + 6R \leq 150$$

$$R \leq 25$$

In the same department, if $R = 0$, then:

$$10T + 6(R) \leq 150$$

$$10T + 6(0) \leq 150$$

$$T \leq 15$$

Similarly, in the IT department, if no tuners are produced,

$$4T + 4R \leq 80$$

$$4(0) + 4R \leq 80$$

$$R \leq 20$$

and, if no receivers are produced,

$$4T + 4R \leq 80$$

$$4T + 4(0) \leq 80$$

$$T \leq 20$$

The four resulting inequalities are graphed in Figure 9.2. The shaded region represents the feasibility space, or production combinations that do not exceed the capacity of either department. The optimal number of products will be defined at one of the four corners of the shaded area—that is, the firm should produce twenty receivers only (point C), fifteen tuners only

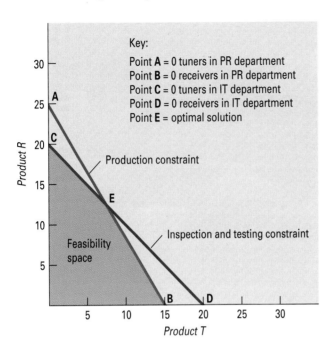

FIGURE 9.2 The Graphical Solution of a Linear Programming Problem

Key:
Point **A** = 0 tuners in PR department
Point **B** = 0 receivers in PR department
Point **C** = 0 tuners in IT department
Point **D** = 0 receivers in IT department
Point **E** = optimal solution

Finding the solution to a linear programming problem graphically is useful when only two alternatives are being considered. When problems are more complex, computers that can execute hundreds of equations and variables are necessary. Virtually all large firms, such as General Motors, Texaco, and Sears use linear programming.

(point B), thirteen receivers and seven tuners (point E), or no products at all. With the constraint that production of both tuners and receivers must be greater than zero, it follows that point E is the optimal solution. That combination requires 148 hours in PR and 80 hours in IT and yields $470 in profit. (Note that if only receivers were produced, the profit would be $400; producing only tuners would mean $450 in profit.)

Unfortunately, the graphical method can optimize only two alternatives and our example was extremely simple. When there are other alternatives being optimized, a complex algebraic method must be employed. Many real-world problems require several hundred equations and variables. Clearly, computers are necessary to execute such sophisticated analyses. Linear programming is a powerful technique, playing a key role in both planning and decision making. It can be used to schedule production, select an optimal portfolio of investments, allocate sales representatives to territories, or produce an item at some minimum cost.[12]

Breakeven Analysis

Linear programming is called a *normative procedure* because it prescribes the optimal solution to a problem. Breakeven analysis is a *descriptive procedure* because it simply describes relationships among variables; then it is up to the manager to make decisions. We can define **breakeven analysis** as a procedure for identifying the point at which revenues start covering their

● **breakeven analysis**
A procedure for identifying the point at which revenues start covering costs

The Warwick, Rhode Island, Police Department might have used breakeven analysis to determine whether installing dictaphone systems in patrol cars would pay off. With the new system, the department experienced a 73 percent reduction in report preparation time, and officers spend the time saved patrolling the community.

associated costs. It might be used to analyze the effects on profits of different price and output combinations or various levels of output.[13]

Figure 9.3 represents the key cost variables in breakeven analysis. Creating most products or services includes three types of costs: fixed costs, variable costs, and total costs. Fixed costs are incurred on existing facilities and production systems regardless of what volume of output is being generated. They include rent or mortgage payments on the building, managerial salaries, and depreciation of plant and equipment. Variable costs vary with the number of units produced, such as the cost of raw materials and direct labor used to make each unit. Total costs are fixed costs plus variable costs. Note that because of fixed costs, the line for total costs never begins at zero.

To determine the breakeven point for profit on sales for a product or service, the manager first must determine both fixed and variable costs. These costs are then combined to show total costs.

FIGURE 9.3 An Example of Cost Factors for Breakeven Analysis

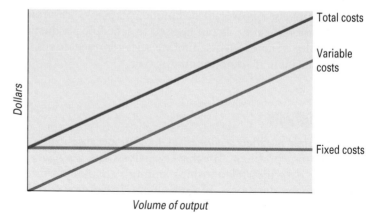

FIGURE 9.4 Breakeven Analysis

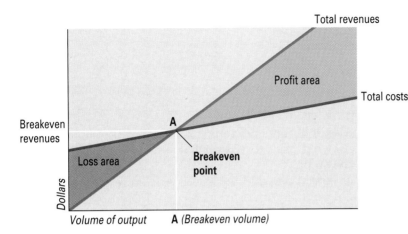

After total costs are determined and graphed, the manager then graphs the total revenues that will be earned on different levels of sales. The regions defined by the intersection of the two graphs show loss and profit areas. The intersection itself shows the breakeven point—the level of sales at which all costs are covered but no profits are earned.

Revenue and profit are other important factors in breakeven analysis. Revenue, the total dollar amount of sales, is computed by multiplying the number of units sold by the sales price of each unit. Profit is then determined by subtracting total costs from total revenues. When revenues and total costs are plotted on the same axes, the breakeven graph shown in Figure 9.4 emerges. The point at which the lines representing total costs and total revenues cross is the breakeven point. If the company represented in Figure 9.4 sells more units than are represented by point A, it will realize a profit; selling below that level will result in a loss.

Mathematically, the breakeven point (expressed as units of production or volume) is shown by the formula

$$BP = \frac{TFC}{P - VC}$$

where

$$BP = \text{breakeven point}$$

$$TFC = \text{total fixed costs}$$

$$P = \text{price per unit}$$

$$VC = \text{variable cost per unit}$$

Assume that you are considering the production of a new garden hoe with a curved handle. You have determined through market research that an acceptable selling price will be $20. You have also determined that the variable costs per hoe will be $15, and you have total fixed costs of $400,000 per year. The question is how many hoes must you sell each year to break even. Using the breakeven model, you find that:

$$BP = \frac{TFC}{P - VC}$$

$$= \frac{400,000}{20 - 15}$$

$$= 80,000 \text{ units}$$

Thus you must sell 80,000 hoes to break even. Further analysis also shows that if you raise your price to $25 per hoe, you need to sell only 40,000 to break even, and so on.

The state of New York used breakeven analysis to evaluate seven different variations of prior approvals for its Medicaid service. Comparisons were conducted of the costs involved in each variation against savings gained from efficiency and improved quality of service. The state found that only three of the variations were cost effective.[14]

Breakeven analysis is a popular and important planning technique, but it also has noteworthy weaknesses.[15] It considers revenues only up to the breakeven point, and it makes no allowance for the time value of money. For example, because the funds used to cover fixed and variable costs could be used for other purposes (such as investment), the organization is losing interest income by tying up its money prior to reaching the breakeven point. Thus managers often use breakeven analysis as only the first step in planning. After the preliminary analysis has been completed, more sophisticated techniques (such as rate-of-return analysis or discounted-present-value analysis) are used. Those techniques can help the manager decide whether to proceed or to divert resources into other areas.

Simulation

● **organizational simulation**
A model of a real-world situation that can be manipulated to discover how it functions

An **organizational simulation** is a model of a real-world situation that can be manipulated to discover how it functions. (The word *simulate* means to copy or to represent.) Simulation is a descriptive rather than a prescriptive technique. Northern Research & Engineering Corp. is an engineering consulting firm that helps clients plan new factories. By using a sophisticated factory simulation model, the firm recently helped a client cut several machines and operations from a new plant and save more than $750,000.

To consider another example, suppose the city of Denver was going to build a new airport. A few of the many issues to be addressed include the number of runways, the direction of those runways, the number of terminals and gates, the allocation of various carriers among the terminals and gates, and the technology and human resources needed to achieve a target frequency of takeoffs and landings. Planners could construct a model to simulate these factors, as well as their interrelationships, and then insert several different values for each factor and observe the probable results.

Simulation problems are in some ways similar to those addressed by linear programming, but simulation is more useful in complex situations characterized by diverse constraints and opportunities. The development of sophisticated simulation models may require the expertise of outside specialists or consultants, and the complexity of simulation almost always necessitates the use of a computer. For these reasons, simulation is most likely to be used as a technique for planning in large organizations that have the required resources.[16]

PERT

PERT, an acronym for Program Evaluation and Review Technique, uses a network to plan projects involving numerous activities and their interrelationships. It was developed by the U.S. Navy to help coordinate the activities of 3,000 contractors during the development of the Polaris nuclear submarine, and it was credited with saving two years of work on the project.[17] It has subsequently been used by most large companies in a variety of ways. The purpose of PERT is to highlight critical time intervals that affect the overall project. There are six basic steps in PERT:

1. Identify the activities to be performed and the events that will mark their completion.

2. Develop a network showing the relationships among the activities and events.

3. Calculate the time needed for each event and the time necessary to get from each event to the next.

4. Identify within the network the longest path that leads to completion of the project. This path is called the critical path.

5. Refine the network.

6. Use the network to control the project.

Suppose that a marketing manager wants to use PERT to plan the test marketing and nationwide introduction of a new product. Table 9.3 identifies the basic steps involved in carrying out this project. The activities are then arranged in a network like the one shown in Figure 9.5. In the figure, each completed event is represented by a number in a circle. The activities are indicated by letters on the lines connecting the events. Notice that some activities are performed independently of one another and others must be performed in sequence. For example, test production (activity a) and test site location (activity c) can be done at the same time, but test site location has to be done before the product can be tested (activities f and g).

The time needed to get from one activity to another is then determined. The normal way to calculate the time between each activity is to average the most optimistic, most pessimistic, and most likely times, with the most likely time weighted by 4. Time is usually calculated with the following formula:

$$\text{Expected time} = \frac{a + 4b + c}{6}$$

PERT is used to plan schedules for projects. It is particularly useful when many activities with critical time intervals must be coordinated. Besides launching a new product, PERT is particularly useful for projects like constructing a new factory or building, remodeling an office, or opening a new store.

TABLE 9.3 Activities and Events for Introducing a New Product

Activities	Events
a. Produce limited quantity for test marketing.	1. Origin of project. 2. Completion of production for test marketing.
b. Design preliminary package.	3. Completion of design for preliminary package.
c. Locate test market.	4. Test market located.
d. Obtain local merchant cooperation.	5. Local merchant cooperation obtained.
e. Ship product to selected retail outlets.	6. Product for test marketing shipped to retail outlets.
f. Monitor sales and customer reactions.	7. Sales and customer reactions monitored.
g. Survey customers in test-market area.	8. Customers in test-market area surveyed.
h. Make needed product changes.	9. Product changes made.
i. Make needed package changes.	10. Package changes made.
j. Mass produce the product.	11. Product mass produced.
k. Begin national advertising.	12. National advertising carried out.
l. Begin national distribution.	13. National distribution completed.

where

a = Optimistic time

b = Most likely time

c = Pessimistic time

critical path
The longest path through a PERT network

The expected number of weeks for each activity in our example is shown in parentheses along each path in Figure 9.5. The **critical path**—or the longest path through the network—is then identified. This path is considered critical because it shows the shortest time that the project can be completed in. In our example, the critical path is 1-2-3-6-7-9-10-11-12-13, totaling 57 weeks. PERT thus tells the manager that the project will take 57 weeks to complete.

The first network may be refined. If 57 weeks to completion is too long a time, the manager might decide to begin preliminary package design before the test products are finished. Or the manager might decide that ten

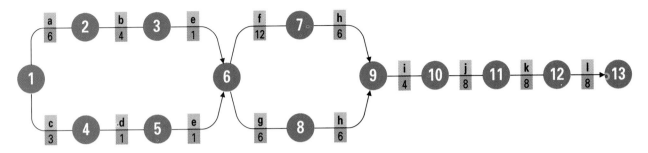

The blue numbers and letters correspond to the numbers and letters used in Table 9.3.

The orange numbers refer to the expected number of weeks for each activity.

weeks rather than twelve is a sufficient time period to monitor sales. If the critical path can be shortened by reallocating resources, so too can the overall duration of the project. The PERT network serves as an ongoing framework for both planning and control throughout the project. For example, the manager can use it to monitor where the project is relative to where it needs to be. Thus if an activity on the critical path takes longer than planned, the manager needs to make up the time elsewhere or accept that the entire project will be late.

Using the information in Table 9.3, the manager can construct a PERT network that portrays activities (shown by arrows) and events (shown by circles). After calculating the most likely time between events, the manager then identifies the critical path, or the longest path through the network.

DECISION-MAKING TOOLS

Managers also use a number of tools that relate more specifically to decision making than to planning. Two commonly used tools are payoff matrices and decision trees.

Payoff Matrix

A **payoff matrix** specifies the probable value of different alternatives depending on different possible outcomes associated with each.[18] To use a payoff matrix, several alternatives must be available, several different events could occur, and the consequences depend on which alternative is selected and on which event or set of events occurs. An important concept in understanding the payoff matrix, then, is probability. A **probability** is the likelihood, expressed as a percentage, that a particular event will or will not occur. If we believe that a particular event will occur 75 times out of 100, we can say that the probability of its occurring is 75 percent, or .75. Probabilities range in value from 0 (no chance of occurrence) to 1.00 (certain occurrence—also referred to as 100 percent). In the business world, there are few probabilities of either 0 or 1.00. Most probabilities that managers use are based on subjective judgment, intuition, and historical data.

● **payoff matrix**
A decision-making tool that specifies the probable value of different alternatives depending on different possible outcomes associated with each

probability
The likelihood, expressed as a percentage, that a particular event will or will not occur

A payoff matrix helps the manager determine the expected value of different alternatives. A payoff matrix is only effective if the manager ensures that probability estimates are as accurate as possible.

FIGURE 9.6 An Example of a Payoff Matrix

		High inflation *(Probability of .30)*	Low inflation *(Probability of .70)*
Investment alternative 1	Leisure products company	−$10,000	+$50,000
Investment alternative 2	Energy enhancement company	+$90,000	−$15,000
Investment alternative 3	Food-processing company	+$30,000	+$25,000

expected value
When applied to alternative courses of action, the sum of all possible values of outcomes due to that action multiplied by their respective probabilities

The **expected value** of an alternative course of action is the sum of all possible values of outcomes owing to that action multiplied by their respective probabilities. These probabilities may be estimated from research or may just be the manager's "best guess" based on experience and intuition. Suppose, for example, that a venture capitalist is considering investing in a new company. If he believes that there is a .40 probability of making $100,000, a .30 probability of making $30,000, and a .30 probability of losing $20,000, the expected value (EV) of this alternative is

$$\begin{aligned} EV &= .40(100{,}000) + .30(30{,}000) + .30(-20{,}000) \\ &= 40{,}000 + 9{,}000 - 6{,}000 \\ &= \$43{,}000 \end{aligned}$$

The investor can then weigh the expected value of this investment against the expected values of other available alternatives. The highest EV signals the investment that should most likely be selected.

For example, suppose another venture capitalist is looking to invest $20,000 in a new business. She has identified three possible alternatives: a leisure products company, an energy enhancement company, and a food-producing company. Because the expected value of each alternative depends on short-run changes in the economy, especially inflation, she decides to develop a payoff matrix. She estimates that the probability of high inflation is .30 and the probability of low inflation is .70. She then estimates the probable returns for each investment in the event of both high and low inflation. Figure 9.6 shows what the payoff matrix might look like (a minus sign indicates a loss). The expected value of investing in the leisure products company is

$$\begin{aligned} EV &= .30(-10{,}000) + .70(50{,}000) \\ &= -3{,}000 + 35{,}000 \\ &= \$32{,}000 \end{aligned}$$

Similarly, the expected value of investing in the energy enhancement company is

$$EV = .30(90,000) + .70(-15,000)$$
$$= 27,000 + (-10,500)$$
$$= \$16,500$$

And, finally, the expected value of investing in the food-processing company is

$$EV = .30(30,000) + .70(25,000)$$
$$= 9,000 + 17,500$$
$$= \$26,500$$

Investing in the leisure products company, then, has the highest expected value.

Other potential uses for payoff matrices include determining optimal order quantities, deciding whether to repair or replace broken machinery, and deciding which of several new products to introduce. Of course, managers must make accurate estimates of the relevant probabilities to effectively use payoff matrices.

Decision Tree

Decision trees are like payoff matrices in that they enhance a manager's ability to evaluate alternatives by making use of expected values. However, they are most appropriate when a number of decisions must be made in sequence.[19]

Figure 9.7 illustrates a hypothetical decision tree. The firm represented wants to begin exporting its products to a foreign market, but limited capacity restricts it to only one market at first. Managers believe that either France or China would be the best alternative to start with. Whichever alternative is selected, sales for the product in that country may turn out to be high or low. In France, there is a .80 chance of high sales and a .20 chance of low sales. The anticipated payoffs in these situations are predicted to be $20 million and $3 million, respectively. In China, the probabilities of high versus low sales are .60 and .40 respectively, and the associated payoffs are presumed to be $25 million and $6 million. As shown in the figure, the expected value of shipping to France is $16,600,000, whereas the expected value of shipping to China is $17,400,000.

The astute reader will note that this part of the decision could have been set up as a payoff matrix. However, the value of decision trees is that we can extend the model to include subsequent decisions. Assume, for example, that the company begins shipping to China. If high sales do in fact materialize, the company must soon make another decision. It might use the extra revenues to (1) increase shipments to China, (2) build a plant close to China to cut shipping costs, or (3) begin shipping to France. Various outcomes are possible for each decision, and each outcome will also have

A number of planning and decision-making tools must be used to ensure successful and timely completion of a major project such as the 1992 world's fair in Seville, Spain, the Universal Exposition. Decision trees are especially appropriate because many decisions must be made in sequence, from ensuring an adequate infrastructure (bridges, highways, and public transportation) to guaranteeing the survival of Chile's sixty-ton iceberg (one of the most talked-about exhibits) in Spain's 100-degree temperatures.

● **decision tree**
A planning tool that extends the concept of a payoff matrix through a sequence of decisions

FIGURE 9.7 An Example of a Decision Tree

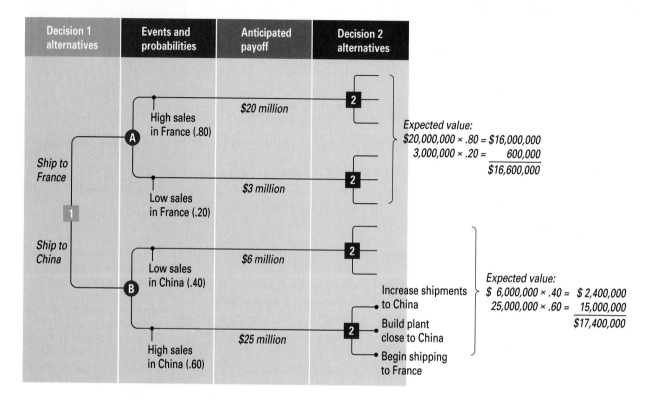

Decision 1 alternatives	Events and probabilities	Anticipated payoff	Decision 2 alternatives

High sales in France (.80) — $20 million — 2

Expected value:
$20,000,000 × .80 = $16,000,000
3,000,000 × .20 = 600,000
$16,600,000

Low sales in France (.20) — $3 million — 2

Ship to France — 1

Ship to China

Low sales in China (.40) — $6 million — 2

B

Increase shipments to China
Build plant close to China
Begin shipping to France

High sales in China (.60) — $25 million — 2

Expected value:
$ 6,000,000 × .40 = $ 2,400,000
25,000,000 × .60 = 15,000,000
$17,400,000

A decision tree extends the basic concepts of a payoff matrix through multiple decisions. This tree shows the possible outcomes of two levels of decisions. The first decision is whether to expand to China or France. The second decision, assuming that the company expands to China, is whether to increase shipments to China, build a plant close to China, or initiate shipping to France.

● **inventory models**
Techniques that help managers decide how much inventory to maintain

both a probability and an anticipated payoff. It is therefore possible to compute expected values through several tiers of decisions. As it is with payoff matrices, determining probabilities accurately is the crucial element in the process. Properly used, however, decision trees can provide managers with a useful road map through complex decision situations.

Other Decision-Making Tools

In addition to payoff matrices and decision trees, a number of other quantitative methods are also available to facilitate decision making.[20]

Inventory Models   **Inventory models** are techniques that help managers decide how much inventory to maintain. For example, Target uses inventory models to help determine how much merchandise to order and when to order it. Inventory consists of both raw materials (inputs) and finished goods (outputs). Polaroid Corp. maintains a supply of chemicals to make film, cartons to pack film in, and packaged film ready to be shipped. For finished goods, too much, as well as too little, inventory is costly: excess inventory ties up capital, whereas a small inventory may result in shortages and customer dissatisfaction. The same holds for raw materials: too much inventory ties up capital, but if a company runs out of resources, work stoppages may occur. Finally, because the process of placing an order for raw materials and supplies has associated costs (such as clerical time, shipping expenses, and higher unit costs for small quantities), it is important to minimize the frequency of ordering. Inventory models help the manager optimize the size of inventory. New innovations in inventory management such as **just-in-time,** or **JIT,** rely heavily on decision-making models. A JIT system involves scheduling materials to arrive in short batches as they are needed, thereby eliminating the need for resources such as a big reserve inventory and warehouse space.[21]

Queuing Models A **queuing model** is intended to help the organization manage waiting lines. We are all familiar with waiting lines: we wait to pay for groceries at The Kroger Co., to buy gas at an Exxon station, when we call American Airlines, Inc., for reservations, and for a teller at Citibank N.A. If the Kroger store manager has only one checkout stand in operation, the store's cost for checkout personnel is very low; however, many customers are upset by the long line that frequently develops. To solve the problem, the store manager could decide to keep twenty checkout stands open at all times. Customers would like the short waiting period, but personnel costs would be very high. The manager would use a queuing model to help determine the optimal number of checkout stands: the number that would balance personnel costs and customer waiting time. Target uses queuing models to determine how many checkout lanes to put in its stores. "Management in Practice" details how L.L. Bean used queuing models to schedule its telephone operators.

Distribution Model A decision facing many marketing managers relates to the distribution of the organization's products. Specifically, the manager must decide where the products should go and how to transport them. Railroads, trucking companies, and air freight companies all have associated shipping costs, and also follow different schedules and routes. Managers must identify the combination of routes that optimizes distribution effectiveness and distribution costs. A **distribution model** helps managers determine this optimal pattern of distribution.

Game Theory **Game theory** was originally developed to predict the effect of one company's decisions on competitors. Models developed from game theory are intended to predict how a competitor will react to various activities that an organization might undertake, such as price changes, promotional changes, and the introduction of new products. If BankAmerica Corp. were considering raising its prime lending rate by 1 percent, it might use a game theory model to predict whether Citicorp would follow suit. If the model revealed that Citicorp would, BankAmerica would probably proceed; otherwise, it would probably maintain the current interest rates. Unfortunately, game theory has not proven as useful as it was originally expected to be. The complexities of the real world combined with the limitation of the technique itself restrict its applicability. Game theory, however, does provide a useful conceptual framework for analyzing competitive behavior, and its usefulness may be improved in the future.

● **just-in-time (JIT)**
An inventory management technique in which materials are scheduled to arrive in small batches as they are needed, eliminating the need for resources such as big reserves and warehouse space

● **queuing model**
A model used to optimize waiting lines in organizations

● **distribution model**
A model used to determine the optimal pattern of distribution across different carriers and routes

● **game theory**
A planning tool used to predict how competitors will respond to different actions the organization might take

artificial intelligence (AI)
A computer program that attempts to duplicate the thought processes of experienced decision makers

Artificial Intelligence A fairly new addition to the manager's quantitative tool kit is **artificial intelligence (AI),** which is essentially a computer program that tries to duplicate the thought processes of experienced decision makers. The most useful form of AI is the expert system.[22] For example, Digital Equipment Corp. has developed an expert system that checks sales orders for new computer systems and then designs preliminary layouts for those new systems. Digital can now ship the computer to a customer in components for final assembly on site. Digital's expert system has enabled it to cut back on its own final assembly facilities.

STRENGTHS AND WEAKNESSES OF PLANNING TOOLS

Like all issues confronting management, planning tools of the type described here have a number of strengths and weaknesses.

Weaknesses and Problems

One weakness of the planning and decision-making tools discussed in this chapter is that they may not always adequately reflect reality. Even with the most sophisticated and powerful computer-assisted technique, reality must often be simplified. Many problems are also not amenable to quantitative analysis because important elements of them are intangible or nonquantifiable. Employee morale or satisfaction, for example, is often a major factor in managerial decisions.

Using these tools and techniques may also be quite costly. For example, only large companies can afford to develop their own econometric models. Even though the computer explosion has increased the availability of quantitative aids, some expense is still involved, and it will take time for many of these techniques to become widely used. Resistance to change also limits the use of planning tools in some settings. If a manager for a retail chain has always based decisions for new locations on personal visits, observations, and intuition, she may be less than eager to begin using a computer-based model for evaluating and selecting sites. Finally, problems may arise when managers have to rely on technical specialists to use sophisticated models. Experts trained in the use of complex mathematical procedures may not understand or appreciate other aspects of management.

Strengths and Advantages

Planning and decision-making tools also offer many advantages. For situations that are amenable to quantification, they can bring sophisticated mathematical processes to bear on planning and decision making. Properly designed models and formulas also help decision makers "see reason." For example, a manager might not be inclined to introduce a new product line simply because he doesn't think it will be profitable. After seeing a forecast predicting first-year sales of 100,000 units coupled with a breakeven analysis

TELEMARKETING DECISIONS AT L. L. BEAN

L. L. Bean, Inc., the outdoor clothing and equipment specialist, gets about two-thirds of its orders over the telephone. It has long relied on mutual loyalty to keep its business growing—the company treats its customers well and the customers keep coming back for more.

This relationship became strained in the mid-1980s, however, when Bean's method of handling customer calls proved inadequate. During peak call hours, 80 percent of Bean's callers got a busy signal, and those customers who did get through often waited ten minutes for an operator. The company calculated that the callers who gave up without ordering represented $10 million per year in lost profit.

So the company turned to management science: Bean hired consultants who used queuing models to choose vendors of shift-scheduling systems and to determine how many telephone lines and operators to use during busy periods. Traditionally, Bean had planned for its holiday peak periods using previous years' levels and aiming for productivity and customer-service goals. The task of hiring operators alone is exceptionally complex. Bean must plan the right mixture of full- and part-time operators, train them, and schedule them.

To determine which of four vendors offered the best operator-scheduling system, the consultants ignored the lists of features that each system offered and instead simulated actual operations of the systems. They used data from previous years' operations at Bean, determined the schedules that each system would recommend based on the data, and then used an economic optimization model to judge which system would yield the most profit. The model calculated the cost of overstaffing or understaffing and the cost of the loss of business from customers who gave up when they didn't reach an operator soon enough. The consultants also compared the systems' abilities to schedule full- and part-time workers.

Tests with the economic optimization model showed that the best scheduling system could save Bean as much as $100,000 over the two-week test period. Bean used similar analyses to calculate the optimum number of telephone lines, operators, and training classes. The results demonstrated that relying on previous experience was costly. The model showed that even though 1989 call volumes were only 6.5 percent higher than 1988 volumes, the company needed to increase its telephone lines by 20 percent and the number of operators by 25 percent in 1989 to achieve maximum profit. The successful use of the model both increased Bean's profit and changed the whole company's attitude about management science.

References: Bruce H. Andrews and Henry Parsons, "L. L. Bean Chooses a Telephone Agent Scheduling System," *Interfaces*, November–December 1989, pp. 1–9; Phil Quinn, Bruce H. Andrews, and Henry Parsons, "Allocating Telecommunications Resources at L. L. Bean, Inc.," *Interfaces*, January–February 1991, pp. 75–91.

showing profitability after only 20,000, however, the manager will probably change his mind. Thus rational planning tools and techniques force the manager to look beyond personal prejudices and predispositions. Finally, the computer explosion is rapidly making sophisticated planning techniques available in a wider range of settings than ever.

The crucial point to remember is that planning tools and techniques are a means to an end, not an end in themselves. Just as a carpenter uses a handsaw in some situations and an electric saw in others, a manager must recognize that a particular model may be useful in some situations but not in others that may call for a different approach. Knowing the difference is one mark of a good manager.

SUMMARY OF KEY POINTS

Managers use a variety of tools and techniques as they develop plans and make decisions. Forecasting is one widely used method. Forecasting is the process of developing assumptions or premises about the future. Managers are often especially concerned about forecasting sales or revenue and technological developments. Time-series analysis and causal modeling are important quantitative forecasting techniques; qualitative techniques are also widely used.

Managers also use other planning tools and techniques in different circumstances. Linear programming helps optimize resources and activities, breakeven analysis helps identify how many products or services must be sold to cover costs, and simulations model reality. PERT helps plan how much time it will take to complete a project.

Other tools and techniques are useful for decision making. Constructing a payoff matrix, for example, helps a manager better assess the expected value of different alternatives. Decision trees are used to extend expected values across multiple decisions. Other popular decision-making tools and techniques include inventory models, queuing models, distribution models, game theory, and artificial intelligence.

A variety of strengths and weaknesses are associated with each of these tools and techniques as well as with their use by a manager. The key to success is knowing when each should and should not be used and knowing how to use and interpret the results that each provides.

DISCUSSION QUESTIONS

Questions for Review

1. What is revenue forecasting? What is technological forecasting?
2. What is time-series analysis?
3. Briefly summarize how a manager can use breakeven analysis.
4. What are the strengths and weaknesses involved in using the various tools and techniques discussed in this chapter?

Questions for Analysis

5. Compare and contrast linear programming and breakeven analysis.
6. Developing a good forecast takes time and resources. Is it possible for an organization to invest too heavily in increasing the accuracy of its forecasts? Why or why not?
7. Is an error at the beginning of a decision tree simply carried throughout the tree at the same value, or is it compounded?

Questions for Application

8. Interview someone in the admissions office at your college or university. Find out how they forecast how many students will apply for admission in the future.

9. Think of a decision that you have recently made or will be making soon. Develop a payoff matrix to determine the expected value of each alternative.

10. Identify a project or activity that you will soon be undertaking. It might be writing a term paper, planning a social event, or repairing your car. Develop a PERT diagram to establish how long it will take to complete the project.

SCHEDULING AIRLINE FLIGHT CREWS

*S*cheduling flight crews for a major airline is a problem of seemingly insoluble complexity. Scheduling the airplanes themselves poses a number of problems, but when the various legal and physical limitations of flight crews are considered, it becomes obvious why the airlines search for a management tool to enable them to create efficient schedules. A linear programming approach has allowed American Airlines, Inc., to save an estimated $18 million dollars yearly compared with its previous method of scheduling.

The basic unit of a flight crew's work is known as a pairing, or round trip from a home base to a destination and back again. Because crew costs are second only to fuel costs as leading direct operating costs for airlines, the airlines have a major incentive to make the pairings as efficient as possible. They must, however, abide by a number of limitations imposed by the Federal Aviation Administration (FAA) and by flight crew contracts.

Ideally, a crew would get off one plane and immediately board another, but because flight delays are so frequent, most airlines plan for up to an hour of ground time for the crews between flights. Usually flight times are built around marketing considerations rather than crew-scheduling considerations. And any time a flight crew must spend a night away from its home base, the airline incurs costs for housing and food. One goal of crew scheduling is to reduce what is known as "pay and credit," the difference between the number of hours a crew member is paid and the hours that that member actually works.

To find the optimum schedules, the airlines use a set-partitioning model, with the rows representing flights to be covered and the columns representing possible crew trips. Because representing the possibilities for a busy airline may require thousands of columns, solving the problem generally requires choosing a subset of the overall scheduling system,

finding the optimum solution for that subset, and then working on other subsets. Even subset operations tend to require a vast amount of computer power. A cost value is associated with each column, and the optimum solution will be represented by that set of columns that minimizes costs while also covering each flight segment once and only once.

Although no one has yet developed a program to find an optimal solution for all of the largest airline's scheduling decisions, consultants working for American Airlines using linear programming software have been able to produce a steady decrease in the airline's ratio of pay and credit to total flying hours. Further refinements may allow the airlines to be confident that they are using all of their human resources most efficiently.

Discussion Questions

1. Is finding the best scheduling solution simply a problem of economic optimization, or do other factors affect management decisions about scheduling?

2. What changes in personnel and training could help airlines alleviate their crew-scheduling problems?

E 3. FAA and union rules contribute to the crew-scheduling difficulties. Do you think the airlines should be allowed to set their own work-hour rules?

References: Ira Gershkoff, "Optimizing Flight Crew Schedules," *Interfaces,* July–August 1989, pp. 29–43; Roy E. Marsten and Fred Shepardson, "Exact Solution of Crew Scheduling Problems Using the Set Partitioning Model: Recent Successful Applications," *Networks,* Vol. 11 (1981), pp. 165–177; Jerrold Rubin, "A Technique for the Solution of Massive Set Covering Problems, with Application to Airline Crew Scheduling," *Transportation Science,* February 1973, pp. 31–48.

PLANNING THE FUTURE OF NEW ZEALAND'S FORESTS

New Zealand's forest plantations cover almost 3 million acres. Until recently, the New Zealand Forest Service controlled these lands, but in 1987 the government decided to sell its commercial forest holdings to private companies. The Forest Service faced a major challenge—to assign a monetary figure to a resource as long-lasting as a forest.

Luckily, the Forest Service had already been working with two different kinds of computer models. Forest estate models facilitate planning for decisions about planting, pruning and thinning, and harvesting. The Forest Service used a forest estate model called Interactive Forest Simulator (IFS), which allows input of the initial state of the forest and of yearly harvesting figures and provides summaries of the consequences of various management strategies. Although IFS is useful for actually managing the forest, it was not flexible enough to answer the many "what-if" questions posed by the attempt to value the forest.

To deal with the more demanding requirements of the forest valuation, a second model was developed to complement IFS. This model, called FOLPI (Forestry-Oriented Linear Programming Interpreter), uses a linear programming model created to work with the data already available in the IFS. One essential feature of FOLPI is that it accepts problems and produces output in forestry terms rather than in mathematical terms with which Forest Service personnel might not be familiar.

The model allowed the Service to project the effects of a number of different factors on the Service's ten different crop types. The forest consists mostly of one species—radiata pine—but the model also needed to account for other species, for regional variations, and for variations in how intensively particular stands had been managed. The model also took into account how the forest value would be affected by the discount rate, volume growth, log prices, costs, replanting assump-

tions, new planting assumptions, and forest-management assumptions.

FOLPI allowed the Service to put particular constraints on all predictions. For instance, the sale of a large volume of the government's forest products would lower log prices; therefore, the Service put an upper limit on the volume to be cut in any one year. More importantly, FOLPI made negotiations between the various parties much easier by showing precisely what long-range effects various policies would produce.

The complementary use of simulation and linear programming models did not by itself make any decisions for the New Zealand Forest Service. But it ensured that the decisions the Service made were based on accurate projections that all parties could have faith in, not rough estimates open for endless dispute.

Discussion Questions

1. Why would it be so important to the New Zealand Forest Service to have accurate predictions of the effects of various policies?

2. Are the problems and solutions in this case unique to forest management, or could they be applied to other products and situations?

E 3. How might these computer models help avoid over-harvesting and consequent erosion and loss of land value that so often plague poorly managed forests?

References: Oscar García, "IFS, An Interactive Forest Simulator For Long-Range Planning," *New Zealand Journal of Forestry Science*, Vol. 11, No. 1 (1981), pp. 8–19; Bruce R. Manley and John A. Threadgill, "LP Use for Valuation and Planning of New Zealand Plantation Forests," *Interfaces*, November–December 1991, pp. 66–79.

Quality as an Organizational Goal

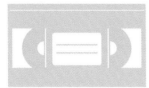

The purpose of this exercise is to help students better understand the relationship between planning and decision making, and product and service quality.

Learning Objectives

After completing this exercise you should have a better understanding of

1. The relationships between planning and decision making and quality.

2. How organizations go about implementing strategies designed to enhance product and service quality.

Preview

Motorola

Motorola, Inc. is the leading U.S. supplier of semiconductors and one of the world's largest makers of mobile radios, telephones, and pagers. The firm has over 100,000 employees and operates manufacturing facilities in ten ten American states, Puerto Rico, Asia, Australia, Canada, Mexico, Latin America, Europe, and the Middle East. Motorola posted 1991 sales of $11.3 billion, profits of $454 million, and owns assets valued at $9.3 billion.

Westinghouse Electric Corporation

Westinghouse Electric Corporation is a diversified company comprised of several major business groups, such as Broadcasting, Energy and Utility Systems, and Financial Services. Westinghouse employs about 116,000 people and has facilities around the world. In 1991, Westinghouse generated $12.8 billion in sales, reported losses totalling slightly over $1 billion, and owns $20 billion in assets. This video exercise focuses on the Commercial Nuclear Fuel Division of Westinghouse.

Globe Metallurgical Inc.

Globe Metallurgical Inc., a Baldrige winner in the small business category, is a privately held manufacturer of silicon metal for the chemical and aluminum industries and iron-based metals for the foundry industry. Based in Cleveland, Globe Metallurgical employs 260 people.

About the Malcolm Baldrige Award

[Curt Reimann, Baldrige Director] thinks the biggest winners may be the employees of quality companies: "All of the award winners are presenting . . . information about the changes in leadership, changes in the culture, changes in the investment in employees, evidence that employees are better off—improved safety, lowered absenteeism, lower turnover, all of the manifestations of employee interest in the work and feelings of contribution." He says companies that apply for the Baldrige "are realizing that in order to gain the respect and the contribution of employees, they have to invest in employees. They have to respect their human dignity, and they have to invest in the long-term, in training and education. They have to be sensitive to morale." There are also pluses for executives, Reimann says. "There is now a discourse taking place between senior executives based on the Baldrige Award . . . because senior executives [from different companies], it turns out, listen to each other more than they listen to quality professionals, and I think that's a very, very healthy development."*

Background Assignment

Go to the library and find articles from 1980 to 1986 about the company assigned to you by your instructor. Look at sources such as *Business Week, Fortune,* and the *Wall Street Journal.* Locate the company's annual sales and profits for each year during the period. If possible, locate copies of your firm's annual reports for the period and review what the reports say about quality. Characterize the environment your company was operating in at the time. What were its threats, problems, challenges?

The Video

The video you are about to watch features Motorola, the Commercial Nuclear Fuel Division of Westinghouse, and Globe Metallurgical Inc., the first recipients of the Malcolm Baldrige National Quality awards, given in 1988. The video briefly examines the steps these firms took to improve quality and how they developed quality improvement systems.

Questions for Discussion

1. What are the similarities and apparent differences in how the three companies went about improving quality?

2. Why is top management commitment to quality improvement so important?

3. Can quality be the basis for a differentiation strategy as discussed in Chapter 7? What happens if all firms in a particular industry start taking this approach?

4. Which of the planning and decision making tools discussed in Chapter 8 are most relevant to quality improvement?

Follow-Up Assignment

Go back to the library and get more recent articles that discuss the performance of your assigned company since it won the Baldrige Award in 1988. If possible, also review corporate annual reports for the last few years to see what top managers have actually said about quality. Have the quality programs continued to succeed? Have changes been instituted?

*Source: Lloyd Dobyns and Clare Crawford-Mason, *Quality or Else.* (Boston: Houghton Mifflin Company, 1991) pp. 179–180. Copyright © Houghton Mifflin Company. Used with permission.

PART

IV

THE ORGANIZING PROCESS

10 *Components of Organization Structure*

11 *Managing Organization Design*

12 *Managing Organization Change*

13 *Managing Human Resources*

Components of Organization Structure

OBJECTIVES

After studying this chapter, you should be able to:

● *Identify the basic building blocks of organizations.*

● *Describe alternative approaches to designing jobs.*

● *Discuss the rationale and the most common bases for grouping jobs into departments.*

● *Describe the basic elements involved in establishing reporting relationships.*

● *Discuss how authority is distributed in organizations.*

● *Discuss the basic coordinating activities undertaken by organizations.*

● *Describe basic ways in which positions within an organization can be differentiated.*

OUTLINE

Building Blocks of Organizations
Designing Jobs
   Job Specialization
   Benefits and Limitations of
     Specialization
   Alternatives to Specialization

Grouping Jobs: Departmentalization
   Rationale for Departmentalization
   Common Bases for Departmentalization

Establishing Reporting Relationships
   The Chain of Command
   Narrow Versus Wide Spans
   Tall Versus Flat Organizations
   Determining the Appropriate Span

Distributing Authority
   The Delegation Process
   Decentralization and Centralization

Coordinating Activities
   The Need for Coordination
   Structural Coordination Techniques

Differentiating Between Positions
   Differences Between Line and Staff
   Administrative Intensity

H. ROSS PEROT left IBM in 1962 to found Electronic Data Systems Inc., or EDS. The basic service EDS provided was handling other businesses' computer operations on a contract basis. EDS prospered and soon became a multibillion-dollar firm.

From the beginning Perot ran EDS with an iron hand: he gave his managers little freedom and autonomy to make decisions without consulting him first. He also mandated strict dress codes. He hired good people, rewarded them handsomely, and expected strong dedication and loyalty in return.

In 1984, General Motors Corp. bought EDS, and Perot became a member of GM's board of directors. As part of the deal, EDS was to assume control of GM's computer operations. At the same time, Perot wanted a say in how GM was being run and often criticized the firm's strategy and approach to doing business. After two years of conflict, GM bought Perot's share of EDS and he left the firm.

Perot's successor, Les Alberthal, quickly set about remaking the organization. His first major task was to complete the integration of EDS into the GM organization, something that had been far more difficult than most people had imagined. Alberthal also began to delegate much more than did Perot, increasing his managers' decision-making latitude, for instance. He also gave managers more freedom in how they dressed, and worked hard to earn (rather than command) the loyalty of EDS employees.

Alberthal's efforts are paying big dividends: since Perot's departure, EDS's annual revenues have grown by more than 25 percent. The firm has also assumed total control of GM's computer operations, and it seems to be handling them very efficiently. In addition, turnover at EDS has dropped dramatically.[1] ●

oss Perot and Les Alberthal each had to make a decision that all CEOs must make—how much decision-making power to keep and how much to give to others. Perot decided to retain most of it for himself; Alberthal decided to give much of it to other managers. Whatever the choice, it is just one of many that managers must make in deciding how to structure an organization.

This chapter discusses many of the critical elements of organization structure that managers can control and is the first of four devoted to organizing, the second basic managerial function identified in Chapter 1. In Part 3, we described managerial planning—deciding what to do. Organizing, the subject of Part 4, focuses on how to do it. We first elaborate on the meaning of organization structure. Subsequent sections explore the basic building blocks that managers use to create an organization.

BUILDING BLOCKS OF ORGANIZATIONS

Imagine asking a child to build a castle with a set of building blocks. He selects a few small blocks and more larger ones. He uses some square ones, some round ones, and some triangular ones. When he finishes, he has his own castle, unlike any other. Another child, presented with the same task, will construct a different castle. The child's activities—choosing a certain combination of blocks and then putting them together in a unique way—are analogous to the manager's job of organizing.

organizing
Deciding how best to group organizational activities and resources

● **organization structure**
The set of building blocks that can be used to configure an organization

Organizing is deciding how best to group organizational activities and resources. Just as the child selects different kinds of building blocks, managers can choose a variety of structural possibilities. And just as the child can assemble the blocks in any number of ways, so too can managers put the organization together in many different ways. In this chapter, our focus is on the building blocks themselves—**organization structure.** In Chapter 11 we focus on how the blocks can be put together—organization design. There are six basic building blocks that managers can use in constructing an organization: designing jobs, grouping jobs, establishing reporting relationships between jobs, distributing authority among jobs, coordinating activities between jobs, and differentiating among jobs. The logical starting point is the first building block—designing jobs for people within the organization.

DESIGNING JOBS

job design
The determination of an individual's work-related responsibilities

The first building block of organization structure is job design. **Job design** is the determination of an individual's work-related responsibilities.[2] For a machinist at Caterpillar, job design might specify what machines are to be operated, how they are to be operated, and what performance standards are expected. For a manager at Caterpillar Inc., job design would involve defining areas of decision-making responsibility, identifying goals and expectations, and establishing appropriate indicators of success. The natural starting point for designing jobs is determining the level of desired specialization.

Job Specialization

Job specialization is the degree to which the overall task of the organization is broken down and divided into smaller component parts. Job specialization evolved from the concept of *division of labor*. Adam Smith, an eighteenth-century economist, described how division of labor was used in a pin factory to improve productivity.[3] One man drew the wire, another straightened it, a third cut it, a fourth ground the point, and so on. Smith claimed that ten men working in this fashion were able to produce 48,000 pins in a day, whereas each man working alone would have been able to produce only 20 pins per day.

More recently, the best example of the impact of specialization is the automobile assembly line pioneered by Henry Ford and his contemporaries. Mass-production capabilities stemming from job specialization techniques have had a profound impact throughout the world. High levels of low-cost production transformed U.S. society during the first several decades of this century into one of the strongest economies in the history of the world.

Job specialization is a normal extension of organizational growth. For example, when Walt Disney started his company he did everything himself—writing cartoons, drawing them, and then marketing them to theaters. As the business grew, he eventually hired others to perform many of these same functions. As growth continued, so too did specialization. For example, as animation artists work on Disney movies today, they may specialize in drawing only a single character. And today, The Walt Disney Company has thousands of different specialized jobs. Clearly, no one person could perform them all.

Benefits and Limitations of Specialization

Job specialization provides four benefits to organizations.[4] First, a worker performing a small, simple task will probably become very proficient at that task. Second, transfer time between tasks may decrease. If employees perform several different tasks, some time may be lost as they stop doing the first task and start doing the next. Third, the more narrowly defined a job is, the easier it may be to develop specialized equipment to assist with that job. Fourth, when an employee who performs a highly specialized job is absent or resigns, the manager should be able to train someone new at relatively low cost. Although specialization is generally thought of in terms of operating jobs, many organizations have extended the basic elements of specialization to managerial and professional levels as well.[5]

On the other hand, job specialization can have negative consequences. The foremost criticism is that workers who perform highly specialized jobs may become bored and dissatisfied. The job may be so specialized that it offers no challenge or stimulation. Boredom and monotony set in, absenteeism rises, and the quality of the work may suffer. Furthermore, the anticipated benefits of specialization do not always occur. For example, a study conducted at Maytag Corporation found that the time spent moving work-in-process from one worker to another was greater than the time needed for the same individual to change from job to job.[6] Thus although some degree of specialization is necessary in all but the smallest organizations, it should not be carried to extremes because of the negative consequences that could result. Managers should be sensitive to situations in which extreme specialization should be avoided. And indeed, there are several alternative approaches to designing jobs that have been developed in recent years.

Alternatives to Specialization

To counter the problems associated with specialization, managers have sought other approaches to job design that achieve a better balance between organizational demands for efficiency and productivity and individual needs for creativity and autonomy. Alternative approaches are job rotation, job enlargement, job enrichment, the job characteristics approach, and work teams.[7]

● **job rotation**
An alternative to job specialization that involves systematically moving employees from one job to another

Job Rotation **Job rotation** involves systematically moving employees from one job to another. A worker in a warehouse might unload trucks on Monday, carry incoming inventory to storage on Tuesday, verify invoices on Wednesday, pull outgoing inventory from storage on Thursday, and load trucks on Friday. Thus the jobs do not change; instead, workers move from job to job. Unfortunately, for this very reason, job rotation has not been very successful in enhancing employee motivation or satisfaction. Jobs that are amenable to rotation tend to be relatively standard and routine. Workers who are rotated to a "new" job may be more satisfied at first, but this soon wanes. Although many companies (among them American Cyanamid Co., Bethlehem Steel Corp., Ford Motor Co., The Prudential Insurance Co. of America, TRW Inc., and Western Electric Company, Incorporated) have tried job rotation, it is most often used today as a training device to improve worker skills and flexibility.

Organizations such as Hallmark set up work teams, or give groups of workers responsibility for performing an interrelated set of jobs, to increase flexibility and save money. By establishing work teams in which artists, writers, lithographers, and merchandisers work together on cards instead of in separate departments, Hallmark has cut a card's development time from two years to one and is better able to respond to changing consumer tastes.

Job Enlargement On the assumption that doing the same basic task over and over is the primary cause of worker dissatisfaction, **job enlargement** was developed to increase the total number of tasks workers perform. As a result, all workers perform a wide variety of tasks, presumably reducing the level of job dissatisfaction. Many organizations have used job enlargement, including IBM, Detroit Edison Co., AT&T, the U.S. Civil Service, and Maytag Corporation. At Maytag, for example, the assembly line for producing washing-machine water pumps was systematically changed so that work that had originally been performed by six workers passing the work sequentially from one person to another was performed by four workers, each of whom assembled a complete pump.[8] Unfortunately, although job enlargement does have some positive consequences, they are often offset by several disadvantages: (1) Training costs usually rise. (2) Unions have argued that pay should increase because the worker is doing more things. (3) In many cases the work remains boring and routine even after job enlargement.

● **job enlargement**
An alternative to job specialization that involves giving the employee more tasks to perform

Job Enrichment A more comprehensive approach, **job enrichment,** assumes that increasing the range and variety of tasks is not sufficient by itself to improve employee motivation.[9] Thus job enrichment attempts to increase both the number of tasks a worker does and the control the worker has over the job. To accomplish this managers remove some controls from the job, delegate more authority to employees, and structure the work in complete, natural units. These changes increase the subordinates' sense of responsibility. Another part of job enrichment is to continually assign new and challenging tasks, thereby increasing the employees' opportunity for growth and advancement. AT&T was one of the first companies to try job enrichment. In one experiment, eight typists in a service unit prepared customer service orders. Faced with low output and high turnover, management determined that the typists felt little responsibility to clients and received little feedback. The unit was changed to create a typing team. Typists were matched with designated service representatives, the task was changed from ten specific steps to three more general steps, and job titles were upgraded. As a result, the frequency of order processing increased from 27 percent to 90 percent, the need for messenger service was eliminated, accuracy improved, and turnover became practically nil.[10] Other organizations that have tried job enrichment include Texas Instruments Incorporated, IBM, and General Foods Corporation. Problems have also been found with this approach, however. For example, careful analysis of jobs and their interdependencies before enrichment is needed but seldom performed, and managers rarely deal with employee preferences when enriching jobs.

● **job enrichment**
An alternative to job specialization that involves increasing both the number of tasks the worker does and the control the worker has over the job

Job Characteristics Approach The **job characteristics approach** is an alternative to job specialization that takes into account the work system and employee preferences.[11] As illustrated in Figure 10.1, the job characteristics approach suggests that jobs should be diagnosed and improved along five core dimensions:

1. *Skill variety:* the number of things a person does in a job
2. *Task identity:* the extent to which the worker does a complete or identifiable portion of the total job
3. *Task significance:* the perceived importance of the task

● **job characteristics approach**
An alternative to job specialization that suggests that jobs should be diagnosed and improved along five core dimensions, taking into account both the work system and employee preferences

The job characteristics approach to job design provides a viable alternative to job specialization. Five core job dimensions may lead to critical psychological states that, in turn, may enhance motivation, performance, satisfaction, absenteeism, and turnover.

F I G U R E 10.1 The Job Characteristics Approach

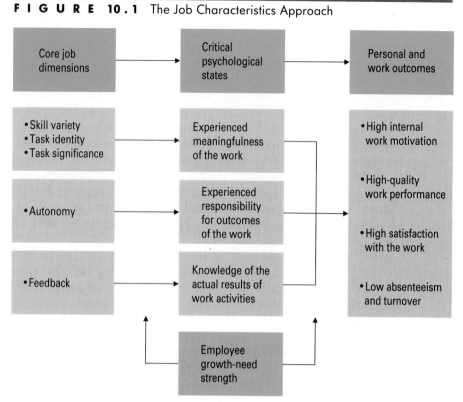

Source: J. R. Hackman and G. R. Oldham, "Motivation Through the Design of Work: Test of a Theory," *Organizational Behavior and Human Performance,* Vol. 16 (1976), pp. 250–279. Copyright © Academic Press, Inc. Reprinted by permission of Academic Press, and the authors.

4. *Autonomy:* the degree of control the worker has over how the work is performed

5. *Feedback:* the extent to which the worker knows how well the job is being performed

The higher a job rates on those dimensions, the more employees will experience various psychological states. Experiencing these states, in turn, presumably leads to high motivation, high-quality performance, high satisfaction, and low absenteeism and turnover. Finally, a variable called growth-need strength is presumed to affect how the model works for different people. People with a strong desire to grow, develop, and expand their capabilities (indicative of high growth-need strength) are expected to respond strongly to the presence or absence of the basic job characteristics; individuals with low growth-need strength are expected not to respond as strongly or consistently.

A large number of studies have been conducted to test the usefulness of the job characteristics approach. The Southwestern Division of Prudential Insurance, for example, used this approach in its claims division. Results included moderate declines in turnover and a small but measurable improvement in work quality. Other research findings have not supported this approach as strongly. Thus although the job characteristics approach is one of the most promising alternatives to job specialization, it is probably not the final answer.[12]

Work Teams Another alternative to job specialization is **work teams.** Under this arrangement, a group of workers is given responsibility for designing the work system to be used in performing an interrelated set of jobs. In the typical assembly-line system, the work flows from one worker to the next, and each worker has a specified job to perform. In a work team, however, the group itself decides how jobs will be allocated. For example, the work team assigns specific tasks to members, monitors and controls its own performance, and has autonomy over work scheduling. We discuss work teams more fully in Chapter 16.

● **work teams**
An alternative to job specialization that allows an entire group to design the work system it will use to perform an interrelated set of tasks

GROUPING JOBS: DEPARTMENTALIZATION

The second building block of organization structure is the grouping of jobs according to some logical arrangement. This process is called **departmentalization.** After establishing the basic rationale for departmentalization, we identify some common bases along which departments are created.

departmentalization
The process of grouping jobs according to some logical arrangement

Rationale for Departmentalization

When organizations are small, the owner-manager can personally oversee everyone who works there. As an organization grows, however, it becomes more and more difficult for the owner-manager to personally supervise all the employees. Consequently, new managerial positions are created to supervise the work of others. The assignment of employees to particular managers is not done randomly. Rather, jobs are grouped according to some plan. The logic embodied in such a plan is the basis for all departmentalization.[13]

Common Bases for Departmentalization

Figure 10.2 presents a partial organizational chart for Apex Computers, a hypothetical firm that manufactures and sells computers and software. The chart shows that Apex uses each of the four most common bases for departmentalization: product, function, customer, and location.

Product Departmentalization **Product departmentalization** involves grouping and arranging activities around products or product groups. Apex Computers has two product-based departments at the highest level of the firm. One is responsible for all activities associated with Apex's personal computer business, and the other handles the software business. Most large businesses adopt this form of departmentalization. The major advantages of product departmentalization are (1) all activities associated with one product or product group can be easily integrated and coordinated; (2) the speed and effectiveness of decision making are enhanced; and (3) the performance of individual products or product groups can be assessed relatively easily and objectively, thereby improving the accountability of departments for

● **product departmental- ization**
Grouping activities around products or product groups

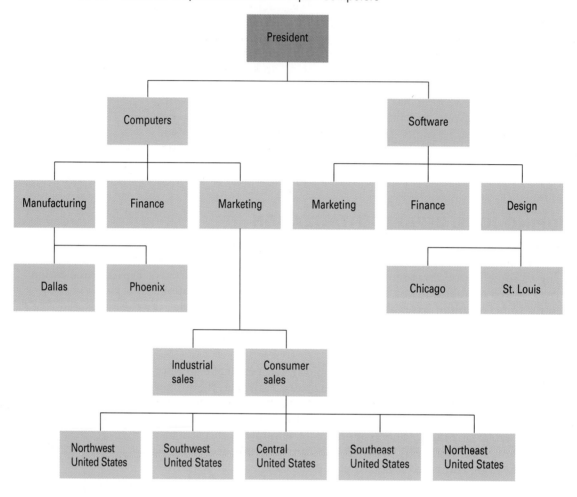

● **functional departmentalization**

Grouping jobs involving the same or similar activities

the results of their activities. Product departmentalization has two major disadvantages. First, managers in each department may focus on their own product or product group to the exclusion of the rest of the organization. Second, administrative costs rise because each department must have its own functional specialists for things like marketing research and financial analysis.

Functional Departmentalization   Another common base for departmentalization is by function.[14] **Functional departmentalization** groups jobs involving the same or similar activities. (The word *function* is used here to mean organizational functions such as finance and production, rather than the basic managerial functions such as planning or controlling.) The computer department at Apex has manufacturing, finance, and marketing departments. This approach is most common in small organizations. The main advantages are that (1) each department can be staffed by experts in that functional area; (2) supervision is facilitated because an individual manager needs to be familiar with only a relatively narrow set of skills; and (3) it is easier to coordinate activities inside of each department. On the other hand, as an organization begins to grow, several disadvantages of this approach may emerge. Decision making tends to become slower and more bureaucratic. Employees may also begin to concentrate too narrowly on their own units and lose sight of the total organizational system. Finally, accountability and performance become increasingly difficult to monitor. For example, it may not be possible to determine whether the failure of a new product is because of production deficiencies or a poor marketing campaign.

Customer Departmentalization Under **customer departmentalization,** the organization structures its activities to respond to and interact with specific customers or customer groups. The lending activities in most banks, for example, are usually tailored to meet the needs of different kinds of customers (i.e., business, consumer, mortgage, and agricultural loans). Figure 10.2 shows that the marketing branch of Apex's computer business has two distinct departments—industrial sales and consumer sales. The industrial sales department handles marketing activities aimed at business customers, whereas the consumer sales department is responsible for wholesaling computers to retail stores catering to individual purchasers. The basic advantage of this approach is that it allows the organization to use skilled specialists to deal with unique customers or customer groups. It takes one set of skills to evaluate a balance sheet and lend a business $50,000 for operating capital and a different set of skills to evaluate an individual's creditworthiness and lend $10,000 for a new car. An organization also requires, however, a fairly large administrative staff to integrate the activities of the various departments. In banks, for example, coordination is necessary to make sure the organization does not overcommit itself in any one area and to handle collections on delinquent accounts from a diverse set of customers.

● **customer departmentalization**
Grouping activities to respond to and interact with specific customers or customer groups

Location Departmentalization **Location departmentalization** groups jobs on the basis of defined geographic sites or areas. The defined sites or areas may range in size from a hemisphere to only a few blocks of a large city. The manufacturing branch of Apex's computer business has two location-based plants—one in Dallas and another in Phoenix. Similarly, the design division of its software unit has two labs, one in Chicago and the other in St. Louis. Apex's consumer sales group has five sales territories corresponding to different regions of the United States. Transportation companies, police departments (precincts represent geographic areas of a city), and the Federal Reserve Bank all use location departmentalization. Its primary advantage is that it enables the organization to respond easily to unique customer and environmental characteristics in the various regions. The organization may need a large administrative staff to keep track of units in scattered locations.

● **location departmentalization**
Grouping jobs on the basis of defined geographic sites or areas

W. R. Grace manufactures its cryovac multilayer films and bags that preserve items such as food in eighteen plants around the world. Location departmentalization enables the company to produce the protective material at locations close to where it will be needed, as this plant in São Paulo, Brazil does.

Other Forms of Departmentalization Although most organizations are departmentalized by function, product, location, or customer, other forms are occasionally used. Some organizations group certain activities by time. One of the machine shops of Baker-Hughes, Incorporated, in Houston, for example, operates on three shifts. Each shift has a superintendent who reports to the plant manager, and each shift has its own functional departments. Time is thus the framework for many organizational activities. Other organizations that use time as a basis for grouping jobs include some hospitals and many airlines. In other situations, departmentalization by sequence is appropriate. Many college students, for instance, must register in sequence: last names starting with A through E in line 1, F through L in line 2, for example. Other areas that may be organized in sequence include credit departments (specific employees run credit checks according to customer name) and insurance claims divisions (by policy number).

Other Considerations Two final points about job grouping remain to be made. First, departments are often called something entirely different—divisions, units, sections, and bureaus are all common synonyms. The higher we look in an organization, the more likely we are to find departments referred to as divisions. At General Motors, for example, EDS is a division. The underlying logic behind all the labels is the same, however: they represent groups of jobs that have been yoked together according to some unifying principle. Second, almost any organization is likely to use multiple bases of departmentalization, depending on level. Although Apex Computer is a hypothetical firm we created to explain departmentalization, it is quite similar to many real organizations in that it uses a variety of bases of departmentalization for different levels and different sets of activities. "Management in Practice" describes how Ryder System, Inc., has recently changed how it groups some of its jobs.

ESTABLISHING REPORTING RELATIONSHIPS

Another basic building block of organizations is the establishment of reporting relationships among positions. Suppose, for example, that the owner-manager of a small business has just hired two new employees, one to handle marketing and one to handle production. Will the marketing manager report to the production manager, will the production manager report to the marketing manager, or will each report directly to the owner-manager? These questions reflect the basic issues involved in establishing reporting relationships, or clarifying the chain of command and the span of management.

The Chain of Command

● **chain of command**
A clear and distinct line of authority among the positions in an organization

The chain of command concept is an old one, first popularized in the early years of this century. For example, early writers about the **chain of command** argued that clear and distinct lines of authority need to be established among all positions in the organization. The chain of command actually has two components. The first, called *unity of command,* suggests that each person within an organization should have a clear reporting relationship to one and only one boss (as we see in Chapter 11, newer models of organization design successfully violate this premise). The second, called the *scalar principle,* suggests that a clear and unbroken line of authority should extend from the lowest to the highest position in the organization. The popular saying "The buck stops here" is derived from this idea—someone in the organization must ultimately be responsible for every decision.

IMPROVING ACCOUNTABILITY AT RYDER

During the past few years it has become apparent that Ryder System's businesses—especially its consumer truck rentals—are disturbingly cyclical and dependent on an economy in which people and goods are constantly on the move. So in slow economic times, Ryder has had to look for new ways to increase revenues and cut costs.

Some of the steps Ryder has taken to become more profitable are familiar. Like many corporations, it had overdiversified, buying into businesses in which it had little or no expertise. So one of Ryder's first moves was to sell more than $430 million of assets, including aircraft-leasing and insurance ventures. To keep pace with rival U-Haul International, Inc.'s rate of updating its fleet, Ryder sold off some of its old fleet and put pressure on truck manufacturers to accept more old trucks as trade-ins.

Ryder's most important move, however, was probably its effort to divide its various businesses into separate units to improve accountability and pinpoint where the company was doing well and where it was losing money. Ryder's vehicle leasing and services division has always been its core business, but it includes three different businesses and three different sets of customers. The consumer truck unit provides small- and medium-sized trucks for people changing their residences or moving small businesses. Commercial truck rentals thrive when business is booming and companies need Ryder's trucks to handle sudden or unusual trucking needs. Its contract carriage operations, on the other hand, provide full-service leasing—truck, driver, and maintenance—to large companies like PepsiCo, Inc., and Kraft General Foods.

Separating the three businesses allowed Ryder to simplify operations and marketing and clarify accountability. Its late-1980s slump showed Ryder that its fortunes were tied to those of the general economy, but separating the three units has highlighted the relative stability of the contract carriage operations. While consumers and business both use fewer trucks during economic hard times, companies like Kraft and Pepsi still need to make their deliveries; the contract carriage operations have grown 10 percent per year since 1985. With layers of old bureaucracy stripped away, Ryder can now more easily see what the problems and opportunities are for its two more cyclical units. As a result, it is now more ready than ever to profit from the next economic expansion.

References: Martha Brannigan, "Ryder Chief Takes Hot Seat in Revamp," *The Wall Street Journal*, June 13, 1991, p. A4; Antonio N. Fins, "How Good A Mechanic Is Tony Burns?" *Business Week*, April 8, 1991, p. 71.

Narrow Versus Wide Spans

Establishing reporting relationships also involves determining how many people will report to each manager. This defines the **span of management** (sometimes called the *span of control*). For years managers and researchers sought to determine the optimal span of management. Should it be relatively narrow (with few subordinates per manager) or relatively wide (many subordinates)? One early writer, A. V. Graicunas, went so far as to quantify problems with the span of management.[15] Graicunas noted that a manager has three kinds of interactions with and among subordinates: direct (the manager's one-to-one relationship with each subordinate), cross (among the subordinates themselves), and group (between groups of subordinates). The number of possible interactions of all types between a manager and subordinates can be determined by the following formula:

$$I = N\left(\frac{2^N}{2} + N - 1\right)$$

● **span of management**
The number of people who report to a particular manager

where I is the total number of interactions with and among subordinates and N is the number of subordinates.

If a manager has only two subordinates, six potential interactions exist. If the number of subordinates increases to three, the possible interactions total eighteen. With five subordinates there are one hundred possible interactions. Although Graicunas offers no prescription for what N should be, his ideas demonstrate how complex the relationships can become when more subordinates are added. The key point is that each additional subordinate adds more complexity than the previous one did. Going from nine to ten subordinates is very different than going from three to four. Another early writer, Ralph C. Davis, described two kinds of spans: an operative span for lower-level managers and an executive span for middle and top managers. He argued that operative spans could approach thirty subordinates, whereas executive spans should be limited to between three and nine (depending on the nature of the managers' jobs, the growth rate of the company, and similar factors). Lyndall F. Urwick suggested that an executive span should never exceed six subordinates, and General Ian Hamilton reached the same conclusion.[16] Today we recognize that the span of management is a crucial factor in structuring organizations but there are no universal, cut-and-dried prescriptions for an ideal or optimal span.[17] Later we summarize some important variables that influence the appropriate span of management in particular situations. First, however, we describe how the span of management affects the overall structure of an organization.

Tall Versus Flat Organizations

Imagine an organization with thirty-one managers and a narrow span of management. As shown in Figure 10.3, the result is a relatively tall organization with five layers of management. With a somewhat wider span of

Industrial contractor Barbara Grogan firmly believes in the flat organization. She credits her success—building a $6 million company in ten years—to high levels of employee productivity, which she encourages with a flat hierarchy and systems to ensure that employees have access to all information. To that end, her new 7,000 square foot office building has no interior doors.

FIGURE 10.3 Tall Versus Flat Organizations

Tall organization

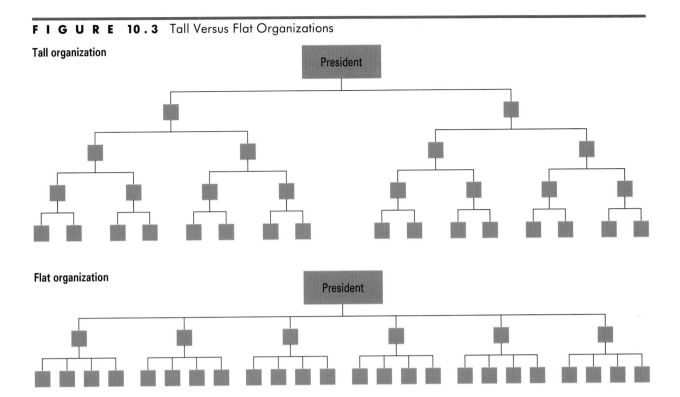

Flat organization

control, however, the flat organization shown in Figure 10.3 emerges. This configuration has only three layers of management.

What difference does it make whether the organization is tall or flat? One early study at Sears, Roebuck and Co. found that a flat structure led to higher levels of employee morale and productivity.[18] It has also been argued that a tall structure is more expensive (because of the larger number of managers involved) and that it fosters more communication problems (because of the increased number of people through whom information must pass). On the other hand, a wide span of management in a flat organization may result in a manager's having more administrative responsibility (because there are fewer managers) and more supervisory responsibility (because more subordinates report to each manager). If these additional responsibilities become excessive, the flat organization may suffer.[19]

Many experts agree that businesses can usually function effectively with fewer layers of organization than they currently have. The Franklin Mint, for example, recently reduced its number of management layers from six to four. At the same time, CEO Stewart Resnick increased his span of management from six to twelve. One reason for this trend is that improved organizational communication networks allow managers to stay in touch with a larger number of subordinates than was possible even just a few years ago.[20] "The Global View" describes how Toyota Motor Corp. has followed this trend.

Wide spans of management result in flat organizations, which may lead to increased employee morale and productivity as well as increased managerial responsibility. Many organizations, including IBM and General Electric, today are moving toward flat structures to improve communication and flexibility.

Determining the Appropriate Span

How do managers determine the appropriate span for their unique situations? Although there is no perfect formula, researchers have identified a

TABLE 10.1 Factors Influencing the Span of Management

1. Competence of supervisor and subordinates (the greater the competence, the wider the potential span)

2. Physical dispersion of subordinates (the greater the dispersion, the narrower the potential span)

3. Extent of nonsupervisory work in manager's job (the more nonsupervisory work, the narrower the potential span)

4. Degree of required interaction (the more required interaction, the narrower the potential span)

5. Extent of standardized procedures (the more procedures, the wider the potential span)

6. Similarity of tasks being supervised (the more similar the tasks, the wider the potential span)

7. Frequency of new problems (the higher the frequency, the narrower the potential span)

8. Preferences of supervisors and subordinates

set of factors that influence the span for a particular circumstance.[21] Some of these factors are listed in Table 10.1. For example, if the manager and subordinates are competent and well trained, a wider span may be effective. Physical dispersion is also important. The more widely subordinates are scattered, the narrower the span should be. On the other hand, if all the subordinates are in one location, the span can be somewhat wider. The amount of nonsupervisory work expected of the manager is also important. Some managers, especially at the lower levels of an organization, spend most or all of their time supervising people. Other managers spend a lot of time doing paperwork, planning, and engaging in other managerial activities. Thus these managers may need a narrower span.

Some job situations also require a great deal of interaction between supervisor and subordinates. In general, the more interaction that is required, the narrower the span should be. Similarly, if there is a fairly comprehensive set of standard procedures, a relatively wide span is possible. If only a few standard procedures exist, however, the supervisor usually has a large role in overseeing day-to-day activities and may find a narrow span more efficient. Task similarity is also important. If most of the jobs being supervised are similar, a supervisor can handle a wide span. When each employee is performing a different task, much of the supervisor's time is spent on individual supervision. Likewise, if new problems that require supervisory assistance arise frequently, a narrow span may be called for. If new problems are relatively rare, though, a wide span can be established. Finally, the preferences of both supervisor and subordinates may affect the optimal span. Some managers prefer to spend little time actively supervising their employees, and many employees prefer to be self-directed. A wide span may be possible in these situations.[22]

AVOIDING THE "LARGE MAN" SYNDROME AT TOYOTA

Toyota Motor Corp. is the leading Japanese automaker and therefore the object of much scrutiny by Americans interested in the Japanese industrial miracle. Toyota's secret has been variously identified as its philosophy of *keizan* (continuous improvement), or its creation of *kanban* (just-in-time production). But while its philosophy and production techiques no doubt contribute to Toyota's tremendous growth, another of its secrets lies in its ability to avoid becoming overwhelmed by the huge, sluggish managerial hierarchy that has plagued its U.S. rivals.

Shoichiro Toyoda, the company's current president and grandson of its founder, recognizes the dangers of becoming too large. He quotes a company saying: "A large man has difficulty exercising his wits fully."* Constantly challenged by smaller, more innovative Honda Motor Co., Ltd., and Nissan Motor Co. Ltd., Toyota keeps rethinking its organizational structure even when enjoying unrivaled success. In 1989, worried that top management was becoming isolated from production workers, Toyota eliminated two layers of middle management, giving some of the displaced managers hands-on work. At the same time, it changed its personnel evaluation systems to focus more on performance and less on seniority and began encouraging workers to address their managers with less formal terms. Only five layers now separate workers from top managers, making teamwork essential.

Typical of the way Toyota uses teams and nontraditional organizational structures is its recent creation of new-model teams. Since 1990, every new Toyota model has been developed by a chief engineer with powers and responsibilities unheard-of in Detroit. U.S. new-model bosses have limited responsibilities, work under specific instructions from product planning and marketing departments, and seldom contact dealers and customers directly. Toyota's chief engineers and their teams, by contrast, determine everything from the dimensions of the car to how it will be made and even who the suppliers will be. They talk directly with car buyers and interview dealers and owners of present models to help them plan new ones. Because the new-model teams have production and marketing issues in mind from the start, their models need fewer design changes, they can be built more efficiently, and the whole process of new-model development can take a year less than it takes U.S. companies. And Toyota has accomplished all this not with new machines and technologies but simply by reorganizing the people it already had.

* Quoted in Alex Taylor, III, "Why Toyota Keeps Getting Better and Better and Better," *Fortune*, November 19, 1990, p. 68.

References: Micheline Maynard, "Overtaking the Big Three on Their Turf," *USA Today*, September 11, 1990, pp. 1B–2B; Alex Taylor III, "Why Toyota Keeps Getting Better and Better and Better," *Fortune*, November 19, 1990, pp. 66+; Joseph B. White, "Toyota Wants More Managers Out on the Line," *The Wall Street Journal*, August 2, 1989, p. A8.

In some organizational settings, other factors may influence the optimal span of management. The relative importance of each factor also varies in different settings. It is unlikely that all eight factors will suggest the same span; some may suggest a wide span, and others may indicate a need for a narrow span. Managers must therefore assess the relative weight of each factor or set of factors when deciding what the optimal span of management is for their organization.

DISTRIBUTING AUTHORITY

authority
Power that has been legitimized by the organization

Another important building block in structuring organizations is the determination of how authority is to be distributed among positions. **Authority** is power that has been legitimized by the organization.[23] Distributing authority is another normal outgrowth of increasing organizational size. For example, when an owner-manager hires a sales representative to market his products, he needs to give the new employee appropriate authority to make decisions about delivery dates, discounts, and so forth. If every decision requires the approval of the owner-manager, he is no better off than he was before he hired the sales representative. The power given to the sales representative to make certain kinds of decisions, then, establishes a pattern of authority—there are some decisions that the sales representative can make alone, some that are to be made in consultation with others, and some on which the sales representative must defer to the boss. Two specific issues that managers must address when distributing authority are delegation and decentralization.

The Delegation Process

● **delegation**
The process by which a manager assigns a portion of his or her total work load to others

Delegation is the establishment of a pattern of authority between a superior and one or more subordinates. Specifically, **delegation** is the process by which a manager assigns a portion of his or her total workload to others.[24]

Reasons for Delegation   The primary reason for delegation is to enable the manager to get more work done. Subordinates help ease the manager's burden by doing major portions of the organization's work. In some instances, a subordinate may have more expertise in addressing a particular problem than the manager does. For example, the subordinate may have had special training in developing information systems or may be more familiar with a particular product line or geographic area. Delegation also helps subordinates develop skills. By participating in decision making and problem solving, subordinates learn more about overall operations and improve their managerial skills.

Steps in the Delegation Process   In theory, as shown in Figure 10.4, the delegation process involves three steps. First, the manager assigns responsibility, or gives the subordinate a job to do. The assignment of responsibility might range from telling a subordinate to prepare a report to placing the person in charge of a task force. Along with the assignment, the person is also given the authority to do the job. The manager may give the subordinate the power to requisition needed information from confidential files or to direct a group of other workers. Finally, the manager establishes

A manager must learn to successfully delegate responsibility to subordinates. Improving communication skills can help managers do this. A manager must not be reluctant to delegate, nor must he or she fear that the subordinate will do the job so well that the manager's advancement is threatened.

F I G U R E   10.4 Steps in the Delegation Process

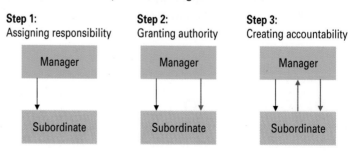

Step 1:
Assigning responsibility

Step 2:
Granting authority

Step 3:
Creating accountability

accountability by the subordinate—that is, the subordinate accepts an obligation to carry out the task assigned by the manager.

These three steps do not occur mechanically, however. Indeed, when a manager and a subordinate have developed a good working relationship, the major parts of the process may be implied rather than stated. The manager may simply mention that a particular job must be done. A perceptive subordinate may realize that the manager is actually assigning the job to her. From past experience with the boss, she may also know, without being told, that she has the necessary authority to do the job and that she is accountable to the boss for finishing the job as "agreed."

Problems in Delegation   Unfortunately, problems often arise in the delegation process. For example, a manager may be reluctant to delegate. Some managers are so disorganized that they are unable to plan work in advance and, as a result, cannot delegate appropriately. Some managers worry that subordinates will do too well and pose a threat to their own advancement. And finally, managers may not trust the subordinate to do the job well. Similarly, some subordinates are reluctant to accept delegation. They may be afraid that failure will result in a reprimand. They may also perceive that there are no rewards for accepting additional responsibility. Or they may simply prefer to avoid risk and, therefore, want the boss to take all responsibility.

Although there are no quick fixes for these problems, improving communication can alleviate them somewhat. Subordinates must understand their own responsibility, authority, and accountability, and the manager must recognize the value of effective delegation. With the passage of time, subordinates should develop to the point where they can make substantial contributions to the organization. At the same time, managers should recognize that a subordinate's satisfactory performance is not a threat to their own career but an accomplishment by both the subordinate who did the job and the manager who trained the subordinate and was astute enough to entrust the subordinate with the project. Ultimate responsibility for the outcome, however, resides with the manager.

Decentralization and Centralization

Just as authority can be delegated from one individual to another, organizations also develop patterns of authority across a wide variety of positions and departments. **Decentralization** is the process of systematically delegating power and authority throughout the organization to middle and lower-level managers. Decentralization is actually one end of a continuum anchored at the other end by **centralization,** the process of systematically retaining power and authority in the hands of higher-level managers. Hence, a decentralized organization is one in which decision-making power and authority are delegated as far down the chain of command as possible. Conversely, in a centralized organization, decision-making power and authority are retained at the higher levels of management. When H. Ross Perot ran EDS he practiced centralization; his successor uses decentralization. No organization is ever completely decentralized or completely centralized; some firms position themselves toward one end of the continuum; some lean the other way.[25]

● **decentralization**
The process of systematically delegating power and authority throughout the organization to middle and lower-level managers

● **centralization**
The process of systematically retaining power and authority in the hands of higher-level managers

Decentralization is the delegation of power and authority to middle- and lower-level managers, and Coca-Cola Enterprises' new decentralized structure enables local managers who understand their market dynamics to make decisions. Coca-Cola is finding that benefits of decentralization include lower costs and the ability to better respond to customers.

What factors determine an organization's position on the decentralization-centralization continuum? One common determinant is the organization's external environment. Usually, the greater the complexity and uncertainty of the environment, the greater is the tendency to decentralize. Another crucial factor is the history of the organization. Firms have a tendency to do what they have done in the past, so there is likely to be some relationship between what an organization did in its early history and what it chooses to do today in terms of centralization or decentralization. The nature of the decisions being made is also considered. The costlier and riskier the decision, the more pressure there is to centralize. Organizations also consider the abilities of lower-level managers. If lower-level managers do not have the ability to make high-quality decisions, there is likely to be a high level of centralization. If lower-level managers are well qualified, top management can take advantage of their talents by decentralizing; in fact, if top management doesn't, talented lower-level managers may leave the organization.

There is no set of clear-cut guidelines for a manager to use in determining whether to centralize or decentralize. Many successful organizations such as Sears and General Electric Co. are quite decentralized. Equally successful firms such as McDonald's Corp. and K mart Corp. have tended to remain centralized. IBM has recently undergone a transformation from using a highly centralized approach to a much more decentralized approach to managing its operations. A great deal of decision-making authority was passed from the hands of a select group of top executives down to six product and marketing groups. The reason for the move was to speed the company's ability to make decisions, introduce new products, and respond to customers.[26] For years, most Japanese firms have been highly centralized. Recently, though, many leading Japanese firms have moved toward decentralization.[27]

COORDINATING ACTIVITIES

A fifth major building block of organization structure is coordination. As discussed earlier, job specialization and departmentalization involve breaking jobs down into small units and then combining those jobs into departments. Once this has been accomplished, the activities of the departments must be linked—systems must be put into place to keep the activities of each department focused on the attainment of organizational goals. This is accomplished by **coordination**—the process of linking the activities of the various departments of the organization.

The Need for Coordination

The primary reason for coordination is that departments and work groups are interdependent—they depend on each other for information and resources to perform their respective activities. The greater the interdependence between departments, the more coordination the organization requires if departments are to be able to perform effectively. There are three major forms of interdependence: pooled, sequential, and reciprocal.[28]

Pooled interdependence represents the lowest level of interdependence. Units with pooled interdependence operate with little interaction—the output of the units is pooled at the organizational level. The Gap, Inc., clothing stores operate with pooled interdependence. Each is considered a department by the parent corporation. Each has its own operating budget, staff, and so forth. The profits or losses from each store are "added together" at the organizational level. The stores are interdependent to the extent that the final success or failure of one store affects the others, but they do not generally interact on a day-to-day basis.

In *sequential interdependence,* the output of one unit becomes the input for another in a sequential fashion. This creates a moderate level of interdependence. At Nissan Motor Co. Ltd., for example, one plant assembles engines and then ships them to a final assembly site at another plant where the cars are completed. The plants are interdependent in that the final assembly plant must have the engines from engine assembly before it can perform its primary function of producing finished automobiles. But the level of interdependence is generally one-way—the engine plant is not necessarily dependent on the final assembly plant.

Reciprocal interdependence exists when activities flow both ways between units. This form is clearly the most complex. Within a Marriott Corporation hotel, for example, the reservations department, front-desk check-in, and housekeeping are all reciprocally interdependent. Reservations has to provide front-desk employees with information about how many guests to expect each day, and housekeeping needs to know which rooms require priority cleaning. If any of the three units does not do its job properly, the others will all be affected.

Structural Coordination Techniques

Given the obvious coordination requirements that characterize most organizations, it follows that many techniques for achieving coordination have been developed. Some of the most useful devices for maintaining coordination among interdependent units are the managerial hierarchy, rules and procedures, liaison roles, task forces, and integrating departments.[29]

Managerial Hierarchy Organizations that use the hierarchy to achieve coordination place one manager in charge of interdependent departments or units. In K mart's distribution centers, major activities include receiving and unloading bulk shipments from railroad cars and loading other shipments onto trucks for distribution to retail outlets. The two groups (receiving and shipping) are interdependent in that they share the loading docks and some equipment. To ensure coordination and to minimize conflict, one manager is in charge of the whole operation.

Rules and Procedures Routine coordination activities can be handled via rules and standard procedures. In K mart's distribution centers, an outgoing truck shipment has priority over an incoming rail shipment. Thus when trucks are to be loaded, the shipping unit is given access to all of the center's auxiliary forklifts. This priority is specifically stated in a rule. But, as useful as rules and procedures often are in routine situations, they are not particularly effective when coordination problems are complex or unusual.

Liaison Role The liaison role of management was introduced in Chapter 1. As a device for coordination, a manager in a liaison role coordinates interdependent units by acting as a common point of contact. This individual may not have any formal authority over the groups but instead simply facilitates the flow of information between units. Two engineering groups working on component systems for a large project might interact through a liaison. The liaison maintains familiarity with each group as well as with the overall project. She can answer questions and otherwise serve to integrate the activities of all the groups.

Task Force A task force may be created when the need for coordination is acute. When interdependence is complex and several units are involved, a single liaison person may not be sufficient. Instead, a task force might be assembled by drawing one representative from each group. The coordination function is thus spread across several individuals, each of whom has special information about one of the groups involved. When the project is completed, task force members return to their original positions. For example, a college overhauling its degree requirements might establish a task force made up of representatives from each department affected by the change. Each person retains her or his regular departmental affiliation and duties but also serves on the special task force. After the new requirements are agreed on, the task force is dissolved.

Integrating Department Integrating departments are occasionally used for coordination. These are somewhat similar to task forces but are established on a more permanent basis. An integrating department generally has some permanent members as well as members who are assigned temporarily from units that are particularly in need of coordination. One study found that successful firms in the plastics industry, which is characterized by complex and dynamic environments, used integrating departments to maintain internal integration and coordination.[30] An integrating department usually has more authority than a task force and may even be given some budgetary control by the organization.

In general, the greater the degree of interdependence, the more attention the organization must devote to coordination. When interdependence is of a pooled or simple sequential nature, the managerial hierarchy or rules and procedures are often sufficient. When more complex forms of sequential or simpler forms of reciprocal interdependence exist, liaisons or task forces may be more useful. When reciprocal interdependence is complex, task forces or integrating departments are needed. Of course, the manager must also rely on her or his own experience and insights when choosing coordination techniques for the organization.

DIFFERENTIATING BETWEEN POSITIONS

The last building block of organization structure that we discuss is differentiating between line and staff positions in the organization. A **line position** is a position in the direct chain of command that is responsible for the achievement of an organization's goals. Line positions include production manager, sales manager, and director of international operations. A **staff position** is intended to provide expertise, advice, and support for line positions. Managers in the legal and market research departments would usually be considered to hold staff positions.

● **line position**
A position in the direct chain of command that is responsible for the achievement of an organization's goals

● **staff position**
Intended to provide expertise, advice, and support for line positions

Differences Between Line and Staff

The most obvious difference between line and staff is purpose—line managers work directly toward organizational goals, whereas staff managers advise and assist. But other distinctions exist as well. One very important difference is authority. Line authority is generally thought of as the formal or legitimate authority created by the organizational hierarchy. Staff authority is less concrete and may take a variety of forms. One form is the authority to advise. In this instance, the line manager can choose whether to seek or to avoid input from the staff; and even when advice is sought, the manager might still choose to ignore it.

Compulsory advice is another form of staff authority: the line manager must listen to the advice but can choose to heed it or ignore it. For example, the CEO is expected to listen to the advice of his financial staff before approving a merger, but may then follow his own beliefs when making the decision. Perhaps the most important form of staff authority is called functional authority—formal or legitimate authority over activities related to the staff member's specialty. For example, a human resources staff manager may have functional authority when there is a question of discrimination in hiring. Conferring functional authority is probably the most effective way to use staff positions because it allows the organization to take advantage of specialized expertise while also maintaining a chain of command.

Administrative Intensity

Organizations sometimes attempt to balance their emphasis on line versus staff positions in terms of administrative intensity. **Administrative intensity** is the degree to which managerial positions are concentrated in staff positions. An organization with a high administrative intensity is one with many staff positions relative to the number of line positions; low administrative intensity reflects relatively more line positions. Although staff positions are important in many different areas, such as law, human resources, and finance, there is a tendency for them to proliferate unnecessarily. All else equal, organizations would like to spend most of their human resources dollars on line managers because by definition they are contributing to the organization's basic goals. A surplus of staff positions represents a drain on an organization's cash and an inefficient use of resources.

Many organizations have taken steps over the past few years to reduce their administrative intensity by eliminating staff positions. CBS has cut hundreds of staff positions at its New York headquarters, and IBM has cut its corporate staff work force from 7,000 to 2,300. Burlington Northern Inc. generates almost $7 billion in annual sales and manages a work force of 43,000 with a corporate staff of only 77 managers![31]

SUMMARY OF KEY POINTS

Organizations are made up of a series of building blocks. The most common of these involve designing jobs, grouping jobs, establishing reporting relationships, distributing authority, coordinating activities, and differentiating between positions.

Job design is the determination of an individual's work-related responsibilities. The most common form is job specialization. Because of various drawbacks to job specialization, managers have experimented with job rotation, job enlargement, job enrichment, the job characteristics approach, and work teams as alternatives.

After jobs are designed, they are grouped into departments. The most common bases for departmentalization are product, function, customer, and location. Each has its advantages and disadvantages. Larger organizations employ multiple bases of departmentalization at different levels.

Establishing reporting relationships starts with the chain of command. The span of management partially dictates whether the organization is relatively tall or flat. In recent years there has been a trend toward flatter organizations. Several situational factors influence the ideal span.

Distributing authority starts with delegation. Delegation is the process by which the manager assigns a portion of his or her total workload to others. Systematic delegation throughout the organization is decentralization. Centralization involves keeping power and authority at the top of the organization. Several factors influence the appropriate degree of decentralization.

Coordination is the process of linking the activities of the various departments of the organization. Pooled, sequential, or reciprocal interdependence among departments is a primary reason for coordination. Managers can draw on several techniques to help achieve coordination.

A line position is a position in the direct chain of command that is responsible for the achievement of an organization's goals. In contrast, a staff position provides expertise, advice, and support for line positions. Administrative intensity is the degree to which managerial positions are concentrated in staff positions.

DISCUSSION QUESTIONS

Questions for Review

1. What is job specialization? What are its advantages and disadvantages?

2. What is meant by departmentalization? Why and how is departmentalization carried out?

3. In what general ways may organizations be shaped? What implications does each of these ways have with regard to the distribution of authority within the organization?

4. How are positions differentiated in organizations? What are the advantages and disadvantages of such differentiation?

Questions for Analysis

5. It is easy to see how specialization can be utilized in manufacturing organizations. How can it be used by other types of organizations such as hospitals, churches, schools, and restaurants? Should those organizations use specialization? Why or why not?

6. Try to develop a different way to departmentalize your college or university, a local fast-food restaurant, a manufacturing firm, or some other organization. What might be the advantages of your form of organization?

7. Which type of position (line, staff, administrative) is most important to an organization? Why? Could an organization function without any of them? Why or why not?

Questions for Application

8. Go to the library and locate organization charts for ten different organizations. Look for similarities and differences among them and try to account for what you find.

9. Contact two very different local organizations (retailing firm, manufacturing firm, church, civic club, etc.), and interview top managers to develop organizational charts for each organization. How do you account for the similarities and differences that you find?

10. How many people does the head of your academic department supervise? The dean of your college? The president of your university or college? Why do different spans of management exist among these officials? How might you find out if the spans are appropriate in size?

REORGANIZING FOR PROFIT IN A SLOW-GROWTH INDUSTRY

When Alcoa (Aluminum Company of America) hired Paul O'Neill as its new CEO in 1987, the company knew it needed revitalization—a new direction or at least a new way to make a profit. For more than a century, aluminum had been Alcoa's only major business, and it still accounts for 85 percent of its revenues. The world's largest aluminum producer, Alcoa makes about 17 percent of the world's aluminum and easily outpaces its U.S. rivals. But just as aluminum once replaced steel in many applications, primarily because it is lighter, aluminum is now being replaced by plastics and ceramics.

The first outsider ever to run the century-old company, O'Neill quickly broke with his predecessor, curtailed Alcoa's moves away from aluminum, and set about developing ways to make Alcoa's business less dependent on the cycles of aluminum profits. Toward that end, Alcoa has entered into joint ventures with partners in Europe and Asia, where aluminum use is growing more steadily.

O'Neill shocked the company when he declared that the top item on his agenda was safety. He was determined to lower the company's already low injury rate to zero. He knew that in the process of investigating why accidents happen, the company would discover ways to improve its work processes and the quality of its products.

Most importantly, O'Neill is trying to transform Alcoa from a company focused on simply selling more aluminum to a loose collection of consumer and industrial aluminum businesses. To do so, he has given twenty-five of Alcoa's unit managers a high degree of authority and accountability in running their own businesses. As Alcoa's Australian unit manager put it, ''We felt liberated.'' Alcoa has long pursued a policy of continuous improvement, but O'Neill believes that Alcoa's managers can achieve more dramatic improvements if they are given more power. So he has radically increased line managers' spending authority. Although he has eliminated some positions at headquarters and in general decentralized Alcoa, he is also demanding that the business units work together better and share more information than they have in the past. The unit managers now report directly to O'Neill and his three-person chairman's council.

Many people have been skeptical of O'Neill's changes, but in his first four years as CEO, Alcoa's return on equity averaged 15 percent, 50 percent greater than in the previous decade. He has challenged all the newly freed unit managers to close by 80 percent the gap between their units and the world leaders within two years. If they can do that, Alcoa may be able to reach O'Neill's own goal of increasing operating profits by $1 billion by 1995.

Discussion Questions

1. Describe one of the structural changes O'Neill has made to Alcoa since he came on board. Were these changes successful for Alcoa? Why or why not?

2. What are the possible drawbacks of reorganizing Alcoa so that the twenty-five unit managers report directly to O'Neill?

E 3. Although Alcoa has the lowest injury rate in the industry, CEO Paul O'Neill announced shortly after arriving that safety was a high priority on his list of improvements. What is the rationale behind this thinking?

References: Michael Schroeder, ''The Recasting of Alcoa,'' *Business Week*, September 9, 1991, pp. 62–64; Thomas Stewart, ''A New Way To Wake Up A Giant,'' *Fortune*, October 22, 1990, pp. 90–103.

CREATING A GLOBAL STRUCTURE AT ICI

*I*mperial Chemical Industries, a manufacturer of chemicals, pharmaceuticals, film, and plastics, used to be known as "Britain's largest industrial company." Nowadays, the only part of the company that seems clearly British is the "Imperial" in its name.

ICI began the metamorphosis into a global company back in 1936, when it started investing in pharmaceutical research and development. Because of its difficulty in making its pharmaceuticals division profitable, the company soon learned a lesson that some of its competitors would not learn until the 1980s: the more it costs to develop a product, the more important it is to have a global market for that product. Developing a drug from the first research to the market may now take more than a decade and cost more than $250 million. No company wants to pay such costs to bring out a drug in one country and then go through the process over again when trying to introduce the drug into another market.

Expanding on this early lesson, ICI gradually built a network of business, manufacturing, and research and development units around the globe. An Australian now runs ICI Americas from Wilmington, Delaware. The formerly all-British board of directors now boasts members from Canada, the United States, Japan, and Germany, and more than one-third of the company's top 180 people are non-British.

ICI's most important changes occurred during a major restructuring in the 1980s. Recognizing that it was employing many more workers than other top chemical companies, ICI laid off one-third of its British work force. Just as important, the company clarified the historically blurry definitions of managerial responsibility and authority.

Before the restructuring, different groups battled to win development money from ICI headquarters. Now a single person heads the company's worldwide efforts to make a particular product successful. Managers who had previously focused their attention solely on maximum production efficiency are now aiming to exploit new markets and create new products. Whole layers of middle managers were eliminated to allow top managers to communicate more directly with operations.

This new focus on products means that the company has dedicated the majority of its resources to support its strongest products and has moved many of its plants and laboratories to the center of the product's market. Four of the nine new business units that the company began in 1983 are outside Great Britain.

These structural changes have allowed ICI to speed up product development and to cut the time it takes to introduce a product to new markets. In the past, it could take five or six years for a drug that succeeded in Great Britain to be introduced in the United States. ICI has cut that period to one or two years, and it hopes eventually to introduce drugs simultaneously around the world.

Discussion Questions

1. Why does product departmentalization make sense for a global company?

2. What new skills would an ICI product manager have to acquire to handle the demands of the new structure?

E **3.** Given the uneven distribution of wealth in countries around the world, can you imagine the dilemmas a company like ICI might face in manufacturing drugs for the world market?

References: Stephanie Cooke, "ICI Wants to Be a Household Word in the U.S.," *Business Week,* September 1, 1986, p. 40; Geoffrey Foster, "The Legacy of Harvey-Jones," *Management Today*, January 1987, pp. 35–86; Jeremy Main, "How to Go Global —And Why," *Fortune*, August 28, 1989, pp. 70–76.

Managing Organization Design

OBJECTIVES

After studying this chapter, you should be able to:

● *Describe the basic nature of organization design.*

● *Identify and explain the two basic universal perspectives on organization design.*

● *Identify and explain several situational influences on organization design.*

● *Discuss how an organization's strategy and its design are interrelated.*

● *Describe the basic forms of organization design that characterize many organizations.*

● *Describe emerging issues in organization design.*

OUTLINE

The Nature of Organization Design

Universal Perspectives on Organization Design
    Bureaucratic Model
    Behavioral Model

Situational Influences on Organization Design
    Core Technology
    Environment
    Organizational Size
    Organizational Life Cycle

Strategy and Organization Design
    Corporate Strategy
    Business Strategy
    Functional Strategy

Basic Forms of Organization Design
    Functional (U-Form) Design
    Conglomerate (H-Form) Design
    Divisional (M-Form) Design
    Matrix Design
    Hybrid Designs

Emerging Issues in Organization Design
    Managing Information
    Global Organizations
    Adapting Organizations

FOR THE PAST several years, The Limited, Inc. has been one of the fastest-growing women's specialty apparel chains in the United States. The keys to its success have been staying in touch with consumer trends and tastes, manufacturing and getting new products into stores quickly, and maintaining tight controls over inventory. The Limited's total sales amounted to more than $5 billion in 1991.

The retail giant is organized around four large divisions. Its cornerstone is The Limited chain, which accounts for almost one-third of the company's total sales. The Limited Express is a chain of smaller stores catering to young women. The Lerner division (Lerner Stores Corp.) focuses on less expensive fashions geared to low-to-middle-income shoppers. Victoria's Secret specializes in lingerie. In addition, The Limited, Inc. owns a number of smaller chains, like Abercrombie & Fitch and Henri Bendel, scattered around the country.

Each of the company's divisions acts as an autonomous entity, taking care of activities such as planning its own stores and developing its own marketing campaigns. Each has its own management team, its own buyers, and its own identity. Not surprisingly, however, this arrangement is occasionally the source of internal conflict and competition. It is not uncommon, for example, for a Limited and Limited Express store in the same shopping mall to carry some of the same products for different prices. Although other chains, such as The Gap, Inc., have started making inroads on The Limited, Inc.'s market share, executives still believe that their formula for success works and have no plans to change it.[1] ●

anagers at The Limited, Inc. have successfully created a large, national retail chain. One of the key ingredients in managing any business is the arrangement of its various pieces into an effective overall design. The Limited, Inc.'s managers have chosen a divisional approach. The divisional design, however, is but one of several different designs they could have chosen to structure the company.

In Chapter 10, we identified the building blocks that go into creating an organization. In this chapter, we explore how the building blocks can be put together to create an overall design for the organization. We first discuss the nature of organization design. We then describe early approaches aimed at identifying universal models of organization design. Situational factors, such as technology, environment, size, and life cycle, are then introduced. Next we discuss the relationship between an organization's strategy and its structure. Basic forms of organization design are described next. We conclude by presenting three related issues in organization design.

THE NATURE OF ORGANIZATION DESIGN

What is organization design? In Chapter 10, we noted that job specialization and span of management are among the common building blocks of organization structure. We also described how the appropriate degree of specialization can vary, as can the appropriate span of management. Not really addressed, however, were questions of how specialization and span might be related to one another. For example, should a high level of specialization be matched with a certain span? And will different combinations of each work best with different bases of departmentalization? These and related issues are associated with questions of organization design.[2]

● **organization design**
The overall pattern of structural components and arrangements used to manage the total organization

Organization design is the overall pattern of structural components and arrangements used to manage the total organization. Thus organization design is a means to implement strategies and plans to achieve organizational goals. As we discuss organization design, keep in mind two important points. First, organizations are not designed and then left intact. Most organizations change constantly as a result of factors such as situations and people. (The processes of organization change are discussed in Chapter 12.) Second, organization design for large organizations is complex and has so many nuances and variations that descriptions of them must be considerably simplified to be described in basic terms.

UNIVERSAL PERSPECTIVES ON ORGANIZATION DESIGN

In Chapter 2, we made the distinction between contingency and universal approaches to solving management problems. (Remember that universal perspectives try to identify the "one best way" to manage organizations, and contingency perspectives suggest that appropriate managerial behavior in a given situation depends on, or is contingent on, unique elements in that situation.)[3] The foundation of what we know today about organization design comes from early universal perspectives: the bureaucratic model and the behavioral model.

Bureaucratic Model

In Chapter 2, we also noted that Max Weber, an influential German sociologist, was a pioneer of classical organization theory. At the core of Weber's writings was the bureaucratic model of organizations.[4] The Weberian perspective suggests that a **bureaucracy** is a model of organization design based on a legitimate and formal system of authority. Many people associate bureaucracy with "red tape," rigidity, and passing the buck. For example, how many times have you heard people refer disparagingly to "the federal bureaucracy"? And many U.S. managers believe that bureaucracy in the Japanese government is a major impediment to U.S. firms' ability to do business there.

Weber viewed the bureaucratic form of organization as logical, rational, and efficient. He offered the model as a framework to which all organizations should aspire; the "one best way" of doing things. According to Weber, the ideal bureaucracy exhibits five basic characteristics:

1. The organization should adopt a distinct division of labor, and each position should be filled by an expert.

2. The organization should develop a consistent set of rules to ensure that task performance is uniform.

3. The organization should establish a hierarchy of positions or offices that creates a chain of command from the top of the organization to the bottom.

● **bureaucracy**
A universal model of organization design based on a legitimate and formal system of authority

Although a bureaucratic model of organization design can help an organization's efficiency, it also has its disadvantages. Companies seeking new-drug approval from the FDA find this out. Because of the enormous amounts of paperwork involved (a fraction of which is shown in the photograph), the FDA exemplifies the inflexibility and rigidity that is often a by-product of a bureaucratic organization design.

4. Managers should conduct business in an impersonal way and maintain an appropriate social distance between themselves and their subordinates.

5. Employment and advancement in the organization should be based on technical expertise, and employees should be protected from arbitrary dismissal.

Perhaps the best examples of bureaucracies today are government agencies and universities. Consider, for example, the steps you must go through and the forms you must fill out to apply for admission to college, request housing, register each semester, change majors, submit a degree plan, substitute a course, and file for graduation. The reason these procedures are necessary is that universities deal with large numbers of people who must be treated equally and fairly. Hence rules, regulations, and standard operating procedures are needed. Some bureaucracies, such as the U.S. Postal Service, are trying to portray themselves as less mechanistic and impersonal. The strategy of the Postal Service is to become more service-oriented as a way to fight back against competitors like Federal Express Corp. and United Parcel Service, Inc.[5]

A primary strength of the bureaucratic model is that several of its elements (such as reliance on rules and employment based on expertise) do, in fact, often improve efficiency. Yet another of its strengths is one we have already noted: because the bureaucratic model was the starting point for much of our current thinking about organizations, it played a foundational role in understanding organization design. Unfortunately, pursuing an ideal bureaucracy can result in several undesired outcomes such as inflexibility, rigidity, and the neglect of human and social processes within the bureaucracy.[6]

Behavioral Model

● **behavioral model**
A universal model of organization design that paralleled the emergence of the human relations school of management thought; the model emphasized developing work groups and interpersonal processes

Another important universal model of organization design was the **behavioral model,** which paralleled the emergence of the human relations school of management thought. Pensis Likert, a management researcher, studied several large organizations to determine what made some more effective than others.[7] He found that the organizations in his sample that used the bureaucratic model of design tended to be less effective than those that used the behavioral model—in other words, paid more attention to developing work groups and were more concerned about interpersonal processes.

System 1
A form of organization design based on legitimate and formal authority; developed as part of the behavioral model of organization design

Likert developed a framework that characterized organizations in terms of eight key processes: leadership, motivation, communication, interactions, decision making, goal-setting, control, and performance goals. Likert believed that all organizations could be placed on a set of dimensions describing each of these eight elements. He argued that the basic bureaucratic form of organization, which he called a **System 1** design, anchored one end of each dimension. The characteristics of the System 1 organization in Likert's framework are summarized in Table 11.1.

System 4
A form of organization design that uses a wide array of motivational processes and promotes open and extensive interaction processes; developed as part of the behavioral model of organization design

Also summarized in this table are characteristics of Likert's other extreme form of organization design, called **System 4,** which was based on the behavioral model. For example, a System 4 organization uses a wide array of motivational processes, and its interaction processes are open and extensive. Other distinctions between System 1 and System 4 organizations are

TABLE 11.1 System 1 and System 4 Organizations

System 1 Organization	System 4 Organization
1. **Leadership process** includes no perceived confidence and trust. Subordinates do not feel free to discuss job problems with their superiors, who in turn do not solicit their ideas and opinions.	1. **Leadership process** includes perceived confidence and trust between superiors and subordinates in all matters. Subordinates feel free to discuss job problems with their superiors, who in turn solicit their ideas and opinions.
2. **Motivational process** taps only physical, security, and economic motives through the use of fear and sanctions. Unfavorable attitudes toward the organization prevail among employees.	2. **Motivational process** taps a full range of motives through participatory methods. Attitudes are favorable toward the organization and its goals.
3. **Communication process** is such that information flows downward and tends to be distorted, inaccurate, and viewed with suspicion by subordinates.	3. **Communication process** is such that information flows freely throughout the organization—upward, downward, and laterally. The information is accurate and undistorted.
4. **Interaction process** is closed and restricted; subordinates have little effect on departmental goals, methods, and activities.	4. **Interaction process** is open and extensive; both superiors and subordinates are able to affect departmental goals, methods, and activities.
5. **Decision process** occurs only at the top of the organization; it is relatively centralized.	5. **Decision process** occurs at all levels through group processes; it is relatively decentralized.
6. **Goal-setting process** is located at the top of the organization; discourages group participation.	6. **Goal-setting process** encourages group participation in setting high, realistic objectives.
7. **Control process** is centralized and emphasizes fixing of blame for mistakes.	7. **Control process** is dispersed throughout the organization and emphasizes self-control and problem solving.
8. **Performance goals** are low and passively sought by managers who make no commitment to developing the human resources of the organization.	8. **Performance goals** are high and actively sought by superiors who recognize the necessity for making a full commitment to developing, through training, the human resources of the organization.

Source: Adapted from Rensis Likert, *The Human Organization* (New York: McGraw-Hill, 1967), pp. 197–211. Used with permission.

---

equally obvious. In between the System 1 and System 4 extremes lie the System 2 and System 3 organizations. Likert argued that System 4 should be adopted by all organizations. He suggested that managers should emphasize supportive relationships, establish high performance goals, and practice group decision making to achieve a System 4 organization. Many organizations attempted to adopt the System 4 design during its period of peak popularity. In 1969, a General Motors plant in the Atlanta area was converted from a System 2 to a System 4 organization. Over a period of three

The behavioral model identifies two extreme types of organization design called System 1 and System 4. The two designs vary in terms of eight fundamental processes. The System 1 design is considered to be somewhat rigid and inflexible.

years, direct and indirect labor efficiency improved, as did tool-breakage rates, scrap costs, and quality.[8]

Like the bureaucratic model, the behavioral approach has both strengths and weaknesses. Its major strength is that it emphasizes human behavior by stressing the value of an organization's employees. Likert and his associates thus paved the way for a more humanistic approach to designing organizations. Unfortunately, the behavioral approach also argues that there is one best way to design organizations—as a System 4. As we see, however, there is strong evidence that there is no one best approach to organization design.[9] What works for one organization may not work for another, and what works for one organization may change as that organization's situation changes. Hence universal models like bureaucracy and System 4 have been largely supplanted by newer models that take contingency factors into account. In the next section, we identify a number of factors that help determine the best organization design for a particular situation.

SITUATIONAL INFLUENCES ON ORGANIZATION DESIGN

The **situational view of organization design** is based on the assumption that the optimal design for any given organization depends on a set of relevant situational factors.[10] Four such factors—technology, environment, size, and organizational life cycle—are discussed here. Another, strategy, is described in the next section.

Core Technology

Technology is the conversion processes used to transform inputs (such as materials or information) into outputs (such as products or services). Most organizations use multiple technologies, but an organization's most important one is called its core technology. Although most people visualize assembly lines and machinery when they think of technology, the term can also be applied to service organizations. For example, a brokerage firm like Dean Witter uses technology to transform investment dollars into income in much the same way that Union Carbide Corp. uses natural resources to manufacture chemical products.

Much of what we know about the link between technology and organization design started with the pioneering work of Joan Woodward.[11] Woodward studied 100 manufacturing firms in southern England. She collected information about such things as the history of each organization, its manufacturing processes, its forms and procedures, and financial data. Woodward expected to find a relationship between the size of an organization and its design, but no such relationship emerged. So she began to seek other explanations for differences. This follow-up analysis led Woodward to classify the organizations according to their technology. Three basic forms of technology were identified by Woodward:

1. *Unit or small-batch technology*. The product is custom-made to customer specifications, or else it is produced in small quantities. Organizations using

this form of technology include a tailor shop like Brooks Brothers (custom suits) and a printing shop like Kinko's (business cards, company stationery).

2. *Large-batch or mass-production technology.* The product is manufactured in assembly-line fashion by combining component parts into another part or finished product. Examples include automobile manufacturers like Subaru and washing-machine companies like Whirlpool Corporation.

3. *Continuous-process technology.* Raw materials are transformed into a finished product by a series of machine or process transformations. The composition of the materials themselves is changed. Examples include petroleum refineries like Exxon Corporation and chemical refineries like The Dow Chemical Co.

These forms of technology are listed in order of their assumed levels of complexity—unit or small-batch technology is presumed to be the least complex and continuous-process technology the most complex. Woodward found that different configurations of organization design were associated with each technology.

As technology became more complex in Woodward's sample, the number of levels of management increased (that is, the organization was taller). The executive span of management also increased, as did the relative size of its staff component. The supervisory span of management, however, first increased and then decreased as technology became more complex, primarily because much of the work in continuous-process technologies is automated. Fewer workers are needed, but the skills necessary to do the job increase. These findings are consistent with the discussion of the span of management in Chapter 10—the more complex the job, the narrower the span should probably be.

At a more general level of analysis, Woodward found that the two extremes (unit or small batch and continuous process) tended to be very similar to Likert's System 4 organization, whereas the middle-range organizations (large batch or mass production) were much more like bureaucracies or System 1. The large-batch and mass-production organizations also had a higher level of specialization.[12] Finally, she found that organizational success was related to the extent to which organizations followed the typical pattern. For example, successful continuous-process organizations tended to be more like System 4 organizations, while less successful firms with the same technology were less like System 4 organizations.

Thus technology clearly appears to play an important role in determining organization design. As future technologies become even more diverse and complex, managers will have to be even more aware of their impact on the design of organizations.[13] We discuss technology more fully in Chapter 20.

General Motors' CEO Robert Stempel is drastically changing the world's largest manufacturing company. By promoting teamwork and delegating—more typical of an organic structure than GM's traditional mechanistic structure—as well as closing assembly plants and factories, cutting both blue- and white-collar jobs, and reorganizing, Stempel hopes to counter rapidly falling sales, productivity, and profits.

Environment

In addition to the various relationships described in Chapter 3, there are a number of specific linkages among environmental elements and organization design. The first widely recognized analysis of environment–organization design linkages was provided by Tom Burns and G. M. Stalker.[14] Like Woodward, Burns and Stalker worked in England. Their first step was identifying two extreme forms of organizational environment:

Mechanistic	Organic
1. Tasks are highly fractionated and specialized; little regard paid to clarifying relationship between tasks and organizational objectives.	1. Tasks are more interdependent; emphasis on relevance of tasks and organizational objectives.
2. Tasks tend to remain rigidly defined unless altered formally by top management.	2. Tasks are continually adjusted and redefined through interaction of organizational members.
3. Specific role definition (rights, obligations, and technical methods prescribed for each member).	3. Generalized role definition (members accept general responsibility for task accomplishment beyond individual role definition).
4. Hierarchic structure of control, authority, and communication. Sanctions derive from employment contract between employee and organization.	4. Network structure of control, authority, and communication. Sanctions derive more from community of interest than from contractual relationship.
5. Information relevant to situation and operations of the organization formally assumed to rest with chief executive.	5. Leader not assumed to be omniscient; knowledge centers identified where located throughout organization.
6. Communication is primarily vertical between superior and subordinate.	6. Communication is both vertical and horizontal, depending on where needed information resides.
7. Communications primarily take form of instructions and decisions issued by superiors, of information and requests for decisions supplied by inferiors.	7. Communications primarily take form of information and advice.
8. Insistence on loyalty to organization and obedience to superiors.	8. Commitment to organization's tasks and goals more highly valued than loyalty or obedience.
9. Importance and prestige attached to identification with organization and its members.	9. Importance and prestige attached to affiliations and expertise in external environment.

Source: Adapted from Tom Burns and G. M. Stalker, *The Management of Innovation* (London: Tavistock, 1961), pp. 119–122. Used with permission.

stable (one that remains relatively constant over time) and unstable (subject to uncertainty and rapid change). Next they studied the designs of organizations in each type of environment. Not surprisingly, they found that organizations in stable environments tended to have a different kind of design from organizations in stable environments. The two kinds of design that emerged, summarized in Table 11.2, were called mechanistic and organic.

A **mechanistic organization,** quite similar to the bureaucratic or System 1 model, was most frequently found in stable environments. Free from uncertainty, organizations structured their activities in rather predictable ways by means of rules, specialized jobs, and centralized authority. Although no environment is completely stable, K mart Corp. and Wendy's

● **mechanistic organization**
A rigid and bureaucratic form of design most appropriate for stable environments

International, Inc., use mechanistic designs. An **organic organization,** on the other hand, was most often found in unstable and unpredictable environments, in which constant change and uncertainty usually dictate a much higher level of fluidity and flexibility. Motorola, Inc. (facing rapid technological change) and The Limited, Inc. (facing constant change in consumer tastes) use organic designs.

These ideas were extended in the United States by Paul R. Lawrence and Jay W. Lorsch.[15] They agreed that environmental factors influence organization design but believed that this influence varies between different units of the same organization. In fact, they predicted that each organizational unit has its own unique environment and responds by developing unique attributes. Lawrence and Lorsch suggested that organizations could be characterized along two primary dimensions. One of these dimensions, **differentiation,** is the extent to which the organization is broken down into subunits. A firm with many subunits is highly differentiated; one with few subunits has a low level of differentiation. The second dimension, **integration,** is the degree to which the various units must work together in a coordinated fashion. For example, if each unit competes in a different market and has its own production facilities, little integration may be needed. Lawrence and Lorsch reasoned that the degree of differentiation and integration needed by an organization depends on the stability of the environments that its subunits faced.[16]

Organizational Size

Size is another factor that affects organization design. Although several definitions of size exist, we define **organizational size** as the total number of full-time or full-time-equivalent employees. A team of researchers at the University of Aston in Birmingham, England, believed that Woodward had failed to find a size-structure relationship because almost all the organizations she studied were relatively small (three-fourths had fewer than 500 employees).[17] Thus they decided to study a wider array of organizations to determine how size and technology both individually and jointly affect an organization's design.

Their primary finding was that technology did in fact influence structural variables in small firms, probably because all their activities tended to be centered around their core technology. In large firms, however, the strong technology-design link broke down, most likely because technology is not as central to ongoing activities in large organizations. The Aston studies yielded a number of basic generalizations: when compared to small organizations, large organizations tend to be characterized by higher levels of job specialization, more standard operating procedures, more rules, more regulations, and a greater degree of decentralization. "Management in Practice" describes how size has benefitted Borden, Inc.

Organizational Life Cycle

Of course, size is not constant. Some small businesses are formed but soon disappear. Others remain as small, independently operated enterprises as long as their owner-manager lives. A few, like Compaq Computer Corpo-

- **organic organization**
A fluid and flexible design most appropriate for unstable and unpredictable environments

differentiation
The extent to which the organization is broken down into subunits

integration
The extent to which the subunits of an organization must work together in a coordinated fashion

- **organizational size**
The number of full-time or full-time-equivalent employees

• **organizational life cycle**
A natural sequence of stages
most organizations pass through
as they grow and mature

ration, Liz Claiborne, Inc., and Reebok International, Inc., skyrocket to become organizational giants. And occasionally large organizations reduce their size through layoffs or divestitures. Although no clear pattern explains changes in size, many organizations progress through a four-stage **organizational life cycle.**[18]

The first stage is the *birth* of the organization. At Compaq, this occurred in 1984 when a handful of Texas Instruments engineers resigned, raised some venture capital, and began to design and build portable computers. The second stage, *youth,* is characterized by growth and the expansion of all organizational resources. Compaq passed through the youth stage in 1985 and entered the third stage, *midlife,* around the beginning of 1986. Midlife is a period of gradual growth evolving eventually into stability. The company remains in midlife today, with sales in excess of $1 billion annually. Compaq has not yet reached the final stage of an organization's life cycle, *maturity.*[19] Maturity is a period of stability, perhaps eventually evolving into decline. Montgomery Ward is an example of a mature organization.

Managers must confront a number of organization design issues as the organization progresses through these stages. In general, as an organization passes from one stage to the next, it becomes bigger, more mechanistic, and more decentralized. It also becomes more specialized, devotes more attention to planning, and takes on an increasingly large staff component. Finally, coordination demands increase, formalization increases, organizational units become geographically more dispersed, and control systems become more extensive. Thus an organization's size and design are clearly linked—and this link is dynamic because of the organizational life cycle.

STRATEGY AND ORGANIZATION DESIGN

Another important determinant of an organization's design is the strategy adopted by its top managers.[20] In general, corporate, business, and functional strategies all affect organization design.

Corporate Strategy

As we noted in Chapter 7, an organization can adopt a variety of corporate strategies. Its choice will partially determine what type of design will be most effective. For example, a firm that pursues an internal growth strategy may need to create large departments for designing and developing new products. If either unrelated or related diversification is used to spur growth, managers will need to decide how to arrange the new units they acquire (we discuss this more fully later). Retrenchment may call for reducing the size of some units or selling off all or parts of some units. Managers must then decide how to redesign the remaining parts of the organization. And a stability strategy may cause the organization to adopt such structural alternatives as wider spans of management and more centralization.

An organization that adopts the portfolio approach must also ensure that its design fits its strategy. For example, each strategic business unit may remain a relatively autonomous unit within the organization. But managers at the corporate level will need to decide how much decision-making lati-

BIG IS BEAUTIFUL AT BORDEN

Large corporate size, once seen as an asset because of the advantages of economies of scale, has become identified with slow-moving, bureaucratic companies like General Motors. According to the new wisdom, huge corporations cannot change quickly enough to keep up with shifts in the global marketplace.

Many large companies, however, are doing just fine. The largest 500 companies in the country, which accounted for 39 percent of corporate after-tax profits in 1954, raked in two-thirds of the U.S. total corporate profits in 1987. Clearly, some companies have found new and profitable ways to be big. Borden, Inc., 135 years old and going strong, is one of them.

During its resurgence in the 1980s, Borden followed some of the conventional wisdom, shedding units that had little to do with its primary business, food, such as its phosphate rock mine and a perfume maker. And it "stuck to its knitting" by continuing to promote its well-known name and Elsie the cow's familiar face to reap profits from its dairy business.

As a new venture, Borden has also moved into non-dairy foods, demonstrating a strategy that takes advantage of the strengths of a large business and the nimbleness of a small one. Borden didn't start making pasta until the late 1970s; now it is the world's largest

producer. At first it ran into great difficulty in getting its Creamette brand accepted locally; pasta lovers tend to be loyal to their favorite regional brand. So rather than try to tear market share from such local favorites as Gioia and Viviano Macaroni Co., Borden bought them and now uses its distribution network to sell Creamette and its local brand against the competition. This strategy has enabled Creamette to become the first national pasta brand and allows Borden to take advantage of economies of scale. Borden now keeps fourteen pasta plants running around the clock. Because it's the largest buyer of durum wheat in the country, it can get lower prices than other buyers. Other pasta makers have to stop production to switch to making specialty pasta shapes, but because of its volume Borden can keep some of its plants making special shapes and sizes full time.

Borden has successfully applied this local-and-national approach to its other new businesses. Even though it is the world's largest dairy producer, Borden can still sell milk in Georgia by claiming to be "Augusta's only hometown dairy." And it works.

References: Walter Guzzard, "Big Can Still Be Beautiful," *Fortune*, April 25, 1988, pp. 50–64; Bill Saporito, "How Borden Milks Packaged Goods," *Fortune*, December 21, 1987, pp. 139–144.

tude to give the heads of each unit (a question of decentralization), how many corporate-level executives will be needed to oversee the operations of various units (a question of span of management), and how much information will be shared among the units (a question of coordination).

Business Strategy

Business strategies affect the design of individual businesses within the organization as well as the overall organization itself. A defender, for example, is likely to be somewhat tall and centralized, have narrow spans of management, and perhaps take a functional approach to departmentalization. Thus it may generally follow the bureaucratic approach to organization design.

In contrast, a prospecting organization is more likely to be flatter and decentralized. With wider spans of management, it tries to be flexible and adaptable in its approach to doing business. A business that uses an analyzer strategy is likely to have an organization design somewhere in between these two extremes (perhaps being a System 2 or 3 organization). Given that a reactor is essentially a strategic failure, its presumed strategy is probably not logically connected to its design.

Competitive strategies can also affect organization design. A firm using a differentiation strategy, for example, may structure departments around whatever it is using as a basis for differentiating its products (i.e., marketing in the case of image, manufacturing in the case of quality). A cost leadership strategy will necessitate a strong commitment to efficiency and control. Thus such a firm may be more centralized as it attempts to control costs. And a firm using a focus strategy may design itself around whatever its focus is directed at (i.e., location departmentalization if its focus is geographic region, customer departmentalization if its focus is customer groups).

Functional Strategy

The relationship between an organization's functional strategies and its design is less obvious and may be subsumed under corporate or business-level concerns. If the firm's marketing strategy calls for aggressive marketing and promotion, separate departments may be needed for advertising, direct sales, and promotion. If its financial strategy calls for low debt, it may need only a small finance department. If production strategy calls for manufacturing in diverse locations, organization design arrangements will need to account for this geographic dispersion. Human resources strategy may call for greater or lesser degrees of decentralization as a way to develop skills of new managers at lower levels in the organization. And research and development strategy may dictate various designs for making the R&D function itself. A heavy commitment to R&D, for example, may require a separate unit with a vice president in charge. A lesser commitment to R&D may be achieved with a director and a small staff.

BASIC FORMS OF ORGANIZATION DESIGN

Because technology, environment, size, life cycle, and strategy can all influence organization design, it should come as no surprise that organizations adopt many different kinds of designs. Most designs, however, fall into one of four basic categories. Others are hybrids based on two or more of the basic forms.

Functional (U-Form) Design

● **functional design**
An organization design based on the functional approach to departmentalization; also called the U-form

The **functional design** is an arrangement based on the functional approach to departmentalization as detailed in Chapter 10. This design has been termed the *U-form* (for unitary) by economist Oliver E. Williamson.[21] Under this arrangement, the members of the organization are grouped into functional departments such as marketing and production. For the organization to operate efficiently, there must be considerable coordination across departments. This integration and coordination are most commonly the responsibility of the CEO. Figure 11.1 shows the U-form design as applied

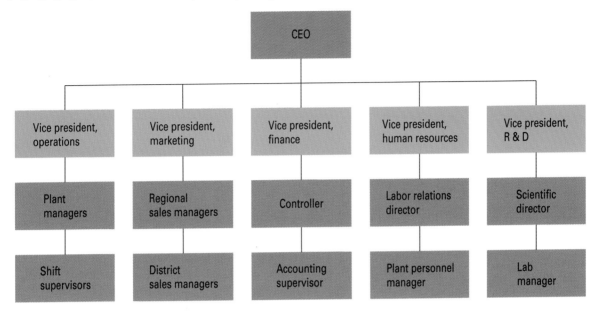

FIGURE 11.1 Functional (U-Form) Design for a Small Manufacturing Company

to the corporate level of a small manufacturing company. In a U-form organization, none of the functional areas can survive without the others. Marketing, for example, needs products from operations to sell and funds from finance to pay for advertising. In general, this approach shares the basic advantages and disadvantages of functional departmentalization. And as we noted in Chapter 10, the U-form design is most commonly used in small organizations because it is fairly easy for an individual CEO to oversee and coordinate the entire organization. As an organization grows, the CEO finds it increasingly difficult to stay on top of all functional areas.

The U-form design is based on functional departmentalization. This small manufacturing firm uses managers at the vice-presidential level to coordinate activities within each functional area of the organization. Note that each functional area is dependent on the others.

Conglomerate (H-Form) Design

Another common form of organization design is the conglomerate, or *H-form*, approach.[22] The **conglomerate design** is used by an organization made up of a set of unrelated businesses. Thus the H-form (for holding) design is essentially a holding company that results from unrelated diversification. This approach is based loosely on the product form of departmentalization. Each business is operated by a general manager who is responsible for its profits or losses, and each general manager functions independently of the others. Pearson PLC, a British firm, uses the H-form design. As illustrated in Figure 11.2, Pearson consists of six business groups. Although its periodicals and publishing operations are related, all its other businesses are unrelated. "The Global View" provides more information about Pearson.

In an H-form organization, a corporate staff usually evaluates the performance of each business, allocates corporate resources across companies, and shapes decisions about buying and selling businesses. The basic shortcoming of the H-form design is the complexity associated with holding diverse and unrelated businesses. Managers usually find it difficult to com-

● **conglomerate design**
An organization design used by an organization comprising a set of unrelated businesses; also called the H-form

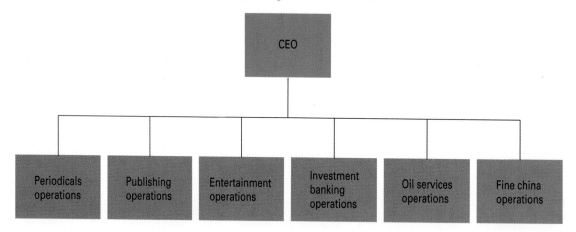

```
                           ┌──────────┐
                           │   CEO    │
                           └────┬─────┘
        ┌──────┬──────┬─────────┼─────────┬──────┬──────┐
   ┌────────┐┌────────┐┌──────────┐┌───────────┐┌─────────┐┌──────────┐
   │Periodicals││Publishing││Entertainment││Investment ││Oil services││Fine china │
   │operations││operations││operations ││banking    ││operations ││operations │
   │          ││          ││           ││operations ││           ││           │
   └────────┘└────────┘└──────────┘└───────────┘└─────────┘└──────────┘
```

Pearson PLC, a British firm, uses the conglomerate form of organization design. This design, which results from a strategy of unrelated diversification, is a complex one to manage. Managers find that comparing and integrating activities among the dissimilar operations are difficult. Companies may abandon this design for another approach, such as the M-form design.

● **divisional design**
An organization design in which multiple businesses in related areas operate within a larger organizational framework; based on the product approach to departmentalization and is also called the M-form

A conglomerate, or H-form, design, is used by an organization such as Tyco that has a group of unrelated businesses. One of Tyco's divisions, its Flow Control Group (made up of the companies Grinnel, Allied, Hersey, and Mueller), is trying to expand internationally. To this end, Tyco acquired Wormald, which gives it access to European, Australian, and Asian office and warehouse space.

pare and integrate activities across a large number of diverse operations. Research by Michael Porter suggests that many organizations that follow this approach achieve only average-to-weak financial performance.[23] Thus although many U.S. firms are still using the H-form design, many are also abandoning it for other approaches.

Divisional (M-Form) Design

In the divisional design, which is becoming increasingly popular, a product form of organization is also used; but, in contrast to the H-form, the divisions are related. Thus the **divisional design,** or *M-form* (for multidivisional), is based on multiple businesses in related areas within a larger organizational framework. This design results from a strategy of related diversification. Some activities are extremely decentralized down to the divisional level; others are centralized at the corporate level.[24] For example,

WHICH WAY FOR PEARSON?

Pearson PLC is a British company with aristocratic roots and an uncertain future. Begun by Samuel Pearson in the mid-nineteenth century as a construction firm, the company achieved extraordinary fame and success under the founder's grandson, Weetman Pearson. It built the first tunnel under the Hudson River and constructed Mexico City's main drainage system, and by the turn of the century it was the world's largest contractor. Weetman was knighted and eventually given the title of viscount, becoming Lord Cowdray.

Even during the peak of Pearson's success as a construction company, Cowdray recognized its limitations and created a holding company (an H-form design) with assets in oil exploration and investment banking as well as construction. After Cowdray's death in 1927, construction lost its importance to Pearson, and Cowdray's heirs continued to build what has been called "a collection of rich men's toys,"* buying such businesses as Madame Tussaud's wax works, French wineries, and makers of fine china. The company's most important investments, however, were in publishing: it owns Britain's premier business newspaper, *The Financial Times,* as well as a number of other periodicals and book publishers.

Its publishing assets made Pearson look like a promising takeover prospect in the 1980s. In 1987, Rupert Murdoch's News Corp. spent $650 million to buy 20 percent of Pearson's stock. Murdoch runs one of the world's biggest publishing conglomerates, and the thought that he would bring his screaming headlines and brash ways to the staid *Financial Times* sent shock waves throughout Pearson. *Times* editors like

to stay as far above the tabloids as possible, sneering even at their main competitor, *The Wall Street Journal,* for pandering too much to the public's taste for human interest stories. The *Times* would rather be read by the important few than by the ordinary many.

If Murdoch had taken control of Pearson, he likely would have sold off many of its nonpublishing assets and used the company's publishing and information subsidiaries to strengthen News Corp.'s worldwide information networks. He had visions of making *The Financial Times* a competitor to *The Wall Street Journal* worldwide, even though Pearson's chief executive for newspapers directly states "I don't believe in a global newspaper."**

Murdoch eventually backed off, selling about half of his Pearson holdings, and Pearson was given some breathing room and a chance to more directly control its own future. But the takeover scare made it clear to Pearson executives that the company needed a coherent design and structure; it could no longer be a collection of "rich men's toys."

*Quoted in Gary Hoover, Alta Campbell, Alan Chai, and Patrick J. Spain (eds.), *Hoover's Handbook of World Business 1992* (Austin, Tex.: The Reference Press, 1991), p. 253.

**Frank Barlow quoted in Allan Dodds Frank and Richard C. Morais, "Watch Out, Dow Jones! Here Comes Rupert Murdoch," *Forbes,* February 22, 1988, p. 35.

References: Allan Dodds Frank and Richard C. Morais, "Watch Out, Dow Jones! Here Comes Rupert Murdoch," *Forbes,* February 22, 1988, pp. 34–35; Gary Hoover, Alta Campbell, Alan Chai, and Patrick J. Spain (eds.), *Hoover's Handbook of World Business 1992* (Austin, Tex.: The Reference Press, 1991), p. 253; Sharon Reier, "A Touch of Class," *Financial World,* November 27, 1990, pp. 42–43.

as shown in Figure 11.3, The Limited, Inc. uses this approach. Each of its divisions is headed by a general manager and operates with reasonable autonomy, but the divisions also coordinate their activities as is appropriate.

The opportunities for coordination and shared resources represent one of the biggest advantages of the M-form design. The Limited's marketing research and purchasing departments are centralized. Thus a buyer can inspect a manufacturer's entire product line, buy some designs for The Lim-

F I G U R E 11.3 Multidivisional (M-Form) Design at The Limited, Inc.

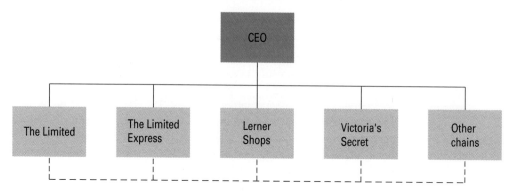

The Limited, Inc., uses the multi-divisional approach to organization design. Although each of its units operates with relative autonomy, they all function in the same general market. This design resulted from a strategy of related diversification. Other firms that use M-form designs include PepsiCo and Woolworth Corporation.

● **matrix design**

An organization design wherein a product-based form of departmentalization is superimposed onto an existing functional arrangement

● **multiple-command structure**

A structure in which an individual reports to both a functional superior and one or more project managers simultaneously

ited chain, others for The Limited Express, and still others for Lerner. The M-form design's basic objective is to optimize internal competition and cooperation. Healthy competition among divisions for resources can enhance effectiveness, but cooperation should also be promoted. Research suggests that the M-form organization that can achieve and maintain this balance will outperform large U-form and all H-form organizations.[25]

Matrix Design

The **matrix design,** another common approach to organization design, is based on two overlapping bases of departmentalization.[26] The foundation of a matrix is a set of functional departments. A set of product groups, or temporary departments, is then superimposed across the functional departments. Employees in a matrix are simultaneously members of a functional department (e.g., engineering) and of a project team. Figure 11.4 shows a basic matrix design. At the top of the organization are functional units headed by vice presidents of engineering, production, finance, and marketing. Each of these managers has several subordinates. Along the side of the organization are a number of positions termed *project manager*. Each project manager heads a project group composed of representatives or workers from the functional departments. Note from the figure that a matrix reflects a **multiple-command structure**—any given individual may report both to a functional superior and to one or more project managers.

The project groups, or teams, are assigned to designated projects or programs. For example, the company might be developing a new product. Representatives are chosen from each functional area to work as a team on the new product. They also retain membership in the original functional group. At any given time, a person may be a member of several teams as well as a member of a functional group. Ford Motor Co. used this approach in creating its popular Taurus automobile. It formed a group called "Team Taurus" made up of designers, engineers, production specialists, marketing specialists, and other experts from different areas of the company. This group facilitated getting a very successful product to the market at least a year earlier than would have been possible using Ford's previous approaches.[27]

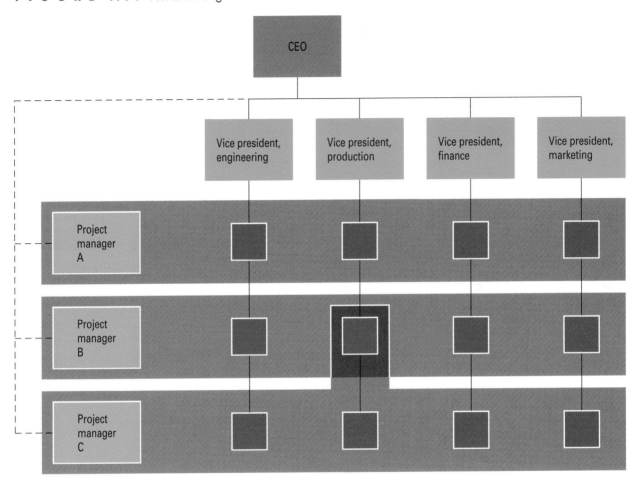

Many organizations have used the matrix design. Notable among them are American Cyanamid Co., Monsanto Company, NCR Corp., The Chase Manhattan Bank, N.A., The Prudential Insurance Co. of America, General Motors Corp., and several state and federal government agencies. Some organizations, however, such as Citibank N.A. and the Dutch firm Philips adopted and then dropped the matrix design. Thus it is important to recognize that a matrix design is not always appropriate. The matrix form of organization design is most often used in one of three situations.[28] First, a matrix may work when there is strong pressure from the environment. For example, intense external competition may dictate the sort of strong marketing thrust that is best spearheaded by a functional department, but the diversity of a company's products may argue for product departments. Second, a matrix may be appropriate when large amounts of information need to be processed. For example, creating lateral relationships by means of a matrix is one effective way to increase the organization's capacity to process information. Third, the matrix design may work when there is

A matrix organization design is created by superimposing a product form of departmentalization onto an existing functional organization. Project managers coordinate teams of employees drawn from different functional departments. Thus a matrix relies on a multiple-command structure.

pressure for shared resources. For example, a company with ten product departments may have resources for only three marketing specialists. A matrix design would allow all the departments to share the company's scarce marketing resource.

Both advantages and disadvantages are associated with the matrix design. Six primary advantages of matrix designs have been observed. First, it enhances flexibility because teams can be created, redefined, and dissolved as needed. Second, because they assume a major role in decision making, team members are likely to be highly motivated and committed to the organization. Third, employees in a matrix organization have considerable opportunity to learn new skills. A fourth advantage of a matrix design is that it provides an efficient way for the organization to take full advantage of its human resources. Fifth, team members retain membership in their functional unit so they can serve as a bridge between the functional unit and the team, enhancing cooperation. Sixth, the matrix design gives top management a useful vehicle for decentralization. Once the day-to-day operations have been delegated, top management can devote more attention to areas such as long-range planning.

On the other hand, the matrix design also has some major disadvantages. Employees may be uncertain about reporting relationships, especially if they are simultaneously assigned to a functional manager and to several project managers. To complicate matters, some managers see the matrix as a form of anarchy in which they have unlimited freedom. Another set of problems is associated with the dynamics of group behavior. Groups take longer than individuals to make decisions, may be dominated by one individual, and may compromise too much. They may also get bogged down in discussion and not focus on their primary objectives. Finally, in a matrix more time may also be required for coordinating task-related activities.[29]

Hybrid Designs

Some organizations use a design that represents a hybrid of two or more of the common forms of organization design. For example, an organization may have five related divisions and one unrelated division, making its design a cross between an M-form and an H-form. Indeed, few companies use a design in its pure form; most firms have one basic organization design as a foundation to managing the business but maintain sufficient flexibility so that temporary or permanent modifications can be made for strategic purposes. Ford, for example, used the matrix approach to design the Taurus, but the company is basically a U-form organization showing signs of moving to an M-form design. As noted earlier, any combination of factors may dictate the appropriate form of design for any particular company.

EMERGING ISSUES IN ORGANIZATION DESIGN

Several issues related to organization design have also emerged over the years. The more important ones are how organizations use their design to manage information, what types of design are used by global organizations, and the importance of organizational flexibility.

Managing Information

As we noted in Chapter 3, organizational environments are becoming increasingly turbulent, complex, and uncertain. As uncertainty increases, the amount of information that the organization has to process also increases. At the same time, breakthroughs in information technology allow managers to process larger quantities of information more and more efficiently. Managers are becoming increasingly aware that these information-processing requirements and capabilities influence organization design.

One implication relates to the span of management and the number of levels of an organization. Innovations in information technology enable a manager to stay in touch with an increasingly large number of managers and subordinates. T. J. Rodgers, CEO of Cypress Semiconductor Corp., uses the firm's information system to check on the progress of each of the 1,500 employees every week. Using this and related approaches, spans of management are likely to widen and organizational levels decrease. And some organizations are using their information-processing capabilities to network with other companies. Pacific Intermountain Express, a large Western trucking company, gives customers access to its own computer network so they can check on the status of their shipments.[30]

Managers can draw on a number of design elements to reduce the need for information processing as well as increase the organization's capacity to process information.[31] One way to decrease information-processing needs is to create **slack resources.** Consider a wholesaler who ships merchandise to various retailers. If the wholesaler carries too little inventory, it runs the risk of losing customers to another wholesaler. The wholesaler can address this by carrying more inventory. The excess inventory represents a slack resource because it enables the wholesaler to be less concerned about projected demand, shipping schedules, and so forth. Slack time can be built into a schedule and contingency (slack) funds into a budget. Of course, additional costs are associated with slack resources. For organization design, the effect of having slack resources depends on the nature of the resources. The wholesaler, for example, will need more employees to handle the new storage facilities.

Creating **self-contained tasks** is another way to reduce information-processing requirements. When an organization moves from functional to product departments, each new unit becomes self-contained, with its own engineers, marketing staff, and so on. Self-containment reduces the need for information processing by reducing the demands on each specialist. Whenever a group needs the expertise of a specialist, it does not have to compete with another unit for that individual's time.

Whereas the preceding two techniques decrease the need to process information, **vertical information systems** allow the organization to process an increased amount of information, which is what Rodgers uses at Cypress. These systems might range from sophisticated computer networks to clerical assistants who organize and summarize information. Creating **lateral relationships** also increases an organization's capacity to process

- **slack resources**
Excess resources used to help an organization decrease its information-processing requirements

- **self-contained tasks**
Independent units used to help an organization decrease its information-processing requirements

- **vertical information systems**
Communication linkages between managers and their subordinates created to help the organization process more information

- **lateral relationships**
Coordination linkages such as liaison roles, task forces, teams, and integrating departments used to help the organization process more information

An emerging trend in all of business is increasing globalization, which is especially apparent these days in the European computer market: Japanese companies such as Fujitsu and Mitsubishi Electric are buying British and Finnish computer firms, thereby increasing Japan's share of the European computer market. IBM is trying to counter this threat and boost its own declining share of European revenues by forming alliances with European computer firms such as Groupe Bull, Siemens, and SGS-Thomson Microelectronics.

information. Basically, lateral relationships are created using any of the coordination techniques described in Chapter 10 (liaison roles, task forces, teams, integrating departments). Then when two interdependent units need to coordinate their activities by sharing information, the existence of a task force facilitates the process. The matrix design also clearly depends on lateral relationships.

Global Organizations

Another emerging issue in organization design is the trend toward the internationalization of business. As we discussed in Chapter 5, most businesses today interact with suppliers, customers, or competitors (or all three) from other countries. The relevant issue for organization design is how to design the firm to most effectively deal with international forces and compete in global markets. For example, consider a moderate-size company that has just decided to "go international." Should it set up an international division, retain its current structure and establish an international operating group, or make its international operations an autonomous subunit?[32]

Figure 11.5 illustrates four of the most common approaches to organization design used for international purposes. The design shown in A is the simplest, relying on a separate international division. Levi Strauss & Co. uses this approach. The design shown in B, used by Ford Motor Corp., is an extension of location departmentalization to international settings. An extension of product departmentalization, with each product manager being responsible for all product-related activities regardless of location, is shown in C. The Procter & Gamble Co. uses a design similar to this one. Finally, the design shown in D, most typical of larger multinational corporations, is an extension of the multidivisional structure with branches located in various foreign markets. Nestlé and Unilever use this type of design.

Adapting Organizations

Finally, many organizations today are creating designs for themselves that maximize their ability to adapt to changing circumstances and to a changing environment. They try to accomplish this by not becoming too compartmentalized or too rigid. As we noted earlier, bureaucratic organizations are hard to change, slow, and inflexible. To avoid these problems, then, organizations can try to be as different from bureaucracies as possible—relatively few rules, general job descriptions, and so forth.

Some organizations today are exploring an approach to organization design that relies almost exclusively on project-type teams, with little or no underlying functional hierarchy. Within such an organization people would float from project to project as necessitated by their skills and the demands of those products. At Cypress Semiconductor, T. J. Rodgers refuses to allow the organization to grow so large that it can't function this way. Whenever a unit or group starts getting too large, he simply splits it into smaller units. Consequently, all units within the organization are small. This allows them to change direction, explore new ideas, and try new methods without dealing with a rigid bureaucratic organizational context. While few organizations have actually reached this level of adaptability,

FIGURE 11.5 Common Organization Designs for International Organizations

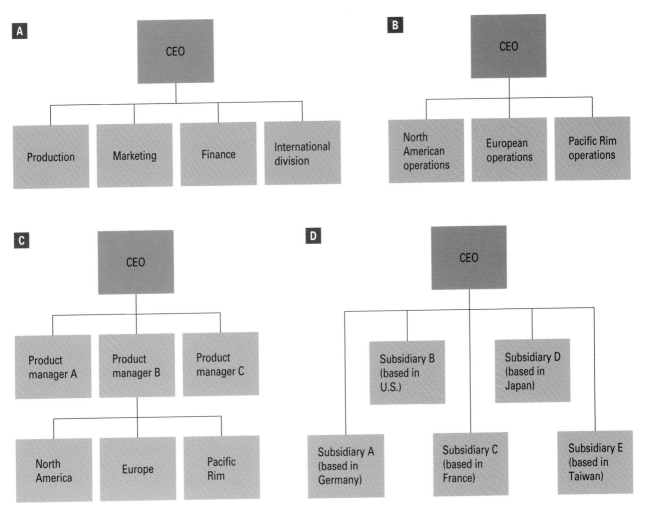

Apple Computer, Inc. and Xerox Corp. are among those moving toward it.[33]

Companies that compete in international markets must create an organization design that fits their own unique circumstances. These four general designs are representative of what many international organizations use. Each is derived from one of the basic forms of organization design.

SUMMARY OF KEY POINTS

Organization design is the overall pattern of structural components and arrangements used to manage the total organization. Two early universal models of organization design were the bureaucratic model and the behavioral model. These models attempted to prescribe how all organizations should be designed.

The situational view of organization design is based on the assumption that the optimal organization design is a function of situational factors. Four important situational factors are technology, environment, size, and organizational life cycle. Each of these factors plays a role in determining how an organization should be designed.

An organization's strategy also helps shape its design. In various ways, corporate, business, and functional strategies all affect organization design.

Many organizations today adopt one of four basic organization designs: functional (U-form), conglomerate (H-form), divisional (M-form), or matrix. Other organizations use a hybrid design derived from two or more of these basic designs.

Three emerging issues in organization design are how organizations use their design to manage information, how international businesses should be designed, and how organizations are maximizing their ability to adapt.

DISCUSSION QUESTIONS

Questions for Review

1. Compare and contrast the bureaucratic and behavioral models of organization design. What are the advantages and disadvantages of each?

2. What are the basic situational factors that affect an organization's design?

3. How are an organization's strategy and its structure related?

4. Describe the basic forms of organization design. Outline the advantages and disadvantages of each.

Questions for Analysis

5. Can bureaucratic organizations avoid the problems usually associated with bureaucracies? If so, how? If not, why not? Do you think bureaucracies are still necessary? Why or why not? Would it be possible to retain the desirable aspects of bureaucracy and eliminate the undesirable ones? Why or why not?

6. The matrix organization design is complex and difficult to implement successfully. Why then do so many organizations use it?

7. Identify common and unique problems in organization design confronted by international businesses when compared with domestic businesses.

Questions for Application

8. What form of organization does your university or college use? What form does your city or town government use? What form is used by other organizations with which you are familiar? What similarities and differences do you see? Why?

9. A question in Chapter 7 asked you to interview the manager of a local small business to determine how (or if) he or she formulates strategy. Interview that same manager again to obtain a description of his or her organization design. Can you identify any links between the manager's strategy and the structure of his or her own organization? Share your findings with the class.

10. Interview members of a local organization (fast-food chain, department store, book store, bank, church, home and school association, etc.) to ascertain how adaptable they perceive their organization to be.

XEROX'S ADAPTIVE ORGANIZATION

According to Professor Paul Lawrence of the Harvard Business School, organizations can choose from a whole spectrum of designs, from the bureaucratic model hierarchy to an "adaptive" structure.* The traditional hierarchy—still the most common organizational structure—remains the design of choice for companies in stable, slow-growth industries like petroleum and forest products. But the more fast-changing an industry is, the more important it is for companies in that industry to be adaptive.

Few industries are more fast-changing than Xerox's, and few companies have been more frustrated at adapting profitably. Xerox researchers developed the photocopier, the personal computer, the laser printer, and the computer "mouse," yet each time the company let most of the fame and profits from these breakthroughs slip away. Therefore it is perhaps no surprise that Xerox is now trying to become a more adaptive organization.

In 1990, Xerox began talking about a new product and a new organizational design, and the similarities between the two may be more than just coincidental. The new machine on which Xerox is pinning so much hope was developed under the in-house name Xenith. For the hefty price tag of $150,000 to $200,000, customers will get a machine that can accept information from paper, computers, pictures, or graphics; store it digitally; manipulate it; and then fax or copy it with unprecedented quality.

This machine was created by a team of Xerox engineers, marketers, and researchers who were charged with the task of beating the rest of the world to the technology that would make copiers obsolete. Now the new Xerox organizational design is trying to destroy altogether the walls that stood for communication boundaries between departments.

In the adaptive organization, everything—departments, reporting relationships, evaluation methods—is more fluid than in a traditional organization. People join together for a specific project, and then move on to work with other people on the next task.

Xerox has already had some notable successes working adaptively on a small scale. It boosted its customer satisfaction from 70 percent to 90 percent by creating a team of people from distribution, accounting, and sales that developed a way to track each copier through the distribution process. A similar cross-departmental team saved Xerox $200 million per year in inventory costs by setting up a system that eliminated the need for departments to keep excess inventory on hand. In both cases, the organization adapted successfully by keeping its eyes on one goal—pleasing the customer, regardless of whether the customer is in-house or outside. The success of the Xenith may demonstrate whether Xerox can become adaptive on a larger scale.

*Brian Dumaine, "The Bureaucracy Busters," *Fortune*, June 17, 1991, p. 38.

Discussion Questions

1. In what other types of industries would an adaptive organization be useful?

2. Why would Xerox's failure to capitalize on its new products show a need for a change in organization design?

E 3. Suppose you are a manager at Xerox, in charge of redesigning a particular department in a more adaptive, flexible way, but it means eliminating the job of an old friend who is part of the hierarchy. What might you do?

References: Brian Dumaine, "The Bureaucracy Busters," *Fortune*, June 17, 1991, pp. 36–50; Laurence Hooper, "Xerox Tries to Shed Its Has-Been Image with Big New Machine," *The Wall Street Journal*, September 20, 1990, pp. A1, A6.

*B*echtel is one of the largest construction and engineering companies in the world. It has built more than 15,000 projects in more than 135 countries. Its long list of projects includes Washington, D.C.'s subway system, San Francisco's Bay Area Rapid Transit system, and Canada's James Bay hydroelectric project.

Until the 1980s, Bechtel thrived on such huge projects and on its high-profile image. Some of its work—such as the construction of nuclear power plants around the world—made Bechtel controversial, and because it is still privately owned and controlled by the Bechtel family, it developed a reputation as a secretive, powerful giant. Its image was most badly tarnished by the revelation that up until the Iraqi invasion of Kuwait, Bechtel was building a petrochemical plant near Baghdad that could have enabled Iraq to make mustard gas. But Bechtel's high-ranking connections around the world—Reagan cabinet members George Schultz and Caspar Weinberger, for instance, used to work for Bechtel—have kept controversy from affecting Bechtel's business.

But what controversy couldn't do, a worldwide construction slump in the mid-1980s could. With less work to do, less credit available, a recession in the United States, and keen competition from huge Japanese contractors, Bechtel began shrinking. First it let go one-half of its 44,000 professionals. Bechtel has had to change every aspect of its organization to be more adaptive and more able to pursue smaller contracts. Its tremendous overhead used to make small jobs inherently unprofitable. But when projects like a $5 billion high-speed railway between Los Angeles and Las Vegas fell through, Bechtel had to find new work in other areas.

Where once the company was primarily builder and engineer, it is now focusing on all aspects of the construction process. It helps clients arrange financing, it has become willing to retain some ownership in the power plants it builds, and it now accepts incentive clauses to land contracts. For instance, it built a power plant for Philadelphia Electric Co. under an arrangement that would have cost Bechtel its basic management fee if it had come in over time or over budget. Instead, the plant was finished under budget and ahead of schedule.

Bechtel is now also specializing in managing and cleaning up mistakes. It successfully smoothed out the problems among the ten British and French contractors working on the English Channel tunnel project. With the decline in nuclear power plant construction, Bechtel has become a leader in decommissioning and cleaning up the plants.

Discussion Questions

1. What changes in organizational design would allow a giant like Bechtel to make competitive bids on smaller projects?

2. What kind of organizational structure would best allow San Francisco–based Bechtel to manage large construction projects around the world?

E **3.** Though Bechtel was following the law when building its chemical plant in Iraq, should it have been concerned about the plant's potentially unethical uses given Iraq's unsteady relationship with the United States and with Kuwait?

References: Gary Hoover, Alta Campbell, and Patrick J. Spain (eds.), *Hoover's Handbook 1991— Profiles of Over 500 Major Corporations* (Austin, Tex.: The Reference Press, 1990), p. 122; G. Pascal Zachary and Susan C. Faludi, "Bechtel, Hurt by Slide in Heavy Construction, Re-Engineers Itself," *The Wall Street Journal*, May 28, 1991, pp. A1, A12.

Managing
Organization Change

OBJECTIVES

After studying this chapter, you should be able to:

● *Describe the nature of organization change, including forces for change and planned versus reactive change.*

● *Discuss the steps in the change process and how to manage resistance to change.*

● *Identify and describe major areas of organization change.*

● *Discuss the assumptions, techniques, and effectiveness of organization development.*

● *Discuss the need for and approaches to organization revitalization.*

OUTLINE

The Nature of Organization Change
  Forces for Change
  Planned Versus Reactive Change

Managing Change in Organizations
  Steps in the Change Process
  Reasons for Resistance to Change
  Overcoming Resistance to Change

Areas of Organization Change
  Changing Strategy
  Changing Structure and Design
  Changing Technology and Operations
  Changing People

Organization Development
  OD Assumptions
  OD Techniques
  The Effectiveness of OD

Organization Revitalization
  The Need for Revitalization
  Approaches to Revitalization

IBM HAS BEEN the dominant firm in its industry for decades. But since the introduction of personal computers more than a decade ago, the industry giant has stumbled and staggered. Many observers say that IBM has grown lethargic—unresponsive to its environment, bureaucratic, and slow to get its new products to market.

The firm recently unveiled a major series of changes that it hopes will solve these problems. At the core of these changes is an overhaul of its organization design. Before the changes, IBM had a monolithic structure, and all major decisions had to be approved by a centralized management committee of top executives. The organization was tall, had narrow spans of management, and little authority was delegated to the lower ranks. A huge group of staff managers was also used to oversee the performance of operating managers.

In its new design, many of IBM's main operations are organized into relatively independent units—almost like smaller firms under a corporate umbrella. Each unit will have almost total responsibility for managing its own affairs. While it must still report its financial performance to corporate management, each unit will now have considerably more control over what it does and how it gets done.

The organization is also attempting to change the way its employees behave and think. For decades IBM had a policy of no layoffs. When it had to cut back, IBM offered generous early retirement programs. While this policy ensured job security, the firm had difficulty ridding itself of marginal employees. But as part of these recent changes, new provisions were put in place to facilitate the dismissal of marginal employees. While it's too soon to measure the effectiveness of these changes, IBM executives think that they have paved the way for a resurgence during the coming years.[1] ●

anagers at IBM have had to grapple with something all managers must eventually confront: the need for change. The environment changed, and the company was forced to change with it. Some might argue that IBM should have changed earlier, and some might argue that the changes were either too substantial or not substantial enough. But regardless of how they would have handled the situation, most experts agree that some change was necessary.

Understanding when and how to implement change is a vital part of management. This chapter describes how organizations manage change. We first examine the nature of organization change and identify the basic issues of managing change. Major areas of change are then identified and described. Finally, we examine two related areas of managerial concern—organization development and organization revitalization.

THE NATURE OF ORGANIZATION CHANGE

● **organization change**
Any substantive modification to some part of the organization

Organization change is any substantive modification to some part of the organization.[2] Thus change can involve virtually any aspect of an organization such as work schedules, bases for departmentalization, span of management, machinery, overall organization design, and people themselves. Keep in mind that any change in an organization may have effects extending beyond the actual area where the change is implemented. For example, when Westinghouse Electric Corp. installed a new computerized production system at one of its plants, employees needed training to operate new equipment, the compensation system was adjusted to reflect new skill levels, the span of management of supervisors was altered, and several related jobs had to be redesigned. Selection criteria for new employees were also changed, and a new quality control system was installed.[3]

Forces for Change

Organizations find it necessary to change when something relevant to the organization either has changed or is going to change. The organization consequently has little choice but to change as well. Indeed, a primary reason for the problems that organizations often face is failure to anticipate or respond properly to changing circumstances. Forces for change may be external or internal to the organization.

External Forces External forces for change derive from the organization's general and task environments. For example, two energy crises, a maturing Japanese automobile industry, floating currency exchange rates, and floating international interest rates, all manifestations of the international dimension of the general environment, have profoundly influenced U.S. automobile companies. New rules of production and competition have forced them to dramatically alter the way they do business.[4] In the political area, new laws, court decisions, and regulations affect organizations. The technological dimension may yield new production techniques that the organization needs to explore. The economic dimension is affected by inflation, the cost of living, and money supplies. The sociocultural dimension, reflecting societal values, determines what kinds of products or services will be accepted in the market.

Because of its proximity to the organization, the task environment is an even more powerful force for change. Competitors influence an organization through their price structures and product lines. When General Motors Corp. offers a rebate on new cars, Ford Motor Co. has little choice but to follow suit. Because customers determine what products can be sold at what prices, organizations must be concerned with consumer tastes and preferences. Suppliers affect organizations by raising or lowering prices or changing product lines. Regulators can have dramatic effects on an organization. For example, if the Occupational Safety and Health Administration (OSHA) rules that a particular production process is dangerous to workers, it can force a firm to close a plant until higher safety standards are met. Unions can force change when they negotiate for higher wages or strike.

Internal Forces A variety of forces inside the organization can cause change. If top management revises the organization's strategy, organization change is likely to result. A decision by an electronics company to enter the home computer market or a decision to increase a ten-year product sales goal by 3 percent would occasion many organization changes. Other internal forces for change may be reflections of external forces. As sociocultural values shift, for example, workers' attitudes toward their jobs may also shift—and workers may demand a change in working hours or working conditions. In such a case, even though the force is rooted in the external environment, the organization must respond directly to the internal pressure it generates.

Planned Versus Reactive Change

Some change is planned well in advance; other change comes about as a reaction to unexpected events. **Planned change** is change that is designed and implemented in an orderly and timely fashion in anticipation of future events. **Reactive change** is a piecemeal response to circumstances as they occur. Because reactive change may be hurried, the potential for poorly conceived and executed change is increased. Planned change is almost always preferable to reactive change.

Southwestern Bell Corp. recently benefitted from planned change. As a result of the deregulation of the telephone industry and the subsequent breakup of AT&T's regional telephone operations, Southwestern Bell had to adapt itself to function as an independent corporation. Top managers developed a comprehensive change plan consisting of 2,000 major activities that needed to be modified or replaced. The change went off remarkably well, with only a few slip-ups along the way.[5]

Caterpillar Inc., on the other hand, is a good example of a firm guilty of reactive change. It recently suffered enormous losses because of a worldwide recession in the construction industry; it took several years to recover. Had managers at Caterpillar anticipated the need for change earlier, they might have been able to respond more quickly. These points become especially telling in view of the frequency of organization change. Most companies

● **planned change**
Change that is designed and implemented in an orderly and timely fashion in anticipation of future events

● **reactive change**
A piecemeal response to circumstances as they develop

When Phillips-Van Heusen Chairman, Lawrence Phillips, anticipated trends in retailing that could affect his clothing business, he planned change in an orderly and timely way. By expanding the company's share of the private-label shirt business, cutting sales to off-price retailers, and opening his own stores in outlet malls, he reduced his company's dependence on increasingly powerful retailers.

or divisions of large companies implement some form of moderate change at least every year and one or more major changes every four to five years.[6] Managers who respond only when they have to are likely to spend a lot of time hastily changing and rechanging things. A more effective approach is to anticipate forces urging change and plan ahead to deal with them.

MANAGING CHANGE IN ORGANIZATIONS

Organization change is a complex phenomenon. A manager cannot simply wave a wand and implement a planned change like magic. Instead, any change must be approached in a systematic and logical fashion for it to have a realistic opportunity to succeed. To carry this off, the manager needs to understand the steps needed for effective change and how to deal with employee resistance to change.[7]

Steps in the Change Process

A number of models or frameworks outlining steps for change have been developed over the years. The Lewin model was one of the first, although a more comprehensive approach is usually more useful.

The Lewin Model   Kurt Lewin, a noted organizational theorist, suggested that every change requires three steps.[8] The first step is *unfreezing:* individuals who will be affected by the impending change must be led to recognize why the change is necessary. Next the *change itself* is implemented. Finally, *refreezing* involves reinforcing and supporting the change so that it becomes a part of the system. For example, one of the changes Caterpillar faced in response to the recession involved a massive work-force reduction. The first step (unfreezing) was convincing the United Auto Workers to support the reduction because of its importance to long-term effectiveness. After this unfreezing was accomplished, 30,000 jobs were eliminated (implementation). Then Caterpillar worked to improve its damaged relationship with its workers (refreezing) by guaranteeing future pay hikes and promising no more cutbacks. As valuable as Lewin's model is in pointing out the importance of planning the change, communicating its value, and reinforcing it after it has been made, the model lacks operational specificity. Thus a more comprehensive perspective is often needed.

A Comprehensive Approach to Change The comprehensive approach to change takes a systems view and delineates a series of specific steps that often lead to more successful change. This expanded model is illustrated in Figure 12.1. The first step is recognizing the need for change. Reactive change might be triggered by events such as employee complaints, declines in productivity or turnover, court injunctions, sales slumps, or labor strikes. Recognition may simply be managers' awareness that change in a certain area is inevitable. The immediate stimulus might be the result of a forecast indicating new market potential, the accumulation of cash surplus for possible investment, or an opportunity to achieve and capitalize on a key technological breakthrough. Managers might also initiate change today because indicators suggest that it will be necessary in the near future.

Managers must then set goals for the change. To increase market share, to enter new markets, to restore employee morale, to settle a strike, and to

FIGURE 12.1 Steps in the Change Process

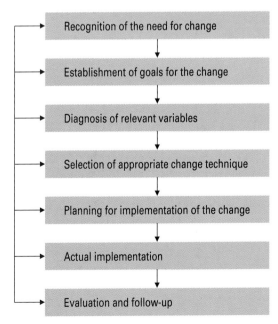

Managers must understand how and why to implement change. A manager who, when implementing change, follows a logical and orderly sequence, such as the one shown here, is more likely to succeed than is a manager whose change process is haphazard and poorly conceived.

identify investment opportunities are all goals for change. Third, managers must diagnose what has brought on the need for change. Turnover, for example, might be caused by low pay, poor working conditions, poor supervisors, or employee dissatisfaction. Thus although turnover may be the immediate stimulus for change, managers must understand its causes to make the right changes. This step is especially critical, because if managers misdiagnose the problem, they are likely to commit resources to implementing an unnecessary change while the real problem remains untreated.

The next step is to select a change technique that will accomplish the intended goals. If turnover is being caused by low pay, the organization may need a new reward system. If the cause is poor supervision, supervisors can be offered interpersonal skills training. (Various change techniques are summarized later in this chapter.) After the appropriate technique has been chosen, managers must plan its implementation. Issues to consider include the costs of the change, its effects on other areas of the organization, and the degree of employee participation that is appropriate for the situation. If the change is implemented as planned, the results should then be evaluated. If the change was intended to reduce turnover, managers must check turnover after the change has been in effect for a while. If turnover is still too high, other changes may be necessary.[9]

Reasons for Resistance to Change

To effectively manage change, managers must understand that resistance often greets change. Managers need to know why people resist change and what can be done about their resistance. When Westinghouse replaced all of its typewriters with computer terminals and personal computers, most people responded favorably, but one manager resisted the change to the point where he began leaving work every day at noon. It was some time before he began staying in the office all day again. Such resistance is common for a variety of reasons.

Uncertainty   Perhaps the biggest cause of employee resistance to change is uncertainty. In the face of impending change, employees may become anxious and nervous. They may worry about their ability to meet new job demands, they may think that their job security is threatened, or they may simply dislike ambiguity. RJR Nabisco, Inc., was recently the target of an extended and confusing takeover battle, and during the entire time employees were nervous about the impending change. *The Wall Street Journal* described them this way: "Many are angry at their leaders and fearful for their jobs. They are swapping rumors and spinning scenarios for the ultimate outcome of the battle for the tobacco and food giant. Headquarters staffers in Atlanta know so little about what's happening in New York that some call their office 'the mushroom complex,' where they are kept in the dark."[10]

Threatened Self-Interests   A change might threaten the self-interests of some managers within the organization, potentially diminishing their power or influence. Managers so affected may fight the change. Managers at Sears, Roebuck and Co. recently developed a plan calling for a new type of store. The new stores would be somewhat smaller than typical Sears stores and would not be located in large shopping malls. Instead they would be located in smaller strip-shopping centers. They would carry clothes and other "soft goods" but not hardware, appliances, furniture, or automotive products. When executives in charge of the excluded product lines heard about the plan, they raised such strong objections that the entire idea was dropped.[11]

Different Perceptions   People may also resist change because their perceptions of the situation differ from the manager's. A manager may make a decision and recommend a plan for change on the basis of her own assessment of a situation. Others in the organization may resist the change because they do not agree with the manager's assessment or perceive the situation differently. When Continental Airlines, Inc., bought Eastern Air Lines, Inc., its managers thought Eastern's labor leaders would agree that labor costs were too high and would submit to contract concessions. Labor, however, perceived the problems to be the result of mismanagement and so refused to give in.[12]

Feelings of Loss   Many changes involve altering work arrangements in ways that disrupt existing social networks. Because social relationships are important, most people resist any change that might adversely affect those relationships. Other intangibles that are threatened by change include power, status, security, familiarity with existing procedures, and self-confidence. For example, Steven Jobs hired John Sculley to bring professional management to Apple. He later found that he did not like Sculley's changes and wanted things as they were before. His own status and self-confidence were being threatened. Jobs tried to oust Sculley, lost a power struggle with the board of directors, and then left himself.[13]

Overcoming Resistance to Change

A manager should not give up in the face of resistance to change. Although there are no certain cures, several techniques at least have the potential to overcome resistance.[14]

Participation   Participation is often the most effective technique for overcoming resistance to change. Employees who participate in planning and implementing a change are better able to understand the reasons for the change. Uncertainty is reduced, and self-interests and social relationships are less threatened. Having had an opportunity to express their ideas and to understand the perspectives of others, employees are more likely to accept the change gracefully. A classical study of participation monitored the introduction of a change in production methods among four groups in a Virginia pajama factory.[15] The two groups that were allowed to fully participate in planning and implementing the change improved their productivity and satisfaction significantly relative to the two groups that did not participate. 3M Company recently attributed $10 million in cost savings to employee participation in several organization change activities.[16]

Education and Communication   Educating employees about the need for and the expected results of an impending change may reduce their resistance. If open communication is established and maintained during the

AT&T's Business Network Sales Division planned to close offices in ten states, giving its salespeople such as John White notebook computers, modems, and printers and having them work out of their homes. AT&T anticipated that some resistance to the change would involve employees' fearing the loss of social relationships, so as part of managing the change, it planned to come up with ways to keep employees connected with one another.

change process, uncertainty can be minimized. Caterpillar used these methods during many of its cutbacks to reduce resistance. First, United Auto Worker representatives were educated about the need for and potential value of the planned changes. Then all employees were told what was happening, when it would happen, and how it would affect them individually.

Facilitation Several facilitation procedures, which include making only necessary changes, announcing those changes well in advance, and allowing time for people to adjust to new ways of doing things, can help reduce resistance to change. One manager at a regional office of The Prudential Insurance Co. of America spent several months systematically planning a change in work procedures and job design. Then, suddenly in a hurry, he came in over a weekend with a work crew and rearranged the office layout. When employees walked in on Monday morning, they were hostile, anxious, and resentful. What was a promising change became a disaster, and the manager had to scrap the entire plan.

Force-Field Analysis Although force-field analysis may sound like something out of a Star Trek movie, it can help overcome resistance to change. In almost any change situation, forces act both for and against the change. To facilitate the change, managers should start by listing each set of forces and then try to remove, or at least minimize some of the forces acting against the change. The forces facilitating the change should outweigh those hindering the change. Suppose, for example, that IBM is considering closing a plant. As shown in Figure 12.2, three factors reinforce the change: IBM needs to cut costs, it has excess capacity, and the plant has outmoded production facilities. At the same time, there is resistance from

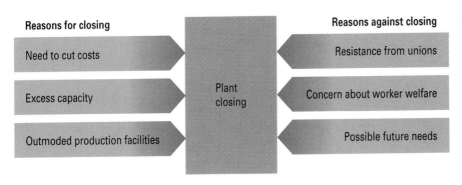

A force-field analysis can help a manager facilitate change. A manager able to identify forces acting both for and against a change can see where to focus efforts to remove barriers to change (such as offering training and relocation to displaced workers). By removing the forces against the change, resistance can be at least partially overcome.

unions, concern for workers being put out of their jobs, and a feeling that the plant might be needed again in the future. IBM might start by convincing the unions that the closing is necessary by presenting profit and loss figures. It could then offer relocation and retraining to displaced workers. And it might shut down the plant and put it in "moth balls" so that it could be renovated later. The three major factors hindering the change are thus eliminated or reduced in importance.

AREAS OF ORGANIZATION CHANGE

We noted earlier that change can involve virtually any part of an organization. In general, however, most change interventions involve organizational strategy, organization structure and design, technology and operations, or people.[17] The most common areas of change within each of these broad categories are listed in Table 12.1.

While change can be directed at any aspect of an organization, most change interventions focus on one of four areas: strategy, organization design, technology/operations, and people. For example, General Motors is currently changing its organization design.

T A B L E   12.1   Areas of Organization Change

Strategy	Organization Structure and Design	Technology and Operations	People
Strategic goals	Job design	Equipment	Abilities/skills
Grand strategy	Departmentalization	Work processes	Performance
Business portfolio	Reporting relationships	Work sequences	Perceptions
Business strategy	Authority distribution	Information systems	Expectations
Functional strategy	Coordination mechanisms	Control systems	Attitudes
Partnerships	Line-staff structure		Values
Internationalization	Overall design		
	Culture		
	Human resource management		

The new Chrysler Technology Center includes a 150,000-square-foot manufacturing operation that will foresee and solve problems before vehicle assembly, and a Scientific Test Facility with five major laboratories. By changing its strategy to emphasize technological advantage, Chrysler hopes to reap the benefits of higher quality, lower costs, and shorter vehicle development times.

Changing Strategy

A change in organizational strategy is an attempt to alter the organization's alignment with its environment. As Table 12.1 shows, the change might focus on any area of strategy. For example, an organization might change its strategic goals or its grand strategy—moving from a growth into a retrenchment mode, for example. A multidivisional corporation might change its portfolio of businesses by buying or selling a business. Or it might alter the strategy for a particular business—for example, dropping a differentiation strategy and adopting a cost leadership strategy. Similarly, a business might choose to change any functional strategy. For example, it might change its posture regarding debt or spending on research and development. Or the organization might decide to enter into a joint venture by means of a partnership or move into international markets. Any of these decisions would reflect a change in the organization's strategy and would be subject to the same considerations as any other change.[18]

Changing Structure and Design

Organization change might also focus on any of the basic components of organization structure or on the organization's overall design. Thus the organization might change the way it designs its jobs or its bases of departmentalization. Likewise it might change reporting relationships or the distribution of authority. For example, we noted in Chapter 10 the trend toward flatter organizations.[19] Coordination mechanisms and line-staff configurations are also subject to change. On a larger scale, the organization might change its overall design. For example, a growing business could decide to drop its functional design and adopt a divisional design. Or it might transform itself into a matrix. Finally, the organization might change any part of its human resources management system, such as its selection criteria, its performance appraisal methods, or its compensation package.[20] "Management in Practice" describes how two large banks are changing their designs to facilitate a merger.

Changing Technology and Operations

Technology is the conversion process used by an organization to transform inputs into outputs. Because of the rapid rate of all technological innovation, technological changes are becoming increasingly important to many organizations.[21] Several areas in which organizations experience technological change are listed in Table 12.1. One major area of change involves equipment. To keep pace with competitors, firms may have to periodically replace existing machinery and equipment with newer models.

A change in work processes or work activities may be necessary if new equipment is introduced or new products are manufactured. In manufacturing industries, the major reason for changing a work process is to accommodate a change in the materials used to produce a finished product. Consider a firm that manufactures battery-operated flashlights. For many years flashlights were made of metal, but now most are made of plastic. A firm might decide to move from metal to plastic flashlights because of consumer

CHANGING ADIDAS ON TWO CONTINENTS

Germany-based Adidas AG sells sports shoes and clothing in 160 countries. The company has a long history of supporting sporting events and training centers and providing teams in developing countries with equipment. Eighty percent of the athletes in the 1988 Olympics games wore Adidas equipment.

But the fortunes of Adidas, and especially of its subsidiary Adidas USA, have floundered over the last decade as companies like Nike, Inc., and Reebok International Ltd. have elbowed their way into Adidas's markets and customers have begun buying athletic shoes for fashion, not for workouts. So during 1991 and 1992, Adidas looked for help on both sides of the Atlantic, with very different results.

In Germany, after months of negotiations, Adi Dassler's four daughters agreed to sell their 80-percent share in the company to Bernard Tapie, a high-profile, controversial Frenchman. The sale outraged some Germans, who objected to a company with a name almost as well-known as Mercedes-Benz being sold to a non-German. Tapie has a reputation for taking over companies, firing their managers and turning them around financially, and then selling them for a profit. In France, Tapie has become a spokesman for unabashed capitalism, using his television appearances and his seat in parliament to spread the gospel of entrepreneurism. Germans were especially afraid that he would move Adidas's high-paying jobs out of Germany, but Tapie promised the Dassler sisters that he would change his freewheeling capitalist style and continue Adidas's support of training centers and teams.

In the United States, meanwhile, Adidas AG has turned over control of Adidas USA to the Contrarian Group, headed by Peter Ueberroth. Ueberroth became famous for his profitable handling of the 1984 Summer Olympics in Los Angeles and his stint as baseball commissioner. He formed the Contrarian Group to function as a management rescue team to help companies that had been battered by the hostile takeovers and junk-bond frenzy of the 1980s. As part of the Adidas USA deal, the Contrarian Group receives a $1 million annual management fee and options to buy 40 percent of Adidas USA and 4 percent of Adidas AG. Ueberroth also received a seat on the board of Adidas AG, and other members of the Contrarian Group took over the top positions at Adidas USA.

Ueberroth's group hopes to become a model for managment in the 1990s, while Tapie carries the stamp of a 1980s financial playboy. The relative fortunes of Adidas AG and Adidas USA should provide some indication of the management directions likely to succeed in the 1990s.

References: E.S. Browning and Terence Roth, "Tapie Seeks Thrill of Victory With Adidas," *The Wall Street Journal,* July 10, 1990, p. A12; John R. Emshwiller, "Peter Ueberroth's Contrarian Group Goes for the Gold in Sport of Corporate Revival," *The Wall Street Journal,* May 10, 1991, p. B1.

organization design, a new set of values, or a company-wide organization development program might all fill this important need.

SUMMARY OF KEY POINTS

Organization change is any substantive modification to some part of the organization. Change can be prompted by internal or external organizational forces. In general, planned change is preferable to reactive change.

Managing the change process is very important. The Lewin model provides a general perspective on the steps in the process, although a comprehensive model is usually more effective. People tend to resist change because of uncertainty, threatened self-interests, different perceptions, and feelings of loss. Participation, education and communication, facilitation, and force-field analysis are methods for overcoming this resistance.

Many different change techniques or interventions are used. The most common ones involve changing strategy, structure and design, technology, and people.

Organization development is concerned with changing attitudes, perceptions, behaviors, and expectations. Its effective use relies on an important set of assumptions. Opinions conflict about the effectiveness of OD techniques.

Revitalization is the infusion of new energy, vitality, and strength into the organization. It is occasionally needed to offset entropy. The basic steps in revitalization are contraction, consolidation, and expansion. Any organization change or development activity could be the basis for revitalization.

DISCUSSION QUESTIONS

Questions for Review

1. What forces or kinds of events lead to organization change? Identify each force or event as planned or reactive change.

2. How is each step in the process of organization change implemented? Are some of the steps likely to meet with more resistance than others? Why or why not?

3. What are the various areas of organization change? In what ways are they similar and in what ways do they differ?

4. Define organization development and organization revitalization. How could a manager assess the effectiveness of an OD effort? A revitalization effort?

Questions for Analysis

5. Could reactive change of the type identified in question 1 have been planned ahead of time? Why or why not? Should all organization change be planned? Why or why not?

6. A company has recently purchased equipment that, when installed, will do the work of 100 employees. The work force of the company is very concerned and is threatening to take some kind of action. If you were the human resources manager, what would you try to do to satisfy all parties concerned? Why?

7. "All organizations need constant revitalization." Can you present a logical counterargument to this statement?

Questions for Application

8. Some people resist change while others welcome change enthusiastically. To deal with the first group, one needs to overcome resistance to change; to deal with the second, one needs to overcome resistance to stability. What advice can you give a manager facing the latter situation?

9. Can a change made in one area of an organization—in technology, for instance—not lead to change in other areas? Why or why not?

10. Find out more about one of the techniques for organization development presented in this chapter. What are the advantages and disadvantages of that technique relative to other techniques?

NAVISTAR PULLS BACK FROM THE BRINK

*I*n 1902, McCormick Harvesting Machine Company merged with two other companies to form International Harvester Co. For the next eighty years, IH on the hood of farm machinery or trucks stood for made-in-the-U.S.A. quality. Therefore, more than just customers and employees worried when the company seemed destined for bankruptcy in the early 1980s: a way of life seemed in doubt.

Harvester's crisis occurred when it was hit by a number of problems at once. The farm crisis was beginning, and foreclosures were becoming common in the United States. A lawsuit alleging a tractor design defect tainted Harvester's reputation for quality. At the same time, IH was suffering through a six-month strike by the United Auto Workers.

Many observers thought that Harvester would survive only with a Chrysler-style infusion of government money. Although it managed to avoid that way out, it emerged from the crisis so altered that it changed its name to Navistar International Corp. Gone was the farm equipment business on which the company had been founded. Gone too were 50,000 of the approximately 65,000 people that IH employed before the crisis. In fact, Navistar survived with just two things: heavy-truck manufacturing and a reputation for quality.

Although many companies in its position might have been tempted to fall back on the past, the only part of its past that Navistar returned to was its history of innovation. To sell his machines, founder Cyrus McCormick became the first in his industry to advertise, to give a warranty with his machines, and to offer credit to his customers. Keeping with such a tradition, Navistar in 1989 offered new models across 85 percent of its product line. While production changeovers necessary to meet a sudden spurt in truck demand meant that Navistar's balance sheet for the year was not impressive, the new models helped the company keep dealers happy and retain its reputation for innovativeness and its share of slightly more than one-fourth of the large-truck market.

Navistar sees the future growth of truck sales coming from overseas, but that doesn't mean that it's planning to export Navistar trucks. In fact, IH sold its overseas businesses as part of the slimming down that changed it into Navistar. But the company thinks that in the future, trucks will be made the way airplanes are now made—with large assemblies coming from different parts of the world.

Meanwhile, Navistar is frustrating Wall Street by not buying back shares, acquiring other companies, or paying out dividends. It is holding onto its cash, planning for the future and ready for the next crisis.

Discussion Questions

1. What advantages does Navistar's plan to participate in making hybrid trucks have over the practice of simply making its own trucks and selling them abroad?

2. Who benefitted from the transformation of International Harvester into Navistar? Who would have benefitted from a government loan that would have kept International Harvester intact?

E **3.** Do you think International Harvester should have taken a large loan from the government to sustain its huge business and save the jobs of those 50,000 people who lost them in the transition to today's Navistar International? Discuss the pros and cons.

References: Marcia Berss, "Jim Cotting's Love Affair with Cash," *Forbes*, March 19, 1990, pp. 50–55; Chet Borucki and Carole K. Barnett, "Restructuring for Self-Renewal," *Academy of Management Executive*, Vol. 4, No. 1, 1990, p. 36; Milton Moskowitz, Michael Katz, and Robert Levering, *Everybody's Business* (San Francisco: Harper & Row, 1980), pp. 624–626.

PREPARING FOR THE EUROPEAN COMMUNITY

The gradual unification of Europe into the European Community, which reached its apex in 1992, is causing changes in every major European company. From a group of small, well-protected markets, Europe is becoming one large market open to worldwide competition. European companies have taken different approaches to cope with these changes.

Undergoing some of the most wrenching changes are Italy's Fiat S.p.A. and the family that controls Fiat, the Agnellis. Fiat is the sixth-largest automaker in the world, but it sells more than 70 percent of its cars to countries that severely restrict Japanese imports: Italy, France, Spain, and Portugal. Italy currently limits Japanese cars to about 2 percent of the Italian market, while in the European Community as a whole, Japanese cars claim 11 percent of the market.

Already, Fiat has felt the heat from outside competition, particularly Ford Motor Co. and Volkswagen AG. Fiat traditionally held 60 percent of the Italian auto market, which allowed it to keep prices and profits high. But now that figure has slipped to less than 48 percent, while in the late 1980s Ford doubled its market share in just three years.

The Agnellis, Italy's premier capitalist family, have long been preparing for the increased competition, using both Fiat's capital and their other holdings to diversify, creating an empire that in some ways imitates the boundary-less European Community itself. More than one-fourth of Fiat's sales come from its businesses unrelated to cars and trucks: telecommunications, railroad, and aerospace equipment; robots; chemicals; publishing; financial services; and retailing.

But while cars will remain Fiat's main business, they don't have to be the keystone of the Agnellis' empire. Through a number of investment companies, the Agnellis are investing in food, hotels, airlines, and other businesses throughout Europe. In a joint venture with a German group, for instance, the Ag-

nellis now own a Paris-based trading company dealing mostly in Far Eastern rubber.

As the family leadership passes from Giovanni Agnelli, at home in Europe and New York, to his younger brother Umberto, who already has links with Japan, the Agnellis are likely to start doing more business in the Far East. Even if Fiat and indeed all of Italy become minor players in the European Community, the Agnellis are likely to remain a strong force in European business.

Discussion Questions

1. What different forces have led Fiat to diversify while so many U.S. companies are selling off unrelated businesses and "sticking to their knitting"?

2. How do you think that the managers at Fiat's plants are dealing with the changes brought on by the formation of the European Community?

E 3. Like automakers in this country, Fiat has an important influence on the health of its native Italian economy. As competition from foreign car makers heats up in 1992 and the future, the Agnelli family may find it increasingly tempting to move away from cars and into other businesses in other countries. Do you think that Fiat has an obligation to its home economy to keep its Italian manufacturing centers alive, even if it may ultimately mean shrinking profits for the company?

References: Guy Collins and Robert L. Simison, "Fiat's Share of Italian Market Hits Skids," *The Wall Street Journal*, May 21, 1991, p. A10; Guy Collins, "Fiat Will Build Major Car Plant in Southern Italy," *The Wall Street Journal*, November 29, 1990, p. A9; John Rossant, "The Agnellis Buy Their Way into Europe '92," *Business Week*, December 16, 1991, pp. 50–52.

Managing Human Resources

OBJECTIVES

After studying this chapter, you should be able to:

● *Describe the environmental context of human resources management, including its strategic importance and its relationship with legal and social factors.*

● *Discuss how organizations attract human resources, including human resources planning, recruiting, and selection, as well as common selection methods.*

● *Describe how organizations develop human resources, including training and development, performance appraisal, and performance feedback.*

● *Discuss how organizations maintain human resources, including the determination of compensation and benefits and career planning.*

● *Discuss labor relations, including how employees form unions and the mechanics of collective bargaining.*

OUTLINE

The Environmental Context of Human Resources Management
    The Strategic Importance of HRM
    The Legal Environment of HRM
    Social Change and HRM

Attracting Human Resources
    Human Resources Planning
    Recruiting Human Resources
    Common Selection Methods

Developing Human Resources
    Training and Development
    Performance Appraisal
    Performance Feedback

Maintaining Human Resources
    Determining Compensation
    Determining Benefits
    Career Planning

Managing Labor Relations
    How Employees Form Unions
    Collective Bargaining

FOOD LION INC. is a highly successful and fast-growing grocery chain based in North Carolina. Founded in 1957, Food Lion struggled for more than a decade and was close to bankruptcy. In 1967, however, managers at Food Lion identified the two factors that would transform the firm into a major retailer. By 1991, Food Lion was operating approximately 800 stores and was the twenty-first largest retailer in the United States.

One reason for Food Lion's success is its relentless focus on lowering prices and cutting costs. All Food Lion stores look just alike, and they all carry the same products. By continually refining its distribution system, building inexpensive and small stores, and carrying primarily food items, the company has been able to cut its costs while maintaining reasonable profit margins.

The other reason for Food Lion's success has been its approach to managing its employees. The firm keeps its labor costs far below the industry average. Each week Food Lion headquarters sends each store its scheduling budget for the next week. This budget mandates the work that each employee must do in forty hours. Store managers must ensure that the work gets done within budget or do it themselves.

Some labor leaders have criticized how Food Lion treats its employees, however. For example, some employees charge that they have been pressured to work overtime without getting paid to meet the scheduling budget. Others claim that managers force them to work relentlessly to meet the budget. Although Food Lion's employees are not unionized, the United Food and Commercial Workers union has recently filed an unfair labor grievance against the firm. On the other hand, managers at Food Lion claim that if employees are caught working without signing in they are subject to dismissal and that all they expect is an honest day's effort for an honest day's pay.[1] ●

uman resources are clearly an integral part of Food Lion's success. Managers at Food Lion argue that they are simply using their human resources fully. Others, however, argue that the firm is exploiting its human resources. Regardless of their position, however, virtually everyone would agree on one thing: an organization that does a poor job of managing its human resources cannot be effective.

This chapter is about **human resources management**—an organization's activities directed at attracting, developing, and maintaining an effective work force. We start by describing the environmental context of HRM. We then discuss how organizations attract human resources. Next we describe how human resources are first developed and then maintained. We conclude by discussing labor relations.

● **human resources management**
The set of organizational activities directed at attracting, developing, and maintaining an effective work force

THE ENVIRONMENTAL CONTEXT OF HUMAN RESOURCES MANAGEMENT

Human resources management takes place within a complex and ever-changing environmental context. Three particularly vital components of this context are HRM's strategic importance and the legal and social environment of HRM.

The Strategic Importance of HRM

Human resources are critical for effective organizational functioning. HRM (or personnel, as it is sometimes called) was once relegated to second-class status in many organizations, but its importance has grown dramatically in the last two decades. Its new importance stems from increased legal complexities, the recognition that human resources are a valuable means for improving productivity, and the awareness today of the costs associated with poor human resources management.[2]

Indeed, managers now realize that the effectiveness of their HR function has a substantial impact on the bottom-line performance of the firm. Poor human resources planning can result in spurts of hiring followed by lay-offs—costly in terms of unemployment compensation payments, training expenses, and morale. Haphazard compensation systems do not attract, keep, and motivate good employees, and outmoded recruitment practices can expose the firm to expensive and embarrassing discrimination lawsuits. Consequently, the chief human resources executive of most large businesses is a vice president directly accountable to the CEO, and many firms are developing strategic HR plans and are integrating those plans with other strategic planning activities.[3]

Even organizations with as few as 200 employees usually have a human resources manager and a human resources department charged with overseeing these activities. Responsibility for HR activities, however, is shared between the HR department and line managers. The HR department may recruit and initially screen candidates, but the final selection is usually made

The Occupational Safety and Health Administration (OSHA) sets standards concerning safety and the prevention of occupational disease. To comply with OSHA standards, a company may have to install expensive equipment or change its production processes. Northern States Power Company, for example, began burning low-sulfur coal and installed emission control equipment to lessen its environmental impact on employees and customers. Janet Anderson and Keith Hanrahan work to ensure that NSP is complying with OSHA standards at the Black Dog Plant in Burnsville, Minn.

by managers in the department where the new employee will work. Similarly, although the HR department may establish performance appraisal policies and procedures, the actual evaluating and coaching of employees is done by their immediate superiors.

The Legal Environment of HRM

A number of laws regulate various aspects of employee-employer relations, especially in the areas of Equal Employment Opportunity, compensation and benefits, labor relations, and occupational safety and health. The major ones are summarized in Table 13.1.

Equal Employment Opportunity   **Title VII of the Civil Rights Act of 1964** forbids discrimination in all areas of the employment relationship. The intent of Title VII is to ensure that employment decisions are made on the basis of an individual's qualifications rather than personal biases. The law has reduced direct forms of discrimination refusing to promote blacks into management, failing to hire men as flight attendants, refusing to hire women as construction workers) as well as indirect forms of discrimination (using employment tests that whites pass at a higher rate than blacks). These requirements have an **adverse impact** on minorities and women when such individuals pass the selection standard at a rate less than 80 percent of the pass rate of majority group members. Criteria that have an adverse impact on protected groups can be used only when there is solid evidence that they effectively identify individuals who are better able than others to do the job.[4] The **Equal Employment Opportunity Commission** is charged with enforcing Title VII.[5]

Title VII of the Civil Rights Act of 1964
Forbids discrimination on the basis of sex, race, color, religion, or national origin in all areas of the employment relationship

adverse impact
When minority group members pass a selection standard at a rate less than 80 percent of the pass rate of majority group members

Equal Employment Opportunity Commission
Charged with enforcing Title VII of the Civil Rights Act of 1964

As much as any area of management, HRM is subject to wide-ranging laws and court decisions. These laws and decisions affect the human resources function in many different areas. For example, AT&T was fined several million dollars for violating Title VII of the Civil Rights Act of 1964.

TABLE 13.1   The Legal Environment of HRM

Area of Regulation

Equal Employment Opportunity

Title VII of the Civil Rights Act of 1964 (as amended by the *Equal Employment Opportunity Act of 1972*): Forbids discrimination in all areas of the employment relationship

Age Discrimination in Employment Act: Outlaws discrimination against people aged 40 through 69

Various Executive Orders, especially *Executive Order 11246 in 1965*: Requires employers with government contracts to engage in Affirmative Action

Pregnancy Discrimination Act: Specifically outlaws discrimination on the basis of pregnancy

Vietnam Era Veterans Readjustment Assistance Act: Extends Affirmative Action mandate to military veterans who served during the Vietnam war

Americans With Disabilities Act: Specifically outlaws discrimination against disabled persons

Compensation and Benefits

Fair Labor Standards Act: Establishes minimum wage and mandated overtime pay for work in excess of 40 hours per week

Equal Pay Act: Requires that men and women be paid the same amount for doing the same jobs

Employee Retirement Income Security Act: Regulates how organizations manage their pension funds

Labor Relations

National Labor Relations Act: Establishes procedures by which employees can establish labor unions and requires organizations to bargain collectively with legally formed unions

Labor-Management Relations Act: Limits union power and specifies management rights during a union organizing campaign

Health and Safety

Occupational Safety and Health Act: Mandates the provision of safe working conditions

---

Age Discrimination in Employment Act
Outlaws discrimination against people aged 40 through 69 years; passed in 1967 and amended in 1978

Affirmative Action
Intentionally seeking and hiring qualified or qualifiable employees from racial, sexual, and ethnic groups that are underrepresented in the organization

The **Age Discrimination in Employment Act,** passed in 1967 and amended in 1978, specifically outlaws discrimination against people aged 40 through 69. Both the Age Discrimination Act and Title VII require passive nondiscrimination, or *Equal Employment Opportunity*. Employers are not required to seek out and hire minorities but they must treat fairly all who apply. Several executive orders, however, require that employers holding government contracts engage in **Affirmative Action**—intentionally seeking and hiring employees from groups that are underrepresented in the organization. These organizations must have a written Affirmative Action plan that spells out employment goals for underutilized groups and how those goals will be met.[6] These employers are also required to act affirmatively in hiring Vietnam-era veterans and qualified handicapped individuals.

Compensation and Benefits Laws also regulate compensation and benefits. The **Fair Labor Standards Act,** passed in 1938 and amended frequently since then, sets a minimum wage and requires the payment of overtime rates for work in excess of forty hours per week. Salaried professional, executive, and administrative employees are exempt from the minimum hourly wage and overtime provisions. The **Equal Pay Act of 1963** requires that men and women be paid the same amount for doing the same jobs. Attempts to circumvent the law by having different job titles and pay rates for men and women who perform the same work are also illegal. However, it is legal to base an employee's pay on seniority or performance, even if it means that a man and woman are paid different amounts for doing the same job. The provision of benefits is also regulated in some ways by state and federal laws. Certain benefits are mandatory—for example, worker's compensation insurance for employees who are injured on the job. Employers who provide a pension plan for their employees are regulated by the **Employee Retirement Income Security Act of 1974 (ERISA).**

Labor Relations Union activities and management's behavior toward unions constitute another heavily regulated area. The **National Labor Relations Act** (also known as the *Wagner Act*), passed in 1935, sets up a procedure for employees of a firm to vote whether to have a union. If they vote for a union, management is required to bargain collectively with the union. The **National Labor Relations Board** was established by the Wagner Act to enforce its provisions. Following a series of severe strikes in 1946, the **Labor-Management Relations Act** (also known as the *Taft-Hartley Act*) was passed in 1947 to limit union power. The law increases management's rights during an organizing campaign. The Taft-Hartley Act also contains the *National Emergency Strike* provision, which allows the president of the United States to prevent or end a strike that endangers national security. Taken together, those laws balance union and management power. Employees can be represented by a properly constituted union, and management can make nonemployee-related business decisions without interference.

Health and Safety The **Occupational Safety and Health Act of 1970** directly mandates the provision of safe working conditions. It requires that employers (1) provide a place of employment that is free from hazards that may cause death or serious physical harm and (2) obey the safety and health standards established by the *Occupational Safety and Health Administration* (OSHA). Safety standards are intended to prevent accidents, whereas occupational health standards are concerned with preventing occupational disease. For example, standards limit the concentration of cotton dust in the air because this contaminant has been associated with lung disease in textile workers. The standards are enforced by OSHA inspections, which are conducted when an employee files a complaint of unsafe conditions or when a serious accident occurs. Spot inspections of plants in especially hazardous

Fair Labor Standards Act
Sets a minimun wage and requires overtime pay for work in excess of forty hours per week; passed in 1938 and amended frequently since then

Equal Pay Act of 1963
Requires that men and women be paid the same amount for doing the same jobs

Employee Retirement Income Security Act of 1974 (ERISA)
Sets standards for pension plan management and provides federal insurance if pension funds go bankrupt

National Labor Relations Act
Passed in 1935 to set up procedures for employees to vote whether to have a union; also known as the Wagner Act

National Labor Relations Board
Established by the Wagner Act to enforce its provisions

Labor-Management Relations Act
Passed in 1947 to limit union power; also known as the Taft-Hartley Act

Occupational Safety and Health Act of 1970
Directly mandates the provision of safe working conditions

industries such as mining and chemicals are also made. Employers who fail to meet OSHA standards may be fined.[7]

Emerging Legal Issues Several other areas of legal concern have emerged during the past few years. One is sexual harassment. Although sexual harassment is forbidden under Title VII, it has received additional attention in the courts recently as more and more victims have decided to publicly confront the problem. The 1991 Supreme Court confirmation hearings for Clarence Thomas brought renewed attention to sexual harassment. "Management in Practice" discusses sexual harassment more fully. Another issue is alcohol and drug abuse. Both alcoholism and drug dependence are seen as major problems today. Recent court rulings have tended to define alcoholics and drug addicts as handicapped, protecting them under the same laws that protect other handicapped people. Finally, AIDS has emerged as an important legal issue. AIDS victims too are most often protected under various laws protecting the handicapped.

Social Change and HRM

Various social changes are affecting how organizations interact with their employees. First, many employment sectors are experiencing a shortage of qualified employees. This is especially true in fields such as engineering, nursing, and computer programming. As a result, organizations are having to rely on part-time workers and spend more on training existing workers for more sophisticated jobs. Second, dual-career families are much more common today than just a few years ago. Organizations are finding that they must make accommodations for employees who are dual career partners. These accommodations may include delaying transfers, offering employment to the spouses of current employees to retain them, and providing more flexible work schedules and benefits packages. A related aspect of social change and HRM, cultural diversity, is covered more fully in Chapter 22.

Employment at will is also becoming an important issue. Although employment at will has legal implications, its emergence as an issue is socially driven. **Employment at will** is a traditional view of the workplace that says organizations can fire an employee for whatever reason they want. Increasingly, however, people are arguing that organizations should only be able to fire people who are poor performers or who violate rules and, conversely, not be able to fire people who report safety violations to OSHA or refuse to perform unethical activities. Several court cases in recent years have upheld this emerging view and have limited many organizations' ability to terminate employees to those cases where there is clear and just cause or as part of an organization-wide cutback.

employment at will
A traditional view of the workplace that says organizations can fire their employees for whatever reason they want; recent court judgments are limiting employment at will

ATTRACTING HUMAN RESOURCES

With an understanding of the environmental context of HRM as a foundation, we are now ready to address its first substantive concern—attracting human resources.

SEXUAL HARASSMENT IN THE WORKPLACE

Few things that go on in a business are as harmful to a company's morale, productivity, and general culture as sexual harassment. Women who feel harassed may resign, file court cases or internal grievances, or simply try to avoid their harassers. But no matter which option a woman chooses, the stress involved and her loss of productivity can hurt her work performance. Harassment forces women to waste their talents. After years of viewing workplace sexual harassment as a trivial charge made only by militant feminists, many businesses are finally realizing that harassment can undermine the effectiveness of a large portion of their work force. And it's illegal.

During the Reagan years, the government loosened many of its regulations governing treatment of employees, but in 1986, the Supreme Court ruled unanimously that sexual harassment violates Title VII of the 1964 Civil Rights Act. The Court said actions can be considered harassment if they are unwelcome and if their severity or persistence create an "abusive working environment."

Americans' awareness of the issue was heightened in 1991, when Anita Hill publicly accused Supreme Court nominee Clarence Thomas, her former boss, of sexual harassment.

Prodded by the 1986 ruling and by the growth of lawsuits and complaints brought to the Equal Employment Opportunity Commission, many companies have begun to treat sexual harassment as a major problem.

At a minimum, companies now spell out harassment policies in their personnel handbooks. More effective steps include sending employees to training sessions and setting up in-house grievance procedures that allow the harassed employee to complain to a third party.

In almost all cases, the key to reducing sexual harassment is education. By now virtually everyone realizes that a boss's ultimatum—sleep with me or forget about your promotion—is harassment. But many men don't know that comments or actions that they may view as "casual" or "all in fun" are threatening to women. And some men have a harder time understanding that repeatedly asking a coworker for a date, remarking on her clothes or physique, telling sexually explicit stories, or posting "girlie" pinups may also "create an abusive working environment" and is therefore illegal.

At the moment, most company policies against harassment are aimed at avoiding lawsuits and resignations of valued employees. Eventually, however, all organizations and employees will need to recognize that an environment that emphasizes women's roles as sex objects undermines their value as employees and colleagues. And that's not good for anyone.

References: Michele Galen, "Ending Sexual Harassment: Business Is Getting the Message," *Business Week*, March 18, 1991, pp. 98–100; Walter Kiechel, III, "The High Cost of Sexual Harassment," *Fortune*, September 14, 1987, pp. 147–152.

Human Resources Planning

The starting point in attracting human resources is planning. Human resources planning, in turn, involves job analysis and forecasting the demand and supply of labor.

Job Analysis **Job analysis** is a systematic analysis of jobs within an organization. A job analysis is made up of two parts. The *job description* lists the duties of a job; the job's working conditions; and the tools, materials, and equipment used to perform it. The *job specification* lists the skills, abilities, and other credentials needed to do the job. Job analysis information is used in many human resources activities. For instance, it is necessary to know about job content and job requirements to develop appropriate selec-

● **job analysis**
A systematized procedure for collecting and recording information about jobs

The first step in attracting human resources is planning. Although a major aspect of a company's human resources planning involves forecasting the supply and demand of labor to meet its needs, planning for some businesses also involves the issue of where their human resources will live once they are hired. Pacific Lumber provides a company town—Scotia, California—for its employees, five hours north of San Francisco. Workers can walk to the lumber mill from their company-provided homes.

Attracting human resources cannot be left to chance if an organization expects to function at peak efficiency. Human resources planning involves assessing trends, forecasting the supply and demand of labor, and then developing appropriate strategies for addressing any differences.

tion methods and job-relevant performance appraisal systems and to set equitable compensation rates.[8]

Forecasting Human Resources Demand and Supply   After managers fully understand the jobs to be performed within the organization, they can start planning for the organization's future human resources needs.[9] Figure 13.1 summarizes the steps most often followed. The manager starts by assessing trends in past human resources usage, future organizational plans, and general economic trends. A good sales forecast is often the foundation, especially for smaller organizations. Historical ratios can then be used to predict demand for employees such as operating employees and sales representatives. Of course, large organizations use much more complicated models to predict their future human resources needs.

Forecasting the supply of labor is really two tasks: forecasting the internal supply (the number and type of employees who will be in the firm at some future date) and forecasting the external supply (the number and type of people who will be available for hiring in the labor market at large). The simplest approach merely adjusts present staffing levels for anticipated turnover and promotions. Again, though, larger organizations use more sophisticated models to make these forecasts. Union Oil Co. of California, for example, has a complex forecasting system for keeping track of the present and future distributions of professionals and managers. The Union Oil sys-

F I G U R E   13.1   Human Resources Planning

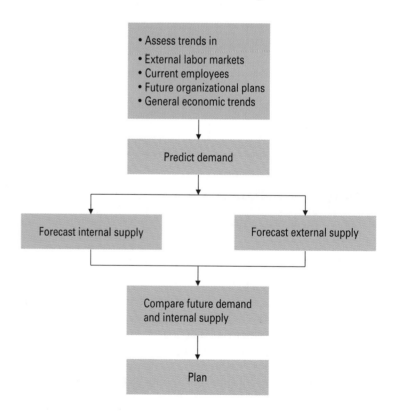

tem can spot areas where there will eventually be too many qualified professionals competing for too few promotions or, conversely, too few good people available to fill important positions.

At higher levels of the organization, managers plan for specific people and positions. The technique most commonly used is the **replacement chart,** which lists each important managerial position, who occupies it, how long he or she will probably stay in it before moving on, and who (by name) is now qualified or soon will be qualified to move into the position. This technique allows ample time to plan developmental experiences for persons identified as potential successors to critical managerial jobs. Charles Knight, CEO of Emerson Electric Co., has an entire room dedicated to posting the credentials of his top 700 executives.[10]

To facilitate both planning and identifying persons for current transfer or promotion, some organizations also have an **employee information system,** or **skills inventory.** Such systems are usually computerized and contain information on each employee's education, skills, work experience, and career aspirations. Such a system can quickly locate all the employees in the organization who are qualified to fill a position requiring, for instance, a degree in chemical engineering, three years of experience in an oil refinery, and fluency in Spanish.

Forecasting the external supply of labor is a different problem altogether. How does a manager, for example, predict how many electrical engineers will be seeking work in Georgia three years from now? To get an idea of the future availability of labor, planners must rely on information from outside sources such as state employment commissions, government reports, and figures supplied by colleges on the number of students in major fields.

Matching Human Resources Supply and Demand   After comparing future demand and internal supply, managers can make plans to deal with predicted shortfalls or overstaffing. If a shortfall is predicted, new employees can be hired, present employees can be retrained and transferred into the understaffed area, individuals approaching retirement can be convinced to stay on, or labor-saving or productivity-enhancing systems can be installed. If the organization needs to hire, the forecast of the external labor supply helps managers plan how to recruit, based on whether the type of person needed is readily available or scarce in the labor market. If overstaffing is expected to be a problem, the main options are transferring the extra employees, not replacing individuals who quit, encouraging early retirement, and laying people off.[11] For example, General Motors Corp. is in the midst of reducing its work force by 74,000.

Recruiting Human Resources

Once an organization has an idea of its future human resources needs, the next phase is usually recruiting new employees. **Recruiting** is the process of attracting qualified persons to apply for the jobs that are open. Where do recruits come from? Some recruits are found internally; others come from outside of the organization.

Internal recruiting means considering present employees as candidates for openings. Promotion from within can help build morale and keep high-

replacement chart
Lists each important managerial position in the organization, who occupies it, how long he or she will probably remain in the position, and who is or will be a qualified replacement

employee information system (skills inventory)
Contains information on each employee's education, skills, experience, and career aspirations; usually computerized

recruiting
The process of attracting individuals to apply for jobs that are open

internal recruiting
Considering current employees as applicants for higher-level jobs in the organization

quality employees from leaving the firm. In unionized firms, the procedures for notifying employees of internal job change opportunities are usually spelled out in the union contract. For higher-level positions, a skills inventory system may be used to identify internal candidates, or managers may be asked to recommend individuals who should be considered. One disadvantage of internal recruiting is its "ripple effect." When an employee moves to a different job, someone else must be found to take his or her old job. In one organization, 454 job movements were necessary as a result of filling 195 initial openings![12]

external recruiting

Getting people from outside the organization to apply for jobs

External recruiting involves attracting persons outside the organization to apply for jobs. External recruiting methods include advertising, campus interviews, employment agencies or executive search firms, union hiring halls, referrals by present employees, and hiring "walk-ins" or "gate-hires" (people who show up without being solicited). Of course, a manager must select the most appropriate methods: he or she might use the state employment service to find maintenance workers but not a nuclear physicist. Private employment agencies can be a good source of clerical and technical employees, and executive search firms specialize in locating top-management talent. Newspaper ads are often used because they reach a wide audience and thus allow minorities "equal opportunity" to find out about and apply for job openings. "The Global View" describes how both Japanese and foreign firms, due to competition for managers, aggressively recruit in Japan.

The organization must also keep in mind that recruiting decisions often go both ways—the organization is recruiting an employee, but the prospective employee is also selecting a job. Thus the organization wants to put its best foot forward, treat all applicants with dignity, and strive for a good person-job fit. Recent estimates suggest that hiring the "wrong" operating employee—one who flops and either quits or must be fired—generally costs the organization $5,000 in lost productivity and training. Hiring the wrong manager can cost the organization as much as $75,000.[13] One generally successful method for facilitating a good person-job fit is through the so-called **realistic job preview (RJP)**.[14] As the term suggests, the RJP involves providing the applicant with a real picture of what it would be like to perform the job that the organization is trying to fill.

realistic job preview (RJP)

Provides the applicant with a real picture of what it would be like to perform the job the organization is trying to fill

Common Selection Methods

Once the recruiting process has attracted a pool of applicants, the next step is to select whom to hire. The intent of the selection process is to gather from applicants information that will predict their job success and then to hire the candidates likely to be most successful. Of course, the organization can only gather information about factors that are predictive of future performance. The process of determining the predictive value of information is called **validation.**

validation

Determining the extent to which a selection device is really predictive of future job performance

Two basic approaches to validation are predictive validation and content validation. *Predictive validation* involves collecting the scores of employees or applicants on the device to be validated and correlating their scores with actual job performance. A significant correlation means that the selection device is a valid predictor of job performance. *Content validation* uses logic and job analysis data to establish that the selection device measures the

DESPERATELY SEEKING JAPANESE MANAGERS

 Most foreign companies trying to do business in Japan have learned by now that hiring Japanese managers can make breaking into Japanese markets much easier. But even after they have conquered trade barriers, overcome cultural differences, and learned to do things the Japanese way, foreign companies face a major hurdle—finding people to hire.

With 1.43 jobs available for every job seeker, even Japanese firms have difficulty filling positions. They have traditionally been much more aggressive than U.S. companies in recruiting Japanese college graduates; according to Motorola, Inc.'s regional director for international staffing, the average Japanese college graduate "receives the equivalent of half a cord of wood in recruitment materials."*

The surplus of jobs and aggressive Japanese recruiters aren't the only problems facing foreign recruiters in Japan. Although traditions are changing, historically the Japanese have viewed leaving a company as the employee's failure, so executive headhunters find luring successful Japanese managers very difficult. Many Japanese are also wary of Western companies because of their perception—often based on fact—that Western companies will simply pull out of the country if they don't fare well initially, leaving workers stranded.

Western recruiters have done well with one group of Japanese workers—women. Traditionally undervalued in their own culture, many Japanese women see more opportunities in working for companies that have Western conceptions of the equality of the sexes. Greater opportunity for advancement and more responsibility attract both women and men to Western companies, along with slightly (10 percent on average) higher pay, shorter work days, vacations, and more personal recognition.

So the battle is on, with educated, English-speaking executives and engineers the top prizes. U.S. companies have learned to be creative in their approaches. Motorola sent its recruitment package in a tall aluminum can so that it wouldn't get lost among mountains of paper. Citicorp staged a foreign-exchange simulation game in Tokyo, giving winners a free trip to Citicorp New York. Japanese companies have fought back by doing such things as flying an executive's mother to Tokyo to convince him not to leave his company.

It's still a tough struggle, but Western companies occasionally do win. A recent survey showed that almost eight percent of students graduating from leading universities chose foreign companies.

*Bill O'Neill quoted in Robert Neff, "When in Japan, Recruit as the Japanese Do—Aggressively," *Business Week*, June 24, 1991, p. 58.

References: Robert Neff, "When in Japan, Recruit as the Japanese Do—Aggressively," *Business Week*, June 24, 1991, p. 58; Edwin Whenmouth, "Hunting Heads in Japan," *Industry Week*, November 4, 1991, p. 34.

---

exact skills needed for successful job performance. The most critical part of content validation is a careful job analysis showing exactly what duties are to be performed. The test is then developed to measure the applicant's ability to perform those duties.

Application Blanks   The first step in selection is usually asking the candidate to fill out an application blank. Application blanks are an efficient method for gathering information about the applicant's previous work history, educational background, and other job-related demographic data. They should not contain questions about areas not related to the job such as gender, religion, or national origin. Application blank data are generally used informally to decide whether a candidate merits further evaluation, and interviewers use application blanks to familiarize themselves with candidates before interviewing them.

Tests Tests of ability, skill, aptitude, or knowledge that is relevant to the particular job are usually the best predictors of job success, although tests of general intelligence or personality are occasionally useful as well. In addition to being validated, tests should be administered and scored in a consistent fashion. All candidates should be given the same directions, should be allowed the same amount of time, and should experience the same testing environment (temperature, lighting, distractions).[15]

Interviews Although a popular selection device, interviews are sometimes poor predictors of job success.[16] For example, biases inherent in the way people perceive and judge others on first meeting affect subsequent evaluations by the interviewer.[17] Interview validity can be improved by training interviewers to be aware of potential biases and by increasing the structure of the interview. In a structured interview, questions are written in advance and all interviewers follow the same question list with each candidate they interview. This procedure introduces consistency into the interview procedure and allows the organization to validate the content of the questions to be asked.[18] For interviewing managerial or professional candidates, a somewhat less-structured approach can be used. Question areas and information-gathering objectives are still planned in advance, but the specific questions vary with the candidates' backgrounds. Trammell Crow Real Estate Investors uses a novel approach in hiring managers. Each applicant is interviewed not only by two or three other managers but also by a secretary or young leasing agent. This provides information about how the prospective manager relates to nonmanagers.[19]

Assessment Centers Assessment centers are rapidly gaining in popularity as a selection tool. They are mainly used to select managers and are particularly good for selecting current employees for promotion. The assessment center is a content-valid simulation of key parts of the managerial job. A typical center lasts two to three days, with groups of six to twelve persons participating in a variety of managerial exercises. Centers may also include interviews, public speaking, and standardized ability tests. Candidates are assessed by several trained observers, usually managers several levels above the job for which the candidates are being considered. Assessment centers are quite valid if properly designed and are fair to members of minority groups and women.[20] For some firms, the assessment center is a permanent facility created for these activities to take place. For other firms, the assessment activities are performed in a multipurpose location, such as a conference room. AT&T pioneered the assessment center concept.

Other Techniques In certain circumstances, organizations also use other selection techniques. Polygraph tests, once popular, are declining in popularity. On the other hand, more and more organizations are requiring that applicants in whom they are interested take physical exams. Drug tests are also increasingly used, especially in situations in which drug-related performance problems could create serious safety hazards.[21] For example, applicants for jobs in a nuclear power plant would likely be tested for drug use. And some organizations even run credit checks on prospective employees.

DEVELOPING HUMAN RESOURCES

Regardless of how effective a selection system is, however, most employees need additional training if they are to grow and develop in their jobs. It is also necessary to evaluate their performance and provide feedback.

Training and Development

In HRM, **training** usually refers to teaching operational or technical employees how to do the job for which they were hired. **Development** refers to teaching managers and professionals the skills needed for both present and future jobs. Most organizations provide regular training and development programs for managers and employees.[22] For example, IBM spends more than $700 million annually on programs and has a vice president in charge of employee education. U.S. business spends more than $30 billion annually on training and development programs away from the workplace. And this figure doesn't include wages and benefits paid to employees while they are participating in such programs.[23]

Assessing Training Needs   The first step in developing a training plan is to determine what needs exist. For example, if employees do not know how to operate machinery required to do their jobs, a training program on how to operate the machinery is clearly needed. On the other hand, when a group of office workers is performing poorly, training may not be the answer. The problem could be motivation, aging equipment, poor supervision, inefficient work design, or a deficiency of skills and knowledge. Only the last could be remedied by training. As training programs are being

● **training**
Teaching operational or technical employees how to do the job for which they were hired

development
Teaching managers and professionals the skills needed for both present and future jobs

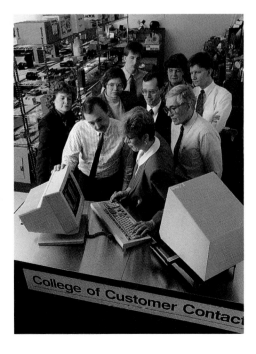

Companies are finding that investing money in training programs pays healthy dividends. The Grainger Division estimates that its new employees gain the equivalent of three to six months of work experience during their one-week training session as the "College of Customer Contact." Because of results such as this, the Division is expanding its Regional Training Center network.

FIGURE 13.2 The Training Process

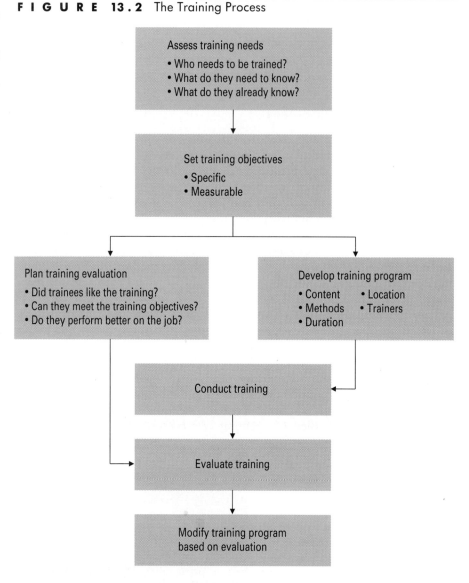

developed, the manager should set specific and measurable goals specifying what participants are to learn. Plans should also be made to evaluate the training program after it has been completed. The training process from start to finish is diagrammed in Figure 13.2.

Common Training Methods As shown in Table 13.2, many different training and development methods are available. Selection of methods depends on many considerations, but perhaps the most important is training content. When the training content is factual material (such as company rules or explanations of how to fill out forms), assigned reading, programmed learning, and lecture methods work well. When the content is interpersonal relations or group decision making, however, firms must use a method that allows interpersonal contact such as role playing or case

TABLE 13.2	Training and Development Methods
Method	**Comments**
Assigned readings	Readings may or may not be specially prepared for training purposes.
Behavior modeling training	Use of a videotaped model displaying the correct behavior, then trainee role playing and discussion of the correct behavior. Used extensively for supervisor training in human relations.
Business simulation	Both paper simulations (such as in-basket exercises) and computer-based business "games" are used to teach management skills.
Case discussion	Real or fictitious cases or incidents are discussed in small groups.
Conference	Small-group discussion of selected topics, usually with the trainer as leader.
Lecture	Oral presentation of material by the trainer, with limited or no audience participation.
On the job	Includes no instruction; casual coaching by more experienced employees; and carefully structured explanation, demonstration, and supervised practice by a qualified trainer.
Programmed instruction	Self-paced method using text or computer followed by questions and answers; expensive to develop.
Role playing	Trainees act out roles with other trainees, such as "boss giving performance appraisal" and "subordinate reacting to appraisal" to gain experience in human relations.
Sensitivity training	Also called T-group and laboratory training, this is an intensive experience in a small group, in which individuals give each other feedback and try out new behaviors. It is said to promote trust, open communication, and understanding of group dynamics.
Vestibule training	Supervised practice on manual tasks in a separate work area where the emphasis is on safety, learning, and feedback rather than productivity.
Interactive video	Newly emerging technique using computers and video technology.

Organizations that engage in training and development activities can select from a variety of different methods. Managers must carefully assess their training and development needs and select the most appropriate method. For example, assigned reading might be effective in teaching new employees about company policies, but on-the-job training might be more effective in teaching current employees how to operate new equipment.

discussion groups. When a physical skill must be learned, methods allowing practice and the actual use of tools and material are needed, as in on-the-job training or vestibule training. (Vestibule training enables participants to focus on safety, learning, and feedback rather than productivity.) Interactive video is also becoming popular. This approach, which relies on a computer-video hookup, is a promising method for combining several training methods such as readings, cases, and drill-and-practice exercises. Xerox Corp., Massachusetts Mutual Life Insurance Co., and Ford Motor Co. have all reported tremendous success with this method.[24]

Evaluation of Training Training and development programs should always be evaluated. Evaluation measures collected at the end of training are easy to get, but actual performance measures collected when the trainee is on the job are more important. Trainees may say they enjoyed the training and learned a lot, but the true test is whether their job performance improves after their training.

Performance Appraisal

● **performance appraisal**
A formal assessment of how well an employee is doing his or her job

When employees are trained and settled into their jobs, one of the next concerns is performance appraisal. **Performance appraisal** is a formal assessment of how well employees are doing their job. Employees' performance should be evaluated regularly for many reasons. One reason is that performance appraisal may be necessary for validating selection devices or assessing the impact of training programs. A second reason is administrative—to aid in making decisions about pay raises, promotions, and training. Still another reason is to provide feedback to employees to help them improve their present performance and plan future careers.

Because performance evaluations often help determine wages and promotions, they must be fair and nondiscriminatory. In the case of appraisals, content validation is used to show that the appraisal system accurately measures performance on important job elements and does not measure traits or behavior that are irrelevant to job performance.[25]

Common Appraisal Methods Two basic categories of appraisal methods commonly used in organizations are objective methods and judgmental methods. *Objective measures* of performance include actual output (i.e., number of units produced), scrappage rate, dollar volume of sales, and number of claims processed. Objective performance measures may be contaminated by "opportunity bias" if some persons have a better chance to perform than others. For example, a sales representative selling snow blowers in Michigan has a greater opportunity than does a colleague selling the same product in Arkansas. Fortunately, it is often possible to adjust raw performance figures for the effect of opportunity bias and thereby arrive at figures that accurately represent each individual's performance.

Another type of objective measure, the special performance test, is a method in which each employee is assessed under standardized conditions. This kind of appraisal also eliminates opportunity bias. For example, GTE Southwest Inc. has a series of prerecorded calls that operators in a test booth answer. The operators are graded on speed, accuracy, and courtesy in handling the calls. Performance tests measure ability but do not measure the extent to which one is motivated to use that ability on a daily basis. (A high-ability person may be a lazy performer except when being tested.) Special performance tests must therefore be supplemented by other appraisal methods to provide a complete picture of performance.

Judgmental methods, including ranking and rating techniques, are the most common way to measure performance. Ranking compares employees directly with each other and orders them from best to worst. Ranking has a number of drawbacks. Ranking is difficult for large groups because the persons in the middle of the distribution may be hard to distinguish from one another accurately. Comparisons of people in different work groups are also difficult. For example, an employee ranked third in a strong group may be more valuable than an employee ranked first in a weak group. Another criticism of ranking is that the manager must rank people on the basis of overall performance, although each person likely has both strengths and weaknesses. Furthermore, rankings do not provide useful information for feedback. To be told that one is ranked third is not nearly so helpful as to be told that the quality of one's work is outstanding, its quantity is satisfactory, one's punctuality could use improvement, and one's paperwork is seriously deficient.

Rating differs from ranking in that it compares each employee with a fixed standard rather than with other employees. A rating scale provides the standard. Figure 13.3 gives examples of three graphic rating scales for a bank teller. Each consists of a performance dimension to be rated (punctuality, congeniality, and accuracy) followed by a scale on which to make the rating. In constructing graphic rating scales, performance dimensions that are relevant to job performance must be selected. In particular, they should focus on job behaviors and results rather than on personality traits or attitudes.

The **Behaviorally Anchored Rating Scale (BARS)** is a sophisticated and useful rating method. Supervisors construct rating scales with associated behavioral anchors. They first identify relevant performance dimensions and then generate anchors—specific, observable behaviors typical of each performance level. An example of a behaviorally anchored rating scale for the dimension "inventory control" is given in Figure 13.4. The other scales in this set, developed for the job of department manager in a chain of specialty stores, include "handling customer complaints," "planning special promotions," "following company procedures," "supervising sales personnel," and "diagnosing and solving special problems." BARS can be effective because it requires that management take proper care in constructing the scales and it provides useful anchors for supervisors to use in evaluating people. It is costly, however, because outside expertise is usually needed and because scales must be developed for each job within the organization.

Behaviorally Anchored Rating Scale (BARS)
A sophisticated rating method in which supervisors construct a rating scale associated with behavioral anchors

Errors in Performance Appraisal   In any kind of rating or ranking system, errors or biases can occur. One common problem is recency error—the tendency to base judgments on the subordinate's most recent performance because it is most easily recalled. Often a rating or ranking is intended to evaluate performance over an entire time period, such as six months or a year, so the recency error does introduce error into the judgment. Other errors include overuse of one part of the scale—being either too lenient or too severe or giving everyone a rating of "average." Halo

Graphic rating scales are a very common method for evaluating employee performance. The manager who is doing the rating circles the point on each scale that best reflects her or his assessment of the employee on that scale. Graphic rating scales are widely used for many different kinds of jobs.

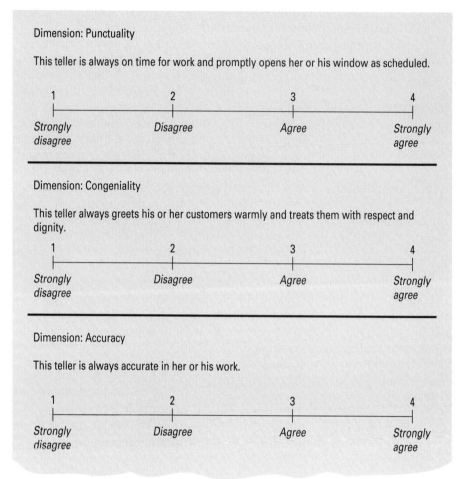

FIGURE 13.3 Graphic Rating Scales for a Bank Teller

Dimension: Punctuality

This teller is always on time for work and promptly opens her or his window as scheduled.

1	2	3	4
Strongly disagree	Disagree	Agree	Strongly agree

Dimension: Congeniality

This teller always greets his or her customers warmly and treats them with respect and dignity.

1	2	3	4
Strongly disagree	Disagree	Agree	Strongly agree

Dimension: Accuracy

This teller is always accurate in her or his work.

1	2	3	4
Strongly disagree	Disagree	Agree	Strongly agree

error is allowing the assessment of an employee on one dimension to "spread" to ratings of that employee on other dimensions. For instance, if an employee is outstanding on quality of output, a rater might tend to give her or him higher marks than deserved on other dimensions. Errors can also occur due to race, sex, or age discrimination, either intentional or unintentional.[26] The best way to offset these errors is to ensure that a valid rating system is developed at the outset, and then to train managers in how to use it.

Performance Feedback

The last step in most performance appraisal systems is giving feedback to subordinates about their performance. This is usually done in a private meeting between the person being evaluated and his or her boss. The discussion should generally be focused on the facts—the assessed level of performance, how and why that assessment was made, and how it can be improved in the future. Feedback interviews are not easy to conduct. Many managers are uncomfortable with the task, especially if feedback is negative and subordinates are disappointed by what they hear. Properly

FIGURE 13.4 Behaviorally Anchored Rating Scale

Job: Specialty store manager
Dimension: Inventory control

7 — Always orders in the right quantities and at the right time

6 — Almost always orders at the right time, but occasionally orders too much or too little of a particular item

5 — Usually orders at the right time, but almost always in the right quantities

4 — Often orders in the right quantities and at the right time

3 — Occasionally orders at the right time, but usually not in the right quantities

2 — Ocassionally orders in the right quantities, but usually not at the right time

Never orders in the right quantities or at the right time

1

Behaviorally anchored rating scales help overcome some of the limitations of standard rating scales. Each point on the scale is accompanied by a behavioral anchor—a summary of an employee behavior that fits that spot on the scale.

training managers, however, can help them conduct more effective feedback interviews.[27]

MAINTAINING HUMAN RESOURCES

After organizations have attracted and developed an effective work force, they must also make every effort to maintain that work force. To do so requires effective compensation and benefits as well as career planning.

Determining Compensation

Compensation is the financial remuneration given by the organization to its employees in exchange for their work. Compensation is an important and complex part of the organization-employee relationship. Basic compensation is necessary to provide employees with the means to maintain a reasonable standard of living. Beyond this, however, compensation also provides a tangible measure of the value of the individual to the organization. If employees do not earn enough to meet their basic economic goals, they will seek employment elsewhere. Likewise, if they believe that their contributions are undervalued by the organization, they may leave or exhibit poor work habits, low morale, and little commitment to the organization. Thus it is clearly in the organization's best interests to design an effective compensation system.[28] A good compensation system can help attract qualified applicants, retain present employees, and stimulate high performance at a cost that is reasonable for one's industry and geographic area.

● **compensation**
The financial remuneration given by the organization to its employees in exchange for their work

To set up a successful system, decisions must be made about wage levels, the wage structure, and the individual wage determination system.

Wage-Level Decision   The wage-level decision is a management policy decision about whether the firm wants to pay above, at, or below the going rate for labor in the industry or the geographic area.[29] Most firms choose to pay near the average. Those that cannot afford more pay below average. Large, successful firms may like to cultivate the image of being "wage leaders" by intentionally paying more than average and thus attracting and keeping high-quality employees. IBM, for example, pays top dollar to get the new employees it wants. The level of unemployment in the labor force also affects wage levels. Pay declines when labor is plentiful and increases when labor is scarce.

Once the wage-level decision is made, managers need information to help set actual wage rates. Managers need to know what the maximum, minimum, and average wages are for particular jobs in the appropriate labor market. This information is collected by means of a wage survey. Area wage surveys can be conducted by individual firms or by local HR or business associations. Professional and industry associations often conduct surveys and make the results available to employers.

job evaluation
An attempt to assess the worth of each job relative to other jobs

Wage-Structure Decision   Wage structures are usually set up through a procedure called **job evaluation**—an attempt to assess the worth of each job relative to other jobs.[30] The simplest method is to rank jobs from those that should be paid the most (for example, the president) to those that should be paid the least (for example, a mail clerk or a janitor). In a small firm with few jobs, this method is quick and practical, but larger firms with many job titles require more sophisticated methods. The next step is setting actual wage rates on the basis of a combination of survey data and the wage structure that results from job evaluation. Jobs of equal value are often grouped into wage grades for ease of administration.

Individual Wage Decisions   After wage-level and wage-structure decisions have been made, the individual wage decision must be addressed. This decision concerns how much to pay each employee in a particular job. Although the easiest decision is to pay a single rate for each job, more typically a range of pay rates is associated with each job. For example, the pay range for an individual job might be $5.85 to $6.39 per hour, with different employees earning different rates within the range. A system is then needed for setting individual rates. This may be done on the basis of seniority (enter the job at $5.85, for example, and increase 10 cents per hour every six months on the job), on the basis of initial qualifications (inexperienced people start at $5.85, more experienced start at a higher rate), or on the basis of merit (raises above the entering rate are given for good performance). Combinations of these bases may also be used.

Determining Benefits

● benefits
Things of value besides compensation that an organization provides to its workers

Benefits are other things of value provided by the organization to its workers. The average company spends an amount equal to more than one-third of its cash payroll on employee benefits. Thus an average employee who is paid $18,000 per year averages about $6,588 more per year in benefits.

Benefits come in several forms. Pay for time not worked includes sick leave, vacation, holidays, and unemployment compensation. Insurance benefits often include life and health insurance for employees and their dependents. Workers' compensation is a legally required insurance benefit that provides medical care and disability income for employees injured on the job. Social security is a government pension plan to which both employers and employees contribute. Many employers also provide a private pension plan to which they and their employees contribute. Employee service benefits include such things as tuition reimbursement and recreational opportunities.

Some organizations have instituted "cafeteria benefits plans," whereby basic coverage is provided for all employees but employees are then allowed to choose which additional benefits they want (up to a cost limit based on salary). An employee with five children might choose medical and dental coverage for dependents; a single employee might prefer more vacation time; and an older employee might elect increased pension benefits. Such a flexible system would be expected to encourage people to stay in the organization and perhaps help the company attract new employees.[31] In recent years, companies have also started offering even more innovative benefits as a way of accommodating different needs. On-site childcare, mortgage assistance, and generous paid leave programs are becoming popular.[32] At the same time, however, J.C. Penney Company, Inc., Chrysler Corp., Allied-Signal Inc., Genentech, and other companies have started eliminating some benefits because of the escalating cost of insurance.[33] Of course, eliminating benefits can create resentment among employees.

A good benefits plan may encourage people to join and stay with an organization, but it seldom stimulates high performance because benefits are tied more to membership in the organization than to performance. To manage their benefits programs effectively, companies should shop carefully, avoid redundant coverage, and provide only those benefits that employees want. Benefits programs should also be explained to employees in plain English so that they can use the benefits appropriately and appreciate what the company is providing.

An organization knows that to attract and keep human resources, it must offer an attractive benefits plan. Employees today want a more diverse package of benefits than in the past, including items such as long-term disability insurance and long-term care insurance. Mary Catherine Sneed, Summit Communications Group vice president, knows that when she is hiring, Summit's total benefits package is an important factor in an employee's decision to take a job with the company.

Career Planning

A final aspect of maintaining human resources is career planning. Few people work in the same jobs their entire career. Some people change jobs within one organization, others change organizations, and many do both. When these movements are haphazard and poorly conceived, both the individual and the organization suffer. Thus it is in everyone's best interest if career progressions are planned in advance. Of course, it is difficult to plan a thirty-year career for a newcomer just joining the organization. But planning can help map out what areas the individual is most interested in and help the person see what opportunities are available within the organization. We discuss managerial career issues more fully in Appendix 1.

MANAGING LABOR RELATIONS

Labor relations is the process of dealing with employees who are represented by an employee association (union). Managing labor relations is an important part of HRM.

● **labor relations**
The process of dealing with employees when they are represented by an employee association (union)

How Employees Form Unions

For a new local union to be formed, several things must occur. First, employees must become interested in having a union. Nonemployees who are professional organizers employed by a national union (such as the Teamsters or United Auto Workers) may generate interest by making speeches and distributing literature outside the workplace. Inside, employees who want a union try to convince other workers of the benefits of a union. The second step is to collect signatures of employees on authorization cards. These cards state that the signer wishes to vote to determine if the union will represent him or her. Thirty percent of the employees in the potential bargaining unit must sign these cards to show the National Labor Relations Board (NLRB) that interest is sufficient to justify holding an election. Before an election can be held, however, the bargaining unit must be defined. The bargaining unit consists of all employees who will be eligible to vote in the election and to join and be represented by the union if one is formed.

The election is supervised by an NLRB representative (or, if both parties agree, the American Arbitration Association—a professional association of arbitrators) and is conducted by secret ballot. If a simple majority of those voting (not of all those eligible to vote) votes for the union, then the union becomes certified as the official representative of the bargaining unit.[34] The new union then organizes itself by officially signing up members and electing officers; it will soon be ready to negotiate the first contract. This process is diagrammed in Figure 13.5. If workers become disgruntled with their union, or if management presents strong evidence that the union is not representing workers appropriately, the NLRB can arrange a decertification election. The results of such an election determine whether the union remains certified.

Organizations usually prefer that employees not be unionized because

April, 1992, brought Mickey Mouse and a powerful wave of American culture to France, with the opening of EuroDisney, 20 miles east of Paris. The opening was hardly smooth: French nationalists protested what they see as an imposition of American taste and culture on their country, and several unions were embroiled in disputes with Disney management. Construction workers threatened to disrupt the opening day's celebrations, due to disagreements over money owed them. Though the park did open and is operating successfully, some disgruntled employees, supported by their unions, are engaged in the grievance process with their employer.

FIGURE 13.5 The Union-Organizing Process

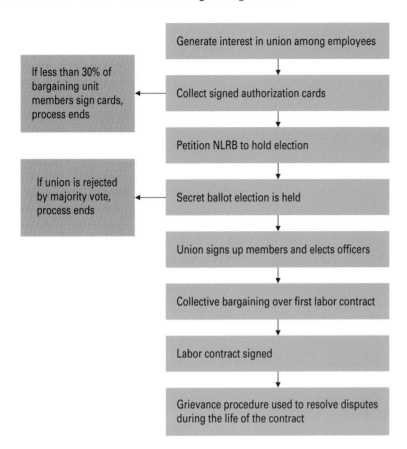

unions limit management's freedom in many areas. Management may thus wage its own campaign to convince employees to vote against the union. It is at this point that "unfair labor practices" are often committed. For instance, it is an unfair labor practice for management to promise to give employees a raise (or any other benefit) if the union is defeated. Experts agree that the best way to avoid unionization is to practice good employee relations all the time—not just when threatened by a union election. Providing absolutely fair treatment with clear standards in the areas of pay, promotion, layoff, and discipline; having a complaint or appeal system for persons who feel unfairly treated; and avoiding any kind of favoritism will help make employees feel that a union is unnecessary.

Collective Bargaining

The intent of **collective bargaining** is to agree on a labor contract between management and the union that is satisfactory to both parties. The contract contains agreements about wages, hours, and other conditions of employment, including promotion, layoff, discipline, benefits, methods of allocating overtime, vacations, rest periods, and the grievance procedure. The process of bargaining may go on for weeks, months, or longer, with representatives of management and the union meeting to make proposals and

collective bargaining
The process of agreeing on a satisfactory labor contract between management and a union

counterproposals. The resulting agreement must be ratified by the union membership. If it is not approved, the union may strike to put pressure on management, or it may choose not to strike and simply continue negotiating until a more acceptable agreement is reached.

grievance procedure
The means by which a labor contract is enforced

The **grievance procedure** is the means by which the contract is enforced. Most of what is in a contract concerns how management will treat employees. When employees feel that they have not been treated fairly under the contract, they file a grievance to correct the problem. The first step in a grievance procedure is for the aggrieved employee to discuss the alleged contract violation with her immediate superior. Often the grievance is resolved at this stage. If the employee still believes that she is being mistreated, however, the grievance can be appealed to the next level. A union official may help an aggrieved employee present her case. If the manager's decision is also unsatisfactory to the employee, additional appeals to successively higher levels are made, until finally all in-company steps are exhausted. The final step is to submit the grievance to *binding arbitration*. An arbitrator is a labor-law expert who is paid jointly by the union and management. The arbitrator studies the contract, hears both sides of the case, and renders a decision that must be obeyed by both parties. The grievance system for resolving disputes about contract enforcement prevents any need to strike during the term of the contract.[35]

SUMMARY OF KEY POINTS

Human resources management is concerned with acquiring, developing, and maintaining the human resources an organization needs. Its environmental context consists of its strategic importance and the legal and social environments that affect human resources management.

Attracting human resources is an important part of the HRM function. Human resources planning starts with job analysis and then focuses on forecasting the organization's future need for employees, forecasting the availability of employees both within and outside the organization, and planning programs to ensure that the proper number and type of employees will be available when needed. Recruitment and selection are the processes by which job applicants are attracted, assessed, and hired. Methods for assessing applicants include application blanks, tests, interviews, and assessment centers. Any method used for selection should be properly validated.

Organizations must also work to develop their human resources. Training and development enable employees to perform their present jobs well and to prepare for future jobs. Performance appraisals are important for determining training needs, deciding pay raises and promotions, and providing helpful feedback to employees. Both objective and judgmental methods of appraisal can be applied, and a good system usually includes several methods. The validity of appraisal information is always a concern because it is difficult to accurately evaluate the many aspects of a person's job performance.

Maintaining human resources is also important. Compensation rates must be fair compared with rates for other jobs within the organization and with rates for the same or similar jobs in other organizations in the labor market. Properly designed incentive or merit pay systems can encourage high performance, and a good benefits program can help attract and retain employees. Career planning is also a major aspect of human resources management.

If a majority of a company's nonmanagement employees so desire, they have the right to be represented by a union. Management must engage in collective bargaining with the union in an effort to agree on a contract. While the contract is in effect, the grievance system is used to settle disputes with management.

DISCUSSION QUESTIONS

Questions for Review

1. What is job analysis and how is it related to human resources planning?

2. Describe recruiting and selection. What are the major sources for recruits? What are the common selection techniques?

3. What is the role of compensation and benefits in organizations? How should the amount of compensation and benefits be determined?

4. What are the basic steps that employees can follow if they wish to create a union?

Questions for Analysis

5. What are the advantages and disadvantages of internal and external recruiting? Which do you feel is best in the long term? Why? Be sure to think about this issue from the standpoint of both the organization and individuals (whether inside or outside of the organization) who might be considered for positions.

6. How do you know if a selection device is valid? What are the possible consequences of using invalid selection methods? How can an organization ensure that its selection methods are valid?

7. Are benefits more important than compensation to an organization? To an individual? Why?

Questions for Application

8. Write a description and specifications for a job that you have held (office worker, checkout clerk, salesperson, lifeguard). Then contact a company with such a job and obtain an actual description and specification from that firm. In what ways are your description and specification like theirs? In what ways are they different?

9. Contact a local organization to determine how that organization evaluates the performance of employees in complex jobs such as middle- or higher-level manager, scientist, lawyer, or market researcher. What problems with performance appraisal can you note?

10. Interview someone who is or has been a member of a union to determine his or her reasons for joining. Would you join a union? Why or why not?

WHAT'S FAIR IN UNION-MANAGEMENT BATTLES?

Nordstrom, Inc., is a Seattle-based department store chain that operates sixty-four stores around the country. The chain is led by four grandchildren of the man who founded it at the turn of the century. Not a discount retailer, Nordstrom lures customers with the exceptional service provided by its salespeople; its fancy touches like an espresso bar and an English-style pub in its new Oak Brook, Illinois, store; and its mammoth shoe department, which features a selection three times that of most department stores.

In 1991, Nordstrom had to contend with more than the recession and the trend toward discount retailers. Its five Seattle-area stores were trying to get rid of, or "decertify," the union—the United Food and Commercial Workers—that had represented their workers for six decades. Although the number of people involved was not large, the battle between an entrenched union and management drew national attention.

Nordstrom made the first move when it demanded during the latest round of contract talks that union membership be made optional. The union maintained that it had struggled to keep Nordstrom's salespeople's pay high, but the company contended that the good pay was the result of its sales-commissions policy. The union fought management's demand not with a strike but with a publicity campaign that clouded the company's reputation at the very time the company was expanding nationally. Among the union's claims was that Nordstrom doesn't pay its salespeople for some of the services they provide, services that have helped Nordstrom build its reputation.

Nordstrom management countered by creating a twenty-four-hour hotline to handle employees' questions and by producing three videos. Two of the films were shown at staff meetings, but one was sent to employees' homes at company expense. While two of the videos featured Nordstrom family members trying to persuade employees to vote against the union, one showed a discussion between professional actors representing the two sides. The union complained that the actor representing the union side fit a negative stereotype of union members.

After the long battle, employees voted against the union. The union said that one of the reasons for its loss was the high employee turnover at the Nordstrom stores. It pointed out that more than half of the employees had been with the company less than 2½ years, implying that these new employees didn't yet know what Nordstrom was like and didn't appreciate what union representation had done for them.

Whatever the courts and the National Labor Relations Board finally decide about the dispute, it stands as a symbol of the declining strength of unions and of the increasingly creative methods that the two sides use to try to sway workers' opinions.

Discussion Questions

1. If you were a Nordstrom employee, how would you make up your mind about union representation? What information would you seek out?

2. Why do you think Nordstrom's management wanted to get rid of the union?

E 3. Do you think that Nordstrom management's techniques were fair in this dispute? What about the union's techniques?

References: Francine Schwadel, "Nordstrom Aim: Midwest Success Amid Recession," *The Wall Street Journal*, April 4, 1991, pp. B1, B2; Francine Schwadel, "Nordstrom Workers Reject Their Union in Voting at Five Seattle-Area Stores," *The Wall Street Journal*, July 22, 1991, p. B3.

CAN JAPANESE AND AMERICANS MIX IN MICHIGAN?

Although all the big Japanese automakers are now producing cars in the United States, Mazda Motor Corporation was the first to do so in the home state of General Motors Corp., Chrysler Corp., and Ford Motor Co. In 1984, Mazda began setting up shop in Flat Rock, Michigan, fifteen miles south of Detroit, on the site of an abandoned Ford plant. Mazda also became one of the few Japanese automakers to accept unions in its plant. Labor and management experts from around the country watched the Mazda experiment develop.

Mazda's first step was to choose its U.S. workers carefully. It has spent about $13,000 per employee to find people who are skilled, motivated, and have an aptitude for learning new work methods. It looks for people who can work as part of a team.

Mazda puts applicants through a five-step screening process during which they are closely monitored as they perform assembly line tasks and practice giving instructions to other workers. Once hired, the new employees go through weeks of training in interpersonal relations and the Japanese philosophy of *kaizen,* or continuous improvement. They also spend time in teams, doing such things as figuring out better ways to put together flashlights and ways to improve a bathtub.

This intensive screening and training is intended to prepare U.S. workers for the Japanese way of doing things and to foster smooth labor-management relations in the plant. Wary of unions, Mazda negotiated with union officials who wanted everything to go well at Mazda in hopes of reducing other Japanese automakers' fear of unions. Even though it tried to screen out potential troublemakers, Mazda ran into difficulty with its U.S. workers on both the labor and management levels.

Between 1986 and 1990, Mazda went through four directors of labor relations, and a number of other top U.S. managers have quit, some of them replaced by Japanese managers. A common complaint among the disgruntled managers is that they believe the Japanese don't really trust them, don't let them make decisions without Japanese supervision, and won't allow them to rise above a certain level in the management hierarchy. Meanwhile, union rank and file voted out the compliant union leaders, replacing them with representatives who demanded better conditions.

On the factory floor, many workers feel that *kaizen* is not much different from the old Detroit practice of continuously speeding up the line. Mazda has made it difficult for workers to make workers' compensation claims, and the issue of attendance shattered the smooth facade of labor-management relations. Mazda has tried to crack down on all forms of absenteeism, which is considerably higher in the United States than in Japan. Clearly both sides will need time to get used to the cross-cultural marriage in Michigan.

Discussion Questions

1. What suggestions would you make to Mazda management to improve labor-management relations in Mazda's Michigan plant?

2. Why do you think Mazda's training in teamwork and *kaizen* hasn't been completely successful?

E 3. Do you think it's wrong for Japanese Mazda managers in MIchigan to expect their U.S. employees to adhere to Japanese-style work routines and policies?

References: William J. Hampton, "How Does Japan Inc. Pick Its American Workers?" *Business Week,* October 3, 1988, pp. 84–88; Gregory A. Patterson, "Mazda-UAW's Michigan Honeymoon Is Over," *The Wall Street Journal,* April 17, 1990, pp. B1, B12.

Designing an Organization Dedicated to Quality

The purpose of this exercise is to help students better understand the relationship between organizing and product and service quality.

Learning Objectives

After completing this exercise you should have a better understanding of

1. The relationships between organizing and quality.

2. How managers can use the organizing function to enhance product and service quality.

Preview

Xerox Corporation

Xerox Corporation is the world's largest and best known manufacturer of photocopying equipment. Xerox markets its products and services in over 130 countries. In 1991, Xerox was the 22nd largest industrial firm in the United States. It generated $17.8 billion in sales and $454 million in profits. Xerox owns $31.6 billion in assets. The winner of the Baldrige Award was Xerox Business Products and Systems (BP&S), one of two Xerox Corp. businesses, based in Stamford, Connecticut.

Milliken & Company

Milliken and Company, Inc. is the largest textile manufacturer in the United States. Milliken has plants in the United States, France, Belgium, and the United Kingdom. Organized into 28 SBUs, the firm makes over 48,000 products. Because Milliken is privately owned, its financial data is not readily available. However, recent estimates suggest that the firm has annual sales of around $2.5 billion.

The Classic Middle Manager Is An Endangered Species

As work becomes less a matter of rigid control and more a matter of cooperation, the need for management declines, which causes its own resistance. Roger Milliken, Chairman and CEO of Milliken & Company says, "It's hard for management to understand that they're not indispensable." Rosabeth Moss Kanter, Editor of *Harvard Business Review* says, "The role of managers is changing dramatically . . . the classic middle managers—supervisors and managers of managers—and people who were sort of built up in an infinite hierarchical progression, they're an endangered species. We're not going to have very many of them anymore." It is worthwhile to remember that middle managers are also workers, who, like those below them, have been doing exactly what they've been told to do by their bosses. And they were hired by their bosses—in incredible numbers.

"More than half of the modern American corporation," Richard Rosecrance, a professor at UCLA, wrote, "consists of workers uninvolved in operations or production work, an astounding fact. . . . The ratio in typical corporations in Japan is about one-sixth of the American figure." He says that applies as well in the military and in public schools. . . . Rosecrance's solution is for workers to take over more management duties to reduce the ratio of managers to operators (or teachers to administrators). He says that needs to happen right away. "In the more distant future," he adds, "the distinction between white and blue collars may disappear."*

Background Assignment

Go to the library and find articles dating from 1985 to 1988 about the company assigned to you by your instructor. Look at sources such as *Business Week, Fortune,* and the *Wall Street Journal.* Locate the company's annual sales and profits for each year during the period. Use these articles to form a general understanding about your company: its environment, competition, strategies, and organizational structure.

The Video

Xerox, BP&S, and Milliken won Baldrige Awards in 1989. Your instructor will now show you a video that explains more about how these two firms achieved this distinction. As you watch the video, pay special attention to how the firms used elements of the organizing function to improve quality.

Questions for Discussion

1. What are the similarities and differences in how Xerox and Milliken went about improving quality? How do they compare to the efforts of Motorola and Westinghouse?

2. Which do you see as an easier avenue for implementing quality enhancement programs, changes in organization design, or changes in human resource management practices?

3. Why must the design of an entire organization become the focus of quality improvement and not just one pocket of an organization's design?

4. Can quality be enhanced without altering organization design or human resource management practices?

Follow-Up Assignment

Return to the library and get more recent articles charting your assigned company's performance since winning the Baldrige award in 1989. Review recent annual reports and note any mention of quality improvement programs. How has quality affected performance? What changes did quality improvement result in for your company? Have these changes paid off?

*Source: Lloyd Dobyns and Clare Crawford-Mason, *Quality or Else.* (Boston: Houghton Mifflin Company, 1991) pp. 116–117. Copyright © Houghton Mifflin Company. Used by permission.

V

THE LEADING PROCESS

14 Motivating Employee Performance

15 Leadership and Influence Processes

16 Managing Interpersonal and Group Processes

17 Managing Communication in Organizations

Motivating Employee Performance

OBJECTIVES

After studying this chapter, you should be able to:

● *Characterize the nature of motivation, including its importance and basic historical perspectives.*

● *Identify and describe the major content perspectives on motivation.*

● *Identify and describe the major process perspectives on motivation.*

● *Describe reinforcement perspectives on motivation.*

● *Identify and describe emerging perspectives on motivation, as well as popular motivational strategies.*

● *Describe the role of organizational reward systems in motivation.*

OUTLINE

The Nature of Motivation
  Importance of Motivation in the
    Workplace
  Historical Perspectives on Motivation

Content Perspectives on Motivation
  Need Hierarchy Approach
  Two-Factor Theory
  Individual Human Needs

Process Perspectives on Motivation
  Expectancy Theory
  Equity Theory

Reinforcement Perspectives on
Motivation
  Kinds of Reinforcement in
    Organizations
  Providing Reinforcement in
    Organizations

Emerging Perspectives on Motivation
  Goal-Setting Theory
  Japanese Approach
  Popular Motivational Strategies

Using Reward Systems to Motivate
Performance
  Effects of Organizational Rewards
  Designing Effective Reward Systems
  New Approaches to Rewarding
    Employees

LINCOLN ELECTRIC IN Cleveland, Ohio, has arguably the most highly motivated workers of any corporation in the United States today: its workers are three times more productive than similar workers in other companies. In addition, Lincoln, which makes industrial electric motors and welding equipment, has gone almost sixty years without losing money and has not had to lay anyone off in more than forty years.

Lincoln's success with its employees is not the result of any fad or new approach. In 1934, its top managers put into effect an incentive pay system to enhance employee motivation. The initial approach was simple—provide a variety of opportunities for employees to earn more money by working harder. Although the system has been refined and expanded over the years, its basic premises are still used today: the harder Lincoln's employees work, the more money they make.

How does the system work? First, base compensation for each employee is tied directly to individual productivity. Workers are paid a specified dollar amount for each acceptable unit they produce. Second, year-end bonuses are given as special rewards. At the end of the year, each worker is evaluated in terms of his or her dependability, ideas, quantity of output, and quality of output. Recent bonuses have averaged 97.6 percent of workers' regular earnings.

Lincoln's success has not gone unnoticed. In the last seven years alone, almost 4,000 managers from other companies have visited Lincoln's Cleveland facilities to learn more about how to motivate employee job performance. Many of them gain new insights into how organizations can convince workers to perform at higher levels. Others, however, leave shaking their heads and arguing that the system won't work for them.[1] ●

*I*t's fairly easy to understand how Lincoln's incentive system works. More difficult, however, is understanding why it works. The answer is rooted in employee motivation. Virtually any organization is capable of having a motivated work force. An organization's managers, however, must figure out how to make a plan like Lincoln's work for them. Lincoln's plan was installed in simpler times, and managers have had decades to fine tune it. Managers today must start with a much more complex view of what people want to motivate them toward higher levels of job performance.

In Chapter 1, we defined the third management function, leading, as the set of processes used to get people to work together to advance the interests of the organization. This chapter is the first of four devoted to those processes, and its major emphasis is on motivating employee job performance. We first examine the nature of employee motivation and then explore the major perspectives on motivation. Newly emerging approaches are then discussed. We conclude with a description of rewards and their role in motivation. The other three chapters in Part 5 discuss other processes involved in the leading function—leadership and influence processes (Chapter 15), interpersonal and group processes (Chapter 16), and communication (Chapter 17).

THE NATURE OF MOTIVATION

● **motivation**
The set of forces that cause people to behave in certain ways

Motivation is the set of forces that cause people to behave in certain ways.[2] On any given day, an employee may choose to work as hard as possible at a job, to work just hard enough to avoid a reprimand, or to do as little as possible and suffer a reprimand. The goal for the manager is to maximize the occurrence of the first behavior and minimize the occurrence of the last one.

Importance of Employee Motivation in the Workplace

Individual performance is generally determined by motivation (the desire to do the job), ability (the capability to do the job), and the work environment (the tools, materials, and information needed to do the job). If an employee lacks ability, the manager can provide training or replace the worker. If there is an environmental problem, the manager can also usually make adjustments to promote higher performance. But if motivation is the problem, the manager's task is more challenging. Individual behavior is a complex phenomenon, and the manager may not be able to figure out why the employee is not motivated and how to change the behavior. Thus motivation is important because it determines performance and because of its intangible nature.[3]

The motivation framework in Figure 14.1 is a good starting point for understanding how motivated behavior occurs. The motivation process begins with a need, or a deficiency. For example, a worker who believes that she is underpaid experiences a deficiency and a need for more income. In

FIGURE 14.1 The Motivation Framework

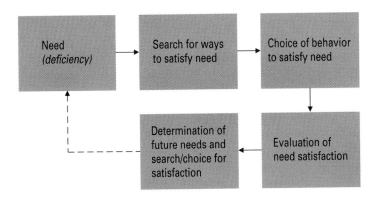

response, the worker searches for ways to satisfy this need, such as working harder to earn a raise or seeking a new job. Next, she chooses an option to pursue. After carrying out the chosen option—working harder and putting in more hours for a reasonable period of time, for example—she then evaluates her success. If her hard work resulted in a pay raise, she probably feels good about her efforts and will continue to work hard. If no raise has been provided, she is likely to try another option such as look for another job.

Historical Perspectives on Motivation

To appreciate what we know about employee motivation, it is helpful to review earlier approaches. In general, motivation theory has evolved through the traditional approach, the human relations approach, and the human resources approach.

Traditional Approach   The traditional approach to employee motivation is best represented by the work of Frederick W. Taylor.[4] As we noted in Chapter 2, Taylor suggested the use of an incentive pay system. He believed that management knew more about the jobs being performed than the workers did, and he assumed that money was everyone's primary motivation. The traditional approach also assumed that work is inherently unpleasant for most people and that the money the employees earn is more important than the nature of the job. Hence people could be expected to perform any kind of job if they were paid enough. Although the role of money as a motivating factor cannot be dismissed, proponents of the traditional approach took a narrow view of the role of monetary compensation and also failed to consider other motivational factors.

Human Relations Approach   The human relations approach (also summarized in Chapter 2) grew out of the work at Western Electric of Elton Mayo and his associates.[5] The human relationists emphasized the role of social processes in the workplace. Their basic assumptions were that employees want to feel useful and important, that employees have strong social needs, and that these needs are more important than money in motivating employees. Advocates of the human relations approach advised managers to make workers feel important and allow them some degree of self-direction and self-control in carrying out routine activities. The illusion of involvement and importance was expected to satisfy workers' basic social needs and result in higher motivation to perform. For example, a manager might allow a work group to appear to participate in making a decision, even though the manager had already determined what the decision would be. Symbolically allowing participation was expected to enhance motivation, even though no real participation took place.

Human Resources Approach Whereas the human relationists believed that the illusion of contribution and participation would enhance motivation, the human resources approach assumes that the contributions themselves are valuable to both employees and organizations. This view assumes that people want to contribute and are able to make genuine contributions. Management's task, then, is to encourage participation and create a work environment that makes full use of the human resources available. This philosophy guides most contemporary thinking about employee motivation. At Ford Motor Co., Westinghouse Electric Corp., Texas Instruments Incorporated, and Hewlett-Packard Co., for example, work teams are solving a variety of problems and making substantive contributions to the organization. Lincoln Electric's philosophy has passed through all three eras as well. "The Global View" discusses how managers in the former Soviet Union often failed to address motivational issues.

CONTENT PERSPECTIVES ON MOTIVATION

● **content perspectives**
Approaches to motivation that try to answer the question "What factor or factors motivate people?"

Content perspectives on motivation focus on the first part of the motivation process—needs and need deficiencies. More specifically, **content perspectives** address the question, "What factors in the workplace motivate people?" Labor leaders often argue that workers can be motivated by more pay, shorter working hours, and improved working conditions. Alternatively, some experts suggest that motivation can be enhanced by providing employees with more autonomy and greater responsibility. Both of these views represent content views of motivation. The former asserts that motivation is a function of pay, working hours, and working conditions; the latter suggests that motivation is a function of autonomy and responsibility. Two widely known content perspectives on motivation are the need hierarchy and the two-factor theory.

Need Hierarchy Approach

Need hierarchies assume that people have a variety of needs that can be arranged in a hierarchy of importance. The best known are Maslow's hierarchy of needs and the ERG theory.

Maslow's hierarchy of needs
A theory suggesting that people must satisfy five groups of needs in order—physiological, security, belongingness, esteem, and self-actualization

Maslow's Hierarchy of Needs Abraham Maslow, a human relationist, argued that people are motivated to satisfy five need levels.[6] **Maslow's hierarchy of needs** is shown in Figure 14.2. At the bottom of the hierarchy are the *physiological needs*—needs such as air, food, and sex that represent

RUSSIAN WORKERS GET A SECOND CHANCE

U.S. citizens have generally held a low opinion of the citizens of the former Soviet Union. The Russian worker has typically been viewed as lazy, unproductive, unmotivated, dishonest, and alcoholic. Now as the governmental and economic systems in that country undergo fundamental changes, Russian workers are getting a second chance—both to earn a better living and to remake their image in Western minds.

Even the staunchest supporter of the Russian citizenry would admit that the old stereotype held some truth—Mikhail Gorbachev conceded that the Soviet Union had a major problem with alcoholism. And worker theft has been such a problem that the Russians have a word for "factory-lifters." But it's doubtful that people in any country would have acted differently given the lack of motivations in the old Soviet system.

Wages were set by bureaucrats in Moscow, and workers had little incentive to be productive, do a good job, or even stay sober. A fired worker could generally find a job at equally poor pay somewhere else. To get more money from the bureaucrats, factory managers would increase their payrolls with unneeded workers. Working next to someone who was in effect paid to be idle certainly didn't motivate a worker to be productive.

Given the low pay, the chronic shortage of goods, and the widespread corruption that meant only top party bosses lived well, many Russians could provide adequately for their families only by doing something illegal. If the only way to feed their families was to steal from the factory where they worked, many U.S. citizens, too, would leave with a pound of sausage in their coats.

The opening of the first McDonald's in Moscow provided the Russian some sense of what work *can* be like. Although other U.S. companies had done business in Russia for years, few had hired Russians to work in conditions similar to those taken for granted in the United States. Russian workers are finding it very different to do a job that actually pleases people, work as part of a team, get encouragement from managers, and eat—legally—the food that they make. The spontaneous cheers of the employees when the McDonald's opens each day symbolize their attitudes. The odds seem excellent that Russian workers will turn out to work as hard as their U.S. counterparts—only the lack of motivation has made them seem different.

References: Vladimir Kvint, "Dead Souls," *Forbes*, May 27, 1991, 96–100; Kevin Maney, "U.S. Ideas Creep Into Soviet Union," *USA Today*, May 11, 1990, pp. B1, B2.

---

basic issues of survival and biological function. These needs must be satisfied before other needs can be considered. In organizations, physiological needs are generally satisfied by adequate wages and the work environment itself, which provides restrooms, adequate lighting, comfortable temperatures, and ventilation. Next are the needs for a stable physical and emotional environment: the *security needs*. Examples include the desire for housing and clothing and the need to be free from worry about money and job security. These needs can be satisfied in the workplace by job continuity (no layoffs), a grievance system (to protect against arbitrary supervisory actions), and an adequate insurance and retirement benefits package (for security against illness and provision of income in later life). The primacy of security needs can be restored, however, when depressed industries and economic decline put people out of work.

Belongingness needs relate to social processes. They include the need for love and affection and the need to be accepted by one's peers. These needs are satisfied for most people by family and community relationships outside of work and friendships on the job. A manager can help satisfy these needs

FIGURE 14.2 Maslow's Hierarchy of Needs

Source: Adapted from Abraham H. Maslow, "A Theory of Human Motivation," *Psychological Review,* Vol. 50, 1943, pp. 370–396.

by allowing social interaction and by making employees feel like part of a team or work group.

Esteem needs actually comprise two different sets of needs: the need for a positive self-image and self-respect and the need for recognition and respect from others. A manager can help address these needs by providing a variety of external symbols of accomplishment such as job titles, nice offices, and similar rewards as appropriate. The manager can also focus on the nature of the work itself, by providing challenging job assignments and opportunities for the employee to feel a sense of accomplishment. At the top of the hierarchy are *self-actualization needs,* which involve realizing one's potential for continued growth and individual development. The self-actualization needs are perhaps the most difficult for a manager to address. Although some argue that the individual must meet these needs entirely from within, a manager can help by promoting a culture in which self-actualization is possible. For instance, a manager could give employees a chance to participate in decision making and the opportunity to learn new skills. This kind of culture might make an employee feel like she has possibilities for advancement to other jobs within the organization.

Maslow suggested that the five need categories constitute a hierarchy. A person is motivated first and foremost to satisfy physiological needs. As long as they remain unsatisfied, the individual is motivated only to fulfill them. When physiological needs are satisfied, they cease to act as primary motivational factors, and the person moves "up" the hierarchy and seeks to satisfy security needs. This process continues until, finally, self-actualization needs are also satisfied.

Maslow's concept of the need hierarchy has a certain intuitive logic and has been accepted by many managers. But research has revealed shortcomings and defects in the theory: five levels of need are not always present, and the order of the levels is not always the same as postulated by Maslow.[7] In addition, people from different cultures are likely to have different need categories and hierarchies. For example, lower-level needs are so critical in Haiti that higher-level needs have little or no relevance.

ERG Theory In response to these and similar criticisms, Clayton Alderfer, in his **ERG theory** of motivation, has proposed an alternative hierarchy of needs.[8] The letters *E, R,* and *G* stand for *existence, relatedness,* and *growth*. This theory collapses the need hierarchy developed by Maslow into three levels. *Existence needs* correspond to Maslow's physiological and security needs. *Relatedness needs* focus on how people relate to their social environment (Maslow's belongingness needs and esteem needs relate to earning the esteem of others). *Growth needs,* the highest level in Alderfer's schema, include the needs for self-esteem and self-actualization.

ERG theory
A theory of motivation suggesting that people's needs are grouped into three possibly overlapping categories—existence, relatedness, and growth

Although the ERG theory assumes that motivated behavior follows a hierarchy in somewhat the same fashion as suggested by Maslow, there are two important differences. First, the ERG theory suggests that more than one level of need can motivate at the same time. For example, it suggests that people can be motivated by a desire for money (existence), friendship (relatedness), and the opportunity to learn new skills (growth) all at once.

Second, the ERG theory includes a *frustration-regression* element, which is missing from Maslow's need hierarchy. Maslow maintained that an individual will remain at one level of need until that need is satisfied. In contrast, ERG theory suggests that if needs remain unsatisfied the individual will become frustrated, regress to a lower level, and begin to pursue lower-level needs again. For example, a worker previously motivated by money (existence needs) may have just been awarded a pay raise sufficient to satisfy those needs. Suppose that he then attempts to establish more friendships to satisfy relatedness needs. If for some reason he finds that it is impossible to become better friends with others in the workplace, he eventually gets frustrated and regresses to being motivated to earn even more money.

The ERG theory is relatively new compared with Maslow's need hierarchy, but research suggests that it may be a more valid account of motivation in organizations.[9] Managers should not, of course, rely too heavily on any one perspective to guide their thinking about employee motivation. The key insights to be gleaned from the need hierarchy view are that some needs may be more important than others and that people may change their behavior after a particular set of needs has been satisfied, such as after a raise in pay.

Two-Factor Theory

Traditional views of job satisfaction assumed that satisfaction and dissatisfaction were at opposite ends of a single continuum. People might be satisfied, dissatisfied, or somewhere in between.

In order to learn more about workplace motivation among professionals and the relationship between satisfaction and dissatisfaction, Frederick Herzberg interviewed 200 accountants and engineers. He asked them to recall occasions when they had been satisfied with their work and highly

The two-factor theory suggests that there are two different dimensions of job satisfaction. A manager who tries to motivate an employee using only hygiene factors such as pay and good working conditions will likely not succeed. To motivate employees and produce a high level of satisfaction, managers must also offer factors such as responsibility and the opportunity for advancement (motivation factors).

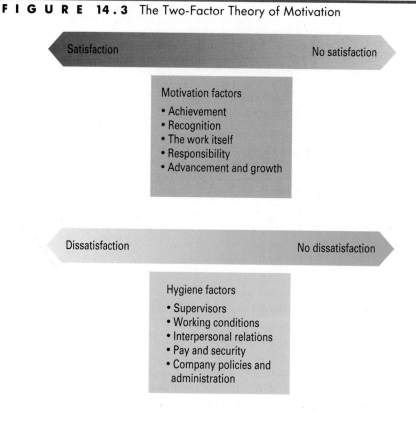

FIGURE 14.3 The Two-Factor Theory of Motivation

Satisfaction   No satisfaction

Motivation factors
- Achievement
- Recognition
- The work itself
- Responsibility
- Advancement and growth

Dissatisfaction   No dissatisfaction

Hygiene factors
- Supervisors
- Working conditions
- Interpersonal relations
- Pay and security
- Company policies and administration

two-f
A theory of motivation suggesting that people's job satisfaction and dissatisfaction are influenced by two independent sets of factors—motivation factors and hygiene factors

motivated and occasions when they had been dissatisfied and unmotivated. Surprisingly, he found that different sets of factors were associated with satisfaction and with dissatisfaction—that is, a person might identify "low pay" as causing dissatisfaction but would not necessarily mention "high pay" as a cause of satisfaction. Instead, different factors, such as recognition or accomplishment, were cited as causing satisfaction.

This finding led Herzberg to conclude that the traditional view of job satisfaction was incomplete. Instead of only one dimension, Herzberg's interviews had identified two different dimensions altogether: one ranging from satisfaction to no satisfaction and the other ranging from dissatisfaction to no dissatisfaction. This perspective is called the **two-factor theory,**[10] and it is shown in Figure 14.3 along with several examples of factors that affect each continuum. Note that the factors influencing the satisfaction continuum—called motivation factors—are related specifically to the work content. The factors presumed to cause dissatisfaction—called hygiene factors—are related to the work environment.

Based on these findings, Herzberg argues that the process of motivating employees consists of two stages. First, managers must ensure that the hygiene factors are not deficient. For example, pay and security must be appropriate, working conditions must be safe, and technical supervision must be acceptable. By providing hygiene factors at an appropriate level, managers do not stimulate motivation but merely ensure that employees are "not dissatisfied." Employees whom managers attempt to "satisfy" through hygiene factors alone will usually do just enough to get by. Thus

Corning Inc. discovered that responding to employees' individual human needs paid off in increased quality. When teams of hourly workers redesigned their factories and decided who should work which jobs, product defects were reduced from 10,000 parts per million to 3 parts per million, and no products have been returned by customers since July 1990. More and more companies are discovering that recognizing employees' needs for achievement, affiliation, and power increases motivation.

managers should proceed to stage two: give employees the opportunity to experience motivation factors such as achievement and recognition. The result is predicted to be a high level of satisfaction and motivation. Herzberg also goes a step further than most theorists and describes exactly how to use the two-factor theory in the workplace. Specifically, he recommends job enrichment, as discussed in Chapter 10. He argues that jobs should be redesigned to provide higher levels of motivation factors.

Although widely accepted by many managers, Herzberg's two-factor theory is not without its critics. One criticism is that the findings in Herzberg's initial interviews can be interpreted in several different ways. Another charge is that his sample was not representative of the general population and that subsequent research often failed to uphold the theory.[11] At the present time, Herzberg's theory is not held in high esteem by researchers in the field. The theory has had a major impact on managers, however, and has played a major role in increasing their awareness of motivation and its importance in the workplace.

Individual Human Needs

In addition to these theories, research has also focused on specific individual human needs that are important in organizations: achievement, affiliation, and power.[12] The **need for achievement,** the best known of the three, is the desire to accomplish a goal or task more effectively than in the past. People with a high need for achievement have a desire to assume personal responsibility, a tendency to set moderately difficult goals, a desire for specific and immediate feedback, and a preoccupation with their task. David C. McClelland, the psychologist who first identified this need, argues that only about 10 percent of the U.S. population have a high need for achievement. In contrast, almost 25 percent of the workers in Japan have a high need for achievement.

Like Maslow's belongingness need, the **need for affiliation** is a desire for human companionship and acceptance. People with a strong need for

need for achievement
The desire to accomplish a goal or task more effectively than in the past

need for affiliation
The desire for human companionship and acceptance

need for power
The desire to be influential in a group and to control one's environment

● process perspectives
Approaches to motivation that focus on why people choose certain behavioral options to fulfill their needs and how they evaluate their satisfaction after they have attained these goals

expectancy theory
A theory suggesting that motivation depends on two things—how much we want something and how likely we think we are to get it

affiliation are likely to prefer (and perform better in) a job that entails a lot of social interaction and offers opportunities to make friends. The need for affiliation is not well understood. The need for power has also received considerable attention as an important ingredient in managerial success.[13] The **need for power** is the desire to be influential in a group and to control one's environment. Research has shown that people with a strong need for power are likely to be superior performers, have good attendance records, and occupy supervisory positions. One study found that managers as a group tend to have a stronger need for power than the general population and that successful managers tend to have stronger needs for power than less-successful managers.[14]

In summary, the major content perspectives on motivation focus on individual needs. Maslow's need hierarchy, the ERG theory, the two-factor theory, and the needs for achievement, affiliation, and power all provide useful insights into factors that cause motivation, but they do not shed much light on the process of motivation. They do not explain why people might be motivated by one factor rather than by another at a given level or how people might go about trying to satisfy their different needs. These questions involve behaviors or actions, goals, and feelings of satisfaction—concepts that are addressed by various process perspectives on motivation.

PROCESS PERSPECTIVES ON MOTIVATION

Process perspectives are concerned with how motivation occurs. Rather than attempt to identify or list motivational stimuli, **process perspectives** focus on why people choose certain behavioral options to satisfy their needs and how they evaluate their satisfaction after they have attained their goals. Popular process perspectives on motivation are expectancy theory and equity theory.

Expectancy Theory

The expectancy theory of motivation has many different forms and labels. We describe its most basic form. Essentially, **expectancy theory** suggests that motivation depends on two things—how much we want something and how likely we think we are to get it. Assume that you are approaching graduation and looking for a job. You see in the want ads that Exxon is seeking a new vice president with a starting salary of $350,000 per year. Even though you might want the job, you will not apply because you realize that you have little chance of getting it. The next ad you see is for someone to scrape bubble gum from underneath theater seats for a starting salary of $4 an hour. Even though you could probably get this job, you do not apply because you do not want it. Then you see an ad for a management trainee for a big company with a starting salary of $25,000. You will probably apply for this job because you want it and because you think you have a reasonable chance of getting it.

The formal expectancy framework was developed by Victor Vroom.[15] Expectancy theory rests on these basic assumptions. It assumes that behav-

According to expectancy theory, people are motivated by how much they want something and how likely they think they are to get it. Some children may not be motivated to do well in school because they do not have the economic resources to attend college. The ''I Know I Can'' program, funded in part by Nationwide Insurance, offers college money to every qualified graduate of Columbus, Ohio, public schools. Having the money to attend college will likely motivate these fifth graders from Windsor Elementary to stay in school.

ior is determined by a combination of forces in the individual and in the environment. It assumes that people make decisions about their own behavior in organizations. It assumes that different people have different types of needs, desires, and goals. And last, it assumes that people make choices from among alternative plans of behavior based on their perceptions of the extent to which a given behavior will lead to desired outcomes.[16]

Figure 14.4 summarizes the basic expectancy model. The model suggests that motivation leads to effort and that effort, combined with employee ability and environmental factors, results in performance. Performance, in turn, leads to various outcomes, each of which has an associated value called its valence.

The expectancy theory of motivation is a complex but relatively accurate portrayal of how motivation occurs. According to this model, a manager must understand what employees want (such as pay, promotions, or status) to begin to motivate them.

F I G U R E   14.4 The Expectancy Model of Motivation

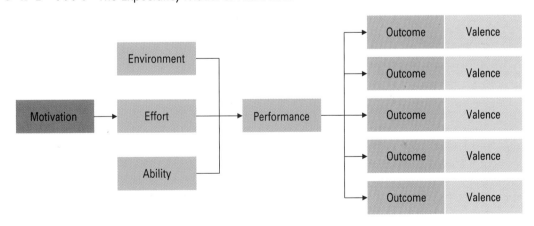

effort-to-performance expectancy
The individual's perception of the probability that his or her effort will lead to high performance

performance-to-outcome expectancy
The individual's perception that her or his performance will lead to a specific outcome

outcomes
Consequences of behaviors in an organizational setting; usually rewards

valence
An index of how much an individual desires a particular outcome (the attractiveness of the outcome to the individual)

Individual's Expectations The most important parts of the expectancy model cannot be shown in the figure, however. These are the individual's expectation that effort will lead to high performance, that performance will lead to outcomes, and that each outcome will have some kind of value.

The **effort-to-performance expectancy** is the individual's perception of the probability that effort will lead to high performance. When the individual believes that effort will lead directly to high performance, expectancy will be quite strong (close to 1.00). If he or she believes that effort and performance are unrelated, the effort-to-performance expectancy is very weak (close to 0). Believing that effort is somewhat but not strongly related to performance carries with it a moderate expectancy (somewhere between 0 and 1).

The **performance-to-outcome expectancy** is the individual's perception that performance will lead to a specific outcome. For example, if an employee believes that high performance *will* result in a pay raise, the performance-to-outcome expectancy is high (approaching 1.00). An employee who believes that high performance *may* lead to a pay raise has a moderate expectancy (between 1.00 and 0). An employee who believes that performance has no relationship with rewards has a low performance-to-outcome expectancy (close to 0).

Expectancy theory recognizes that a person's behavior results in a variety of **outcomes,** or consequences, in an organizational setting. A high performer, for example, may get bigger pay raises, faster promotions, and more praise from the boss. On the other hand, she may also be subject to more stress and incur resentment from co-workers. Each of these outcomes also has an associated value, or **valence**—an index of how much an individual values a particular outcome. If the individual wants the outcome, its valence is positive; if the individual does not want the outcome, its valence is negative; and if the individual is indifferent to the outcome, its valence is zero.

The outcome and valence aspect of expectancy theory goes beyond the content perspectives on motivation. Different people have different needs, and they try to satisfy these needs in different ways. For an employee who has a high need for achievement and a low need for affiliation, the pay raise and promotions just cited as outcomes of high performance might have positive valences, the praise and resentment zero valences, and the stress a negative valence. For an employee with a low need for achievement and a high need for affiliation, the pay raise, promotions, and praise might all have positive valences, whereas both resentment and stress could have negative valences.

Conditions for Motivated Behavior For motivated behavior to occur, three conditions must be met. First, the effort-to-performance must be greater than zero (the person must believe that if effort is expended, high performance will result). The performance-to-outcome expectancy must also be greater than zero (the individual must believe that if high performance is achieved, certain outcomes will follow). And the sum of the valences for the outcomes must be greater than zero. (One or more outcomes may have negative valences if they are more than offset by the positive valences of other outcomes. For example, the attractiveness of a pay raise, a promotion, and praise from the boss may outweigh the unattractiveness of more stress and resentment from co-workers.) Expectancy theory suggests that when these conditions are met, people are motivated.

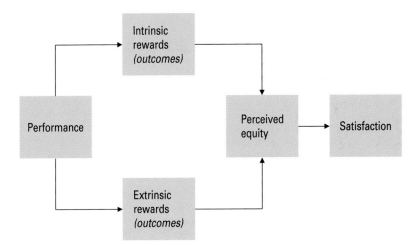

The Porter-Lawler extension of expectancy theory suggests that if performance results in equitable rewards, people will be more satisfied. Thus performance can lead to satisfaction. Managers must therefore be sure that any system of motivation includes rewards that are fair, or equitable, for all.

Source: Edward E. Lawler, III, and Lyman W. Porter, "The Effect of Performance on Job Satisfaction," *Industrial Relations,* October 1967, p. 23. Used with permission of the University of California.

Porter-Lawler Extension   An interesting extension of expectancy theory has been proposed by Porter and Lawler.[17] Recall from Chapter 2 that the human relationists assumed that employee satisfaction causes good performance. We also noted that research has not supported such a relationship. Porter and Lawler suggest that there may indeed be a relationship between satisfaction and performance but that it goes in the opposite direction—that is, high performance may lead to high satisfaction. Figure 14.5 summarizes Porter and Lawler's logic that performance results in both extrinsic (pay and promotions) and intrinsic (self-esteem and accomplishment) rewards. The employee evaluates the equity, or fairness, of the rewards relative to the effort expended and the level of performance attained. If the rewards are perceived to be equitable, the individual is satisfied.

Implications for Managers   Managers trying to improve the motivation of their subordinates can follow a series of steps to implement the basic ideas of expectancy theory. First, figure out the outcomes, or rewards each employee is likely to want. Second, decide what kinds and levels of performance are needed to meet organizational goals. Then make sure that the desired levels of performance are attainable. Also make sure that desired outcomes, or rewards, and desired performance are linked. Next, analyze the complete situation for conflicting expectancies, and ensure that the rewards are large enough. Finally, make sure that the total system is equitable (fair to all).[18] These issues are explored in more detail later in this chapter when we discuss organizational reward systems.

A&P has had considerable success with expectancy theory. At its Philadelphia stores, A&P workers took a 25-percent pay cut, but they can now earn large bonuses by working more efficiently. Each worker knows what needs to be done to earn a bonus. Employees are earning more money than before, yet the stores are also achieving higher levels of profitability.[19] Lincoln Electric's incentive system is also clearly consistent with expectancy theory.

Expectancy theory also has limitations. Although the theory makes sense and has been generally supported by empirical research, it is quite difficult to apply.[20] To really use the complete theory in the workplace, for example, a manager must identify all the potential outcomes for each employee, determine all relevant expectancies, and then balance everything somehow to maximize employee motivation.

Equity Theory

After needs have stimulated the motivation process and an action that is expected to satisfy those needs is chosen, the individual assesses the fairness, or equity, of the resultant outcome. Much of our current thinking on equity has been shaped by the theories of motivation developed by J. Stacy Adams. Adams's **equity theory** of motivation contends that people are motivated to seek social equity in the rewards they receive for performance.[21] Equity is an individual's belief that the treatment he or she is receiving is fair relative to the treatment received by others.

According to equity theory, outcomes from a job include pay, recognition, promotions, social relationships, and intrinsic rewards. To get these rewards, the employee makes inputs to the job, such as time, experience, effort, education, and loyalty. The theory suggests that people view their outcomes and inputs as a ratio and then compare their ratio to someone else's. This other "person" may be someone in the work group or a group average or composite. The process of comparison looks like this:

$$\frac{\text{Outcomes (self)}}{\text{Inputs (self)}} \overset{?}{=} \frac{\text{Outcomes (other)}}{\text{Inputs (other)}}$$

Both the formulation of the ratios and comparisons between them are subjective and are based on individual perceptions. As a result of comparisons, three conditions may result: the individual may feel equitably rewarded, under-rewarded, or over-rewarded. A feeling of equity will result when the two ratios are equal. This may occur even when the other person's outcomes are greater than the individual's own outcomes—provided that the other's inputs are also proportionately greater. Suppose that Mark has a high school education and earns only $15,000. He may still feel equitably treated relative to Susan, who earns $20,000, because she has a college degree.

People who feel under-rewarded try to reduce the inequity by decreasing inputs (exerting less effort), increasing outcomes (asking for a raise), distorting the original ratios by rationalizing, trying to get the other person to change her or his outcomes or inputs, leaving the situation, or changing the object of comparison. An individual may also feel over-rewarded relative to another person. For example, a newly-hired employee who starts at a higher salary than some long-standing employees may feel over-rewarded. This is not likely to be terribly disturbing to most people, but research suggests that some people who experience inequity under these conditions are somewhat motivated to reduce it.[22] Under such a circumstance, the person might increase his inputs by exerting more effort, reduce his outcomes by producing fewer units (if paid on a per unit basis), distort the original ratios by

equity theory
Theory suggesting that people are motivated to seek social equity in the rewards they receive for performance

rationalizing, or try to reduce the inputs or increase the outcomes of the other person.

Implications for Managers The single most important idea for managers to remember from equity theory is that if rewards are to motivate employees, they must be perceived as being equitable and fair. If a person achieves rewards as a result of performance and regards these rewards as equitable, satisfaction will result. A second implication is that managers need to consider the nature of the "other" to whom the employee is comparing herself or himself. In recent years, for example, the number of dual-career couples has increased dramatically, and husband-and-wife equity comparisons have ruined both marriages and careers.[23] The research support for equity theory is mixed.[24] The concepts of equity and social comparisons are certainly important for the manager to consider, but managers should not rely on only this framework when managing employee motivation.

REINFORCEMENT PERSPECTIVES ON MOTIVATION

A third element of the motivational process addresses why some behaviors are maintained over time and why other behaviors change. As we have seen, content perspectives deal with needs, and process perspectives explain why people choose various behaviors to satisfy needs and how they evaluate the equity of the rewards they get for those behaviors. Reinforcement perspectives explain the role of those rewards as they cause behavior to change or remain the same over time. Specifically, **reinforcement theory** argues that behavior that results in rewarding consequences is likely to be repeated, whereas behavior that results in punishing consequences is less likely to be repeated. This approach to explaining behavior was originally tested on animals, but B. F. Skinner and others have been instrumental in demonstrating how it also applies to human behavior.[25]

● **reinforcement theory**
Approach to motivation that argues that behavior that results in rewarding consequences is likely to be repeated, whereas behavior that results in punishing consequences is less likely to be repeated

Kinds of Reinforcement in Organizations

In organizational settings, managers can use four basic kinds of reinforcement: positive reinforcement, avoidance, punishment, and extinction.[26] These are summarized in Table 14.1. Two kinds of reinforcement strengthen or maintain behavior, and two weaken or decrease behavior. **Positive reinforcement,** which strengthens behavior, is a reward or a positive outcome after a desired behavior is performed. When a manager observes an employee doing an especially good job and offers praise, the praise serves to positively reinforce the behavior of good work. Other positive reinforcers in organizations include pay raises, promotions, and awards. Employees who work at General Electric Co.'s customer service center receive clothing, sporting goods, and even trips to Disney World as rewards for outstanding performance.[27] **Avoidance** also strengthens desired behavior. An employee may come to work on time to avoid a reprimand. In this instance, the employee is motivated to perform the behavior of punctuality to avoid an unpleasant consequence that is likely to follow tardiness.

positive reinforcement
A method of strengthening behavior by offering rewards or positive outcomes after a desired behavior is performed

avoidance
A method of strengthening behavior in which the employee avoids unpleasant consequences that would result if the behavior were not performed

A manager who wants the best chance of reinforcing a behavior would likely offer the employee a positive reinforcement after a variable number of behaviors (variable ratio reinforcement). For example, the manager could praise the employee after the third, sixth, fourth, ninth, and so on credit card application received.

TABLE 14.1   Elements of Reinforcement Theory

Arrangement of the Reinforcement Contingencies

1. **Positive reinforcement.** Strengthens behavior by providing a desirable consequence.

2. **Avoidance.** Strengthens behavior by allowing escape from an undesirable consequence.

3. **Punishment.** Weakens behavior by providing an undesirable consequence.

4. **Extinction.** Weakens behavior by not providing a desirable consequence.

Schedules for Applying Reinforcement

1. **Fixed interval.** Reinforcement applied at fixed time intervals, regardless of behavior.

2. **Variable interval.** Reinforcement applied at variable time intervals, regardless of behavior.

3. **Fixed ratio.** Reinforcement applied after a fixed number of behaviors, regardless of time.

4. **Variable ratio.** Reinforcement applied after a variable number of behaviors, regardless of time.

punishment
A means of weakening undesired behaviors by providing negative outcomes or unpleasant consequences when the behavior is performed

Punishment is used by some managers to weaken undesired behaviors. When an employee is loafing, coming to work late, doing poor work, or interfering with the work of others, the manager might resort to reprimands, discipline, or fines. The logic is that the unpleasant consequence will reduce the likelihood that the employee will choose that particular behavior again. Given the counterproductive side effects of punishment (such as resentment and hostility), it is often advisable to use positive reinforcement if possible. Avoidance and punishment are obviously related. If an employee comes to work on time to avoid a reprimand, avoidance is operating. But if the employee is late and receives a reprimand, this is punishment because it will presumably change the employee's behavior.

extinction
A means of weakening undesired behaviors in which a manager simply ignores or does not reinforce that behavior

Extinction can also be used to weaken behavior, especially behavior that has previously been rewarded. When an employee tells an off-color joke and the boss laughs, the laughter reinforces the behavior and the employee may continue to tell off-color jokes. By simply ignoring this behavior and not reinforcing it, the boss can cause the behavior to subside and eventually become "extinct."

Providing Reinforcement in Organizations

fixed-interval schedule
Provides reinforcement at fixed intervals of time regardless of behavior, such as regular weekly paychecks

Not only is the kind of reinforcement important, but so is when or how often it occurs. Various strategies for providing reinforcement are also listed in Table 14.1. The **fixed-interval schedule** provides reinforcement at fixed intervals of time, regardless of behavior. The weekly or monthly paycheck is a good example of this schedule. This method provides the least incentive for good work because employees know they will be paid regularly regardless of their effort. A **variable-interval schedule** also uses time as the basis for reinforcement, but the time interval varies from one reinforcement to the next. This schedule is appropriate for praise or other rewards based on

variable-interval schedule
Provides reinforcement at varying intervals of time, such as occasional visits by the supervisor

visits or inspections. When employees do not know when the boss is going to drop by, they tend to maintain a reasonably high level of effort all the time.

A **fixed-ratio schedule** gives reinforcement after a fixed number of behaviors, regardless of the time that elapses between behaviors. This results in an even higher level of effort. For example, when Sears, Roebuck and Co. is recruiting new credit-card customers, salespersons get a small bonus for every fifth application returned from their department. Under this arrangement, motivation will be high because each application gets the employee closer to the next bonus. A manager using the **variable-ratio schedule,** the most powerful schedule in terms of maintaining desired behaviors, varies the number of behaviors needed for each reinforcement. A supervisor who praises an employee for her second order, the seventh order after that, the ninth after that, then the fifth, and then the third is using a variable-ratio schedule. The employee is motivated to increase the frequency of the desired behavior because each performance increases the probability of receiving a reward. Of course, a variable-ratio schedule is difficult (if not impossible) to use for formal rewards such as pay because it would be too complicated to keep track of who was rewarded when.

fixed-ratio schedule
Provides reinforcement after a fixed number of behaviors regardless of the time that elapses between behaviors, such as a bonus for every fifth sale

variable-ratio schedule
Provides reinforcement after varying numbers of behaviors are performed, such as the use of compliments by a supervisor on an irregular basis; this is the most powerful schedule in terms of maintaining desired behaviors

EMERGING PERSPECTIVES ON MOTIVATION

In addition to the established models and theories of motivation, two promising emerging perspectives are goal-setting theory and the Japanese approach.

Goal-Setting Theory

Goal-setting theory suggests that a manager and subordinate together set goals for the subordinate on a regular basis.[28] These goals should be moderately difficult, specific, and of a type that the employee will accept and commit to accomplishing. Managers should directly link rewards to the subordinate's reaching the goals. Goal-setting theory helps the manager tailor rewards to individual needs, clarify expectancies, maintain equity, and provide reinforcement on a systematic basis. Thus it provides a comprehensive framework for integrating the other approaches. In all likelihood, goal-setting theory will become increasingly popular in organizations.[29]

Japanese Approach

The so-called Japanese approach, which is not really a theory or model but a philosophy of management, is increasing in popularity. In many ways, it extends from the human resources perspective. The basic goal underlying the Japanese approach is to bring management and workers together as partners. Historically, in the United States the management-worker relationship has ranged from antagonistic to merely indifferent. In Japan, however, managers and workers see themselves as one group, and the result is that everyone is highly committed and motivated. A good example of the Japanese approach in the United States is Domino's Pizza. Domino's em-

Increasingly, organizations are setting goals related to improving quality. Laquita S. Swartz, a vice president for First of America Bank-Indianapolis, is developing programs to improve customer service, employee morale, and interdepartmental cooperation. Setting employee goals around programs such as these helps a manager link employee rewards directly to the achievement of the goal.

ployees are called team members, team leaders, or coaches. A large percentage of the company's profits is distributed back to workers; all employees own stock; and all employees work together toward Domino's best interests.[30] "Management in Practice" details how Steelcase uses this approach as well.

Popular Motivational Strategies

Managers trying to motivate their employees can adopt specific motivational strategies derived from one or more theories discussed in the previous sections. **Behavior modification,** or **OB Mod** (for organizational behavior modification), is a technique for applying the concepts of reinforcement theory in organizational settings.[31] An OB Mod program starts by specifying behaviors that are to be increased (such as producing more units) or decreased (such as coming to work late). These target behaviors are then tied to specific reinforcements. Although many organizations (such as The Procter & Gamble Co., Warner-Lambert Company, and Ford) have used OB Mod, the best-known application has been at Emery Air Freight. Management believed that the containers used to consolidate small shipments into fewer, larger shipments were not being packed efficiently. Through a system of self-monitored feedback and rewards, Emery increased container usage from 45 percent to 95 percent and saved more than $3 million during the first three years of the program.[32]

Many organizations also use a **modified workweek** for employees as a strategy for increasing motivation. The modified workweek helps employees satisfy higher-level needs and provides an opportunity to fulfill several needs simultaneously. One alternative is the *compressed workweek,* in which people work forty hours in less than the traditional five full workdays. Most commonly, people work ten hours a day for four days. Another popular plan is the *flexible work schedule.* In this approach, employees are required to work during a certain period called core time and can choose what other hours to work. Thus an individual can come in early and leave early, come in late and leave late, or come in early, take a long lunch, and leave late. Allowing employees to work at home or to share jobs with others is also becoming popular. Working at home is especially useful for writers and others using computers. Job sharing allows two persons to work part-time while the organization still gets the benefit of a full-time "worker."[33] Many companies, including John Hancock Mutual Life Insurance Co., ARCO, General Dynamics, Metropolitan Life Insurance Co., and IBM have experimented successfully with one or more of these modifications. By allowing employees some independence in terms of when they come to work and when they leave, managers acknowledge and show "esteem" for the employees' ability to exercise self-control.

Changing the nature of the task-related activities of work, using any of the alternatives to job specialization described in Chapter 10, is also being used more and more as a motivational technique. More precisely, job rotation, job enlargement, job enrichment, the job characteristics approach, and autonomous work groups can all be used as part of a motivational program. A number of studies have shown that improving the design of work may increase motivation. One study at Texas Instruments Incorporated, for example, found that job design resulted in decreased turnover and improved employee motivation.[34]

● **behavior modification** (or **OB Mod** for organizational behavior modification) A technique for applying the concepts of reinforcement theory in organizational settings

● **modified workweek** A strategy for increasing motivation by helping employees satisfy higher-order needs through the use of alternative work schedules

MOTIVATING THE WORK FORCE OF THE FUTURE

 Demographers predict that the work force will grow during the 1990s more slowly than it has at any time since the 1930s. And 60 percent of the people entering the work force in this decade will be women. Companies therefore can't count indefinitely on an unlimited labor supply, and to get the best employees, they may need to adopt policies that appeal especially to women. Because women, even more than men, are often torn between work and family responsibilities, appealing to women's needs often means being more flexible about how employees mix their work and their family life.

Steelcase, Inc., the country's number-one office furniture maker, is among the leaders in offering solutions to family-versus-work conflicts. At the heart of all its approaches is an appreciation for the uniqueness of every employee's situation and a recognition that no one company policy is going to suit every worker. The key to Steelcase's motivational system is flexibility.

About one-fifth of Steelcase's 2,000 office workers are on flextime. Within some limits they are free to set their own hours as long as they work a total of forty hours each week. Forty workers share twenty jobs, getting half a week or every other week off. Both kinds of flexible schedules allow employees to inte-grate better their jobs and families, creating their own work weeks to complement their family schedules.

Steelcase is also one of the leaders in offering "cafeteria style" benefits plans. Employees are allotted a certain amount of money each year for benefits, and they get to choose how to spend those dollars. The company offers a number of medical, dental, and insurance plans, and if employees don't use all of their benefits allotments paying for such plans, they can receive the balance in cash or put it into various kinds of savings accounts.

Although such programs are not always successful, they generally benefit both company and employees. The flexibility allows Steelcase to keep its turnover low; workers who could make more money elsewhere stay on at Steelcase because of the way their Steelcase jobs fit their lifestyles. Flexible benefits programs can actually save companies money over more traditional programs, and they generally make employees happier too. Such flexibility even seems to reduce calls for unionization and stimulate productivity. It is likely to be a common theme in organizations' attempts to motivate the workers of the future.

References: Bob Cohn, "A Glimpse of the 'Flex' Future," *Newsweek*, August 1, 1988, pp. 38–39; Janice Castro, "Home Is Where the Heart Is," *Time*, October 3, 1988, pp. 46–53.

Finally, many organizations today are using empowerment and participation to boost motivation. When workers have more power and are allowed to participate more fully, they are able to pursue various needs that are important to them as individuals. Likewise, the actual activities themselves also facilitate the process of motivation, and achieving valued rewards as a result of contributing to the organization provides positive reinforcement.

USING REWARD SYSTEMS TO MOTIVATE PERFORMANCE

Aside from these types of strategies, an organization's reward system is its most basic tool for managing employee motivation. An organizational **reward system** is the formal and informal mechanisms by which employee performance is defined, evaluated, and rewarded.

● **reward system**
The formal and informal mechanisms by which employee performance is defined, evaluated, and rewarded

Effects of Organizational Rewards

Organizational rewards can affect attitudes, behaviors, and motivation. Thus managers must clearly understand and appreciate their importance.

Effect of Rewards on Attitudes Although employee attitudes such as satisfaction are not a major determinant of job performance, they are nonetheless important. They contribute to (or discourage) absenteeism and affect turnover, and they help establish the culture of the organization. We can draw some major generalizations about employee attitudes and rewards.[35] First, employee satisfaction is influenced by how much is received and how much the individual thinks should be received. Second, employee satisfaction is affected by comparisons with what happens to others. Third, employees often misperceive the rewards of others. When an employee believes that someone else is making more money than that person really makes, the potential for dissatisfaction increases. Fourth, overall job satisfaction is affected by how satisfied employees are with both the external and the fundamental rewards they derive from their jobs. Drawing from the content theories and expectancy theory, this conclusion suggests that behavior is the result of a variety of needs and may be channeled toward a variety of goals.

Effect of Rewards on Behaviors An organization's primary purpose in giving rewards is to influence employee behavior. Rewards affect employee satisfaction, which, in turn, plays a major role in determining whether an employee will remain on the job or seek a new job. Reward systems also influence patterns of attendance and absenteeism; and, if rewards are based on actual performance, employees tend to work harder to earn those rewards.

Effect of Rewards on Motivation Reward systems are clearly related to the expectancy theory of motivation. The effort-to-performance expectancy is strongly influenced by the performance appraisal that is often a part of the reward system. An employee is likely to put forth extra effort if he or she knows that performance will be measured, evaluated, and rewarded. The performance-to-outcome expectancy is affected by the extent to which the employee believes that performance will be followed by rewards. Finally, as expectancy theory predicts, each reward or potential reward has a somewhat different value for each person. One person may want a promotion more than benefits; someone else may want a stress-free job instead of increased responsibility.

Designing Effective Reward Systems

Experts agree that the elements of an effective reward system have four major characteristics.[36] First, the reward system must meet the needs of the individual for basic necessities. These needs include the physiological and security needs identified by Maslow and Alderfer and the hygiene factors identified by Herzberg. Next, the rewards should compare favorably with those offered by other organizations. Unfavorable comparisons with people in other companies could result in feelings of inequity and perhaps the loss of valuable employees. Third, the distribution of rewards within the organization must be equitable. When some employees feel underpaid com-

Au Bon Pain's Ron Shaich and Louis Kane, co-chairmen of the elite fast-food bakeries, have a simple program for motivating employees: Employees participating in the partner/manager program agree to a salary of $500 a week minimum and 35 percent of the store's profits once the store's goals have been met. This program, which has been the subject of case studies by Harvard University, Boston University, and Boston College professors, reduces employee burnout and turnover and encourages managers to be entrepreneurial.

pared with others in the organization, the probable results are low morale and poor performance. (People are more likely to compare their situation with that of others in their own organization than with that of outsiders.) Finally, the reward system must recognize that different people have different needs and will choose different paths to satisfy those needs. Both content theories and expectancy theory contribute to this conclusion. Insofar as possible, a variety of rewards and a variety of methods for achieving them should be made available to employees.

New Approaches to Rewarding Employees

Organizational reward systems have traditionally been either a fixed rate (hourly or monthly) or an incentive system. In a fixed-rate system, hourly employees are paid a specific wage (based on job demands, experience, or other factors) for each hour they work, and salaried employees receive a fixed sum of money on a weekly or monthly basis. Although some reductions may be made for absences, the amount is usually the same regardless of whether the employee works less than or more than a normal amount of time.

From a motivational perspective, such rewards can be tied more directly to performance through merit pay raises. In a **merit system,** employees get different pay raises at the end of the year, depending on their overall job performance.[37] When the organization's performance appraisal system is appropriately designed, merit pay is a good system for maintaining long-term performance. Increasingly, however, organizations are experimenting with various kinds of incentive systems. An **incentive system** attempts to reward employees in proportion to what they do. A piece-rate pay plan is a good example of an incentive system. In a factory manufacturing luggage, for example, each worker may be paid fifty cents for each handle and set of locks installed on a piece of luggage. Hence the employee has an incentive

merit system
A reward system whereby employees get different pay raises at the end of the year depending on their overall job performance

incentive system
A reward system whereby employees get different pay amounts at each pay period in proportion to what they do

to work hard: the more units produced, the higher the pay. Four increasingly popular incentive systems are profit sharing, gain sharing, lump-sum bonuses, and pay for knowledge.[38]

Profit sharing provides a varying annual bonus to employees based on corporate profits. This system unites workers and management in working toward the same goal—higher profits. However, there can be equity problems in deciding how to allocate the profits. Ford, USX Corporation, and Alcoa all have profit-sharing plans. Gain sharing is a group-based incentive system in which all group members get bonuses when predetermined performance levels are exceeded. Although this system facilitates teamwork and trust, it may also focus workers too narrowly on attaining the specific goals needed for the bonus while neglecting other parts of their jobs.

Lump-sum bonuses give each employee a one-time cash bonus instead of a base salary increase. The organization can control its fixed costs by not increasing base salaries; however, employees sometimes feel resentful that they may not get an increase in the future. Aetna Life and Casualty Co., Timex Group Ltd., and The B. F. Goodrich Co. have successfully used this approach. Finally, pay-for-knowledge systems focus on paying the individual rather than the job. Under a traditional arrangement two workers doing the same job are paid the same rate, regardless of their skills. Under a pay-for-knowledge system people are advanced in pay grade for each new skill or set of skills they learn. This approach increases training costs but also results in a more highly skilled work force. Schoolteachers often receive higher pay for increased training. General Foods Corporation and Texas Instruments have also experimented with this method and have had favorable results.

SUMMARY OF KEY POINTS

Motivation is the set of forces that cause people to behave in certain ways. Motivation is an important consideration of managers because it, along with ability and environmental factors, determines individual performance. Approaches to motivation have evolved from the traditional view through the human relations approach to the human resources view.

Content perspectives on motivation are concerned with what factor or factors cause motivation. Popular content theories include Maslow's need hierarchy, the ERG theory, and Herzberg's two-factor theory. Other important needs are the needs for achievement, affiliation, and power.

Process perspectives on motivation deal with how motivation occurs. Expectancy theory suggests that people are motivated to perform if they believe that their effort will result in high performance, that this performance will lead to rewards, and that the positive aspects of the outcomes outweigh the negative aspects. Equity theory is based on the premise that people are motivated to achieve and maintain social equity.

The reinforcement perspective focuses on how motivation is maintained. Its basic assumption is that behavior that results in rewarding consequences is likely to be repeated, whereas behavior resulting in negative consequences is less likely to be repeated. Reinforcement contingencies can be arranged in the form of positive reinforcement, avoidance, punishment, and extinction, and they can be provided on fixed-interval, variable-interval, fixed-ratio, or variable-ratio schedules.

Two newly emerging approaches to employee motivation are goal-setting theory and the Japanese approach. Popular motivational strategies include behavior modification, modified workweeks, work redesign, and participation programs to enhance motivation.

Organizational reward systems are the primary mechanisms managers have for managing motivation. Properly designed systems can improve attitudes, motivation, and behaviors. Effective reward systems must provide sufficient rewards on an equitable basis at the individual level. Contemporary reward systems include merit systems and various kinds of incentive systems.

DISCUSSION QUESTIONS

Questions for Review

1. What are the basic historical perspectives on motivation?

2. Summarize the basic differences among content, process, and reinforcement perspectives on motivation.

3. In what ways are the emerging perspectives on motivation like the content, process, and reinforcement perspectives? In what ways are they different?

4. What are the similarities and differences between the motivational strategies described in this chapter?

Questions for Analysis

5. Compare and contrast the different content theories. Can you think of any ways in which the theories are contradictory?

6. Expectancy theory seems to make a great deal of sense, but it is complicated. Some people argue that its complexity reduces its value to practicing managers. Do you agree or disagree?

7. Offer examples other than those from this chapter to illustrate positive reinforcement, avoidance, punishment, and extinction.

Questions for Application

8. Think about the worst job you have held. What approach to motivation was used in that organization? Now think about the best job you have held. What approach to motivation was used there? Can you base any conclusions on this limited information? If so, what?

9. Interview both managers and workers (or administrators and faculty) from a local organization. What views of or approaches to motivation seem to be in use in that organization?

10. Can you locate any local organizations that have implemented or are implementing any of the motivational strategies discussed in this chapter? If so, interview a manager and a worker to obtain their views on the program.

WAKING UP BANKAMERICA

*L*ike most big U.S. banks, BankAmerica Corp. had a rough time in the 1980s when the real estate market began to go soft, the financial bubble created by the leveraged buy-out boom collapsed, and Third World countries began to default on a growing number of loans. In 1990, however, BankAmerica, the country's second-largest bank, reported a net income of more than $1.1 billion, more than twice as much as Citicorp, the nation's largest bank. The credit for the turnaround goes largely to Richard Rosenberg, now the bank's CEO, and his approach to consumer banking.

Even during difficult times, consumer banking tends to be profitable. Before the recent interest rate decline, BankAmerica paid an average of 6.7 percent interest to its depositors, while charging customers 18 percent for credit card borrowing and 10 percent or more for home equity loans.

Rosenberg knew all this when he came to BankAmerica in 1987 to head its retail division. But he found the division in poor shape: the bank's impressive network of branch offices wasn't being used efficiently, and morale was terrible—employees were embarrassed to tell friends where they worked.

Initially, Rosenberg spent much of his time visiting branch offices, convincing them that they really were doing a good job and that they could turn a profit. He got managers to be aggressive in finding customers and learning what they needed. And when people did good work, Rosenberg praised them with a telephone call or a handwritten note.

To encourage the selling of profitable products, Rosenberg linked bonuses to the branch's ability to attract new customers and sell new products. Instead of giving incentives for cutting costs or simply doing their jobs, the bank now rewards branches and their employees for exceeding their sales goals.

Reviving an idea he had used with success at Wells Fargo & Company, Rosenberg created the Alpha account, a package deal that includes a savings and checking account and a line of credit as well as a statement that shows all these activities in simplified form. The bank charges less for these services bundled together than separately, and the idea quickly caught on—52,000 Alpha accounts were opened in the first three weeks.

As for morale, the bank's thirty-one California districts now hold recognition dinners every quarter during which branches and employees are rewarded for outstanding performances. Gleeful winners give the branch cheer, asserting their superiority to other branches.

These morale boosters and marketing gimmicks may raise eyebrows in the staid world of banking. But they have helped make BankAmerica the healthiest big bank in the country, and that may motivate a little imitation.

Discussion Questions

1. What motivators mentioned in the chapter did Rosenberg use to increase employee performance?

2. Why do you think Rosenberg was able to motivate BankAmerica's employees to turn the bank around?

E 3. Although banks are service organizations, they are also profit seekers. Do you think that there should be an imposed limit on the amount of profit banks can reap from their customers?

References: Gary Hector, "It's Banquet Time for BankAmerica," *Fortune*, June 3, 1991, pp. 69–75; John W. Milligan, "Can Bank of America Become America's Bank?" *Institutional Investor*, March 1991, pp. 46–50.

A Japanese make[r] [of equip]ment, Hitachi Ltd.'s a[ttitude toward its em]ployees shows that m[otivation is not an] isolated corporate goal [separate from strate]gies and programs. Ins[tead, motivation is an] outgrowth of an organi[zation's culture.]

Hitachi believes in t[he importance of its em]ployees and stresses te[amwork throughout its] operations. It rewards g[roup as well as indi]vidual achievements an[d tries to break down] the traditional barriers b[etween workers and] bosses. Most importantly, it motivates employees simply by listening to them, taking them seriously, and following up on their suggestions and requests.

Kazumitsu Minami, president of Hitachi Consumer Products of America, objects to being called the employees' "godfather," but has earned the title because he keeps his door open, and he listens. In the privacy of his office, employees tell him about family problems, worry about finances, and gripe about the assembly line. Sometimes all they want is a sympathetic ear, but when they want action, Minami tries to provide it.

In 1986, for instance, a number of workers asked to shift the television production line to a four-day week. Minami took the request seriously, reviewed it with managers and groups of employees, and finally allowed employees to vote on it. A majority of employees want to stick to the traditional work week.

At that point, most executives would have dropped the idea, rightfully feeling that they had already done a lot to respond to the unhappy employees. But Minami didn't want to let the matter rest just because only a minority of employees favored the four-day week. So when the company began building videocassette recorders on a new assembly line, Minami put it on a four-day work week and invited workers from other lines to transfer and take advantage of the new schedule.

This kind of attention to people, taking a long-range view, comes as no surprise to people who have followed Hitachi's development. The company's president, Katsushige Mita, describes himself as a *nobushi* or mountain priest. He is known for being ascetic and idealistic and for his ability to disentangle himself from the details of the day and see the big picture. That's the kind of vision necessary for a high-tech company to recognize that its people are more important to its success than its technology. Such a broad vision has also put Hitachi in the forefront of a series of new joint ventures between Japanese and U.S. computer chipmakers who once battled each other in fierce competitive secrecy. Hitachi has shown that it values innovation in many different areas, from its relationships with other organizations to its treatment of its workers.

Discussion Questions

1. If Hitachi needed to justify the way it deals with its employees, how could it measure the effects of its policies on motivation?

2. How could the boss's willingness to listen to employees' personal problems contribute to the employees' motivation?

E 3. How is Kazumitsu Minami's leadership style an example of a socially responsible behavior on the part of Hitachi toward its employees?

References: Henry Eason, "The Corporate Immigrants," *Nation's Business,* April 1987, pp. 12–19; "The Mountain Priest," *Fortune,* August 3, 1987, p. 42; Otis Port and Todd Mason, "What's Behind the Texas Instruments–Hitachi Deal," *Business Week,* January 16, 1989, pp. 93–96; Stephen Kreider Yoder and James P. Miller, "Hitachi, GM Unit Team Up to Buy National Semiconductor Subsidiary," *The Wall Street Journal,* February 28, 1989, p. B4.

Leadership and Influence Processes

OBJECTIVES

After studying this chapter, you should be able to:

- *Describe the nature of leadership and distinguish leadership from management.*

- *Discuss and evaluate the trait approach to leadership.*

- *Discuss and evaluate models of leadership focusing on behaviors.*

- *Identify and describe the major situational approaches to leadership.*

- *Identify and describe two new perspectives on leadership.*

- *Discuss political behavior in organizations and how it can be managed.*

OUTLINE

The Nature of Leadership
  The Meaning of Leadership
  Leadership Versus Management
  Power and Leadership

The Search for Leadership Traits

Leadership Behaviors
  Michigan Studies
  Ohio State Studies
  Leadership Grid

Situational Approaches to Leadership
  LPC Theory
  Path-Goal Theory
  Vroom-Yetton-Jago Model
  Other Situational Approaches

New Perspectives on Leadership
  Substitutes for Leadership
  Transformational Leadership

Political Behavior in Organizations
  Common Political Behaviors
  Managing Political Behavior

THURMAN JOHN RODGERS, who founded Cypress Semiconductor in 1983 at the age of 35, believes that his primary task is to create a work environment in which creative and motivated people can flourish. To do this, he encourages people to take risks and rewards them handsomely when they succeed. In addition, he works hard at avoiding bureaucratic hurdles and other organizational characteristics that he thinks lead to poor performance in other businesses.

Cypress Semiconductor Corp. is a fast-growing electronics firm based in California's fabled silicon valley. In its first year of operations Cypress generated around $3 million in sales. By 1992, its sales had increased to more than $300 million, making it one of the fastest growing companies in the world.

In his role as CEO of Cypress, Rodgers is clearly a manager. He sets goals for the firm, oversees its structural configuration, motivates its employees, and maintains adequate control. But Rodgers also goes far beyond these basic management functions as he leads his firm toward ever greater heights.

He has developed an elaborate information system that allows him to monitor the performance of each of his 1,500 employees on a weekly basis. But he argues that he is not looking for people to punish. Instead, Rodgers identifies people who are not performing well and then meets with them to find out how he can help them do better.

While not everyone is comfortable in a system such as this, most employees at Cypress think Rodgers is an incredible manager. They also recognize that his behavior goes far beyond that of a typical manager, however. Indeed, they are more apt to describe him as their leader than as their boss.[1] ●

A leader's roles are to influence the group's goals, motivate behavior, and help define group culture. The only female president of a major U.S. professional sports team, Susan O'Malley uses pep talks and a team motto of "You Gotta Believe" in her role as motivator. Washington Bullets owner chose 30-year-old O'Malley to lead the franchise because "she has a wonderful, wonderful way with people and is a tremendous achiever."

● **leadership**

As a process, the use of noncoercive influence to shape the group's or organization's goals, motivate behavior toward the achievement of those goals, and help define group or organization culture; as a property, the set of characteristics attributed to individuals who are perceived to be leaders

leaders

People who can influence the behaviors of others without having to rely on force; those accepted by others as leaders

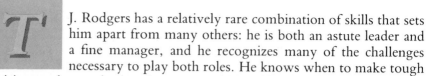

J. Rodgers has a relatively rare combination of skills that sets him apart from many others: he is both an astute leader and a fine manager, and he recognizes many of the challenges necessary to play both roles. He knows when to make tough decisions, when to lead and encourage his employees, and when to stand back and let them do their jobs. And thus far, his firm has reaped big payoffs from his efforts.

This chapter examines people like Rodgers more carefully—by focusing on leadership and its role in management. We characterize the nature of leadership and trace through the three major approaches to studying leadership—traits, behaviors, and situations. After examining newly emerging perspectives on leadership, we conclude by describing another approach to influencing others—political behavior in organizations.

THE NATURE OF LEADERSHIP

In Chapter 14, we described employee motivation. From the manager's standpoint, trying to motivate people is an attempt to influence their behavior. In many ways, leadership too is an attempt to influence the behavior of others. In this section, we first define leadership, then differentiate it from management, and conclude by relating it to power.

The Meaning of Leadership

Leadership is both a process and a property.[2] As a process, leadership is the use of noncoercive influence to shape the group's or organization's goals, motivate behavior toward the achievement of those goals, and help define group or organization culture.[3] As a property, leadership is the set of characteristics attributed to individuals who are perceived to be leaders. Thus **leaders** are people who can influence the behaviors of others without having to rely on force; leaders are people whom others accept as leaders.

Leadership Versus Management

From these definitions, it should be clear that leadership and management are related, but they are not the same. A person can be a manager, a leader, both, or neither.[4] Some of the basic distinctions between the two are summarized in Table 15.1. At the left side of the table are four elements that differentiate leadership from management. The two columns show how each element differs when considered from a management and a leadership point of view. For example, when executing plans, managers focus on monitoring results, comparing them with goals, and correcting deviations. In contrast, the leaders focus on energizing people to overcome bureaucratic hurdles to help reach goals. Thus when T. J. Rodgers monitors the performance of his employees he is playing the role of manager. But when he inspires them to work harder at achieving their goals, he is a leader.

Organizations need both management and leadership if they are to be effective. Leadership is necessary to create change, and management is nec-

TABLE 15.1 Distinctions Between Management and Leadership

Activity	Management	Leadership
Creating an agenda	**Planning and budgeting.** Establishing detailed steps and timetables for achieving needed results; allocating the resources necessary to make those needed results happen	**Establishing direction.** Developing a vision of the future, often the distant future, and strategies for producing the changes needed to achieve that vision
Developing a human network for achieving the agenda	**Organizing and staffing.** Establishing some structure for accomplishing plan requirements, staffing that structure with individuals, delegating responsibility and authority for carrying out the plan, providing policies and procedures to help guide people, and creating methods or systems to monitor implementation	**Aligning people.** Communicating the direction by words and deeds to all those whose cooperation may be needed, so as to influence the creation of teams and coalitions that understand the vision and strategies and accept their validity
Executing plans	**Controlling and problem solving.** Monitoring results vs. plan in some detail, identifying deviations, and then planning and organizing to solve these problems	**Motivating and inspiring.** Energizing people to overcome major political, bureaucratic, and resource barriers to change by satisfying very basic, but often unfulfilled, human needs
Outcomes	Produces a degree of predictability and order, and has the potential to consistently produce major results expected by various stakeholders (e.g., for customers, always being on time; for stockholders, being on budget)	Produces change, often to a dramatic degree, and has the potential to produce extremely useful change (e.g., new products that customers want, new approaches to labor relations that help make a firm more competitive)

Source: Reprinted with permission of The Free Press, a Division of Macmillan, Inc., from *A Force for Change* by John P. Kotter, Inc.

essary to achieve orderly results. Management in conjunction with leadership can produce orderly change, and leadership in conjunction with management can keep the organization properly aligned with its environment. "The Global View" describes how Jan Carlzon, CEO of Scandinavian Airlines, has adroitly combined leadership and management.

Power and Leadership

To fully understand leadership, it is necessary to understand power. **Power** is the ability to affect the behavior of others. One can have power without actually using it. For example, a football coach has the power to bench a player who is not performing up to par. The coach seldom has to use this power because players recognize that the power exists and work hard to keep their starting positions. In organizational settings, there are usually five kinds of power: legitimate, reward, coercive, referent, and expert power.[5]

Legitimate Power **Legitimate power** is power granted through the organizational hierarchy; it is the power accorded people occupying a particu-

While management and leadership are related, they are also distinct constructs. Managers and leaders differ in how they go about creating an agenda, developing a rationale for achieving the agenda, executing plans, and in the types of outcomes they achieve.

power
The ability to affect the behavior of others

legitimate power
Power granted through the organizational hierarchy; it is the power defined by the organization that is to be accorded people occupying particular positions

lar position as defined by the organization. A manager can assign a subordinate tasks, and a subordinate who refuses to do them can be reprimanded or even fired. Such outcomes stem from the manager's legitimate power as defined and vested in her or him by the organization. Legitimate power, then, is authority. All managers have legitimate power over their subordinates. The mere possession of legitimate power, however, does not by itself make someone a leader. Some subordinates follow only orders that are strictly within the letter of organizational rules and policies. If asked to do something not in their job description, they refuse or do a poor job. The manager of such employees is exercising authority but not leadership.

reward power

The power to give or withhold rewards, such as salary increases, bonuses, promotions, praise, recognition, and interesting job assignments

Reward Power **Reward power** is the power to give or withhold rewards. Rewards that a manager may control include salary increases, bonuses, promotion recommendations, praise, recognition, and interesting job assignments. In general, the greater the number of rewards a manager controls and the more important the rewards are to subordinates, the greater is the manager's reward power. If the subordinate sees as valuable only the formal organizational rewards provided by the manager, then he or she is not a leader. If the subordinate also wants and appreciates the manager's informal rewards like praise, gratitude, and recognition, however, then the manager is also exercising leadership.

coercive power

The power to force compliance by means of psychological, emotional, or physical threat

Coercive Power **Coercive power** is the power to force compliance by means of psychological, emotional, or physical threat. In the past physical coercion in organizations was relatively common. In most organizations today, however, coercion is limited to verbal reprimands, written reprimands, disciplinary layoffs, fines, demotion, and termination. Some managers occasionally go so far as to use verbal abuse, humiliation, and psychological coercion in an attempt to manipulate subordinates. (Of course, most people would agree that these are not appropriate managerial behaviors.) James Dutt, former CEO of Beatrice Company, once told a subordinate that if his wife and family got in the way of his working a twenty-four-hour-day seven days a week, he should get rid of them.[6] The more punitive the elements under a manager's control and the more important they are to subordinates, the more coercive power the manager possesses. On the other hand, the more a manager uses coercive power, the more likely he is to provoke resentment and hostility and the less likely he is to be seen as a leader.

referent power

The personal power that accrues to someone based on identification, imitation, loyalty, or charisma

Referent Power Compared with legitimate, reward, and coercion power, which are relatively concrete and grounded in objective facets of organizational life, **referent power** is abstract. It is based on identification, imitation, loyalty, or charisma. Followers may react favorably because they identify in some way with a leader, who may be like them in personality, background, or attitudes. In other situations, followers might choose to imitate a leader with referent power by wearing the same kinds of clothes, working the same hours, or espousing the same management philosophy. Referent power may also take the form of charisma, an intangible attribute of the leader that inspires loyalty and enthusiasm. Thus a manager might have referent power, but it is more likely to be associated with leadership.

LEADING SAS INTO THE BIG LEAGUES

Scandinavian Airlines System (SAS) is dwarfed by a number of U.S. airlines and not exactly a household word in the United States. Yet any casual reader of U.S. business magazines knows the face of Jan Carlzon, SAS's CEO. Carlzon's service innovations, detailed in his autobiography *Moments of Truth,* his attempts to make SAS into a global airline, and his own personal charisma have made Carlzon a hero in his native Sweden and a leader admired throughout the world.

After the deregulation of European airlines in 1992, Carlzon believes that large carriers will elbow smaller ones out of business, as happened in the United States in the years following deregulation. Carlzon plans for his airline to be one of the survivors.

When Carlzon took over SAS, he was worried about surviving not into the next century but into the next year. Because of its high union wages, Carlzon knew his airline couldn't compete in the fare wars. So he looked to his company's strength—his well-paid work force and Scandinavia's worldwide reputation for quality. And he staked the company's survival on its ability to attract business customers, many of whom are less concerned with a flight's cost than with its amenities.

To turn itself into a business traveler's dream, SAS devoted up to 60 percent of its seats to EuroClass, a business class with wide leather seats and VIP treatment. It also went all-out to improve its customers' experiences on the ground. It made agreements with other airlines so that SAS's reach would be worldwide. It linked itself to hotels around the world, improved its lounges, and made more computers and fax machines available to business customers who want to work while they wait.

Most importantly, Carlzon set out to change the way his employees deal with customers. "We used to fly planes," he says, "now we transport people."* Carlzon sees the most important employee-customer interactions—which he calls "moments of truth"—as occurring during check-in and boarding and any time a problem arises. If employees handle such moments well, he reasons, travelers will feel good about the airline and will return to it. So SAS gave its employees the power to handle such difficult moments themselves, making a refund or offering free drinks without a lot of red tape.

Like other airlines, SAS hit some turbulence in the early 1990s. But industry observers are betting that Carlzon can get his airline back on course again.

*Quoted in Michael Maccoby, "Three Firms That Changed," *Research Technology Management,* January–February 1990, p. 44.

References: Kenneth Labich, "An Airline that Soars on Service," *Fortune,* December 31, 1990, pp. 94–96; Michael Maccoby, "Three Firms that Changed," *Research Technology Management,* January–February 1990, pp. 44–45; John Marcom, Jr., "Moment of Truth," *Forbes,* July 8, 1991, pp. 83–86.

Expert Power   **Expert power** is derived from information or expertise. A manager who knows how to interact with an eccentric but important customer, a scientist who is capable of achieving an important technical breakthrough that no other company has dreamed of, and a secretary who knows how to unravel bureaucratic red tape all have expert power over anyone who needs that information. The more important the information and the fewer the people who have access to it, the greater is the degree of expert power possessed by any one individual. In general, people who are both leaders and managers tend to have a lot of expert power.

Using Power   How does a manager or leader use power? Several methods have been identified. One method is the *legitimate request,* which is based on legitimate power. The manager requests that the subordinate comply be-

expert power
The personal power that accrues to someone based on the information or expertise that they possess

cause the subordinate recognizes that the organization has given the manager the right to make the request. Most day-to-day interactions between manager and subordinate are of this type. Another use of power is *instrumental compliance,* which is based on the reinforcement theory of motivation. In this form of exchange, a subordinate complies to get the reward the manager controls. Suppose that a manager asks a subordinate to do something outside the range of the subordinate's normal duties, such as working extra hours on the weekend, terminating a relationship with a long-standing buyer, or delivering bad news. The subordinate complies and, as a direct result, reaps praise and a bonus from the manager. The next time the subordinate is asked to perform a similar activity, that subordinate will recognize that compliance will be instrumental in her getting more rewards. Hence the basis of instrumental compliance is clarifying important performance-reward contingencies.

A manager is using *coercion* when she suggests or implies that the subordinate will be punished, fired, or reprimanded if he does not do something. *Rational persuasion* occurs when the manager can convince the subordinate that compliance is in the subordinate's best interest. For example, a manager might argue that the subordinate should accept a transfer because it would be good for the subordinate's career. In some ways, rational persuasion is like reward power except that the manager does not really control the reward.

Still another way a manager can use power is through *personal identification.* A manager who recognizes that she has referent power over a subordinate can shape the behavior of that subordinate by engaging in desired behaviors: the manager consciously becomes a model for the subordinate and exploits personal identification. Sometimes a manager can induce a subordinate to do something consistent with a set of higher ideals or values through *inspirational appeal.* For example, a plea for loyalty represents an inspirational appeal. Referent power plays a role in determining the extent to which an inspirational appeal is successful because its effectiveness depends at least in part on the persuasive abilities of the leader.

A dubious method of using power is through *information distortion.* The manager withholds or distorts information to influence subordinates' behavior. For example, if a manager has agreed to allow everyone to participate in choosing a new group manager but subsequently finds one individual whom she really prefers, she might withhold some of the credentials of other qualified applicants so that the desired member is selected. This use of power is dangerous. It may be unethical, and if subordinates find out that the manager has deliberately misled them, they will lose their confidence and trust in that manager's leadership.[7]

THE SEARCH FOR LEADERSHIP TRAITS

The first organized approach to studying leadership analyzed the personal, psychological, and physical traits of strong leaders. The trait approach assumed that some basic trait or set of traits existed that differentiated leaders from nonleaders. If those traits could be defined, potential leaders could be identified. Researchers thought that leadership traits might include intelligence, assertiveness, above-average height, good vocabulary, attractive-ness, self-confidence, and similar attributes.[8]

During the first several decades of this century, hundreds of studies were conducted in an attempt to identify important leadership traits. For the most part, the results of the studies were disappointing. For every set of leaders who possessed a common trait, a long list of exceptions was also found, and the list of suggested traits soon grew so long that it had little practical value. Alternative explanations usually existed even for relations between traits and leadership that initially appeared valid. For example, it was ob-served that many leaders have good communication skills and are assertive. Rather than those traits being the cause of leadership, however, successful leaders may begin to display those traits after they have achieved leadership positions.

Although most researchers gave up trying to identify traits as predictors of leadership ability, many people still explicitly or implicitly adopt a trait orientation.[9] For example, politicians are all too often elected on the basis of personal appearance, speaking ability, or an aura of self-confidence.[10]

LEADERSHIP BEHAVIORS

Spurred on by their lack of success in identifying useful leadership traits, researchers soon began to investigate other variables, especially the behav-iors or actions of leaders. The new hypothesis was that effective leaders somehow behaved differently than less-effective leaders. Thus the goal was to develop a fuller understanding of leadership behaviors.

Michigan Studies

Researchers at the University of Michigan, led by Rensis Likert, began studying leadership in the late 1940s.[11] Based on extensive interviews with

Browning-Ferris Industries' District Manager Bill Davis exemplifies employee-centered leader behav-ior: he believes that keeping em-ployees excited about their jobs means keeping them informed. To this end, he sees himself as a coach who develops teamwork among his employees by sharing success and recognizing drivers who get the highest marks from customers.

both leaders (managers) and followers (subordinates), this research identified two basic forms of leader behavior: job centered and employee centered. Managers using **job-centered leader behavior** pay close attention to subordinates' work, explain work procedures, and are keenly interested in performance. Managers using **employee-centered leader behavior** are interested in developing a cohesive work group and ensuring that employees are satisfied with their jobs. Their primary concern is the welfare of subordinates.

- **job-centered leader behavior**

The behavior of leaders who pay close attention to the job and work procedures involved with that job

- **employee-centered leader behavior**

The behavior of leaders who develop cohesive work groups and ensure employee satisfaction

The two styles of leader behavior were presumed to be at the ends of a single continuum. Although this suggests that leaders may be extremely job-centered, extremely employee-centered, or somewhere in between, Likert studied only the two end styles for contrast. He argued that employee-centered leader behavior generally tended to be more effective. We should also note the similarities between Likert's leadership research and his Systems 1 through 4 organization design (discussed in Chapter 11). Job-centered leader behavior is consistent with the System 1 design (rigid and bureaucratic), whereas employee-centered leader behavior is consistent with the System 4 design (organic and flexible). When Likert advocates moving organizations from System 1 to System 4, he is also advocating a transition from job-centered to employee-centered leader behavior.

Ohio State Studies

At about the same time that Likert was beginning his leadership studies at the University of Michigan, a group of researchers at Ohio State also began studying leadership.[12] The extensive questionnaire surveys conducted during the Ohio State studies also suggested that there are two basic leader behaviors or styles: initiating-structure behavior and consideration behavior. When using **initiating-structure behavior,** the leader clearly defines the leader-subordinate role so that everyone knows what is expected, establishes formal lines of communication, and determines how tasks will be performed. Leaders using **consideration behavior** show concern for subordinates and attempt to establish a friendly and supportive climate. The behaviors identified at Ohio State are similar to those described at Michigan, but there are important differences. One major difference is that the Ohio State researchers did not interpret leader behavior as being one-dimensional: each behavior was assumed to be independent of the other. Presumably, then, a leader could exhibit varying levels of initiating structure and at the same time varying levels of consideration.

- **initiating-structure behavior**

The behavior of leaders who define the leader-subordinate role so that everyone knows what is expected, establish formal lines of communication, and determine how tasks will be performed

- **consideration behavior**

The behavior of leaders who show concern for subordinates and attempt to establish a warm, friendly, and supportive climate

At first, the Ohio State researchers thought that leaders who exhibit high levels of both behaviors would tend to be more effective than other leaders. A study at International Harvester Co. (now Navistar International Corp.), however, suggested a more complicated pattern.[13] The researchers found that employees of supervisors who ranked high on initiating structure were high performers but expressed low levels of satisfaction and had a high absence rate. Conversely, employees of supervisors who ranked high on consideration had low performance ratings but high levels of satisfaction and few absences from work. Later research isolated other variables that make consistent prediction difficult and determined that situational influences also occurred. (This body of research is discussed in the section on Situational Approaches to Leadership.)

Leadership Grid

In Chapter 12 we discussed an organization development technique called the Leadership Grid.[14] The Grid can also be seen as a model of leadership based on two forms of leader behavior: **concern for people** (similar to employee-centered and consideration behavior) and **concern for production** (similar to job-centered and initiating-structure behaviors). By combining the two forms of behavior, the Grid offers a way to analyze leader behavior in organizations. Note that the Grid, like the Michigan and Ohio State frameworks, implies that maximum concern for both people and production—in this case, the 9,9 coordinates—is the one generally appropriate combination of leader behaviors.

concern for people
That part of the Managerial Grid that deals with the human aspects of leader behavior

concern for production
That part of the Managerial Grid that deals with the job and task aspects of leader behavior

The leader-behavior theories have played an important role in the development of contemporary thinking about leadership. In particular, they urge us not to be preoccupied with what leaders are (the trait approach) but to concentrate on what leaders do (their behaviors). Unfortunately, these theories also make universal prescriptions about what constitutes effective leadership. When we are dealing with complex social systems composed of complex individuals, few if any relationships are consistently predictable, and certainly no formulas for success are infallible. Yet the behavior theorists tried to identify consistent relationships between leader behaviors and employee responses in the hope of finding a dependable prescription for effective leadership. As we might expect, they often failed. Other approaches to understanding leadership were therefore needed. The catalyst for these new approaches was the realization that, although interpersonal and task-oriented dimensions might be useful to describe the behavior of leaders, they were not useful for predicting or prescribing it. The next step in the evolution of leadership theory was the creation of situational models.[15]

SITUATIONAL APPROACHES TO LEADERSHIP

Situational models assume that appropriate leader behavior varies from one situation to another. The goal of a situational theory, then, is to identify key situational factors and to specify how they interact to determine appropriate leader behavior. Before discussing the three major situational theories, we should first discuss an important early model that laid the foundation for subsequent developments. In a 1958 study of the decision-making process, Robert Tannenbaum and Warren H. Schmidt proposed a continuum of leadership behavior. Their model is much like the original Michigan framework.[16] Besides purely job-centered behavior (or "boss-centered" behavior, as they termed it) and employee-centered ("subordinate-centered") behavior, however, they identified several intermediate behaviors that a manager might consider. These are shown on the leadership continuum in Figure 15.1.

This continuum of behavior moves from the one extreme of having the manager make the decision alone to the other extreme of having the employees make the decision with minimal guidance. Each point on the contin-

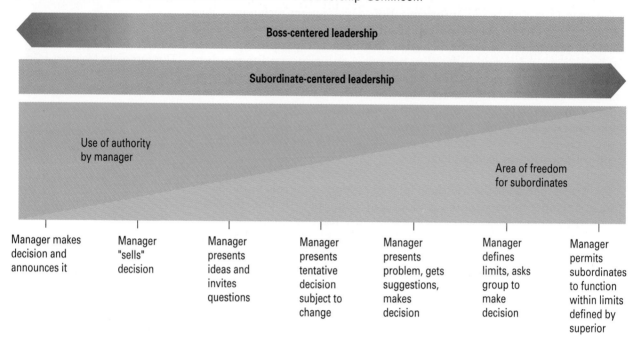

F I G U R E   15.1 Tannenbaum and Schmidt's Leadership Continuum

Boss-centered leadership

Subordinate-centered leadership

Use of authority by manager

Area of freedom for subordinates

| Manager makes decision and announces it | Manager "sells" decision | Manager presents ideas and invites questions | Manager presents tentative decision subject to change | Manager presents problem, gets suggestions, makes decision | Manager defines limits, asks group to make decision | Manager permits subordinates to function within limits defined by superior |

The Tannenbaum and Schmidt leadership continuum was an important precursor to modern situational approaches to leadership. The continuum identifies seven levels of leadership that range between the extremes of boss-centered and subordinate-centered leadership.

uum is influenced by characteristics of the manager, subordinates, and the situation. Managerial characteristics include the manager's value system, confidence in subordinates, personal inclinations, and feelings of security. Subordinate characteristics include the subordinates' need for independence, readiness to assume responsibility, tolerance for ambiguity, interest in the problem, understanding of goals, knowledge, experience, and expectations. Situational characteristics that affect decision making include the type of organization, group effectiveness, the problem itself, and time pressures. Although this framework pointed out the importance of situational factors, it was only speculative. It remained for others to develop more comprehensive and integrated theories. In the following sections, we describe the three most important and most widely accepted situational theories of leadership: the LPC theory, the path-goal theory, and the Vroom-Yetton-Jago model.

LPC Theory

LPC theory
A theory of leadership that suggests that the appropriate style of leadership varies with situational favorableness

The **LPC theory,** developed by Fred Fiedler, was the first true situational theory of leadership.[17] As we will discuss later, LPC stands for least preferred co-worker. Beginning with a combined trait and behavior approach, Fiedler identified two styles of leadership: task-oriented (analogous to job-centered and initiating-structure behavior) and relationship-oriented (similar to employee-centered and consideration behavior). He went beyond the earlier behavioral approaches by arguing that the style of behavior is a reflection of the leader's personality, and that most personalities fall into one of his two categories, task-oriented or relationship-oriented by nature. Fiedler measures leader style by means of a controversial questionnaire called the **least preferred co-worker (LPC)** measure. To use the measure, a manager or leader is asked to describe the specific person with whom he or she is able to work least well—the LPC—by filling in a set of sixteen scales anchored at each end by a positive or negative adjective. For example, three of the sixteen scales are:

Helpful __ __ __ __ __ __ __ __ Frustrating
    8 7 6 5 4 3 2 1

Tense __ __ __ __ __ __ __ __ Relaxed
    1 2 3 4 5 6 7 8

Boring __ __ __ __ __ __ __ __ Interesting
    1 2 3 4 5 6 7 8

least preferred co-worker (LPC)

The measuring scale that asks leaders to describe the person with whom he or she is able to work least well

The leader's LPC score is then calculated by adding up the numbers below the line checked on each scale. Note in these three examples that the higher numbers are associated with the positive qualities (helpful, relaxed, and interesting), whereas the negative qualities (frustrating, tense, and boring) have low point values. A high total score is assumed to reflect a relationship orientation and a low score a task orientation on the part of the leader. The LPC measure is controversial because researchers disagree about its validity. Some question exactly what an LPC measure reflects and whether the score is an index of behavior, personality, or some other factor.[18]

Favorableness of the Situation   The underlying assumption of situational models of leadership is that appropriate leader behavior varies from one situation to another. According to Fiedler, the key situational factor is the favorableness of the situation from the leader's point of view. This factor is determined by leader-member relations, task structure, and position power. *Leader-member relations* refer to the nature of the relationship between the leader and the work group. If the leader and the group have a high degree of mutual trust, respect, and confidence, and if they like one another, relations are assumed to be good. If there is little trust, respect, or confidence, and if they do not like each other, relations are poor. Naturally, good relations are more favorable.

Task structure is the degree to which the group's task is well defined. The task is structured when it is routine, easily understood, and unambiguous and when the group has standard procedures and precedents to rely on. An unstructured task is nonroutine, ambiguous, complex, with no standard procedures or precedents. You can see that high structure is more favorable for the leader, whereas low structure is less favorable. For example, if the task is unstructured, the group will not know what to do and the leader will have to play a major role in guiding and directing its activities. If the task is structured, the leader will not have to get so involved and can devote time to nonsupervisory activities. *Position power* is the power vested in the leader's position. If the leader has the power to assign work and to reward and punish employees, position power is assumed to be strong. But if the leader must get job assignments approved by someone else and does not administer rewards and punishment, position power is weak and it is more difficult to accomplish goals. From the leader's point of view, strong position power is clearly preferable to weak position power. However, position power is not as important as task structure and leader-member relations.

FIGURE 15.2 The Least-Preferred Co-Worker Theory of Leadership

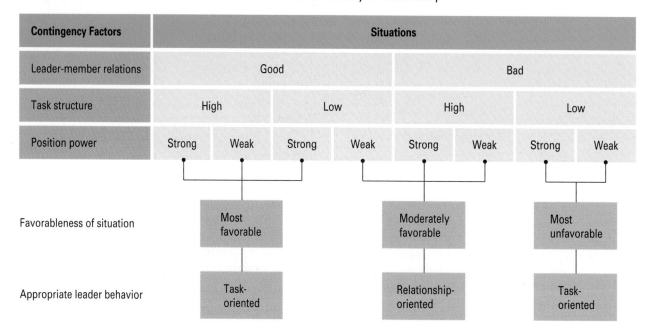

Favorableness and Leader Style   Fiedler and his associates conducted numerous studies linking the favorableness of various situations to leader style and the effectiveness of the group.[19] The results of these studies—and the overall framework of the theory—are shown in Figure 15.2. To interpret the model, look first at the situational factors at the top of the figure: good or bad leader-member relations, high or low task structure, and strong or weak leader-position power can be combined to yield eight unique situations. For example, good leader-member relations, high task structure, and strong leader-position power (at the far left) are presumed to define the most favorable situation; bad leader-member relations, low task structure, and weak leader-power (at the far right) are the least favorable. The other combinations reflect intermediate levels of favorableness.

Below each set of situations is shown the degree of favorableness and the form of leader behavior found to be most strongly associated with effective group performance for those situations. When the situation is most or least favorable Fiedler has found that a task-oriented leader is most effective. When the situation is only moderately favorable, however, a relationship-oriented leader is predicted to be most effective.

Flexibility of Leader Style   Fiedler argued that, for any given individual, leader style is essentially fixed and cannot be changed: leaders cannot change their behavior to fit a particular situation because it is linked to their particular personality traits. Thus when a leader's style and the situation do not match, Fiedler argued that the situation should be changed to fit the leader's style. When leader-member relations are good, task structure low, and position power weak, the leader style most likely to be effective is relationship-oriented. If the leader is task-oriented, a mismatch exists. According to Fiedler, the leader can make the elements of the situation more congruent by structuring the task (by developing guidelines and procedures, for instance) and increasing power (by requesting additional authority or by other means).

Fiedler's contingency theory has been attacked on the grounds that it is not always supported by research, that his findings are subject to other interpretations, that the LPC measure lacks validity, and that his assumptions about the inflexibility of leader behavior are unrealistic.[20] However, Fiedler's theory was one of the first to adopt a situational perspective on leadership. It has helped many managers recognize the important situational factors they must contend with, and it has fostered additional thinking about the situational nature of leadership.

Path-Goal Theory

The path-goal theory of leadership—associated most closely with Martin Evans and Robert House—is a direct extension of the expectancy theory of motivation discussed in Chapter 14.[21] Recall that the primary components of expectancy theory included the likelihood of attaining various outcomes and the value associated with those outcomes. The **path-goal theory** of leadership suggests that the primary functions of a leader are to make valued or desired rewards available in the workplace and to clarify for the subordinate the kinds of behavior that will lead to goal accomplishment and valued rewards—that is, the leader should clarify the paths to goal attainment.

● **path-goal theory**
A theory of leadership suggesting that the primary functions of a leader are to make valued or desired rewards available in the workplace and to clarify for the subordinate the kinds of behavior that will lead to those rewards

Leader Behavior   The most fully developed version of path-goal theory identifies four kinds of leader behavior. *Directive leader behavior* is letting subordinates know what is expected of them, giving guidance and direction, and scheduling work. *Supportive leader behavior* is being friendly and approachable, showing concern for subordinate welfare, and treating members as equals. *Participative leader behavior* is consulting subordinates, soliciting suggestions, and allowing participation in decision making. *Achievement-oriented leader behavior* is setting challenging goals, expecting subordinates to perform at high levels, encouraging subordinates, and showing confidence in subordinates' abilities.

In contrast to Fiedler's theory, path-goal theory assumes that leaders can change their style of behavior to meet the demands of a particular situation. For example, when encountering a new group of subordinates and a new project, the leader may be directive in establishing work procedures and in outlining what needs to be done. Next, the leader may adopt supportive behavior to foster group cohesiveness and a positive climate. As the group becomes familiar with the task and as new problems are encountered, the leader may exhibit participative behavior to enhance group members' motivation. Finally, achievement-oriented behavior may be used to encourage continued high performance. "Management in Practice" discusses how Sam Walton used achievement-oriented leader behavior to exhort his employees to work even harder.

Situational Factors   Like other situational theories of leadership, path-goal theory suggests that appropriate leader style depends on situational factors. Path-goal theory focuses on the situational factors of personal characteristics of subordinates and environmental characteristics of the workplace.

Important personal characteristics include the subordinates' perception of their own ability and their locus of control. If people perceive that they are lacking in ability, they may prefer directive leadership to help them understand path-goal relationships better. If they perceive themselves to have a lot of ability, however, employees may resent directive leadership. Locus of control is a personality trait. People who have an internal locus of control believe that what happens to them is a function of their own efforts and behavior. Those who have an external locus of control assume that fate, luck, or "the system" determines what happens to them. A person with an internal locus of control may prefer participative leadership, whereas a person with an external locus of control may prefer directive leadership. Managers can do little or nothing to influence the personal characteristics of subordinates, but they can shape the environment to take advantage of these personal characteristics by providing rewards and structuring tasks, for example.

Environmental characteristics include factors outside the subordinate's control. Task structure is one such factor. When structure is high, directive leadership is less effective than when structure is low. Subordinates do not usually need their boss to continually tell them how to do an extremely routine job. The formal authority system is another important environmental characteristic. Again, the higher the degree of formality, the less directive is the leader behavior that will be accepted by subordinates. The nature of the work group also affects appropriate leader behavior. When the work group provides the employee with social support and satisfaction, supportive leader behavior is less critical. When social support and satisfaction cannot be derived from the group, the worker may look to the leader for this support.

The basic path-goal framework as illustrated in Figure 15.3 shows that different leader behaviors affect subordinates' motivation to perform. Personal and environmental characteristics are seen as defining which behaviors lead to which outcomes. The path-goal theory of leadership is a dynamic and incomplete model. The original intent was to state the theory in general terms so that future research could explore a variety of interrelationships and modify the theory. Research that has been done suggests that the path-goal theory is a reasonably good description of the leadership process and that future investigations along these lines should enable us to discover more about the link between leadership and motivation.[22]

The path-goal theory of leadership suggests that managers can use four types of leader behavior to clarify subordinates' paths to goal attainment. Personal characteristics of the subordinate and environmental characteristics within the organization both must be taken into account when determining which style of leadership will work best for a particular situation.

FIGURE 15.3 The Path-Goal Framework

Subordinates' personal characteristics
- Perceived ability
- Locus of control

Leader behaviors
- Directive
- Supportive
- Participative
- Achievement-oriented

Environmental characteristics
- Task structure
- Authority system
- Work group

Subordinates' motivation to perform

A NATION'S RETAIL LEADER

Sam Walton was one of the great business leaders in the United States, and without question, the nation's best retailer. In 1991, his chain, WalMart Stores, Inc., passed Sears, Roebuck and Co. and K mart Corp. to become the nation's largest retailer, with more than $32 billion in revenues. For two decades it has grown at a pace that other companies only dream about, and recently Wal-Mart has been dominating lists of the nation's most admired companies.

Sam Walton himself was such a plain-spoken, down-home character that if he appeared in a television situation comedy, viewers would probably complain that he was unrealistic and corny. His and Wal-Mart's base is Arkansas (not New York or Los Angeles), he was most often seen in a Wal-Mart baseball cap, and he drove an old pickup with cages for his quail dogs in back. His first slogan was "We care."

But one of the secrets of Walton's success is that he *did* care, and he managed to convince his employees—called "associates"—not only that he was sincere, but that they should care too, about the company and its customers. Walton passed on his philosophy during his pizza lunches with associates and his Saturday morning pep rallies with managers. And he addressed all of the company's more than 215,000 employees at once by way of a sophisticated satellite television system. Walton was not comfortable with high technology, but he did recognize that technology is essential for keeping communication and distribution costs down. Even though he appeared with the help of a television signal that had traveled through space, he still rambled on about his dogs before delivering the day's inspirational message.

Although Walton's personality and the corporate culture built around it were powerful motivators, Wal-Mart doesn't rely on them alone to keep people working hard. The company has a variety of profit-sharing plans, including bonuses for every associate in a store that keeps "shrinkage"—merchandise lost to theft and damage—below the company's average.

Other empires have crumbled when their leaders died or retired, and some worry about the fate of Wal-Mart now that Walton is no longer at the helm. The Walton trait that may be hardest to duplicate was his refusal to be satisfied, his hunger to find a better way. But Wal-Mart executives are optimistic: they believe that the corporate culture is so strong and the principles on which it is founded are so well-accepted that the company can carry on without Sam Walton. No doubt Sears and K mart hope they're wrong.

References: Janice Castro, "Mr. Sam Stuns Goliath," *Time*, February 25, 1991, pp. 62–63; John Huey, "Wal-Mart: Will It Take Over the World?" *Fortune*, January 30, 1989, pp. 52–61.

Vroom-Yetton-Jago Model

The **Vroom-Yetton-Jago (VYJ) model** predicts what kinds of situations call for what degrees of group participation. The VYJ model, then, sets norms or standards for including subordinates in decision making. The model was first proposed by Victor Vroom and Philip Yetton in 1973 and was revised and expanded in 1988 by Vroom and Arthur G. Jago.[23] The VYJ model is somewhat narrower than the other situational theories in that it focuses on only one part of the leadership process—how much decision-making participation to allow subordinates.

● **Vroom-Yetton-Jago (VYJ) model**
Predicts what kinds of situations call for what degrees of group participation

Basic Premises The VYJ model argues that decision effectiveness is best gauged by the quality of the decision and by employee acceptance of the decision. Decision quality is the objective effect of the decision on performance. Decision acceptance is the extent to which employees accept and are committed to the decision. To maximize decision effectiveness, the VYJ

TABLE 15.2   Decision Styles in the Vroom-Yetton-Jago Model

Decision Style	Definition
AI	Manager makes the decision alone.
AII	Manager asks for information from subordinates but makes the decision alone. Subordinates may or may not be informed about what the situation is.
CI	Manager shares the situation with individual subordinates and asks for information and evaluation. Subordinates do not meet as a group, and the manager alone makes the decision.
CII	Manager and subordinates meet as a group to discuss the situation, but the manager makes the decision.
GII	Manager and subordinates meet as a group to discuss the situation, and the group makes the decision.

A = autocratic; C = consultative; G = group

Source: Reprinted from *Leadership and Decision-making* by Victor H. Vroom and Philip W. Yetton by permission of the University of Pittsburgh Press. © 1973 by the University of Pittsburgh Press.

model suggests that, depending on the situation, managers adopt one of five decision-making styles. As summarized in Table 15.2, there are two autocratic styles (AI and AII), two consultative styles (CI and CII), and one group style (GII).

The situation that is presumed to dictate an appropriate decision-making style is defined by a series of questions about the characteristics or attitudes of the problem under consideration. To address the questions, the manager uses one of four decision trees. Two of the trees are used when the problem affects the entire group, and the other two are appropriate when the problem relates to an individual. One of each is to be used when the time necessary to reach a decision is important, and the others are to be used when time is less important but the manager wants to develop subordinates' decision-making abilities.

Figure 15.4 shows the tree for time-driven group problems. The problem attributes defining the situation are arranged along the top of the tree and are expressed as questions. To use the tree, the manager starts at the left side of it and asks the first question. Thus the manager first decides whether the problem involves a quality requirement—that is, whether there are quality differences in the alternatives and if they matter. The answer determines the path to the second node, where the manager asks another question. The manager continues in this fashion until a terminal node is reached and an appropriate decision style is indicated. Each prescribed decision style is assigned to protect the original goals of the process (decision quality and subordinate acceptance) within the context of the group versus individual and time versus development framework.

Evaluation   The original version of the VYJ model has been widely tested. Indeed, one recent review concluded that it had received more scientific

FIGURE 15.4 Time-Driven Group Problem Decision Tree for VYJ Model

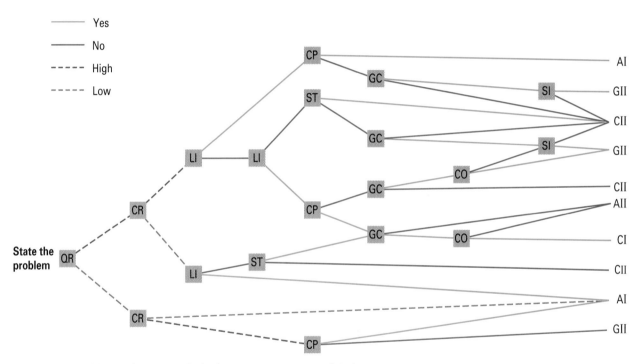

QR Quality requirement: How important is the technical quality of this decision?

CR Commitment requirement: How important is subordinate commitment to the decision?

LI Leader's information: Do you have sufficient information to make a high-quality decision?

ST Problem structure: Is the problem well structured?

CP Commitment probability: If you were to make the decision by yourself, is it reasonably certain
    that your subordinate(s) would be committed to the decision?

GC Goal congruence: Do subordinates share the organizational goals to be attained in solving this problem?

CO Subordinate conflict: Is conflict among subordinates over preferred solutions likely?

SI Subordinate information: Do subordinates have sufficient information to make a high-quality decision?

Source: Reprinted from *The New Leadership* by Victor H. Vroom and Arthur G. Jago. Prentice-Hall, 1988. Used by permission of the authors.

support than any other leadership theory.[24] The inherent complexity of the model presents a problem for many managers, however. Even the original version was criticized because of its complexity, and the revised VYJ model is far more complex than the original. To aid managers, computer software has been developed to facilitate their ability to define their situation, answer the questions about problem attributes, and develop a strategy for decision-making participation.[25]

Managers can use this decision tree to obtain insights into how much subordinates should participate in the decision-making process. To use this tree, the manager asks a series of questions about the problem situation. The answers to each question lead the manager through the tree. At each endpoint is a recommended decision style (see Table 15.2) that is predicted to enhance decision quality and acceptance.

Other Situational Approaches

In addition to the major theories, other situational models have been developed in recent years. We discuss the vertical-dyad linkage model and the life cycle model.

Eberhard von Kuenheim, chief executive of Bavarian Motor Works (BMW), reveres old-world craftsmanship, and he sets exacting standards of quality for employees, suppliers, and dealers alike. Every BMW apprentice serves up to three years, foremen are trained in the latest quality techniques, suppliers are rigorously audited, and dealers are reviewed for service and customer approval. His high standards (setting challenging goals, expecting subordinates to perform at high levels) are characteristic of achievement-oriented leader behavior.

vertical-dyad linkage (VDL) model

Stresses that leaders have different kinds of relationships with different subordinates

Vertical-Dyad Linkage Model The **vertical-dyad linkage (VDL) model** stresses that leaders have different kinds of relationships with different subordinates.[26] Each manager-subordinate relationship represents one vertical dyad. The model suggests that leaders establish special working relationships with a handful of subordinates called the in-group. Other subordinates remain in the out-group. Those in the in-group receive more of the manager's time and attention and also tend to be better performers. Early research on this model is quite promising.

life cycle theory

A model suggesting that appropriate leader behavior depends on the maturity of the follower

Life Cycle Theory Another well-known situational theory is the **life cycle theory,** which suggests that appropriate leader behavior depends on the maturity of the followers.[27] In this context, maturity includes motivation, competence, and experience. The theory suggests that as followers become more mature, the leader needs to gradually move from a high level of task orientation to a low level. Simultaneously, employee-oriented behavior should start low, increase at a moderate rate, and then decline again. This theory is well-known among practicing managers, but it has received little scientific support from researchers.[28]

NEW PERSPECTIVES ON LEADERSHIP

Because of its importance to organizational effectiveness, leadership continues to be the focus of a great deal of research and theory building. New approaches that have attracted much attention are the concepts of substitutes for leadership and transformational leadership.

Substitutes for Leadership

substitutes for leadership

A concept that identifies situations in which leader behaviors are neutralized or replaced by characteristics of subordinates, the task, and the organization

The concept of **substitutes for leadership** was developed because existing leadership models and theories do not account for situations in which leadership is not needed.[29] They simply try to specify what kind of leader behavior

Transformational leadership transmits a sense of mission, stimulates learning experiences, and inspires new ways of thinking. In today's fast-changing business environment, transformational leaders are becoming increasingly important; and few industries are as turbulent as the airlines. Southwest Airlines' CEO Herbert Kelleher, by instituting flexible work rules and a generous profit-sharing plan, enabled Southwest to be one of the few carriers to post a 1991 profit. Kelleher's antics also boost productivity—he has been known to dress up as Elvis.

is appropriate. The substitute concepts, however, identify situations in which leader behaviors are neutralized or replaced by characteristics of the subordinate, the task, and the organization. For example, when a patient is delivered to a hospital emergency room, the professionals on duty do not wait to be told what to do by a leader. Nurses, doctors, and attendants all go into action without waiting for directive or supportive leader behavior from the emergency-room supervisor.

Characteristics of the subordinate that may serve to neutralize leader behavior include ability, experience, need for independence, professional orientation, and indifference toward organizational rewards. For example, employees with a high level of ability and experience may not need to be told what to do. Similarly, a subordinate's strong need for independence may render leader behavior ineffective. Task characteristics that may substitute for leadership include routineness, the availability of feedback, and intrinsic satisfaction. When the job is routine and simple, the subordinate may not need direction. When the task is challenging and intrinsically satisfying, the subordinate may not need or want social support from a leader.

Organizational characteristics that may substitute for leadership include formalization, group cohesion, inflexibility, and a rigid reward structure. Leadership may not be necessary when policies and practices are formal and inflexible, for example. Similarly, a rigid reward system may rob the leader of reward power and thereby decrease the importance of the role. Preliminary research has provided support for the concept of substitutes for leadership.[30]

Transformational Leadership

Another new perspective on leadership has been called by a number of labels: charismatic leadership, inspirational leadership, symbolic leadership, and transformational leadership. We use the term **transformational leadership** and define it as leadership that goes beyond ordinary expectations by transmitting a sense of mission, stimulating learning experiences, and inspiring new ways of thinking.[31] Because of rapid change and turbulent environments, transformational leaders are increasingly being seen as vital to the success of business.

transformational leadership
Leadership that goes beyond ordinary expectations by transmitting a sense of mission, stimulating learning experiences, and inspiring new ways of thinking

A recent popular-press article identified seven keys to successful leadership: trusting one's subordinates. developing a vision, keeping cool, encouraging risk, being an expert, inviting dissent, and simplifying things.[32] Although this list was the result of a simplistic survey of the leadership literature, it is nevertheless consistent with the premises underlying transformational leadership. So, too, are recent examples cited as effective leadership. Take, for example, the case of General Electric Co. When Jack Welch assumed the position of CEO, GE was a lethargic behemoth composed of more than one hundred businesses. Decision making was slow, and bureaucracy stifled individual initiative. Welch stripped away the bureaucracy, streamlined the entire organization, sold dozens of businesses, and bought many new ones. He literally recreated the organization, and today GE is one of the most admired and profitable firms in the world. Transformational leadership was the basis for all of Welch's changes.[33] Other transformational leaders are John Scully at Apple and Lee Iacocca at Chrysler. Given both its theoretical appeal and its practical importance, the notion of transformational leadership is destined to become even more popular.

POLITICAL BEHAVIOR IN ORGANIZATIONS

● **political behavior**
The activities carried out for the specific purpose of acquiring, developing, and using power and other resources to obtain one's preferred outcomes

Another common influence on behavior is politics and political behavior. **Political behavior** describes activities carried out for the specific purpose of acquiring, developing, and using power and other resources to obtain one's preferred outcomes.[34] Political behavior may be undertaken by managers dealing with their subordinates, subordinates dealing with their managers, and managers and subordinates dealing with others at the same level. In other words, it may be directed upward, downward, or laterally. Decisions ranging from where to locate a manufacturing plant to where to put the company coffeepot are subject to political action. In any situation, individuals may engage in political behavior to further their own ends, to protect themselves from others, to further goals they sincerely believe to be in the organization's best interest, or to simply acquire and exercise power. And power may be sought by individuals, by groups of individuals, or by groups of groups.

While political behavior is difficult to study because of its sensitive nature, one survey found that many managers believed that politics influenced salary and hiring decisions in their firms. Many also believed that the incidence of political behavior was greater at the upper levels of their organizations and less at the lower levels. More than one-half of the respondents felt that organizational politics was bad, unfair, unhealthy, and irrational but most suggested that successful executives have to be good politicians and be political to "get ahead."[35]

Common Political Behaviors

Research has identified four basic forms of political behavior widely practiced in organizations.[36] One form is *inducement,* which occurs when a manager offers to give something to someone else in return for that individual's support. For example, a product manager might suggest to another product manager that she will put in a good word with his boss if he supports a new marketing plan that she has developed. A second tactic is *persuasion,* which relies on both emotion and logic. An operations manager wanting to construct a new plant on a certain site might persuade others to support his goal on grounds that are objective and logical (land is less expensive, taxes are lower) as well as subjective and personal.

A third political behavior involves the *creation of an obligation.* For example, one manager might support a recommendation made by another manager for a new advertising campaign. Although he may really have no opinion on the new campaign, he may think that by going along he is incurring a debt from the other manager and will be able to "call in" that debt when he wants to get something done and needs additional support. Finally, *coercion* is the use of force to get one's way. For example, a manager may threaten to withhold support, rewards, or other resources as a way to influence someone else.

Managing Political Behavior

By its very nature, political behavior is tricky to approach in a rational and systematic way. But managers can handle political behavior so that it does not do excessive damage. First, managers should be aware that even if their actions are not politically motivated, others may assume that they are. Second, by providing subordinates with autonomy, responsibility, challenge, and feedback, managers reduce the likelihood of political behavior by subordinates. Third, managers should avoid using power if they want to avoid charges of political motivation. Fourth, managers should get disagreements out in the open so that subordinates will have less opportunity for political behavior, using conflict for their own purposes. Finally, managers should avoid covert activities. Behind-the-scene activities give the impression of political intent even if none really exists.[37] Other guidelines include clearly communicating the bases and processes for performance evaluation, tying rewards directly to performance, and minimizing competition among managers for resources.[38]

Of course, those guidelines are a lot easier to list than they are to implement. The well-informed manager should not assume that political behavior does not exist or, worse yet, attempt to eliminate it by issuing orders or commands. Instead, the manager must recognize that political behavior exists in virtually all organizations and that it cannot be ignored or stamped out. It can, however, be managed in such a way that it will seldom inflict serious damage on the organization. It may even play a useful role in some situations.[39] For example, a manager may be able to use his or her political influence to stimulate a greater sense of social responsibility or to heighten awareness of the ethical implications of a decision.

SUMMARY OF KEY POINTS

As a process, leadership is the use of noncoercive influence to shape the group's or organization's goals, motivate behavior toward the achievement of those goals, and help define group or organization culture. As a property, leadership is the set of characteristics attributed to those who are perceived to be leaders. Leadership and management are often related but are also different. Managers and leaders use legitimate, reward, coercive, referent, and expert power.

The trait approach to leadership assumes that some basic trait or set of traits differentiates leaders from nonleaders. The leadership-behavior approach to leadership assumes that the behavior of effective leaders is somehow different from the behavior of nonleaders. Research at the University of Michigan and Ohio State identified two basic forms of leadership behavior—one concentrating on work and performance and the other concentrating on employee welfare and support. The Managerial Grid attempts to train managers to exhibit high levels of both forms of behavior.

Situational approaches to leadership recognize that appropriate forms of leadership behavior are not universally applicable and attempt to specify situations in which various behaviors are appropriate. The LPC theory suggests that a leader's behaviors should be either task-oriented or relationship-oriented depending on the favorableness of the situation. The path-goal theory suggests that directive, supportive, participative, or achievement-oriented leader behaviors may be appropriate, depending on the personal characteristics of subordinates and the environment. The Vroom-Yetton-Jago model maintains that leaders should vary the extent to which they allow subordinates to participate in making decisions as a function of problem attributes. The vertical-dyad linkage model and the life cycle theory are two new situational theories.

Emerging leadership perspectives are the concept of substitutes for leadership and the role of transformational leadership in organizations.

Political behavior is another influence process frequently used in organizations. Managers can take steps to limit the effects of political behavior.

DISCUSSION QUESTIONS

Questions for Review

1. Could someone be a manager but not a leader? A leader but not a manager? Both a leader and a manager? Explain.

2. What were the major findings of the Michigan and Ohio State studies of leadership behaviors? Briefly describe each group of studies and compare and contrast their findings.

3. What are the situational approaches to leadership? Briefly describe each and compare and contrast their findings.

4. Describe two new perspectives on leadership. How can they be integrated with existing approaches to leadership?

Questions for Analysis

5. How is it possible for a leader to be both task-oriented and employee-oriented at the same time? Can you think of other forms of leader behavior that would be important to a manager? If so, share your thoughts with your class.

6. When all or most of the leadership substitutes are present, does the follower no longer need a leader? Why or why not?

7. Why should members of an organization be aware that political behavior may be going on within the organization? What might occur if they were not aware?

Questions for Application

8. What traits seem best to describe student leaders? Military leaders? Business leaders? Political leaders? Religious leaders? What might account for the similarities and differences in your lists of traits?

9. Think about a decision that would affect you as a student. Use the Vroom-Yetton-Jago model to decide whether the administrator making that decision should involve students in the decision. Which parts of the model seem most important in making that decision? Why?

10. How do you know if transformational leadership is present in a group or organization? Could transformational leadership ever lead to dysfunctional outcomes for individuals or organizations? If so, why? If not, why not?

A Leader on the Move

*T*hough only fifty years old in 1992, Michael Walsh has evolved a philosophy of leadership made convincing by his successes, first as a football player at Stanford, then in law, and finally in a series of major corporations. In Walsh's view, a leader must be enormously energetic to make decisions, change processes, and convince everyone that the new way is the best way. As an outsider moving into important positions, first at Cummins Engine, then at Union Pacific, and finally at Tenneco Inc., Walsh sometimes had to do with energy what he could not do with expertise. But that outsider status also was a valuable asset, especially at Union Pacific, where elements of the company were so involved in political competition with other units that they had almost completely lost sight of the goal of pleasing customers.

According to Walsh, a leader has to have a keen eye for which parts of a company look promising and which are losers. This doesn't mean that only high-growth and high-margin businesses can have leaders; rather a leader must start with what the company has and separate its strengths from its weaknesses. At Tenneco, which has six major businesses ranging from auto parts to natural gas pipelines, Walsh has to decide how to balance the flow of attention and cash to each operation. Ideally, he hopes to find ways that the businesses complement each other.

Walsh has a reputation for being a cost cutter, but he thinks that term conveys the wrong emphasis. He likens what he tries to do in a company to what good athletes do. Athletes train to reach performance goals, and in doing so usually lose any excess body fat. But that doesn't mean they set out to lose weight.

Few would disagree with Walsh's emphasis on good judgment and his ability to motivate and evaluate people. But Walsh also believes in acting with a speed that would disturb some executives. He feels that a leader often must make a decision first and ask ques-

tions later. This attitude may be a legacy from his days at Union Pacific, where he headed the railroad group, only one of the businesses owned by the parent holding company. He knew that he had to show the parent company good results quickly.

Leaders must also be able to set priorities for their entire organization, and to Walsh's mind the number-one priority must be pleasing the customer. Many of his actions at Union Pacific—like cutting six layers of management between himself and superintendents—seem like textbook "downsizing" moves, but they were in fact motivated by his desire to please customers. When the railroad superintendents had to get three signatures to spend more than $100, their work was sluggish. Now superintendents can spend up to $25,000 on their own.

At the rate he's going, Walsh may revive three or four more companies before he retires. But if his successes continue, he may need to take time out to write a book about his approach to leadership.

Discussion Questions

1. Do you agree that leaders must often act first and ask questions later? What are the dangers of this approach?

2. Do you think most leaders would accept the analogy of a lean company to a lean athlete? What does this analogy imply a business leader should *not* do?

E 3. Walsh has held four major positions in a dozen years. Do you think a good leader should show loyalty to a particular organization and stay with it for more than a few years?

References: Andrew Kupfer, "An Outsider Fires Up A Railroad," *Fortune*, December 18, 1989, pp. 133–146; Nora E. Field, "'Success Depends on Leadership,'" *Fortune*, November 18, 1991, pp. 153–154.

Kim Woo-Choong, Chairman of Daewoo, Korea's fourth-largest business group, is going against the flow. While many companies are trying to decentralize, giving more responsibility to low-level managers, Kim is moving in the opposite direction, taking control back into his own hands. Whether his centralization of power is viewed as a step backwards or a step into the future will depend largely on his ability to reverse Daewoo's recent fortunes.

Kim founded Daewoo, the newest of Korea's four big business conglomerates (*chaebol*) in 1967, and by 1988 it included twenty-eight companies involved in trade, financial services, construction, and the manufacture of everything from machine guns to ships to fax machines. As his business grew, Kim, like many entrepreneurs-turned-corporate-leaders, gradually gave up control of many Daewoo companies and spent much of his time traveling around the world, looking for new markets.

But trouble began brewing for the *chaebol* in the late 1980s under Korean President Roh Tae-Woo. At a time when former President Chun Doo Hwan's close ties with the *chaebol* were the subject of sensational televised hearings, Roh decided to end the government's support of the four big groups and give smaller companies a chance to compete.

Changes in the government's support were not Kim's only problem. The increase in democracy in South Korea and violent strikes by some workers ended years of cheap and docile Korean labor. Some of Korea's trade barriers have begun to come down, the currency has been revalued, and the debt that the *chaebol* built up while amassing market share has now become a burden. From a Western perspective, the *chaebol* were overdiversified and poorly managed.

In 1990, Kim began what he calls a "revolution" at Daewoo. In early January, 5,000 of Daewoo's top managers came to the Seoul Hilton International for their yearly meeting with the chairman, but the usual spirit of self-congratulation was missing. Many of them had already received letters from Kim criticizing their "poor performance and easy-going manner." Scores were "retired."

Under Kim's pressure, Daewoo's bureaucracies began to change. At Daewoo's subsidiary, Seoul Hilton International, 200 middle managers lost their jobs, while the Daewoo trading company cut one-third of its middle managers.

Kim actually began the changes himself when he took charge of Daewoo Shipbuilding during its crisis in 1988. He saved $8 million a year simply by ending the company policy of providing workers with free haircuts. And he slashed thousands of positions. His reputation grew, as Daewoo Shipbuilding turned itself around and began showing a profit.

Kim's personal takeover of power may seem old-fashioned to managers in the United States, but observers have been impressed by his ability to shrink the bureaucracy and make companies profitable again. And if anyone can revive the image of the corporate leader as a driven, tireless, one-man show, it is Kim.

Discussion Questions

1. Why do you think Kim Woo-Choong is choosing a leadership strategy the opposite of that advocated by many U.S. business leaders?

2. What are Kim Woo-Choong's strengths as a leader?

E 3. Do you think that concentrating power and decision-making in the hands of one person could pose problems?

References: Laxmi Nakarmi, "At Daewoo, A 'Revolution' at the Top," *Business Week*, February 18, 1991, pp. 68–69; Laxmi Nakarmi, "Korea's Conglomerates Face Life Without a Safety Net," *Business Week*, November 28, 1988, p. 51.

Managing Interpersonal and Group Processes

OBJECTIVES

After studying this chapter, you should be able to:

● *Describe the interpersonal nature of organizations.*

● *Define and identify types of groups in organizations and discuss reasons people join groups and the stages of group development.*

● *Identify and discuss four essential characteristics of mature groups.*

● *Explain how organizations create and manage teams.*

● *Discuss interpersonal and intergroup conflict in organizations*

OUTLINE

The Interpersonal Nature of Organizations
    Interpersonal Dynamics
    Outcomes of Interpersonal Behaviors

Groups in Organizations
    Types of Groups
    Why People Join Groups
    Stages of Group Development

Characteristics of Mature Groups
    Role Structures
    Behavioral Norms
    Cohesiveness
    Informal Leadership

Using Teams in Organizations
    Creating Work Teams
    Managing Work Teams

Interpersonal and Intergroup Conflict
    Causes of Conflict
    Managing Conflict

FREDERICK SMITH FIRST proposed the idea of a private overnight mail delivery service in a term paper. His Yale professor awarded him a grade of "C" and suggested that the idea would never work. Undeterred by this pessimism, Smith went ahead with his plans and, in 1973, launched Federal Express Corp.

After a slow start, Federal Express has grown to become a multinational organization with its own fleet of 255 planes and 34,000 computerized delivery vans and offices around the globe. Annual sales at Federal Express exceed $5 billion, and the firm is considered to be one of the best-managed organizations in the United States.

In recent years, however, competitors such as United Parcel Service, Inc. (UPS) and Airborne Express and new technology, most notably facsimile machines, have combined to slow Federal Express's growth. To fight back, the firm has begun looking for new and innovative ways to compete even more effectively and to lower costs.

One major new initiative at Federal Express has been to create hundreds of work teams. Work teams are groups of workers who concentrate on identifying new and more efficient ways to get things done. Each team has between five and ten members. So far, work teams have helped Federal Express cut service errors by almost 15 percent. One team found a glitch in the firm's billing system that was costing the company more than $2 million a year.[1] ●

anagers at Federal Express recognized and took advantage of what many experts are increasingly seeing as a tremendous resource for all organizations—the power of groups. Rather than operate as individuals reporting to a supervisor, employees at Federal Express now function as members of a group. Group members schedule their own work hours, assign themselves to jobs, and rotate across jobs as a way to learn new skills.

This chapter is about processes that lead to and follow from activities like those at Federal Express. We begin by characterizing the interpersonal nature of organizations. We then introduce basic concepts of group dynamics. Subsequent sections explain the characteristics of mature groups and the use of teams in organizations. We conclude with a discussion of interpersonal and intergroup conflict.

THE INTERPERSONAL NATURE OF ORGANIZATIONS

In Chapter 1, we noted how much of a manager's job involves scheduled and unscheduled meetings, telephone calls, and related activities. Indeed, managers spend most of their time interacting with other people, both inside and outside the organization. The schedule that follows is a typical day for the president of a Houston-based company, part of a larger firm headquartered in California. He kept a log of his activities for several different days so you could better appreciate the nature of managerial work.

8:00–8:15 A.M. Arrive at work; review mail sorted by secretary.

8:15–8:30 A.M. Read *The Wall Street Journal*.

8:30–9:15 A.M. Meet with labor officials and plant manager to resolve minor labor disputes.

9:15–9:30 A.M. Review internal report and dictate correspondence for secretary to type.

9:30–10:00 A.M. Meet with two marketing executives to review advertising campaign.

10:00–noon Meet with company executive committee to discuss strategy, budgetary issues, and competition (this committee meets weekly).

12:00–1:15 P.M. Lunch with the financial vice president and two executives from another subsidiary of the parent corporation. Primary topic of discussion is the Houston Oilers football team.

1:15–2:00 P.M. Meet with human resources director and assistant about a recent OSHA inspection; establish a task force to investigate the problems identified and suggest solutions.

2:00–2:30 P.M. Conference call with four other company presidents.

2:30–3:00 P.M. Meet with financial vice president about a confidential issue that came up at lunch (unscheduled).

3:00–3:30 P.M. Work alone in office.

3:30–4:15 P.M. Meet with a group of sales representatives and the company purchasing agent.

4:15–5:30 P.M. Work alone in office.

5:30–7:00 P.M. Play racquetball at nearby athletic club with marketing vice president.

This manager spent most of his time working and interacting with other people. And this compressed daily schedule does not include several brief telephone calls, brief conversations with his secretary, and brief conversations with other managers. Clearly, interpersonal relations are a pervasive part of all organizations and a vital part of all managerial activities.[2]

Interpersonal Dynamics

The nature of interpersonal relations in an organization is as varied as the individual members themselves. At one extreme, interpersonal relations can be personal and positive. This occurs when the two parties know each other, have mutual respect and affection, and enjoy interacting with one another. Two managers who have known each other for years, play golf together on weekends, and are close personal friends will likely interact at work in a positive way. At the other extreme, interpersonal dynamics can be personal but negative. This is most likely when the parties dislike one another, do not have mutual respect, and do not enjoy interacting with one another. Suppose that a manager has fought openly for years to block another manager's promotion. The other manager, however, eventually gets promoted to the same rank. When the two of them must interact, it will most likely be in a negative manner.

Most interactions fall between these extremes, as members of the organization interact professionally and focus primarily on accomplishing goals. The interaction concerns the job at hand, is relatively formal and structured, and is task-directed. Two managers may respect each other's work and

Interpersonal relations in an organization take on a new dimension when the business partners are married to each other. Entrepreneurial couples, or "copreneurs," face unique challenges, as Norman and Eva Campbell, who together run an insulation firm, found out. The constant togetherness, for example, can be both an advantage and one of the greatest sources of conflict.

recognize each other's professional competence. However, they may also have few common interests and little to talk about besides the job they are doing. These different types of interaction may occur between individuals, between groups, or between individuals and groups, and they can change over time. The two managers in the second scenario, for example, might decide to bury the hatchet and adopt a detached, professional manner. The two managers in the third example might find that they have interests in common and evolve to a personal and positive interaction.

Outcomes of Interpersonal Behaviors

Interpersonal behaviors can cause a variety of things to happen. Recall from Chapter 14, for example, that numerous perspectives on motivation suggest that people have social needs. Interpersonal relations in organizations can be a primary source of need satisfaction for many people. People with a strong need for affiliation find that high-quality interpersonal relations are an important positive element in the workplace. When this same person is confronted with poor-quality working relationships, however, the effect can be just as great in the other direction.

Interpersonal relations also serve as a solid basis for social support. Suppose that an employee receives a poor performance evaluation or is denied a promotion. Others in the organization can lend support because they share a common frame of reference—an understanding of the causes and consequences of what happened.[3] Good interpersonal relations throughout an organization can also be a source of synergy. People who support one another and who work well together can accomplish much more than people who do not support one another and who do not work well together. At Federal Express, one factor cited for the success of the group-based method of organization was that everyone was committed to cooperation and to making the new approach work. Another outcome, implied earlier, is conflict—people may leave an interpersonal exchange feeling angry or hostile. Conflict is discussed later in the chapter. Still another outcome is the formation of groups, discussed next.

GROUPS IN ORGANIZATIONS

group
Two or more persons who interact regularly to accomplish a common purpose or goal

Groups are a ubiquitous part of organizational life and the basis for much of the work that gets done. They evolve both inside and outside the normal structural boundaries of the organization. We define a **group** as two or more persons who interact regularly to accomplish a common purpose or goal.[4] Note that the individuals must interact regularly to be considered a group. This interaction need not always follow the same pattern, but it must occur. The purpose of a group may range from preparing a new advertising campaign to informally sharing information to making important decisions to fulfilling social needs.[5] "The Global View" describes how one Japanese organization makes extensive use of groups to meet its goals.

Types of Groups

In general, organizations include functional groups, task groups, and informal or interest groups.[6] These are illustrated in Figure 16.1.

ODS—An Experiment in Group Processes

Life at Japan's ODS Corporation must sometimes seem as though it was created by a researcher in organizational behavior who wants to study group processes. ODS's employees spend as much as seven hours per week in meetings—team meetings about special projects, section meetings that discuss sales, managers' meetings that formulate strategies, weekly meetings in which all employees discuss company rules, and marathon meetings every April and October.

Nothing, it seems, is beyond the scope of these meetings. At the annual three-day salary meeting, when sessions can stretch far into the night, employees argue that they or their co-workers have been rated too low on the latest salary rankings. The company's 250 employees can debate the evaluations in all seven of the job and personality categories, and they can change the ratings. Employees also decide who to appoint to the company's board of directors and how to divide the company's profits.

And the company *is* profitable, despite the hundreds of employee-hours spent each week in meetings. ODS does research, advertising, and consulting for other companies, designing products and creating logos for giants like Sony Corp. Its success has won ODS respect in Japan, even though many of founder Takahiro Yamaguchi's ideas, especially about communication, violate the traditions of Japanese business and culture.

The Japanese people have long been known for their reliance on nonverbal communication; they are more apt to sense or feel what someone is thinking than to ask a direct question or provide a direct answer. To most Japanese, therefore, Yamaguchi's approach is decidedly Western and somewhat suspect. While Yamaguchi wouldn't deny that his communication style owes much to the non-Japanese, he insists that his goals are to make into a reality ideas that other Japanese companies merely preach. Japanese companies are world-famous for their participatory management and for instilling in workers the sense that what's good for the company is good for the worker. Yet Yamaguchi accuses Japanese corporate leaders of being isolated from their employees, many of whom are dissatisfied.

If workers are truly to identify their own happiness with the company's success, Yamaguchi says, management must be flexible and adaptable. He believes that the interpersonal harmony that Japanese workers are known for can be made real only if conflicts are aired, as they are at ODS. His employees say that Yamaguchi lives his own philosophies, giving his time and energy to his employees. And it's his philosophy, as much as his company's research and creativity skills, that brings customers to ODS.

References: Michael Berger, "Now the Japanese Bring Democracy to Salary Reviews," *International Management*, October 1986, pp. 58–60; Phyllis Birnbaum, "What Makes Salaryman Run?" *Across the Board*, June 1988, pp. 14–21; Yumiko Ono, "Sick of Meetings? Then ODS Is Not the Place for You," *The Wall Street Journal*, September 12, 1989, p. A-8.

Functional Groups A **functional group** is a group created by the organization to accomplish a number of on-going organizational purposes with an unspecified time horizon. The marketing department of K mart Corp., the management department of Memphis State University, and the nursing staff of the Mayo Clinic are functional groups. K mart's marketing department, for example, seeks to plan effective advertising campaigns, increase sales, run in-store promotions, and develop a unique identity for the company. The new work teams at Federal Express are also functional groups. The functional group remains in existence after it attains its current objectives.[7]

● **functional group**
A group created by the organization to accomplish a number of organizational purposes; its time horizon is indefinite

Task Groups A **task group** is a group created by the organization to accomplish a relatively narrow range of purposes. Most committees and

● **task group**
A group created by the organization to accomplish a relatively narrow range of purposes within a stated or implied time horizon

Within any given organization there are many different types of groups. In this hypothetical organization, a functional group is shown within the red boundary, a task group within the purple boundary, and an informal group within the orange boundary.

F I G U R E   16.1 Types of Groups in Organizations

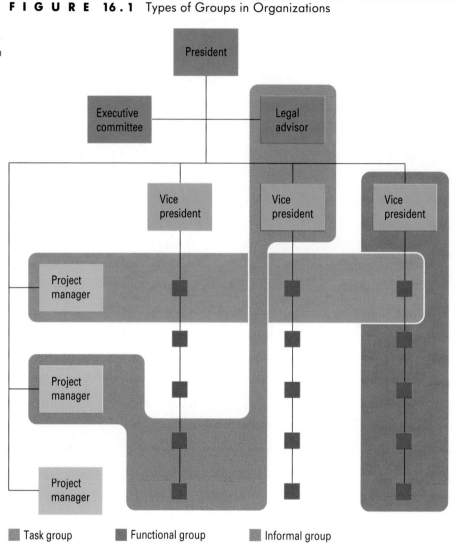

■ Task group   ■ Functional group   ■ Informal group

task forces are task groups. The organization specifies which group an employee is to work with and assigns a relatively narrow set of goals, such as developing a new product or evaluating a proposed grievance procedure. The time horizon for accomplishing these purposes is either specified (a committee may be asked to make a recommendation within sixty days) or implied (the project team will disband when the new product is developed). For example, Ford Motor Co. used a task force to design its Taurus automobile. When the design was completed, the task force was dissolved.

● **informal or interest group**
A group created by its members for purposes that may or may not be relevant to those of the organization; its time horizon is unspecified

Informal or Interest Groups An **informal or interest group** is created by its members for purposes that may or may not be relevant to organizational goals. It has an unspecified time horizon. A group of employees who lunch together every day may discuss how to improve productivity, how to embezzle money, or local politics and sports. As long as the group members enjoy eating together, they will probably continue to do so. When

An organization creates a task group to accomplish a narrow purpose, and Sony formed such a group to develop a personal computer as small as a pocket diary. The hand-held computer needed to be powerful enough to read, store, and manipulate handwritten Japanese characters. The task group was made up of a dozen engineers and had one year to develop the complete product design for the computer. Although the project took twice as long as scheduled, the PalmTop was introduced to the market in 1990.

lunches cease to be pleasant, they will seek other company or a different activity. Informal groups can be a powerful force that managers must not ignore. One writer described how a group of employees at a furniture factory subverted their boss's efforts to increase production. They tacitly agreed to produce a reasonable amount of work but not to work too hard. One man kept a stockpile of completed work hidden as a back-up in case he got too far behind. In another example, a group of automobile workers described how they left out gaskets and seals and put soft-drink bottles inside doors.[8] Of course, informal groups can also be a positive force, as demonstrated several years ago when Delta Air Line, Inc.'s employees worked together to buy a new plane for the company to show their support. We pay special attention to informal groups throughout this chapter.

Why People Join Groups

People join groups for a variety of reasons. They join functional groups simply by virtue of joining organizations. People accept employment to earn money or to practice their chosen profession. Once inside the organization, they are assigned to jobs and roles and thus become members of functional groups. People in existing functional groups are told, are asked, or volunteer to serve on committees, task forces, and teams. People join informal or interest groups for a variety of reasons, most of them quite complex.[9]

Interpersonal Attraction One reason that people form informal or interest groups is that they are attracted to each other. Many different factors contribute to interpersonal attraction.[10] When people see a lot of each other, pure proximity increases the likelihood that interpersonal attraction will develop. Attraction is increased when people have similar attitudes, personalities, or economic standings.

Group Activities   People may also be motivated to join a group because the activities of the group appeal to them. People enjoy activities such as jogging, playing bridge, bowling, discussing poetry, playing war games, and flying model airplanes. Many of these activities are more enjoyable to participate in as a member of a group, and most require more than one person. A person may join a bowling team not because of any noticeable attraction to other group members but simply because being a member of the group allows that person to bowl, an activity she enjoys. Of course, if the level of interpersonal attraction of the group is very low, a person may forgo the activity rather than join the group. Many large firms like Exxon Corporation and Apple Computer, Inc., have a league of football, softball, or bowling teams.

Group Goals   The goals of a group may also motivate people to join. The Sierra Club, which is dedicated to environmental conservation, is a good example of this kind of interest group. Various fund-raising groups are another illustration. Members may or may not be personally attracted to the other fund raisers, and they probably do not enjoy the activity of knocking on doors asking for money, but they join the group because they subscribe to its goal. Workers join unions like the United Auto Workers because they support its goals.

Need Satisfaction   People may join a group to satisfy their need for affiliation. New residents in a community may join the Newcomers Club partially as a way to meet new people and partially just to be around other people. Likewise, newly divorced people often join support groups for companionship.

Instrumental Benefits   People may also join groups because membership is sometimes seen as instrumental in providing other benefits. For example, it is fairly common for college students entering their senior year to join several professional clubs or associations because listing such memberships on a résumé is thought to enhance the chances of getting a good job. Similarly, a manager might join a certain racquet club not because she is attracted to its members (although she might be) and not because of the opportunity to play tennis (although she may enjoy it). The Club's goals are not relevant and her affiliation needs may be satisfied in other ways. She may feel that being a member of this club, however, will lead to important and useful business contacts. The racquet club membership is instrumental in establishing those contacts. Membership in civic groups such as Kiwanis and Rotary may be solicited for similar reasons.

Stages of Group Development

Imagine the differences between a collection of five persons who have just been brought together to form a group and another group that has functioned like a well-oiled machine for years. Members of a new group are unfamiliar with how they will function together and are tentative in their interactions. In a group with considerable experience, members are familiar with one another's strengths and weaknesses and are more secure in their role in the group. The new group is generally considered to be immature;

Mutual acceptance
Members get acquainted,
test interpersonal behaviors

*Slow
evolution to
next stage*

Communication and decision making
Members develop group structure
and patterns of interaction

*Burst of
activity to
next stage*

Motivation and productivity
Members share acceptance
of roles, sense of unity

*Slow
evolution to
next stage*

Control and organization
Members enact roles, direct
effort toward goal attainment
and performance

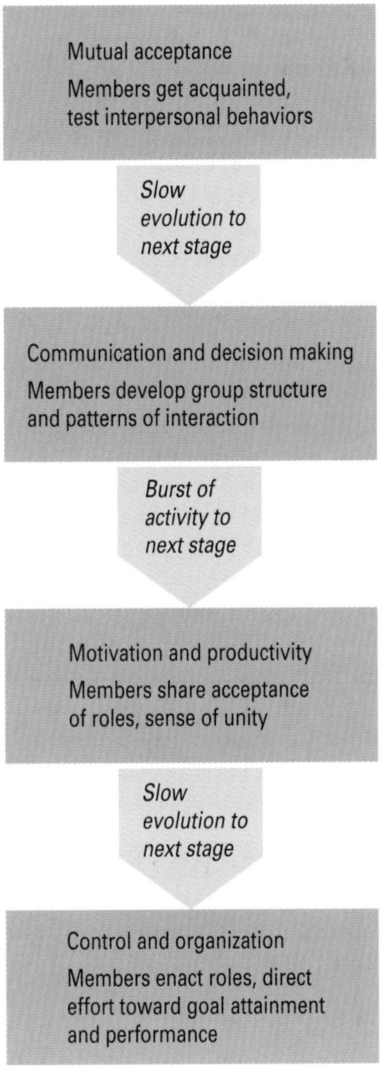

As groups mature, they tend to evolve through four distinct stages of development. Managers must understand that it may take group members time to become acquainted, accept each other, develop a group structure, and become comfortable with their roles in the group before they can begin to work directly to accomplish goals.

the older group, mature. To progress from the immature phase to the mature phase, a group must go through certain stages of development, as shown in Figure 16.2.[11]

In the first stage, *mutual acceptance,* group members get acquainted and begin to test which interpersonal behaviors are acceptable and which are unacceptable to the other members. Members are very dependent on others at this point to provide cues about what is acceptable. Group members establish basic ground rules, and a tentative group structure may emerge. At Reebok International Ltd., for example, a merchandising group was created to handle its new sportswear business. The group leader and his team members were barely acquainted and had to spend a few weeks getting to know one another.

The second stage of development, *communication and decision making,* is often slow to emerge. During this stage the group may lack unity and interaction patterns may be uneven. At the same time, some members of the group may begin to exert themselves and become recognized as the group leaders or at least to play a major role in shaping the group's agenda. In Reebok's group, some members advocated a rapid expansion into the marketplace; others argued for a slower entry. Each faction fought for control of the group so that its preferred strategy would be adopted.

The third stage of development, called *motivation and productivity,* usually begins with a burst of activity. During this stage each person begins to recognize and accept her or his role and to understand the roles of others. Members also begin to accept one another and to develop a sense of unity. The group may also temporarily regress to the previous stage. For example, the group might begin to accept one particular member as the leader. If this person later violates important norms and otherwise jeopardizes his or her claim to leadership, conflict might re-emerge as the group rejects this leader and searches for another. Reebok's group decided on a rapid expansion. Those group members who "lost" still recognized their roles and began to develop a sense of unity.

Control and organization, the final stage of group development, is slow to develop. The group really begins to focus on the problem at hand. The members enact the roles they have accepted, interaction occurs, and efforts are directed toward attaining the group's goals. The basic structure of the group is no longer an issue but has become a mechanism for accomplishing the purpose of the group. Reebok's decision was not the right one. Poor quality and late deliveries plagued the sportswear line from the beginning. Eventually a new group leader was appointed, the group started all over again, and has finally achieved target quality and delivery standards.[12]

CHARACTERISTICS OF MATURE GROUPS

As groups mature and pass through the stages of development, they begin to take on four characteristics—a role structure, norms, cohesiveness, and informal leadership.

Role Structures

● **role**
The part each person plays in helping the group reach its goals; includes task specialist and socioemotional roles

role structure
The set of defined roles and interrelationships among those roles that the group members define and accept

Each individual in a group has a part—or **role**—to play, in helping the group reach its goals. Some people, for example, are leaders, some do the work, and some interact with other groups. A person who takes on a *task-specialist role* concentrates on getting the group's task accomplished; a group member who takes on a *socioemotional role* provides social and emotional support to others in the group. A few people, usually the leaders, perform both roles; a few others may do neither. The group's **role structure** is the set of defined roles and interrelationships among those roles that the group members define and accept. Each of us belongs to many groups—work groups, classes, families, and social organizations—and therefore plays multiple roles.[13]

Role structures emerge as a result of role episodes, as shown in Figure 16.3. The process begins when group members expect an individual to adopt a certain role in the expected role. The expected role gets translated

FIGURE 16.3 The Development of a Role

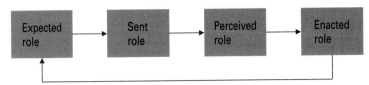

into the sent role—the messages and cues that group members use to communicate the expected role to the individual. The perceived role is what the individual perceives the sent role to mean. Finally, the enacted role is what the individual actually does in the role. The enacted role, in turn, influences future expectations the group has of the individual. In a new group, role episodes for all members unfold simultaneously. And role episodes seldom unfold this easily. When major disruptions occur, individuals may experience role ambiguity, conflict, or overload.

Role Ambiguity **Role ambiguity** arises when the sent role is unclear. Suppose a new department manager is told that he is responsible for promoting individual employees but should get involved in employee development. He will likely expand role ambiguity because these functions are closely related. Role ambiguity can stem from poor job descriptions, vague instructions from a supervisor, or unclear cues from co-workers. The result of role ambiguity is likely to be a subordinate who does not know what to do, which can be a major problem for both the individual experiencing it and the organization that expects the employee to perform.

role ambiguity
Arises when the sent role is unclear and the individual does not know what is expected

Role Conflict **Role conflict** occurs when the messages and cues of the sent role are clear but contradictory or mutually exclusive.[14] Research has shown that conflict may occur in a variety of situations and lead to a variety of adverse consequences, including stress, poor performance, and rapid turnover.[15] One common form is *interrole conflict*—conflict between roles. For example, if a person's boss says that to get ahead one must work overtime and on weekends, and the same person's spouse says that more time is needed at home with the family, interrole conflict may result.[16] In a matrix organization, interrole conflict often arises between the roles one plays in different task groups as well as between task group roles and one's permanent role in a functional group.

role conflict
Occurs when the messages and cues of the sent role are clear but contradictory or mutually exclusive

Conflicting demands from different sources within the context of the same role may cause *intrarole conflict*. A manager's boss may tell her that she needs to put more pressure on subordinates to follow new work rules. Her subordinates, however, may indicate that they expect her to get the rules changed. Thus the cues are in conflict, and the manager may be unsure about which course to follow. *Intrasender conflict* occurs when a single source sends clear but contradictory messages. This might arise if the boss says one morning that there can be no more overtime for the next month but after lunch tells someone to work late that same evening. *Person-role conflict* results from a discrepancy between the role requirements and the individual's personal values, attitudes, and needs. If a person is told to do something unethical or illegal, or if the work is distasteful (for example, firing a close friend), person–role conflict is likely. Role conflict of all varieties is of particular concern to managers.

Role Overload A final consequence of a weak role structure is **role overload,** which occurs when expectations for the role exceed the individual's capabilities. When a manager gives an employee several major assignments at once while increasing the person's regular workload, the employee will probably experience role overload. An individual who takes on too many roles at one time may also experience role overload. For example, a person trying to work extra hard at his job, run for election to the school board, serve on a committee in church, coach Little League baseball, maintain an active exercise program, and be a contributing member to his family will probably encounter role overload.

Implications In a functional or task group, the manager can take steps to avoid role ambiguity, conflict, and overload. Having clear and reasonable expectations and sending clear and straightforward cues go a long way toward eliminating role ambiguity. Consistent expectations that take into account the employee's other roles and personal value system may minimize role conflict. Role overload can be avoided simply by recognizing the individual's capabilities and limits. Communication between managers and subordinates can go a long way toward resolving role-related problems. In friendship and interest groups, role structures are likely to be less formal; hence the possibility of role ambiguity, conflict, or overload may not be so great. If one or more of these problems occurs, however, they may be difficult to handle. Because roles in friendship and interest groups are less likely to be partially defined by a formal authority structure or written job descriptions, the individual cannot turn to these sources to clarify a role.

Behavioral Norms

Norms are standards of behavior that the group accepts for its members. Most committees, for example, develop norms governing their discussions. A person who talks too much is perceived as doing so to make a good impression or to get his or her own way. Other members may not talk much to this person, may not sit nearby, may glare at the person, and may otherwise "punish" the individual for violating the norm. Norms, then, define the boundaries between acceptable and unacceptable behavior.[17] Some groups develop norms that limit behavior to "make life easier" for the group. In general, these norms are counterproductive: don't make more than two comments in a committee discussion, or don't produce any more than you have to. Other groups may develop norms that set minimum levels of participation. These norms are intended to encourage motivation, commitment, and high performance: don't come to meetings unless you've read the reports to be discussed, or produce as much as you can. Eastman Kodak Company has successfully used group norms to reduce injuries in some of its plants.[18]

Norm Generalization The norms of one group cannot always be generalized to another group. Some academic departments, for example, have a norm that suggests that male faculty members wear a coat and tie on teaching days. People who fail to observe this norm are "punished" by sarcastic

● role overload
Occurs when expectations for the role exceed the individual's capabilities to perform

● norms
Standards of behavior that the group accepts and expects of its members

remarks or even formal reprimands. In other departments the norm may be jeans and casual shirts, and the person unfortunate enough to wear a tie may be punished just as vehemently. Even within the same work area, similar groups can develop different norms. One work group may strive always to produce above its assigned quota; another may maintain productivity just below its quota. Being friendly and cordial to its supervisor may be one group's norm; that of another group may be to remain aloof and distant. Some differences are due primarily to the composition of the groups.

Norm Variation Norms can also vary within a group. A common norm is that the least senior member of a group is expected to perform unpleasant or trivial tasks for the rest of the group: wait on customers who are known to be small tippers (in a restaurant), deal with complaining customers (in a department store), or handle the low commission line of merchandise (in a sales department). Certain individuals, especially leaders, may violate some norms. If the group is going to meet at 8 o'clock, anyone arriving late will be chastised for holding things up. Occasionally, however, the leader may arrive a few minutes late. As long as this does not happen too often the group will probably not do anything.

Norm Conformity Several factors, one of which is factors associated with the group, contribute to norm conformity. For example, some groups may exert more pressure for conformity than others. The initial stimulus that prompts behavior can also affect conformity. The more ambiguous the stimulus (for example, news that the group is going to be transferred to a new unit), the more pressure there is to conform. Individual traits determine the individual's propensity to conform (for example, more intelligent people are often less susceptible to pressure to conform). Finally, situational factors such as group size and unanimity influence conformity.

As an individual learns the group's norms, he can do several different things. The most obvious is to adopt the norms. For example, the new male professor who notices that all the other men in the department dress up to teach can also start wearing a suit. A variation is to try to obey the "spirit" of the norm while retaining individuality. The professor may recognize that the norm is actually to wear a tie; thus he might succeed by wearing a tie with his sport shirt, jeans, and sneakers. If the individual ignores the norm, several things can happen. At first the group may increase its communication with the deviant individual to try to bring her back in line. If this does not work, communication may decline. Over time, the group may begin to exclude the individual from its activities and, in effect, ostracize the person.

Finally, we briefly consider another aspect of norm conformity—**socialization,** or the generalized norm conformity that occurs as a person makes the transition from being an outsider to being an insider. A newcomer to an organization, for example, gradually begins to learn the norms about such things as dress, working hours, and interpersonal relations. As the newcomer adopts these norms, she is being socialized into the organizational culture. Some organizations, like Texas Instruments Incorporated, work to actively manage the socialization process; others leave it to happenstance.[19]

socialization
Generalized norm conformity that occurs as a person makes the transition from being an outsider to being an insider of a group (such as an organization)

Cohesiveness

● **cohesiveness**
The extent to which members are loyal and committed to the group; the degree of mutual attractiveness within the group

Yet another important group characteristic is its cohesiveness. **Cohesiveness** is the extent to which members are loyal and committed to the group. Members of a highly cohesive group work well together, support and trust one another, and are generally effective at achieving their chosen goal. In contrast, a group that lacks cohesiveness is not very coordinated, and its members do not necessarily support one another fully; this group may have a difficult time reaching its goals. Of particular interest to managers are the factors that increase and reduce cohesiveness and the consequences of group cohesiveness. These are listed in Table 16.1.

Factors That Increase Cohesiveness   One of the strongest factors that can increase the level of cohesiveness in a group is intergroup competition. When two or more groups are in direct competition (for example, three sales groups competing for top sales honors or two football teams competing for a conference championship), each group is likely to become more cohesive. Additionally, just as personal attraction plays a role in causing a group to form, so too does attraction seem to enhance cohesiveness. Cohesiveness can also be increased by favorable evaluation of the entire group by outsiders. Thus a group's winning a sales contest or a conference title or receiving recognition and praise from a superior will tend to increase cohesiveness. Similarly, if all the members of the group agree on their goals, cohesiveness is likely to increase. And the more frequently members of the group interact with each other, the more likely the group is to become cohesive. A manager who wants to foster a high level of cohesiveness in a group might establish some form of intergroup competition, assign members to the group who are likely to be attracted to one another, provide opportunities for success, establish goals that all members are likely to accept, and allow ample opportunity for interaction.

Cohesiveness is the extent to which members are loyal and committed to the group, and the Minnesota Twins' reward for its cohesiveness was winning the 1991 World Series. Members of cohesive groups such as sports teams work well together, support and trust one another, and are generally effective at achieving their goal. One of the strongest factors that increases a group's cohesiveness is competition between groups—such as the hard fought seven-game series between the Twins and the Atlanta Braves.

TABLE 16.1	Factors That Influence Group Cohesiveness
Factors That Increase Cohesiveness	**Factors That Reduce Cohesiveness**
Intergroup competition	Group size
Personal attraction	Disagreement on goals
Favorable evaluation	Intragroup competition
Agreement on goals	Domination
Interaction	Unpleasant experiences

Several different factors can potentially influence the cohesiveness of a group. For example, a manager can establish intergroup competition, assign compatible members to the group, create opportunities for success, establish acceptable goals, and foster interaction in order to increase cohesiveness. Other factors can be used to decrease cohesiveness.

Factors That Reduce Cohesiveness Group cohesiveness tends to decline as a group increases in size as well as when members of a group disagree on what the goals of the group should be. For example, when some members believe that the group should maximize output and others think that output should be restricted, cohesiveness declines. Intragroup competition also reduces cohesiveness. When members are competing among themselves, they focus more on their own actions and behaviors than on those of the group. Additionally, domination by one or more persons in the group may cause overall cohesiveness to decline. Other members may feel that they are not being given an opportunity to interact and contribute, and they may become less attracted to the group as a consequence. Finally, unpleasant experiences that result from group membership may reduce cohesiveness. A sales group that comes in last in a sales contest, an athletic team that sustains a long losing streak, and a work group reprimanded for poor-quality work may all become less cohesive as a result of their unpleasant experience.

Consequences of Cohesiveness In general, as groups become more cohesive their members tend to interact more frequently, conform more to group norms, and become more satisfied with the group. (Note that cohesiveness and interaction frequently each affect the other—cohesiveness increases interactions, which in turn, further increase cohesiveness.) Cohesiveness may also influence group performance. Performance however, is also influenced by the group's performance norms. Figure 16.4 shows how cohesiveness and performance norms interact to help shape group performance.

When both cohesiveness and performance norms are high, performance should be high because the group wants to perform at a high level (norms) and its members are working together toward that end (cohesiveness). When norms are high and cohesiveness is low, performance will be moderate. Although the group wants to perform at a high level, its members are not necessarily working well together. When norms are low, performance will be low, regardless of whether group cohesiveness is high or low. The least desirable situation occurs when low performance norms are combined with high cohesiveness. In this case all group members embrace the standard

Group cohesiveness and performance norms interact to determine group performance. From the manager's perspective, high cohesiveness combined with high performance norms are the best situation, while high cohesiveness and low performance norms are the worst situation. Managers who can influence the level of cohesiveness and performance norms can greatly improve the effectiveness of a work group.

FIGURE 16.4 The Interaction Between Cohesiveness and Performance Norms

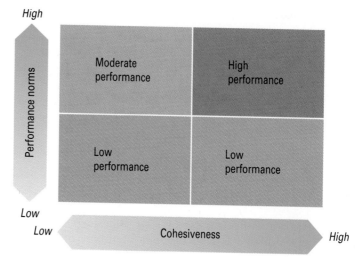

of restricting performance (owing to the low performance norm), and the group is united in its efforts to maintain that standard (owing to the high cohesiveness). If cohesiveness were low, the manager might be able to raise performance norms by establishing high goals and rewarding goal attainment or by bringing in new group members who were high performers. But a highly cohesive group is likely to resist these interventions.[20]

Informal Leadership

Most functional and task groups have a formal leader—that is, one appointed by the organization. Because friendship and interest groups are formed by the members themselves, however, any formal leader must be elected or designated by the members. Although some groups do designate such a leader (a softball team may elect a captain, for example), many do not. Moreover, even when a formal leader is designated, the group may also look to others for leadership. An **informal leader** is a person who engages in leadership activities but whose right to do so has not been formally recognized. The formal and the informal leader in any group may be the same person, or they may be different people. We noted earlier the distinction between the task-specialist and socioemotional roles within groups. An informal leader is likely to be a person capable of carrying out both roles effectively. If the formal leader can fulfill one role but not the other, an informal leader often emerges to supplement the formal leader's functions. If the formal leader cannot fill either role, one or more informal leaders may emerge to carry out both sets of functions.

Is informal leadership desirable? In many cases informal leaders are quite powerful because they draw from referent or expert power. When they are working in the best interest of the organization, they can be a tremendous asset. Notable athletes such as David Robinson, Joe Montana, and Nolan Ryan are classic examples of informal leaders. When informal leaders work counter to the goals of the organization, however, they can cause major

● **informal leader**
A person who engages in leadership activities but whose right to do so has not been formally recognized by the organization or group

difficulties. Such leaders may lower performance norms, instigate walkouts or wildcat strikes, or otherwise disrupt the organization.

USING TEAMS IN ORGANIZATIONS

Organizations are increasingly making use of work teams to get work done. We described Federal Express's experiences with teams in our opening incident. Other firms that are making extensive use of teams include Texas Instruments, General Mills, Inc., 3M, The Procter & Gamble Co., and Digital Equipment Corp.

Creating Work Teams

In an organization, a **team** is a group of workers that serves as a unit, often with little or no supervision, to carry out organizational functions. Earlier forms of teams included autonomous work groups and quality circles. Today, teams are sometimes called self-managed teams, cross-functional teams, or high-performance teams. Organizations create teams for a variety of reasons. They give more responsibility for task performance to the workers who are actually performing the tasks. They also empower workers by giving them greater authority and decision making freedom. In addition, they allow the organization to capitalize on the knowledge and motivation of its workers. Finally, teams enable the organization to shed its bureaucracy and promote flexibility and responsiveness. "Management in Practice" describes how one organization went about creating teams.

team
A group of workers that serves as a unit, often with little or no supervision, to carry out organizational functions

Managing Work Teams

Of course, teams are not appropriate for all situations. In general, they are most useful when the tasks to be performed are complex and involve high

Organizations form teams for a variety of reasons, including increasing worker responsibility and giving workers greater authority and decision-making freedom. Additionally, by forming a cross-functional team to examine quality improvement, AT&T was able to capitalize on the knowledge and motivation of team members (clockwise from lower right) Laura McPhee, Steve Holloman, Wayne Simpson, Frank Mezta, Bob Ringen, Cliff Slaby, and Jack Dreams.

levels of interdependence: the team itself serves as a mechanism for coping with complexity and for managing interdependencies.[21]

When an organization decides to use teams, it is essentially implementing a major form of organization change, as discussed in Chapter 12. Thus management must follow a logical and systematic approach to planning and implementing teams into an existing organization design. Management must also recognize that resistance may be encountered, most likely from first-line managers who will be giving up much of their authority to the team. Many organizations find that they must change the whole philosophy of such managers away from being a supervisor to being a coach or facilitator.[22]

After teams are in place, managers should continue to monitor their contributions and how effectively they are functioning. In the best circumstance, teams will become very cohesive groups with high performance norms. To achieve this state, the manager can use any or all of the techniques described earlier for enhancing cohesiveness. If implemented properly, and with the support of the workers themselves, performance norms will likely be relatively high. That is, if the change is properly implemented, the team participants will understand the value and potential of teams and the rewards they may get as a result of their contributions.

INTERPERSONAL AND INTERGROUP CONFLICT

Throughout this chapter, we have addressed a variety of interpersonal relationships that occur in organizations. Another important type of relationship is **conflict**, or a disagreement between two or more persons or groups. Organizational conflict results from disagreement between individual employees, work groups, or departments. The management of conflict is of considerable importance to all organizations. Union Carbide Corp., for example, once sent 200 of its managers to a three-day workshop on conflict management. The managers engaged in a variety of exercises and discussions to learn whom they were most likely to have conflict with and how they should try to resolve it.[23]

Most people associate antagonism, hostility, unpleasantness, and dissension with conflict. Indeed, most people, including managers and management theorists, have traditionally viewed conflict as a problem to be avoided.[24] In recent years, however, we have come to recognize that although conflict can be a major problem, certain kinds of conflict may be beneficial. The general relationship between conflict and performance is suggested in Figure 16.5. Complacency and stagnation may set in when conflict is absent, and performance may suffer. A moderate level of conflict can spark motivation, creativity, innovation, and initiative. Too much conflict can produce undesirable results such as hostility and lack of cooperation. Managers must find and maintain the optimal level of conflict that fosters the highest level of performance. Thus managers need to be concerned with the management of conflict within their organizations. The starting point for management is understanding the causes of conflict.

TEAMING UP TO SAVE A PRODUCT

The United States used to lead the world in the making of machine tools, and Cincinnati Milacron used to lead the United States, especially in plastics-molding machinery. But Japanese competition and Milacron's response to it—giving up on some of the low end of the product line—soon threatened Milacron's market share and reputation. The company fought back with a new machine called Vista and a new way of developing its products—teamwork.

Sales of plastics-molding machinery have been growing well. (If you're trying to imagine what such machinery does, think of manufacturing one of Milacron's most famous products, the 2-liter plastic soft drink bottle.) But in the mid-1980s, as U.S. companies were being driven out of the market, two Milacron executives got together and figured out what characteristics a new machine would need to compete with Japanese products. They decided that a new machine would have to be 40 percent less expensive than its predecessors, 40 percent faster and more effective, and developed in a year, one-half the normal development period.

Milacron put together a team of ten, with people from purchasing, marketing, inventory, manufacturing, and engineering. They moved their offices close together and reported directly to the vice president. They kept logs of their work so future teams could learn from their successes and failures. They agreed not to talk about their project with outsiders, to ease members' worries about being ridiculed for suggesting ideas outside their expertise. They met as a group only once a week and avoided making decisions during that meeting. They wanted decisions made quickly, whenever problems arose.

The group began by interviewing prospective customers and looking at competing machines. Group members made common-sense decisions that might have been rejected if they had been working through normal departmental channels. For instance, they decided to work with the metric rather than the English system of measurement, and they strove to use readily available, U.S.-made parts and to cut down the number of parts as much as possible. Instead of searching for inexpensive parts, they looked for sensible, inexpensive ways to put those parts together.

The result? Vista outsold its predecessor by 2.5 times in its first year of production. It uses 50 percent fewer parts and costs 40 percent less. And those team log books left Milacron with a legacy that the company is not likely to ignore.

References: "Cincinnati Milacron Benchmarks Flexible Manufacturing Systems Via Computer Modeling," *Industrial Engineering,* March 1991, pp. 24–83; Peter Nulty, "The Soul of An Old Machine," *Fortune,* May 21, 1990, pp. 67–72; John Teresko, "Two Builders Look For A New Image," *Industry Week,* January 21, 1991, p. 42.

Causes of Conflict

Some of the causes of conflict in organizations are the result of organizational design; others pertain to the individual or the group.

Interdependence   In Chapter 10, we described three forms of group interdependence: pooled, sequential, and reciprocal. Just as increased interdependence increases coordination problems, it also increases the potential for conflict. For example, recall that in sequential interdependence work is passed from one unit to another. Conflict may arise if the first group is turning out too much work (the second group will get behind), too little work (the second group cannot meet its goals), or work of poor quality. At a Penney's department store, conflict arose because stockroom employ-

Either too much or too little conflict can be dysfunctional for an organization. In either case performance may be low. However, an optimal level of conflict that sparks motivation, creativity, innovation, and initiative can result in higher levels of performance. T. J. Rodgers, CEO of Cypress Semiconductor, maintains a moderate level of conflict in his organization as a way of keeping people energized and motivated.

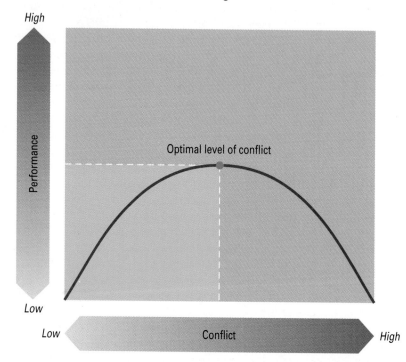

F I G U R E 16.5 The Nature of Organizational Conflict

ees were slow in delivering merchandise to the sales floor so that it could be priced and shelved.

Differences in Goals Different departments have different goals, and these goals may be incompatible. A marketing goal of maximizing sales, achieved partially by offering a wide variety of sizes, shapes, colors, and models, may conflict with a production goal of minimizing costs, achieved partially by long production runs of a limited number of items. We noted earlier the problems at Reebok when some people wanted to introduce the new sportswear line as quickly as possible, while others wanted to be more deliberate.

Resource Competition Most organizations—especially universities, hospitals, government agencies, and businesses in depressed industries—have limited resources, and conflict may therefore arise from competition for them. In one New England town, the public works department and the library recently battled over funds from a federal construction grant.

Interpersonal Dynamics Conflict may arise from interpersonal dynamics. The most general situation is the so-called personality clash—when two people distrust each other's motives, dislike one another, or for some other reason simply can't get along. New management trainees may resent having to learn routine administrative duties, whereas senior managers may believe that it is necessary for them to learn the business from the ground up. Some people are extremely competitive, so conflict may arise when two managers are vying for a promotion. There is an ongoing high level of conflict between H. Ross Perot and his old friends at Electronic Data Systems Inc. After Perot sold EDS to General Motors Corp., he eventually resigned and started a new company to compete with his old firm. When he left EDS, he signed a contract agreeing not to compete for a specified time and in specified areas. Perot contends that his new company lives up to that agreement; EDS maintains otherwise. The result has been name calling, insults, lawsuits, and countersuits—with the end nowhere in sight. Strong personalities have played a major role in these battles.[25]

Managing Conflict

To best cope with conflict, a manager can stimulate it in constructive ways, avoid it before it arises, and resolve it if it does happen.[26]

Encouraging Conflict Conflict can often be stimulated by placing employees or groups in competitive situations. Recall, for example, the number of "disagreements" you have observed between two football, baseball, basketball, or hockey teams. Managers can establish sales contests, bonuses, or other competitive stimuli to spark competition. Another useful method for stimulating conflict is to bring in outsiders. Outsiders can shake things up and stimulate a certain level of conflict. The Beecham Group, a British company, hired an American as its CEO expressly to change how the company did business.[27] Finally, a manager can stimulate conflict by changing established procedures. For example, a university president announced that all vacant staff positions could be filled only after written justification had received his approval. Conflict resulted because this reduced the authority of department heads. Most requests were okayed, but department heads had to think through their staffing needs and a few unnecessary positions were eliminated.

Reducing Conflict When a manager wants to reduce or avoid conflict, he or she has several alternatives. One is to expand the resource base. Suppose that a top manager receives two budget requests for $100,000 each. If she has only $180,000 to distribute, the stage is set for conflict. If both proposals are worthwhile, it may be possible for the manager to come up with the extra $20,000 from some other source and thereby avoid difficulty. Pooled, sequential, and reciprocal interdependencies (as discussed in Chapter 10) can all result in conflict, so the manager should use an appropriate technique for enhancing coordination and reducing the probability that conflict will arise. Techniques for coordination (described in Chapter 10) include making use of the managerial hierarchy; relying on rules and procedures; and enlisting liaison persons, task forces, and integrating departments. At the Penney store mentioned earlier, the conflict was addressed by providing salespeople with clearer forms on which to specify what merchandise they needed and in what sequence. Differences in goals can also be a potential source of conflict. Managers can sometimes focus the employees' attention on higher-level, or supraordinate, goals as a way of eliminating lower-level conflict. When labor unions such as the United Auto Workers recognize that they must make wage concessions to ensure survival of the industry, industry survival is considered a supraordinate goal. The immediate goal may be higher wages for union members, but the members realize that

Every organization experiences conflict, and uncertain economic conditions give rise to more than usual, as Apple Computer discovered. Its decision to eliminate 1,500 jobs fueled worker protests, led by Apple engineer and activist Rick Eames and the 500-member protest group Employees for One Apple. What will it take to resolve this conflict? Eames believes that getting management to consult employees before deciding issues that affect them will be a step in the right direction.

without the automobile industry they would not even have jobs. Another way to avoid conflict is through the management of interpersonal dynamics. A manager who has two valuable subordinates, one a chain smoker and the other a vehement antismoker, should avoid requiring them to work together in a confined space.

Resolving Conflict Despite everyone's best intentions, conflict is still inevitable in any organization. If it is harmful, attempts must be made to resolve it. Compromise can work if it is used with care, but even in most compromise situations someone wins and someone loses. Budget problems may be amenable to compromise because of their objective nature. Assume, for example, that additional resources are not available, the manager has only $180,000 to divide, and each of two groups claims to need $100,000. If the manager believes that both projects warrant funding, she can allocate $90,000 to each, and the two groups' having at least been treated equally may still the conflict. The confrontation approach to conflict resolution—also called interpersonal problem solving—involves bringing the parties together to confront the conflict. The parties discuss the nature of their conflict and attempt to reach an agreement or a solution. Confrontation requires a reasonable degree of maturity on the part of the participants, and the manager must structure the situation carefully. If handled well, this approach can be an effective means of resolving conflict. Some techniques for avoiding conflict may be used to resolve conflict. If conflict arises from incompatible personalities, the manager might transfer one or both parties to other units. If conflict stems from group interdependence, the manager might realize that he is using an inappropriate coordination technique and shift to another.

SUMMARY OF KEY POINTS

Interpersonal dynamics occur throughout an organization. They may be positive and personal, detached and professional, or negative and personal. Several outcomes result from interactions with other people, including need satisfaction, social support, synergy, conflict, and group formation.

A group is two or more persons who interact regularly to accomplish a common purpose or goal. General kinds of groups in organizations are functional groups, task groups, and informal or interest groups. People join functional or task groups to pursue a career. Their reasons for joining informal or interest groups include interpersonal attraction, group activities, group goals, need satisfaction, and potential instrumental benefits. The stages of group development include mutual acceptance, communication and decision making, motivation and productivity, and control and organization.

Four important characteristics of mature groups are role structures, group norms, group cohesiveness, and informal leadership. Role structures define task and socioemotional specialists and may be victimized by role ambiguity, role conflict, or role overload. Group norms are standards of behavior for group members. Group cohesiveness is the extent to which members are loyal and committed to the group and to one another. Several factors can increase or reduce group cohesiveness. The relationship between performance norms and cohesiveness is especially important. Informal leaders are those leaders whom the group members themselves choose to follow.

More and more organizations are using teams. A team is a group of workers that functions as a unit, often with little or no supervision, to carry out organizational functions. Implementing teams is a form of organization change. Ideally, teams will be cohesive and have high performance norms.

Conflict can be either a constructive or a destructive force in organizations. Conflict can arise from several different circumstances. Managers can stimulate constructive forms of conflict in certain situations. It is also possible to avoid or resolve conflict through the use of several techniques.

DISCUSSION QUESTIONS

Questions for Review

1. What is a group? Describe the several different types of groups and indicate the similarities and differences between them.

2. Why do people join groups? Do all groups develop through all of the stages discussed in this chapter? Why or why not?

3. Describe the characteristics of mature groups. How might the management of a mature group differ from the management of groups that are not yet mature?

4. Describe the nature and causes of conflict in organizations. Is conflict always bad? Why or why not?

Questions for Analysis

5. Is it possible for a group to be more than one type at the same time? If so, under what circumstances? If not, why not?

6. Think of several groups of which you have been a member. Why did you join each? Did each group progress through the stages of development discussed in this chapter? If not, why not?

7. Do you think teams are a valuable new management technique that will endure, or are they just a fad that will be replaced with something else in the near future?

Questions for Application

8. See if you can locate local organizations that regularly use groups in their operations. What kinds of groups are being used? How are they being used? Is that use effective? Why or why not?

9. Try to find out if a local business is using teams. If so, talk to a manager or team participant at the company and learn about their experiences.

10. Would a manager ever want to stimulate conflict in his or her organization? Why or why not? Interview several managers of local business organizations to obtain their views on the use of conflict and compare them to your answer to this question.

CHRYSLER LEARNS FROM ITS VIPER TEAM

*I*n many ways, the Dodge Viper is a throwback to the muscle cars of yesteryear. Its chief selling points are its graceful racing-car lines and its mammoth 400-horsepower engine. Although demand for the cars was high even before they became available, Chrysler is planning to make only 3,000 each year. Even with a $50,000 price tag, the Viper is not going to make a major contribution to Chrysler's bottom line. The way Chrysler created the Viper, however, represented a big breakthrough for the company and gave some indication of the way U.S. car making will evolve in the 1990s. The key factor was teamwork.

Chrysler unveiled a prototype of the Viper during the January 1989 international auto show. It was a big hit. They set a goal of getting Vipers on the street in three years, two years less than the normal time frame.

To meet such a deadline, Chrysler realized it would have to use simultaneous engineering techniques. That meant putting the development of the car in the hands of a team of marketing, engineering, and manufacturing specialists; suppliers who would make the Viper's parts; and six workers who actually built the prototypes. The team included only eighty-five members, hundreds fewer than are responsible for most new cars.

The makeup of the team meant that the Viper didn't have to go through costly and time-consuming re-engineering once the marketing and manufacturing people got their hands on the design. Just as important was the inclusion of suppliers. About 90 percent of the Viper's parts come from suppliers, compared to about 70 percent for the average Chrysler. Using their own expertise rather than following a designer's specifications, suppliers came up with innovative products, like a "press bent" windshield that eliminates the distortion usually associated with radically curved glass. Chrysler likes that particular innovation so much it is using it on other car lines.

On the factory floor, the Viper is handled by the same kind of teamwork. It is hand built by craftspeople who all share the same general job classification and can trade off functions when necessary. Altogether, Chrysler says that developing the Viper cost about one-tenth as much as redesigning a standard car model.

A high-priced, impractical car, the Viper is never going to do for Chrysler what its minivans did. But it is drawing people to the showroom. And it has improved Chrysler's morale by demonstrating that U.S. car makers can develop a new model as quickly and as cheaply as the Japanese.

Discussion Questions

1. What drawbacks are there to the kind of teams that developed the Viper? Why haven't automakers always used them?

2. Under what conditions can a supplier become part of a manufacturer's team?

E 3. In addition to facing tough orders from top management for a shorter schedule than usual, Team Viper had fewer people than the average Chrysler new-car team, with more people performing a wider variety of tasks. Such conditions could have opened the door to risky shortcuts, and no doubt caused the team members considerable stress. On the other hand, being part of a highly visible experimental project can be very motivating. Are such demands too great to be placed on workers, or can the Viper project be considered a success in new car development methods?

References: James R. Healey, "Deliberately Crude Model Roars Appeal," *USA Today*, November 12, 1991, pp. 1B, 2B; James R. Healey, "Team Concept Cuts Time," *USA Today*, November 12, 1991, p. 2B; David Woodruff, "The Racy Viper Is Already a Winner for Chrysler," *Business Week*, November 4, 1991, pp. 36–38.

FORD AND MAZDA TEAM UP

*D*espite the apparent rancor between Japanese and U.S. car makers, Ford Motor Co. and Mazda Motor Corporation have been working together so effectively that their alliance is providing a blueprint for similar joint ventures.

The alliance began in 1979, when Ford acquired a 25-percent share of Mazda. Since then, they have worked together on a number of products: Ford often provides marketing and finance expertise and Mazda contributes its manufacturing and product-development skills. The relationship has made Ford the best-selling foreign car brand in Japan.

Of course, any such alliance must face a number of obstacles, both competitive and cultural. Even when they agree to share, they often have difficulties simply communicating. Ford executives get impatient with the Japanese style of giving extended explanations and Mazda's Japanese team working in the Louisville plant on the Explorer/Navajo project had some uneasy moments when the doors and windows closed and the lights went off—until someone explained the U.S. tradition of April Fool's Day.

The alliance's greatest success so far has been the redesigned Ford Escort, known as the CT20, which went on sale in mid-1990. Ford had originally planned for the 1991 Escort to be a "global car," with one design that could be manufactured in a number of different places. In 1983, it enlisted Mazda's help in designing a somewhat less ambitious car to be sold in North America and Asia.

Ford quickly put together a team that knew Mazda's methods. The team's leader, Toshiaki Saito, a Japanese who had come to Ford fresh from design school, soon had Ford's approval for the CT20's styling, and he moved his team to Hiroshima to work with Japanese engineers.

Over the next few months, the team negotiated constantly about everything from the size of the license-plate recess to the design of roof rails. When it looked as though the design would go way over budget, the team decided to find ways to use even more U.S.-made parts, which would ultimately cut costs. Mazda persuaded Ford to use Mazda's approach with suppliers, reducing their number as much as possible and enlisting their aid in building the prototypes on regular assembly lines with the actual parts, rather than having a specialty shop build them.

But this and other problems were ironed out, and the careful planning and months of negotiation paid off. The CT20 underwent 60-percent fewer last-minute design changes than the average Ford and came in on time, on budget, and working better than expected. Score one for teamwork.

Discussion Questions

1. How would you choose and train a team of U.S. Ford workers who were going to Japan to work with Mazda?

2. What kinds of cultural problems did the Ford-Mazda team have to overcome?

E **3.** Even while Ford was hailing the success of the jointly developed Escort, it was joining other U.S. car makers in blasting Japanese automakers, including Mazda, for "dumping" minivans in the United States at artificially low prices. Do you think it's ethical of Ford to work with a company it accuses of illegal trade practices? Or do you think that the Ford-Mazda alliance is an issue separate from Mazda's dumping practices with its Japanese-made cars?

References: James B. Treece, "How Ford and Mazda Shared the Driver's Seat," *Business Week*, March 26, 1990, pp. 94–95; James B. Treece and Karen Lowry Miller, "The Partners," *Business Week*, February 10, 1992, pp. 102–107.

Managing Communication in Organizations

OBJECTIVES

After studying this chapter, you should be able to:

● *Describe the role and importance of communication in the manager's job.*

● *Identify the basic forms of interpersonal communication and cite advantages and disadvantages of each.*

● *Identify general forms of group and organizational communication and cite characteristics of each.*

● *Discuss behavioral elements of communication.*

● *Describe how the communication process can be improved.*

● *Discuss how organizational communication can be managed.*

OUTLINE

Communication and the Manager's Job
   A Definition of Communication
   The Role of Communication in
     Management
   The Communication Process

Forms of Interpersonal
Communication
   Oral Communication
   Written Communication
   Choosing the Right Form

Forms of Group and Organizational
Communication
   Vertical Communication
   Horizontal Communication
   Communication Networks
   The Grapevine
   Other Forms of Communication

Behavioral Elements of
Communication
   Perception
   Nonverbal Communication

Improving Communication
Effectiveness
   Barriers to Communication
   Overcoming Barriers to Communication

Managing Organizational
Communication
   Formal Information Systems
   Electronic Communication

CAN A FUNDAMENTAL concern for communication translate into revenues of $50 million? Brook Furniture Rental's CEO Bob Crawford thinks it has. Brook is a fast-growing residential and business furniture leasing firm whose profit margins exceed those of any other firm in the industry.

Crawford believes that his focus on communication is critical to his firm's success. In particular, Crawford works hard to create a culture where employees can speak freely, question decisions made by others, and offer suggestions and criticism. He thinks that employees are the best source of new ideas in any organization and wants to make sure that those ideas are brought to light.

Crawford also puts a premium on listening skills. He argues that the ability to listen is one of a manager's most critical skills. To drive home this point, he regularly sponsors workshops for all of his staff to help them develop their own listening skills. The workshops are intended to help managers learn to better listen to both their employees and to customers.

Crawford also does a number of other things to keep lines of communication open. For example, he often conducts training programs for new employees himself. This allows him to present the company "story" personally and to answer important questions. For another, he frequently accompanies sales representatives on their calls with Brook's customers. Crawford argues, again, that this promotes effective communication between the company and its customers.[1] ●

anagers around the world agree that most of their job is spent communicating. Managers must communicate with others to convey their vision and goals for the organization. And it is essential for others to communicate with them so that they will better understand what's going on in their environment and how they and their organizations can become more effective.

This chapter explores communication from the perspectives of both managers and organizations. We begin by examining communication in the context of the manager's job. We then identify and discuss forms of interpersonal, group, and organizational communication. After discussing behavioral elements of communication, we describe how organizational communication can be effectively managed.

COMMUNICATION AND THE MANAGER'S JOB

A manager's typical day includes doing desk work, attending scheduled meetings, placing and receiving telephone calls, reading correspondence, answering correspondence, attending unscheduled meetings, and walking around the company.[2] Most of these activities involve communication. In fact, managers usually spend more than one-half of their time on some form of communication. Communication always involves two or more persons, so behavioral processes such as motivation, leadership, and group dynamics all come into play.

A Definition of Communication

Imagine three managers working in an office building. The first is all alone but is nevertheless yelling for a subordinate to come help. No one appears, but he continues to yell. The second is talking on the telephone to a subordinate, but static on the line causes the subordinate to misunderstand some important numbers being provided by the manager. As a result, the subordinate sends 1,500 crates of eggs to 150 Fifth Street, when he should have sent 150 crates to 1500 Fifteenth Street. The third manager is talking in her office with a subordinate who clearly hears and understands what is being said. Each of these managers is attempting to communicate but with different results.

communication

The process of transmitting information from one person to another

Communication is the process of transmitting information from one person to another.[3] Did any of our three managers communicate? The last did and the first did not. How about the second? In fact, she did communicate: she transmitted information, and information was received. The problem was that the message transmitted and the message received were not the same. The words spoken by the manager were distorted by static and noise. **Effective communication,** then, is the process of sending a message in such a way that the message received is as close in meaning as possible to the message intended. Although the second manager engaged in communication, it was not effective.

effective communication

The process of sending a message in such a way that the message received is as close in meaning as possible to the message intended

Our definition of effective communication is based on the ideas of meaning and consistency of meaning. Meaning is the idea that the person who initiates the communication exchange wishes to convey. In effective communication, the meaning is transmitted in such a way that the receiving person understands it. For example, consider these messages:

1. The high today will be only 40 degrees.
2. It will be cold today.
3. Ceteris paribus.
4. Xn1gp bo5cz4ik ab19.

You probably understand the first statement. The second statement may seem clear at first, but it is somewhat less clear than the first statement because cold is a relative condition and the word can mean different things to different people. Fewer still understand the third statement because it is written in Latin. None of you understands the last statement because it is written in a secret code that your author developed as a child.

The Role of Communication in Management

We noted earlier the variety of activities that fill a manager's day. Meetings, telephone calls, and correspondence are all a necessary part of every manager's job—and all clearly involve communication. On a typical Monday, Nolan Archibald, CEO of Black & Decker Corp., attended five scheduled meetings and two unscheduled meetings; had fifteen telephone conversations; received twenty-nine letters, memos, and reports; and dictated ten letters.[4] The opening incident also underscores the role of communication in management.

To better understand the linkages between communication and management, recall the variety of roles that managers must fill. Each of the ten basic managerial roles discussed in Chapter 1 (see Table 1.2) would be impossible to fill without communication.[5] Interpersonal roles involve interacting with supervisors, subordinates, peers, and others outside the organization. Decisional roles require managers to seek out information to use in making decisions and then communicate those decisions to others. Informational roles focus specifically on acquiring and disseminating information.

Communication also relates directly to the basic management functions of planning, organizing, leading, and controlling. Environmental scanning, integrating planning-time horizons, and decision making, for example, all necessitate communication. Delegation, coordination, and organization change and development also involve communication. Developing reward systems and interacting with subordinates as a part of the leading function would be impossible without some form of communication. And communication is essential to establishing standards, monitoring performance, and taking corrective actions as a part of control. Clearly, then, communication is a pervasive part of virtually all managerial activities.

The Communication Process

Figure 17.1 illustrates how communication generally takes place between people. The process of communication begins when one person (the sender) wants to transmit a fact, idea, opinion, or other information to someone

Effective communication is essential to the success of any group. In a meeting of Humana's service enhancement team, this speaker is transmitting her message both orally and in writing to reinforce her message. This team, made up of fourteen managers, concluded that the quality of customer service is essential to competitive advantage. Humana must now effectively communicate this finding not only to its employees but also to the public.

else (the receiver). This fact, idea, or opinion has meaning to the sender, whether it be simple and concrete or complex and abstract. For example, Linda Porter, a marketing representative at Xerox Corp., recently landed a new account and wanted to tell her boss about it. This fact represented meaning.

The next step is to encode the meaning into a form appropriate to the situation such as words, facial expressions, gestures, or even artistic expressions and physical actions. For example, Porter might have said, "I just landed the Acme account," "We just got some good news from Acme," or "I just spoiled Canon's day." She might have given her boss the "thumbs-up" sign, or a number of other things. She actually chose the second message. Clearly, the encoding process is influenced by situational factors such as the content of the message and the familiarity of sender and receiver.

After the message has been encoded, it is transmitted through the appropriate channel or medium. The channel by which this encoded message is being transmitted to you is the printed page. Common channels in organizations include meetings, memos, letters, reports, and telephone calls. Linda Porter might have written her boss a note, called him on the telephone, or dropped by his office to convey the news. Because both she and her boss were out of the office when she got the news, she called and left a message for him.

After the message is received, it is decoded back into a form that has meaning for the receiver. As noted earlier, the consistency of this meaning can vary dramatically. On hearing about the Acme deal, the sales manager at Xerox might have thought, "This'll mean a big promotion for both of us," "This is great news for the company," or "She's blowing her own horn too much again." His actual feelings were closest to the second statement. Often the meaning prompts a response, and the cycle is continued when a new message is sent by the same steps back to the original sender. The manager might have called the sales representative to offer congratula-

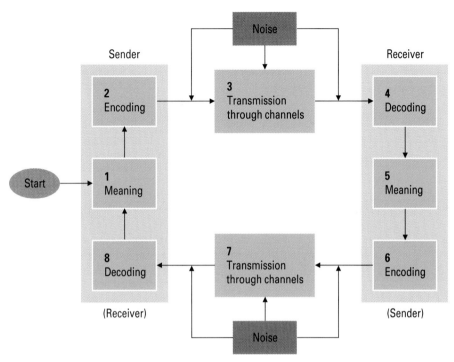

The numbers indicate the sequence in which steps take place.

As the figure shows, noise can disrupt the communication process at any step. Managers must therefore understand that a conversation in the next office, a fax machine out of paper, and the receiver's worries may all thwart the manager's best attempts to communicate.

tions, written her a personal note of praise, or sent a formal letter of acknowledgment. Porter's boss wrote her a personal note.

"Noise" may disrupt communication anywhere along the way. Noise can be the sound of someone coughing, a truck driving by, or two people talking nearby. It can also include disruptions such as a letter being lost in the mail, a telephone line going dead, or one of the participants in a conversation being called away before the communication process is completed. If the note written by Porter's boss had gotten lost, she might have felt unappreciated. As it was, his actions positively reinforced not only her efforts at Acme but also her effort to keep him informed.

FORMS OF INTERPERSONAL COMMUNICATION

Managers need to understand several kinds of communication. Oral and written communication are primarily interpersonal; thus we discuss them together here. Other forms of organizational communication are covered in the next section.

Oral Communication

Oral communication takes place in face-to-face conversation, group discussions, telephone calls, and other circumstances in which the spoken word

● **oral communication**
Face-to-face conversation, group discussions, telephone calls, and other circumstances in which the spoken word is used to transmit meaning

The two basic forms of interpersonal communication are oral and written communication. Each has its own unique advantages and disadvantages. Managers should consider using oral communication, for example, when their message is personal, nonroutine, and brief. But they might consider written communication when the message is impersonal, routine, and long.

TABLE 17.1 Interpersonal Communication

Form	Advantages	Disadvantages
Oral	1. Promotes feedback and interchange 2. Is easy to use	1. May suffer from inaccuracies 2. Leaves no permanent record
Written	1. Tends to be more accurate 2. Provides a record of the communication	1. Inhibits feedback and interchange 2. Is more difficult and time consuming

is used to express meaning. Henry Mintzberg demonstrated the importance of oral communication when he found that most managers spend between 50 and 90 percent of their time talking to people.[6] Oral communication is so prevalent for several reasons. As summarized in Table 17.1, the primary advantage of oral communication is that it promotes prompt feedback and interchange in the form of verbal questions or agreement, facial expressions, and gestures. Oral communication is also easy (all the sender needs to do is talk), and it can be done with little preparation (though careful preparation is advisable in certain situations). The sender does not need pencil and paper, computer, or other equipment. In one survey, 55 pecent of the executives sampled felt that their own written communication skills were fair or poor, so they chose oral communication to avoid embarrassment![7]

Oral communication also has drawbacks. It may be inaccurate if the speaker chooses the wrong words to convey meaning or leaves out pertinent details, if noise disrupts the process, or if the receiver forgets part or all of the message. In a two-way discussion, there is seldom time for a thoughtful, considered response or for introducing many new facts, and there is no permanent record of what has been said. In addition, although most managers are comfortable talking to people individually or in small groups, few enjoy speaking to large audiences.[8]

Written Communication

● **written communication**
Memos, letters, reports, notes, and other circumstances in which the written word is used to transmit meaning

Although to "put it in writing" can overcome many of oral communication's problems, **written communication** is not as common as one might imagine, nor is it a mode of communication much respected by managers. One sample of managers indicated that only 13 percent of the mail they received was of immediate use to them.[9] More than 80 percent of the managers who responded to another survey indicated that the written communication they received was of fair or poor quality.[10]

The biggest single drawback of written communication is that it inhibits feedback and interchange (see Table 17.1). When one manager sends another manager a letter, it must be written or dictated, typed, mailed or routed, received, opened, and read. If the message is misunderstood, it may take several days for it to be recognized, let alone rectified. A telephone call could settle the whole matter in just a few minutes. Thus written communication is also usually more difficult and time consuming than oral communication.

Of course, written communication offers some advantages. Because the sender can take the time to collect and assimilate the information and can draft and revise it before it is transmitted, it is often quite accurate. It also provides a permanent record of the exchange: the receiver can take the time to read it carefully and can refer to it repeatedly, as needed. For these reasons, written communication is generally preferable when important details must be relayed. At times it is important to one or both parties to have a written record available as evidence of exactly what took place. Julie Regan, founder of Toucan-Do, an importing company based in Honolulu, relies heavily on formal business letters when establishing contacts and buying merchandise from vendors in Southeast Asia. She believes that such letters give her an opportunity to carefully think through what she wants to say, to tailor her message to each individual, and to avoid misunderstandings later.

Choosing the Right Form

Which form of interpersonal communication should the manager use? The best medium will be determined by the situation. Oral communication is often preferred when the message is personal, nonroutine, and brief. Written communication is usually best when the message is more impersonal, routine, and longer.[11] The manager can also combine media to capitalize on the advantages of each. For example, a quick telephone call to set up a meeting is easy and gets an immediate response. Following up the call with a reminder note helps ensure that the recipient will remember the meeting, and it provides a record of the meeting having been called. Recent breakthroughs in electronic communication have facilitated just such actions. As we discuss more fully later, mobile telephones, facsimile machines, and computer networks blur the differences between oral and written communication and help each be more effective.

The form of interpersonal communication is determined by the situation. Organizations that have branch offices in many and faraway locations, such as Mrs. Fields Cookies, are finding that electronic communication systems are ideal for communications between the branches and top management. Chairman Randy Fields sees the computer as the most powerful management tool available: it eliminates layers of management and enables top managers to keep in close touch with employees.

FORMS OF GROUP AND ORGANIZATIONAL COMMUNICATION

In addition to the two pure forms of interpersonal communication just described, managers are concerned about other varieties of organizational communication. Each of these involves oral or written communication, but each also extends to broad patterns of communication across the organization. As shown in Figure 17.2, these forms of communication are vertical and horizontal communication, communication networks, and the grapevine.

Vertical Communication

Vertical communication is communication that flows both up and down the organization, usually along formal reporting lines—that is, it is the communication that takes place between people and those above and below them in the organization. Vertical communication may involve only two people, or it may flow through several different organizational levels.

● **vertical communication**
Communication that flows up and down the organization, usually along formal reporting lines; it takes place between managers and their subordinates and may involve several different levels of the organization

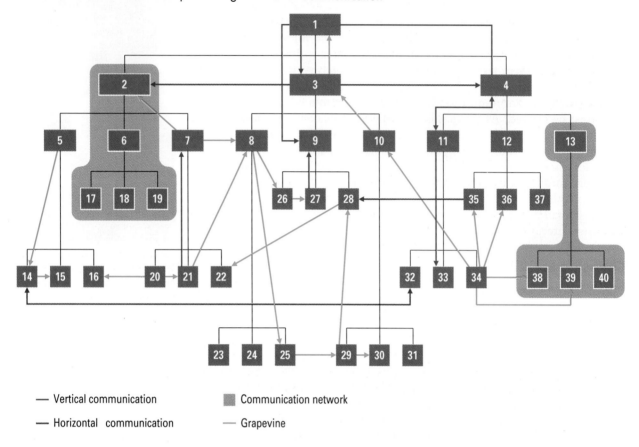

— Vertical communication

— Horizontal communication

■ Communication network

— Grapevine

Group and organizational communication can take a variety of forms. In this organization, vertical communication is shown by red arrows and horizontal communication is shown by purple arrows. Communication networks are enclosed by orange borders, and the grapevine is shown by blue arrows.

Upward Communication Upward communication consists of messages from subordinates to superiors, usually from subordinates to their direct superior, then to that person's direct superior, and so on up the hierarchy. In Figure 17.2, the exchange between manager 27 and manager 9, manager 4 and manager 1, and manager 21 and manager 7 is of this type. Occasionally, a message might by-pass a particular superior. The typical content of upward communication is requests, information that the lower-level manager thinks is important to the higher-level manager, responses to requests from the higher-level manager, suggestions, complaints, and financial information. Research has shown that upward communication is more subject to distortion than is downward communication. Subordinates are likely to withhold or distort information that makes them look bad. The greater the degree of difference in status between superior and subordinate and the greater the degree of distrust, the more likely the subordinate is to suppress or distort information.[12] For example, when Harold Geneen was CEO of ITT Corp., subordinates routinely withheld information about problems from him if they thought the news would make him angry and if they thought they could solve the problem themselves without his ever knowing about it.[13] (Later in the chapter we discuss ways to improve communication.)

Downward Communication Downward communication occurs when information flows down the hierarchy from superiors to subordinates. In Figure 17.2, downward communication is taking place between managers 1 and 3, 1 and 9, and 11 and 33. The typical content of these messages is directives on how something is to be done, the assignment of new responsibilities, performance feedback, and general information that the higher-level manager thinks will be of value to the lower-level manager. Vertical communication can, and usually should, be two-way. For example, in Figure 17.2, managers 4 and 11 are engaged in a dialogue about something.

Horizontal Communication

Whereas vertical communication involves a superior and a subordinate, **horizontal communication** involves colleagues and peers at the same level of the organization. For example, an operations manager might communicate to a marketing manager that inventory levels are running low and that projected delivery dates should be extended by two weeks. Horizontal communication probably occurs more among managers than among nonmanagers. In Figure 17.2, horizontal communication is taking place between managers 2, 3, and 4, managers 28 and 35, and managers 14 and 32.

Horizontal communication serves a number of purposes. It facilitates coordination among interdependent units. For example, a manager at Motorola, Inc., was recently researching the strategies of Japanese semiconductor firms in Europe. He found a great deal of information that was relevant to his assignment. He also uncovered some additional information that was potentially important to another department; so he passed it along to a colleague in that department, who used it to improve his own operations.[14] Horizontal communication can also be used for joint problem solving, as when two plant managers at Westinghouse Electric Corp. got together to work out a new method to improve productivity. Finally, horizontal communication plays a major role in work teams with members drawn from several departments.

- **horizontal communication**
Communication that flows laterally within the organization; it involves colleagues and peers at the same level of the organization and may involve people from several different organizational units

Communication Networks

A **communication network** is the pattern through which the members of a group communicate. In Figure 17.2, managers 2, 6, 17, 18, and 19 constitute a communication network and so do managers 13, 38, 39, and 40. Researchers studying group dynamics have discovered several typical networks in groups consisting of three, four, and five members. Representative networks among members of five-member groups are shown in Figure 17.3.[15] In the wheel pattern, all communication flows through one central person (person 1) who is probably the group's leader. The wheel is the most centralized network because one person receives and disseminates all information. The Y pattern is slightly less centralized—two persons (1 and 2) are close to the center. The chain offers a more even flow of information among members, although two people (the ones at each end) interact with only one other person. This path is closed in the circle pattern. Finally, the all-channel network, the most decentralized, allows a free flow of information among all group members. Everyone participates equally, and the group's leader, if there is one, is not likely to have excessive power.

- **communication network**
The pattern through which the members of a group communicate

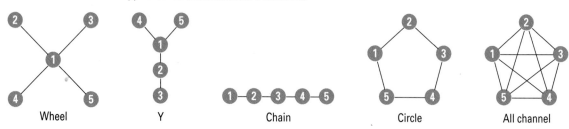

FIGURE 17.3 Types of Communication Networks

Wheel	Y	Chain	Circle	All channel

Research on communication networks has identified five basic networks for five-person groups. These vary in terms of information flow, position of the leader, and effectiveness for different types of tasks. Managers might strive to create centralized networks when group tasks are simple and routine. Alternatively, managers can foster decentralized groups when group tasks are complex and nonroutine.

There are some interesting connections between the type of network and group performance. When the group's task is relatively simple and routine, centralized networks tend to perform with greatest efficiency and accuracy. The dominant leader facilitates performance by coordinating the flow of information. When a group of accounting clerks is logging incoming invoices and distributing them for payment, for example, one centralized leader can coordinate things efficiently. When the task is complex and nonroutine, such as making a major decision about organizational strategy, decentralized networks tend to be most effective because open channels of communication permit members to interact and efficiently share relevant information. Managers should recognize the effects of communication networks on group and organizational performance and should try to structure networks appropriately.

The Grapevine

● **grapevine**

An informal communication network among people in an organization; it can permeate an entire organization and does not always follow formal communication channels

The **grapevine** is an informal communication network that can permeate an entire organization. Grapevines are found in all organizations except the very smallest, but they do not always follow the same patterns as, nor do they necessarily coincide with, formal channels of authority and communication. Figure 17.2 illustrates three grapevines. One starts with manager 7, who passes information on to managers 2 and 8. Manager 2 tells no one else, but manager 8 passes the information on to 26, who subsequently tells 27. The second grapevine is short, running from manager 5 to 14 to 17. The third grapevine, starting with manager 34, is considerably longer and more complex.

Research has identified several kinds of grapevines.[16] The two most common are illustrated in Figure 17.4. The gossip chain occurs when one person spreads a message—most likely personal information—to many other people. Each one, in turn, may either keep the information confidential or pass it on to others. The other common grapevine is the cluster chain, in which one person passes the information to a selected few individuals. Some of the receivers pass the information to a few other people; the rest keep it to themselves.

There is some disagreement about how accurate the information carried by the grapevine is, but research is increasingly finding it to be fairly accurate, especially when the information is based on fact rather than speculation. One recent study found that the grapevine may be between 75 and 95 percent accurate.[17] That same study also found that informal communication is increasing in many organizations for two basic reasons. One contributing factor is the recent increase in merger, acquisition, and takeover

FIGURE 17.4 Common Grapevine Chains Found in Organizations

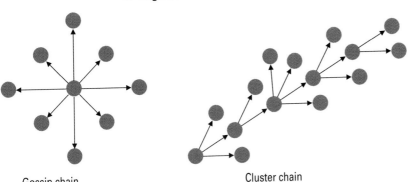

Gossip chain
(One person tells many)

Cluster chain
(Many people tell a few)

SOURCE: Based on Keith Davis and John W. Newstrom, *Human Behavior at Work: Organizational Behavior*, 8th ed. (New York: McGraw-Hill, 1989). Reproduced with permission.

The two most common grapevine chains in organizations are the gossip chain (in which one person communicates messages to many others) and the cluster chain (in which many people pass messages to a few others).

activity. Because such activity can greatly affect the people within an organization, it follows that they may spend more time talking about it.[18] The second contributing factor is that as more and more corporations move facilities from inner cities to suburbs, employees tend to talk less and less to others outside the organization and more and more to each other.

Attempts to eliminate the grapevine are fruitless, but fortunately the manager does have some control over it. By maintaining open channels of communication and responding vigorously to inaccurate information, the manager can minimize the damage the grapevine can do. The grapevine can actually be an asset. By learning who the key people in the grapevine are, for example, the manager can partially control the information they receive and use the grapevine to sound out employee reactions to new ideas such as a change in human resources policies or benefits packages. The manager can also get valuable information from the grapevine and use it to improve decision making.

Other Forms of Communication

A few other kinds of group and organizational communication warrant note. One that has become especially popular lately is **management by wandering around.**[19] The basic idea is that some managers keep in touch with what's going on by walking around the company talking with immediate subordinates, subordinates far down the organizational hierarchy, delivery people, customers, and anyone else who is involved with the company in some way. Bill Marriott, Jr., for example, frequently visits the kitchens, loading docks, and custodial work areas whenever he tours a Marriott hotel. He claims that by talking with employees throughout the hotel, he gets new ideas and has a better feel for the entire company. "Management in Practice" also describes how John Amerman, CEO of Mattel Inc., uses this approach.

Another form of organizational communication is the informal interchange that takes place outside the normal work setting, usually in the context of informal or interest groups. Employees attending the company

management by wandering around
An approach to communication that involves the manager walking around the company and having spontaneous conversations with subordinates, delivery people, customers, and anyone else who is involved with the company

Hyatt Hotels takes the concept of management by wandering around one step further: once a year, top management participates in In-Touch Day, a program to get them familiar with day-to-day routines and problems of Hyatt employees. Managers work in jobs such as bellmen, chambermaids, and carpenters to learn the realities of the hotel business. Vice president of human resources Myrna Hellerman, in charge of implementing the program, has folded napkins, made pastry, and served food.

perception
The set of processes people use to receive and interpret information from their environment

picnic, playing on the company softball team, or taking fishing trips together will almost always spend part of their time talking about work. For example, Texas Instruments Incorporated engineers at the Lewisville, Texas, facility often frequent a local bar in town after work. On any given evening, they talk about the Dallas Cowboys, the company's newest government contract, the weather, their boss, the company's stock price, local politics, and problems at work. There is no set agenda, and the topics of discussion vary from group to group and from day to day. Still, the social gatherings serve an important role. They promote a strong culture and enhance understanding of how the organization works.

BEHAVIORAL ELEMENTS OF COMMUNICATION

To a certain extent, the grapevine, management by wandering around, and informal communication are behavioral in nature. Two other important behavioral elements, perception and nonverbal communication, can also be a part of all organizational communication.

Perception

Perception is the set of processes that people use to receive and interpret information from their environment. Perception includes not only the five senses but also awareness, meaning, and interpretation. Perception plays a major role in receiving and decoding information. Each of us is constantly bombarded with information from the environment. Everywhere we turn we encounter information—so much information that we cannot handle it all. To illustrate, answer the following questions:

1. What color shirt was worn by the last person you saw?
2. What was the last song you heard on the radio?
3. Exactly how much did you pay for the tank of gas you most recently purchased?
4. When you were last watching television, how many commercials did you see?

For managers, the daily barrage of information takes the form of sales forecasts, economic indexes, memos, letters, reports, telephone calls, and conversations. As shown in Figure 17.5, perception acts as a filter that screens out information that is trivial or that we do not want to know.

Two basic perceptual processes are perceptual organization and selective perception. Selective perception allows us to screen out information, while perceptual organization helps us group information.

FIGURE 17.5 Basic Perceptual Processes

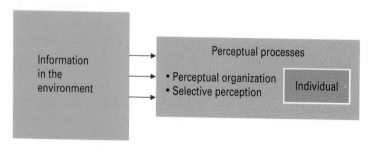

ROBERT HORTON TALKS BRITISH PETROLEUM BACK TO LIFE

Winston Churchill once chose British Petroleum Co. p.l.c. to fuel the Royal Navy, and for years the company coasted on past glory and its huge oil reserves. But when BP began to see its own fuel gauge dropping, it turned to Robert B. Horton, a man famous for his ability to tell good news or bad to one person or thousands.

BP has long relied on its huge but dwindling oil reserves in Prudhoe Bay, Alaska, and the North Sea. But under Horton, BP has radically altered the way it spends its oil exploration money, investing in risky, "frontier" drilling. To succeed in its innovative strategy, BP must be lean and flexible and able to make decisions quickly. New structure must accompany the new strategy.

BP chose Horton to shake things up because he spent the 1980s as the company's top trouble-shooter, earning the nickname "Horton the Hatchet." First he turned around the company's refining and chemical division, then he trimmed the fat from Standard Oil of Ohio. He has the invaluable skill of carrying out his "hatchet" duties without creating too much resentment.

Horton spends about half of his time on internal and external communication. He is so adept at dealing with people one-on-one that he had a videoconferencing studio installed near his office so he could talk directly to BP employees in nineteen offices around the world. He likes videoconferencing because, he says, it "is very efficient for business meetings, and helps save the health of executives because it cuts down on travel."* The company's far-flung offices are also linked by a computerized message system.

Horton saw how necessary restructuring was when he returned to Britain from Cleveland and viewed BP with fresh eyes. He was appalled at the poor communication and the levels of distrust and second-guessing in the old, slow-moving bureaucracy. In his first year, Horton cut corporate staff from about 2,500 to less than 380 and worked to decentralize responsibility; increase trust, openness, and teamwork; and involve employees in directing the changes. Responding to employee criticisms, Horton abolished six of BP's eleven bureaucratic layers and divided the work previously done by eighty standing committees among individuals and small, flexible teams that report directly to Horton or to the heads of the company's four major divisions. Now that so many people can easily get the chief's ear, ideas and decisions should flow with the speed and clarity necessary for the company to be an innovator into the next century.

* Quoted in Faye Rice, "Champions of Communication," *Fortune,* June 3, 1991, p. 120.

References: "BP Signals a New Direction," *Petroleum Economist,* April 1990, p. 106; Peter Nulty, "Batman Shakes BP to Bedrock," *Fortune,* November 19, 1990, pp. 155–162; Faye Rice, "Champions of Communication," *Fortune,* June 3, 1991, pp. 111–120.

many as 7 million Americans use telephones, computers, and couriers to work outside their conventional offices.[33]

Cellular telephones and facsimile machines have made it even easier for managers to communicate with one another. Many now use cellular telephones to make calls while commuting to and from work; some carry the telephones in briefcases so they can receive calls while at lunch. Facsimile machines make it easy for people to use written communication and get rapid feedback.

Psychologists, however, are beginning to associate some problems with these communication advances. For one thing, managers who are seldom in their "real" offices are likely to fall behind in their fields and be victimized by organizational politics because they are not present to keep in touch with what's going on and to protect themselves. They drop out of the organizational grapevine and miss out on much of the informal communication that takes place. Moreover, the use of electronic communication at the expense of face-to-face meetings and conversations makes it hard to build a strong culture, develop solid working relationships, and create a mutually supportive atmosphere of trust and cooperativeness. Overload can also result because managers are easily accessible with cellular phones and fax machines for conferences and reviewing material.[34]

SUMMARY OF KEY POINTS

Communication is the process of transmitting information from one person to another. Effective communication is the process of sending a message in such a way that the message received is as close in meaning as possible to the message intended. Communication is a pervasive and important part of the manager's job. The communication process consists of a sender encoding meaning and transmitting it to one or more receivers, who receive the message and decode it into meaning. In two-way communication the process continues with the roles reversed. Noise can disrupt any part of the overall process.

Interpersonal communication focuses on communication among a small number of people. Two important forms of interpersonal communication, oral and written, both offer unique advantages and disadvantages. Thus the manager should weigh the pros and cons of each when choosing a medium for communication.

There are a variety of forms of organizational communication. Vertical communication between superiors and subordinates may flow upward or downward, although two-way communication is generally preferable. Horizontal communication involves peers and colleagues at the same level in the organization. Communication networks are recurring patterns of communication among members of a group. The grapevine is the informal communication network among people in an organization.

Two behavioral elements of communication are perception and nonverbal communication. Perception consists of the processes that individuals use to receive and interpret information from the environment. Selective perception and perceptual organization are important elements of perception. Nonverbal communication includes facial expressions, body movements, physical contact, gestures, and inflection and tone.

Managing the communication process necessitates recognizing the barriers to effective communication and understanding how to overcome them. It is possible for both sender and receiver to learn and practice effective techniques for improving communication. Organizations also use both managerial and operational approaches to managing communication. Electronic communication, represented by computer networks, word-processing systems, cellular telephones, facsimile machines, and the like, is likely to have a profound effect on managerial and organizational communication in the years to come.

DISCUSSION QUESTIONS

Questions for Review

1. Define communication. What are the components of the communication process?

2. At what points in the communication process can problems occur? Give examples of communication problems and indicate how they might be prevented or alleviated.

3. Describe three different communication networks. Which type of network seems to most accurately describe the grapevine? Why?

4. What are the behavioral elements of communication? Identify five examples of nonverbal communication that you have recently observed.

Questions for Analysis

5. Is it possible for an organization to function without communication? Why or why not?

6. Which form of interpersonal communication is best for long-term retention? Why? Which form is best for getting across subtle nuances of meaning? Why?

7. In terms of the barriers most likely to be encountered, what are the differences between horizontal and vertical communication in an organization? How might a formal information system be designed to reduce such barriers?

Questions for Application

8. What forms of communication have you experienced today? What form of communication is involved in a face-to-face conversation with a friend? A telephone call from a customer? A traffic light or crossing signal? A picture of a cigarette in a circle with a slash across it? An area around machinery defined by a yellow line painted on the floor?

9. Interview a local manager to determine what forms of communication are used in his or her organization. Arrange to observe that manager for a couple of hours. What forms of communication did you observe?

10. How are electronic communication devices likely to affect the communication process in the future? Why? Interview someone from a local organization who uses electronic communications to see if she or he feels as you do.

A DEVASTATING RUMOR

*U*sually management rejoices when it learns that people are spreading the word about one of its products. Word-of-mouth publicity can be more effective than any ad at raising the public's interest in a product and attracting what is often called a "cult following." But sometimes "the word on the street" can have just the opposite effect.

In 1990, a new soft drink, Tropical Fantasy, suddenly became popular in the poor inner-city neighborhoods of New York and other Northeastern cities. Its 20-ounce bottles sold for $.49, giving consumers 25 percent more to drink for 40 percent less money than they would normally get from Coke or Pepsi. Soon Tropical Fantasy was nudging the big two off shelves in neighborhood stores.

But then the rumors started. According to crude fliers distributed around New York City, Tropical Fantasy was made by the Ku Klux Klan and contained "stimulants to sterilize the black man, and who knows what else!!!!" The fliers contained two effective claims, one true, one false. The true claim was that the soda was sold mostly in poor neighborhoods. "You won't find them downtown. . . . Look around. . ." the flier proclaimed. The false claim was that the television show "20/20" had said something about Tropical Fantasy, a lie that no doubt gave credibility to the rest of the flier.

In truth, Tropical Fantasy is bottled by Brooklyn Bottling, a family-run business. The soda helped bring the company back from the brink of bankruptcy, but the company dropped its sales projections for Tropical Fantasy from $15 million to $9 million after the rumors started. And though the Brooklyn district attorney is looking into the matter, Brooklyn Bottling may never know who set out to destroy it.

One theory is that the local soft-drink workers' union didn't like the amount of business going to Brooklyn Bottling, a non-union shop. Other people point the finger at the giants in the soda business, Coke and Pepsi. Tropical Fantasy's success meant that sales of other sodas dropped 25 percent or more. Store owners report that salespeople from the big two threatened to take away their "cold boxes" where sodas are stored or to stop giving them credit if they continued to sell Tropical Fantasy. But so far all efforts to trace the fliers to a single source have failed.

Tropical Fantasy is just the latest in a string of products that have suffered because of rumors or sabotage. Corona beer fought rumors that it contained urine, and Wendy's had to convince people that its hamburgers did not contain worm meat. Experts say that to fight such rumors, companies must send memos to employees, have managers talk to their staff, call press conferences as soon as the rumor goes public, and buy factual ads if the rumor refuses to die. But for Brooklyn Bottling, such steps are too late.

---

1. What elements of organization communication seem to have been at work in the Tropical Fantasy case?

2. What steps do you think Brooklyn Bottling should have taken as soon as it became aware of the rumors?

E 3. If you were a local soda distributor, which steps do you think it would be fair to take to limit a new soda's popularity: lowering your price below cost to win back market share; threatening to take away a store's cold case; threatening to stop giving a store credit; helping to spread rumors about a competing product?

References: Alix M. Freedman, "Rumor Turns Fantasy Into Bad Dream," *The Wall Street Journal*, May 10, 1991, pp. B1, B4; Larry Light, "Killing a Rumor Before It Kills a Company," *Business Week*, December 24, 1990, p. 23.

*S*ome of the communication skills necessary to hold a top spot in a global company are obvious—fluency in more than one language, for instance, seems crucial. But negotiating skills are also becoming increasingly important. A successful corporate leader may have to be, as BASF Corporation's chairman J. Dieter Stein puts it, "an ambassador to both sides."*

Stein has a difficult job, trying to make coherence out of diversity on a number of different levels. Until recently, BASF AG, BASF Corp.'s "parent," was a purely German company, with no non-Germans in top positions. The company's close ties with the German government have given it a checkered past. One of BASF's scientists, Fritz Haber, received a Nobel prize for his research on ammonia in 1919, but his work with poison gases later led to his being charged as a war criminal. Though non-Germans are working their way up in BASF's ranks, Stein still must deal with a strongly nationalistic parent company.

So one of Stein's jobs is to manage relations between Germany's BASF and BASF Corp. of North America. BASF Corp. does only about one-fifth as much business as its parent company, but it has been growing quickly, and Stein estimates that it will be close to the parent in size by the end of the decade. Such growth will necessitate a change in the way BASF AG views its North American relations.

At the same time, Stein must work to create a cohesive identity for BASF Corp.'s holdings; BASF Corp. has grown by buying companies that produce chemicals, pigments, flavors and fragrances, and paint and inks. Although none of these businesses is foreign to a chemist like Stein, he must use his skills to make sure that BASF Corp. makes the most of the overlapping strengths of its businesses.

Stein got a lesson in the skills of his new job when he first came to the United States in 1985 and found that his colleagues took his freely voiced opinions as orders, not as part of an interchange of ideas. He quickly let others know of his intent and also established a reputation as a good listener who could hear both sides, analyze their positions, and then make a firm decision.

Although Stein began as a chemist and once turned down a promotion to the patent department because he didn't want to do paperwork, his career changed in 1980 when he became the top human resources person for BASF's worldwide operations outside of its home base. The job was new for Stein and for BASF, so Stein had to create his duties as he went. Part of his job was to identify and help develop talent from around the world, an experience that showed him how important cross-cultural contact was becoming.

*Quoted in W. David Gibson, "He Carries an All-Purpose Portfolio for BASF in the U.S.," *Chemical Week*, November 30, 1988, p. 86.

Discussion Questions

1. Do you think some background in human resources management is essential for any top executive in a global company?

2. What particular skills might Stein need to play his role of "ambassador" between the North American and German branches of BASF?

3. What dilemmas might a company that has had strong ties to its government in the past face?

References: W. David Gibson, "He Carries an All-Purpose Portfolio for BASF in the U.S.," *Chemical Week*, November 30, 1988, pp. 86–88; Gary Hoover, Alta Campbell, and Patrick J. Spain (eds.) *Hoover's Handbook 1991—Profiles of Over 500 Major Corporations* (Austin, TX: The Reference Press, 1990), p. 115.

Achieving Quality Through Worker Empowerment

The purpose of this exercise is to help students better understand the important role for leaders in motivating workers to achieve improvements in product and service quality.

Learning Objectives

After completing this exercise you should have a better understanding of

1. The relationships between leading and quality.

2. How managers and organizations can use the leading process to enhance product and service quality.

Preview

Cadillac

Cadillac is the premium car division of General Motors. GM itself, the largest corporation in the world, had 1991 sales of $123.8 billion but lost $4.5 billion. During the mid-1980s, GM compromised Cadillac's image by making it more like the firm's other brands. Later in that same decade, however, efforts were made to revitalize Cadillac and restore its image.

IBM

To many people IBM is synonymous with computers. IBM is a major player in all segments of the computer industry, from laptops to mainframes. In 1991 IBM generated sales of approximately $65 billion but lost $2.8 billion. IBM has over $92 billion in assets. IBM Rochester (Minnesota), manufacturer of intermediate computer systems and disk storage products, is the focus of this video exercise.

Federal Express

Federal Express has been credited largely with inventing the overnight package delivery business. Federal Express reported revenues in 1991 of $7 billion and earned profits of $116 million.

Wallace Co.

Wallace Co. is a family-owned, pipe-and-valve distributor to the refining, chemical, and petrochemical industries. Based in Houston, the company's annual sales are $88 million. Wallace was founded in 1942 by Chairman John Wallace's father, C.S. Wallace. The company employs 200 people.

Leaders, Not Managers

Laurence Osterwise at IBM says that the idea is to excite creativity, sharing with employees the concepts, techniques, and tools they need. "I think, if anything," he says, "one of our competitive advantages [in the United States] is our people's ingenuity and innovative spirit, and we've got to find out how to most effectively foster that." That can be done better by leaders than by managers. "It's fairly clear," he says, "and should have been obvious to everyone, that people would rather be led than managed and empowered as opposed to controlled." Osterwise says empowerment "starts with the authority, the responsibility, then the accountability. It causes people to be more thoughtful when they really get that authority and responsibility and more dedicated and committed." But that requires extensive training, since to give people power without the skills to use it, Osterwise says, "will . . . lead to anarchy and disaster."*

Background Assignment

Go to the library and find articles on your assigned company spanning the period from 1984 to 1989. If you are in a Federal Express group, look for a couple of articles that focus specifically on Frederick Smith, the firm's founder and CEO. Try also to locate annual reports for your company during the 1984–1989 period, identifying central themes and issues. Use this information to form an understanding of your company's circumstances at this time: its environment, competition, and strategies.

The Video

In 1990 Cadillac, IBM Rochester, Federal Express, and Wallace were the four firms to win Baldrige awards for product or service quality. Your instructor will now show you a video that provides some general information about how these firms won this award. Compare the background information given about each company with what you have discovered through your own research.

Questions for Discussion

1. Teamwork seems to be a common thread in quality improvement programs. Why?

2. What about Frederick Smith makes him a good leader?

3. What are the basic similarities and differences in enhancing product quality versus enhancing service quality?

4. Some critics question whether small firms such as Wallace should pursue the Baldrige award because it takes so much time. Do you think this is a legitimate concern?

5. What is meant by the phrase "leading, not managing"?

Follow-Up Assignment

Return to the library and find more recent articles analyzing your company's performance since it won the Baldrige award in 1990. Also locate recent annual reports and note any references to quality programs, or to the use of work teams in the organization. How have quality improvements affected performance? What changes have taken place at your assigned company?

*Source: Lloyd Dobyns and Clare Crawford-Mason, *Quality or Else.* (Boston: Houghton Mifflin Compay, 1991) p. 157. Copyright © Houghton Mifflin Company. Used with permission.

THE CONTROLLING PROCESS

18 The Nature of Control

19 Managing Quality, Productivity, and Operations

20 Managing Technology and Innovation

21 Managing Information Systems

The Nature of Control

OBJECTIVES

After studying this chapter, you should be able to:

● *Describe the nature of control in organizations, including its purpose, importance, areas, responsibilities, and the planning-controlling link.*

● *Identify and explain the general steps in the control process.*

● *Identify and explain major forms of operations control and describe why organizations use multiple control systems.*

● *Discuss two general approaches to organizational control.*

● *Describe strategic control.*

● *Discuss how managers can effectively manage the control process.*

● *Describe major issues in choosing a style of control.*

OUTLINE

Control in Organizations
    Purpose of Control
    Areas of Control
    Importance of Control
    Responsibilities for Control
    The Planning-Controlling Link

Steps in the Control Process
    Establishing Standards
    Measuring Performance
    Comparing Performance Against
      Standards
    Evaluation and Action

Forms of Operations Control
    Preliminary Control
    Screening Control
    Postaction Control
    Multiple Control Systems

Forms of Organizational Control
    Bureaucratic Control
    Clan Control

Strategic Control

Managing the Control Process
    Developing Effective Control Systems
    Understanding Resistance to Control
    Overcoming Resistance to Control

Choosing a Style of Control

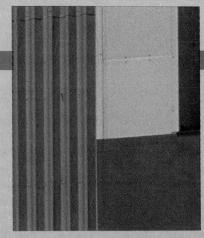

BOMBAY CO. WAS founded by two entrepreneurs in 1975 as a mail order company. Its name was selected to evoke images of the British Empire during its apex. The firm did poorly and was soon sold to Tandy Brands. At the time, Tandy was a small conglomerate with diverse holdings. But Tandy's managers had been looking for a specialty retailer to take center stage and they decided that Bombay Co. fit the bill.

Tandy's management sold many of its other businesses, changed the firm's name to Bombay Co. Inc., and put an expansion plan into place. Today several hundred Bombay Co. stores are located in malls throughout North America. The firm now has annual sales of well over $100 million and posted 1990 profits of more than $12 million.

What has accounted for Bombay's success? For one thing, the firm keeps focusing on its target market of young professionals. It offers high-quality Victorian-style furniture at moderate prices, most of which it buys from manufacturers in South Korea and Taiwan. Customers buy products directly from a Bombay store and assemble them at home with their own tools. This allows Bombay to devote much less space to inventory than is required of other furniture stores.

An important measure of retail performance is sales-per-square-foot; a Bombay store's is generally around $300. This figure is 15 percent higher than at comparable stores in malls and four times the average for a traditional furniture store not in a mall. By combining a tightly focused product line with a solid marketing strategy and effective cost control, Bombay is likely to continue its rapid growth and continued profitability.[1] ●

B ombay Co.'s managers have achieved considerable success. Major factors contributing to this success have been their ability to keep focused on what they want to do and to hold costs within acceptable limits. These factors, part of the control function of management, help keep organizations on track toward generating profits for owners and accomplishing its basic goals.

We noted in Chapter 1 that control focuses on monitoring and evaluating the activities of an organization. This chapter is the first of four devoted to the control function of management. We begin by exploring the nature of control and discussing the purpose, importance, and areas of control as well as who is responsible for control. We then discuss the general steps in the control process—establishing standards, measuring performance, comparing performance against standards, and evaluation and action—and the major forms of operations control. Subsequent sections address forms of organizational control, strategic control, how managers can make control systems effective, and major issues to consider when choosing a method of control. The other chapters in Part 6 cover operations management, productivity, and quality; managing technology and innovation; and managing information systems. Appendix 2 provides coverage of tools for budgetary and financial control.

CONTROL IN ORGANIZATIONS

● **control**

The regulation of organizational activities in such a way as to facilitate goal attainment

We define **control** as the regulation of organizational activities to facilitate goal attainment. Managers at Bombay Co. focus their control efforts on managing their product line and its associated costs. As a result, the firm remains very profitable.

Purpose of Control

Without control, an organization would have no indication of how well it was performing in relation to its goals. The purpose of control is to provide managers with an assessment of where the organization is in comparison to where it is supposed to be at a certain point in time and in terms of one or more indicators of performance. For example, Federal Express Corp. has a performance goal of delivering 99 percent of its packages on time. If on-time deliveries fall to 97 percent, managers know that they have a problem. On the other hand, an on-time rate of 99.5 percent would indicate that the company is doing better than expected.

Areas of Control

Organizational control can focus on any area of an organization. Two useful ways of identifying areas of control are in terms of resource focus and level.

Resource Focus   Financial, physical, human, and information resources, as shown in Figure 18.1, are also the focus of control. The management process itself involves efficiently and effectively combining these resources

The control of financial resources is central to the process of organizational control because of both its importance in its own right as well as its relationship to the other areas. Lack of control of physical resources (e.g., improper inventory management), human resources (e.g., hiring unqualified persons), and information resources (e.g., lack of market information) will all affect the organization's financial resources.

into appropriate outputs. Control of physical resources includes inventory management (stocking neither too few nor too many units in inventory), quality control (maintaining appropriate levels of output quality), and equipment control (having the proper kinds of buildings, office equipment, and so on). Control of human resources includes selection and placement activities, training and development, performance appraisal, and compensation levels. Control of information resources involves sales and marketing forecasting, environmental analysis, public relations, production scheduling, and economic forecasting.

Financial resources are at the center of Figure 18.1 because they, in addition to being organizational resources in their own right, are related to the control of all the other resources. Pure financial control does exist: one aspect is ensuring that the organization always has enough cash on hand to meet its obligations but does not have excess cash sitting idle. But financial control extends to the other three kinds of resources as well: excess inventory leads to storage costs; poor selection of employees leads to termination and rehiring expenses; and inaccurate sales forecasts lead to disruptions in cash flows and other financial effects. Financial issues, then, tend to pervade most control-related activities.[2]

Level   Control can also be classified by level. Operations control is control focused on one or more operating systems within an organization. Quality control is one type of operations control. Organizational control is concerned with the overall functioning of the organization. Strategic control is concerned with how effectively the organization understands and aligns itself with its environment.[3] We discuss these levels of control more fully later in this chapter.

Importance of Control

Given the basic purpose of control and how pervasive its use is in the organization, an organization without effective control is not likely to achieve its goals: control is therefore essential to an organization's success. Control helps an organization adapt to changing conditions, limits the compounding of errors, helps an organization cope with complexity, and helps minimize costs.

By measuring the actual costs of each step of its timber-cutting processes, Weyerhaeuser is able to discover and quantify delays and inefficiencies. Like an increasing number of organizations, Weyerhaeuser is using a new accounting technique—ABC analysis—to help it discover the real costs of its business processes. ABC analysis differs from traditional cost-management systems because overhead costs are assigned where they are incurred instead of spread evenly over all products and processes.

Changing Conditions In today's complex and turbulent environment, all organizations must contend with change.[4] Between the time a goal is established and the time it is reached, many things can happen in the organization and its environment to disrupt movement toward the goal or even to change the goal itself. A properly designed control system can help managers anticipate, monitor, and respond to changing circumstances. For example, Metalloy, a forty-six-year-old family-run metal-casting company, recently signed a contract to make engine-seal castings for NOK, a Japanese parts maker. Metalloy was satisfied when its first 5,000-unit production run yielded 4,985 acceptable castings and only 15 defective ones. NOK, however, was quite unhappy and insisted that Metalloy raise its standards. Managers at Metalloy had not kept abreast of changing quality standards.[5]

Compounding of Errors A small mistake or error by itself does not often seriously damage the health of an organization. With the passage of time, however, a small error uncorrected may accumulate and become extremely serious. For example, Whistler Corporation, a large radar-detector manufacturer, was faced with such rapidly escalating demand that it essentially stopped worrying about quality. Its defect rate rose from 4 percent to 9 percent to 15 percent and eventually reached 25 percent. One day, a manager realized that 100 of the firm's 250 employees were spending all of their time fixing defective units, and $2 million worth of radar detectors were awaiting repair. An adequate control system would have kept the problem from reaching such proportions.[6]

Organizational Complexity When a firm purchases only one raw material, produces but one product, has a simple structure, and enjoys constant demand for its product, its managers can probably maintain control with a notepad and pencil. But in an organization that produces many products from myriad raw materials, has a large market area and a complicated organization structure, and operates in a competitive environment, it is difficult (if not impossible) to maintain adequate control without an elaborate control system. Emery Air Freight was quite effective until it bought Purolator Courier Corporation. The "new" Emery that resulted from the acquisition was much more complex than the "old" one, but no new controls were added. Consequently, Emery began to lose money and market share, costs increased, and service deteriorated. The firm barely survived and even today has not regained its former level of profitability.

Minimizing Costs Effective control can eliminate waste, lower costs, and improve output per unit of input. For example, managers at Georgia-Pacific Corporation recently replaced the blades in their sawmills with thinner blades that take a smaller "bite" out of logs. The wood that is saved by the new blades each year can fill 800 railcars.[7] Bombay Co.'s low operating costs are also attributable to its effective control.[8]

Responsibilities for Control

Given the wide array of control systems and concerns in organizations, who exactly is responsible for managing control? Traditionally, managers have determined the kinds of control that will be used, actually implemented control systems, and take appropriate actions based on the information provided by those control systems.

Most large organizations also have one or more specialized managerial positions called controller. The controller is responsible for helping line managers with their control activities, coordinating the organization's overall control system, and gathering and assimilating relevant information. Many businesses that use a divisional form of organization design have one controller for the corporation and one for each division. The increased importance of the controller is reflected in the large number of controllers who climb farther up the managerial ranks. Recent chief executive officers of Cooper Industries, Singer, FMC Corporation, CPC International Inc., General Motors Corp., Pfizer Inc., and Fruehauf were all former controllers.

More and more organizations are involving operating employees in their control systems. Managers are finding that employee participation, as discussed in Chapter 14, can increase organizational effectiveness. Whistler Corporation increased employee involvement in an effort to eliminate its quality problems. The quality-control unit was abolished, and all employees were subsequently made responsible for product quality. As a result, Whistler eliminated its quality problems and is now highly profitable once again.

The Planning-Controlling Link

Managers must establish a tight linkage between planning and control. As indicated in Chapter 1, planning is usually the first part of the management process. The organizing and leading functions get the actual work of the organization done, and the controlling function is directly tied back into planning. For example, management plans to increase market share by 2 percent in each of the next seven years. At the end of year 1, as expected, market share has increased 2 percent. This performance, as measured by the control system, tells management that it should continue with the existing plan. At the end of year 2, market share has increased only 1 percent. This performance tells management that some adjustment is needed to steer the firm back toward its desired rate of growth. At the end of year 3, the control system reveals that the firm is exceeding its projected 2-percent growth rate by so much that a new plan is needed.

The organization continuously cycles back and forth between planning and controlling. The manager makes plans and then uses the control system to monitor progress toward fulfillment of those plans. The control system, in turn, tells the manager that things are going as they should (the current plan should be maintained), that things are not going as they should (the current plan should be modified), or that the situation has changed (a new plan should be developed). Bombay Co. does a good job of linking planning and control. Managers, for example, plan new store openings and make sales projections. Buyers use that information to order new merchandise, and other managers keep abreast of information such as ongoing sales patterns and current inventories.

STEPS IN THE CONTROL PROCESS

Regardless of the type or number of control systems needed by an organization, there are four general steps in any control process.[9] They are illustrated in Figure 18.2.

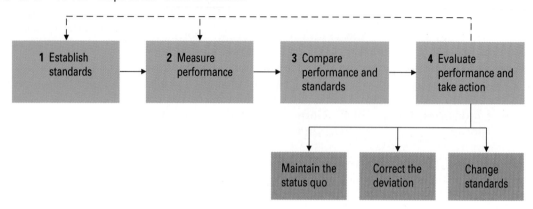

Establishing Standards

Having an effective control system can help ensure that an organization achieves its goals. Implementing a control system, however, is a systematic process that generally proceeds through four interrelated steps.

● **standard**
A target against which subsequent performance is to be compared

The first step in the control process is establishing standards. A **standard** is a target against which subsequent performance is to be compared. Standards for a fast-food restaurant like McDonald's Corp. might include the following:

1. A minimum of 95 percent of all customers will be greeted within three minutes of their arrival.

2. Precooked hamburgers will not sit in the warmer more than five minutes before they are served to customers.

3. All empty tables will be cleaned within five minutes after they have been vacated.

As much as possible, standards established for control purposes should be derived from the organization's goals and, like objectives, be expressed in measurable terms. Note that standard 1 for a fast-food restaurant has a time limit of three minutes and an objective target of 95 percent of all customers. In standard 2, the objective target is implied: "all" precooked hamburgers. On a broader level, control standards also reflect organizational strategy. A control standard for a retailer might be the goal of increasing annual sales volume by 25 percent within five years. A hospital might aim to increase its patient recovery rate to 98 percent within six years. A university might adopt a standard, or goal, of graduating 80 percent of its student athletes within five years of their initial enrollment by the year 1996. In short, control standards can be as narrow or as broad as the level of activity to which they apply. Further, they must also follow logically from organizational goals and objectives.

A final aspect of establishing standards is to decide which performance indicators are relevant. When a new product is introduced, its manufacturer should have some idea in advance whether the first month's sales will accurately indicate long-term growth or whether sales will take awhile to gather momentum. Similarly, when a retailer adopts a standard of increasing sales by 12 percent next year, management should have some idea whether to expect even growth of 1 percent per month or growth of 2 percent for the first ten months and 10 percent during the Christmas season. If the former,

a 1 percent increase during the first six months is cause for alarm; if the latter, a 1 percent increase by July is probably acceptable. Sharper Image Corp., an upscale specialty shop, recently set two performance standards for yearly sales: that same-store sales (i.e., sales from stores already in operation) should increase by 5 percent from the previous year and that overall sales, including revenues from new stores, should increase by 25 percent. Those sales-increase levels represent both a goal and a standard, and management viewed each as a relevant indicator of performance.[10]

Measuring Performance

The second step in the control process is measuring performance. In this context, **performance** refers to those activities that managers are attempting to control. The measurement of performance is constant and ongoing for most organizations, and for control to be effective, relevant performance measures must be valid. When a manager is concerned with controlling sales, daily, weekly, or monthly sales figures represent actual performance. A production manager might measure performance in terms of unit cost, quality, or volume. The performance of employees—or output—may be measured in terms of quality or quantity. Measuring performance is not always easy. A research and development scientist at Merck & Co., Inc., for example, may spend years working on a single project before achieving a major breakthrough. A manager who takes over a business that is on the brink of failure may need months or even years to turn things around. Nevertheless, some performance indicators can usually be developed. The scientist's progress can be partially assessed by peer review. Valid performance measurement, however difficult to obtain, is essential to maintain effective control. At the end of its fiscal year, Sharper Image measured its total sales and sales for each individual store. The results indicated

● **performance**
In a control context, activities that managers are attempting to control

that although overall sales did indeed reach the desired 25 percent level of increase, same-store sales actually declined by 7 percent.

Comparing Performance Against Standards

The third step in the control process is to compare measured performance against the standards developed in step 1. Performance may be higher than, lower than, or the same as the standard. Management must decide how much leeway is permissible before taking remedial action. In some cases comparison is easy. Each product manager at General Electric Co. has a goal of being either number 1 or number 2 in her or his market. Determining whether this standard has been met is relatively simple. At Sharper Image, comparisons were also fairly easy to make—one standard was met and the other was not.

In other settings, however, comparisons are less clear-cut. Assume that each of three sales managers has a goal of increasing sales by 10 percent during the year. At the end of the year, one manager has increased sales by 9.9 percent, another by 9.3 percent, and the third by 8.7 percent. For the most part, deciding whether each has met the standard is a management decision that must be based on many relevant factors, including the absolute dollar amounts involved and any mitigating circumstances. Although none of the three sales managers attained the precise goal of 10 percent, one was very close. Another may have met with unexpected competition from a new company. These and other relevant factors must be considered. Comparisons must also be made as often as necessary. For long-run and high-level standards, comparisons may be appropriate annually. In other circumstances, however, comparisons are more frequent. For example, a business with a cash shortage may need to monitor its on-hand cash reserves on a daily basis. When Emery Air Freight was on the brink of bankruptcy, its managers checked the company's cash reserves virtually every day.

Evaluation and Action

The final step in the control process is to evaluate performance (by means of the comparisons made in step 3) and then take appropriate action. This evaluation draws heavily on a manager's analytic and diagnostic skills, which were discussed in Chapter 1. After evaluation, one of three actions is usually appropriate.

Maintain the Status Quo Doing nothing, or maintaining the status quo, is generally appropriate when performance more or less measures up to the standard. If the standard for cost reductions this year is 4 percent and we have achieved a reduction of 3.99 percent, we are clearly on the right track. At Sharper Image, new-store sales were doing even better than expected, so no action was deemed necessary regarding their performance.

Correct the Deviation Likely, some action will be needed to correct a deviation from the standard. If the cost-reduction standard is 4 percent and we have thus far managed only a 1 percent reduction, something must be done to get us back on track. We may need to motivate our employees to work harder or supply them with new machinery. Managers at Sharper

Image saw a clear problem with their same-store sales and took corrective action immediately. They increased advertising, brought in new products, and started paying more attention to their product mix. In some situations, companies may be doing better than anticipated but still need to correct the deviation. For example, when Gillette Co. recently introduced its new Sensor razor, demand for its blades was so high that merchants could not keep them in stock. As a result, Gillette temporarily cut back on its advertising to avoid irritating customers.

Change Standards Yet another response to the outcome of comparing performance to standards is to change the standards. The standard may have been too high or too low to begin with, which becomes apparent if large numbers of employees exceed the standard by a wide margin or if no one ever meets the standard. In other situations, a standard may need to be adjusted because circumstances have changed. A sales-increase standard of 10 percent may have to be modified when a new competitor comes on the scene. Given new market conditions, the old standard of 10 percent may no longer be realistic. One cause cited for Sharper Image's problems is increased competition from other specialty chains as well as department stores. Thus the company may need to reassess its standard and adopt a lower one to better reflect the realities of its marketplace.

FORMS OF OPERATIONS CONTROL

We now turn our attention to the three levels of control practiced by most organizations. This section describes operations control systems. The next two sections address organizational and strategic control. As shown in Figure 18.3, operations control can take one of three forms—preliminary, screening, and postaction. The three forms vary primarily in terms of where they occur in relation to the transformation processes used by the organization.[11]

F I G U R E 18.3 Forms of Operations Control

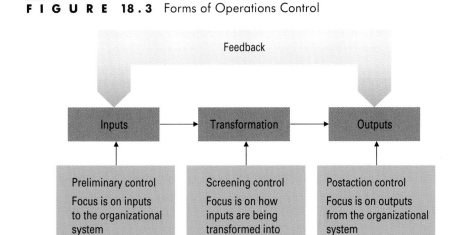

Inputs → Transformation → Outputs

Feedback

Preliminary control
Focus is on inputs to the organizational system

Screening control
Focus is on how inputs are being transformed into outputs

Postaction control
Focus is on outputs from the organizational system

Most organizations develop multiple control systems that incorporate all three basic forms of control. For example, the publishing company that produced this book screens inputs by hiring only qualified persons, typesetters, and printers (preliminary control). In addition, quality is checked during the transformation process such as after the manuscript is typeset (screening control), and the outputs—printed and bound books—are checked before they are shipped from the bindery (postaction control).

A new concept in preliminary control (which concentrates on inputs to the system) is executive education. By sending its managers to school, an organization hopes to improve the quality of its human resources. But some companies are not satisfied with the business school's curriculum and are customizing programs with schools willing to meet their needs. The University of Michigan, which has customized courses for Ford, Upjohn, and General Electric, has been ranked number one by employers.

Preliminary Control

● **preliminary control** (also called **steering control** or **feedforward control**)
Attempts to monitor the quality or quantity of financial, physical, human, and information resources before they actually become part of the system

Preliminary control (also called **steering control** or **feedforward control**) concentrates on inputs to the system early in the overall process. Preliminary control attempts to monitor the quality or quantity of financial, physical, human, and information resources before they become part of the system.[12] Firms like The Procter & Gamble Co. and General Mills, Inc., hire only college graduates for their management training programs—and only after several interviewers and other selection criteria have been satisfied. Thus they control the quality of human resources entering the organization. Bombay Co. specifies strict quality standards when it orders new furniture. Television networks like ABC and CBS refuse to accept certain kinds of advertising. And the Associated Press verifies the accuracy of its news stories before they are released.

Screening Control

● **screening control** (also called **yes/no control** or **concurrent control**)
Relies heavily on feedback processes during the transformation process

Screening control (also called **yes/no control** or **concurrent control**) occurs during the transformation process. Screening control relies heavily on feedback processes. Suppose that a manager of a manufacturing plant establishes a number of checkpoints along the assembly line. As the product moves along the line, it is periodically checked to make sure that all of the components assembled so far are working properly. This is screening control because the product is being controlled during the transformation process itself. Such control systems are also an effective way to promote employee participation and catch problems early in the transformation process. For example, Corning Incorporated recently adopted such a system for use in manufacturing television glass. Under its old system, finished television screens were casually inspected only after they were finished, and more than 4 percent of them were later returned by customers because of tiny defects. Under Corning's new system, the glass screens are inspected at

Postaction Control

Postaction control focuses on the outputs of the organization after the transformation process is complete. Corning's old system was postaction control—a final inspection was made only after everything was done. Even though Corning abandoned postaction control, it is useful and effective in certain situations, such as when a product or service is fairly simple and routine. If a product can be manufactured in only two or three steps, postaction control may be the most effective method. Although postaction control is generally not so useful as preliminary or screening control, it can be effective in two important ways. It provides management with information for future planning. For example, when a quality check of finished goods indicates an unacceptably high defect rate, the manager knows that the causes must be determined and corrected. Postaction control also provides a basis for rewarding employees. Recognizing that an employee has exceeded her sales goals (planned outputs) by a wide margin, for example, may alert the manager that a bonus or promotion is in order.[14]

● **postaction control**
Monitors the outputs or results of the organization after the transformation process is complete

Multiple Control Systems

Most organizations cannot survive by using only one form of operational control; thus most firms adopt multiple controls. For example, Ford Motor Co. uses preliminary control by hiring only qualified employees and specifying required quality standards when ordering parts from other manufacturers. It also uses numerous screening controls by checking the quality of various components of its cars as they are being assembled. A final inspection and test drive as each car rolls off the assembly line is part of the company's postaction control system. "Management in Practice" discusses an actual example of how multiple control systems are used.

FORMS OF ORGANIZATIONAL CONTROL

We noted earlier that organizations practice various kinds of control over their overall design and operating systems. Two dominant forms of organizational control are bureaucratic control and clan control.[15] Figure 18.4 shows eight elements on which the two differ. A few organizations may fall at one extreme or the other, but most have tendencies toward one form and characteristics of both.

Bureaucratic Control

Bureaucratic control is a form of organizational control characterized by formal and mechanistic structural arrangements. As Figure 18.4 shows, the goal of bureaucratic control is to extract employee compliance. Organizations that use it rely on strict rules and a rigid hierarchy, concentrate on

● **bureaucratic control**
A form of organizational control characterized by formal and mechanistic structural arrangements

Element	Bureaucratic control	Clan control
Goal of control approach	Employee compliance	Employee commitment
Degree of formality	Strict rules, formal controls, rigid hierarchy	Group norms, culture, self-control
Performance expectations	Directed toward minimum levels of acceptable performance	Directed toward enhanced performance above and beyond the minimum
Organization design	Tall structure, top-down influence	Flat structure, shared influence
Reward system	Directed at individual performance	Directed at group performance
Participation	Limited and formal	Extended and informal

Organizational control generally falls somewhere between the two extremes of bureaucratic and clan control. NBC Television uses bureaucratic control, whereas Levi Strauss uses clan control.

ensuring that people meet minimally acceptable levels of performance, and have a tall structure. Moreover, they focus their rewards on individual performance and allow only limited and formal employee participation. NBC television approaches organizational control in ways that reflect many elements of bureaucratic control. Management has established numerous rules to regulate employee travel, expense accounts, and so forth. A new performance appraisal system goes to great lengths to specify minimally acceptable levels of performance, and rewards are based on individual contributions. In addition, many employees have argued that they have too small a voice in how the organization is managed. The organization's structure is considerably taller than those of the other major networks.[16]

Clan Control

● **clan control**
An approach to organizational control based on informal and organic structural arrangements

Clan control is an approach to organizational control based on informal and organic structural arrangements. As indicated in Figure 18.4, its goal is employee commitment. Accordingly, it relies heavily on group norms, a strong corporate culture, and self-control of behavior. The focus of performance is not so much on minimally acceptable levels, but rather on how people can enhance their levels of performance beyond minimum levels. Organizations using this approach are usually relatively flat and encourage shared influence. Rewards are often directed at group performance, and participation is widespread. Levi Strauss & Co. practices clan control. Much

MAKING IT BIG IN THE COMPUTER BARGAIN BUSINESS

 The secret to the success of Gateway 2000 seems almost absurdly simple: sell a product that's as good as any other company's, but price it below competing models. Coming up with such an approach is the easy part. The trick is carrying it out well enough to make a profit. By keeping tight control of its costs and learning as it expands, Gateway 2000 has followed its philosophy well enough to give its giant competitors headaches.

Gateway sells IBM-compatible personal computers over the phone. It buys parts as inexpensively as it can, assembles them, and ships its products in boxes painted to look like the Holstein cows you might see near the company's headquarters in North Sioux City, South Dakota. In 1991, it sold more computers than any other mail-order company—around 230,000. All this from a company that started with $10,000 in 1985 by men who are just now entering their thirties.

President and founder Ted Waitt is a good salesman; cofounder Mike Hammond knows the technical side of the business. While Hammond searches for the best values in components, Waitt steers the company through the minefields of a fiercely competitive business. Selling directly to customers allows Gateway to avoid retailers' markups and to lower its prices at will, without angering retailers. Gateway has, in fact, been lowering prices every two months. Other successful mail-order companies, like Dell Computer, have turned to manufacturing their own components or doing their own research and development, expensive ventures that Waitt wants to stay away from.

Gateway's out-of-the-way location also helps keep costs down. South Dakota has no personal or corporate income taxes, and because of the low cost of living, Gateway can pay assemblers as little as $5.50 an hour, though that figure gets augmented by monthly bonuses. Gateway's facilities are far from luxurious—during busy times, half-assembled computers sit on carts in the hallways.

Waitt has also been smart enough to realize that the company's tremendous growth requires changes at the top. He has hired outsiders to revamp the company's decision-making and assembly processes. Though he wants to sell more computers to corporate clients, he doesn't plan to create a field sales force to do so. "The biggest challenge," he says, "is adding the bureaucracy it takes to run the company without becoming fat, lazy, inflexible—bureaucratic."* Again, the theory sounds simple, but with Gateway's tight controls, it works.

*Quoted in Andrew Kupfer, "The Champ of Cheap Clones," *Fortune*, September 23, 1991, p. 120.

References: John M. Dodge, "Lean PC Prices Help Gateway Fatten Corporate Customer List," *PC Week*, June 24, 1991, pp. 1, 8; Andrew Kupfer, "The Champ of Cheap Clones," *Fortune*, September 23, 1991, pp. 116–120; Robert L. Scheier and Michael R. Zimmerman, "Gateway at Crossroads After Losing Top Execs," *PC Week*, February 24, 1992, p. 165.

---

of the work of the company is accomplished by groups and teams. Thus group norms help facilitate high performance, and rewards are subsequently provided to the best-performing groups and teams. The company's culture reinforces contributions to the overall team effort, and employees are very loyal to the organization. Levi's has a flat structure and power is widely shared. Participation is also encouraged in all areas of operation.[17]

STRATEGIC CONTROL

Strategic control—the third level of control practiced by organizations—is aimed at ensuring that the organization is maintaining an effective align-

● **strategic control**
Control aimed at ensuring that the organization is maintaining an effective alignment with its environment and moving toward achieving its strategic goals

F. Kenneth Iverson, CEO of steel manufacturer Nucor Corp., has demonstrated considerable ability in the area of strategic control. He implemented a German technological advance to turn scrap steel and iron into quality sheet steel using about half the labor and energy other processes use. With this process Nucor is not only competing effectively with other minimills but is proving to be formidable competition for integrated steelmakers such as USX and LTV.

ment with its environment and moving toward achieving its strategic goals.[18] Because the study of strategic control is still in its infancy, there are no generally accepted models or theories. In general, however, as we noted in Chapter 7, the implementation of strategy generally involves structure, leadership, technology, human resources, and information and control systems. Thus it follows that strategic control should focus on these five areas to ensure that strategy has been and is being effectively implemented. For example, the organization should periodically examine its structure to determine whether it is facilitating its strategic goals. Suppose that a firm using a functional (U-form) design has a goal of growing at a rate of 20 percent per year but is currently growing at a rate of 10 percent per year. Close examination might reveal that the firm's current structure is constraining growth by slowing decision making and inhibiting innovation. This examination could also suggest that adopting a divisional (M-form) design is more likely to facilitate the desired growth (for example, by speeding decision making and promoting innovation).[19]

Management should focus strategic control on the extent to which the five areas of strategy implementation are facilitating the accomplishment of the organization's strategic goals. If they are, the organization should respond in the same way as with other forms of control—maintain the status quo. If, on the other hand, one or more of the methods of implementation are inhibiting the attainment of goals, it should be changed. Consequently, the firm might find it necessary to alter its structure, replace important leaders, adopt new technology, modify its human resource policies, or change its information and operational control systems.[20] For example, the board of directors at Borden, Inc., realized that the company was not meeting its strategic goals and was not providing its stockholders with an adequate return on their investment. The board brought in a new CEO (change in leadership), Romeo Ventres, who then changed the company's structure (from an H-form to an M-form), implemented a variety of new manufacturing techniques to enhance productivity (change in technology), brought

NO LONGER JUST ITALY'S OIL COMPANY

 Gabriele Cagliari knows the benefits and pitfalls of running a state-owned organization. His company, ENI, was formed in 1953 as an arm of Italy's Ministry of State Participation, and it controls more than 50 percent of Italy's oil market. But as it gradually pulls away from government control, ENI needs to become a powerful international competitor, which means playing by rules very different from those dreamed up by Italy's politicians.

Like most government-controlled enterprises, ENI has traditionally made efficiency and corporate strategy secondary to political goals. Like the U.S. Defense Department trying to close military bases, ENI has had to make sure that it doesn't offend powerful politicians, and its decisions have been influenced by issues such as which areas of the country were suffering the worst unemployment.

In the 1980s, ENI took the first big step on the road to becoming an efficient company that could compete worldwide by cutting its work force by more than one-third. Cagliari is looking at further cuts and at selling off unprofitable pieces of ENI's Italian businesses. The government's 1991 decision to give up control of ENI and sell shares publicly made some of Cagliari's political decisions easier, but they also made the need for efficiency more pressing.

Ironically, ENI has had an easier time preparing abroad for its new roles. In 1990, ENI passed Fiat as Italy's most profitable company, and Cagliari has been increasing the company's visibility and reputation by entering into joint agreements around the world. ENI has formed partnerships with the Venezuelan oil company to build a methanol plant; with a Japanese company it is building a refinery in Iran; and it is working to expand into Eastern Europe, setting up its first gas stations in Moscow and Hungary.

Cagliari has been successful at guiding ENI in part because of his background. A chemical engineer, Cagliari knows the technical parts of ENI's businesses, a knowledge that helps him make decisions about ENI's billion-dollar joint ventures and buyouts. He also speaks fluent English from a five-year stay in the United States and is consciously making himself into a global manager. His success at ENI may well become a model as other European countries sell off their national companies and the companies' managers try to get their often-bloated charges under control.

References: John Rossant, "Can a Pumped-Up ENI Get Into Fighting Trim?," *Business Week*, May 27, 1991, pp. 76–77; Dev George, "Italy's ENI Group to be Privatized?", *Offshore*, December, 1991, p. 9.

---

in several new managers (change in human resources), installed a new management information system to help him keep track of all areas of the organization's operations (change in information systems), and mandated new levels of product quality (change in operational control). As a result, Borden became much more competitive and profitable.[21] "The Global View" discusses another example of effective strategic control.

MANAGING THE CONTROL PROCESS

Understanding the steps and levels of control is necessary if a manager truly wants to have effective control. Managers must also understand how to develop an effective control system as well as overcome occasional resistance to control.

By cutting the number of parts in its 1992 Seville touring sedan by 20 percent, Cadillac designed a car that is less prone to worker error, easier to build, and higher quality. By effectively linking its planning and control systems, Cadillac could simplify the car's design, and is now better able to quantify and control such functions as worker error.

Developing Effective Control Systems

What constitutes an effective control system? Control systems tend to be most effective when they are integrated with planning and are flexible, accurate, timely, and objective.

Integration with Planning   We noted earlier that control should be linked with planning. In general, the more explicit and precise this linkage is, the more effective the control system will be. The most important factor in effectively integrating planning and control is to account for control as plans are developed. For example, as part of the planning process, goals should be set that can be converted into standards to reflect how well the plan is being realized. For example, managers at Champion Spark Plug Company recently decided to broaden their product line to include a full range of automotive accessories—a total of twenty-one new products altogether. As a part of this plan, managers decided in advance what level of sales they wanted to realize from each product for each of the next five years, and they established those sales goals as standards against which actual sales would be compared. Thus by considering their control system as they developed their plan, managers at Champion did an excellent job of tying planning and control together.[22]

Flexibility   An effective control system must be flexible enough to accommodate change. Consider an organization whose diverse product line requires seventy-five different raw materials. The company's inventory control system must be able to manage and monitor current levels of inventory for all seventy-five materials. When a change in product line changes the number of raw materials needed, or when the required quantities of any materials change, the control system should be able to accommodate the revised requirements. Designing and implementing a new control system would be an unnecessary expense. Champion had to revise one of its standards when one of its biggest customers, Montgomery Ward, decided to not stock the full line of Champion products.

Accuracy   Control systems must also be designed in such a way to ensure that the information they rely on is accurate. This seems obvious, but it is surprising how many managers base decisions on inaccurate information. Sales representatives in the field may hedge their sales estimates to make themselves look good. Production managers may hide costs to meet their targets. Human resources managers may overestimate their minority recruiting prospects to meet Affirmative Action goals. In each case upper management receives inaccurate information. Denied accurate measurement and reporting of performance, managers may take inappropriate action, and the results of inaccurate information can be quite dramatic. If sales estimates are artificially high, a manager might either cut advertising (thinking it is no longer needed) or increase advertising (to further build momentum). In either case the action may not be appropriate. Similarly, having been fed artificially low production costs, a manager who is unaware of the hidden costs may quote a sales price much lower than desirable. Or an executive may speak out publicly on the effectiveness of the company's minority recruiting, only to find out later that the number of prospects has been overestimated.

Timeliness   An effective control system must provide performance information in a timely way. Timeliness does not necessarily mean fast; it simply means that information is provided as often as is suitable for the activities being controlled. Champion has a wealth of historical data on its spark-plug sales and so needs new information on a regular but not necessarily constant basis. For its new products, however, managers took steps to get sales feedback on a more frequent basis. In a retail store, managers usually need daily sales results for activities such as overseeing cash flow and adjusting advertising and promotion. Physical inventory counts, however, may be taken only quarterly or even annually. When a new product comes on the market, managers may need frequent sales reports to gauge public acceptance. For older, more established products, sales reports are needed less often. In general, the more uncertain and unstable the situation, the more frequently measurement is needed; the more stable the situation, the less often it is needed.

Objectivity   To the extent possible, the information provided by the control system should be objective. Consider a human resources manager who asks two plant managers to submit reports summarizing their respective plants' human resources situations. One manager notes that morale at his plant is "okay," that grievances are "about where they should be," and that turnover is "under control." The other reports that absenteeism at her plant is running at 4 percent, that sixteen grievances have been filed this year (compared with twenty-four last year), and that turnover is 12 percent. Which manager's report is more useful? Of course, managers need to look beyond the numbers when making decisions. When a sales representative is posting impressive sales increases every month, or when a production manager is cutting costs consistently, upper-level managers should be pleased. One way to increase sales, however, is to offer unauthorized discounts, make unrealistic guarantees about product performance, or promise early delivery dates. Costs can be cut by decreasing quality or putting unreasonable pressure on employees. For obvious reasons, those techniques may not be in the best interests of the organization. The control system should therefore provide objective information to the manager for evaluation and action, but the manager must take appropriate precautions in interpreting it.

Understanding Resistance to Control

Properly designed control systems are useful and effective, but many people still resist control. Some common reasons for resistance are overcontrol, inappropriate focus, rewards for inefficiency, and accountability.

Overcontrol   Occasionally, organizations make the mistake of overcontrol—they try to control too many things. This becomes especially problematic when the control relates directly to employee behavior. If an organization tells its employees when to come to work, where to park, when to have morning coffee, and when to leave for the day, it is exerting considerable control over their daily activities. Yet many organizations find it necessary to impose these rules. Troubles arise when additional, unnecessary controls are added. Employees who are told how to dress, what they can and cannot put on their desks, and how to wear their hair, are likely to feel overcontrolled. Employees at Chrysler Corp. used to complain because if they drove a non-Chrysler vehicle they were forced to park in a distant parking lot. Drivers of Chrysler products, however, were allowed to park close to the building. If controls are perceived as excessive, employees resist them.

Inappropriate Focus Employees may resist a control system whose focus is inappropriate. The control system may be too narrow, or it may focus too much on quantifiable variables and leave no room for analysis or interpretation. A sales standard that encourages high-pressure tactics to maximize short-run sales may do so at the expense of goodwill from long-term customers. Such a standard is too narrow. A university reward system that encourages faculty members to publish large numbers of articles but fails to consider the quality of the work is also inappropriately focused.

Rewards for Inefficiency Imagine two operating departments that are approaching the end of the fiscal year. One department expects to have $5,000 of its budget left over (because it was efficient); the second is already $3,000 in the red (because it was inefficient). A high ranking bureaucrat, looking only at the numbers, may cut the new budget for department 1 ("They had money left, so they obviously got too much to begin with"), and increase the budget for department 2 ("They obviously haven't been getting enough money"). Thus department 1 is punished for being efficient and department 2 is rewarded for being inefficient. (No wonder departments commonly hasten to deplete their budgets as the end of the year approaches!) People naturally resist this kind of control, because the rewards and punishments associated with spending and conserving are unfair.

Accountability Some people resist control because effective control systems create accountability. When people have the responsibility to do something, effective controls allow managers to determine whether they successfully discharge that responsibility. If standards are properly set and performance is accurately measured, managers not only know when problems arise but also which departments and even which individuals are responsible. Some people, especially those who are not doing a good job, do not want to answer for their mistakes and therefore resist control. The issue of accountability is becoming even more sensitive today as organizations become more adept at monitoring employees. For example, American Express Company has a computer system that provides daily information on how many calls each of its operators handles. And not surprisingly, some of the operators are unhappy with the system.

Overcoming Resistance to Control

Managers overcome resistance to control by ensuring the effectiveness of controls, encouraging participation, using MBO, and developing a good blend of checks and balances.

Create Effective Controls Perhaps the best way to overcome resistance to control is to create effective control to begin with. If control systems are properly integrated with an organization's planning system and if the controls are flexible, accurate, timely, and objective, the organization should not fall victim to the problems of overcontrol, incorrect focus, or rewarding inefficiency. Those employees who fear accountability most (because they are poor performers) will perhaps be held even more accountable for their performance.

Encourage Participation Chapter 12 noted that participation can help overcome resistance to change. By the same token, employees who are involved with planning and implementing the control system are less likely to resist it. For instance, employee participation in planning, decision making, and quality control at the Chevrolet Gear Axle plant in Detroit has resulted in increased employee concern for quality and a greater commitment to meeting standards.[23]

Use MBO Management by objectives, as discussed in Chapter 6, can also overcome employee resistance to control. When MBO is used properly, employees help establish their own goals. These goals, in turn, become standards against which their performance will be measured. Employees also know in advance that their rewards will be based on the extent to which they achieve and maintain those goals and standards. MBO, then, is a vehicle for facilitating the integration of planning and control.

Use Checks and Balances Maintaining a system of checks and balances can also overcome employee resistance to control. Suppose that a production manager argues that he failed to meet a certain cost standard because of the increased prices of raw materials. A properly designed inventory control system will either clearly support or clearly refute the production manager's explanation. Or suppose that an employee who has been fired for excessive absences argues that she has not been absent "for a long time." The human resources control system should have records on the matter. Multiple standards and information systems provide checks and balances for control. Resistance declines because the system of checks and balances serves to protect employees as well as management. For example, if the production manager's argument about the rising cost of raw materials is supported by the inventory control records, he or she will not be held solely accountable for failing to meet the cost standard. Instead, action should be taken to correct the problems of raw materials cost.

CHOOSING A STYLE OF CONTROL

How should a manager develop a style of control? One approach to selecting a style of control bases the decision on four factors: management style, organizational style, performance measures, and employee desire to participate.[24] Table 18.1 suggests four questions about these factors that managers can ask themselves. Management styles are presumed to be either participative (consulting with subordinates) or directive (telling others what to do). Organizational style, which is a composite of culture, structure, and reward systems, can be participative (participative decision making throughout the

In selecting a control system, managers should assess their managerial style and characteristics of the organization, its performance measurement system, and their employees. By answering these questions and using the decision tree in Figure 18.6, managers can gain useful information to use in selecting a style of control.

TABLE 18.1 Questions to Ask When Choosing a Control Strategy

1. **In general, what kind of managerial style do I have?**

   Participative: I frequently consult my subordinates on decisions, encourage them to disagree with my opinion, share information with them, and let them make decisions whenever possible.

   Directive: I usually take most of the responsibility for and make most of the major decisions, pass on only the most necessary job-relevant information, and provide detailed and close direction for my subordinates.

2. **In general, what kind of culture, structure, and reward system does my organization have?**

   Participative: Employees at all levels of the organization are used to participating in decisions and influencing the course of events. Managers are clearly rewarded for developing employees' skills and decision-making capacity.

   Nonparticipative: Most important decisions are made by a few people at the top of the organization. Managers are not rewarded for developing employee competence or encouraging employees to participate in decision making.

3. **How accurate and reliable are the measures of key areas of subordinate performance?**

   Accurate: Measures are reliable, all major aspects of performance can be adequately measured, changes in measures accurately reflect changes in performance, measures cannot be easily sabotaged or faked by subordinates.

   Inaccurate: Not all important aspects of performance can be measured, measures often do not pick up on important changes in performance, good performance cannot be adequately defined in terms of the measures, measures can be easily sabotaged.

4. **Do my subordinates desire to participate and respond well to opportunities to take responsibility for decision making and performance?**

   High desire to participate: Employees are eager to participate in decisions, can make a contribution to decision making, and want to take more responsibility.

   Low desire to participate: Employees do not want to be involved in many decisions, do not want additional responsibility, and have little to contribute to decisions being made.

Source: Reprinted by permission of the *Harvard Business Review*. An exhibit from "Fit Control Systems to Your Management Style" by Cortlandt Cammann and David A. Nadler (January–February 1976). Copyright © 1976 by the President and Fellows of Harvard College; all rights reserved.

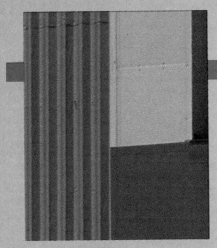

WHEN GENERAL ELECTRIC receives an order to deliver a custom-made industrial circuit-breaker box, it delivers a high quality product in only three days. This time frame is remarkable when you consider that not long ago, GE needed three weeks to fill a comparable order. Even more incredible is that during the three-week era, General Electric had six plants making the boxes. Now they're all made at a single facility.

The key to General Electric's radical improvements has been an entirely new approach to designing and manufacturing products. In the old days (circa 1985), each circuit-breaker box was custom designed. Using as many as 28,000 unique parts, each box was then assembled by hand. Now, however, each box is designed by a computer using specifications supplied by the customer. And the boxes now use only 1,275 parts.

To speed up the process used to design and build the boxes, General Electric totally revamped its approach to designing and manufacturing products. In its circuit-breaker business, for example, General Electric learned that bureaucratic "red tape" at the supervisory level was causing delays. To address this problem, the firm eliminated virtually all supervisory and quality-control positions.

General Electric also decided to close five of the six plants making the boxes and concentrate all production at a single facility. All decisions are now made on the shop floor by the plant's 129 workers, and they make them faster and better than their managers did before the change. Product quality has improved dramatically, while productivity has increased by 20 percent. The plant used to have a two-month backlog of orders; the backlog now hovers around two days.[1] ●

anagers at General Electric have reaped huge payoffs from improving quality and productivity. And they have done so through an area that many organizations used to take for granted—operations management. Quality and productivity have become major determinants of organizational success or failure today. In this chapter we explore first quality and then productivity in detail. We then introduce operations management and its role in improving quality and productivity. Two critical areas of operations management—designing operations systems and using operations systems—are then discussed.

MANAGING QUALITY

Quality has become a central issue in managing organizations today. The catalyst for its emergence as a mainstream management concern was foreign business, especially Japanese. And nowhere was it more visible than in the auto industry. During the energy crisis in the late 1970s, many people bought Toyotas, Hondas, and Nissans because they were more fuel efficient than U.S. cars. Consumers soon found, however, that not only were the Japanese cars more fuel efficient, they were also of higher quality than U.S. cars. Parts fit together better, the trim work was neater, and the cars were more reliable. Thus, after the energy crisis subsided, Japanese cars remained formidable competitors because of their reputations for quality.[2]

The Meaning of Quality

quality
The totality of features and characteristics of a product or service that bear on its ability to satisfy stated or implied needs

The American Society for Quality Control defines **quality** as the totality of features and characteristics of a product or service that bears on its ability to satisfy stated or implied needs.[3] Quality has several different attributes. Table 19.1 lists eight basic dimensions that determine the quality of a particular product or service. For example, a product that has durability and is reliable is of higher quality than a product with less durability and reliability.

Quality is also relative. For example, a Lincoln Continental is a higher-grade car than a Ford Taurus, which, in turn, is a higher-grade car than a Ford Escort. The difference in quality stems from differences in design and other features. The Escort, however, is considered a high-quality car relative to its engineering specifications and price. Likewise, the Taurus and Continental may also be high-quality cars, given their standards and prices. Thus quality is both an absolute and a relative concept.

Quality is relevant for both products and services. While its importance for products like cars and computers was perhaps recognized first, service firms ranging from airlines to restaurants have also come to see that quality is a vitally important determinant of their success or failure. Service quality has become a major competitive issue in U.S. industry today.

The Importance of Quality

To help underscore the importance of quality, the U.S. government created the Malcolm Baldrige Award, named after the former Secretary of Commerce who championed quality in U.S. industry. The award, administered by an agency of the Commerce Department, is given annually to firms that

1. **Performance.** A product's primary operating characteristic. Examples are automobile acceleration and a television set's picture clarity.
2. **Features.** Supplements to a product's basic functioning characteristics, such as power windows on a car.
3. **Reliability.** A probability of not malfunctioning during a specified period.
4. **Conformance.** The degree to which a product's design and operating characteristics meet established standards.
5. **Durability.** A measure of product life.
6. **Serviceability.** The speed and ease of repair.
7. **Aesthetics.** How a product looks, feels, tastes, and smells.
8. **Perceived quality.** As seen by a customer.

Source: Reprinted by permission of *Harvard Business Review*. An exhibit from "Competing on the Eight Dimensions of Quality," by David A. Garvin, *Harvard Business Review* (November/December 1987). Copyright © 1987 by the President and Fellows of Harvard College; all rights reserved.

achieve major improvements in the quality of their products or services. Recent winners of the Baldrige Award include Motorola and the Cadillac Division of General Motors. "Management in Practice" provides a summary of the major contributions to quality management by its foremost pioneers.

Beyond these general reasons, quality is also an important concern for individual managers and organizations for three very specific reasons: competition, productivity, and costs.[4]

Competition Quality has become one of the most competitive points in business today. Among Ford, Chrysler, and General Motors Corp., each argues, for example, that its cars are higher in quality than the cars of the others. IBM, Apple Computer Inc., and Digital Equipment Corp. stress the quality of their products as well. Indeed, it seems that virtually every U.S. business has adopted quality as a major point of competition. Thus a business that fails to keep pace may find itself falling behind not only foreign competition but also other U.S. firms.

Productivity Managers have come to recognize that quality and productivity are related. In the past, many managers thought that they could increase output (productivity) only by decreasing quality. Managers today have learned the hard way that such an assumption is almost always wrong. If a firm installs a meaningful quality enhancement program, three things are likely to result. First, the number of defects is likely to decrease, causing fewer returns from customers. Second, because the number of defects goes down, resources (materials and people) dedicated to reworking flawed output will be decreased. Third, because making employees responsible for quality reduces the need for quality inspectors, the organization is able to produce more units with fewer resources.

Costs Improved quality also lower costs. Poor quality results in higher returns from customers, high warranty costs, and lawsuits from customers

THE QUALITY REVOLUTION

The word quality is turning up everywhere these days, from television commercials to the jackets of best-selling books. Of course, not everyone jumping onto the quality bandwagon can really brag about significant improvements in the products they make or the services they provide. But all this talk about quality *does* reflect a real and significant change in the ways companies around the world are doing their work. Although the Japanese were interested in the thinking of American quality theorists long before American companies began to pay attention to these men, the ideas of W. Edwards Deming, Philip B. Crosby, Joseph M. Juran, and Armand V. Feigenbaum have caught on in classrooms and workplaces everywhere. We are in the midst of a quality revolution.

Most quality experts would agree that if a single day marks the beginning of the quality revolution, it is May 16, 1924, when Walter A. Shewhart wrote a memo to his superiors at Bell Labs. The memo concerned ways to use statistics to improve the quality of the telephones Bell was making. More than 5,000 of the 40,000 employees making telephone equipment in a plant near Chicago were inspectors; the company was spending a lot of money weeding out bad products. Shewhart wanted to reduce all this wasted effort.

Of the four leading American quality experts, **W. Edwards Deming** relies most on statistics and control charts. He met Shewhart in 1938 and applied his statistical methods to train census bureau clerks in the 1930s and engineers and technicians making military materiel during the second World War. After the war, he was invited to give a series of lectures to Japanese business leaders, and his effect on Japanese business was so profound that to this day the highest award for quality in Japan is the Deming Prize.

Deming's approach to quality is philosophical and far-reaching. Although he doesn't think that it is possible to make perfect products every time, he believes in continuously working to improve, and like the other quality experts he focuses on changes in the work process rather than in the product. Rejecting the widely held belief that worker sloppiness is at the core of quality problems, Deming blames almost all lapses of quality on the system created by management. He calls workers "the experts," because they best understand work processes, and he has a reputation for being very hard on managers who want to escape the blame for poor quality.

Unlike Deming, **Philip B. Crosby** is an executive, and he believes perfect is possible; he spread his message of "Zero Defects" and "do it right the first time" through Western Electric and Martin Marietta. After his book *Quality Is Free* became a bestseller in 1979, Crosby quit his job at ITT, and began setting up quality schools around the world. He believes it is possible to measure the cost of poor quality, and that such measurements are necessary in order to combat the notion that quality is expensive. He advocates that quality is not only free, but easy.

Joseph M. Juran, like Deming, knew Shewhart and has become a hero in Japan. Juran got his start in the inspection department of a Western Electric factory, working for the same organization Shewhart and Deming worked for, though they worked in different departments. Whereas

Deming believes that a commitment to quality requires a transformation of the entire organization, Juran feels that managing for quality is akin to managing for finance, a matter of emphasis. Juran also believes that some competition within the organization can be useful, in contrast to Deming, who thinks that competition among workers or work groups is harmful because it detracts from total cooperation.

Armand V. Feigenbaum became General Electric's top quality expert at the age of 24 and made his mark worldwide by publishing a book and articles about Total Quality Control in the early 1950s. He stresses that working to improve quality is an important way to lower costs; like Crosby, he fights the myth that maintaining quality is expensive. In fact, he says that investing in quality improvement pays better dividends than any other investment a company can make.

Despite their differences, today's leading quality experts agree on a number of things: that the push for quality must begin at the top, that workers are generally not to blame for poor quality, that poor quality is more expensive than high quality, and that technological improvements or instituting small parts of a quality agenda—like quality circles—doesn't result in high quality. They don't exactly agree on a definition of quality, but they do all accept that the definition must take into account what will satisfy today's customers—and tomorrow's.

References: William E. Conway, *The Quality Secret: The Right Way to Manage* (Nashua, NH: Conway Quality Inc., 1992); Lloyd Dobyns & Clare Crawford-Mason, *Quality or Else* (Boston: Houghton Mifflin, 1991).

injured by faulty products. Future sales are lost because of disgruntled customers. An organization with quality problems often has to increase inspection expenses just to catch defective products. We noted in Chapter 18 how Whistler Corporation was using 100 of its 250 employees just to fix poorly assembled radar detectors.[5]

Total Quality Management

Once an organization makes the decision to enhance the quality of its products and services, it must then decide how to implement this decision. The most pervasive approach to managing quality has been called **total quality management,** or **TQM**—a real and meaningful effort by an organization to change its whole approach to business to make quality a guiding factor in everything the organization does. Figure 19.1 highlights the major ingredients in TQM.

● **total quality management (TQM)**
A strategic commitment by top management to change its whole approach to business to make quality a guiding factor in everything it does

Strategic Commitment The starting point for TQM is a strategic commitment by top management. Such commitment is important for several reasons. First, the organizational culture must change to recognize that quality is not just an ideal but is instead an objective goal that must be pursued. Second, a decision to pursue the goal of quality carries with it some real costs—for expenditures such as new equipment and facilities. Thus without a commitment from top management, quality improvement will prove to be just a slogan or gimmick, with little or no real change.

F I G U R E 19.1 Total Quality Management

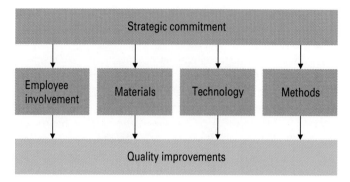

Employee Involvement Employee involvement is another critical ingredient in TQM. Virtually all successful quality enhancement programs involve making the person responsible for doing the job responsible for making sure it is done right.[6] By definition, then, employee involvement is a critical component in improving quality. Work teams, discussed in Chapter 16, are common vehicles for increasing employee involvement.

Technology New forms of technology are also useful in TQM programs. Automation and robots, for example, can often make products with higher precision and better consistency than can people. Investing in higher-grade machines capable of doing jobs more precisely and reliably often improves quality. For example, AT&T has achieved notable improvements in product quality by replacing many of its machines with new equipment.[7]

Materials Another important part of TQM is improving the quality of the materials that organizations use. Suppose that a company that assembles stereos buys chips and circuits from another company. If the chips have a high failure rate, consumers will return defective stereos to the company whose nameplate appears on them, not to the company that made the chips. The stereo firm then loses in two ways: refunds back to customers, and a damaged reputation. As a result many firms have increased the quality requirements they impose on their suppliers as a way of improving the quality of their own products.

Methods Improved methods can improve product and service quality. Methods are operating systems used by the organization during the actual transformation process. American Express Company, for example, has found ways to cut its approval time for new credit cards from twenty-two to only eleven days. This results in improved service quality.[8] Another important method for improving quality, statistical quality control, is discussed later.

MANAGING PRODUCTIVITY

While the current focus on quality by U.S. companies is a relatively recent phenomenon, managers have been aware of the importance of productivity for several years. The stimulus for this attention was a recognition that the gap between productivity in the United States and productivity in other industrialized countries was narrowing. In this section we describe the meaning of productivity and underscore its importance. After summarizing recent productivity trends, we suggest ways that organizations can increase their productivity.

The Meaning of Productivity

In a general sense, **productivity** is an economic measure of efficiency that summarizes the value of outputs relative to the value of the inputs used to create them.[9] Productivity can be and often is assessed at different levels of analysis and in different forms.

productivity
An economic measure of efficiency that summarizes what is produced relative to resources used to produce it

Levels of Productivity   By level of productivity we mean the units of analysis used to calculate or define productivity. For example, aggregate productivity is the total level of productivity achieved by a country. Industry productivity is the total productivity achieved by all the firms in a particular industry. Company productivity, just as the term suggests, is the level of productivity achieved by an individual company. Unit and individual productivity refer to the productivity achieved by a unit or department within an organization and the level of productivity attained by a single person.

Forms of Productivity   There are many different forms of productivity. Total factor productivity is defined by the following formula:

$$\text{Productivity} = \frac{\text{Outputs}}{\text{Inputs}}$$

Total factor productivity is an overall indicator of how well an organization uses all of its resources, such as labor, capital, materials, and energy to create all of its products and services. The biggest problem with total factor productivity is that all the ingredients must be expressed in the same terms—dollars (it is difficult to add hours of labor to number of units of a raw material in a meaningful way). Total factor productivity also gives little insight into how things can be changed to improve productivity. Consequently, most organizations find it more useful to calculate a partial productivity ratio. Such a ratio uses only one category of resource. For example, labor productivity could be calculated by this simple formula:

$$\text{Labor productivity} = \frac{\text{Outputs}}{\text{Direct labor}}$$

This method has two advantages. First, it is not necessary to transform the units of input into some other unit. Second, this method provides managers with specific insights into how changing different resource inputs affects productivity. Suppose that an organization can manufacture 100 units of a particular product with twenty hours of direct labor. The organization's labor productivity index is 5 (or 5 units per labor hour). Now suppose that worker efficiency is increased (through one of the ways to be discussed later in this chapter) so that the same twenty hours of labor results in the manufacture of 120 units of the product. The labor productivity index increases to 6 (6 units per labor hour), and the firm can see the direct results of a specific managerial action.

The Importance of Productivity

Managers consider it important that their firms maintain high levels of productivity for a variety of reasons. Firm productivity is a primary determinant of an organization's level of profitability and, ultimately, its ability to survive. If one organization is more productive than another, it will have more products to sell at lower prices and have more profits to reinvest in other areas. Productivity also partially determines people's standards of living within a particular country. At an economic level, businesses consume resources and produce goods and services. The goods and services created within a country can be used by that country's own citizens or exported for sale in other countries. The more goods and services the businesses within a country can produce, the more goods and services the country's citizens will have. Even goods that are exported result in financial resources flowing back into the home country. Thus the citizens of a highly productive country are likely to have notably higher standards of living than are the citizens of a country with low productivity.

Productivity Trends

The United States has the highest level of productivity in the world. For example, Japanese workers produce only about 73 percent as much as U.S. workers, while German workers produce about 82 percent as much.[10] An alarming trend began in the 1960s, however, and continued into the 1980s. During this time, the rate of productivity growth in the United States slowed, especially in comparison to the rates in other industrialized countries. That is, while U.S. workers continued to be the most productive workers in the world, their counterparts in Japan, Germany, and similar countries began to close the gap.

This trend was a primary factor in the decisions made by U.S. businesses to retrench, retool, and become more competitive in the world marketplace. For example, General Electric's dishwasher plant in Louisville has cut its inventory requirements by 50 percent, reduced labor costs from 15 percent to only 10 percent of total manufacturing costs, and cut product development time in half.[11] The chapter-opening incident clearly documents major productivity gains in another GE business. As a result of these and other efforts, productivity trends have now leveled out and U.S. workers are generally maintaining their lead in most industries.

Several factors have been cited to account for the productivity slowdowns recorded during the 1960s and 1970s.[12] First, the composition of the U.S. work force has undergone major changes. After World War II more and more of the general population went to college. Thus postwar gains in productivity were at least partially attributable to higher levels of education. Later, as the proportion of workers with higher education leveled off, productivity gains also tended to level off. Another factor is that the work force absorbed many new and inexperienced employees during the last decade, as more and more women and younger workers joined the work force.

A second contributing factor was a decline in the quality of U.S. production facilities relative to facilities in the rest of the world. Generally, existing factories continued to operate as they had in years past, while companies in other countries were investing heavily in new and highly efficient facilities. For example, in 1990 the average U.S. plant was almost eighteen years old. Its counterpart in Japan was less than twelve years old.

A final contributor was the tremendous growth of the service sector in the United States. While this sector grew, its productivity levels did not. One part of this problem relates to measurement. For example, it is fairly easy to calculate the number of tons of steel produced at a Bethlehem Steel mill and divide it by the number of labor hours used; it is more difficult to determine the output of an attorney or a Certified Public Accountant. Still, virtually everyone agrees that improving service-sector productivity is the next major hurdle facing U.S. business.

Improving Productivity

How does a business or industry improve its productivity? Numerous specific suggestions made by experts generally fall into two broad categories: improving operations and increasing employee involvement.

Improving Operations   One way that firms can improve operations is by spending more on research and development. R&D spending helps identify new products, new uses for existing products, and new methods for making products. Each of these contributes to productivity. For example, Bausch & Lomb almost missed the boat on extended-wear contact lenses because the company had neglected R&D. When it became apparent that its major competitors were almost a year ahead of Bausch & Lomb in developing the new lenses, management made R&D a top-priority concern. As a result, the company made several scientific breakthroughs, shortened the time needed to introduce new products, and greatly enhanced both total sales and profits—and all with a smaller work force than the company used to employ.[13] Even though other countries are greatly increasing their R&D spending, the United States continues to be the world leader in this area.[14]

Dodge Viper is not the car of the year because it is snazzy or sporty or red—though here it is all three. Rather, accolades go to Chrysler for meeting its goal of producing a car from start to finish in less than thirty-six months. The development effort was restricted to 85 people and $70 million. By comparison, Chrysler spent $600 million revamping the minivan in 1991. Suggestions for improving productivity fall into two categories: improving operations and increasing employee involvement. Chrysler utilized both.

Another way firms can boost productivity through operations is by reassessing and revamping their transformation facilities. The opening incident describes how one of GE's modernized plants does a better job than six antiquated ones. Just building a new factory is no guarantee of success, but IBM, Ford Motor Co., Allen-Bradley, Caterpillar Inc., and many other businesses have achieved dramatic productivity gains by revamping their production facilities. Facilities refinements are not limited to manufacturers. In recent years, many McDonald's restaurants have added drive-through windows, and many are moving soft-drink dispensers out to the restaurant floor so that customers can get their own drinks. Each of these moves is an attempt to increase the speed with which customers can be served, and thus to increase productivity.

Increasing Employee Involvement   The other major thrust in productivity enhancement has been toward employee involvement. We noted earlier that participation can enhance quality. So, too, can it boost productivity. Examples of this involvement are an individual worker being given a bigger voice in how she does her job, a formal agreement of cooperation between management and labor, and total involvement throughout the organization. Recall how GE eliminated most of the supervisors at its remaining circuit-breaker plant and put control in the hands of workers.

Another method popular in the United States is increasing the flexibility of an organization's work force by training employees to perform a number of different jobs. Such cross-training allows the firm to function with fewer workers because workers can be transferred easily to areas where they are most needed. For example, the Lechmere department store in Sarasota, Florida, encourages workers to learn numerous jobs within the store. One person in the store can operate a forklift in the stockroom, serve as a cashier, or provide customer service on the sales floor. At a Motorola plant, 397 of 400 employees have learned at least two skills under a similar program.

Rewards are essential to making employee involvement work. Firms must reward people for learning new skills and using them proficiently. At Motorola, for example, workers who master a new skill are assigned for five days to a job requiring them to use that skill. If they perform with no defects, they are moved to a higher pay grade, and then they move back and forth between jobs as they are needed. If there is a performance problem, they receive more training and practice. This approach is fairly new, but preliminary indicators suggest that it can increase productivity significantly. Many unions resist such programs because they threaten job security and reduce a person's identification with one skill or craft.[15]

MANAGING QUALITY AND PRODUCTIVITY THROUGH OPERATIONS MANAGEMENT

We noted earlier that both quality and productivity can be enhanced through various elements of operations. But what exactly are operations? And how are they managed? **Operations management** is the set of managerial activities used by an organization to transform resource inputs into products and services.[16] When IBM buys electronic components, assembles them into computers, and then ships them to customers, it is relying on operations

● **operations management**
The total set of managerial activities used by an organization to transform resource inputs into products, services, or both

management. When a Pizza Hut Inc. employee orders food and paper products and then combines dough, cheese, and tomato paste to create a pizza, he or she is using operations management.

The Importance of Operations

Operations is an important functional concern for organizations because efficient and effective management of operations goes a long way toward ensuring quality and productivity. Inefficient or ineffective operations management, on the other hand, will almost inevitably lead to lower levels of both quality and productivity. In an economic sense, operations management provides utility, or value, of one type or another, depending on the nature of the firm's products or services. If the product is a physical good, such as a Yamaha motorcycle, operations provides form utility by combining many dissimilar inputs (sheet metal, rubber, paint, combustion engines, and human craftsmanship) to produce the desired output. The inputs are converted from their incoming forms into a new physical form. This conversion is typical of manufacturing operations and essentially reflects the organization's technology.

In contrast, the operations activities of American Airlines Inc. provide time and place utility through its services. The airline transports passengers and freight according to agreed-on departure and arrival places and times. Other service operations, such as a Coors Brothers Beer distributorship or The Gap Inc. retail chain, provide place and possession utility by bringing the customer and products made by others together. Although the organizations in these examples produce different kinds of products or services, their operations processes share many important features.[17]

Manufacturing and Production

Because manufacturing once dominated U.S. industry, the entire area of operations management used to be called production management. **Manufacturing** is a form of business that combines and transforms resources into tangible outcomes that are then sold to others. The Goodyear Tire & Rubber Company is a manufacturer because it combines rubber and chemical compounds and uses blending equipment and molding machines to ultimately create tires. Broyhill is a manufacturer because it buys wood and metal components, pads, and fabric and then combines them into furniture.

During the 1970s, manufacturing entered a long period of decline in the United States, primarily because of foreign competition. U.S. firms had grown lax and sluggish, and new foreign competitors came onto the scene with new equipment and much higher levels of efficiency. For example, steel companies in the Far East were able to produce high-quality steel for much lower prices than were U.S. companies like Bethlehem Steel and U.S. Steel (now USX Corporation). Faced with a battle for survival, many companies underwent a long and difficult period of change by eliminating waste and transforming themselves into leaner and more efficient and responsive entities. They reduced their work forces dramatically, closed antiquated or unnecessary plants, and modernized their remaining plants. In recent years, their efforts have started to pay dividends as U.S. business has regained its competitive position in many different industries. Although manufacturers from other parts of the world are still formidable competitors

manufacturing
A form of business that combines and transforms resource inputs into tangible outcomes

In response to foreign competition, U.S. manufacturing companies have gone through a process of eliminating waste and becoming more efficient and responsive to customer needs. Springs Industries has invested $500 million in the past five years to improve quality and productivity. Its new wide-screen printing technology enables it to ensure high quality on small production runs, resulting in less inventory and more flexibility.

service organization
An organization that transforms resources into services

speed
The time needed by the organization to get its activities, including developing, making, and distributing products or services accomplished

and U.S. firms may never again be competitive in some markets, the overall picture is much better than it was just a few years ago. And prospects continue to look bright.[18]

Service Operations

During the decline of the manufacturing sector, a tremendous growth in the service sector kept the U.S. economy from declining at the same rate.[19] A **service organization** is one that transforms resources into an intangible output and creates time or place utility for its customers. For example, Merrill Lynch Co. Inc. makes stock transactions for its customers, Avis leases cars to its customers, and your local hairdresser cuts your hair. In 1947, the service sector was responsible for less than half of the U.S. gross national product (GNP). By 1975, however, this figure reached 65 percent, and by 1991 it approached 73 percent. The service sector was responsible for almost 90 percent of all new jobs created in the United States during the 1980s.[20] Managers have come to see that many of the tools, techniques, and methods that are used in a factory are also useful to a service firm. For example, managers of automobile plants and hair salons each have to decide how to design their facility, identify the best location for it, determine optimal capacity, make decisions about inventory storage, set procedures for purchasing raw materials, and set standards for productivity and quality.

The Role of Operations in Organizational Strategy

It should be clear by this point that operations management is very important to organizations. Beyond its direct impact on quality and productivity, it also directly influences the organization's overall level of effectiveness. Obviously, then, operations management needs to be addressed at every level, starting at the top. For example, the deceptively simple strategic decision whether to stress high quality regardless of cost, lowest possible cost regardless of quality, or some combination of the two, has numerous important implications. A highest-possible quality strategy will dictate state-of-the-art technology and rigorous control of product design and materials specifications. A combination strategy might call for lower-grade technology and less concern about product design and materials specifications. Just as strategy affects operations management, so too does operations management affect strategy. Suppose that a firm decides to upgrade the quality of its products or services. The organization's ability to implement the decision is dependent in part on current production capabilities and other resources. If existing technology will not permit higher-quality work and if the organization lacks the resources to replace its technology, increasing quality to the desired new standards will be difficult.

A recent survey identified speed as the number-one strategic issue confronting managers in the 1990s.[21] **Speed** is the time needed by the organization to get something accomplished, and it can be emphasized in any area, including developing, making, and distributing products or services. The opening incident provides an example of the kinds of breakthroughs organizations like General Electric are achieving. Table 19.2 identifies a number of basic suggestions that have helped companies increase the speed of their operations. For example, GE found it better to start from scratch with a remodeled plant. GE also wiped out the need for approvals by eliminating

T A B L E 19.2   Guidelines for Increasing the Speed of Operations

1. Start from scratch (it's usually easier than trying to do what the organization does now faster).
2. Minimize the number of approvals needed to do something (the fewer people who have to approve something, the faster it will get done).
3. Use work teams as a basis for organization (teamwork and cooperation work better than individual effort and conflict).
4. Develop and adhere to a schedule (a properly designed schedule can greatly increase speed).
5. Don't ignore distribution (making something faster is only part of the battle).
6. Integrate speed into the organization's culture (if everyone understands the importance of speed, things will naturally get done quicker).

Source: Adapted from Brian Dumaine, "How Managers Can Succeed Through Speed," *Fortune*, February 13, 1989, pp. 54–59. The Time Inc. Magazine Company. All rights reserved.

Many organizations today are using speed for competitive advantage. These are six common guidelines that organizations follow when they want to shorten the time they need to get things accomplished. While not every manager can do each of these things, most managers can do at least some of them. Increasing speed will give organizations a strategic advantage and help them compete more effectively.

most managerial positions, and set up teams as a basis for organizing work. Stressing the importance of the schedule helped Motorola, Inc. build a new plant and start production of a new product in only eighteen months.

Distribution is equally important. Benetton Group SPA, for example, has only one warehouse to serve 5,000 stores in sixty countries. But the state-of-the-art facility, which cost $30 million to build, ships 230,000 pieces of clothing daily—and employs only eight persons! And, finally, organizations must instill an appreciation for speed in their corporate culture. Honda Motor Co. Ltd., for example, started supporting Formula One car racing only a few years ago. But since new engineers have been rotating through the Formula One team, the entire organization has placed a higher value on speed.

DESIGNING OPERATIONS SYSTEMS

The problems faced by operations managers as they attempt to improve quality and productivity revolve around the acquisition and utilization of resources for conversion. Their goals include both efficiency and effectiveness. A number of issues and decisions must be addressed as operations systems are designed.[22] The most basic ones are technology (covered in Chapter 20), product-service mix, capacity, and facilities.

Product-Service Mix

A natural starting point in designing operations systems to enhance quality and productivity is determining the **product-service** mix. This decision flows from corporate, business, and marketing strategies. Managers have to make a number of decisions about their products and services, starting with how many and what kinds to offer. The Procter & Gamble Co., for example, makes regular, tartar-control, and gel formulas of Crest toothpaste and packages them in several different sizes of tubes and pumps. Decisions also have to be made regarding the level of quality desired, the

product-service mix
How many and what kinds of products, services (or both) to offer

optimal cost of each product or service, and exactly how each is to be designed. GE, for example, reduced the number of parts in its industrial circuit breakers from 28,000 to 1,275. The whole process involved product design. "The Global View" summarizes how Suchard mishandled several Brach products.

Capacity

● capacity
The amount of products, services, or both that can be produced by an organization

The **capacity** decision involves choosing the amount of products, services, or both that can be produced by the organization. Determining whether to build a factory capable of making 5,000 or 8,000 units per day is a capacity decision. So, too, is deciding whether to build a restaurant with 100 or 150 seats or a bank with five or ten teller stations. The capacity decision is truly a high-risk one because of the uncertainties of future product demand and the large monetary stakes involved. An organization that builds capacity exceeding its needs may commit resources (capital investment) that will never be recovered. Many firms made this mistake during the 1960s and 1970s. Alternatively, an organization can build a facility with a smaller capacity than expected demand. Doing so may result in lost market opportunities, but it may also free capital resources for use elsewhere in the organization.

A major consideration in determining capacity is demand. A company operating with fairly constant monthly demand might build a plant capable of producing an amount each month roughly equivalent to its demand. But if its market is characterized by seasonal fluctuations, building a smaller plant to meet normal demand and then adding extra shifts during peak periods might be the most effective choice. Likewise, a restaurant that needs 150 seats for Saturday night but never needs more than 100 at any other time during the week would probably be foolish to expand to 150 seats. During the rest of the week, it must still pay to light, heat, cool, and clean the excess capacity.

Facilities

● facilities
The physical locations where products or services are created, stored, and distributed

● location
The physical positioning or geographic site of facilities

● layout
The physical configuration of facilities, the arrangement of equipment within facilities, or both

● product layout
A physical configuration of facilities arranged around the product; used when large quantities of a single product are needed

Facilities are the physical locations where products or services are created, stored, and distributed. Major decisions pertain to location and layout.

Location   **Location** is the physical positioning or geographic site of facilities, and must be determined by the needs and requirements of the organization. A company that relies heavily on railroads for transportation needs to be located close to rail facilities. GE decided that it did not need six plants to make circuit breakers, so it invested heavily in automating one plant and closed the other five. Different organizations in the same industry may have different facilities requirements. Benetton uses only one distribution center for the entire world, whereas K mart Corp. has several distribution centers in the United States alone. A retail business must choose its location very carefully to be convenient for consumers.

Layout   The choice of physical configuration, or the **layout,** of facilities is closely related to other operations decisions. The three entirely different layout alternatives shown in Figure 19.2 help demonstrate the importance of the layout decision. A **product layout** is appropriate when large quantities of a single product are needed. It makes sense to custom design a

A NOT-SO-SWEET BUSINESS FOR A FOREIGNER

Klaus Jacobs, a Swiss billionaire, understands European eating habits and how to appeal to the European sweet tooth. He expanded his family's coffee business into a major force in the European candy market by buying two famous Swiss brands, Suchard and Tobler, in 1982. To get better U.S. distribution for his fancy candies, in 1987 Jacobs bought E. J. Brach Corp., an eighty-three-year-old Chicago-based company that held about two-thirds of the U.S. market for candy sold in bags.

Jacobs's control of Brach was such a failure that when Philip Morris bought most of Jacobs's holdings in 1990, it refused to buy Brach. Jacobs knew candy, but he didn't understand U.S. distribution systems, retailers, or candy-eating habits.

Examples of Jacobs's confusion are numerous. While U.S. consumers concentrate their candy buying at Halloween, Christmas, Valentine's Day, and Easter, Europeans tend to eat candy year-round. So under Jacobs, Brach failed to run its holiday promotions. The United States has more stores and more types of stores than Jacobs was used to. When Jacobs reduced the product line from 1,700 items to 400, a move that made sense from some angles, he overlooked the reason that Brach had been making all those products in a wide variety of sizes. Grocery,

drug, and discount stores that might be selling Brach in the same mall needed different products with different profit margins. In essence, U.S. retailers buy a product line, not individual products, and when Brach no longer offered the full range of products that they wanted, retailers began buying from other suppliers.

For two years, Brach's sales and market share plummeted, until Jacobs in effect admitted his mistake, brought back some of the Brach executives he had fired, and put Peter Rogers, a veteran of the U.S. candy business, in charge. Rogers reversed most of Jacobs's decisions, beefing up Brach's product line again and trying to provide everything that retailers needed. While keeping its own sales personnel to handle large national accounts, Brach turned over its regional accounts to candy brokerage firms, recognizing that it didn't have the sales force to compete head-to-head with candy giants like Mars and Hershey.

The re-Americanization of Brach slowly took effect, and the company's balance sheets began showing profits again in the 1990s. Chances are a company selling candy to U.S. consumers will never again miss a Valentine's Day promotion.

References: Amy Feldman, "Arrogance Goeth Before a Fall," *Forbes*, September 30, 1991, pp. 82–87; Merrill Goozner, "Brach Cuts Much of its Sales Force," *Chicago Tribune*, March 16, 1991, p. C1.

---

straight-line flow of work for a product when a specific task is performed at each workstation as each unit flows past. Most assembly lines use this format. For example, IBM's personal computer factories use a product layout.

Process layouts are used in operations settings that create or process a variety of products. Auto repair shops and healthcare clinics are good examples. Each car and each person is a separate "product." The needs of each incoming job are diagnosed as it enters the operations system, and the job is routed through the unique sequence of workstations needed to create the desired finished product. In a process layout, each type of conversion task is centralized in a single workstation or department. All welding is done in one designated shop location, and any car that requires welding is moved to that area. This setup is in contrast to the product layout, in which several different workstations may perform welding operations if the conversion task sequence so dictates.

The **fixed-position layout** is used when the organization is creating a few very large and complex products. Aircraft manufacturers like The Boe-

● **process layout**
A physical configuration of facilities arranged around the process; used in facilities that create or process a variety of products

● **fixed-position layout**
A physical configuration of facilities arranged around a single work area; used for the manufacture of large and complex products such as airplanes

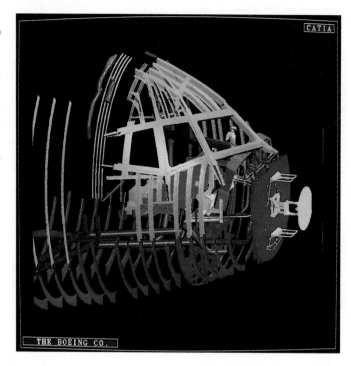

When an organization, such as the Boeing Co., creates a few large and complex products, it uses a fixed-position layout. Before actual production on the Boeing 777 airliner could begin, 7,000 specialists linked by eight mainframe computers and 2,800 computer workstations designed the aircraft. The 777 is the largest product ever designed completely by computer.

ing Co. and shipbuilders like Newport News use this method. An assembly line capable of moving a 747 would require an enormous plant, so instead the airplane itself remains stationary, and people and machines move around it as it is assembled.

USING OPERATIONS SYSTEMS

After operations systems have been properly designed, they must then be put into use by the organization. Their basic functional purpose is to control transformation processes to ensure that relevant goals are achieved in areas such as quality and costs. Operations has a number of special purposes within this control framework, including purchasing and inventory management.

Operations Management as Control

One way of using operations management as control is to coordinate it with other functions. Monsanto Company, for example, established a consumer products division that produces and distributes fertilizers and lawn chemicals. To facilitate control the operations function was organized as an autonomous profit center. Monsanto finds this effective because its manufacturing division is given the authority to determine not only the costs of creating the product but also the product price and the marketing programs.

In terms of overall organizational control, a division like the one used by Monsanto should be held accountable only for the activities over which it has decision-making authority. It would be inappropriate, of course, to make operations accountable for profitability in an organization that stresses sales and market share over quality and productivity. Misplaced accountability results in ineffective organizational control, to say nothing of hostil-

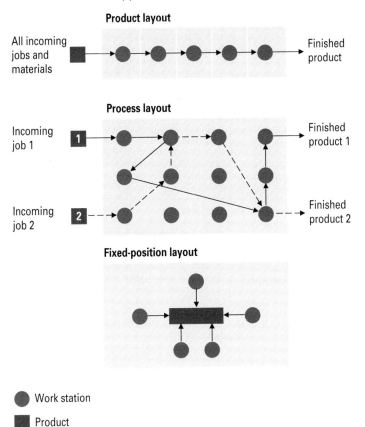

Product layout

All incoming jobs and materials

Finished product

Process layout

Incoming job 1

Finished product 1

Incoming job 2

Finished product 2

Fixed-position layout

● Work station

■ Product

When a manufacturer produces large quantities of a product (such as cars or computers) it may arrange its facilities into an assembly line (product layout). In a process layout, the work (such as patients in a hospital or custom pieces of furniture) moves through a variety of workstations. Locomotives and bridges are both manufactured in a fixed position layout.

ity and conflict. Depending on the strategic role of operations, then, operations managers are accountable for different kinds of results. For example, in an organization using bureaucratic control, accountability will be spelled out in rules and regulations. In a clan system, it is likely to be understood and accepted by everyone.

Within operations, managerial control ensures that resources and activities achieve primary goals such as a high percentage of on-time deliveries, low unit-production cost, or high product reliability. Any control system should focus on the elements that are most crucial to goal attainment. For example, firms in which product quality is a major concern (as it is at Rolex Co.) might adopt a screening control system to monitor the product as it is being created. If quantity is a pressing issue (as it is at Timex Group Ltd.), a postaction system might be used to identify defects at the end of the system without disrupting the manufacturing process itself.

Purchasing Management

Purchasing management is concerned with buying the materials and resources needed to create products and services.[23] Thus the purchasing manager for a retailer like Sears, Roebuck is responsible for buying the merchandise the store will sell. The purchasing manager for a manufacturer buys raw materials, parts, and machines needed by the organization. Large companies like GE, IBM, and Westinghouse have large purchasing departments.

● **purchasing management**
Buying materials and resources needed to produce products and services

The manager responsible for purchasing must balance a number of constraints. Buying too much ties up capital and increases storage costs. Buying too little might lead to shortages and high reordering costs. The manager must also make sure that the quality of what is purchased meets the organization's needs, that the supplier is reliable, and that the best financial terms are negotiated.

Many firms have recently changed their approach to purchasing as a means to lower costs and improve quality and productivity. In particular, rather than relying on hundreds or even thousands of suppliers, many companies are reducing their number of suppliers and negotiating special production-delivery arrangements. For example, the Honda plant in Marysville, Ohio, found a local business owner looking for a new opportunity. They negotiated an agreement whereby he would start a new company to mount car stereo speakers into plastic moldings. He delivers finished goods to the plant three times a day, and Honda buys all he can manufacture. Thus he has a stable sales base, Honda has a local and reliable supplier, and both companies benefit.[24]

Inventory Management

● **inventory control**
Managing the organization's raw materials, work-in-process, finished goods, and products in transit

Inventory control, also called materials control, is essential for effective operations management.[25] The four basic kinds of inventories are *raw materials, work-in-process, finished-goods,* and *in-transit* inventories. As shown in Table 19.3, the sources of control over these inventories are as different as their purposes. Work-in-process inventories, for example, are made up of partially completed products that need further processing; they are controlled by the shop floor system. In contrast, the quantities and costs of finished-goods inventories are under the control of the overall production scheduling system, which is determined by high-level planning decisions.

JIT is a recent breakthrough in inventory management. With JIT inventory systems, materials arrive just as they are needed. JIT therefore helps an organization control its raw materials inventory by reducing the amount of space it must devote to storage.

TABLE 19.3   Inventory Types, Purposes, and Sources of Control

Type	Purpose	Source of Control
Raw materials	Provides the materials needed to make the product	Purchasing models and systems
Work-in-process	Enables overall production to be divided into stages of manageable size	Shop-floor control systems
Finished goods	Provides ready supply of products on customer demand and enables long, efficient production runs	High-level production scheduling systems in conjunction with marketing
In-transit (pipeline)	Distributes products to customers	Transportation and distribution control systems

In-transit inventories are controlled by the transportation and distribution systems.

Like most other areas of operations management, inventory management changed notably in recent years. One particularly important breakthrough is the **just-in-time (JIT) method.** First popularized by the Japanese, the JIT system reduces the organization's investment in storage space for raw materials and in the materials themselves. Historically, manufacturers built large storage areas and filled them with materials, parts, and supplies that would be needed days, weeks, and even months in the future. A manager using the JIT approach orders materials and parts more often and in smaller quantities, thereby reducing investment in both storage space and actual inventory. The ideal arrangement is for materials to arrive just as they are needed—or just in time.

Recall our example about the small firm that assembles stereo speakers for Honda and delivers them three times a day, making it unnecessary for Honda to carry large quantities of the speakers in inventory. In an even more striking example, Johnson Controls Inc. makes automobile seats for Chrysler Corp. and ships them by small truckloads to a Chrysler plant seventy-five miles away. Each shipment is scheduled to arrive two hours before it is needed. Clearly, the JIT approach requires high levels of coordination and cooperation between the company and its suppliers. If shipments arrive too early, Chrysler has no place to store them. If they arrive too late, the entire assembly line may have to be shut down, resulting in enormous expense. When properly designed and used, the JIT method controls inventory very effectively.

> **just-in-time (JIT) method**
> An inventory system that has necessary materials arriving as soon as they are needed (just in time) so that the production process is not interrupted

Operations Control Techniques

Several specialized techniques have been developed to facilitate operations control. These include materials requirements planning, statistical quality control, and the economic order quantity. (PERT, discussed in Chapter 9, is also used for control.)

Materials Requirements Planning   An important part of operations management is determining what materials and services are necessary to do the work of the organization. Consider a contractor who is about to construct a new house. One of the basic materials needed will be 2- × 4-inch lumber for framing the walls. The contractor will determine in advance how much lumber will be required. Of course, if the 2 × 4's are delivered too early, they may be stolen or scattered. But construction will be delayed if they are delivered too late. The process of determining how much lumber to buy and when to have it delivered is an operations issue. In recent years, attention has focused on a new approach to this activity called **materials requirements planning (MRP).**[26]

The first step in an MRP system is to specify the materials and parts needed for production and operations. These materials and parts are generally listed in a document called a *bill of materials (BOM)*. The BOM for a pizza parlor might include flour, tomato paste, cheese, various toppings, napkins, and soft-drink syrup. The BOM for a complex product like an automobile or airplane lists thousands of parts. The next step is to determine inventory on hand—the organization does not want to order more materials than it needs. The manager using the MRP system then establishes ordering

> **materials requirements planning (MRP)**
> A system that integrates production and inventory control

and delivery schedules for materials and parts that are needed. A fast-food restaurant like McDonald's Corp. gets daily delivery of perishables such as hamburger meat from a local supplier. Delivery time for an advanced guidance system for a fighter plane might be months or years.

One of the great advantages of an MRP system is its ability to juggle delivery schedules and lead times effectively. When hundreds of parts are needed in different quantities and delivery times range from a day to several months, coordination is impossible for individual managers. But an MRP system can arrange things so that parts and materials are ordered in such a way as to arrive on schedule. The computer-generated reports usually initiate the ordering of parts and materials. In sophisticated systems, the computer may even be programmed to place the order automatically. Many large manufacturing firms like Westinghouse, Texas Instruments, Boise-Cascade, and Lockheed have made effective use of MRP systems.

statistical quality control (SQC)
A set of specific statistical techniques that can be used to monitor quality: includes acceptance sampling and in-process sampling

Statistical Quality Control Another increasingly useful operations management control technique is **statistical quality control (SQC).** As the term suggests, SQC is primarily concerned with managing quality. Moreover, it is a set of specific statistical techniques that can be used to monitor quality.[27] Acceptance sampling involves sampling finished goods to ensure that quality standards have been met. Acceptance sampling is effective only when the correct percentage of products that should be tested (for example, 2, 5, or 25 percent) is determined. This decision is especially important when the test renders the product useless. Flash cubes, wine, and collapsible steering wheels, for example, are consumed or destroyed during testing. Another SQC method is in-process sampling. In-process sampling involves evaluating products during production so that needed changes can be made. The painting department of a furniture company might periodically check the tint of the paint it is using. The company can then adjust the color as necessary to conform to customer standards. The advantage of in-process sampling is that it allows problems to be detected before they accumulate.

economic order quantity (EOQ)
A mathematically determined quantity of what should be ordered to optimize the costs of carrying inventory, placing orders, and stocking out

Economic Order Quantity Another control technique used by many firms, especially small ones, is the **economic order quantity (EOQ).** The EOQ is a mathematically determined quantity of how much should be ordered to optimize the costs of carrying inventory, placing orders, and stocking out. The EOQ formula is

$$EOQ = \sqrt{\frac{2RS}{C}}$$

where R = yearly requirement of what is being ordered
S = ordering or setup cost
C = carrying costs per unit

For example, if we use 4,500 units per year, if setup costs are $20, and if carrying costs are $.50 per unit, then each order should be for 600 units.

SUMMARY OF KEY POINTS

Quality is a major consideration for all managers today. Quality is important because it affects competition, productivity, and costs. Total quality management is a comprehensive, organization-wide effort to enhance quality through a variety of avenues.

Productivity is also a major concern to managers. Productivity is a measure of how efficiently an organization is using its resources to create products or services. The United States still leads the world in individual productivity, but other industrialized nations are catching up.

Quality and productivity are often addressed via operations management, the set of managerial activities that organizations use in creating their products and services. Operations management is important to both manufacturing and service organizations. It plays an important role in an organization's strategy.

The starting point in operations management is designing operations systems. Key areas of concern are product and service design, capacity, facilities, and technology.

After an operations system has been designed and put into place, it serves a critical role in control. Major areas of interest during the use of operations systems are purchasing and inventory management. Several specialized techniques are available to help managers control operations.

DISCUSSION QUESTIONS

Questions for Review

1. What is quality? Why is it so important today?

2. What is productivity? How can it be increased?

3. What is the relationship of operations management to overall organizational strategy? Where do productivity and quality fit into that relationship?

4. What are the major components of operations systems? How are they designed?

Questions for Analysis

5. How might the management functions of planning, organizing, and leading relate to the management of quality and productivity?

6. Some people argue that quality and productivity are inversely related; as one goes up, the other goes down. How can that argument be refuted?

7. Is operations management most closely linked to corporate-level, business-level, or functional strategies? Why or in what way?

Questions for Application

8. Interview local managers in different kinds of organizations (business, service, religious) to determine how they deal with quality and productivity.

9. Consider your college or university as an organization. How might it go about developing a TQM program?

10. Go to the library and locate information on several different organizations' uses of operations management. What similarities and differences do you find? Why do you think those similarities and differences exist?

GENERAL MOTORS KEEPS SEARCHING FOR THE SECRET

*D*uring the last decade General Motors Corp. seems finally to have accepted that business as usual will no longer work. After years of steady growth, GM began faltering in the 1970s with the first oil crises and the invasion of less expensive, more efficient, and better-built Japanese cars. By 1991, GM's North American operations were losing $6 billion a year and announcing layoffs of thousands of employees. Worse still, the company hasn't found the secret to turning things around.

One problem that has long plagued the auto-making giant is simply its size: GM is often cited as the perfect example of the bloated, slow-moving corporation. Its recent layoffs and factory closings are part of an ongoing attempt to become leaner and more efficient, a program that is expected to save $5 billion annually through 1995.

GM has also belatedly jumped on the quality bandwagon and is building cars that have fewer defects and that hold up better than they used to. The Japanese, however, have also been improving and by some measurements are actually widening the quality gap.

After studying Japanese corporations, GM began imitating many aspects of the Japanese production system. When it built a new $1.2 billion factory in Orion Township, Michigan, in the early 1980s, GM thought robotics might be the key, and it installed 170 robots in the plant. It also imitated the Japanese practice of reducing the number of job categories and encouraging workers to become proficient at a number of different tasks. Despite these innovations, the Orion plant still ranks among the company's worst in product quality.

Ironically, one of GM's few success stories takes place at an older factory in Oklahoma City. In 1990, one of the plant's products, the Pontiac 6000, ranked higher than any other U.S. car on J. D. Power's list of trouble-free cars. One reason is the plant's own version of just-in-time manufacturing. The factory has radically reduced inventory, and the plant manager proudly shows off an open space the size of a high school gym that used to be full of parts waiting to be worked on. The "synchronous manufacturing" or "lean production" system doesn't use backup machines and quality control workers; parts keep moving through the plant from station to station, and if a machine breaks, workers quickly alert repair teams. They can't simply switch to another machine or work on a backlog of parts.

The lean production system accounts for part of the Oklahoma City plant's relative success, but just as important are the unusually good relations between workers and management. At the Orion plant, distrust is epidemic, sometimes breaking into violence. Although the secrets to GM's profitability still seem elusive, the Oklahoma City plant's experience indicates that the company needs to look at old lessons as well as new ones.

Discussion Questions

1. How might the use of robots be related to the Orion plant's problems with labor-management relations?

2. What problems are likely to arise when a factory tries to introduce piecemeal changes in production techniques?

E 3. In deciding which plants to close, how heavily should GM consider the effects a closing will have on a particular community and its workers?

References: Gregory A. Patterson, "Two GM Auto Plants Illustrate Major Role of Workers' Attitudes," *The Wall Street Journal,* August 29, 1991, pp. A1, A4; Bradley A. Stertz, "Big Three Boost Car Quality but Still Lag," *The Wall Street Journal,* March 27, 1989, pp. B1, B8; David Woodruff, "GM Can't Downshift Fast Enough," *Business Week,* December 30, 1991, p. 37.

Although few people living in the United States have heard of Kyocera Corporation, four surveys in recent years have listed Kyocera as the company that Japanese executives most admire for its entrepreneurial and technological progress. Much of the basic technology for its most important products—industrial ceramics—was pioneered by a U.S. company, but Kyocera officials now estimate that 90 percent of the products Kyocera makes originated in its own laboratories, where "amoebas" are in control.

The driving force behind Kyocera, Kazuo Inamori, has been making a name for himself as an entrepreneur and an innovator ever since he got a doctorate in chemical engineering and went to work for Sofu Industries. Rejecting the Japanese tradition of deference to superiors, he argued with his research director at Sofu, quit, and founded Kyoto Ceramics in 1959. (The name was soon shortened to Kyocera.) Now the head of a company with more than $2.5 billion in sales each year, Inamori is still breaking the rules.

Inamori's U.S.–style entrepreneurial bent is combined with some typically Japanese elements, like the regimented early morning employee exercises in the parking lot, and with some ideas that are purely Inamori's own, like "amoebas." Kyocera's amoebas take the concept of autonomous work teams to its logical extreme. They form and dissolve according to the needs of a particular project, and they can include from two to hundreds of people. Every supervisor and virtually every executive is in charge of an amoeba. Each amoeba makes its own decisions about purchases and suppliers, although it needs permission to spend money.

This kind of financial responsibility makes amoebas very cost conscious because the boss can find out at any time how the amoeba is doing, and he does not hesitate to lecture amoebas whose work is not going well. As is traditional in Japan, everyone is expected to work for the benefit of the group, so the heads of even top-performing amoebas are rewarded only with points toward promotions. The amoebas are so successful in making high-quality products at a low cost that in some of Kyocera's best product lines, like ceramic semiconductor-chip packages, the company has eliminated almost all of its competitors.

Kyocera's name is not yet as well known as Sony's or Toyota's partly because of the kinds of products it makes and partly because its products often appear with other companies' names on them. Now that the company is selling under its own name, Inamori is going to have to increase his company's visibility and name recognition. But that may not be too hard, given the company's excellent reputation among corporate U.S. buyers.

Discussion Questions

1. What aspects of the unique amoeba work groups help them produce high-quality products?

2. Would amoebas work in any organization? Why or why not?

E 3. The amoebas in Kyocera's U.S. plants don't work quite as well as those in Japan because U.S. workers often resist giving up their own interests for the group's. Debate the pros and cons of the pure Japanese-style amoebas versus the more individual-focused, U.S. tendency.

References: Gene Bylinsky, "The Hottest High-Tech Company in Japan," *Fortune*, January 1, 1990, pp. 82–88; "Cult of Personality," *Business Month*, August 1990, pp. 42–44; Stanford Diehl and Stan Wszola, "Laser Printers Get Personal," *BYTE*, July 1990, pp. 138–156.

Managing Technology and Innovation

OBJECTIVES

After studying this chapter, you should be able to:

- *Discuss technology and the organization and describe some examples of manufacturing and service technology.*

- *Discuss attributes of creative individuals and outline steps in the creative process.*

- *Describe the innovation process, forms of innovation, and some reasons that organizations fail to innovate.*

- *Describe how organizations can promote innovation.*

OUTLINE

Technology and the Organization
    Manufacturing Technology
    Service Technology

Creativity and Innovation
    The Creative Individual
    The Creative Process

Organizational Innovation
    The Innovation Process
    Forms of Innovation
    Failure to Innovate

Promoting Innovation in Organizations
    Reward System
    Intrapreneurship
    Organizational Culture

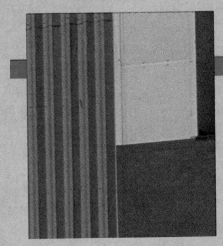

FROM ITS BEGINNING in 1946, Sony's fundamental goal has been innovation. Its founders—three Japanese engineers—set about creating an organization that would put a premium on new ideas and new ways of designing and manufacturing consumer electronic products.

Many of Sony's early products were big successes both at home and abroad. The firm produced the first Japanese tape recorder in 1950 and was a pioneer in the development of the transistor radio. Sony also helped develop the technology used in today's color televisions. But not every Sony innovation was a hit. An electric seat warmer and an electric rice cooker, for example, were both major flops.

Today, Sony is still one of the most innovative firms in the world. Its engineers create approximately 1,000 new products each year—an average of four every business day. Around 800 of these are extensions or refinements of existing products such as the addition of a new feature to a television set or a new way of designing a stereo component unit. The other 200 are new products altogether. Among Sony's more important products over the last several years are the VCR, the compact disc player, and the personal stereo (Walkman).

What is Sony's secret? How is it able to consistently generate new products? For one thing, the firm seeks creative engineers who don't focus too narrowly on one special area of research. Sony's management believes that by hiring open-minded and curious people, it fosters a culture that embraces new ideas and challenges people to continually seek new products and ways to improve existing ones. For another, the firm's basic way of managing itself helps promote innovation. For example, engineers who hear about a new product being developed in another group can apply for membership to that group without checking with their boss first. If the group invites someone new to join, that person's boss is expected to approve the transfer without hesitation. This method helps engineers stay involved in a number of different projects while also promoting competition for new ideas as a way of attracting new members to the group.[1] ●

$\mathcal{S}$ony has proven itself a master at managing the dual challenges of technology and innovation. Sony relies on innovation in its constant search for new ideas for products and, at the same time, keeps up with evolving technologies that enable it to more efficiently produce existing products. All organizations must monitor the technology they are using to maintain efficiency. And they must work to foster innovation if they are to remain competitive in their product or service offerings.

technology
The set of processes and systems used by organizations to convert resources into products or services

In Chapter 3 we defined **technology** as the set of processes and systems used by organizations to convert resources into products or services. Here we are interested in technology as a form of control that combines and changes resources into products or services. Given that technology is a form of control, organizations must stay abreast of changes in available technology to be able to take advantage of the newest, most efficient ways of operating.

innovation
The managed effort of an organization to develop new products or services or new uses for existing products or services

Innovation is the managed effort of an organization to develop new products or services or new uses for existing products or services. Innovation is also a form of control in that it helps the organization remain abreast of its competitors.

We begin by discussing technology and its uses within the organization. Next we look at the innovative process in organizations; specifically, the management of creativity and creative individuals and ways organizations can cultivate innovation.

TECHNOLOGY AND THE ORGANIZATION

Both manufacturing and service firms must monitor technological developments. Changes in technology have affected all aspects of how companies do business.

Manufacturing Technology

In Chapter 11 we discussed the research of Joan Woodward, who identified three forms of technology—unit or small batch, large batch or mass production, and continuous process.[2] She proposed that each form of technology is associated with a specific type of organization structure. New forms of technology not considered by Woodward are automation and computer-assisted manufacturing.

automation
The process of designing work so that it can be completely or almost completely performed by machines

Automation **Automation** is the process of designing work so that it can be completely or almost completely performed by machines. Automated machines operate quickly and make few errors, so they can increase a firm's output and improve products and services. Automation can also foster innovation by making it easier to create new forms of products and services. And indeed, many automated processes are themselves innovations.

Automation is the most recent step in the development of machines and machine-controlling devices. Machine-controlling devices have been around since the 1700s. James Watt, a Scottish engineer, invented a mechan-

A firm might decide to automate its facilities because automated machines speed up production and reduce errors. TRW, with one of Germany's most highly automated plants, is enjoying the benefits of reduced costs, decreased waste, and improved quality. Automation is not enough, however; TRW has found that it is managers' and employees' dedication to continuous improvement that make the benefits of automation possible.

ical speed control to regulate the speed of steam engines in 1787. The Jacquard loom, developed in 1805 by the French inventor Joseph Marie Jacquard, was controlled by paper cards with holes punched in them. Early accounting and computing equipment was controlled by similar punched cards.

Early forms of automatic machines were primitive, and the use of automation was relatively slow to develop. The big move to automate factories began during World War II, when the shortage of skilled workers and the development of high-speed computers combined to bring about a tremendous interest in automation. Programmable automation (the use of computers to control machines) was introduced during this era, far outstripping conventional automation (the use of mechanical or electromechanical devices to control machines).[3] The automobile industry began to use automatic machines for a variety of jobs. In fact, the term *automation* was coined in the 1950s by the automobile industry. The chemical and oil-refining industries also began to use computers to regulate production. Programmable automation presents the greatest opportunities and challenges for management today.

Automation relies on feedback, information, sensors, and a control mechanism. Feedback is the flow of information from the machine back to the sensor. Sensors are the parts of the system that gather information and compare it with some preset standards. The control mechanism is the device that sends instructions to the automatic machine. These elements are illustrated by the example in Figure 20.1. A thermostat has sensors that monitor air temperature and compare it to a preset low value. If the air temperature falls below the preset value, the thermostat sends an electrical signal to the furnace, turning it on, and the furnace heats the air. When the sensors detect that the air temperature has reached a value higher than the low preset value, the thermostat stops the furnace. The last step (shutting off the furnace) is known as feedback, a critical component of any automated operation.

All automation includes feedback, information, sensors, and a control mechanism. A simple thermostat is an example of automation. Another example is Benetton's distribution center in Italy. Orders are received, items pulled from stock and packaged for shipment, and invoices are prepared and transmitted with no human intervention.

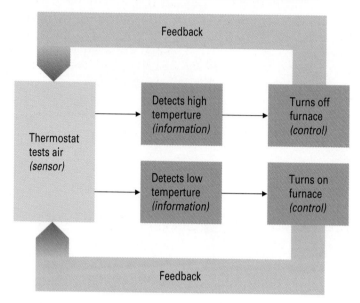

F I G U R E   20.1   A Simple Automatic Control Mechanism

Feedback

Thermostat tests air *(sensor)*

Detects high temperture *(information)*

Turns off furnace *(control)*

Detects low temperture *(information)*

Turns on furnace *(control)*

Feedback

The impact of automation on people in the workplace is complex. People may lose their jobs to automation, and not all companies are able to help displaced workers find new jobs. Thus the human costs of automation are sometimes high. In the long term, however, more jobs may be created than are lost. Some of these jobs may be related to servicing automated equipment, others may arise from overseas market expansion due to more efficient production, and still others may be in support functions. In the electronics industry, for example, the rising demand for products has led to increasing employment opportunities despite the use of automation. In contrast, in the coal industry, although the output per miner has risen dramatically from the 1950s on, the demand for coal has decreased, so productivity gains resulting from automation have lessened the need for miners. Consequently, many minors have lost their jobs, and the industry has not been able to absorb them.

Computers and Manufacturing   Current extensions of automation generally revolve around computer-aided design and computer-aided manufacturing. **Computer-aided design (CAD)** is the use of computers to design parts and products and to simulate performance so that prototypes need not be constructed. Using CAD, McDonnell Douglas Corp. studies hydraulic tubing in DC-10s, Japan's automative industry speeds up car design, General Electric Co. changes the design of circuit breakers, and Benetton Group SPA designs new styles and products. Oneida Ltd. used CAD to design a new spoon in only two days.[4] **Computer-aided manufacturing (CAM)** is the use of computers to plan and control manufacturing processes. A CAM system is especially useful when products or parts are re-ordered frequently because the computer can maintain better control over ordering, routing, assembling, and shipping products. Toyota makes extensive use of CAM in producing its line of Lexus luxury automobiles.

● **computer-aided design (CAD)**
The use of computers to design parts and products and to simulate performance so that prototypes need not be constructed

● **computer-aided manufacturing (CAM)**
The use of computers to plan and control manufacturing processes

When CAD is linked with CAM (CAD/CAM; also known as **computer-integrated manufacturing** or **CIM**), the computer controlling production shares the design computer's information and is able to have machines with the proper settings ready when production is needed. All design, testing, and manufacturing activities are controlled by computer. Computers adjust machine placements and settings automatically to enhance both the complexity and the flexibility of scheduling. Because the computer can access the company's other information systems, CIM is a powerful and complex management control tool.[5]

In **flexible manufacturing systems (FMS),** robotic work units or work-stations, assembly lines, robotic carts, or some other form of computer-controlled transport system moves material as needed from one part of the system to another. IBM's manufacturing facility in Lexington, Kentucky, relies on an FMS to coordinate and integrate automated production and materials-handling facilities.[6]

These systems are not without disadvantages, however.[7] Because of their tremendous complexity, CAD systems are not always reliable. CIM systems are so expensive that they raise the breakeven point for firms using them, and the firm must be able to operate at high levels of production and sales to afford the systems.[8] Additionally, a firm converting to any one of these systems undergoes fundamental change, which generates resistance.

Robotics   One of the newest trends in manufacturing technology is robotics. A **robot** is any artificial device that is able to perform functions ordinarily thought to be appropriate for human beings. *Robotics* refers to the science and technology of the construction, maintenance, and use of robots. The use of industrial robots has steadily increased since 1980 and is expected to continue to increase slowly as more companies recognize the benefits that accrue to users of industrial robots.

Robots were first used for welding and this area continues to be the one in which robots are most frequently used. Other applications include materials handling, machine loading and unloading, painting and finishing, assembly, casting, and machining applications such as cutting, grinding, polishing, drilling, sanding, buffing, and deburring. Chrysler Corp., for instance, replaced about 200 welders with fifty robots on an assembly line and increased productivity about 20 percent.[9] Robots are increasingly being used for inspection work: they can check for cracks and holes and, when equipped with vision systems, perform visual inspections.

The robots used by small manufacturers are lighter, faster, stronger, and more intelligent than those used in heavy manufacturing and are the types that more and more organizations will be using in the future.[10] An upholstery shop uses a robot to slice carpeting to fit the inside of custom vans. A novelties company uses a robot to stretch balloons flat so that they can be spray-painted with slogans. At a jewelry company, a robot holds class rings while they are engraved by a laser.

Robots are also beginning to be used increasingly for service applications. The Dallas Police Department used a robot to apprehend a suspect who had barricaded himself in an apartment building. When the robot smashed a window and reached its mechanical arm into the building, the suspect panicked and ran outside. At the Long Beach Memorial Hospital in California, brain surgeons are assisted by a robot arm that drills into the patient's skull

● **computer-integrated manufacturing (CIM)**
The integration of CAD with CAM (also known as CAD/CAM), in which the computer controlling production shares the design computer's information and is able to have machines with the proper settings ready when production is needed

● **flexible manufacturing systems (FMS)**
Robotic work units or work-stations, assembly lines, robotic carts, or some other form of computer-controlled transport system that moves material as needed from one part of the system to another

robot
Any artificial device that is able to perform functions ordinarily thought to be appropriate for human beings

with excellent precision.[11] Some newer applications involve remote work. For example, the use of robot submersibles controlled from the surface can help divers in remote locations. Surveillance robots fitted with microwave sensors can do things that a human guard cannot do such as "see" through nonmetallic walls and in the dark. In other applications, automated farming (agrimation) uses robot harvesters to pick fruit.[12]

Of course, there are also disadvantages associated with robots. First of all, robots are somewhat inflexible. They are designed and programmed for a specific set of tasks, such as combining four subcomponents to construct a certain product. Any change in tasks or assembly procedures may require that the robot be completely reprogrammed or, worse yet, scrapped and replaced with a new one. Robots are also expensive. If a worker calls in sick it may be a simple matter to have someone else fill in temporarily, but if a robot malfunctions it may cause major problems and inconvenience.

Service Technology

Service technology is also changing rapidly. It, too, is moving increasingly toward automated systems and procedures. In banking, for example, new technological breakthroughs have led to automated teller machines, debit cards, and made it much easier for customers to manage their own accounts via a modem and home computer. Some people now have their paychecks deposited directly into a checking account from which many of their bills are then automatically paid. And credit card transactions by Visa USA Inc. customers are recorded and billed electronically.

Hotels use increasingly sophisticated technology to accept and record room reservations. For example, again using their own computers, customers can book a reservation with some hotels without ever talking to a person. Universities use new technologies such as CD-ROM to electronically store and provide access to books, scientific journals, government reports, and articles. Hospitals and other healthcare organizations use new forms of service technology to manage patient records, dispatch ambulances, and monitor vital signs. Restaurants use technology to record and fill customer orders, order food and supplies, and prepare food. Given the increased role that service organizations are playing in today's economy, even more technological innovations are likely to be developed in the years to come.

A manufacturing or service organization's developing or creating a technology represents one of the most fundamental innovations in any organization. And every change to that technology represents still more innovation. Thus no discussion of technology is complete without also considering innovation's conceptual complement, creativity.

CREATIVITY AND INNOVATION

creativity
An individual's ability to generate new ideas or conceive of new perspectives on existing ideas

Creativity is an individual's ability to generate new ideas or conceive of new perspectives on existing ideas. An organization must have creative employees if it is to develop new products, services, or technologies (or new uses for existing ones)—that is, if it is to be innovative. Thus the concepts of creativity and innovation are related but they are not the same: creativity is an individual process that may or may not occur in an organization, and innovation is an organizational activity aimed at managing and stimulating the creativity of employees.[13] A new product or service that results from these activities is also sometimes referred to as an innovation. Thus, innovation can refer either to a process or something that results from that process.

The Creative Individual

Organizations that aim to introduce new and exciting products and services into the marketplace must have creative employees. What makes a person creative? How do people become creative? How does the creative process work? Although psychologists have not yet discovered complete answers to these questions, examining a few general patterns can help us understand the sources of individual creativity. Numerous researchers have focused their efforts on attempting to describe the common attributes of creative individuals. These attributes generally fall into three categories: background experiences, personality traits, and cognitive abilities.[14]

Background Experiences Background experiences are the events that people live through during childhood and young adulthood. Researchers have noticed that many creative individuals were raised in an environment in which creativity was valued.[15] Mozart, one of the greatest composers of all time, was raised in a family of musicians and began composing and performing music at age 6. Pierre and Marie Curie, great scientists in their own right, also raised a daughter, Irene, who won the Nobel Prize in chemistry. Thomas Edison's renowned creativity was nurtured by his mother. People with very different background experiences than these, however, are also creative. The African American abolitionist and writer

Organizations know that it is not enough to hire creative people; creativity must be encouraged, often by providing the proper environment. To this end, most of the world's major automakers—including the Big Three—have established design departments near Los Angeles. Successful California designs include the Mazda Miata and Toyota's Celica and Previa. An example of the creativity being unleashed at Mercedes is Michael Ma's Tatanka, a fantasy car inspired by the American buffalo.

Creative employees are extremely important to an organization because they supply innovative ideas for products and services. But creativity is not only valued in the area of product development: creative marketing ideas are equally important. During recessionary times, Estée Lauder president Robin Burns is trying innovative marketing ideas such as testing mini "stores within stores" and distributing videos advertising Spellbound perfume with *Elle* magazine.

cognitive abilities
A person's power to think intelligently and to analyze situations and data effectively

● **preparation**
The necessary education and training to enable a person to be creative; the first part of the creative process

Frederick Douglass was born into slavery in Tuckahoe, Maryland, with very limited opportunities for education. Nonetheless, Douglass became one of the most influential figures of his era. His powerful oratory and creative thinking helped lead to the Emancipation Proclamation, which ended slavery in the United States.

Personality   A variety of personality traits have been linked with individual creativity. The personality traits shared by most creative people are broad interests, an attraction to complexity, high levels of energy, independence and autonomy, strong self-confidence, and a strong belief that one is, in fact, creative.[16] Individuals who have these personality characteristics are more likely to be creative than people who do not have them.

Cognitive Abilities   **Cognitive abilities** are a person's power to think intelligently and to analyze situations and data effectively. Research suggests that intelligence may be a precondition for individual creativity, which means that although most creative people are highly intelligent, not all intelligent people necessarily are creative.[17] Creativity is also linked with the ability to think divergently and convergently. Divergent thinking is a skill that allows people to see differences between situations, phenomena, or events. Convergent thinking is a skill that allows people to see similarities between situations, phenomena, or events. Creative people are generally very skilled at both divergent and convergent thinking.[18]

Some of the decisions made by Lee Iacocca after he assumed the presidency of Chrysler illustrate the interplay between divergent and convergent thinking. When he joined Chrysler, the company was losing millions of dollars, laying off employees, and on the verge of bankruptcy. Once the organization was stabilized financially with the help of government loans, Iacocca turned to improving Chrysler's products. The first task was to catalog what a range of different customers might want in a car in terms of size, performance, cost, and styling. Describing these diverse and sometimes contradictory customer needs is an example of divergent thinking. One of Iacocca's insights was that it might be possible to meet all these different customer needs by manufacturing different versions of one basic automobile design. This design became known as the "K-car." Iacocca used convergent thinking to find a common solution to numerous problems.[19]

The Creative Process

Although creative people often report that ideas seem to come to them "in a flash," individual creative activity actually tends to progress through a series of stages.[20] Figure 20.2 summarizes the major stages of the creative process. While not all creative activity follows these four stages, much of it does.

Preparation   The creative process normally begins with a period of **preparation,** which may include education and formal training. In Edison's time a highly creative person with a high school education or less could make important creative contributions to technology. Many inventors during that time were self-taught. Because relatively little was known about science and technology, creative people could be less well trained and less well

FIGURE 20.2 The Creative Process

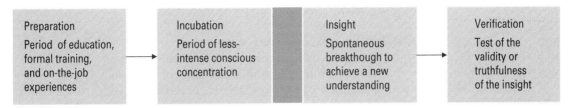

Preparation	Incubation	Insight	Verification
Period of education, formal training, and on-the-job experiences	Period of less-intense conscious concentration	Spontaneous breakthough to achieve a new understanding	Test of the validity or truthfulness of the insight

educated and still be highly successful. Because of the growth in science and technology over the last century, we now know a great deal more about both how the world works and how to apply this knowledge to engineer new products and services. Formal education and training is usually the most efficient way of becoming familiar with this vast amount of research and knowledge. Thus scientists today generally have a Ph.D. degree.

Moreover, the requirement for increased preparation through formal education and training is not limited to the physical and life sciences such as physics, chemistry, and biology. The economic and business world has also grown more sophisticated over the years. To make a creative contribution to business management or business services, individuals must usually receive formal training and education in business. This is one reason for the increasing demand for undergraduate and masters-level business education. Formal business education can be an effective way for an individual to get "up to speed" and begin making creative contributions as quickly as possible. Experiences that scientists and managers have on the job after they complete formal training can also contribute to the creative process. In an important sense, the education and training of creative people never really ends. It continues as long as they remain interested in the world and curious about the way things work.

Incubation   The second phase of the creative process is incubation. **Incubation** is a period of less-intense conscious concentration during which the creative person is able to let the knowledge and ideas acquired during preparation mature and develop. From the outside, it may look like nothing is happening—few major breakthroughs occur during incubation. Slowly, however, often subconsciously, the creative individual is linking ideas and generating new concepts.

Incubation is often helped along by pauses in concentrated rational thought. Some creative people rely on reading and listening to music to provide a "break" from thinking, and some rely on sleep. Yet others depend on physical activity such as jogging or swimming to supply the needed pause. While out rowing one day, David Morse, a research scientist at Corning Incorporated, hit on the answer to a long-sought-after product improvement. Morse had a special interest in a new line of cookware called Visions. These glass pots and pans had many advantages over traditional cookware, but no one at Corning had yet succeeded in putting a nonstick surface on the glass. Looking for a solution to this problem, Morse put in many long days in the laboratory, but it was during his hours of rowing that the ideas and concepts that would enable him to devise a nonstick

While the creative process is anything but mechanical and predictable, it often follows these general steps. Managers need to understand that adequate training is a necessary part of preparation, for example. They also need to recognize that developing good ideas may take time. Not all ideas will work, of course, but most are still worth verifying.

● **incubation**
A period of less-intense conscious concentration during which the knowledge acquired during preparation is allowed to mature and develop; the second part of the creative process

coating began to come together and mature. Morse may never have been able to solve this technical problem if he had not taken the time to let his ideas incubate.[21]

● insight
A spontaneous breakthrough leading to new insight into a problem or situation; the third part of the creative process

Insight   Usually occurring after preparation and during incubation, **insight** is a spontaneous breakthrough in which the creative person achieves a new understanding of some problem or situation. Insight represents a coming together of all the scattered thoughts and ideas that were maturing during incubation. It may occur suddenly or develop slowly over time. Insight can be triggered by some external event, such as a new experience or an encounter with new data that forces the person to think about old issues and problems in new ways, or it can be a completely internal event in which patterns of thought finally coalesce in ways that generate new understanding. One manager's insight led to a complete restructuring of Citibank N.A.'s Back Room Operations, or BRO. BRO is the enormous amount of paperwork that a bank must process to serve its customers, such as listing checks and deposits, updating accounts, and preparing bank statements. BRO had historically been managed as if it were part of the regular banking operation. When John Reed assumed responsibility for BRO, he realized that it was actually more like manufacturing than banking. Reed's insight was that BRO could be managed as a "paper manufacturing" process. Based on this insight, he hired former manufacturing managers from Ford Motor Co. and other automobile companies. By reconceptualizing the nature of BRO, Reed was able to substantially reduce the costs of these operations for Citibank.[22]

verification
Experiments, practical trials, or the development of a prototype (or all three) to test the validity or truthfulness of an insight; the fourth part of the creative process

Verification   Once an insight has occurred, **verification** determines the validity or truthfulness of the insight. For many creative ideas, verification includes scientific experiments to determine whether the insight actually leads to the expected results. David Morse's insight concerning how to put a nonstick coating on glass pots was verified by such experiments. Morse's idea set in motion several important experiments and practical trials to discover the best way to apply the nonstick surface. Without these experiments and trials, Morse's idea would have remained an interesting concept, with little practical application.

Verification may also include the development of a product or service prototype. A prototype is one (or a small number) of products built just to see if the ideas behind this new product actually work. Product prototypes are rarely sold to the public, but are valuable to verify the insights developed in the creative process. Once the new product or service is developed, verification in the marketplace is the ultimate test of the creative idea behind it. "Management in Practice" provides further insights into the creative processes that went into the development of the Infiniti automobile.

ORGANIZATIONAL INNOVATION

For an organization to successfully introduce new products and services, individual creativity must be linked with innovation. Innovative organizations are able to attract, nurture, and develop creative employees and, in turn, to take advantage of the new products and services they create.

INFINITI'S CREATIVE DESIGNERS

How do automakers go about designing a new car model? For Nissan Motor Co. Ltd.'s Infiniti division, the question is a particularly important one. The Infiniti cars are Nissan's attempt to capture a portion of the luxury car market once dominated by Mercedes-Benz and BMW. Nissan introduced Infiniti in 1989 with a series of ads that never showed the car itself but relied on scenes of pussy willows and rock gardens to get across a sense of the new model's "philosophy." So when Infiniti prepared to introduce a new model, the J30, in 1991, it wanted something special. And to get the right design, it turned not to Tokyo but to its own U.S. design studio, Nissan Design International (NDI).

NDI already had a good track record for Nissan. Its 1987 Pulsar NX, which could be easily converted from a coupe to a convertible to a wagonback, won the Japan Car of the Year award. And unlike many automakers' design studios, NDI accepts commissions from other companies, getting innovative ideas from very un-automotive products. It has designed audio tweeters, outboard motors, and a computer whose manufacturer wanted "a piece of art."

Perhaps because of this non-auto input, NDI doesn't follow a standard route for designing its cars, simply taking a basic car design and playing with minor parts of it to change the style. The design for the Infiniti J30, in fact, started with an egg and an arched line, doodled by young designer Doug Wilson. The gentle slopes of the J30 design reminded many people of the look of old Jaguars, proving that there's nothing truly new in shapes, but giving just the right hint of old-fashioned class. Nissan executives liked the sloping rear end, but hated the front. While U.S. car buyers tend to view cars from the side, Japanese view the front as a face, with "eyes" (headlights), a "mouth" (the grill), and an expression all its own. Nissan top brass accepted the J30 design, but insisted on enlarging the eyes and shrinking the mouth to make the "face" more expressive.

The development of the J30 doesn't present a formula for managing creativity, but it does include a number of elements important to virtually any design. The designers knew their audience and the effect they wanted to have, they took a step back from the product to see it with fresh eyes, they worked with old and new ideas, and, like any designers working in the real world, they were ready to compromise.

References: Larry Armstrong, "It Started with an Egg," *Business Week*, December 2, 1991, pp. 142–146; Stuart Elliott, "Toyota, Nissan Enlist Big Guns of Advertising," *USA Today*, July 24, 1989, pp. B1, B2.

The Innovation Process

Organizations with creative employees often possess numerous ideas for many new products and services as well as several product prototypes that verify their insights. To turn these ideas and prototypes into real products and services that can be sold to customers, however, an organization must marshall other resources to develop and sell the innovation. The process of developing, applying, launching, growing, and managing the maturity and decline of a creative idea is called the *organizational innovation process.*[23] This process is depicted in Figure 20.3.

Development   Most ideas do not emerge from the creative process ready to be instantly transformed into new products or services. Development is the stage in which an organization evaluates, modifies, and improves on a creative idea before turning that idea into a product or service to sell. Development occurs after a creative insight is verified and, where appropriate, product prototypes are built. Parker Brothers, for example (manu-

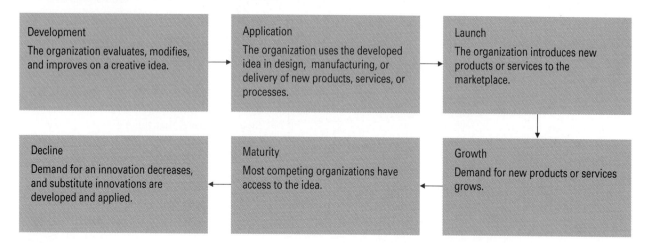

Development
The organization evaluates, modifies, and improves on a creative idea.

Application
The organization uses the developed idea in design, manufacturing, or delivery of new products, services, or processes.

Launch
The organization introduces new products or services to the marketplace.

Decline
Demand for an innovation decreases, and substitute innovations are developed and applied.

Maturity
Most competing organizations have access to the idea.

Growth
Demand for new products or services grows.

Organizations actively seek to manage the innovation process. These steps illustrate the general life cycle that characterizes most innovations today. Of course, as with creativity, the innovation process will suffer if it is approached too mechanically and rigidly.

facturers of the board games Monopoly, Risk, and Life), was working to develop an indoor volleyball game. Its designers created a foam ball that was so appealing that the firm decided to scrap plans for the volleyball game and to sell the ball alone. Parker Brothers will never know how well the volleyball game would have sold, but the Nerf ball and numerous related products that were later developed have generated millions of dollars in revenues for the company.[24]

Application Even after development, the idea has yet to be applied to real products or services. Application is the stage in which an organization takes a developed idea and uses it in the design, manufacturing, or delivery of new products, services, or processes. At this point the idea emerges from the laboratory and is transformed into tangible goods or services. One example of application is the use of radar-based focusing systems in Polaroid Corp.'s instant cameras. The idea of using radio waves to discover the location, speed, and direction of moving objects was first applied extensively by Allied forces during World War II. As radar technology developed over the following years, its electrical components became smaller and more streamlined. Researchers at Polaroid saw radar's potential and applied this well-developed technology in a new way.[25]

Launch Launch is the stage in which an organization introduces new products or services to the marketplace. The key question is not, "Does the idea work?" but, "Will customers want to purchase the new product or service?" History is full of creative ideas that did not generate enough interest among customers to be successful. Some notable failures include Sony's seat warmer, the Edsel automobile (with its notoriously homely front end), the movie *Bonfire of the Vanities* (which never attracted audience enthusiasm and lost millions of dollars), and Polaroid's SX-70 instant camera (which cost $3 billion to develop but never sold well). Thus despite individual creativity, development, and application, new products and services may still fail at the launch phase of innovation.[26]

Growth Once an idea has been successfully launched, it then enters the stage of growth, where demand for the new product or service increases.

This is a period of high economic performance for an organization because demand for the product or service is often greater than supply. Organizations that fail to anticipate this demand may unintentionally limit their growth, as Gillette Co. did by underestimating demand for its Sensor razor blades. At the same time, overestimating demand for a new product or service can be just as detrimental to performance. Many "Western wear" retailers overestimated demand after the popularity of the John Travolta movie *Urban Cowboy* suddenly—but very briefly—increased demand for cowboy boots, shirts, and other Western-style clothes. Many stores lost money after purchasing a great deal of Western-wear inventory that took years to sell.

Maturity   After a period of growing demand, an innovative product or service often enters a period of maturity. Maturity is the stage in which most organizations in an industry have access to the idea and are applying it in approximately the same way. The technological application of an innovation during this stage can be very sophisticated. Because most firms have access to the innovation, however, either because they have developed it themselves or have copied it from others, it does not provide competitive advantage to any one of them. The time that elapses between development and maturity varies depending on the particular product or service. Whenever an innovation or its implementation involves complex, rare, or difficult-to-imitate skills (such as a complicated manufacturing process or highly sophisticated teamwork), moving from the growth phase to the maturity phase takes a long time. Strategic imitation may then be delayed, and the organization may enjoy a period of sustained competitive advantage.

One innovation that has taken a long time to move from growth to maturity (and may not have matured even yet) is the user-friendliness of Apple Computer Inc.'s Macintosh computer. When the Macintosh was first introduced, it immediately provided a level of user-friendliness that was unique in the personal computer industry. Over the years, efforts to make other types of PCs as user-friendly as the Macintosh have not succeeded, and customers who wanted to purchase user-friendly PCs were limited to the Macintosh. Only recently has Microsoft Corp.'s Windows software begun to offer effective user-friendliness in non-Macintosh computers.

When an innovation or its implementation does not depend on complex, rare, or difficult-to-imitate skills, then the time between the growth and maturity phases can be brief. In the market for computer memory devices, for example, technological innovation by one firm can be very quickly duplicated by other firms because the skills needed to design and manufacture these electronic devices are widespread. Computer memory devices thus move very rapidly from growth to maturity. Similarly, personal stereos and other consumer electronics products also move quickly from growth to maturity.

Decline   Decline is the stage during which demand for an innovation decreases and substitute innovations are developed and applied. An organization does not gain a competitive advantage from an innovation at maturity, so it must encourage its creative scientists, engineers, and managers to begin looking for new ideas. Thus the individual creative process depicted in Figure 20.2 begins again and again leads to the innovation process. It is this continued search for competitive advantage that usually leads new products and services from the creative process through maturity and finally to decline.

Forms of Innovation

Innovations can be radical or incremental, technical or managerial, and product or process.

Radical Versus Incremental Innovations   **Radical innovations** are new products or technologies that completely replace the existing products or technologies in an industry. Organizations that implement radical innovations fundamentally shift the nature of competition and the interaction of firms within their environments. **Incremental innovations** are new products or processes that modify existing products or technologies. The implementation of incremental innovations alter, but do not fundamentally change, competitive interaction in an industry.

Many radical innovations have been introduced by organizations over the last several years. Compact discs are replacing long-playing vinyl records, and high-definition television seems likely to replace regular television (both black and white and color) in the near future. Whereas radical innovations like these tend to be visible and public, incremental innovations actually are more numerous. One example is General Motors Corp.'s aerodynamic minivan, the Lumina. Manufacture of this van pioneered the use of plastic autobody panels and employed a new process for forming the front windshield. Although the van's exterior is innovative, the engine, drive train, and other mechanical parts are standard.

Radical innovations have higher potential for economic return than do incremental innovations: an organization that is able to successfully launch a radical innovation will have an important competitive advantage. Associated with this higher economic potential, however, is greater economic risk and uncertainty. Economic risk exists when, at the time a decision is made, several outcomes are possible and the probability of each occurring is known. Economic uncertainty exists when, at the time a decision is made, both the range of possible outcomes and their likelihood of occurring are not known. Highly risky and uncertain radical innovations have a much greater chance of failing to meet expectations than do less risky and uncertain incremental innovations. In general, the riskier and more uncertain an innovation, the greater the potential economic return must be to balance the risks the organization bears.

Technical Versus Managerial Innovations   **Technical innovations** are changes in a product's or service's physical appearance, performance, or manufacturing processes. Many of the most important innovations over the last fifty years have been technical. For example, the serial replacement of the vacuum tube with the transistor, the transistor with the integrated circuit, and the integrated circuit with the microchip has greatly enhanced the power, ease of use, and operating speed of a wide variety of electronic products. Not all innovations developed by organizations are technical, however. **Managerial innovations** are changes in the processes of managing the way products and services are conceived, created, and delivered to

---

● **radical innovations**
New products, services, or technologies that completely replace existing ones

● **incremental innovations**
New products, services, or technologies that modify existing ones

● **technical innovations**
Changes in a product's or service's physical appearance, performance, or manufacturing processes

● **managerial innovations**
Changes in the processes of managing the way products and services are conceived, created, and delivered to customers

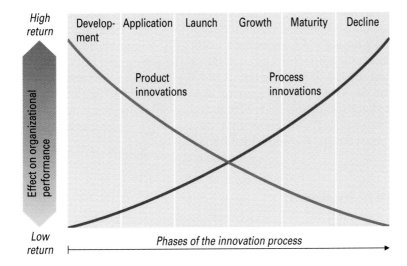

F I G U R E   20.4   Effects of Product and Process Innovation on Economic Return

High return

Effect on organizational performance

| Develop-ment | Application | Launch | Growth | Maturity | Decline |

Product innovations

Process innovations

Low return

Phases of the innovation process

As the innovation process moves from development to decline, the economic return from product innovations gradually declines. In contrast, the economic return from process innovations increases during this same process.

customers. Managerial innovations do not necessarily affect the physical appearance or performance of products or services directly, but they can. Many Japanese firms have used managerial innovations to improve the quality of their products or services. One of the most important of these innovations developed in the last thirty years, called the quality circle, helped Oki Electronics become one of the premier electronics companies in the world. Organizations that have been able to incorporate quality circles, in which small groups of concerned workers discuss how to improve product quality and implement total quality management, have found that quality improves dramatically and the costs of operations decrease.[27] (Total quality management is discussed more fully in Chapter 19.)

Product Versus Process Innovations   Two important types of technical innovations are product and process innovations. **Product innovations** are changes in the physical characteristics or performance of existing products or services or the creation of brand new products or services. **Process innovations** are changes in the way products or services are manufactured, created, or distributed. The implementation of robotics, as discussed earlier, is a process innovation. Whereas managerial innovations generally affect the broader context of organization-wide development and the way the organization is managed, process innovations more directly affect technology itself.

As Figure 20.4 shows, the effect of product and process innovations on economic return depends on the stage of the innovation process. During development, application, and launch, product innovations are particularly important because the innovation's physical attributes and capabilities most affect organizational performance. Later on, as an innovation enters the phases of growth, maturity, and decline, an organization's ability to develop process innovations such as fine tuning manufacturing, increasing product quality, and improving product distribution becomes important to maintaining economic return.

● **product innovations**
Changes in the physical characteristics or performance of existing products or services or the creation of brand new products or services

● **process innovations**
Changes in the way products or services are manufactured, created, or distributed

Japanese organizations have often excelled at process innovation. The market for 35mm cameras was dominated by German and other European manufacturers when, in the early 1960s, Japanese organizations such as Canon and Nikon began making cameras. Some of these early Japanese-made products were not very successful, but these companies continued to invest in process innovations and eventually were able to increase quality and decrease manufacturing costs. Now the Japanese dominate the world-wide market for 35mm cameras, and the Germans, because they did not maintain the same pace of process innovation, are struggling to maintain market share and profitability. By focusing efforts on refining the manufacturing process, organizations that do not have a competitive advantage when innovations are introduced may develop a competitive advantage over time.

Failure to Innovate

To remain competitive in today's economy, an organization must be both creative and innovative. And yet, many organizations are not successful at bringing out new products and services, or do so only after innovations created by others are very mature. Organizations fail to innovate for at least three reasons.

Lack of Resources   Implementing an innovation strategy can be expensive in terms of dollars, time, and energy. If a firm does not have sufficient money to fund a program of innovation or does not currently employ the creative individuals it needs to be innovative, it may find itself lagging behind in innovation. Even highly innovative organizations cannot develop or launch every new product or service its employees think up. For example, numerous other commitments in the electronic instruments and computer industry forestalled Hewlett-Packard Co. from investing in Steve Jobs's and Steve Wozniak's idea for a personal computer. With infinite

Companies are learning that lack of resources, failure to recognize opportunities, and resistance to change are not the only barriers to innovation. Organizations must also learn to manage their "intellectual capital" in order to be innovative. One way to foster this is to create an organization that shares knowledge. Polaroid's CEO I. Mac-Allister Booth found that using an interdisciplinary team to create a new medical imaging system, Helios, cut development time for the product in half.

resources of money, time, and technical and managerial expertise, HP might have entered this market early. Because the firm did not have this flexibility, however, it had to make some difficult choices about which innovations to invest in.

Failure to Recognize Opportunities Because organizations cannot pursue all innovations, they need to develop the capability to carefully evaluate ideas and to select the ones that hold the greatest potential. To obtain a competitive advantage, an organization usually must make investment decisions before an innovation reaches maturity. But, as just suggested, the earlier the investment, the greater the risk. If organizations are not skilled at recognizing and evaluating opportunities, they may be overly cautious and fail to invest in innovations that turn out later to be successful for other firms.

Resistance to Change Many organizations tend to resist change. Innovation means giving up old products and old ways of doing things in favor of new products and new ways of doing things. These kinds of changes can be personally difficult for managers and other members of an organization. As we described in more detail in Chapter 12, resistance to change can slow the innovation process.

PROMOTING INNOVATION IN ORGANIZATIONS

A wide variety of ideas for promoting innovation in organizations have been developed over the years. "The Global View" discusses how many U.S. firms are trying to tap into Japanese innovations. More specific ways for promoting innovation are described in the following sections.

Reward System

An organization uses its reward system to encourage and discourage certain behaviors by employees. Important components of the reward system include salaries, bonuses, and perquisites. Managers can also use the reward system to promote creativity and innovation by providing financial and nonfinancial rewards to people and groups that develop innovative ideas. Once the members of an organization understand that they will be rewarded for creative activities, they are more likely to work creatively. With this end in mind, Monsanto Company gives a $50,000 award each year to the scientist or group of scientists that develops the biggest commercial breakthrough.

Not only must organizations reward creative behavior, they also must avoid punishing employees when creativity does not result in highly successful innovations. It is the nature of the creative and innovation processes that many new product ideas will simply not work out in the marketplace. Each process is fraught with too many uncertainties to generate positive results every time. An individual may have prepared herself to be creative, but an insight may elude her. Or managers may attempt to apply a developed innovation only to recognize that it does not work. Indeed, some organizations assume that if all their innovative efforts succeed, they are probably not taking enough risks in research and development. At 3M Company, nearly 60 percent of the creative ideas suggested each year do not succeed in the marketplace.

Organizations need to be very careful in responding to innovation failure. If innovation failure is caused by incompetence, systematic errors, or managerial sloppiness, an organization should respond appropriately, perhaps by withholding raises or reducing promotion opportunities. Creative people who develop an innovation that simply does not work out, however, should not be punished for failure. If they are, they will probably not be creative in the future. A punitive reward system will discourage people from taking risks and therefore reduce the organization's ability to obtain competitive advantages. To avoid punishing failure inappropriately, a manager must thoroughly understand the creative individual's skills and capabilities and the goal the individual was attempting to accomplish. By developing this understanding, a manager will be able to distinguish among creative activities that simply did not work out and managerial incompetence, stupidity, or poor judgment.

Intrapreneurship

intrapreneurs
Individuals or groups that, similar to entrepreneurs, develop a new product or business; unlike entrepeneurs, however, they function in the context of a larger organization

Intrapreneurship also helps organizations encourage innovation. **Intrapreneurs** are similar to entrepreneurs, except that they develop a new product or business in the context of a larger organization. To successfully use intrapreneurship to encourage creativity and innovation, the organization must find one or more individuals to perform three entrepreneurial roles.[28] The *inventor* actually conceives of and develops the new idea, product, or

Microsoft's Bill Gates has developed an organizational culture that supports creative and innovative activity by keeping design teams small and creating a working environment that fosters individual creativity. The design team shown here is responsible for developing "multimedia computing"—the integration of sound, moving pictures, still pictures, and text in the personal computer.

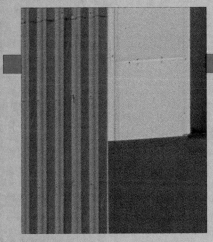

WESTINGHOUSE ELECTRIC CORP. has manufactured everything from light bulbs to nuclear reactors. After a major restructuring in the 1980s, the firm emerged with seven operating groups: Broadcasting, Electronic Systems, Environmental Systems, Financial Services, Industries, Power Systems, and the Knoll Group. How does Westinghouse manage such a diverse and complex set of businesses? One important way that the firm copes with its diversity and complexity is electronic communication.

The heart of Westinghouse's communication network is an electronic mail system. The system uses 6,000 personal computers to link 10,700 employees and 1,000 customers. The system allows any Westinghouse manager to retrieve vital information, transmit and receive messages, and file reports from anywhere in the world. Experts estimate that the system has increased white-collar productivity at the firm by 6 percent a year since the early 1980s.

Another cog in Westinghouse's information network is an elaborate expert system. This system helps manage several complex operating systems within the firm. For example, it helps monitor the company's power plant in Orlando, Florida. The information it provides allows managers there to make adjustments in the plant, anticipate changes in power demand, and switch the flow of electricity from one network to another without interrupting service.[1] ●

*I*n recent years businesses like Westinghouse have recognized that they need better ways to manage their information. Information comes in a variety of forms and in large quantities. If organizations aren't careful, they can lose control of how they manage the information that they need to conduct business efficiently and effectively.

This chapter is about advances made by organizations in managing information. We describe the role and importance of information to managers, the characteristics of useful information, and information management as control. We identify the basic building blocks of information systems and discuss the general and specific determinants of information system needs. We then look at the primary kinds of information systems used in organizations and describe how these information systems are managed and their impact on organizations. Finally, we highlight recent advances in information management.

INFORMATION AND THE MANAGER

Information has always been an integral part of every manager's job. Its importance, however, and therefore the need to manage it continue to grow at a rapid pace. Its growing importance stems from the increasing complexity of organizations' environments and the ever-growing amount of information created by that complexity. To appreciate this trend, we need to understand the role of information in the manager's job, characteristics of useful information, and the nature of information management as control.[2]

The Role of Information in the Manager's Job

In Chapters 1 and 17 we highlighted the role of communication in the manager's job. Given that information is a vital part of communication, it follows that management and information are closely related. Indeed, management itself can be conceptualized as a series of steps involving the reception, processing, and dissemination of information. As illustrated in Figure 21.1, the manager is constantly bombarded with data and information (we note the difference between the two later).

Suppose that Bob Henderson is an operations manager for a large manufacturing firm. During a normal day, Bob receives a great many pieces of information from both formal and informal conversations and meetings, telephone calls, personal observation, letters, reports, memos, and trade publications. A report from a subordinate explains exactly how to solve a pressing problem, so he calls the subordinate and tells him to put the solution into effect immediately. He scans a copy of a report prepared for another manager, sees that it has no relevance to him, and discards it. He sees a *Wall Street Journal* article that he knows Sara Ferris in marketing should see, so he passes it on to her. He files yesterday's production report because he knows that he won't need to analyze it for another week. He observes a worker doing a job incorrectly and realizes that the incorrect method is associated with a mysterious quality problem that someone told him about last week.

Archaeologists in charge of excavating the Viking village of Birka, west of Stockholm, Sweden, needed a reliable method of tracking and recording excavated articles. Monarch Marketing Systems developed an inventory system using all-weather bar code labels, which archaeologist Solveig Brunstedt applies to items from the dig. The bar codes enable archaeologists to quickly and easily record data, which can then be compiled into useful information about Viking life long ago.

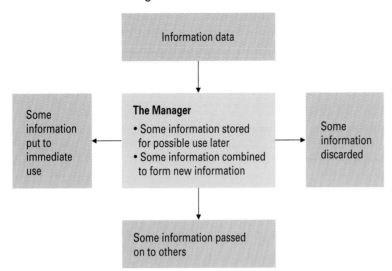

Information data

The Manager
• Some information stored for possible use later
• Some information combined to form new information

Some information put to immediate use

Some information discarded

Some information passed on to others

Managers who receive information and data must decide what to do with it. Some is stored for possible later use, while other information is combined to form new information. Subsequently, some is used immediately, some is passed on to others, and some is discarded.

A major part of processing information is differentiating between data and information. **Data** are raw figures and facts reflecting a single aspect of reality. The facts that a plant has thirty-five machines, that each machine is capable of producing 1,000 units per day, that current and projected future demand for the units is 30,000 per day, and that workers sufficiently skilled to run the machines make $15 an hour are data. **Information** is data presented in a way or form that has meaning. Thus interpreting these four pieces of data provides information—the plant has excess capacity and is therefore incurring unnecessary costs. Information provides a basis for action. Based on this information, the plant manager might decide to sell four machines (keeping one as a back-up) and transfer five operators to other jobs.[3]

The grocery industry has made good use of this distinction in its drive to automate inventory and checkout facilities. The average Kroger grocery store, for example, carries 21,000 items. With the use of computerized scanning machines at the checkout counters, sales figures for any product are available daily. These figures alone are data and have little meaning in their pure form. Information is compiled from this data by another computerized system. Using this system, managers can identify how any given product or product line is selling in any number of stores over any period of time.[4]

data
Raw figures and facts reflecting a single aspect of reality

● **information**
Data presented in a way or form that has meaning

Characteristics of Useful Information

What factors differentiate information that is useful from information that is not useful? In general, useful information is accurate, timely, complete, and relevant.[5]

Accurate   For information to be of real value to a manager, it must be accurate. **Accurate information** provides a valid and reliable reflection of reality. A Japanese construction company recently bought information from a consulting firm about a possible building site in London. The Japanese

● **accurate information**
Provides a valid and reliable reflection of reality

were told that the land, which would be sold in a sealed bid auction, would attract bids of close to $250 million. They were also told that the land currently held an old building that could easily be demolished. Thus the Japanese bid $255 million—$90 million more than the next-highest bid. A few days later, the British government declared the building historic, preempting any thought of demolition. Clearly, the Japanese acted on information that was less than accurate.[6]

● **timely information**
Available in time for appropriate managerial action

Timely Information also needs to be timely. **Timely information** must be available in time for appropriate managerial action; it does not necessarily have to be available fast. What constitutes timeliness is a function of the situation facing the manager. When Marriott Corporation was gathering information for its proposed Fairfield Inn project, managers projected a six-month window for data collection. They believed that six months would give them time to get all of the information they needed while not delaying the project too much. In contrast, Marriott's computerized reservation and accounting system can provide a manager today with last night's occupancy level at any Marriott facility.[7]

● **complete information**
Provides the manager with all of the facts and details he or she needs

Complete **Complete information** gives the manager all the facts and details he or she needs; it must tell a complete story for it to be useful. If it is less than complete, the manager is likely to get an inaccurate or distorted picture of reality. For example, managers at Kroger used to think that house brands were more profitable than national brands because they yielded higher unit profits. On the basis of this information, they gave house brands a lot of shelf space and centered a lot of promotional activities around them. As Kroger's managers became more adept at understanding their information, however, they realized that national brands were actually more profitable over time because they sold many more units than house brands during any given period of time. Hence, while a store might sell ten cans of Kroger coffee in a day with a profit of 25 cents per can (total profit of $2.50), it would also sell fifteen cans of Maxwell House with a profit of 20 cents per can (total profit of $3.00).

● **relevant information**
Assures managers that the information is useful to them in their particular circumstances for their particular needs

Relevant **Relevant information** is useful to a manager, depending on his or her particular needs and circumstances. Operations managers need information on costs and productivity, human resources managers need information on hiring needs and turnover rates, and marketing managers need information on sales projections and advertising rates. As Wal-Mart Stores, Inc., contemplates expansion into other countries, it may begin to gather information about factors such as local regulations and customs. But the information isn't really relevant until the decision is made to begin international expansion.[8]

Information Management as Control

The manager needs to see information management as a vital part of the organization's control process.[9] As already noted, managers receive much more data and information than they need or can use. Accordingly, deciding how to handle each piece of data and information is essentially a form of control.

FIGURE 21.2 Information Management as Control

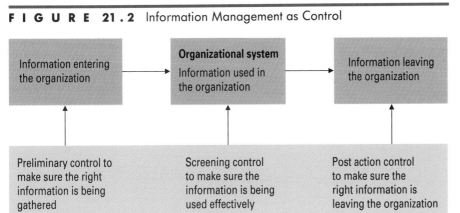

Information entering the organization	**Organizational system** Information used in the organization	Information leaving the organization
Preliminary control to make sure the right information is being gathered	Screening control to make sure the information is being used effectively	Post action control to make sure the right information is leaving the organization

Information management can be a part of the control system via preliminary, screening, and/or postaction control mechanisms. Since information from the environment is just as much a resource as raw materials or finances, it must be monitored and managed to promote its efficient and effective utilization.

The control perspective on information management is illustrated in Figure 21.2. Information enters, is used by, and leaves the organization. For example, Marriott took great pains to get all the information it needed to plan for and enter the economy lodging business. Once this preliminary information was gathered, it was made available in the proper form to everyone who needed it. In general, the effort to ensure that information is accurate, timely, complete, and relevant is a form of screening control. Finally, Marriott took steps to see that its competitors did not learn about its plans until the last possible minute. It also wanted to time and orchestrate news releases, public announcements, and advertising for maximum benefit. These efforts thus served a postaction control function.

BUILDING BLOCKS OF INFORMATION SYSTEMS

Information systems are generally either manual or computer-based. All information systems have five basic parts. Figure 21.3 diagrams these parts for a computer-based system. The *input medium* is the device that is used to add data and information into the system. For example, the optical scanner at Kroger enters point-of-sale information. Data can also be entered with a keyboard.

The data that are entered into the system typically flow first to a *processor,* which is that part of the system capable of organizing, manipulating, sorting, or performing calculations with the data. Most systems also have one or more *storage devices*—a place where data can be stored for later use. Floppy disks, hard disks, magnetic tapes, and optical disks are commonly used storage devices. As data are transformed into useable information, the resultant information must be communicated to the appropriate person by means of an *output medium.* Common devices used to display output are video displays, printers, and other computers.

Finally, the entire information system is operated by a *control system*—most often software of one form or another. Simple systems in smaller organizations can use off-the-shelf software. MicroSoft Word, WordPer-

Computer-based information systems generally have five basic components—an input medium, a processor, an output medium, a storage device, and a control system. Non-computer based systems use parallel components for the same basic purposes.

FIGURE 21.3 Building Blocks of a Computer-Based Information System

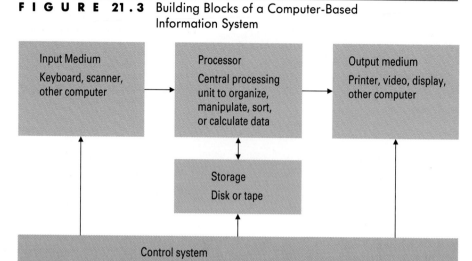

fect, and Word Star are popular word processing programs. Lotus 1-2-3 and Excel are popular spreadsheet programs, and dBASE III is frequently used for database management. Of course, elaborate systems of the type used by large businesses require a special customized software, hardware, or both. Linking computers together into a network increases the complexity of the system.

As we noted earlier, information systems need not be computerized. Many small organizations still function quite well with a manual system using paper documents (input medium), routing slips (processor), file folders and cabinets (storage devices), and typewriters (output medium). Increasingly, however, even small businesses are abandoning their manual systems for computerized ones. As hardware prices continue to drop and software becomes more and more powerful, computerized information systems will likely be within the reach of any business that wants to have one.

DETERMINANTS OF INFORMATION SYSTEM NEEDS

What determines whether an organization needs an information system, and how do these factors help define the organization's information management needs? In general, the key factors that determine these needs fall into two categories: organizational determinants and managerial determinants.[10] These are illustrated in Figure 21.4.

Organizational Determinants

The organization's environment and size generally help define its information management needs.

Environment In Chapters 3 and 11 we noted that an organization's environment affects it in many different ways, one of which is as a determinant of its information management needs. In general, the more uncertain and complex the environment, the greater is the need to formally manage information. Given that virtually all organizations face at least some degree of uncertainty, it can be argued that all organizations need to worry about managing their information. An organization like Hewlett-Packard Co. or IBM, however, that operates in an extremely uncertain environment has very strong needs for elaborate information management.

Size Size is another general determinant of an organization's information management needs. If all else is equal, the larger an organization is, the greater are its needs to manage its information systematically. Thus General Motors Corp. has greater information management needs than does its Cadillac division alone, and each has greater needs than does a single Cadillac dealership. The effects of organizational size can also be either slightly constrained or greatly accentuated by the diversity of the organization. A large organization that is essentially a single division, for example, has less pressure for information management than does a firm of the same size that comprises several different divisions.

Managerial Determinants

Two managerial factors also serve to define the information management needs of an organization. These managerial determinants are the area and level of the manager within the organization.

Area Each of an organization's basic functional areas (like finance, operations, marketing, or human resources) has a unique set of information man-

---

F I G U R E 21.4 Determinants of an Organization's Information-Processing Needs

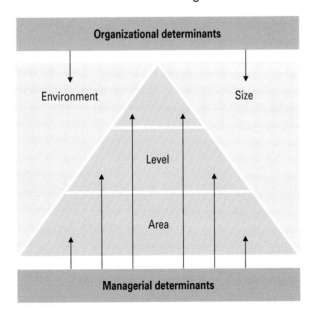

Information processing needs are determined by such organizational factors as the environment and the organization's size and such specific managerial factors as their area and level in the organization.

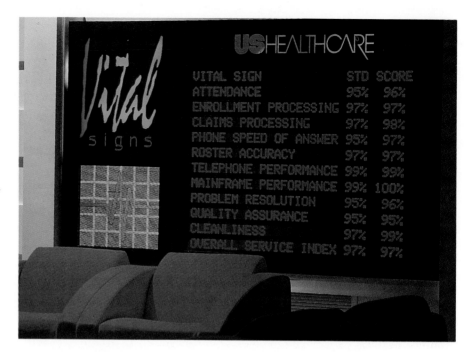

U.S. Healthcare, like more and more organizations today, is measuring the achievement of its service quality goals. But employees' supervisors are not the only ones who have access to these measurements: the company installed an electronic information board in the Customer Service Center that displays goals and measurements of activities such as average speed of answering telephone calls and resolving problems. Employees share in a bonus incentive fund when high standards are met.

agement needs. Human resources managers, for example, need information such as complete demographic data on all current employees, job-grade information, and Affirmative Action statistics. Marketing managers need data on current prices, market share, and advertising expenditures.

A related factor determining an organization's information management needs is the extent to which the managers in various areas within an organization are integrated and coordinated. If each acts totally on its own and coordination is handled by the managerial hierarchy, each area can survive with its own information system. But if managers in different areas are expected to coordinate their activities, then their information systems need to be coordinated. For example, the marketing system may be updated to include a projection for 10 percent more sales next year than previously expected. An integrated information system could use that information to provide the operations manager with an indication that additional output will be needed, to provide the human resources manager with an indication of how many additional workers will be needed, and to provide the financial manager with an indication of how much additional working capital will be needed to support higher wage and materials costs.

Level   A manager's level within the organization also helps determine the information management requirements of the organization. Managers at the top of the organization need broad, general kinds of information across a variety of time frames to help them with strategic planning. Middle managers need information of somewhat more specificity and with a shorter time frame. Lower-level managers need highly specific information with a very short time frame. For example, the vice president of marketing at General Mills, Inc., might want to know projected demand for eight different cereal products over the next five years. A divisional sales manager might need to know projected demand for two of those cereal products for the next one-year period. A district sales manager might need to know how much of one cereal is likely to be sold next month.

BASIC KINDS OF INFORMATION SYSTEMS

Organizations that use information systems, especially large organizations, often find that they need several kinds of systems to manage their information effectively. The most general kinds of information systems are transaction-processing systems, management information systems, decision support systems, and executive information systems.[11]

Transaction-Processing Systems

Transaction-processing systems are the first computerized form of information system many businesses adopt. A **transaction-processing system (TPS)** is a system designed to handle routine and recurring transactions within the business. Visa USA Inc. uses a TPS to record charges to individual credit accounts, credit payments made on the accounts, and send monthly bills to customers. In general, a TPS is most useful when the organization has a large number of highly similar transactions to process. Thus most forms of customer billings, bank transactions, and point-of-sale records are amenable to this form of information system. The automated scanners at Kroger that record each unit sold and its price are a form of TPS.

A TPS is especially helpful in aggregating large amounts of data into more manageable forms of information summaries. For example, a bank manager probably cares little about any given Visa transaction recorded for any single cardholder. More useful is information such as the average number of purchases made by each cardholder, their average daily balances, and average monthly finance charges assessed. In general, a TPS is most useful to lower-level managers. Even though TPS was the first approach to computerizing information management, it is still of considerable use and relevance to many organizations. Many of these organizations, however, have also found it necessary to develop more sophisticated systems.

● **transaction-processing system (TPS)**
A system designed to handle routine and recurring transactions with a business

Management Information Systems

The next step in the evolution of information management is generally called the **management information system (MIS).** An MIS is a system that gathers comprehensive data, organizes and summarizes it in a form that is of value to functional managers, and then provides those same managers with the information that they need to do their work. Figure 21.5 shows how such a system might work.

An MIS for a manufacturing firm might develop a computerized inventory system that keeps track of both anticipated orders and inventory on hand. A marketing representative talking to a customer about anticipated delivery dates can "plug into the system" and get a good idea of when an order can be shipped. The plant manager can also use the system to help determine how much of each of the firm's products to manufacture next

● **management information system (MIS)**
A system that gathers comprehensive data, organizes and summarizes it in a form of value to managers, and provides those managers with the information they need to do their work

FIGURE 21.5 A Basic Management Information System

A basic management information system relies on an integrated database. Managers in various functional areas can access the database and get information they need to make decisions. For example, operations managers can access the system to determine sales forecasts by marketing managers, and financial managers can check human resource files to identify possible candidates for promotions into the finance department.

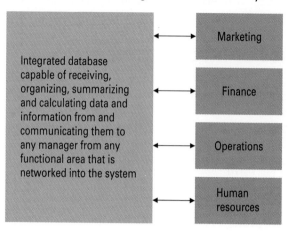

week or next month. Seminole Manufacturing Co., which supplies Wal-Mart with men's pants, uses a variation on the standard MIS called an EDE—electronic data exchange. The EDE system allows Seminole to tie directly into Wal-Mart's computerized inventory system to check current sales levels and stock on hand. Wal-Mart can also transmit new orders directly into Seminole's system—and managers there are ready to start working on it. As a result, delivery times have been cut in half and sales are up 31 percent.[12]

Decision Support Systems

● **decision support system (DSS)**

A system that automatically searches for, manipulates, and summarizes information needed by managers for use in making specific decisions

An increasingly common information system is called a **decision support system (DSS).** A DSS is an elaborate and quite powerful system that can automatically search for, manipulate, and summarize information needed by managers for specific decisions. A DSS is much more flexible than a traditional MIS and can help managers cope with nonroutine problems and decisions.[13]

A manager might be interested in knowing the likely effects of a price increase for a particular product sold by the firm. Thus she might query the DSS to determine the potential outcomes for price increases of 5, 7, and 10 percent. The DSS knows the pricing history for the product, the prices charged by competitors, their most recent price changes, the effects of price on sales, seasonal variations in demand and price, inflation rates, and virtually any other relevant information that might have already been determined. The system then calculates projected sales, market share, and profit profiles for each of the potential price-increase levels and provides them to the manager.

Decision support systems are extremely complex. They take considerable time and resources to develop and more time and resources to maintain and to teach managers how to effectively use them. They also seem to hold considerable potential for improving the quality of information available to managers making important decisions. "Management in Practice" describes how Frito-Lay, Inc., uses its decision support system to gain competitive advantage.

THE CHIPMAKER TURNS TO ITS SCANNERS

Frito-Lay, Inc., a division of PepsiCo, Inc., is the country's largest chipmaker. It produces about 40 percent of the $12.6 billion worth of salty snacks that U.S. snackers consume each year, and it accounts for about 42 percent of PepsiCo's profits. But it's not easy being number one and supporting all of the company's 240 products. Regional brands come out with new products and suddenly take a bite out of market share, while high-volume competitors like Anheuser-Busch, Inc.'s, Eagle Snacks discount their products and start a price war. Frito-Lay executives must stay on their toes.

That's why Frito was the first in its business to turn to decision support software to help it make marketing decisions. Ever since bar-code scanners became commonplace in U.S. supermarkets, virtually unlimited data have been available on what is selling where. The problem has been that this data in its raw form is virtually useless; marketing executives had to pour over reams of computer printouts looking for facts that might point to trends. Because such work was so time-consuming, much of the "instant" data got wasted or was analyzed too late.

Frito-Lay's Executive Information System has changed all that. It not only gathers the information rapidly but displays it in the most useful form and even flags figures that may be particularly important. The com-

pany's 10,000 salespeople use their handheld terminals to enter information daily, and the company's computer screens display how Frito's top 100 product lines are doing in 400,000 stores nationwide. The program graphs sales with color codes: red means a steep sales drop, yellow a slowdown, green a surge. The program also provides data about competitors' products, which promotions are working, and whether store displays are attracting customers.

Although Frito-Lay can't yet say how the system has affected its profit picture, management boasts that it saves each salesperson a day of paperwork per week. And it's easy to imagine how this well-digested information could help Frito-Lay fine-tune its marketing strategies. Now the company can tell in days rather than months how a discounting promotion is affecting sales, and it can spot a competitor's challenge before it does too much damage. Some analysts worry that making today's decisions based on yesterday's sales may lead to too much focus on short-term profits. But PepsiCo seems to like the system and is already expanding it to gather information on soft drink sales. The software may even pave the way for joint Frito-Pepsi promotions.

References: Stephanie Anderson Forest, "Chipping Away at Frito-Lay," *Business Week*, July 22, 1991, p. 26; Jeffrey Rothfeder and Jim Bartimo, "How Software Is Making Food Sales a Piece of Cake," *Business Week*, July 2, 1990, pp. 54–55.

Executive Information Systems

Executive information systems are the newest form of information system. An **executive information system (EIS)** is a system designed to meet the special information-processing needs of top managers. Because many top managers lack basic computer skills and because they need highly specialized information not readily available in other kinds of systems, many executives were reluctant to use their organizations' information system.

Executives don't need technical knowledge to use an EIS; they are constructed to be user-friendly. Such systems generally use icons and symbols and require few commands. The information they provide allows managers to bypass details and get directly to overall trends and patterns that may affect strategic decision making. It summarizes information rather than provides specific details. Thus, an EIS is both more powerful but easier to use than other systems. It also tailors the information to the specific needs of the manager.[14]

executive information system (EIS)
A system designed to meet the special information-processing needs of top managers

MANAGING INFORMATION SYSTEMS

By now, the value and importance of information systems should be apparent. Important questions must still be answered, however. How are such systems developed, and how are they used on a day-to-day basis? This section provides insights into these issues and related areas.

Establishing Information Systems

Several basic steps are involved in creating an information system, and these are outlined in Figure 21.6.[15] The first step is to determine the information needs of the organization and to establish goals for what is to be achieved with the proposed system. It is absolutely imperative that the project have full support and an appropriate financial commitment from top management if it is to be successful. Once the decision has been made to develop and install an information system, a task force is usually formed to oversee everything. Target users must be well represented on such a task force.

Next, three tasks can be done simultaneously. One task is to assemble a database. Most organizations already possess the information they need for an information system, but it is often not in the correct form. The Pentagon is spending large sums of money to transform all of its paper records into computer records. Many other branches of the government are also working hard to computerize their data.[16]

While the database is being assembled, the organization also needs to determine its hardware needs and acquire the appropriate equipment. Some systems rely solely on one large mainframe computer; others are increasingly using personal computers. Equipment is usually obtained from large manufacturers like IBM, Wang, Unisys Corporation, and Digital Equipment Corporation. Finally, software needs must also be determined and an

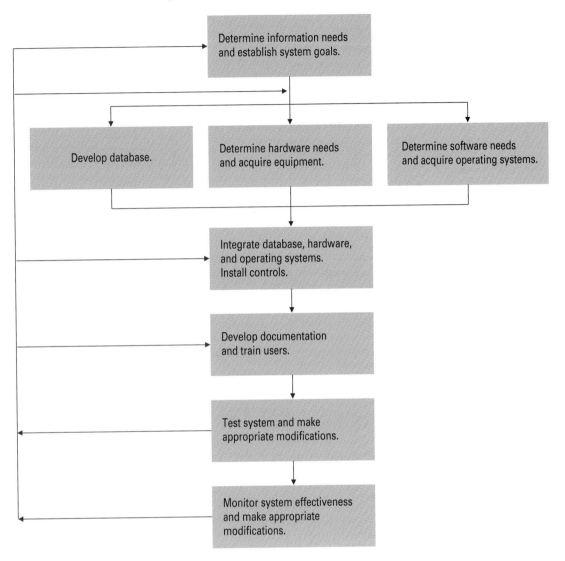

Establishing an information system is a complex procedure. Managers must realize, however, that the organization's information management needs will change over time, and some steps of the process may have to be done again in the future.

appropriate operating system obtained. Again, off-the-shelf packages will sometimes work, although most companies find it necessary to do some customization to suit their needs.

The actual information system is created by integrating the database, the hardware, and the software. (The mechanics of doing this are beyond the scope of this discussion.) The company, however, usually has to rely on the expertise of outside consulting firms along with the vendors who provided the other parts of the system to get it all put together. During this phase, activities include installation of equipment, stringing of cables between units, entering of data into the system, and installation and testing of the operating system. During this phase, system controls are also installed. A control is simply a characteristic of the system that limits certain forms of access or limits what a person can do with the system. For example, top managers may want to limit access to certain sensitive data to a few key people. These people may be given private codes that must be entered before the data are made available. Those who install and test the system must ensure that data cannot be accidentally erased by someone who happens to press the wrong key.

The next step is to develop documentation of how the system works and train people to use it. Documentation is the manuals, computerized help programs, diagrams, and instruction sheets that teach people how to use the system. In addition to documentation, training sessions, which allow people to practice using the system under the watchful eyes of experts, are also common.

The system must then be tested and appropriate modifications made. Regardless of how well planned an information system is, glitches will almost certainly appear. For example, the system may be unable to generate a report that needs to be made available to certain managers. Or the report may not be in the appropriate format. Or certain people may be unable to access data that they need to get other information from the system. In most cases, the consultants or internal group that installed the system will be able to make such modifications as the need arises.

An organization's information management needs will change over time. Hence, although the glitches get straightened out and the information system is operating normally, modifications may still be needed in the future. For example, after Black & Decker Corp. acquired General Electric Co.'s small-appliance business, it had to overhaul its own information system to accommodate all the new information associated with its new business. Information management is a continuous process.

Integrating Information Systems

In large and complex organizations, information systems must also be integrated. Integration may involve linking different information systems within the same organization or different organizations altogether.[17] Within an organization, for example, the marketing system and the operations system may need to communicate with one another. "The Global View" discusses how Merrill Lynch has integrated its information systems to better manage its worldwide operations.

Linking systems is not easy.[18] A company might install its first information system in operations using a Wang system. A couple of years later, it might put a system into marketing but decide to use IBM equipment. When a decision is made still later to integrate the two systems, differences in technology and operating systems might make such integration difficult or even impossible.

One way that this problem can be overcome is to develop everything at once. Unfortunately, doing so is expensive, and sometimes managers simply can't anticipate today exactly what their needs will be tomorrow. Another method is to adopt a standard type of system at the beginning so that subsequent additions fit properly. Even then, however, breakthroughs in information system technology may still make it necessary to change approaches in midstream.

Using Information Systems

The real test of the value of an information system is how it can be used. Ideally, an information system should be simple to use and nontechnical— that is, one should not have to be a computer expert to use the system. In

MERRILL LYNCH TRADES AROUND THE WORLD

The stock market crash of October 19, 1987, caused many changes in the financial world, but perhaps none was more important than the realization that the stock market was now global. Brokers used to assume that the markets in London and Tokyo took their cue from Wall Street, but the waves of panic selling that swept around the globe on Black Monday convinced everyone that no stock market could be considered in isolation any longer. The realization came to U.S. brokers none too soon, for whereas stock markets in the United States represented 58 percent of worldwide stock value in 1975, they represent only about one-third of it today.

Big U.S. brokers like Merrill Lynch & Co., Inc., obviously want to profit from the globalization of the stock market, and information technologies are their most important resource. Merrill Lynch spends as much as $1.5 billion each year on information technologies, and it entered the 1990s with a mandate to simplify its information systems and radically improve their productivity. One part of its goal is to create computer "platforms" that will allow any Merrill Lynch employee to access any one of the eight or more major databases that the company uses. The company hopes that by making it easier for employees to do their work, such technology advances will increase productivity and eventually lower overall costs.

Now at Merrill Lynch offices around the world, brokers keep track of local and international developments and pass information on to other parts of the company. All of Merrill's trades go through one of two IBM supercomputers in Manhattan, machines that are so important that the company keeps another one ready to fill in if one of the main computers goes down. With their terminals giving them information on all major exchanges, Merrill Lynch brokers follow events around the world. Will German banks really lower their interest rates? Will the bullish opening of the London market turn into a rally?

Ironically, with billions of dollars worth of sophisticated technology at their disposal, many Merrill Lynch brokers still rely principally on the telephone. Brokers in New York talk constantly to their colleagues in London and Tokyo, trying to use their professional hunches to gauge how individual markets will do and how they will affect each other. As good as information technology now is, it hasn't yet made obsolete the need for human dialogue.

References: Bryan Burrough, Craig Forman, and Kathryn Graven, "How Merrill Lynch Moves Its Stock Deals All Around the World," *The Wall Street Journal*, November 9, 1987, pp. 1, 8; Elaine M. Koerner, "Integrating Information Systems for Competitive Advantage at Merrill Lynch," *Long-Range Planning*, April 1990, pp. 27–34.

---

theory, a manager should be able to access a modern information system by turning on a computer and pressing certain keys in response to menu prompts. The manager should also be able to enter appropriate new data or request that certain kinds of information be provided. The requested information might first be displayed on a computer screen or monitor. After the manager is satisfied, the information can then be printed out or stored in the system for future use.[19]

The Travelers Corporation has made effective use of its information system by hiring a team of trained nurses to review health-insurance claims. The nurses tap into the company's regular information system and analyze the medical diagnoses provided with each claim. They can use this information to determine whether a second opinion is warranted before a particular surgical procedure is approved. They enter their decision directly into the system. When the claim form is printed out, it contains a provision that spells out whether the claimant must seek a second opinion before proceeding with a particular treatment.[20]

A company's information system should be easily accessible by everyone who needs to use it. Employees access Sun Life's information system through the Command Centre, and Nazir Kassam and Lana Sam are among those who answer as many as 160 queries a day. The Command Centre, which is staffed seven days a week, 24 hours a day, is responsible for the management of Sun Life's International Voice and Data network as well as the running of daily production and on-line systems.

THE IMPACT OF INFORMATION SYSTEMS ON ORGANIZATIONS

Information systems are clearly an important part of most modern organizations. Their effects are felt in a variety of ways. In particular, information systems affect performance, the organization itself, and people within the organization. Information systems also have clear limits to what they can do.

Performance Effects

Information systems are installed because management thinks that they will make the organization more effective and efficient. During the 1980s, for example, almost 40 percent of all capital spending by U.S. companies was on information systems technology—close to one trillion dollars.[21] Has the expenditure been worthwhile? Some experts say yes, whereas others have their doubts. Although information systems can speed up an organization's ability to crunch numbers and generate documents, it is difficult to measure whether the increased speed is justified in light of the enormous costs involved. Many organizations, including General Electric, K mart Corp., and American Airlines, Inc., claim that their information systems have made them enormously successful. Indeed, there seems to be a growing consensus that information systems do pay for themselves over time, although it may take years for the system to pay its own way. Westinghouse firmly believes that its commitment to information systems has paid huge dividends.

A highly effective system was developed by the U.S. Forest Service. The Forest Service used to have a policy of attacking every forest fire by 10 A.M. the day after it was reported. Costs could run as high as $10 million for a major fire. The service now uses computer models as a part of its information system to determine how important containment really is. For example, rivers often provide a natural barrier that stops fires from spreading.

An Idaho blaze was determined to fit just such a pattern. Under the old plan, the Fire Service would have spent an estimated $3.7 million to extinguish the blaze. But understanding how a river would halt the fire's spread resulted in expenses of only $400,000. Information is made available to firefighters in the field through hand-held programmable computers tied into a master information system.[22] Although not every organization will be as satisfied as the Forest Service with its information system, more and more firms are telling comparable success stories.

Organizational Effects

Information systems affect the organization's basic structure and design. These effects generally happen in two ways. First, most organizations find it useful to create a separate unit to handle the information management system; some even create a new top-management position, usually called the chief information officer, or CIO.[23] This manager and her or his staff is responsible for maintaining the information system, upgrading it as appropriate, finding new uses for it, and training people in its use.

The second way in which information affects organizations is by allowing managers to eliminate layers in the managerial hierarchy. As detailed in Chapter 10, information systems allow managers to stay in touch with large numbers of subordinates, thereby eliminating the need for so many layers of hierarchical control. IBM, for example, eliminated a layer of management because of improved efficiencies achieved through its information management system. Some experts have suggested that in the future managers will be able to coordinate as many as 200 subordinates at one time.[24]

Behavioral Effects

Information systems affect the behaviors of people in organizations both positively and negatively. On the plus side, information systems usually improve individual efficiency. Some people also enjoy their work more because they have fun using the new technology. As a result of computerized bulletin boards and electronic mail, groups can form across organizational boundaries.

Negative effects include isolation: information systems enable people to have everything they need to do their jobs without interacting with others. Managers can work at home easily, with the possible side effects of making them unavailable to others who need them or removing them from important parts of the social system. Computerized working arrangements also tend to be much less personal than other methods. For example, a computer-transmitted "pat on the back" will likely mean less than one given in person. Researchers are just beginning to determine how individual behaviors and attitudes are affected by information systems.

Information System Limitations

Managers must also recognize the limits of information systems.[25] Several of these are listed in Table 21.1. First, as already noted, information systems are expensive and difficult to develop. Thus organizations may try to cut corners or install a system in such a piecemeal fashion that its effectiveness suffers.

While information systems play a vital role in modern organizations, they are not without their limitations. In particular, there are six basic limitations to information systems. For example, one major limitation of installing an information system is cost. For a large company, an information system might cost several million dollars.

TABLE 21.1   Limitations of Information Systems

1. Information systems are expensive and difficult to develop and implement.
2. Information systems are not suitable for all tasks or problems.
3. Managers sometimes rely on information systems too much.
4. Information provided to managers may not be as accurate, timely, complete, or relevant as it appears.
5. Managers may have unrealistic expectations of what the information system can do.
6. The information system may be subject to sabotage, computer viruses, or downtime.

Information systems simply are not suitable for some tasks or problems. Complex problems requiring human judgment must still be addressed by human beings. Information systems are often a useful tool for managers, but they can seldom actually replace managers. Managers also may come to rely too much on information systems. As a consequence, the manager may lose touch with the real-world problems he or she needs to be concerned about.

Information may not be as accurate, timely, complete, or relevant as it appears. People have a strong tendency to think that because a computer performed the calculations, the answer must be correct—especially if the answer is calculated to several decimal places. If the initial information was flawed, however, all resultant computations using it will be flawed as well.

Managers sometimes have unrealistic expectations about what information systems can accomplish. They may believe that the first stage of implementation will result in a full-blown communication network that a child could use. When the manager comes to see the flaws and limits of the system, she or he may become disappointed and as a result not use the system effectively. Finally, the information system may be subject to sabotage, computer viruses, or downtime. Disgruntled employees have been known to deliberately enter false data.[26] And a company that relies too much on a computerized information system may find itself totally paralyzed in the event of a simple power outage.

RECENT ADVANCES IN INFORMATION MANAGEMENT

Because of the enormous promise of information systems, and despite their occasional limitations, work continues to uncover new and even more sophisticated approaches to managing information. This section highlights some of the most interesting ones.

Telecommunications

● **telecommunications**
The use of electronic media to communicate over distances; includes the telephone, telegraph, electronic bulletin boards, and facsimile machines

One area in which great strides have been made is **telecommunications.** Several forms of telecommunications have been or are being developed.

Videoconferencing allows people in different locations to see and talk to one another. For example, Sam Walton often used teleconferences to talk directly with Wal-Mart employees during their normal Saturday morning meetings.[27] Electronic mail systems allow managers to send messages to one another through computer linkups. People "post" messages on electronic bulletin boards for other interested people to read. Voice messaging allows voice messages to be stored and transferred between computers.

Networks and Expert Systems

Advances continue to be made in the area of networking. Even computer systems with very different operating systems are increasingly able to communicate with one another. Although there are still a variety of "standard" operating systems, as each is more finely developed it can interface with others more and more effectively.

Expert systems are also becoming more and more practical. An **expert system** is an information system created to duplicate, or at least imitate, the thought processes of a human being.[28] The starting point in developing an expert system is to identify all the "if-then" contingencies that pertain to a given situation. These contingencies form the knowledge base for the system. For example, Table 21.2 summarizes the knowledge base for a hypothetical firm's pricing policy. The facts and if-then contingencies outlined in the table determine the pricing policy. Statements 3, 5, and 7 in boldface type represent the current situation facing the company. Thus a manager could query the system with the question "What is price policy?" The system would respond, "Price policy is increase price." When the manager asked why, the system would answer, "Price policy is increase price because margin is low and demand is strong."

Organizations have developed considerably more complex and useful expert systems. For example, Campbell Soup Company developed an expert system to recreate the thought processes of one of its key managers, Aldo Cimino. Cimino was so familiar with operations of the seven-story soup kettles used to cook soup that the company feared no one else could

● **expert system**
An information system created to duplicate or imitate the thought processes of a human being

Air traffic controllers rely on the telephone network for the information they need. If this network were to fail, the controllers could no longer locate each airliner in the sky. U.S. West Communications has developed a system to instantly reroute service to another network in case of failure. The Self-Healing Network Service ensures that air traffic controllers have continuous access to vital information.

TABLE 21.2   An Example Knowledge Base for a Firm's Pricing Policy

Factual Knowledge
Price is $50.00.
Cost is $45.00.
Demand is 1,121.
Margin is (price − cost).

Process Knowledge
1. If margin is high and demand is weak, then price-policy is decrease-price.
2. If margin is normal and demand is steady, then price-policy is maintain-price.
3. **If margin is low and demand is strong, then price-policy is increase-price.**
4. If margin is greater-than 25, then margin is high.
5. **If margin is less-than 10, then margin is low.**
6. If margin is-not high and margin is-not low, then margin is normal.
7. **If demand is greater-than 1,100, then demand is strong.**
8. If demand is less-than 900, then demand is weak.
9. If demand is-not strong and demand is-not weak, then demand is steady.

Source: David B. Paradice and James F. Courtney, Jr., "Intelligent Organizations," *Texas A&M Business Forum*, Fall 1988, pp. 18–22. Reprinted with permission.

learn the job as well as he. So it hired Texas Instruments Incorporated to study his job, interview him and observe his work, and create an expert system that could mimic his experience. The resultant system, containing more than 150 if-then rules, helps operate the kettles today.[29]

SUMMARY OF KEY POINTS

Information is a vital part of every manager's job. For information to be useful, it must be accurate, timely, complete, and relevant. Information management is best conceived of as part of the control process.

Information systems contain five basic components: input medium, processor, storage device, output medium, and control system. Whereas the form will vary, both manual and computerized information systems have these components.

An organization's information management requirements are determined organizationally by its environment and size, and managerially by the manager's area and level in the organization. Each factor must be weighed in planning an information system.

Basic kinds of information systems are transaction-processing systems, basic management information systems, decision support systems, and executive information systems. Each provides certain types of information and is most valuable for specific types of managers.

Managing information systems involves first deciding how to establish the information systems. Of course, this step actually involves a wide array of specific activities and steps. The systems must then be integrated. Finally, managers must be able to use them.

Information systems affect organizations in a variety of ways. Major influences are on performance, the organization itself, and behavior within the organization. Managers should also understand that information systems have limitations so they do not have unrealistic expectations.

Recent advances in information systems include breakthroughs in telecommunications, networks, and expert systems. Each promises to further enhance an organization's ability to more effectively manage information.

DISCUSSION QUESTIONS

Questions for Review

1. What are the characteristics of useful information? How can information management aid in organizational control?

2. What are the building blocks of information systems? How are they related to one another?

3. What is a management information system (MIS)? How can such a system be used to benefit an organization?

4. What is an expert system? Do such systems have any important potential for use by business organizations? Why or why not?

Questions for Analysis

5. In what ways is an information system like an inventory control system or a production control system? In what ways is it different from those?

6. It has been said that the information revolution now occurring is like the industrial revolution in terms of the magnitude of its impact on organizations and society. What leads to such a view? Why might that view be an overstatement?

7. Is it possible for the chief information officer of an organization to become too powerful? If so, how might the situation be prevented? If not, why not?

Questions for Application

8. Interview a local business manager about the use of information in his or her organization. How is information managed? Does the organization use a computer system? How well does the information system seem to be integrated with other aspects of organizational control?

9. Your college or university library deals in information. What kind of information system does it use? Is it computerized? How might the information system be redesigned to be of more value to you?

10. Go to the library and see if you can locate a reference to the use of an expert system in a business firm. If you can, share it with the class. Why might this be a difficult assignment?

BUILDING RETAILING'S NEXT SUPERSTAR

By now most U.S. consumers are familiar with Wal-Mart, the Arkansas-based retailing phenomenon. But the Waltons aren't the only Arkansas family to build a wildly successful retail chain at a time when many once-prospering retailers are going out of business. William Dillard and his family are not nearly as rich as the Waltons, and though their chain—Dillard's—does about $3 billion of business each year, that's only one-tenth of Wal-Mart's revenues. But Dillard's is beginning to generate the same kind of interest that Wal-Mart has, in part because of its financial track record: 25 percent compound annual growth in earnings per share and 37 percent annual return to investors over the last decade.

It may surprise people used to the down-home image of the Arkansas businessman, but William Dillard can attribute much of his company's success to its reliance on advanced computer technology. A computer system links Dillard's 194 stores, allowing executives to find out almost instantly how any product is doing in any of the company's stores. With a few keystrokes someone at headquarters can find out how many Union Bay brand jeans have been sold, not just that week or that month, but that morning.

This quick access to information has allowed Dillard's to create a program called Quick Response that gets new stock to the company's stores in record time and eliminates the need for any human intervention. All merchandise carries a bar code, and when the code is scanned at the checkout register, the sales information is sent instantly to the company's IBM mainframe computer in Little Rock. The information is collected and passed on electronically to Dillard's warehouses and vendors, and the necessary replacement items can be on their way to the appropriate stores within days, still without anyone getting involved.

The Quick Response network allows Dillard's to keep its stores unusually well-stocked and to ensure that customers seldom leave the store frustrated because they can't find the right size or color.

This kind of loyalty extends to vendors as well. Dillard's tends to find one supplier for a particular item and stick with that company, even through difficult times. Such close relations irritate companies that would like to sell to Dillard's, but as Alex Dillard puts it, "We believe in building relationships, and that takes time."* Suppliers like to sell to Dillard's not just because of this loyalty but because the Quick Response system allows them to lower their own inventories.

Other retailers have been skeptical about Dillard's ability to grow beyond its small-town roots, but their numbers are diminishing. Dillard's has been buying them up.

*Quoted in Susan Caminiti, "A Quiet Superstar Rises in Retailing," *Fortune*, October 23, 1989, p. 169.

Discussion Questions

1. Why don't more retailers use something like Dillard's Quick Response program?

2. How does the Quick Response system help Dillard's sell its merchandise? What limitations does it impose?

E 3. How great a role should loyalty play in choosing the right vendor, as opposed to product quality and price?

References: Susan Caminiti, "A Quiet Superstar Rises in Retailing," *Fortune*, October 23, 1989, pp. 167–174; Carol Hymowitz and Thomas F. O'Boyle, "Two Disparate Firms Find Keys to Success in Troubled Industries," *The Wall Street Journal*, May 29, 1991, pp. A1, A9; Gretchen Morgenson, "A Midas Touch," *Forbes*, February 4, 1991, p. 42.

INFORMATION SYSTEMS KEY TO PACKAGE DELIVERY COMPETITION

*F*ederal Express invented overnight delivery. United Parcel Service was once the dominant private package service. Now the two giants are competing in each other's turf, each offering to move parcels of just about any size, anywhere, as fast as customers need them. The stakes in this competition are high, and to gain advantage the two companies have been turning to increasingly sophisticated information systems.

UPS has spent $1.4 billion on computerization. At the heart of its system is its own version of the bar code, called a dense code, which can hold twice as much information as a normal bar code in a fingerprint-like swirl that takes up less than a square inch. With a dense code on every package, scanners on conveyors or in delivery trucks can read a package's origin, destination, contents, and price without anyone having to contact headquarters.

A small subsidiary in Los Angeles recently experimented with an entire electronic tracking system. Tracking devices allow headquarters to know where all the company's vehicles are at any time and to send messages to a particular vehicle. Such devices allow drivers to get directions electronically and carry a computerized clipboard to record transactions. If UPS can successfully transfer this system to its huge fleet, UPS drivers may one day present package recipients with the traditional "sign at the X" clipboard, plug the clipboard into a central computer, and send all the transaction information, including a copy of each customer's signature, to headquarters.

Federal Express employees use their own hand-held "Supertrackers" to record information about packages. At Federal's central hub in Memphis, the company is phasing in a Ramp Management Advisory System (RMAS) to make more efficient the tracking and launching of its scores of daily flights. RMAS uses expert system technology running on Unix-based workstations. Each aircraft appears on the screen as a different icon, and the icon's colors change when its status changes. The ground and maintenance crews can tap into the network to get scheduling information. Reports of flight activity, which used to take two hours to write up, are now completed in minutes.

Behind the big two, other companies are growing quickly with their own technological innovations. DHL Airways, for instance, controls only about 2 percent of the market, but it is working to create its own integrated information network which has already allowed it to make great strides. No one in the package delivery industry can afford to be technologically complacent.

Discussion Questions

1. With the big companies investing so much money in new technology, do you think a smaller company could use simpler technology and underbid Federal and UPS? How might such a company operate?

2. How do customers directly benefit from these advances in information technology?

E **3.** Do you think the drivers and package sorters at companies like UPS and Federal Express will benefit or suffer from these advances?

References: "Federal Express Corp.," *Transportation & Distribution*, Vol. 32, No. 5, p. 66; Thomas Hoffman, "Will Open Systems Deliver at DHL?," *InformationWeek*, February 24, 1992, p. 20; Maryfran Johnson, "Expert Systems Put FedEx in Flight," *Computerworld*, November 18, 1991, p. 45; Kenneth Labich, "Big Changes at Big Brown," *Fortune*, January 18, 1988, pp. 56–64; Todd Vogel, "Can UPS Deliver the Goods in a New World?," *Business Week*, June 4, 1990, pp. 80–82.

Updating The Old "Quality Control"

The purpose of this exercise is to help students better understand how total quality management has changed the traditional thinking about the control function.

Learning Objectives

After completing this exercise you should have a better understanding of

1. The relationships between control and quality.

2. How managers and organizations can use the controlling process to enhance product and service quality.

Preview

Zytec Corp.

Zytec Corp., formerly a unit of Magnetic Peripherals Inc., was founded as an independent firm in 1984 when its senior managers purchased the business via a leveraged buyout. Zytec makes power supplies for computers and other electronic equipment. Based in Eden Prairie, Minnesota, Zytec employs around 750 workers. From its very beginning, Zytec managers approached all phases of business operations with the philosophy of total quality management.

Solectron Corp.

Solectron Corp. provides customized integrated manufacturing services for manufacturers in the electronics industry. The firm was founded in 1977 by an immigrant from Taiwan and a second-generation Japanese American. Today Solectron employs over 3,300 people and has operations at eight California sites. In 1991, Solectron generated $265 million in sales, of which $9 million was profit.

Marlow Industries

Marlow Industries, based in Dallas, was started in 1973. Marlow makes customized thermoelectric coolers—devices that monitor and control the temperature of electronic equipment. The firm employs about 160 people and has annual sales of over $12 million.

Doing Things Right the First Time

"Quality control, quality assurance and all these things, diligently applied," Philip Crosby says, "still produced material that did not meet the contract, did not meet the requirements, always had variations. . . . I went to Juran courses and Deming courses and everybody else courses, and what I learned was that the best thing you can do is contain it. All dams leak. . . . But that was not satisfactory to the management that I had. They didn't want to always play catch-up, they didn't want to always play defense. They wanted to know why couldn't we make what it was we said we were going to make. . . . It finally dawned on me about prevention . . .

prevention was always sort of a far-out thing in industry, but my education was medical, and in medicine, prevention is the whole thing. It's okay to fix, but it's better to stay well. . . . I began to see that the problem was management, not the workers." Crosby says management accepted the statistical theory that a few things will always be bad and the business school theory that to try to get everything right would be too expensive. "I thought, 'It must be cheaper to do things right the first time.'"*

Background Assignment

Go to the library and find articles on your assigned company for the years spanning 1985 to 1990. Though these firms are all somewhat small, you should be able to find enough background information for this exercise. From the information you gather, characterize your assigned company's situation during the 1985–1990 period. Describe its environment, threats, and challenges.

The Video

In 1991, Zytec, Solectron, and Marlow Industries were the three Baldrige winners. Your instructor will show you a video that provides some general information about how these firms were selected for the award.

Questions for Discussion

1. Can an organization improve quality by focusing on one of the basic managerial functions, or must all of them be involved?

2. Zytec, Solectron, and Marlow are all relatively new and relatively small organizations. This combination of winners is very different from that of previous years. Can you think of any possible explanations?

3. To date only one firm (Federal Express) has won a Baldrige award in the service category. Why do you think most winners are manufacturers?

4. Assuming you have completed all of the video exercises in this book, what are some of the common themes and practices which appear to characterize all of the Baldrige award winners?

Follow-Up Assignment

Return to the library and get more recent articles charting your assigned company's performance since winning the Baldrige award in 1991. Review recent annual reports and note any mention of quality improvement programs. How has quality affected performance? What changes did quality improvement result in for your company? Have these changes paid off?

*Source: Lloyd Dobyns and Clare Crawford-Mason, *Quality or Else.* (Boston: Houghton Mifflin Company, 1991) p. 65. Copyright © Houghton Mifflin Company. Used with permission.

SPECIAL
CHALLENGES OF
MANAGEMENT

22 *Managing Cultural
Diversity*

23 *Entrepreneurship and New
Venture Formation*

Appendix **1** *Managerial
Careers*

Appendix **2** *Tools for
Budgetary and Financial Control*

Managing Cultural Diversity

OBJECTIVES

After studying this chapter, you should be able to:

● *Discuss the nature of cultural diversity, including its meaning and associated trends.*

● *Identify and describe the major dimensions of diversity in organizations.*

● *Discuss the primacy impact of diversity on organizations.*

● *Describe individual and organizational strategies and approaches to coping with diversity.*

● *Discuss the six characteristics of the fully multicultural organization.*

OUTLINE

The Nature of Cultural Diversity
   The Meaning of Cultural Diversity
   Reasons for Increasing Diversity

Dimensions of Diversity
   Age Distributions
   Gender
   Ethnicity
   Other Dimensions of Diversity

The Impact of Diversity on Organizations
   Diversity in Other Countries
   Diversity as a Force for Social Change
   Diversity as a Competitive Advantage
   Diversity as a Source of Conflict

Managing Diversity in Organizations
   Individual Strategies for Dealing with
    Diversity
   Organizational Approaches to Managing
    Diversity

Toward the Multicultural Organization

AVON PRODUCTS, INC., headquartered in New York, is the largest cosmetics firm in the United States. For many years the firm concentrated on direct selling spearheaded by a cadre of thousands of saleswomen who went door-to-door pushing the firm's fragrances and cosmetics. The firm's slogan, "Avon calling," was widely recognized throughout the United States. Avon still earns almost 95 percent of its revenues from its direct sales operations.

In 1987 Avon decided to enter the retail cosmetics business. Its first effort culminated in the acquisition of the line of Giorgio fragrances that same year. Giorgio's Red was the top-selling fragrance in the United States in 1990. Avon is also concentrating more and more on foreign markets, recently entering markets in Eastern Europe and China. Much of the firm's future growth promises to come from abroad.

For years, Avon has had an effective Affirmative Action program that allowed the firm to identify and hire qualified minority employees. But recently, the firm became alarmed that while it was hiring many minority employees, they were not advancing in the organization very fast and many of them were leaving for better opportunities elsewhere.

To help cope with this problem, Avon created networks of black, Hispanic, and Asian employees. Each network meets regularly, publishes a newsletter for the employees it represents, and presents their interest to top management. So far, Avon's approach seems to be paying off. Its retention rate has improved, for example, and several minority group members have been promoted to higher levels in the organization. But perhaps most important, white male managers in the firm say that they are developing a better understanding of what others value and how to better work with minority group members for the benefit of everyone.[1] ●

ike most organizations in the world today, Avon has seen tremendous change in the composition of its work force during the last several decades. Once dominated by white male managers, the firm now employs people at a variety of organizational levels from a diverse set of cultural backgrounds. And like other organizations today, Avon has encountered more than a few challenges as it has addressed the variety of issues and opportunities created by its increasingly diverse work force.

This chapter is about diversity in today's workplace. We begin by exploring the meaning and nature of cultural diversity. We then identify and discuss several common dimensions of diversity. The impact of diversity on the organization is then explored. We then address how diversity can be managed for the betterment of individuals and organizations. Finally, we characterize the fully multicultural organization.

● **cultural diversity**
Exists in a group or organization whose members differ from one another along one or more important dimensions such as age, gender, or ethnicity

The globalization movement—the increasing number of firms that have businesses, suppliers, or customers in other countries— contributes to increased cultural diversity in organizations. Dow, with half of its sales, assets, and employees located outside of the U.S., sees worldwide access to gifted researchers as a major benefit of globalization. More than eleven countries are represented at Dow's Los Angeles Operations.

THE NATURE OF CULTURAL DIVERSITY

Cultural diversity has become an important issue in many organizations, both in the United States and abroad. A logical starting point, then, is to establish the meaning of cultural diversity and to then examine why such diversity is increasing today.

The Meaning of Cultural Diversity

Cultural diversity exists in a group or organization whose members differ from one another along one or more important dimensions.[2] Diversity can be conceptualized as a continuum. If everyone in the group or organization is exactly like everyone else, there is no cultural diversity whatsoever. But if everyone is different along every imaginable dimension, total diversity exists. Of course, these extremes are more hypothetical than real. Most organizations are characterized by a level of diversity somewhere between these extremes. Therefore, diversity should be thought of in terms of degree or level of diversity along relevant dimensions, not as an absolute phenomenon wherein a group or organization is or is not diverse.

These dimensions might include gender, age, or ethnic origin. A group comprising five middle-aged white male U.S. executives has relatively little diversity. If one member leaves and is replaced by a young white female executive, the group becomes a bit more diverse. If another member is replaced by an older black executive, diversity increases some more. And when a third member is replaced by a Japanese executive, the group becomes even more diverse.

Reasons for Increasing Diversity

As we noted earlier, organizations today are becoming increasingly diverse along many different dimensions. Several different factors account for these trends and changes, and four of the more important ones are illustrated in Figure 22.1.

FIGURE 22.1 Reasons for Increasing Diversity

| Legislation and legal action | | Changing demographics in the labor force |

Increasing diversity in organizations

| Increased awareness that diversity improves the quality of the work force | | The globalization movement |

Cultural diversity is increasing in most organizations today for four basic reasons. These reasons promise to make diversity even greater in the future. For example, Digital Equipment's Boston plant has 350 employees. These employees come from 44 countries and speak 19 languages.

Changing demographics in the labor force is contributing to increased diversity. As more women and minorities enter the labor force, for example, the available pool of talent from which organizations hire employees has changed in both size and composition. If talent within each segment of the labor pool is evenly distributed (for example, if the percentage of very talented men in the work force is the same as the percentage of very talented women in the work force), it follows logically that, over time, proportionately more women and proportionately fewer men will be hired by an organization.[3]

A related factor contributing to diversity is the increased awareness by organizations that they can improve the overall quality of their work force by hiring and promoting the most talented people available. By casting a broader net in recruiting and looking beyond traditional sources for new employees, organizations are finding better qualified employees from many different segments of society. Thus organizations are finding that diversity can be a source of competitive advantage.[4]

Legislation and legal actions that have forced organizations to hire more broadly have also increased diversity. Before 1964, organizations in the United States were essentially free to discriminate against women, blacks, and other minorities. Thus most organizations were dominated by white men. But over the last thirty years or so, various laws have outlawed discrimination against these and other groups. As we detailed in Chapter 13, organizations must hire and promote people today solely on the basis of their qualifications.

A final factor contributing to increased diversity in organizations is the globalization movement. Organizations that have opened offices and related facilities in other countries have had to learn to deal with different customs, social norms, and mores. Strategic alliances and foreign ownership are also contributing as managers today are increasingly likely to have job assignments in other countries, to work with foreign managers within their own countries, or both. As employees and managers move from assignment to assignment across national boundaries, organizations and their subsidiaries

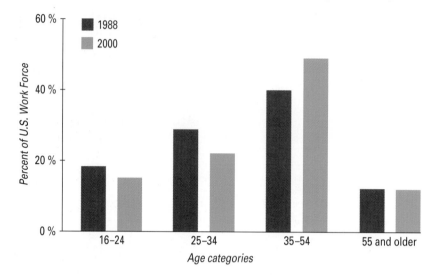

FIGURE 22.2 Age Distribution Trends in the U.S. Work Force

Source: *Occupational Outlook Handbook* (U.S. Bureau of Labor Statistics: Washington D.C., 1990–1991), pp. 8–12.

within each country become more diverse. Thus, both patterns of diversity within other countries and increased diversity as a result of cross-national transfers of employees are important factors that serve to increase diversity.

DIMENSIONS OF DIVERSITY

As indicated earlier, many different dimensions of diversity can be used to characterize an organization. In this section we discuss age, gender, ethnicity, and other dimensions of diversity.

Age Distributions

The average age of the U.S. work force is gradually increasing and will continue to do so for the next several years. Figure 22.2 presents age distributions for U.S. workers in 1988 and projected age distributions for the year 2000.

Several factors are contributing to this pattern. For one thing, the baby-boom generation (the unusually large number of people who were born in the twenty-year period after World War II) continues to age. Declining birth rates among the post-baby-boom generations simultaneously account for smaller percentages of new entrants into the labor force. Another factor that contributes to the aging work force is improved health and medical care: people are able to remain productive and active for longer periods of time. Combined with higher legal limits for mandatory retirement, more and more people are working beyond the age at which they might have retired just a few years ago.[5]

A quality improvement team at Corning that surveyed women employees discovered that lack of career support and child-care programs, unequal pay, and sexual harassment were common complaints. Addressing these issues, Corning implemented child care, part-time hours, training programs, and formal sexual harassment procedures. Corning's director of diversity Dawn M. Cross said, "For us it was a cost of doing business. There were artificial barriers resulting in many employees being underutilized."

How does this trend affect organizations? Older workers tend to have more experience, may be more stable, and can make greater contributions to productivity than younger workers. On the other hand, despite improvements in health and medical care, older workers are likely to require higher levels of insurance coverage and medical benefits. The declining labor pool of younger workers will continue to pose problems for organizations as they find fewer potential new entrants into the labor force.[6]

Gender

More and more women are entering the work force, and organizations have subsequently experienced changes in the relative proportions of male and female employees. In the United States, for example, the percentage of male employees will shrink from 55 percent in 1988 to 53 percent by the year 2000. Simultaneously, the percentage of female employees will increase from 45 percent in 1988 to 47 percent by the year 2000.[7]

These trends aside, a major gender-related problem that many organizations face today is the so-called glass ceiling. The **glass ceiling** describes a barrier that keeps many women from advancing to top management positions in many organizations. This ceiling is a barrier that is difficult to break, but it is also so subtle as to be hard to see. Indeed, although women comprise almost 45 percent of all managers, there are only two female CEOs among the 1000 largest businesses in the United States. Similarly, the average pay of women in organizations is lower than that of men. While the pay gap is gradually shrinking, inequalities are still present nonetheless.[8]

Why does the glass ceiling exist? One reason is that some male managers are still reluctant to promote female managers.[9] Another is that many talented women choose to leave their jobs in larger organizations and start their own businesses. Still another reason is that some women choose to suspend or slow their career progression to have children.[10]

glass ceiling
A barrier that exists in some organizations that presumably keeps women from advancing to top management positions

Ethnicity

● **ethnicity**
The ethnic composition of a group or organization

Yet another major dimension of cultural diversity in organizations is **ethnicity,** or the ethnic composition of a group or organization. Within the United States, most organizations reflect varying degrees of ethnicity comprising whites, blacks, Hispanics, and Asians. Figure 22.3 shows the ethnic composition of the U.S. work force in 1988 and as projected for the year 2000 in terms of these ethnic groups.[11]

The biggest projected changes involve whites and Hispanics. In particular, the percentage of whites in the work force is expected to drop from 79 percent to 74 percent. At the same time, the percentage of Hispanics is expected to climb from 7 percent to 10 percent. The percentages of blacks and Asians and others are expected to climb only about 1 percent each.

As are women, black, Hispanic, and Asian people are generally underrepresented in the executive ranks of most organizations today. And their pay is similarly lower. But also as for women, the differences are gradually disappearing as organizations fully embrace equal employment opportunity and recognize the higher overall level of talent available to them.[12]

Other Dimensions of Diversity

In addition to age, gender, and ethnicity, organizations are also confronting other dimensions of diversity. Country of national origin is a dimension of diversity that can be especially important for global organizations, particularly when different languages are involved. Handicapped and physically challenged employees are also increasingly important in many organizations. Single parents, dual career couples, gays and lesbians, people with special dietary preferences (e.g., vegetarians), and people with different po-

The U.S. work force is becoming ever more diverse along most dimensions of race and ethnicity. The most significant trend suggests that whites will comprise a significantly smaller percentage of the work force by the year 2000 than was the case as recently as 1988. Most growth is in the Hispanic sector. Modest growth in the percentage of black and Asian workers is also expected. Managers will have to become ever more sensitive to the needs, expectations, and aspirations of a multicultural work force.

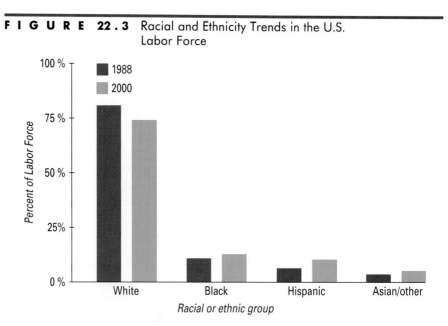

FIGURE 22.3 Racial and Ethnicity Trends in the U.S. Labor Force

Source: *Occupational Outlook Handbook* (U.S. Bureau of Labor Statistics: Washington D.C., 1990–1991), pp. 8–12.

Women make up 40 percent of the labor force in Japan, and the largest group of working women are part-time workers. Some are high school graduates who work briefly before getting married; others are middle aged and return to work after raising children. Most women work at jobs that are low paying and have little future. Junko Yoda is an exception: she is a vice president in the Tokyo office of an American bank. Only 1 percent of all Japanese working women—about 160,000—are in managerial positions.

litical ideologies and viewpoints represent major dimensions of diversity in today's organizations.[13]

THE IMPACT OF DIVERSITY ON ORGANIZATIONS

There is no question that organizations are becoming ever more diverse. But what is the impact of this diversity on organizations? As we see, diversity provides both opportunities and challenges for organizations. Diversity also plays a number of important roles in organizations today.

Diversity in Other Countries

How does the increasing diversity in U.S. organizations compare with diversity in other countries? In the paragraphs that follow we first examine diversity in European countries and then in Japan.

Diversity in Europe Although European organizations face the same aging work force as their U.S. counterparts, they tend to have less diversity in terms of gender: most European firms have even fewer women executives than do U.S. firms. Because equal employment legislation and the feminist movement each came to Europe later than to the United States, large numbers of European women did not begin to pursue professional careers until just a few years ago. Although this pattern is changing, the relative percentage of women in managerial positions in Europe is somewhat less than is found in U.S. organizations.

In contrast to U.S. organizations, however, European firms are considerably more diverse in terms of national origin because Europe comprises many relatively small nations. Companies in Europe have long been accustomed to doing business in a variety of countries. And for decades, managers have moved from country to country, either for promotions within their firm or for jobs in new firms. As a result, many European companies have a rich tradition of diversity. "The Global View" discusses the European diversity experience in more detail.

Diversity in Japan Japanese organizations also have their own unique diversity profiles that in some ways resemble those found in European organizations. For example, the Japanese also have an aging work force and they employ relatively few women, especially in managerial positions. The traditional career path for Japanese women who finished school was to work a few years in clerical positions and then "drop out" to raise a family. Until recently, few ever returned to the work force.

United States firms in Japan are a major reason that career opportunities for women are changing in that country. Fighting an acute labor shortage in Japan, U.S. firms like IBM and Motorola, Inc., started offering women leaving to have children a guaranteed job later if they wished to return to work. To the surprise of many traditional Japanese managers, large numbers of women have indeed chosen to return to work after a few years. Now, many Japanese organizations have begun to make similar offers.

Whereas the number of women managers in Japan lags behind the United States and mirrors the situation in Europe, Japanese organizations have little diversity of other forms and varieties. For example, because the borders to Japan were long closed to immigrants, there is little diversity in Japanese firms in terms of ethnicity and national origin. Most Japanese managers tend to be Japanese nationals. The Japanese are also only beginning to make accommodations for physically challenged employees and similar groups.

Diversity in Other Parts of the World Although the United States, Japan, and Europe represent the major economic centers in the world today, other areas of Pacific Asia including South Korea, Taiwan, Hong Kong, and neighboring countries are becoming increasingly important. In general, diversity in these countries mirrors that of Japan—little ethnic diversity because of restrictive immigration laws, relatively few women because of social norms, and an aging work force. But in Australia, which has had more open immigration policies, ethnic diversity in the work force is perhaps as great as in any other single country in the world today. Canada also has a relatively diverse work force, but Mexico tends to have relatively little diversity. Few accessible statistics exist for assessing diversity in most other countries.

The message of these diversity patterns for managers in international businesses is both simple and complex. The simple message is that managers must be prepared to confront a variety of diversity issues when conducting business in other countries. While some of the dimensions—age and gender, for instance—are equally relevant, they also must be considered within the cultural context of the particular country. The complex message is that while understanding and addressing diversity issues within a single country are difficult enough, coping with them across many different countries greatly magnifies the role of diversity in the organization.

ENCOURAGING DIVERSITY IN EUROPE

 For most European companies, managing cultural diversity has long been a necessity. With the formation of the European Community in 1992, legal barriers disappeared and the countries officially recognized their own interdependence. But many forward-thinking companies and individuals had been preparing for 1992 for a long time.

Europe's managers for the 1990s are a different breed than the current directors and CEOs who rebuilt Europe after World War II. Born after the War, today's managers were often raised to feel that all of Europe was their home country. Many spent the summers of their teen years traveling from Scandinavia to the Mediterranean, making friends in many countries and improving their language skills. They have fewer national and corporate loyalties and prejudices than their parents had, and they're likely to feel at ease far from their home towns.

With such people playing increasingly important roles in European companies, it's no surprise that many of these companies have recognized the value of cultural diversity. As Luis Carlos Collazos, human resources director of Hewlett-Packard Spain puts it, "It's beneficial for our company to be diverse in terms of cultures and personal profiles because it enriches the organization and keeps it in better touch with the market and society."* To benefit from such enrichment, Hewlett-Packard participates in the Inter-Europe Student Exchange Program, in which students go to work for HP units outside their own country. "From different realities and visions comes an organization that's more energetic and dynamic,"** Collazos says.

Other European managers would agree. Amadeus Global Travel Distribution, a holding company owned by leading European airlines, boasts representation from thirty-two different countries on its staff of 650. "We foment internationalism within the company,"† says Amadeus's Miguel Benzo. The company offers three-day seminars in which its upper-level managers learn to lead multicultural teams and interact with people from other cultures on all levels of the corporate hierarchy. Language isn't a problem because everyone at Amadeus is fluent in English.

As advanced as some European companies are in accepting and encouraging cultural diversity, many still have two major weak spots—attitudes toward women and toward the estimated eight million "guest workers" who provide much of the unskilled labor in Europe. The next step for many companies will be allowing women to escape the staff positions in which they've traditionally been trapped and accepting non-Europeans in the work force as thoroughly as they now accept people from Finland to Greece.

*Quoted in Barry Louis Rubin, "Europeans Value Diversity," *HRMagazine*, January 1991, p. 41.

**Quoted in Rubin, p. 41.

†Quoted in Rubin, p. 40.

References: Richard I. Kirkland, Jr., "Europe's New Managers," *Fortune*, September 29, 1986, pp. 56–60; Barry Louis Rubin, "Europeans Value Diversity," *HRMagazine*, January 1991, pp. 38–41, 78.

Diversity as a Force for Social Change

Diversity in an organization can be a major force for social change as the composition of an organization's work force gradually comes to fully mirror the composition of its surrounding labor market. For example, a manager in an organization who learns to effectively interact with a diverse set of people at work will be better equipped to deal with a diverse set of people in other settings. And conversely, a person who is comfortable interacting in a variety of diverse settings should have little problem in dealing with diversity at work. Thus diversity in organizations both facilitates and is facilitated by social change in the environment.

Many organizations today are finding that diversity can be a source of competitive advantage. A variety of arguments have been developed to support this viewpoint. For example, a black sales representative for Revlon helped that firm improve its packaging and promotion for its line of darker skin tone cosmetics.

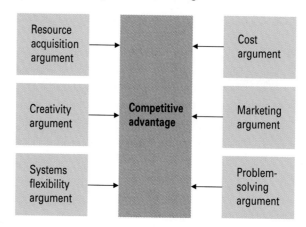

F I G U R E   22.4 How Diversity Promotes Competitive Advantage

Organizations also affect social change through the images they use to promote themselves and their products. An organization that runs print ads showing nothing but white male executives in its workplace conveys a certain image of itself. In contrast, an organization that uses diverse people as representatives conveys a different image. During its coverage of the 1992 Winter Olympic Games in France, CBS used two co-anchors to announce its telecasts—one male (Tim McCarver) and one female (Paula Zahn). The network also used black, French, Asian, and British announcers for specific events. There was also a fairly even mix of male and female announcers during the telecasts.

Diversity as a Competitive Advantage

Many organizations are also finding that diversity can be a source of competitive advantage in the marketplace. In general, six arguments have been proposed for how diversity contributes to competitiveness.[14] These are illustrated in Figure 22.4.

The *cost argument* suggests that organizations that learn to cope with diversity generally have higher levels of productivity and lower levels of turnover and absenteeism. Those organizations that do a poor job of managing diversity, on the other hand, have lower productivity and higher levels of turnover and absenteeism. Because each of these factors directly affects costs, the former organization is more competitive than the latter. Ortho Pharmaceutical Corporation estimates that it has saved $500,000 by lowering turnover among women and ethnic minorities.[15]

The *resource acquisition argument* for diversity suggests that organizations effectively managing diversity become known among women and minorities as good places to work and are thus better able to attract qualified employees from among these groups. Given the increased importance of these groups in the overall labor force, organizations that can attract talented employees from all segments of society are likely to be more competitive.

The *marketing argument* suggests that organizations with diverse work forces are better able to understand different market segments than are less diverse organizations. For example, a cosmetics firm like Avon that wants to sell its products to women and blacks can better understand how to create and effectively market such products if women and black managers arc available to provide input into aspects of marketing such as product development, design, packaging, and advertising.[16]

The *creativity argument* for diversity suggests that organizations with diverse work forces are generally more creative and innovative than are less diverse organizations. The members of an organization dominated by one population segment generally adhere to norms and ways of thinking that reflect that segment. Moreover, they have little insight or stimulus for new ideas that might be derived from different perspectives. The diverse organization, in contrast, is characterized by multiple perspectives and ways of thinking and is therefore more likely to generate new ideas and ways of doing things.

Related to the creativity argument is the *problem-solving argument*. Diversity carries with it an increased pool of information. In virtually any organization, there is some information that everyone has and other information that is unique to each individual. In an organization with little diversity, there is less unique information. But in a more diverse organization, there is more unique information. Thus because a wider variety of information can be used to solve a problem, the probability is greater that better solutions will be identified.

Finally, the *systems flexibility argument* for diversity suggests that organizations must be more flexible to manage a diverse work force. As a direct consequence, the overall organizational system becomes more flexible. As we discussed in Chapters 3 and 11, organizational flexibility enables the organization to better respond to changes in its environment. Thus by effectively managing diversity within its work force, an organization simultaneously becomes better equipped to address its environment.

Diversity as a Source of Conflict

Unfortunately, diversity in an organization can also become a major source of conflict, which can arise for a variety of reasons. Conflict can arise when an individual thinks that someone has been hired, promoted, or fired because of her or his diversity status. For example, suppose a male executive loses a promotion to a woman. If he believes that she was promoted because the organization simply wanted to have more female managers rather than because she was the better candidate for the job, he will likely feel resentful toward both her and the organization itself.

Conflict can also be caused by misunderstood, misinterpreted, or inappropriate interactions between people of different groups. For example, suppose a male executive tells a sexually explicit joke to a new female executive. He may intentionally be trying to embarrass her, he may be clumsily trying to show her that he treats everyone the same, or he may be trying to make her feel like part of the team. Regardless of his intent, however, if she finds the joke offensive she will justifiably feel anger and hostility. These feelings may be directed only at the offending individual or more generally toward the entire organization if she believes that its culture facilitates such behaviors. And of course, sexual harassment itself is both unethical and illegal.

Conflict can also arise as a result of other elements of diversity. For example, suppose a U.S. manager publicly praises a Japanese employee's outstanding work. The manager's action stems from the dominant cultural belief in the United States that such recognition is important and rewarding. But because the Japanese culture places a much higher premium on group loyalty and identity than on individual accomplishment, the employee will likely feel ashamed and embarrassed. Thus a well-intentioned action may backfire and result in unhappiness.

Conflict may also arise as a result of fear, distrust, or individual prejudice. Members of the dominant group in an organization may worry that newcomers from other groups pose a personal threat to their own positions in the organization. For example, managers in U.S. firms taken over by Japanese firms have sometimes been resentful or hostile to Japanese managers assigned to work with them. People may also be unwilling to accept people who are different from themselves. And personal bias and prejudices are still very real among some people today and can lead to potentially harmful conflict.[17]

MANAGING DIVERSITY IN ORGANIZATIONS

Because of the tremendous potential that diversity holds for competitive advantage as well as the possible consequences of diversity-related conflict, much attention has been focused in recent years on how individuals and organizations can better manage diversity.[18] In the sections that follow we first discuss individual strategies for dealing with diversity and then summarize organizational approaches to managing diversity.

Individual Strategies for Dealing with Diversity

Individuals themselves can contribute to an organization's effort to manage diversity by striving for understanding, empathy, tolerance, and communication.[19]

Understanding Some managers have taken the basic concepts of equal employment opportunity to an unnecessary extreme. They know that by law they cannot discriminate against people on the basis of characteristics such as gender and race. Thus in following this mandate they come to believe that they must treat everyone the same.

But this belief can cause problems when it is translated into workplace behaviors among people after they have been hired. People are not the same, and whereas they need to be treated fairly and equitably, managers must understand that differences among people do, in fact, exist. Thus any effort to treat everyone the same, without regard to their fundamental human differences, will only lead to problems. It is therefore important for managers to understand that cultural factors cause people to behave in different ways and that these differences should be accepted.

Empathy Related to understanding is empathy: people should try to understand the perspective of others. For example, suppose a Japanese woman joins a group that has traditionally been made up of Hispanic men. Each man may be a little self-conscious as to how to act toward its new member and may be interested in making her feel comfortable and welcome. But they may be able to do this even more effectively by empathizing with how she may feel. For example, she may feel disappointed or elated about her new assignment, she may be confident or nervous about her position in the group, and she may be experienced or inexperienced in working with male colleagues. By learning more about these and similar circumstances, the existing group members can further facilitate their ability to work together effectively.

Tolerance   Another individual approach to dealing with diversity is tolerance. Even though managers learn to understand diversity, and even though they may try to empathize with others, they may still not accept or enjoy some aspect of behavior on the part of others. For example, one organization recently reported that it was experiencing considerable conflict among its U.S. and Israeli employees. The Israeli employees seemed to argue about every issue that arose. The U.S. managers preferred a more harmonious way of conducting business and became uncomfortable with the conflict. Finally, after considerable discussion it was learned that many Israeli employees simply enjoy arguing and just see it as part of getting work done. The firm's U.S. employees still do not enjoy the arguing, but they are willing now to tolerate it as a fundamental cultural difference between themselves and their colleagues from Israel.[20]

Communication   A final individual approach to dealing with diversity is communication. Diversity problems may become magnified because people are afraid or otherwise unwilling to openly discuss issues that relate to diversity. For example, suppose a younger employee, meaning no harm, has a habit of good-naturedly kidding an elderly colleague about her age. But the older employee may find the jokes offensive. If the two do not communicate, the jokes will continue and the resentment will grow. Eventually, what started as a minor problem may erupt into a much bigger one.

For communication to work, it must be two-way. If a person wonders if a certain behavior on her or his part is offensive to someone else, the curious individual should probably just ask. Similarly, someone offended by the behavior of another person should explain to the offending individual how the behavior is perceived and request that it be stopped. As long as such exchanges are handled in a friendly, low-key, and nonthreatening way, they will generally have a positive outcome. Of course, if the same message is presented in an overly combative manner or if a person continues to engage in offensive behavior after having been asked to stop, problems will only escalate. At this point, third parties within the organization may have to intervene. And in fact, most organizations today have one or more systems in place to address questions and problems that arise as a result of diversity. We now turn our attention to various ways that organizations can better manage diversity.

Organizational Approaches to Managing Diversity

Although individuals play an important role in managing diversity, a major effort must come from the organization itself. Through its various policies and practices people in the organization come to understand what behaviors are and are not appropriate. Diversity training is an even more direct method for managing diversity. The organization's culture is the ultimate context from which diversity must be addressed.

Organizational Policies   The starting point in managing diversity is the policies that an organization adopts that directly or indirectly affect how people are treated. The extent to which an organization embraces the premise of equal employment opportunity, for example, will to a large extent determine the potential diversity within an organization. But the organization that follows the law to the letter and only practices passive discrimination is very different from the organization that actively seeks a diverse and varied work force.

Another aspect of organizational policies that affects diversity is how the organization addresses and responds to problems that arise from diversity. For example, consider a case of sexual harassment. If the organization's policies put an excessive burden of proof on the individual being harassed and invoke only minor sanctions against the guilty party, it is sending a clear signal as to the importance of such matters. But the organization with a balanced set of policies for addressing questions like sexual harassment sends its employees a different message as to the importance of diversity and individual rights and privileges.

Indeed, perhaps the major policy through which an organization can reflect its stance on diversity is its mission statement. If the organization's mission statement articulates a clear and direct commitment to diversity, everyone who comes into contact with that mission statement will grow to understand and accept the importance of diversity, at least to that particular organization.

Organizational Practices   Organizations can also help manage diversity through a variety of ongoing practices and procedures. Avon's creation of networks for various groups represents one example of an organizational practice that fosters diversity. In general, because diversity is characterized by differences among people, organizations can more effectively manage that diversity with flexible rather than rigid practices and procedures.

Benefits packages, for example, can be structured so as to better accommodate individual situations. An employee who is part of a dual career couple and who has no children may require relatively little insurance (perhaps his spouse's employer provides more complete coverage) and would like to be able to schedule vacations to coincide with those of his spouse. A single parent may need a wide variety of insurance coverage and prefer to schedule his vacation time to coincide with school holidays.

An organization can also accommodate diversity by offering flexible working hours. Differences in family arrangements, religious holidays, and cultural events may dictate that employees have some degree of flexibility in when they work. A single parent may need to leave the office every day at 4:30 to pick up the children from their day-care center. An organization that truly values diversity will make every reasonable attempt to accommodate such a need.

Organizations can also facilitate diversity by making sure that there is diversity in its key committees and executive teams. Even if diversity exists among the organization's employees, if it does not reflect diversity in groups

When Monsanto found that, despite its efforts to hire more women and minorities, an increasing number of both were leaving the company. It began a series of managing-diversity programs, one of which is the "Consulting Pairs" program. This program trains employees to act as in-house consultants on race and gender issues, and the trained employees spend as much as 20 percent of their work time helping others with diversity issues.

like committees and teams it implies that diversity is not a fully ingrained element of its culture. In contrast, if all major groups and related work assignments reflect diversity, the message is a quite different one.

Diversity Training   Many organizations are finding that diversity training is an effective way to manage diversity and minimize its associated conflict. More specifically, **diversity training** is training that is specifically designed to better enable members of an organization to function in a diverse workplace. This training can take a variety of forms. For example, many organizations find it useful to help people learn more about their similarities to and differences from others. Men and women can be taught to work together more effectively and can gain insights into how their own behaviors affect and are interpreted by others. In one organization, a diversity training program helped male managers gain insights into how various remarks could be interpreted as being sexist. In the same organization, female managers learned how to point out their discomfort with those remarks without appearing overly hostile.[21]

Similarly, white and black managers may need training to better understand each other. Managers at Mobil Corporation noticed that four black colleagues never seemed to eat lunch together. After a diversity training program, they came to realize that the black managers felt that if they ate together, their white colleagues would be overly curious about what they might be talking about. Thus they avoided close associations with one another because they feared calling attention to themselves.[22]

Some organizations even go so far as to provide language training for their employees as a vehicle for managing diversity. Motorola, for example, provides English language training for its foreign employees on assignment in the United States. At Pace Foods in San Antonio, with a total payroll of 350 employees, staff meetings and employee handbooks are translated into Spanish for the benefit of the company's 100 Hispanic employees.[23] "Man-

● **diversity training**
Training that is specifically designed to better enable members of an organization to function in a diverse workplace

agement in Practice" provides details about how Digital Equipment Corp. helps manage diversity for its employees.

Organizational Culture The ultimate test of an organization's commitment to managing diversity is its culture. Regardless of what managers say or put in writing, unless they fundamentally believe that diversity is valued, it cannot ever become truly an integral part of an organization. An organization that really wants to promote diversity must shape its culture so that it clearly underscores top management commitment to and support of diversity in all of its forms throughout every part of the organization. With top management support, however, reinforced with a clear and consistent set of organizational policies and practices, diversity can become a basic part of an organization.

TOWARD THE MULTICULTURAL ORGANIZATION

● **multicultural organization**

An organization that has achieved high levels of diversity, is able to fully capitalize on the advantages of diversity, and has few diversity-related problems

Many organizations today are grappling with cultural diversity. We noted back in Chapter 5 that although many organizations are becoming increasingly global, no truly global organization exists. In similar fashion, whereas organizations are becoming ever more diverse, few true multicultural organizations exist. The **multicultural organization** has achieved high levels of diversity, is able to fully capitalize on the advantages of the diversity, and has few diversity-related problems.[24] One recent article described six basic characteristics of such an organization.[25] These characteristics are illustrated in Figure 22.5.

First, the multicultural organization is characterized by *pluralism:* every group represented in an organization works to better understand every other group. Thus black employees try to understand white employees, and white employees try just as hard to understand their black colleagues. In addition, every group represented within an organization has the potential to influence the organization's culture and its fundamental norms.

Second, the multicultural organization achieves *full structural integration.* Full structural integration suggests that the diversity within an organization will be a complete and accurate reflection of the organization's external labor market. If around half of the labor market is female, then about half of the organization's employees will be female. Moreover, this same proportion is reflected at all levels of the organization. There are no glass ceilings or other subtle forms of discrimination.

Third, the multicultural organization achieves *full integration of the informal networks:* there are no barriers to entry and participation in any organizational activity. For example, people enter and exit lunch groups, social networks, communication grapevines, and other informal aspects of organizational activity without regard to age, gender, ethnicity, or other dimension of diversity.

Fourth, the multicultural organization is characterized by an *absence of prejudice and discrimination.* No traces of bias exist, and prejudice is eliminated. Discrimination is not practiced in any shape, form, or fashion, not because it is illegal, but because employees lack prejudice and bias. People

THE SLOW RISE OF JAPAN'S SALARYWOMAN

*T*he dedication, hard work, and loyalty of Japanese male employees—often called "salarymen"—is legendary and one of the main reasons behind Japan's economic success. But there are no longer enough salarymen to go around. Unemployment in Japan hovers around 2 percent, college graduates are often deluged with job offers, and Japan has to import foreign workers to do much of the country's low-status work. And there's no relief in sight—the average Japanese woman has only 1.57 children, and that rate is falling.

To combat this shortage of skilled workers, Japan has begun to turn to its women. The role of women in Japanese society has been governed by tradition: Japanese women stay at home. In an attempt to get more women into the labor force and up the corporate ranks, the Japanese government in 1986 passed a law barring discrimination on the basis of gender. That was only the first step.

About 40 percent of the Japanese work force is now female, but only about 1 percent of those women hold managerial positions. Most still work as "office ladies," and the average Japanese woman brings home only $.57 for every dollar that her husband makes. The 1986 law did not establish penalties for violators, so discrimination still exists at all levels.

As is often true in arguments about discrimination, it is difficult to establish a clear cause-and-effect relationship. Companies say that they don't give women responsibility and status because they invest so much in training each employee that they lose money if the employee doesn't stay at least ten years. Many of the women argue that they leave precisely because they aren't given the opportunities afforded their male colleagues.

The changes in Japanese law haven't led to more rapid changes in the workplace in part because the laws were, in effect, trying to change cultural traditions rather than reflect changes already made. A recent survey revealed that more Japanese than U.S. women feel they are treated unfairly at work because of their gender. Yet Japanese women feel much less need for change or for organized women's movements than do U.S. women.

Few Japanese women complain about their situation. Perhaps this silence is a result of the weight of their traditional roles. Or it may be because the hard-working lifestyle of "salarymen" is unappealing to them. As one woman pointed out, "Japanese men are such workaholics."*

*Quoted in Yumiko Ono, "Women's Movement in Corporate Japan Isn't Moving Very Fast," *The Wall Street Journal*, June 6, 1991, pp. A1, A14.

Discussion Questions

1. What similarities and differences do you see between the ways U.S. and Japanese companies treat women employees?

2. Do you think the Japanese government might be more successful at improving the status of women workers if it stressed the diversity advantages that women bring to the workplace rather than emphasizing the economic necessity of hiring women?

E 3. United States companies who do business in Japan—and in societies more restrictive of women, such as Saudi Arabia—must face the question of whether to treat women employees the way they are traditionally treated in the host country or the way they would be treated in the United States. Which approach do you think is more ethical? more practical?

References: Karen Lowry Miller, "The 'Mommy Track,' Japanese-Style," *Business Week*, March 11, 1991, p. 46; Yumiko Ono, "Women's Movement in Corporate Japan Isn't Moving Very Fast," *The Wall Street Journal*, June 6, 1991, pp. A1, A14.

Entrepreneurship and New Venture Formation

23

OBJECTIVES

After studying this chapter, you should be able to:

● *Characterize the nature of entrepreneurship.*

● *Discuss small business and its role in the U.S. economy.*

● *Identify the major causes of small-business success and failure.*

● *Describe the major issues in starting a small business.*

● *Discuss the major elements of managing a small business.*

● *Discuss entrepreneurship in large businesses.*

OUTLINE

The Nature of Entrepreneurship

The Importance of Small Business
   The Impact of Small Business
   Major Areas of Small Business
   Small Business and the Global Economy

Small Business Successes and Failures
   Common Causes of Success
   Common Causes of Failure

Business Plan

Issues of Ownership
   Approaches to Starting a Business
   Forms of Ownership
   Sources of Financing

Managing the Small Business
   Planning in the Small Business
   Organizing in the Small Business
   Leading in the Small Business
   Controlling in the Small Business

Entrepreneurship in Large Businesses

SAMUEL FORTE DROPPED out of school during the Depression and went to work for a jewelry manufacturer in Rhode Island. After a few years he left and started his own business. He named his firm Fort Jewelry, dropping the *e* because he knew most people would spell it that way.

His first product was cheap (10 cents) wedding bands that he sold to U.S. sailors heading for Cuba. Forte gradually expanded and was soon making a wide variety of costume jewelry. He later dropped the "jewelry" from the firm's name because thieves were stealing his packages. His company is known today as Fort Inc.

In 1950 a customer asked Forte to create a decorative enamel emblem that could be glued to a spoon handle. The customer was buying inexpensive spoons from Japan, affixing emblems, and selling them as souvenirs. Forte offered to make the entire spoon. This new venture took off, and Fort soon dropped the rest of his product line altogether.

Today, Fort controls about 60 percent of the U.S. market for souvenir spoons. Still family owned and headed by seventy-three-year-old Samuel, the firm manufactures about six million spoons a year. At any given time, the firm has about eighty different styles available. Various styles commemorate states, cities, and tourist attractions. Revenues from the spoons are more than $4.5 million a year.

Retailers love the spoons because they can mark up the price at least four times above what they pay and still have an inexpensive novelty. Customers like them because they are relatively inexpensive, are linked with places they have visited, and do not seem as common as a tee-shirt or other souvenir. Fort has recently begun to expand its product line. Today it affixes enamel emblems to a number of other products including key chains, thimbles, and letter openers.[1] ●

amuel Forte did what thousands of other people do every year: he identified an opportunity and tried to capitalize on it by starting a new business. Like Forte, many of those who try succeed in creating a new enterprise. Many others, however, fail. Some of those who fail try again, and they often succeed the second or perhaps the third time. Henry Ford went bankrupt twice before succeeding with the Ford Motor Co.

This chapter is about entrepreneurship and small business management. We first explain the nature of entrepreneurship and discuss its importance. We then discuss major causes of small business success and failure. Next we describe how a new business is started. After discussing how small businesses are managed, we examine entrepreneurship in large businesses.

THE NATURE OF ENTREPRENEURSHIP

● **entrepreneurship**
The process of organizing, operating, and assuming the risk of a business venture

entrepreneur
Someone who engages in entrepreneurship; someone who organizes, operates, and assumes the risk of his or her business venture

Entrepreneurship is the process of organizing, operating, and assuming the risk of a business venture.[2] An **entrepreneur** is someone who engages in entrepreneurship. Hence a business owner who hires a professional manager to run his business and then turns to other interests is not an entrepreneur. Although he is assuming the risk of the venture, he is not actively involved in organizing or operating it. Likewise, a professional manager whose job is running someone else's business is not an entrepreneur. Although she may be organizing and operating the enterprise, she is assuming no personal risk for its success or failure.

Entrepreneurship involves starting a business and maintaining an active role in its management. Figure 23.1 illustrates three general prospects for a

A new business may face any number of growth possibilities. Three general growth patterns are rapid and dramatic growth, slow and steady growth, and gradual decline. Although few firms follow path 1, those that do have a number of problems brought on by their rapid growth. These problems include a lack of experience, managerial growth, a shortage of qualified managers, and several difficulties of maintaining adequate control.

F I G U R E   23.1   General Paths Taken by New Ventures

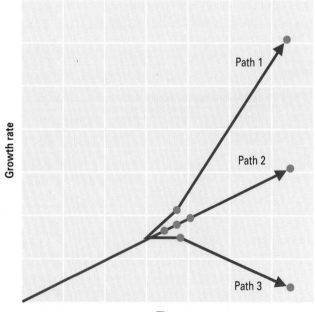

business after it is first established. A business following path 1, the least common one, has an initial period of modest growth followed by tremendous growth that transforms it into a large business. Sun Microsystems Inc., Reebok International Ltd., Blockbuster Entertainment Corp., Compaq Computer Corporation, and Liz Claiborne, Inc. took this path.[3] More common is path 2: companies reach a basic level of sales and profitability required to support their continued existence and then either stabilize at that level or continue to grow at a modest rate. Many local small businesses that have been around for several years—an automobile repair shop, a newspaper distributorship, an independent video rental store, for example—have taken this path. Many other businesses follow path 3. These businesses survive for a while, perhaps even several years, but eventually fail.

Entrepreneurs themselves may also follow a number of paths. Some, like Wayne Huizenga of Blockbuster Entertainment, remain with their company as the firm grows. Others, like Steven Jobs of Apple Computer, Inc., leave after several years and start new ventures (Jobs started NeXT, Inc., a computer company). Still others sell the business as soon as it turns profitable and start another. Some leave the business and go to work for someone else or retire.[4]

THE IMPORTANCE OF SMALL BUSINESS

What is a small business? There are actually many different definitions, but the most widely quoted ones are those of the U.S. **Small Business Administration (SBA).** Created in 1953 by Congress, the SBA's purpose is twofold: to improve the managerial skills of entrepreneurs and to help them borrow money. The SBA has drafted definitions of "smallness" to fit virtually every industry; a partial list appears in Table 23.1. Notice that some indicators go far beyond what many people think of as small. For example, a petroleum refiner with 1,500 employees probably boasts sales of several million dollars each year. For the sake of simplicity, we define a **small business** as one that is independently owned and operated and has little influence over its environment relative to a large business. For example, a large refiner like Exxon or British Petroleum can affect the price of gasoline worldwide by adjusting its own prices or by increasing or decreasing supply. But a small independent gasoline retailer can have virtually no effect on gasoline prices.

Small Business Administration (SBA)
Created by Congress in 1953 to improve the managerial skills of entrepreneurs and help them borrow money

● **small business**
A business that is independently owned and operated and that has relatively little influence over its environment

The Impact of Small Business

Small business plays a major role in the U.S. economy. More than 99 percent of the nation's 17 million businesses are small. Their effects are felt in a number of areas, including financial performance, innovation, job creation, new-business formation, and contributions to big business.

Financial Performance   There are far more small businesses than large ones. Evidence also suggests that small business outperforms big business financially. On average, for example, small manufacturers earn a higher return on owners' equity than do large manufacturers for two main reasons. First, small business in many manufacturing industries can respond more

The Small Business Administration (SBA) provides different definitions of what constitutes "smallness" for firms in different industries. These differences are presumably associated with relative difference in capital investment, differences in industry structure, and similar factors.

T A B L E 23.1 SBA Standards of Size for Selected Industries

Manufacturers	Fewer Employees Than
Petroleum refining	1,500
Electronic computers	1,000
Macaroni and spaghetti	500

Wholesalers	Fewer Employees Than
Sporting goods	500
Furniture	500
Paints and varnishes	500

Retailers	Annual Sales Less Than
Grocery stores	$13.5 million
Automobile agencies	11.5 million
Restaurants	10.0 million

Services	Annual Sales Less Than
Computer-related services	$12.5 million
Accounting services	4.0 million
Television repair	3.5 million

Source: "U.S. Small Business Administration: Small Business Size Standards," *Federal Register,* Vol. 49, No. 28 (Washington, D.C.: U.S. Government Printing Office, February 9, 1984), pp. 5024–5048.

rapidly and at less cost than can big business to the quickening rate of change in products and services, processes, and markets. Second, small business has become more attractive to aggressive and highly motivated individuals.[5] Such characteristics enable these entrepreneurs to take risks, foster innovation, and remain flexible—all of which can contribute to higher profit margins. In any event, small business has a positive impact on national economic performance in terms of gross national product, growth rates, and other indicators.

Innovation Entrepreneurs and small business also play a major role in innovation. Entrepreneurs are responsible for the personal computer, the transistor radio, the photocopying machine, the jet engine, and the instant photograph. Their ingenuity also gave us the pocket calculator, power steering, automatic transmission, air conditioning, and even the nineteen-cent ballpoint pen. Clearly, society benefits from the presence of small businesses: their resourcefulness and ingenuity have spawned new industries and contributed a great many innovative ideas and technological breakthroughs.[6]

Job Creation Small businesses create more new jobs than do larger businesses. Throughout the 1980s, for example, firms with fewer than one hundred employees created more than one-half of all new private-sector jobs in the United States.[7] The U.S. Department of Commerce found that small, young, high-technology businesses created new jobs at a much faster rate than did larger, older businesses. Such small businesses (especially those in chemistry and electronics) generate demand for people with a high degree of scientific or engineering knowledge. Clean Harbors, Inc., a Boston-based pollution control firm, has created around 500 jobs in the New England area, and Reebok has created more than 2,000 jobs in the last eight years.

New-Business Formation   Another indicator of the importance of small business is the record number of businesses formed each year since 1960. New incorporations hit the 600,000 mark for the first time in 1983.[8] This figure is more than four times 1960's total, and the pace continued through the 1980s and into the 1990s. Although some of the new corporations are mature businesses that were born as sole proprietorships or partnerships and have only recently incorporated, many more small businesses are created each year than are larger ones.

Contributions to Big Business   A final reason small businesses have such an enormous impact is their contributions to big business. Big businesses buy more of their inputs from small businesses than from other big businesses. General Motors Corp., for example, buys from more than 25,000 suppliers, most of them small businesses. Small businesses can create and deliver specialized products more efficiently than can larger businesses because their smallness gives them added flexibility. Small businesses also play an important role in distributing and selling the products of larger businesses to consumers.[9] Some of the reasons for these patterns are explored in the following section.

Major Areas of Small Business

In general, small businesses tend to do well in service, retail, and wholesale industries. They often do not perform well in manufacturing.

Service   Service organizations are perhaps the most common type of small business because they may require a fairly small capital investment to get started. A certified acountant, for example, can go into business just by establishing an office and advertising his or her services. Small businesses such as video rental shops, hair salons, and auto repair shops have flourished in recent years.

Retail   Retail businesses are another popular area for small business. Small business is especially effective in the area of specialty retailing—retail establishments that cater to certain customer groups like golfers, college students, and people who do their own automobile repairs. Many large retail chains allow individual stores to be run by entrepreneurs who have signed franchise agreements.

Wholesale   Wholesaling, which is dominated by small businesses, involves buying products from large manufacturers and reselling the products to retailers. Small businesses are effective in this area because they are flexible and can develop the personal working relationships necessary to coordinate large numbers of sellers and buyers.

Manufacturing   Manufacturing is the one area in which small businesses often perform more poorly than do larger businesses. Starting a manufacturing firm almost always requires a large initial investment in plant and equipment. Thus few small businesses can afford to manufacture automobiles, refrigerators, or televisions. Still, some small businesses have succeeded in manufacturing, especially in the computer industry; Compaq, Dell Computer Corp., Sun Microsystems, and Compucon Systems are examples of such companies.[10]

Agriculture   Agriculture is in transition. Small family farms were among the first small businesses, and until recently they were among the most successful. Economies of scale, high equipment prices, and increased competition from abroad, however, have forced many small farmers to sell their land. They are being replaced by giant agribusiness enterprises and corporate farms.

Small Business and the Global Economy

Many people equate international business with big business. In reality, however, many small firms have prospered by carving out a niche in the global economy. As "The Global View" discusses more fully, for example, many small U.S. firms are succeeding as exporters. Many small businesses are also finding that they can secure financing more easily from foreign investors. For example, the Japanese invested almost $250 million in small businesses in the United States in 1990 alone.[11] In addition, small businesses are thriving in other countries. In Germany, for instance, firms employing fewer than 500 persons account for more than two-thirds of that country's gross national product and employ 80 percent of the German work force.[12]

SMALL BUSINESS SUCCESSES AND FAILURES

Although many new businesses started each year succeed, many more fail. In this section we discuss common reasons for small-business success and failure.

Common Causes of Success

Many ingredients contribute to small-business success, but the most common ones are hard work, drive, and dedication on the part of the entrepreneur; market demand for the product or service being offered; managerial competence; and luck.[13]

Hard Work, Drive, and Dedication   Important to the success of any small business is the entrepreneur's hard work, drive, and dedication. To succeed, an individual must have a strong desire to work independently and be willing to put in long hours.[14] Samuel Forte clearly had such drive. In general, successful entrepreneurs tend to be reasonable risk-takers, self-confident, hardworking, goal setters, and innovators.[15]

Market Demand   For any business to succeed, there must be sufficient demand for its product or service. If a college community of 50,000 citizens

YOU DON'T HAVE TO BE BIG TO GO OVERSEAS

Traditionally, U.S. start-up companies felt they needed to grow up before they thought about foreign customers. There were enough potential American buyers for most products, and the costs and difficulties of exporting seemed prohibitive. But with the coming of the global marketplace, all that has changed, and many small companies treat the whole world as though it were their neighborhood.

Momenta Corporation, for instance, was raising money from Taiwan and setting up operations in Japan, Taiwan, and Singapore within its first year of operations. Like many other small companies, Momenta discovered that it could find cheap investment capital more easily overseas. National and local governments from Singapore to Scotland lure new companies by offering loans, tax breaks, and grants.

The U.S. government, always concerned about the trade imbalance, is eager to encourage small U.S. companies to look for markets overseas. No one is exactly sure what percentage of exports come from small companies, but in 1985 the Small Business Administration (SBA) estimated that half of U.S.-made manufacturing exports came from companies with fewer than 500 employees. The SBA tries to match U.S. companies with foreign partners and distributors and provide expertise that will help ease companies' worries about trade barriers.

Having taken the first steps to sell abroad, small businesses face the next big question of whether to move any of their facilities abroad. This issue has become particularly urgent for companies that rely on exports to Europe, where the creation of the European Community threatens some companies with trade barriers. Some small business, like New Jersey's Filament Fiber Technology, have already set up plants in Europe to circumvent future protectionist pressures. Other companies point to high European wages and the relatively low value of the dollar in arguing that now is not the time to set up shop in Paris.

The decisions facing a small business owner require keen self-scrutiny and market analysis. A company that makes a highly specialized product for a niche market may have to sell overseas to expand production. But a company whose management team is still learning how to make a profit in the U.S. may find itself dangerously overextended if it tries to grow in two places at once. The risks are real, but no U.S. entrepreneur of the 1990s can afford to ignore the opportunities.

References: Udayan Gupta, "Small Firms Aren't Waiting to Grow Up to Go Global," *The Wall Street Journal*, December 5, 1989, p. B2; William J. Holstein, "Should Small U.S. Exporters Take the Big Plunge?," *Business Week*, October 12, 1988, pp. 64–68; Barbara Marsh, "Small Business Isn't So Little In Export Trade," *The Wall Street Journal*, August 18, 1989, pp. B1, B2; Jeanne Saddler, "U.S. Intensifies Effort to Urge Small Firms to Export," *The Wall Street Journal*, June 16, 1989, p. B2.

and 15,000 students has only one pizza parlor, there is probably sufficient demand for more. If there are already fifteen pizza parlors in operation, however, a new one will have to serve especially good pizza or offer something unique if it is to succeed. Liz Claiborne's clothing business was successful because there was unmet demand for clothing for working women.

Managerial Competence   Regardless of the level of demand, the entrepreneur must also possess basic managerial competence. She needs to understand how to select a location, what kinds of facilities are needed, how to acquire financing, and how to manage people. The entrepreneur must also understand how to manage growth, control costs, and make difficult choices and decisions. An entrepreneur who has a product for which there is tremendous demand might be able to survive for a while without manage-

Ingredients common to entrepreneurial success are hard work, market demand, and managerial competence. Allene Graves had all of these going for her when she opened The Answer Temps (TAT), a Washington, D.C., temporary employment agency. After working in the private sector for 15 years, Graves began her business in 1987. Clients include the Department of Consumer and Regulatory Affairs, and TAT's revenues topped $400,000 in 1991.

rial skills. Over time, however, and under normal circumstances, the small-business owner who lacks basic competence is unlikely to succeed.

Luck   Some small businesses succeed, at least in part, because of pure luck. One reason Fort Inc. prospered is because someone sought out Samuel Forte to make a special product. Had that individual never contacted Forte, the firm might well have kept making nothing more than costume jewelry. And it might very well have failed.

Common Causes of Failure

Basic causes of small-business failure are managerial incompetence or inexperience, neglect, weak control systems, and undercapitalization.[16]

Managerial Incompetence or Inexperience   Just as competence contributes to success, so does incompetence contribute to failure. The entrepreneur may lack the basic skills or experience to recognize problems and to make hard decisions. She may have no experience hiring and evaluating employees, dealing with bankers, or negotiating contracts. Or he may do a poor job of dealing with suppliers or customers.

Neglect   Some entrepreneurs fail because they neglect some aspect of operations. For example, they may get into business because of their impressions of its glamour and excitement. But as they experience the drudgery and sweat that go with entrepreneurship, they may be tempted to ignore key areas like inventory control and collections. Beyond operations, they may also ignore customer dissatisfaction, worker unrest, or financial difficulties—preferring to think that things will improve on their own. Or they may spend so much time on some area, such as marketing (because they enjoy it so much) that they inadvertently ignore or neglect other areas. Regardless of the reason, neglect can lead to major problems.

Ineffective Control Systems   Small businesses can be ruined by ineffective control systems. If control systems do not provide adequate information on a timely basis, the entrepreneur may be in trouble before he knows it. For example, too many slow-paying customers can dramatically weaken a small business's cash flow. So, too, can excess inventory, employee theft, poor-quality products, plummeting sales, and insufficient profit margins. If the control system does not alert the entrepreneur to problems such as these, or alerts the entrepreneur too late, recovery may be difficult or impossible.

Undercapitalization   A small business may fail because it is undercapitalized, or has too few funds to survive start-up and growth. A rule of thumb is that an entrepreneur should have sufficient funds when starting out to be able to live with no business income for one year.[17] Items that should be covered by these funds include all living expenses, the business's operating expenses, and unexpected contingencies. An entrepreneur who is planning to pay next month's rent from a new business's profits may be courting disaster. An entrepreneur in College Station, Texas, recently invested $95,000 to open a new Mexican food restaurant with plush facilities, top-of-the-line decor, and an extravagant office for himself. He closed the restaurant in less than a month because he lacked the funds to meet his payroll and pay his suppliers. If he had spent less on carpeting and had waited a few months before outfitting his office with oak paneling, he might have succeeded.

BUSINESS PLAN

Entrepreneurs must do a thorough job of planning to bring an idea for a product or service to fruition. At one time, it was possible to succeed in business simply by putting in long hours and working hard. Although long hours and hard work may still be important, increasingly complex technology, markets, and other environmental factors necessitate paying attention to planning. A **business plan,** in this context, is a document prepared by an entrepreneur in preparation for opening a new business.[18]

business plan
A document prepared by an entrepreneur in preparation for opening a new business

The very act of preparing a business plan forces prospective entrepreneurs to crystallize their thinking about launching their business successfully—from the moment they decide to go into business through the moment they open for business. In essence, the business plan forces them to develop their business on paper before investing time and money in it. The idea of a business plan is not new. Big business has been engaged in planning for years. What is new is the growing use of specialized business plans by entrepreneurs, mostly because creditors and investors whom they approach for money demand such plans. These pressures are healthy: a business plan makes entrepreneurs aware of what it will take to succeed as well as gives investors and creditors information on which to decide whether to help finance the small business.

A business plan should describe the match between the entrepreneur's abilities and the requirements for producing and marketing a particular product or service. It should define strategies for production and marketing, legal aspects and organization, and accounting and finance. In particular, it should answer four basic questions: (1) What does the entrepreneur want? (2) What are the entrepreneur's strengths? (3) What are the most workable ways of achieving the entrepreneur's goals? (4) What does the entrepreneur expect in the future?

F I G U R E   23.2 A PERT Diagram for Business Planning

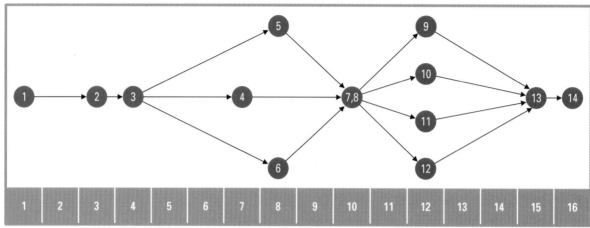

Weeks

1. Decide to go into business
2. Analyze yourself
3. Choose product or service
4. Research the market
5. Forecast sales revenues

6. Select site
7. Develop production plan
8. Develop marketing plan
9. Develop organizational plan
10. Develop legal plan

11. Develop insurance plan
12. Develop accounting plan
13. Develop financial plan
14. Write cover letter

Source: Nicholas C. Siropolis, *Small Business Management: A Guide to Entrepreneurship,* 4th ed. (Boston: Houghton Mifflin, 1990), p. 166. Copyright © 1990 by Houghton Mifflin Company.

Business planning involves a number of very specific activities and events, as shown in this PERT diagram. Following a logical and systematic process such as this will enhance the chances for success.

The PERT diagram in Figure 23.2 shows the complexity of planning a new business. Notice that the development of a business plan consists of a set of specific activities focusing on such things as marketing research and marketing mix, location, and production. Of these activities, perhaps none is more pivotal than marketing research—the systematic and intensive study of all the facts, opinions, and judgments that concern the successful marketing of a product or service. Clearly, the more entrepreneurs know about their markets, the greater are their chances of serving customers uniquely and at a profit. Often, the entrepreneur must be different to be better than the competition.

Figure 23.2 also demonstrates the sequential nature of many of the decisions that must be made. For example, entrepreneurs cannot forecast sales revenues without first researching markets. In fact, the sales forecast is one of the most important elements in the business plan: without it, estimating intelligently the size of a plant, store, or office is all but impossible. Nor is it possible to determine how much inventory to carry or how many employees to hire. Another important activity is financial planning, which translates all other activities into dollars. Generally, the financial plan is made up of a cash budget, an income statement, balance sheets, and a breakeven chart. The most important of these statements is the cash budget because it tells entrepreneurs how much money they need both before and after they open for business.

ISSUES OF OWNERSHIP

A number of critical issues must be addressed when starting a business. Whether to start a business from scratch, how to organize the ownership of the business, and how to obtain financing are all issues that must be decided.

Approaches to Starting a Business

The first questions an entrepreneur must address when planning a business is whether to buy an existing business or start a new one. A related question is whether to seek a franchising agreement or remain independent.

Buying an Existing Business   Buying an existing business offers a clear set of advantages: historical records show exactly how much revenue and profit have been generated, the kind of cash flow to expect, and so forth. The entrepreneur also gets existing supplier, distributor, and customer networks and has to do less guesswork about what to expect. On the negative side, the entrepreneur inherits whatever problems the business may already have and may be forced to accept contractual agreements prepared by others.

Starting a New Business   Starting a new business from scratch allows the entrepreneur to avoid the problems of an existing business. A great deal of excitement is often associated with opening a new enterprise. The entrepreneur has the opportunity to choose suppliers, bankers, lawyers, and employees without worrying about existing agreements or contractual arrangements. On the negative side, more uncertainty is involved in starting a new business than in taking over an existing one. The entrepreneur will have less information about projected revenues and cash flow, will have to build a customer base from zero, and may be forced to accept unfavorable credit terms from suppliers. It is also harder for a new business to borrow money because the bank has little or no experience with it.

Franchising   An alternative that is increasingly pursued today is a **franchising** agreement. The entrepreneur pays a parent company (the franchiser) a flat fee or a share of the income from the business, and in return, the franchisee uses the company's trademarks, products, formulas, and business plan. Franchising may reduce the entrepreneur's risks because parent companies often provide advice and assistance. They also provide proven methods, training, financial support, and an established identity and image. Few McDonald's Corp. franchises fail.

   On the negative side, franchises may be expensive. A McDonald's franchise costs several hundred thousand dollars. The franchisee is often restricted in what she or he can do. A McDonald's franchisee cannot change the formula for a milkshake or alter the preparation of Big Macs. Some franchise agreements are difficult to terminate. Despite the drawbacks, franchising is growing by leaps and bounds. It presently accounts for one-third of U.S. retail sales, and that figure is expected to climb to one-half by the end of this century.[19]

franchising
The payment by an entrepreneur to a parent company of a fee or a share of the income (or both) to use the name and some resources of that parent company

Forms of Ownership

Depending on the outcome of the previous decision, the entrepreneur needs to decide what form of ownership is best for the new business. There are a number of alternatives, each with its own strengths and weaknesses.[20]

sole proprietorship
The most popular form of legal ownership; an organization that is owned by a single individual

Sole Proprietorship   About 70 percent of U.S. businesses are **sole proprietorships.** The major advantages of a sole proprietorship are that the individual entrepreneur has total freedom over how he conducts the business, it's simple to start, start-up costs are low, and the proprietor's business profits are taxed as ordinary income. However, the proprietor has unlimited liability (his or her personal assets are at risk to cover business debts), it may be difficult to raise money, the business ends when the proprietor retires or dies, and there is no one else to rely on. Sears, Roebuck and Co. was started as a sole proprietorship by Richard Sears.

partnership
A form of business ownership in which two or more persons agree to work together as joint owners of the business

Partnership   A **partnership** is the agreement of two or more persons to work together as owners of a business. There are many varieties of partnerships. The least popular form of ownership, partnerships are often used in accounting, legal, and architectural firms. They provide a larger pool of talent and money than do sole proprietorships, are easy to form, and offer the same tax benefits as sole proprietorships. They offer unlimited liability, however, they cease to exist when the partnership is dissolved, and disagreements between partners are common. Richard Sears added Alvah Roebuck as a partner when his business became too big for him to manage alone.

corporation
A legal entity created under the law; independent of any single individual

Corporation   A **corporation** is a legal entity created under the law and is independent of any single individual. Most large organizations use the corporation as their basis for ownership. A corporation can borrow money, enter into contracts, own property, sue, and be sued. Its owners are the people who buy its stock. Advantages of incorporating are that the corporation is responsible for its own liabilities, so the owners have limited liability; there is continuity in the event of retirement or death; and corporations can often borrow money easily. However, there are more start-up costs, regulation, and taxation (the corporation pays taxes on its profits, and then stockholders pay taxes on their dividends). As Sears, Roebuck and Co. grew into a big business, its owners chose to incorporate. Of course, many small businesses incorporate so that the entrepreneur can avoid the liability problem and capitalize on the various other benefits (assuming, of course, they offset the costs).

Other Forms of Ownership   An entrepreneur may also adopt one of a few special forms of ownership. Master limited partnerships and S-corporations are forms of ownership that provide many of the advantages of corporations without double taxation. A cooperative may be organized when many small entrepreneurs band together to conduct business on a unified basis. Ocean Spray Cranberry, for example, is a cooperative that comprises 700 cranberry growers and 100 citrus growers.

Sources of Financing

An important issue confronting all entrepreneurs is where to get the money to open and operate the business. As we noted earlier, the entrepreneur

Entrepreneur Susan Michaels (middle), formerly a television talk show host, used savings and the investments of others to finance A Grand Affair, her formal-wear rental business. Besides using several years' savings, she recruited minority partner Alexa Palmer (right), who invested $30,000. Michaels's husband, Michael Steinway (left), is also part owner of the business.

should not rely on anticipated profits. Personal resources (savings and money borrowed from friends or family) are the entrepreneur's most common source of funds. Personal resources are often the most important source because they underscore and reinforce the entrepreneur's personal commitment to the venture. Many entrepreneurs take advantage of various lending programs and assistance provided by lending institutions and government agencies.[21] Government programs are especially interested in helping women and minority entrepreneurs. Another common source of funds is venture capitalists. A **venture capitalist** is someone who actively seeks to invest in new businesses in return for a share of ownership or profits. The advantage of this approach is access to a large resource base with fewer restrictions than might be imposed by the government or a bank. The entrepreneur, however, must give up a share of the profits or share ownership.[22]

venture capitalist
Someone who actively seeks to invest in new businesses in return for a share of the ownership, profits, or both

MANAGING THE SMALL BUSINESS

Until just a few years ago, the conventional wisdom among managers and researchers was that management concepts and approaches were applicable to all businesses regardless of size. Now, however, people generally agree that an entrepreneur managing a small business faces a different set of circumstances altogether, and these circumstances dictate a different approach to management. Thus planning, organizing, leading, and controlling must be approached from a special perspective when they are to be applied to a small business.

Planning in the Small Business

Planning is crucial to an entrepreneur's success, yet perhaps no other function is more ignored. Many entrepreneurs think that planning is done only by giant corporations such as General Motors or IBM, and because planning is not a tangible activity, it might be forgotten in the face of checking the quality of raw materials and signing for a bank loan.[23] Entrepreneurs must be careful to guard against these two beliefs, as failing to plan can undermine the potential success of their venture before it even starts.

The basic planning context for the typical small business is much simpler than that faced by a larger firm. Its environment is usually much simpler: it usually has fewer regulators to contend with, its task environment is more easily identified, and its planning horizon is somewhat shorter. Moreover, its set of tactical, action, and contingency plans is likely to be smaller and more easily managed. This relative simplicity should not be overstated. For example, although a large business has a more complex planning task, it also has many more people involved in planning. The entrepreneur frequently does all planning alone. Moreover, the entrepreneur may be able to tolerate fewer errors in forecasts and plans than can managers employed by large organizations.

The entrepreneur must plan for the life cycle stages through which the small business will likely pass. By assuming that planning takes place only before startup, an entrepreneur may be contributing to his or her own failure. An entrepreneur's failure to continue planning is often the reason so many small businesses grow erratically, stand still, or fail.

Many small businesses exhibit a general pattern of growth that passes through predictable stages.[24] In the *acceptance* stage, entrepreneurs generally struggle to break even. They are usually close enough to the business to spot obstacles and act quickly to remove them. For example, without some contracts in hand, an entrepreneur who leases factory space to make vinegar expects the first few months to be lean. It will probably take some time to "debug" the vinegar-making equipment and ensure that the vinegar it makes uniformly meets the quality standards of prospective customers; to make vinegar with negligible waste and at low cost; and to convince prospective customers, especially food chains, to buy the vinegar, generally on a trial basis. Meanwhile, with sales limping along, the cash drain becomes severe as bills and wages must be paid. There is little relief until the marketplace begins to accept the vinegar. Then and only then do cash inflows begin to match and finally overtake cash outflows—perhaps months after startup.

The *breakthrough* stage follows. During the acceptance stage, the rate of growth has been so slow that it may pass unnoticed. But in the breakthrough stage, growth is so fast that entrepreneurs may fail to keep up with it. Unprepared, they may make wrong decisions or fail to act. Sales revenues continue to spiral upward, and problems begin to surface that need attention. For example, problems may arise with cash flow (Will we have the necessary cash to pay the bills?), production (Are we keeping costs down in ways that are consistent with making a high-quality product?), quality (Are we making good on our guarantee of uniform high quality?), and delivery (Are we delivering promptly on all customer orders?). At the same time, competition may become more severe.

In the face of the pressures of the breakthrough stage, entrepreneurs may hastily apply ill-conceived solutions to problems. For example, if sales begin to level off or slip, they may add too many specialists such as an accountant, a quality-control analyst, and a customer service representative. As a result, costs go up, squeezing profits further. Meanwhile, entrepreneurs try to regain the successful techniques and procedures they lost shortly after breakthrough, and the cycle of growth begins to repeat itself as they pass through the *maturity* stage.

The best way to head off the problems that accompany growth is to continue updating the business plan. For example, continuing to update the financial plan will alert entrepreneurs to cash-flow problems. Here the cash budget is especially useful because it will alert them to future cash shortages.[25]

Organizing in the Small Business

Given the high level of environmental uncertainty that exists in business today, few entrepreneurs have the skills needed to succeed on their own. Until World War II, the business world had few regulations, few taxes, few big competitors, few records, and no computers; simplicity, however, has since given way to complexity. Major corporations such as AT&T and E. I. du Pont de Nemours & Co. employ thousands of specialists. Du Pont, for example, has more than 600 marketing researchers, most of whom have at least a master's degree. This degree of expert help is clearly beyond the reach of most entrepreneurs, but they do need help to survive and grow. As a starting point, they must identify the kinds of help they need. The business plan, which should be continually updated as the business grows, can help them identify these areas.[26]

Defining Skill Needs   With limited resources, entrepreneurs often have no choice but to define their organization in terms of skills rather than in terms of persons. Even though they cannot afford to hire a full-time accountant or a full-time marketing researcher, they must organize their business as though they could afford such specialists. Only by going through such a procedure can they ensure that needed skills have not been overlooked.

Suppose that a chemical engineer has just invented a new process to make fiber glass–reinforced plastic for sports cars like the Corvette. This process is faster and cheaper than the present one. Ready to exploit his invention, the chemical engineer decides to go into business for himself. To start, he must define the specific skills needed to make his business a reality. Using the business plan and following the outline shown in Figure 23.2, he might determine the skills needed for the business with the skill needs assessment shown in Table 23.2. Notice in the table that the engineer himself is best qualified to complete six of the steps. For the rest, he recognizes that he must rely on outside experts. Such help may come from a variety of sources. As shown in Figure 23.3, entrepreneurs like the chemical engineer need outside professional help from accountants, bankers, professors, insurance agents, and lawyers. We will say more later about the outside management help that is available.

Job Descriptions   The manager must also establish job descriptions (described in Chapter 13) that spell out who does what, who has what authority, and who reports to whom. Job descriptions ensure that problems such as people not knowing exactly what their job involves and to whom they report are avoided.

Organization Charts   Charting all the positions and interrelationships can be very useful for a small business. The small-business manager should

TABLE 23.2 Identifying Skill Needs

Step Number	Description of Step	Skill Needed	Expert Best Suited to Meet Need	
			Entre-preneur	Other
1	Decide to go into business	Knowledge of self	✓	
2	Analyze yourself		✓	
3	Pick product or service		✓	
4	Research the market	Knowledge of marketing research		Marketing researcher
5	Forecast sales revenues			Marketing researcher
6	Select site			Marketing researcher
7	Develop production plan	Knowledge of chemical engineering	✓	
8	Develop marketing plan	Knowledge of marketing		Advertising account executive
9	Develop organizational plan	Knowledge of skill needs	✓	
10	Develop legal plan	Knowledge of law		Lawyer
11	Develop insurance plan	Knowledge of insurance		Insurance agent
12	Develop accounting plan	Knowledge of accounting		Accountant
13	Develop financial plan	Knowledge of finance		Loan officer
14	Write cover letter	Knowledge of venture	✓	

Source: Nicholas C. Siropolis, *Small Business Management: A Guide to Entrepreneurship,* 4th ed. (Boston: Houghton Mifflin, 1990), p. 307. Copyright © 1990 by Houghton Mifflin Company. Used with permission.

recognize, however, that organization charts have their limitations. Although they symbolize how an entrepreneur plans to do the work, few small businesses run precisely the way their organization charts indicate. In a growing business, a chart may soon become outdated or unpredictable events may change the course of an entrepreneur's plans. For these and other reasons, organization charts should be evaluated and revised at least once a year. Organization charts are also limited in that they cannot show how all the jobs within a small business are related. To try to do so would result in a chart with solid and broken lines crisscrossing the page in undecipherable confusion. A good organization chart is a simple one that highlights only the jobs and lines of authority that are crucial to the goals of the small business. An organization chart must communicate if it is to be effective.

The main value of an organization chart may be that the very act of putting one together forces entrepreneurs to crystallize their thinking about what work must be done and how it should be done to make the business profitable. Without such forethought, organization charts will have little value.

Management Help Another aspect of organizing in the small business is to identify sources of assistance. Since the 1950s, the idea that small businesses need management assistance has become increasingly widespread.

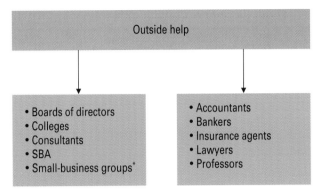

*Generally with chambers of commerce.

Source: Nicholas C. Siropolis, *Small Business Management: A Guide to Entrepreneurship*, 4th ed. (Boston: Houghton Mifflin, 1990), p. 294. Copyright © 1990 by Houghton Mifflin Company. Used with permission.

Entrepreneurs generally need help from a variety of outside sources. Some of these sources provide free assistance, while others charge for their services. Nevertheless, these charges are usually a good investment. Entrepreneurs who need assistance but are unwilling to seek help are likely to fail.

Table 23.3 lists the many sources of management help now offered at little or no cost to entrepreneurs, either before or after they go into business for themselves. Because of the depth of management sophistication needed to launch a high-technology business such as microcomputer manufacture, services differ depending on whether the business is high technology or low technology.

Table 23.3 lists not only federal help but also help from such sources as community colleges and universities, chambers of commerce, and organizations made up of small businesses. Heading the list is the SBA. Since it was founded in 1953, the SBA has helped hundreds of thousands of small businesses. Most entrepreneurs have the mistaken view that all the SBA does is lend money or guarantee repayment of loans made by commercial banks. Even more important are the SBA's efforts to help entrepreneurs manage better. Any entrepreneur can spend money. The SBA's programs help them spend wisely.

The SBA offers entrepreneurs four major management assistance programs: Service Corps of Retired Executives (SCORE), Active Corps of Executives (ACE), Small Business Institute (SBI), and Small Business Development Center (SBDC). All four programs offer management help at no charge to the entrepreneur. SCORE tries to match the expert to the need. If an entrepreneur needs a marketing plan but does not know how to put one together, the SBA tries to find a SCORE counselor with marketing knowledge and experience to help. SBI taps the talents available at colleges and universities. This program involves not only professors of business administration but also students working for advanced degrees. Under a professor's guidance, such students work with entrepreneurs to help solve their management problems.

Leading in the Small Business

Of all the traits that entrepreneurs must possess if they are to be effective leaders, perhaps none is so vital as the willingness to pursue excellence day in and day out. The entrepreneur must set the tone that motivates employ-

TABLE 23.3   Sources of Help for Entrepreneurs

Management Help Offered by	Where Available	Before They Go into a Business Whose Technology Is		After They Go into a Business Whose Technology Is	
		High	Low	High	Low
U.S. Small Business Administration counseling by					
Staff	N				✓
Service Corps of Retired Executives	N				✓
Active Corps of Executives	N				✓
Small Business Institute	N				✓
Small Business Development Center	S	✓		✓	✓
Prebusiness workshops	N		✓		
Nonaccredited courses and seminars	N		✓		
Publications	N		✓		✓
U.S. Department of Commerce					
Seminars and workshops	N			✓	✓
Publications	N	✓	✓	✓	✓
Other federal agencies (example: IRS[a])					
Seminars and workshops	N				✓
Publications	N				✓
State, county, and local governments					
Counseling	S				✓
Seminars and workshops	S				✓
Publications	S				✓
Local development corporations and the like					
Counseling	N				✓
Seminars and workshops	N				✓
Universities					
Accredited courses	S	✓	✓	✓	✓
Nonaccredited courses and seminars	S				✓
Publications	S	✓	✓	✓	✓
Counseling	S				✓
Community colleges					
Accredited courses	S				✓
Nonaccredited courses and seminars	N				✓
Counseling	S				✓
Small-business groups (example: NFIB[b])					
Seminars and workshops	S				✓
Counseling	S				✓
Publications	N				✓
Large corporations (example: Bank-America Corp.)					
Publications	N		✓		✓
Counseling	S				✓
Trade associations					
Publications	N			✓	✓
Seminars and workshops	N			✓	✓

[a]U.S. International Revenue Service.
N = nationally; S = some parts of nation.
[b]National Federation of Independent Business.

CEO Cecil Ursprung (bottom left), of Reflexite Corp. (makers of reflective material used in road signs) believes employees should have power over decisions affecting their work. Under Ursprung's unusual leadership style, Reflexite has achieved amazing growth. Central to his philosophy is the company's employee stock ownership plan. Employees, who own 59 percent of Reflexite's stock, feel a sense of proprietorship and long-term commitment to the company and its profitability.

ees to excel. As noted by the famed football coach Vince Lombardi, "You don't try to win some of the time. You don't try to do things right some of the time. You do them right all of the time."[27]

One way that entrepreneurs can motivate employees to excel is to have high expectations. Entrepreneurs who expect excellence from employees often receive it. Only highly motivated employees are likely to make and sell superior products that cause customers to develop loyalty to the business. Entrepreneurs generally want their employees to be loyal to the business, too, but they should guard against expecting blind loyalty regardless of how they treat their employees and through good times and bad. True loyalty is the employee's working up to his or her capabilities and doing the best possible job in the pursuit of excellence. In essence, true loyalty is loyalty to the job, not to the entrepreneur.

Besides motivating employees to excel, entrepreneurs must also work toward helping employees satisfy their own personal goals while at the same time performing organizational responsibilities effectively. Managers can do several things along these lines. First, entrepreneurs must help their employees become achievers. The attitude that employees do not care about deriving satisfaction from their jobs can lead to such problems as absenteeism and high turnover, shoddy workmanship, and a decline in employees' motivation to work.

Second, just as coaches must be close to their players to be effective as leaders, so must entrepreneurs be close to their employees. Teams that win consistently have coaches that know their jobs and have a knack for communicating that knowledge to players. Players see their assignments clearly because the coach helps them understand what is expected of them. They know how to carry out their assignments because the coach has meticulously laid out the game plan and the plays to use against the competition. They carry out their assignments with precision because the coach has created an atmosphere of fairness, confidence, and camaraderie.

Creating such a work atmosphere is difficult. No two players—or employees—are exactly alike. What appeals to one may repel another. Because all employees are unique and complex, entrepreneurs must understand their needs to help them do their best.

Third, entrepreneurs, as leaders, can help employees achieve status and gain a positive opinion of themselves and their jobs. They may do so by sharing decision-making responsibilities with employees, giving employees greater responsibility as soon as they are ready for it, taking employees' ideas and suggestions to heart, and judging employees rigorously on merit and rewarding them accordingly.

Entrepreneurs who follow these suggestions are more likely to succeed than those who do not. By building up employees' self-image and improving their status, entrepreneurs are likely to grow as leaders themselves.

Controlling in the Small Business

Discussion of the control function brings us full circle. Without control, the other three managerial functions—planning, organizing, and leading—are meaningless because only by practicing control can entrepreneurs tell how effective the other three functions are. It is never enough just to set goals and then organize and lead to meet those goals. Entrepreneurs must measure their progress at frequent intervals and make adjustments based on those measurements. To do that, they need information that tells them whether their goals are being met. "Management in Practice" summarizes how one unique small business makes effective use of control.

Despite its importance, control tends to be ignored by many entrepreneurs. One reason may be that entrepreneurs believe that control is a function practiced only by big business. With this attitude, it is hardly surprising that so many entrepreneurs find themselves in trouble from the start. They fail to see that control is simply the process by which they may assure themselves that their actions, as well as those of their employees, conform to plans and policies.

Especially vital is accounting information, which may be useful in several ways. As a means of communication, it helps inform employees of the actions that the entrepreneur wishes them to take. As a means of motivation, it helps motivate employees in such a way that they will do what the entrepreneur wants them to do. As a means of getting attention, it signals the existence of problems that require investigation and possibly action. As a means of checking up, it helps the entrepreneur assess how well employees are doing their jobs. Such an appraisal of performance can lead to salary increases, promotion, reassignment, or corrective action of various kinds.

The key element of the control process is the information that allows entrepreneurs to compare actual performance with planned performance. This information allows them to measure not only their performance but also the propriety of their goals and actions and, if need be, to adjust them. To illustrate the importance of control to the small business, consider the example of one small contracting firm. Elling Brothers Mechanical Contractors specializes in the design and installation of piping systems. The company moved into the installation of custom and made-to-order systems and, after losing $250,000 on small cost overruns that escalated and snowballed over the course of a fifteen-month job, realized that tighter control was needed. Following a set of guidelines developed by a consultant, Elling

NEW LIFE FOR AN OLD PARK

The Breakers hotel on Lake Erie, between Toledo and Cleveland, is a relic of turn-of-the-century life. It was built in 1905 as a lakefront resort, and neighboring Cedar Point amusement center was added the following year to bring more guests to the hotel. Among the hotel's famous visitors were John D. Rockefeller and Annie Oakley. Football legend Knute Rockne is supposed to have practiced passing on the Breakers' lawn during time off from his lifeguarding duties.

Like many such resorts, the Breakers and Cedar Point suffered from changes in demographics and travel patterns, and in the 1970s their controlling company, Cedar Fair, became the target of takeover interest. Finally in 1981, Britain's Pearson, Plc., joined Cedar Fair executives in a leverage buyout. Six years later, the company became a publicly traded master limited partnership, and in less than ten years the value of Pearson's investment had risen $200 million. In fact, Cedar Fair's profit margins reached 29 percent in 1991, twice those of Disney World.

Much of the credit for transforming a has-been company into the Disney World of Ohio goes to Richard Kinzel, who began working at Cedar Fair in 1972. Through a carefully controlled program of expanding the attractions without expanding costs, Kinzel has been able to keep four million people a year happy and make a good profit even though the park is open only about one-third of the year.

Because the park is a summer-only business, it employs only sixty year-round staff members. Most of the summer work is done by college students earning $5 or $6 an hour. To keep those smiles on repeat-customers' faces, Kinzel makes sure that the park is spotless, and every year the park opens a new ride. It now boasts the world's highest and fastest roller coasters and constantly branches into new forms of entertainment such as Adventure Golf and a Grand Prix go-kart track.

Cedar Point's relatively inexpensive accommodations are also part of the attraction. Guests can still stay at the 400-room Breakers, and in 1990, Cedar Point added a new hotel without adding new management to run it. The company has been doing so well that it recently bought two parks in Pennsylvania, and even during recession years when attendance slipped slightly, per capita spending went up. Cedar Point is not yet on the same scale as Disney's parks, but it could probably teach Disney some lessons.

References: Lisa Gubernick, " 'Terror With A Smile,' " *Forbes*, September 2, 1991, pp. 64–65; United Press International, "Cedar Fair Attendance Falls 4 Percent," October 2, 1990; United Press International, "Cedar Fair to Buy Pennsylvania Parks," January 23, 1992; United Press International, "Cedar Fair Says Economy Didn't Hurt Earnings, Revenue," January 21, 1992.

implemented a new accounting control system that saved the company from going under.[28]

ENTREPRENEURSHIP IN LARGE BUSINESSES

Strictly speaking, entrepreneurship requires the entrepreneur to run the business, but in recent years there has been a keen interest in injecting an entrepreneurial spirit into large organizations.[29] Managers have come to realize that an organization can become lethargic and susceptible to a takeover or attack by competitors. In Chapter 20 we described the concept of the intrapreneur—someone who develops an idea within the context of a large organization. The roles of intrapreneur and entrepreneur are similar. The biggest substantive difference is that the intrapreneur works within a broader context and the entrepreneur assumes more personal risk.

Kodak's Zebras—the 1,500 employees who make black and white film have worked, since 1989, in a horizontal structure known as "the flow." A 25-member leadership team watches the flow, measuring end-of-process tallies such as productivity. The self-directed teams have doubled productivity and improved morale because, in the entrepreneurial fashion, they "own" the process and therefore have the power to make the changes that are needed.

Organizations often go to great lengths in their attempts to maintain an entrepreneurial spirit as they grow. For example, Toys 'Я' Us has become a huge business, but the company views each store as an independent small business beneath a corporate umbrella. Store managers are held personally responsible for the performance of their stores, and they receive large rewards if they perform well. The goal is to create a sense of hundreds of small businesses rather than one big one.[30] More and more large businesses are recognizing the value of this model. Thus entrepreneurial zeal and spirit represent an important contribution made by small business to the nation's economy in general and to large business in particular.

SUMMARY OF KEY POINTS

Entrepreneurship is the process of organizing, operating, and assuming the risk of a business venture. An entrepreneur is someone who engages in entrepreneurship. A new enterprise established by an entrepreneur can grow rapidly, remain stable, or decline.

A small business is one that is independently owned and operated and has relatively little influence over its environment. Small businesses are important because of their financial performance, innovation, job creation, new-business formation levels, and contributions to big business. Many small businesses are present in the service, retailing, and wholesaling sectors; there are fewer of them in manufacturing.

Four common determinants of small-business success are hard work, drive, and dedication on the part of the entrepreneur; market demand for the product or service being offered; managerial competence; and luck. Four basic causes of failure are managerial incompetence or inexperience, neglect, weak control systems, and undercapitalization.

When starting a new business, the entrepreneur must consider a number of issues, including preparing a well-conceived business plan (which is a document prepared by an entrepreneur in preparation for opening a new business) and making a decision regarding ownership. Other important considerations involve the issues of franchising and whether to buy an existing business or start a new one.

Entrepreneurs must plan, organize, lead, and control just like their counterparts in larger businesses. Each managerial function, however, has unique aspects relevant more to small businesses than to larger ones.

DISCUSSION QUESTIONS

Questions for Review

1. What is an entrepreneur? What is entrepreneurship? How do they differ?

2. What is a small business? Why do you think definitions vary so much from industry to industry?

3. What factors contribute to small business success?

4. List some reasons for the failure of small businesses. How would you sum up these reasons into one catch-all reason?

Questions for Analysis

5. Managing a small company is different from managing a large corporation. What are some of the major differences? Can you think of any not mentioned in the text?

6. The U.S. Department of Commerce and U.S. Office of Management and Budget have stated that major inventions are just as likely to be developed in small businesses as in large companies with complete research and development divisions. Why do you think that this is so?

7. A friend of yours with no college background has started a small business and has decided to take some courses to gain a better background in business. What courses would you recommend to your friend? Why?

Questions for Application

8. Locate and interview the owner of a small business who is also the founder of the business. Why did the interviewee establish the company? What big problems did he or she face in getting it started? What current problems is he or she facing? Would the interviewee do it again?

9. Get together with two other members of your class and try to come up with an idea for a new company. How would you go about establishing the company? How would it be organized? Who will have what responsibility? What would be your business strategy? Do you think that you could get the business to succeed? Why or why not?

10. Go to the library and locate material on three different entrepreneurs. In what ways are they similar and different? Why are they similar? Why are they different?

BLUE BELL BLOSSOMS

When the Brenham Creamery Company of Brenham, Texas, began making ice cream in 1911, it churned out only two gallons a day, and the ice cream didn't make it very far from the creamery. Eighty years later, with its name changed to Blue Bell Creameries, the company still bills itself as "the little creamery in Brenham." But its peak output now tops 100,000 gallons a day, and although it has only recently begun to show up outside of its home state, Texans are so fond of it that it has become the nation's second-biggest brand of ice cream, after Breyers.

Blue Bell's growth has been carefully planned and controlled by the Kruse family. E. F. Kruse became plant manager in 1919, and his sons Ed and Howard still run the privately owned company. Expansion hasn't been just a matter of running ads in new places and filling grocers' warehouses with ice cream. Blue Bell's success depends in large measure on its ability to maintain its image as a "little creamery," not an easy job when three out of five scoops sold in Texas are Blue Bell's.

Before Blue Bell began looking beyond Texas's borders, it had solidly established itself in its home base and developed the manufacturing capability and the product variety to allow it to compete with national brands. At first the company was reluctant to let visitors see that the "little creamery" had a huge, ultramodern facility, but that fear proved groundless. Blue Bell's labs have also kept up with the times. During a given year, Blue Bell makes as many as thirty-nine flavors. It was quick to appeal to diet-conscious ice cream lovers, offering the country's first half-gallon dairy dessert with NutraSweet.

With its products virtually saturating the Texas market, Blue Bell began moving into Oklahoma and Louisiana in 1989. The company persuaded supermarkets to sell Blue Bell by explaining that Blue Bell's turnover rate is almost three times that of the average ice cream, meaning more profit for the supermarkets. Blue Bell also owns its own distribution system and delivers directly to the store, not to a warehouse, helping to ensure that the ice cream stays fresh.

Getting the word out to the public has meant spending $100,000 or so on advertising in each new market. And newspaper stories, such as one in the New Orleans *Times-Picayune* that focused on Blue Bell's country roots, certainly helped. Within three months of its arrival in New Orleans, Blue Bell had already claimed a 33-percent market share.

So far, Blue Bell has managed to grow big without losing the benefits of being small. Despite its size and tremendous growth, it is still selling itself as the small town creamery that can boast that Monday night's milking is ice cream on its way to the store by Wednesday.

Discussion Questions

1. What lessons does Blue Bell's success offer for small business owners who want to expand?

2. Do you think that being privately owned is an advantage or a disadvantage for a company like Blue Bell?

E 3. Do you think Blue Bell is guilty of false advertising when it bills itself as the "little creamery" despite its continued expansion into the national market? Or is this part of the legitimate image-making all companies engage in when they try to sell their products?

References: Steve Hill, "Bigger Markets Won't Affect Little Creamery in Brenham," *Bryan–College Station Eagle*, March 25, 1990, pp. A1, 6a; Toni Mack, "The Ice Cream Man Cometh," *Forbes*, January 22, 1990, pp. 52–56; C. Kevin Swisher, "Just Desserts," *Texas Highways*, August 1991, pp. 12–17.

SOGETI AND THE FUTURE OF SOFTWARE

When most people think of computer software, they envision word-processing programs like WordPerfect, spreadsheet programs like 1-2-3, and companies like Microsoft Corp. and Lotus Development Corp. But when analysts say that world spending on software and related services has now topped spending on hardware, they don't have in mind the off-the-shelf packages that you buy for your home computer. The bulk of the programming performed around the world is done for particular companies that have unique software needs.

Sogeti, a French company with revenues topping $2 billion, is positioned as well as any company in the world to take advantage of this growing need for software, service, and support. By far the largest computer-services group in Europe, Sogeti recently entered into an agreement with Daimler-Benz AG, solidifying its position as one of the Continent's fastest-growing and most prestigious companies.

The company is the brainchild of Serge Kampf, who left General Electric Co.'s computer business, Groupe Bull, in 1967. Sogeti began what's known as a "body shop," a collection of computer-service temporaries. Its programmers were scattered in groups throughout France, held together mostly by a good reputation and tight financial controls. They did much of the work on France's computerized telephone directory, which allows users to find any number in France or buy seats in airplanes and theaters from one of its terminals.

Although Kampf continues to control the company from his home in Grenoble, France, Sogeti has recently been branching out, buying Britain's leading computer-services firm as well as two management-consulting companies in the United States. This last purchase gives some clues as to Sogeti's vision of the future of computer services. More companies are asking management consultants not just for ways to motivate employees or build teams but for help doing tasks that require computers.

Sogeti also provides systems integration, which is an entire package of hardware and software that performs a complete function such as handling all billings for a company. Most hardware manufacturers are delighted to provide such integration, but Sogeti offers more objective advice, without ties to any particular hardware.

Finally, Sogeti, like Electronic Data Systems Inc., offers facilities management, or handling all of a company's computer needs the way outside contractors now handle all of a company's construction or janitorial needs. For many companies, the day of the in-house computer expert may be passing.

Kampf's formula for success seems simple enough: hire good people, let them work in their own way, build a solid reputation, and plan to fill tomorrow's needs, not yesterday's. Already, a business magazine has labeled him "The Napoleon of Software."

Discussion Questions

1. What things might hamper Sogeti's ability to grow?

2. How would Kampf's entrepreneurial skills need to differ from those of someone who starts a company to build a better personal computer?

3. Sogeti's services cover a broad range. Which of the specific services Sogeti offers might be useful to two firms which have just merged?

References: Linda Lewis, "Daimler–Benz Takes Sogeti Stake in Services Strategy," *Computer World,* August 5, 1991, p. 71; John Marcom, Jr., "The Napoleon of Software," *Forbes,* June 24, 1991, pp. 112–116.

Managerial Careers

OUTLINE

The Nature of Managerial Careers

Career Management
   Individual Career Planning
   Organizational Career Planning

Special Issues in Careers
   Women and Minorities
   Dual-Career Couples
   Career Transitions

*E*llen Marram received her MBA from Harvard in 1970 and then accepted a position as a marketing assistant at Lever Bros. Co. Two years later she moved to Johnson & Johnson and then went to Standard Brands in 1977. That company was acquired by Nabisco Brands Inc. in 1981. Marram stayed on and has since received four promotions. Today, she is president of the company's $1.2 billion-a-year grocery products' division (maker of such products as Fleischmann's margarine and Nabisco Cream of Wheat). Her unit has 4,000 employees, and her salary is almost $300,000 per year. Marram has earned a reputation as a shrewd manager and will likely be a candidate one day for the top spot at a major corporation.[1]

The work experiences of Ellen Marram are both common and unique. Most managers today graduate from college and go on to work for an organization. They sometimes leave their original employer and work for someone else. They also occasionally get promoted. Other managers, such as Donald Peterson, former CEO of Ford Motor Co., have some of the same experiences, like college and promotions. But Peterson spent virtually his whole working life at Ford. This appendix provides some insight into managerial careers.

THE NATURE OF MANAGERIAL CAREERS

A person's **career** is the set of work-related experiences, behaviors, and attitudes encountered throughout his or her working life. One person may spend his entire career doing the same kind of work for the same company. Another may work for a number of different companies in a number of different jobs. Still another may open her own business and never work for someone else. Each of these patterns represents a career in its fullest sense.[2] This contrasts sharply with the notion of a job—a single work assignment performed for an organization.

Perhaps the key distinction between a job and a career is the level of psychological involvement by the employee. When employees think of their work only in terms of what they have to do between 8 A.M. and 5 P.M. every day and how much they are paid for doing it, and they do not consider what they will be doing next year or the year after or how important the work itself is to them, they are viewing their work as simply a job. When individuals view their work in the context of a career, however, they are much more involved with what they do. They view their career with a long-term outlook and recognize that it comprises a sequence of steps that, taken together, will engage their entire working lives. And although money is important, it is only one of many things (including promotion opportunities, recognition, and personal satisfaction) that influence their behavior.

Figure A1.1 illustrates the general stages people go through in their careers. The first stage, which usually occurs during the first few years of the individual's adult life, is called **exploration.** Through a long period of self-examination (based on observations of others, part-time jobs, talking to other people, and educational courses), the person gradually decides that

career
A set of work-related experiences, behaviors, and attitudes encountered throughout working life

exploration
The first stage of one's career; usually occurs during the first few years of an individual's adult life

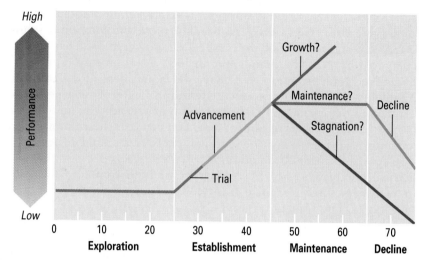

FIGURE A1.1 Common Career Stages

Source: Adapted from *Careers in Organizations,* by Douglas T. Hall. Copyright © 1976 by Scott, Foresman and Co. Reprinted by permission.

she may want to be an engineer, a doctor, a manager, or an artist and begins to prepare. The exploration stage continues even after the person finishes school and takes her first job. The chosen career may not live up to expectations, or the person may decide to work a few years and then return to graduate, medical, or law school.

Most people eventually settle on a career and then proceed into the **establishment** stage. During this phase, the individual is likely to receive occasional promotions and reassignments. Although changes may still occur, at this stage the person generally knows what she or he is interested in and starts to establish an occupational identity.[3] Even though Ellen Marram changed jobs several times early in her career, she always worked for consumer products firms. Such job changes are common during this phase. Few people spend their whole careers with the same organization.

The next phase, which starts around the age of 45 for the average person, is called the **maintenance,** or midcareer, stage. During this time, several things are possible. Some people continue on an upward track toward an upper-level management position. These managers are likely to be groomed for specific openings at the highest levels of the organization. Others reach a plateau—a position where they are likely to remain for the rest of their career.[4] Managers on a plateau often serve as mentors for younger managers. Still others begin to stagnate and decline. Those in this group find themselves increasingly less valued by the organization and may be subject to demotion, termination, or early retirement.

The final career stage for most people is **decline** or disengagement. During this stage, the person can look ahead and see the end of her or his career. She or he begins to plan for retirement and gradually starts to psychologically withdraw from the organization. Many top executives stay on for a while after their formal retirement, however, to work as advisers and to

establishment
Second stage of one's career during which an individual is likely to receive occasional promotions and reassignments

maintenance
The midcareer stage during which some people continue on an upward career track, others reach a plateau

decline
The disengagement stage during which a person begins to plan for retirement and gradually starts to psychologically withdraw from an organization

help train their replacements. And more and more "retired" managers, not content to relax at home, are starting new careers late in life. For example, when he retired at the age of sixty-three after thirty years as an insurance agent, Thomas S. Duck founded the Ugly Duckling Rent-a-Car company in Tucson. Today he has more than 600 outlets and annual revenues of $85 million.[5]

CAREER MANAGEMENT

Given this basic understanding of how careers unfold, and given the importance of a career, you should not be surprised to learn that managing career dynamics is important to both individuals and organizations.

Individual Career Planning

Career planning must start with the individual.[6] After all, only the individual truly knows what he or she wants from life and work. However, people must avoid overplanning. For example, some people set specific goals as to when they want to be promoted, and they identify specific jobs that they want to have as they progress up the organizational ladder. Such rigidity promises disappointment if the promotion is delayed and may cause the person to miss an opportunity to have an exciting new job. Walter Wriston, former CEO of Citibank N.A., held several jobs on his way to the top spot—and not one of them had even existed when he joined the bank! Thus it is important to achieve a balance between knowing generally what you want and how to go about getting it and being rigidly fixed on a specific goal with an inflexible timetable and agenda. Two important tools for achieving this balance are personal assessment and mentor relationships.

Personal Assessment   Personal assessment is learning about yourself—your aspirations, strengths, and weaknesses—and about career opportunities. Many people argue that choosing a career in an area you enjoy is important. For example, Debbi Fields enjoyed baking cookies more than anything else. After several years of frustration while searching for a career, she decided to open a store and sell her cookies. Today, Mrs. Fields Inc. is a multi-million-dollar business with hundreds of Mrs. Fields Cookies stores around the world. The starting point in individual career management is learning about oneself. This inner exploration can be achieved through analysis of the kinds of part-time work you have enjoyed, the courses you have enjoyed, and an honest assessment of what you want from life. University counseling centers offer tests and aptitude profiles that can provide useful insights.

Coupled with this kind of assessment is determining what kind of organization you want to be a part of. Some people want to work for a large company like Xerox Corp. or Digital Equipment Corp. because it provides security and prestige. Others want to work in a smaller organization. Still others want to start their own business to be independent.[7] And, of course, preferences and options often change over the course of a career. It may be necessary to work for a big company at first to save enough money to launch your own business later.

You should try to be realistic about your options. If you are a small adult with limited athletic skills, you are not likely to succeed as a professional football player. You might, however, be successful as a coach or trainer. If your grades are mediocre and you have no aptitude for science, you are unlikely to gain admittance to medical school and should therefore not be too committed to a career as a doctor. But you might succeed as a medical administrator.

Another important element of personal assessment is learning about opportunities. A field that is growing and expanding provides more opportunities than one that is shrinking. Some fields are more difficult to break into than are others. Consider, for example, the hundreds of young people who trek to Hollywood to become movie stars. Only a few succeed. Many fields, like medicine, university teaching, and law, require extra years of formal education. You must decide what is best for you and what sacrifices you are willing to make to reach your goals; only then, with realistic expectations, can you set out to reach them.

Mentor Relationships   Another useful tool for managing one's career is mentor relationships. A mentor is a senior manager who acts as a sponsor, advocate, and teacher for a younger and less experienced new manager, sometimes called a protégé.[8] Mentors are usually in the maintenance stage of their own careers. The mentor-protégé relationship is usually informal and can be initiated by either party. The younger manager may ask the mentor for advice or assistance, or the senior manager may recognize special traits in the younger manager and start taking special interest in his or her performance. During the mentor-protege relationship, the mentor teaches and counsels the protege about performance-related issues, organizational politics, and other important matters. If the mentor thinks it appropriate, he or she also helps advance the protégé's career by telling others how good the protégé's work is and recommending her or him for new job assignments.[9]

Johnson & Johnson, Jewel Food Stores, Federal Express Corp., AT&T Bell Laboratories, Colgate-Palmolive Co., and other organizations have formal mentor programs. Colgate-Palmolive CEO Reuben Marks is a firm believer in the importance of mentor relationships. Besides taking part in the formal program within his company, Marks also participates in another program in which he serves as a mentor to disadvantaged minority youths.[10]

Organizational Career Planning

Mentoring can be either an individual or an organizational approach to career planning. Other techniques are more purely organizational.[11] Table A1.1 summarizes several career-planning programs used by U.S. companies. AT&T, BankAmerica Corp., General Electric Co., General Foods Corporation, and Sears, Roebuck and Co. all have formal career-management programs for employees. Each attempts to help employees understand career options and limits within the company, identify their individual priorities and potential, and develop general strategies for achiev-

TABLE A1.1	Organizational Career Planning Techniques
Technique	**Description**
Career management program	Formal and comprehensive program to help organizations and individuals understand career dynamics within the organization
Career counseling	Formal method for providing employees with counseling and advice about their careers
Career-pathing	Identification of logical and coherent progressions of jobs that individuals might choose to pursue
Career resources planning	Application of planning methods to help people and organizations understand and predict when specific jobs might be open and when specific individuals might be prepared to fill them
Career information systems	Formal information system that makes some or all of the information from the above-mentioned techniques highly accessible to employees

ing a good match between what the organization and the individual want and need.

Increasingly, organizations are also confronting the interrelationships of career management and the globalization of the business world. Nestlé SA and other organizations have a cadre of international managers who have been trained to accept work assignments anywhere in the world. Because of both the costs of overseas assignments and the important role that such assignments can play in a person's career, organizations are paying increased attention to incorporating foreign experiences into key managers' careers.[12]

SPECIAL ISSUES IN CAREERS

Recent years have seen the advent of new career issues for managers to contend with. These issues include opportunities for women and minorities, dual-career couples, and career transitions.

Women and Minorities

Most people are generally aware of the dramatic changes in recent years in the number of women and minorities pursuing professional careers of all types, but especially as managers. In 1972, only 4 percent of those receiving M.B.A. degrees were women, and women held only 20 percent of U.S. management and administrative positions. By 1987, those figures increased to 33 and 37 percent, respectively.[13]

Nevertheless, women still experience various forms of discrimination, often subtle; although some have made it to the upper echelons, there are still few women in the top-management ranks of large U.S. companies. Many companies, however, recognize the importance of women managers to organizational success and are actively working to help them attain top positions.[14]

The situation of minorities is less positive. Even though many organizations have hired large numbers of black managers, for example, few have moved into meaningful top-management positions.[15] And there are very few Hispanic managers in U.S. business. Still, progress is being made, and the minority communities have success stories they can be proud of. Reginald F. Lewis, for example, is a successful black entrepreneur. His TLC Group is one of the largest investment companies on Wall Street. Its biggest deal to date was purchasing Beatrice Company for $985 million a few years ago.[16]

Dual-Career Couples

The entry of more and more women into the workplace has created an issue that organizations must increasingly confront—the dual-career couple. A dual-career couple exists when both partners in a relationship are pursuing careers. The tensions and problems caused by two careers range from the mundane to the traumatic. For example, with both partners working, there are relatively simple problems of coordination like buying groceries and scheduling vacations. More important, however, are questions about who will stay home with a sick child (especially if the illness is long-term) and what will happen if one partner is transferred to another city.[17] Some couples decide that one partner's career will take precedence over the other's; some couples manage with a "commuter" marriage.

Some organizations are becoming sensitive to the needs and problems faced by dual-career couples. General Motors provides counseling and referral services for the spouse of a transferred employee. IBM provides child care assistance and provides all employees with up to a year of unpaid leave for child care at home. Merck & Co., Inc., provides child care, flexible working hours, and work-at-home options to dual-career couples. Still, most businesses are just beginning to address the problem.[18]

Career Transitions

Most people go through a series of stages in the course of their careers. Transitions through these stages may be either planned or unplanned.

Planned Transition A planned transition occurs when the individual or the organization knows about a change in advance and can plan for it. Candidates for top-management positions often know about new job assignments several months in advance, for example, and can carefully plan things associated with the new assignment. Even middle- and lower-level managers often have some advance word about transfers or promotions.

Unplanned Transition Unplanned transitions occur when the individual or the organization has little or no advance warning about a career change.

For example, a death or unexpected resignation can prompt a promotion with no advance warning. Corporate restructurings, unexpected layoffs and terminations, mergers, acquisitions, and takeovers can create circumstances in which managers previously secure in their jobs find themselves out of work.[19] Some organizations do little to help in these circumstances, but more and more firms provide outplacement assistance to terminated employees. Outplacement assistance, usually administered by a specialized service firm, helps the employee cope with the problem and locate new employment. Such services are likely to become increasingly common.[20]

Tools for Budgetary and Financial Control

OUTLINE

Budgetary Control
  Types of Budgets
  Fixed and Variable Costs in Budgets
  Developing Budgets
  Zero-Base Budgets
  Strengths and Weaknesses of Budgets

Other Tools of Financial Control
  Financial Statements
  Ratio Analysis
  Financial Audits
  Using Financial Control Techniques
    Effectively

n this appendix we examine a number of tools for budgetary and financial control. We first provide an overview of control techniques and methods. We then discuss budgets and budgetary control and other tools of financial control.

Control techniques and methods can be thought of as tools that help managers assess how effectively they are moving toward goals. Control techniques and methods provide performance-related information that managers can compare against standards. Managers interpret the information provided by control techniques and determine what, if any, actions are necessary. As we noted in Chapter 18, financial control is at the heart of all other areas of control. Not surprisingly, then, financial control techniques pervade most other forms of control.

BUDGETARY CONTROL

Budgeting is the process of expressing a set of planned activities for a coming time period in numerical terms; a **budget** is therefore a plan expressed in numerical terms.[1] Organizations may establish budgets for work groups, departments, divisions, or the whole organization. The usual time period for a budget is one year, although breakdowns of budgets by the quarter or month are also common. Budgets are generally expressed in financial terms, but they may occasionally be expressed in units of output, time, or other quantifiable factors.

Budgets are the foundation of most control systems. Because of their quantitative nature, they provide yardsticks for measuring performance, and they facilitate comparisons across departments, between levels in the organization, and from one time period to another. Budgets serve four primary purposes. They help managers coordinate resources and projects (because they use a common denominator, usually dollars). They help define the standards needed in all control systems. They provide clear and unambiguous guidelines about the organization's resources and expectations, and they facilitate performance evaluations of managers and units.

Types of Budgets

Most organizations develop and make use of three different kinds of budgets—financial, operating, and nonmonetary.

Financial Budgets   A **financial budget** summarizes where the organization expects to get its cash for the coming time period and how it plans to use it. Usual sources of cash include sales revenues, short- and long-term loans, sale of assets, and issuance of new stock. For example, Sears, Roebuck and Co. recently modified its financial budgets to reflect an expected drop in sales revenues and special income from the sale of the Sears Tower in Chicago. Common uses of cash are to pay expenses, repay debt, purchase new assets, add to retained earnings, and pay dividends to stockholders.

One special type of financial budget is the **cash-flow budget.** This budget, sometimes just called a **cash budget,** is a projection of all sources of cash

budgeting
The process of expressing a set of planned activities for a coming time period in numerical terms

budget
A plan expressed in numerical terms

financial budget
Summarizes where the organization expects to get its cash for the coming time period and how it plans to use it

cash-flow budget or cash budget
A projection of all sources of cash income and cash expenditures in monthly, weekly, or even daily periods

income and cash expenditures in monthly, weekly, or even daily periods. Its purpose is to ensure that the organization is able to meet its current obligations. For example, the owner of a small business who has a $10,000 payroll and a $1,000 utility bill due on the last day of every month must make sure that he has sufficient cash on hand to meet those obligations.

Another type of financial budget, the **capital expenditures budget,** deals with major assets such as a new plant, machinery, or land. Companies often finance such major expenditures by borrowing large amounts of money (through long-term loans or bonds); thus the capital expenditures budget is quite important. All organizations, even giants like Exxon Corporation and General Electric Co., pay close attention to these budgets because of the large investments usually reflected within them.

The **balance sheet budget** forecasts the organization's assets and liabilities in the event all other budgets are met. Hence it serves as an overall control framework to ensure that other budgets mesh properly and yield results that are in the best interests of the organization. This budget is also called the master budget by some organizations.

Operating Budgets A second major category of budgets consists of **operating budgets.** An operating budget is an expression of the organization's planned operations. An operating budget outlines what qualities of products and services the organization intends to create and what resources will be used to create them.

A **sales** or **revenue budget** focuses on income the organization expects to receive from normal operations. First, sales are forecast for the period being budgeted. Then the selling price of each item is determined. These two amounts are combined to create the revenue budget. If a firm expects to sell 1,000 products at $10 each and 5,000 at $5 each, its sales budget is $12,500. For a government organization, the revenue budget might specify the anticipated influx of tax dollars. A nonprofit hospital would base its revenue budget on revenue such as anticipated contributions and grants. Sales or revenue budgets are important because they help the manager understand what the future financial position of the organization will be.

An **expense budget** outlines the anticipated expenses of the organization in the coming time period. For example, a manager who has a telephone expense budget of $12,000 a year knows that the unit can spend about $1,000 a month on telephone calls. The expense budget also points out upcoming expenses so that the manager can prepare for them. A **profit budget** focuses on anticipated differences between sales or revenues and expenses. If budgeted sales are $1 million and budgeted expenses are $700,000, the manager has a budgeted profit of $300,000. If budgeted sales and expenses are too close together, the profit budget may not be acceptable because the resultant profit is too small. In that case, managers may take steps to increase the sales budget (such as cutting prices or raising sales quotas) or cut the expense budget (such as reducing inventory costs or improving scrappage rates).

Nonmonetary Budgets A nonmonetary budget is a budget expressed in terms that are not financial, such as units of output, hours of direct labor, machine hours, or square-foot allocations. Nonmonetary budgets are generally used at the lower levels of an organization because they are especially

capital expenditures budget
A type of financial budget which deals with major assets such as a new plant, machinery, or land

balance sheet budget
Forecasts the organization's assets and liabilities in the event that all other budgets are met

operating budget
An expression of the organization's planned operations

sales or revenue budget
An outline of the income the organization expects to receive from normal operations

expense budget
An outline of the anticipated expenses of the organization in the coming time period

profit budget
Focuses on anticipated differences between sales or revenues and expenses

helpful to managers at that level. For example, a plant manager can probably schedule work more effectively knowing that he or she has 8,000 labor hours to allocate in a week, rather than $76,451 in wages that can be spent.

Fixed and Variable Costs in Budgets

Regardless of their purpose, most budgets must account for three kinds of costs—fixed, variable, and semivariable.[2] **Fixed costs** are expenses that the organization incurs whether it is in operation or not. A retailer may pay a fixed monthly rent regardless of how many days the store is open. Other fixed costs may include property taxes, minimum utility bills, and some salaries. For example, Kimberly-Clark Corporation must pay rent for its office space, managerial salaries, interest on its bonded indebtedness, warehouse storage costs, and various state and federal taxes whether it makes 1,000 or 100,000 boxes of Kleenex tissues today.

Variable costs are costs that vary according to the scope of operations. The best example of a variable cost is the cost of raw materials used in production. If $2 worth of material is used in making each unit, costs for ten units are $20, costs for forty units are $80, and so on. Other variable costs include travel expenses, sales taxes, and utility expenses above base rates. Kimberly-Clark's variable costs for Kleenex include the costs to make the tissues themselves (paper, dye, etc.), the decorator boxes they are packaged in, and the large cases boxes are placed in for shipping.

Semivariable costs vary as well, but in a less direct way. Advertising, for example, varies according to season and competition. Other major semivariable costs include direct labor, equipment and plant repairs, and maintenance. Kimberly-Clark, for example, recently boosted its television advertising efforts for its disposable diapers in response to a new campaign launched by The Procter & Gamble Co. When developing a budget, managers must accurately account for all three categories of costs. Fixed costs are usually the easiest to deal with. Rent, for example, is almost always governed by a lease and cannot change until the lease expires. Variable costs can often be forecast—but with less precision—from projected operations. Semivariable costs are the most difficult to predict because they are likely to vary, but not in direct relation to operations. For these costs, the manager must often rely on experience and judgment. Some forecasting techniques are also useful for estimating semivariable costs.

Finally, we should note that many U.S. firms are reassessing the manner in which they assign costs to different products. Historically, most fixed costs were assigned on the basis of materials and labor hours needed to produce a given product. Unfortunately, such procedures introduce error into the cost estimates of particular products. For example, Continental Can makes lids for beer cans. The machines, labor, and materials used to make the lids have not changed for years; there is virtually no waste, and productivity is extremely high. New versions of the same product, however, require more expensive machines, computer-assisted design, and higher setup costs. Yet because the actual time and materials needed to make both types of lid are the same, each is budgeted at the same unit cost. Because of these and related shortcomings, managers are looking for new ways to determine the various costs that must be accounted for in budgets.[3]

fixed costs
Expenses that the organization incurs whether it is in operation or not

variable costs
Costs that vary according to the scope of operations

semivariable costs
Costs that vary but not in direct relation to operations

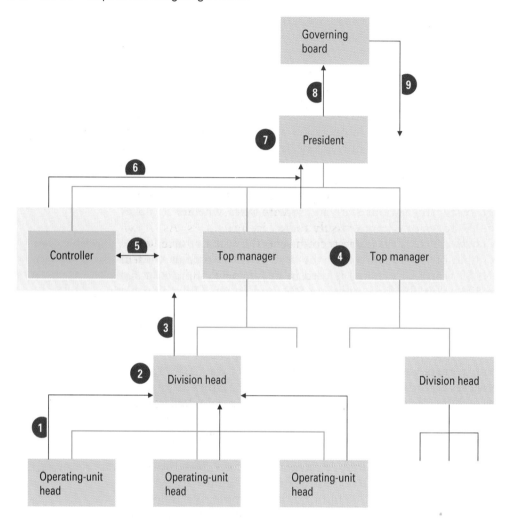

Developing Budgets

Budgets have traditionally been developed by top management and the controller and then imposed on lower-level managers. Some organizations still follow this pattern, but many contemporary organizations now allow lower-level managers to participate in the process. The typical course of a budget preparation is illustrated in Figure A2.1. As a starting point, top management generally issues a call for budget requests. The request is often accompanied by a general indication of overall patterns that the budgets may expect to take. For example, if sales are expected to drop next year, managers may be told up front to prepare for some cuts in operating budgets.

In step 1 of the actual process, the heads of each operating unit submit their budget requests to their division head. These operating-unit heads might be department managers in a manufacturing or wholesaling firm or program directors in a social service agency. The division heads might be plant managers, regional sales managers, or college deans.

The division head integrates and consolidates the various budget requests from the operating-unit heads into one overall division budget request (step 2). Overlapping or inconsistent requests are corrected at this stage. In a college budget, two department heads might each request five new word processors at a cost of $2,000 each. The dean, however, might be aware that the manufacturer grants a 10 percent discount on orders of ten or more systems, so he would forward a request of $18,000 rather than $20,000 for the ten word processors. Similarly, if a regional sales manager notices that one sales manager's budget request assumes a 15 percent increase in product price while another assumes a 12 percent increase, she would need to resolve the inconsistency. A great deal of interaction between managers usually takes place as the division head works to integrate and coordinate the budgetary needs of the various departments.

In step 3, division budget requests are forwarded to a budget committee, which is usually composed of top managers with line authority. In businesses, the committee members are likely to be vice presidents. As shown in Figure A2.1 (step 4), budget requests from several divisions are reviewed at this stage, and once again duplications and inconsistencies are corrected. A university's business college and its speech department might both request funds to develop a new course in business communication. Campus administrators would have to eliminate this duplication. Similarly, the news and the entertainment divisions of a television network might both request funds for a news-magazine show like "60 Minutes" or "Good Morning, America." The budget committee would resolve this overlap.

Step 5 of the process involves interaction between the budget committee and the controller. The interaction can take a variety of forms. All budgets could pass from the committee to the controller for further evaluation and approval. Or the controller could be a member of the budget committee. Or the controller might evaluate the budget requests before they ever go to the budget commmittee.

In step 6, the final budget is sent to the president or CEO for approval. After his or her scrutiny (step 7), it is then passed on to the board of directors or other governing board for review (step 8). Final budgets are then communicated back to the divisions and operating units. As budget requests pass through these various stages, it is almost certain that some changes will be made. The money that a unit ultimately has available may be more than, less than, or the same as what it initially requested.

The budgetary process has been described here in very general terms. Endless variations are possible. Many organizations have budget departments that assist managers in preparing and evaluating budget requests. Occasionally, top management provides initial guidelines on what resources are available so that lower-level managers will have some sense of what is realistic to ask for. Mechanisms are also needed for revising budgets during their term if necessary. For example, if demand for a firm's products were to jump unexpectedly, a plant manager should be able to request additional funds to pay for the overtime labor needed to meet this demand.

This "bottom-up" approach to budgeting is often advocated because it has two primary strengths. First, individual unit managers are likely to be more familiar than anyone else with their own needs. They can call attention to special situations that top management may not be aware of and will probably include all the important elements in developing their own budgets. Second, managers are more likely to "live with" and try to meet a budget if they had a hand in developing it.

Zero-Base Budgets

Zero-base budgeting (ZBB) was pioneered at Texas Instruments Incorporated in 1970 and popularized by President Jimmy Carter when he used it in the federal government in the late 1970s.[4] The basic idea underlying ZBB is quite simple. Under a conventional budgeting system, yearly budgets start with the previous year's budget and are then adjusted up (in most cases) or down. The manager concentrates on justifying any additional funding. The existing budget is considered a given, and debate centers on the merits of the proposed changes. Under a ZBB system, however, each budgeting unit begins with a clean slate each year. The entire budget—not just the adjustments to an existing budget—must be justified.

The first step in ZBB is to break down the activities of the organization into "decision packages." Each package represents an activity or set of activities and specifies the costs and benefits and the consequences if the package is not approved. Decision packages are then ranked in order of importance. Finally, funds are allocated to each decision package according to its relative rank. The higher the rank, the greater is the probability of full funding; the lower the rank, the more likely the activity is to be dropped or only partially funded.

In a relatively short period of time, ZBB has been adopted by a variety of organizations, including Xerox Corp., Ford Motor Co., Westinghouse Electric Corp., Playboy Enterprises, and many federal and state agencies. Ford attributes millions of dollars in savings to zero-base budgeting, and Xerox enjoyed a substantial boost in profits following a shift to ZBB.[5] The primary advantage to ZBB is that it helps maintain vitality by constantly assessing and questioning existing programs. It also facilitates the development of new programs. The process of continual justification necessitates more paperwork, however, and managers may resort to inflating the importance of their programs to maintain funding. ZBB will probably be used even more widely in the future as a technique for organizational control.

Strengths and Weaknesses of Budgets

Budgets offer a number of advantages, but they have potential drawbacks as well. On the plus side, budgets facilitate effective control. By placing dollar values on operations, managers can monitor operations better and pinpoint problem areas. Second, budgets facilitate coordination and communication between departments. In a sense, unit budgets are like pieces of a puzzle that fit together to yield an overall picture. By expressing diverse activities in terms of a common denominator (dollars), different units can better communicate with one another. Budgets also help maintain records of organizational performance. Finally, budgets are a natural complement to planning. The link between planning and control was examined in earlier chapters. As managers plan and then develop control systems, budgets are often a natural next step because they provide feedback to the planners as to how accurate the predictions were.

On the other hand, some managers apply budgets too rigidly. They fail to acknowledge that changing circumstances may justify budget adjustments. Moreover, the process of developing budgets can be very time consuming. This is especially true when organizations adopt ZBB. Finally, budgets may limit innovation and change. When all available funds are allocated to specific operating budgets, it may be impossible to get additional funds to take advantage of an unexpected opportunity.[6]

OTHER TOOLS OF FINANCIAL CONTROL

Although budgets are the most common means of financial control, other tools are also used. These include financial statements, ratio analysis, and financial audits.

Financial Statements

A **financial statement** is a profile of some aspect of an organization's financial circumstances. There are commonly accepted and required ways for preparing and presenting financial statements.[7] The two financial statements prepared and used by virtually all organizations are a balance sheet and an income statement.

financial statement
A profile of some aspect of an organization's financial circumstances

Balance Sheet   The **balance sheet** is a listing of the assets and liabilities of the organization at a particular point in time, usually the end of the organization's fiscal year. An abbreviated example of the balance sheet for a small clothing store, Campus Clothing, Inc., is shown in Table A2.1. It is divided into current assets (assets that are relatively liquid, or easily converted into cash), fixed assets (assets that are longer-term in nature and less liquid), current liabilities (debts and other obligations that must be paid in

balance sheet
A listing of the assets and liabilities of the organization at a particular point in time

TABLE A2.1   Sample Balance Sheet for a Small Clothing Shop

Campus Clothing, Inc.
Balance Sheet
December 31, 1992

Current assets		Current liabilities	
Cash	$ 10,000	Accounts payable	$ 60,000
Accounts receivable	10,000	Accrued expenses	20,000
Inventory	140,000	Long-term liabilities	150,000
	160,000		230,000
Fixed assets		Owners' equity	
Land	60,000	Common stock	200,000
Building and equipment	400,000	Retained earnings	190,000
	460,000		390,000
Total current and fixed assets	$620,000	Total liabilities and equity	$620,000

Campus Clothing, Inc.
Income Statement
For Year Ending December 31, 1992

Gross sales		$806,000
Less returns	6,000	
Net sales		800,000
Less expenses and cost of sales:		
Expenses	120,000	
Depreciation	40,000	
Cost of goods sold	400,000	560,000
Operating profit		240,000
Other income		20,000
Interest expense	30,000	
Taxable income		230,000
Less taxes	115,000	
Net income		115,000

the near future), long-term liabilities (debts that are payable over an extended period of time), and owners' (or stockholders') equity (the owners' claim against the assets). The sum of all current and fixed assets must equal the sum of all liabilities and equity.

income statement
Captures performance over a period of time

Income Statement Whereas the balance sheet reflects a snapshot profile of an organization's financial position at a single point in time, the **income statement** captures performance over a period of time. The time period for income statements is usually one year and coincides with the firm's fiscal year. Table A2.2 provides a simplified income statement for Campus Clothing, Inc. In general, the income statement adds up all income to the organization and then subtracts all expenses, debts, and liabilities. The "bottom line" of the statement represents net income, or profit. Information from the balance sheet and income statement is used in computing the important financial ratios.

Ratio Analysis

The financial statements of an organization provide some useful information to managers, owners, and other interested parties. Information from financial statements is used to calculate several different ratios that provide even more insights.

liquidity ratios
A measure of how liquid, or how easily converted into cash an organization's assets are

Liquidity Ratios Several **liquidity ratios** are used to learn how liquid (how easily converted into cash) an organization's assets are. The most common of these, the current ratio, is current assets divided by current liabilities. For Campus Clothing, this is 160,000 divided by 80,000, or 2. This ratio of 2:1 is generally regarded as acceptable. It indicates how many dollars of liquid assets are available for each dollar of current liability. Creditors consider the current ratio a good index of an organization's ability to pay its bills on time.

Debt Ratios **Debt ratios** reflect an organization's ability to meet long-term financial obligations. One common debt ratio is total liabilities divided by total assets. This ratio for Campus Clothing is 230,000 divided by 620,000, or .37. This indicates that the company has approximately 37 cents in liabilities for every dollar of its assets. The higher this ratio, the poorer credit risk the organization is perceived to be. If management were to ask for a loan of $60,000, for example, the bank would recognize that, even if the store were to go out of business, there would still be enough money left to repay the loan after all other debts were paid. Another common debt ratio is the debt-to-equity ratio.

debt ratio
A measure of an organization's ability to meet long-term financial obligations

Return on Assets A third important financial ratio is return on assets (ROA). The ROA is the percentage return to investors on each dollar of assets that they own. It serves as a yardstick for investors and managers to gauge which of several investment opportunities is most profitable. The common formula for ROA is

return on assets
The percentage return to investors on each dollar of assets that they own

$$\frac{\text{Net income}}{\text{Total assets}} = \text{ROA}$$

For Campus Clothing, net income is $115,000 and it has $620,000 in total assets. Hence ROA is

$$\frac{115,000}{620,000} = .19$$

For each dollar invested by Campus Clothing, the company earns 19 cents, a return of 19 percent per year. This is generally considered a good return by most investors.

Other Ratios Liquidity ratios, debt ratios, and return on assets are widely used forms of financial analysis. Another frequently used ratio is return on investment (ROI). ROI is determined by dividing owners' equity into net income. This ratio represents the return to the investor from each dollar of equity. For Campus Clothing, net income is $115,000 and owners' equity is $390,000. Hence ROI is

$$\frac{115,000}{390,000} = .29$$

Other ratios are also of interest to managers and investors. Coverage ratios help in estimating the organization's ability to cover interest expenses on borrowed capital. Operating ratios focus on functional areas rather than on the total organization. For example, inventory turnover (cost of goods sold divided by average daily inventory) reflects how efficiently the organization is forecasting sales and ordering merchandise. Profitability ratios reflect the relative effectiveness of an organization. For example, profits of $5 million are quite good on sales of $20 million (.25) but are poor on sales of $100 million (.05).

Financial Audits

audits
Independent appraisals of an organization's accounting, financial, and operational systems

Whereas most control techniques also have other purposes, audits are used almost exclusively for control. **Audits** are independent appraisals of an organization's accounting, financial, and operational systems. The two major types of financial audits are the external audit and the internal audit.

External Audits   **External audits** are financial audits conducted by experts who are not employees of the organization.[8] External audits are typically concerned with the extent to which the organization's accounting procedures and financial statements are compiled in an objective and verifiable fashion. Certified public accountants (CPAs) are usually engaged for this purpose. Their main objective is not to prepare financial documents and reports but to verify for stockholders, the IRS, and other interested parties the accuracy of the methods by which those documents and reports have been prepared by financial managers and accountants within the organization.

External audits are almost always extremely thorough. In some cases, auditors even count physical inventory to verify that it agrees with what is shown on the balance sheet. The reason for this precision is that auditors who make mistakes will have their reputations damaged and may even have their licenses revoked. External audits are so important that publicly held corporations are required by law to have external audits on a regular basis to ensure investors that the corporations' financial reports are reliable.

internal audit
The process of verifying the accuracy of financial and accounting procedures used by the organization, conducted by employees of the organization

Internal Audits   Whereas external audits are conducted by external accountants, an **internal audit** is handled by employees of the organization. Its primary objective is the same as that of an external audit—to verify the accuracy of financial and accounting procedures used by the organization. Internal audits also focus on the efficiency and appropriateness of the financial and accounting procedures. In some cases, an accounting system may be technically correct but inefficient. Both external and internal audits verify the accuracy of reports, but only the internal audit is concerned with efficiency.

Large organizations such as Dresser Industries, The Dow Chemical Co., and Eastman Kodak Company have internal auditing staffs. These staffs spend all their time conducting audits of different divisions and functional areas of the organizations. Smaller organizations may assign accountants to an internal audit group on a temporary or rotating basis. Because the staff members who conduct internal audits are permanently on the organization's payroll, internal audits tend to be expensive. However, employees may be familiar with the organization and can point out other aspects of the accounting system besides its technical correctness. For example, a simple change in accounting procedures can sometimes provide managers with more or better information about the financial status of the organization. External auditors may be more objective than employees and have more specialized skills. They are also generally less expensive than a full-time auditing staff.

Using Financial Control Techniques Effectively

To use budgets and other financial control techniques effectively, managers need to keep certain things in mind. Foremost among them is to remember that they are tools. Just as a good hammer and saw can help a carpenter construct a house, so too can a good financial control system help a manager be effective.

In addition, financial controls work most effectively if they are integrated with other information systems of the type discussed in Chapter 21. Financial information is often an important input into other information systems, and those same systems, in turn, are most effective when they can process and provide financial information back to managers. For example, a good information system can tell a manager exactly what current assets and liabilities are. This up-to-date information might then be provided to a banker from whom the firm is attempting to borrow money.

Chapter Notes

Chapter 1

1. "Hit 'em Hardest With the Mostest," *Forbes*, September 16, 1991, pp. 48–51; Gary Hoover, Alta Campbell, and Patrick J. Spain, eds., *Hoover's Handbook—Profiles of Over 500 Major Corporations* (Austin, Tex: The Reference Press, 1990), p. 503; "No-Frills Firm Flies Against the Ordinary," *USA Today*, August 24, 1989, pp. B1, B2.

2. William G. Scott and David K. Hart, *Organizational America* (Boston: Houghton Mifflin, 1979); and Page Smith, *The Rise of Industrial America* (New York: McGraw-Hill, 1984).

3. Frederick W. Taylor, *Shop Management* (New York: Harper & Row, 1903), p. 21.

4. Rosabeth Moss Kanter, "The New Managerial Work," *Harvard Business Review*, November–December 1989, pp. 85–92.

5. Fred Luthans, "Successful vs. Effective Real Managers," *The Academy of Management Executive*, May 1988, pp. 127–132.

6. Alex Taylor III, "How a Top Boss Manages His Day," *Fortune*, June 19, 1989, pp. 95–100.

7. William Whitely, "Managerial Work Behavior: An Integration of Results from Two Major Approaches," *Academy of Management Journal*, June 1985, pp. 344–362.

8. Thomas A. Stewart, "GE Keeps Those Ideas Coming," *Fortune*, August 12, 1991, pp. 41–49.

9. See Patricia Sellers, "Does the CEO Really Matter?" *Fortune*, April 22, 1991, pp. 80–94.

10. Henry Mintzberg, *The Nature of Managerial Work* (New York: Harper & Row, 1973); see also Ford S. Worthy, "How CEOs Manage Their Time," *Fortune*, January 18, 1988, pp. 88–97.

11. Rosemary Stewart, "Middle Managers: Their Jobs and Behaviors," in Jay W. Lorsch, ed., *Handbook of Organizational Behavior* (Englewood Cliffs, N.J., Prentice-Hall, 1987), pp. 385–391.

12. "Caught in the Middle," *Business Week*, September 12, 1988, pp. 80–88.

13. Kenneth Labich, "Making Over Middle Managers," *Fortune*, May 8, 1989, pp. 58–64.

14. Steven Kerr, Kenneth D. Hill, and Laurie Broedling, "The First-Line Supervisor: Phasing Out or Here to Stay?" *Academy of Management Review*, January 1986, pp. 103–117; Leonard A. Schlesinger and Janice A. Klein, "The First-Line Supervisor: Past, Present, and Future," in Lorsch, ed., *Handbook of Organizational Behavior*, pp. 358–369.

15. *The Corporate Elite* (special issue of *Business Week*, 1990).

16. *The Corporate Elite* (special issue of *Business Week*, 1990).

17. *The Corporate Elite* (special issue of *Business Week*, 1990).

18. *The Corporate Elite* (special issue of *Business Week*, 1990).

19. *The Corporate Elite* (special issue of *Business Week*, 1990).

20. "Benefit of B.A. Is Greater Than Ever," *The Wall Street Journal*, August 17, 1988, p. 21.

21. *The Corporate Elite* (special issue of *Business Week*, 1990).

22. Mintzberg, *The Nature of Managerial Work*.

23. Robert L. Katz, "The Skills of an Effective Administrator," *Harvard Business Review*, September–October 1974, pp. 90–102.

24. Andrew Kupfer, "How to Be a Global Manager," *Fortune*, March 14, 1988, pp. 52–58.

25. Mintzberg, *The Nature of Managerial Work*.

26. "U.S. Corporations With the Biggest Foreign Revenues," *Forbes*, July 22, 1991, p. 286.

27. James L. Perry and Hall G. Rainey, "The Public-Private Distinction in Organization Theory: A Cri-

tique and Research Strategy," *Academy of Management Review,* April 1988, pp. 182–201; see also Ran Lachman, "Public and Private Sector Differences: CEOs' Perceptions of Their Role Environments," *Academy of Management Journal,* September 1985, pp. 671–680.

Chapter 2

1. Gary Hoover, Alta Campbell, and Patrick J. Spain, eds., *Hoover's Handbook—Profiles of Over 500 Major Corporations* (Austin, Tex.: The Reference Press, 1990), p. 584; "In Wake of Cost Cuts, Many Firms Sweep Their History Out the Door," *The Wall Street Journal,* December 21, 1987, p. 21; "Wells Fargo Initiates Talks About a Merger With Security Pacific," *The Wall Street Journal,* January 22, 1991, pp. A1, A4.

2. Alan M. Kantrow, ed., "Why History Matters to Managers," *Harvard Business Review,* January–February 1986, pp. 81–88.

3. "Profiting from the Past," *Newsweek,* May 10, 1982, pp. 73–74.

4. Jeffrey Pfeffer, "The Theory-Practice Gap: Myth or Reality?" *The Academy of Management Executive,* February 1987, pp. 31–33.

5. "Can Andy Grove Practice What He Preaches?" *Business Week,* March 16, 1987, pp. 68–69; "Intel to Motorola: Race Ya," *Business Week,* March 13, 1989, p. 42.

6. See also Alan L. Wilkins and Nigel J. Bristow, "For Successful Organization Culture, Honor Your Past," *The Academy of Management Executive,* August 1987, pp. 221–227.

7. Daniel Wren, *The Evolution of Management Theory,* 3rd ed. (New York: Wiley, 1987); Daniel Wren, "Management History: Issues and Ideas for Teaching and Research," *Journal of Management,* Summer 1987, pp. 339–350; Page Smith, *The Rise of Industrial America* (New York: McGraw-Hill, 1984).

8. Marilyn Wellemeyer, "Books Bosses Read," *Fortune,* April 27, 1987, pp. 145–148.

9. William G. Scott, "The Management Governance Theories of Justice and Liberty," *Journal of Management,* June 1988, pp. 277–298.

10. Lex Donaldson, "The Ethereal Hand: Organizational Economics and Management Theory," *Academy of Management Review,* July 1990, pp. 369–381.

11. Wren, *The Evolution of Management Theory.*

12. Charles Babbage, *On the Economy of Machinery and Manufactures* (London: Charles Knight, 1832).

13. Wren, *The Evolution of Management Theory.*

14. Wren, *The Evolution of Management Theory.*

15. Frederick W. Taylor, *Principles of Scientific Management* (New York: Harper and Brothers, 1911).

16. Charles D. Wrege and Amedeo G. Perroni, "Taylor's Pig-Tale: A Historical Analysis of Frederick W. Taylor's Pig-Iron Experiment," *Academy of Management Journal,* March 1974, pp. 6–27; Charles D. Wrege and Ann Marie Stoka, "Cooke Creates a Classic: The Story Behind Taylor's Principles of Scientific Management," *Academy of Management Review,* October 1978, pp. 736–749.

17. Edwin A. Locke, "The Ideas of Frederick W. Taylor: An Evaluation," *Academy of Management Review,* January 1982, pp. 14–20. See also Stephen J. Carroll and Dennis J. Gillen, "Are the Classical Management Functions Useful in Describing Managerial Work?" *Academy of Management Review,* January 1987, pp. 38–51.

18. Henri Fayol, *General and Industrial Management,* trans. J. A. Coubrough (Geneva: International Management Institute, 1930).

19. Max Weber, *Theory of Social and Economic Organizations,* trans. T. Parsons (New York: Free Press, 1947); Richard M. Weis, "Weber on Bureaucracy: Management Consultant or Political Theorist?" *Academy of Management Review,* April 1983, pp. 242–248.

20. Chester Barnard, *The Functions of the Executive* (Cambridge, Mass.: Harvard University Press, 1938).

21. Hugo Munsterberg, *Psychology and Industrial Efficiency* (Boston: Houghton Mifflin, 1913).

22. Wren, *The Evolution of Management Theory,* pp. 256–264.

23. Elton Mayo, *The Human Problems of an Industrial Civilization* (New York: Macmillan, 1933); Fritz J. Roethlisberger and William J. Dickson, *Management and the Worker* (Cambridge, Mass.: Harvard University Press, 1939).

24. For a recent commentary on the Hawthorne studies, see Lyle Yorks and David A. Whitsett, "Hawthorne, Topeka, and the Issue of Science versus Advocacy

in Organizational Behavior," *Academy of Management Review*, January 1985, pp. 21–30.

25. Barry M. Staw, "Organizational Psychology and the Pursuit of the Happy/Productive Worker," *California Management Review*, Summer 1986, pp. 40–53.

26. Abraham Maslow, "A Theory of Human Motivation," *P ychological Review*, July 1943, pp. 370–396.

27. Douglas McGregor, *The Human Side of Enterprise* (New York: McGraw-Hill, 1960).

28. Cynthia D. Fisher, "On the Dubious Wisdom of Expecting Job Satisfaction to Correlate with Performance," *Academy of Management Review*, October 1980, pp. 607–612.

29. Paul R. Lawrence, "Historical Development of Organizational Behavior," in Jay W. Lorsch, ed., *Handbook of Organizational Behavior* (Englewood Cliffs, N.J.: Prentice-Hall, 1987), pp. 1–9. See also Larry L. Cummings, "Toward Organizational Behavior," *Academy of Management Review*, January 1978, pp. 90–98.

30. See Gregory Moorhead and Ricky W. Griffin, *Organizational Behavior*, 3rd ed. (Boston: Houghton Mifflin, 1992) for a recent review of current developments in the field of organizational behavior.

31. Wren, *The Evolution of Management Thought*, Chapter 21.

32. Norman Gaither, *Production and Operations Management*, 5th ed. (Fort Worth: The Dryden Press, 1992).

33. For a recent review of operations management, see Everett E. Adam, Jr., and Ronald J. Ebert, *Production and Operations Management: Concepts, Models, and Behavior*, 4th ed. (Englewood Cliffs, N.J.: Prentice-Hall, 1989).

34. For more information on systems theory in general, see Ludwig von Bertalanffy, C. G. Hempel, R. E. Bass, and H. Jonas, "General Systems Theory: A New Approach to Unity of Science," I–VI *Human Biology*, Vol. 23, 1951, pp. 302–361. For systems theory as applied to organizations, see Fremont E. Kast and James E. Rosenzweig, "General Systems Theory: Applications for Organizations and Management," *Academy of Management Journal*, December 1972, pp. 447–465. For a recent update, see Donde P. Ashmos and George P. Huber, "The Systems Paradigm in Organization Theory: Correcting the Record and Suggesting the Future," *Academy of Management Review*, October 1987, pp. 607–621.

35. Monci Jo Williams, "Synergy Works at American Express," *Fortune*, February 16, 1987, pp. 79–80.

36. "European Banks, Insurance Firms Search for Synergies," *The Wall Street Journal*, April 26, 1989, p. A10.

37. Fremont E. Kast and James E. Rosenzweig, *Contingency Views of Organization and Management* (Chicago: Science Research Associates, 1973).

38. "The Mess at Continental," *Business Week*, August 5, 1991, p. 24.

39. William Ouchi, *Theory Z—How American Business Can Meet the Japanese Challenge* (Reading, Mass.: Addison-Wesley, 1981). For a recent analysis of Theory Z, see Jeremiah J. Sullivan, "A Critique of Theory Z," *Academy of Management Review*, January 1983, pp. 132–142.

40. William Bowen, "Lessons from Behind the Kimono," *Fortune*, June 15, 1981, pp. 247–250.

41. Thomas J. Peters and Robert H. Waterman, Jr., *In Search of Excellence* (New York: Harper & Row, 1982).

42. Kenneth E. Aupperle, William Acar, and David E. Booth, "An Empirical Critique of *In Search of Excellence*: How Excellent Are the Excellent Companies?" *Journal of Management*, Winter 1986, pp. 499–512; Michael A. Hitt and R. Duane Ireland, "Peters and Waterman Revisited: The Unended Quest for Excellence," *The Academy of Management Executive*, May 1987, pp. 91–98.

43. See Tom Peters, "Restoring American Competitiveness: Looking for New Models of Organizations," *The Academy of Management Executive*, May 1988, pp. 103–109.

Chapter 3

1. "Batten Down the Hatches and Rev Up the Jacuzzis," *Business Week*, August 19, 1991, pp. 88–89; "Carnival Cruise Lines May Seek a Buyer For Gaming Venture," *The Wall Street Journal*, October 11, 1991, p. A12.

2. See Jay B. Barney and William G. Ouchi, eds., *Organizational Economics* (San Francisco: Jossey-Bass, 1986), for an overview of current thinking about linkages between economics and organizations.

3. Robert H. Hayes and Ramchandran Jaikumar, "Manufacturing's Crisis: New Technologies, Obsolete Organizations," *Harvard Business Review,* September–October 1988, pp. 77–85.

4. "Regulation Rises Again," *Business Week,* June 26, 1989, pp. 58–59.

5. See Richard M. Steers and Edwin L. Miller, "Management in the 1990s: The International Challenge," *The Academy of Management Executive,* February 1988, pp. 21–23; and Richard I. Kirkland, Jr., "Entering a New Age of Boundless Competition," *Fortune,* March 14, 1988, pp. 40–48.

6. Philip M. Rosenzweig and Jitendra V. Singh, "Organizational Environments and the Multinational Enterprise," *Academy of Management Journal,* June 1991, pp. 340–361.

7. See Ian C. MacMillan, "Controlling Competitive Dynamics by Taking Strategic Initiative," *The Academy of Management Executive,* May 1988, pp. 111–118, for an interesting view of influencing competitors.

8. "National Firms Find That Selling to Local Tastes Is Costly, Complex," *The Wall Street Journal,* July 9, 1987, p. 17. See also Regis McKenna, "Marketing in an Age of Diversity," *Harvard Business Review,* September–October 1988, pp. 88–95.

9. Susan Helper, "How Much Has Really Changed Between U.S. Automakers and Their Suppliers?" *Sloan Management Review,* Summer 1991, pp. 15–28.

10. "Many Businesses Blame Governmental Policies for Productivity Lag," *The Wall Street Journal,* October 28, 1980, pp. 1, 22.

11. Grant T. Savage, Timothy W. Nix, Carlton J. Whitehead, and John D. Blair, "Strategies for Assessing and Managing Organizational Culture," *The Academy of Management Executive,* May 1991, pp. 61–75.

12. "Time Warner Feels the Force of Stockholder Power," *Business Week,* July 21, 1991, pp. 58–59.

13. Rob Norton, "Who Owns This Company, Anyhow?" *Fortune,* July 29, 1991, pp. 131–142.

14. John J. Curran, "Companies That Rob the Future," *Fortune,* July 4, 1988, pp. 84–89.

15. "More Competitors Turn to Cooperation," *The Wall Street Journal,* June 23, 1989, p. B1.

16. Jeremy Main, "The Winning Organization," *Fortune,* September 26, 1988, pp. 50–60.

17. Idalene F. Kesner, "Directors' Characteristics and Committee Membership: An Investigation of Type, Occupation, Tenure, and Gender," *Academy of Management Journal,* March 1988, pp. 66–84; Jeffrey Kerr and Richard A. Bettis, "Boards of Directors, Top Management Compensation, and Shareholder Returns," *Academy of Management Journal,* December 1987, pp. 645–664.

18. Marsha Sinetar, "Building Trust into Corporate Relationships," *Organizational Dynamics,* Winter 1988, pp. 73–79.

19. Terrence E. Deal and Allan A. Kennedy, *Corporate Cultures: The Rights and Rituals of Corporate Life* (Reading, Mass.: Addison-Wesley, 1982).

20. Gurney Breckenfield, "The Odyssey of Levi Strauss," *Fortune,* March 22, 1982, pp. 110–124. See also "Levi Strauss . . . at $3 Billion Plus," *Daily News Record,* October 10, 1988, p. 44.

21. Jay B. Barney, "Organizational Culture: Can It Be a Source of Sustained Competitive Advantage?" *Academy of Management Review,* July 1986, pp. 656–665.

22. "Hewlett-Packard's Whip-Crackers," *Fortune,* February 13, 1989, pp. 58–59.

23. William Ouchi, *Theory Z—How American Business Can Meet the Japanese Challenge* (Reading, Mass.: Addison-Wesley, 1981); Thomas J. Peters and Robert H. Waterman, Jr., *In Search of Excellence* (New York: Harper & Row, 1982).

24. James D. Thompson, *Organizations in Action* (New York: McGraw-Hill, 1967).

25. Michael E. Porter, *Competitive Strategy: Techniques for Analyzing Industries and Competitors* (New York: Free Press, 1980).

26. Ian I. Mitroff, Paul Shrivastava, and Firdaus E. Udwadia, "Effective Crisis Management," *The Academy of Management Executive,* August 1987, pp. 283–292.

27. "Getting Business to Think About the Unthinkable," *Business Week,* June 24, 1991, pp. 104–107.

28. For recent discussions of how these processes work, see Barbara W. Keats and Michael A. Hitt, "A Causal Model of Linkages Among Environmental Dimensions, Macro Organizational Characteristics, and Performance," *Academy of Management Journal,* Septem-

ber 1988, pp. 570–598; and Danny Miller, "The Structural and Environmental Correlates of Business Strategy," *Strategic Management Journal*, Vol. 8, 1987, pp. 55–76.

29. "Why the Street Isn't Moved by Tenneco's Big Move," *Business Week*, September 26, 1988, pp. 130–133.

30. Tom Burns and G. M. Stalker, *The Management of Innovation* (London: Tavistock, 1961).

31. Keats and Hitt, "A Causal Model of Linkages Among Environmental Dimensions, Macro Organizational Characteristics, and Performance."

32. MacMillan, "Controlling Competitive Dynamics by Taking Strategic Initiative."

33. David B. Yoffie, "How an Industry Builds Political Advantage," *Harvard Business Review*, May–June 1988, pp. 82–89.

34. Arie Y. Lewin and John W. Minton, "Determining Organizational Effectiveness: Another Look, and an Agenda for Research," *Management Science*, May 1986, pp. 513–538; Kim S. Cameron, "Effectiveness as Paradox: Consensus and Conflict in Conceptions of Organizational Effectiveness," *Management Science*, May 1986, pp. 539–553.

35. E. Yuchtman and S. Seashore, "A Systems Resource Approach to Organizational Effectiveness," *American Sociological Review*, Vol. 32, 1967, pp. 891–903.

36. Cameron, "Effectiveness as Paradox."

37. B. S. Georgopoules and A. S. Tannenbaum, "The Study of Organizational Effectiveness," *American Sociological Review*, Vol. 22, 1957, pp. 534–540.

38. Cameron, "Effectiveness as Paradox."

Chapter 4

1. "Suddenly, Green Marketers Are Seeing Red Flags," *Business Week*, February 25, 1991, pp. 74–76; Jaclyn Fierman, "The Big Muddle in Green Marketing," *Fortune*, June 3, 1991, pp. 91–101; "Environmentalists, State Officers See Red as Firms Rush to Market 'Green' Products," *The Wall Street Journal*, March 13, 1990, pp. B1, B5.

2. See Thomas M. Garrett and Richard J. Klonoski, *Business Ethics*, 2nd ed. (Englewood Cliffs, N.J.: Prentice-Hall, 1986), for a review of the different meanings of the word *ethics*.

3. "Kazuo Wada's Answered Prayers," *Business Week*, August 26, 1991, pp. 66–67.

4. See Thomas M. Jones, "Ethical Decision Making by Individuals in Organizations: An Issue-Contingent Model," *Academy of Management Journal*, June 1991, pp. 366–395.

5. John Huey, "Wal-Mart—Will It Take Over the World?" *Fortune*, January 30, 1989, pp. 52–61.

6. Patricia Sellers, "Getting Customers to Love You," *Fortune*, March 13, 1989, pp. 38–49.

7. "How Don Sheelen Made a Mess That Regina Couldn't Clean Up," *Business Week*, February 12, 1990, pp. 46–50.

8. Linda Klebe Trevino, "Ethical Decision Making in Organizations: A Person-Situation Interactionist Model," *Academy of Management Review*, July 1986, pp. 601–617; Bart Victor and John B. Cullen, "The Organizational Bases of Ethical Work Climates," *Administrative Science Quarterly*, Vol. 33, 1988, pp. 101–125.

9. Anne B. Fisher, "Who's Hurt by Salomon's Greed?" *Fortune*, September 23, 1991, pp. 71–72.

10. "What Led Beech-Nut Down the Road to Disgrace," *Business Week*, February 22, 1988, pp. 124–128.

11. "The Dark Side of Japan Inc." *Newsweek*, January 9, 1989, p. 41.

12. Archie B. Carroll, "In Search of the Moral Manager," *Business Horizons*, March–April 1987, pp. 7–15; William D. Litzinger and Thomas E. Schaefer, "Business Ethics Bogeyman: The Perpetual Paradox," *Business Horizons*, March–April 1987, pp. 16–21.

13. "Businesses Are Signing Up for Ethics 101," *Business Week*, February 15, 1988, pp. 56–57; "Ethics on the Job: Companies Alert Employees to Potential Dilemmas," *The Wall Street Journal*, July 14, 1986, p. 17.

14. Sir Adrian Cadbury, "Ethical Managers Make Their Own Rules," *Harvard Business Review*, September–October 1987, pp. 69–73.

15. Jerry W. Anderson, Jr. "Social Responsibility and the Corporation," *Business Horizons*, July–August 1986, pp. 22–27.

16. See Archie Carroll, *Business and Society: Ethics and Stakeholder Management* (Cincinnati: Southwestern,

1989), for a review of the evolution of social responsibility.

17. "Big Trouble at Allegheny," *Business Week*, August 11, 1986, pp. 56–61.

18. Edwin M. Epstein, "The Corporate Social Policy Process: Beyond Business Ethics, Corporate Social Responsibility, and Corporate Social Responsiveness," *California Management Review*, Spring 1987, pp. 99–114.

19. "A Mail-Order Romance: Land's End Courts Unseen Customers," *Fortune*, March 13, 1989, pp. 44–45.

20. Alan Farnham, "Holding Firm on Affirmative Action," *Fortune*, March 13, 1989, pp. 87–88.

21. "Ashland Just Can't Seem to Leave its Checkered Past Behind," *Business Week*, October 31, 1988, pp. 122–126.

22. Jeremy Main, "Here Comes the Big New Cleanup," *Fortune*, November 21, 1988, pp. 102–118.

23. "Ashland Just Can't Seem to Leave its Checkered Past Behind."

24. Nancy J. Perry, "The Education Crisis: What Business Can Do," *Fortune*, July 4, 1988, pp. 71–81.

25. Anthony H. Bloom, "Managing Against Apartheid," *Harvard Business Review*, November–December 1987, pp. 49–56.

26. For discussions of this debate, see Abby Brown, "Is Ethics Good Business?" *Personnel Administrator*, February 1987, pp. 67–74; Jean B. McGuire, Alison Sundgren, and Thomas Schneeweis, "Corporate Social Responsibility and Firm Financial Performance," *Academy of Management Journal*, December 1988, pp. 854–872; "Business Ethics for Sale," *Newsweek*, May 9, 1988, p. 56; Kenneth E. Aupperle, Archie B. Carroll, and John D. Hatfield, "An Empirical Examination of the Relationship Between Corporate Social Responsibility and Profitability," *Academy of Management Journal*, June 1985, pp. 446–463; and Margaret A. Stroup, Ralph L. Neubert, and Jerry W. Anderson, Jr., "Doing Good, Doing Better: Two Views of Social Responsibility," *Business Horizons*, March–April 1987, pp. 22–25.

27. "Doing Well by Doing Good," *Business Week*, December 5, 1988, pp. 53–57.

28. "Ashland Just Can't Seem to Leave its Checkered Past Behind."

29. "Fast-Food Chains Draw Criticism for Marketing Fare as Nutritional," *The Wall Street Journal*, April 6, 1987, p. 23.

30. "Make the Punishment Fit the Corporate Crime," *Business Week*, March 13, 1989, p. 22.

31. "Should Business Be Forced to Help Bring Up Baby?" *Business Week*, April 6, 1987, p. 39.

32. "How to Win Friends and Influence Lawmakers," *Business Week*, November 7, 1988, p. 36.

33. "How to Win Friends and Influence Lawmakers."

34. Steven L. Wartick and Philip L. Cochran, "The Evolution of the Corporate Social Performance Model," *Academy of Management Review*, October 1985, pp. 758–769; Jerry W. Anderson, Jr., "Social Responsibility," *Business Horizons*, July–August 1986, pp. 22–27; and Epstein, "The Corporate Social Policy Process: Beyond Business Ethics, Corporate Social Responsibility, and Corporate Social Responsiveness."

35. Anderson, "Social Responsibility and the Corporation."

36. "Corporate Giving Is Flat, and Future Looks Bleaker," *The Wall Street Journal*, October 17, 1988, p. B1.

37. "Unfuzzing Ethics for Managers," *Fortune*, November 23, 1987, pp. 229–234.

38. Janelle Brinker Dozier and Marcia P. Miceli, "Potential Predictors of Whistle-Blowing: A Prosocial Behavior Perspective," *Academy of Management Review*, October 1985, pp. 823–836; Janet P. Near and Marcia P. Miceli, "Retaliation Against Whistle Blowers: Predictors and Effects," *Journal of Applied Psychology*, February 1986, pp. 137–145.

Chapter 5

1. Christopher Knowlton, "Europe Cooks Up a Cereal Brawl," *Fortune*, June 3, 1991, pp. 175–179; "Winning the War of Battle Creek," *Business Week*, May 13, 1991, p. 80; "Nestle To Help General Mills Sell Cereals in Europe," *The Wall Street Journal*, December 1, 1989, p. B5.

2. Richard M. Steers and Edwin L. Miller, "Management in the 1990s: The International Challenge," *The Academy of Management Executive*, February 1988, pp. 21–22; David A. Ricks, Brian Toyne, and Zaida Mar-

tinez, "Recent Developments in International Management Research," *Journal of Management,* June 1990, pp. 219–254.

3. For a more complete discussion of forms of international business, see Arvind Phatak, *International Dimensions of Management,* 2nd ed. (Boston: Kent, 1989).

4. "Help Wanted from the Multinationals," *Business Week,* February 29, 1988, pp. 68–70.

5. "The Stateless Corporation," *Business Week,* May 14, 1990, pp. 98–104.

6. Philip M. Rosenzweig and Jitendra V. Singh, "Organizational Environments and the Multinational Enterprise," *Academy of Management Review,* April 1991, pp. 340–361.

7. John Labate, "Gearing Up For Steady Growth," *Fortune,* July 29, 1991, pp. 83–102; "The *Fortune* Global 500," *Fortune,* July 29, 1991, pp. 237–280.

8. "U.S. Corporations With the Biggest Foreign Revenues," *Forbes,* July 22, 1991, pp. 286–288.

9. John D. Daniels and Lee H. Radebaugh, *International Business,* 6th ed. (Reading, Mass.: Addison-Wesley, 1992).

10. Kenichi Ohmae, "The Global Logic of Strategic Alliances," *Harvard Business Review,* March–April 1989, pp. 143–154.

11. "The Magnet of Growth in Mexico's North," *Business Week,* June 6, 1988, pp. 48–50; "Will the New Maquiladoras Build a Better Manana?" *Business Week,* November 14, 1988, pp. 102–106.

12. Allen J. Morrison, David A. Ricks, and Kendall Roth, "Globalization Versus Regionalism: Which Way For the Multinational?" *Organizational Dynamics,* Winter 1991, pp. 17–29.

13. Ben L. Kedia and Rabi S. Bhagat, "Cultural Constraints on Transfer of Technology Across Nations: Implications for Research in International and Comparative Management," *Academy of Management Review,* October 1988, pp. 559–571; Carla Rapoport, "Japan's Growing Global Reach," *Fortune,* May 22, 1989, pp. 48–56.

14. Louis Kraar, "The Growing Power of Asia," *Fortune,* October 7, 1991, pp. 118–131.

15. "Where Killers and Kidnappers Roam," *Fortune,* September 23, 1991, p. 8.

16. Daniels and Radebaugh, *International Business.*

17. John Paul Newport, Jr., "Texas Faces Up to a Tougher Future," *Fortune,* March 13, 1989, pp. 102–112.

18. "Firms Address Worker's Cultural Variety," *The Wall Street Journal,* February 10, 1989, p. B1.

19. "You Don't Have to be a Giant to Score Big Overseas," *Business Week,* April 13, 1987, pp. 62–63.

20. "Famous Bakery Keeps Business Thriving," *Corsicana Daily Sun,* June 9, 1991, p. 1C.

Chapter 6

1. "Where Did They Go Wrong?" *Business Week* (special issue on quality), October 25, 1991, pp. 34–38; "A 1990 Reorganization at Hewlett-Packard Already Is Paying Off," *The Wall Street Journal,* July 22, 1991, pp. A1, A10; "It's Still a Difficult Environment," *The Wall Street Journal,* August 5, 1991, pp. 42–44; "Hewlett-Packard Rethinks Itself," *Business Week,* April 1, 1991, pp. 76–79.

2. This framework is inspired by numerous sources: George Steiner, *Top Management Planning* (New York: Macmillan, 1969); John E. Dittrich, *The General Manager and Strategy Formulation* (New York: Wiley, 1988); Henry Mintzberg, "Crafting Strategy," *Harvard Business Review,* July–August 1987, pp. 66—75; Michael E. Porter, *Competitive Advantage* (New York: Free Press, 1985); Charles W. L. Hill and Gareth R. Jones, *Strategic Management: An Analytical Approach,* 2nd ed. (Boston: Houghton Mifflin, 1992).

3. Max D. Richards, *Setting Strategic Goals and Objectives,* 2nd ed. (St. Paul, Minn.: West, 1986).

4. See Robert D. Pritchard, Philip L. Roth, Steven D. Jones, Patricia J. Galgay, and Margaret D. Watson, "Designing a Goal-Setting System to Enhance Performance: A Practical Guide," *Organizational Dynamics,* Summer 1988, pp. 69–78, for a discussion of how goals affect motivation.

5. Carol Davenport, "America's Most Admired Corporations," *Fortune,* January 30, 1989, pp. 68–94.

6. John A. Pearce, II, and Fred David, "Corporate Mission Statements: The Bottom Line," *The Academy of Management Executive,* May 1987, p. 109.

7. Nancy J. Perry, "Will Sony Make It In Hollywood?" *Fortune,* September 9, 1991, pp. 158–166.

8. "Nike Catches Up with the Trendy Frontrunner," *Business Week*, October 24, 1988, p. 88.

9. "Optima Moves Quickly into Ranks of Top Credit Cards," *The Wall Street Journal*, October 4, 1988, p. B1.

10. See Hill and Jones, *Strategic Management*.

11. H. Donald Hopkins, "Long-Term Acquisition Strategies in the U.S. Economy," *Journal of Management*, Vol. 13, No. 3, 1987, pp. 557–572.

12. Ronald Henkoff, "How to Plan for 1995," *Fortune*, December 31, 1990, pp. 70–79.

13. "Hamish Maxwell's Big Hunger," *Business Week*, October 31, 1988, pp. 24–26; Ronald Henkoff, "Deals of the Year," *Fortune*, January 30, 1989, pp. 162–170.

14. "Hamish Maxwell's Big Hunger."

15. Hill and Jones, *Strategic Management*.

16. Peter Lorange and Balaji S. Chakravarthy, *Strategic Planning Systems*, 2nd ed. (Englewood Cliffs, N.J.: Prentice-Hall, 1989).

17. Carla Rapoport, "The World's Most Valuable Company," *Fortune*, October 10, 1988, pp. 92–104.

18. Richard I. Kirkland, Jr., "Outsider's Guide to Europe in 1992," *Fortune*, October 24, 1988, pp. 121–127.

19. Robert D. Gilbreath, "Planning for the Unexpected," *The Journal of Business Strategy*, Vol. 8, 1987, pp. 44–49.

20. Gilbreath, "Planning for the Unexpected." See also Donald C. Hambrick and David Lei, "Toward an Empirical Prioritization of Contingency Variables for Business Strategy," *Academy of Management Journal*, December 1985, pp. 763–788.

21. James Brian Quinn, Henry Mintzberg, and Robert M. James, *The Strategy Process* (Englewood Cliffs, N.J.: Prentice-Hall, 1988).

22. Vasudevan Ramanujam and N. Venkatraman, "Planning System Characteristics and Planning Effectiveness," *Strategic Management Journal*, Vol. 8, 1987, pp. 453–468.

23. Gary Hector, "Yes, You *Can* Manage Long Term," *Fortune*, November 21, 1988, pp. 64–76; "Coca-Cola Starts Drive to Pull Diet Coke Ahead of Pepsi," *The Wall Street Journal*, January 24, 1989, p. B1.

24. Henry Mintzberg, "Crafting Strategy," *Harvard Business Review*, July–August 1987, pp. 66–75.

25. Bill Saporito, "Ganging Up on Black & Decker," *Fortune*, December 23, 1985, pp. 63–72; John Huey, "The New Power in Black & Decker," *Fortune*, January 2, 1989, pp. 89–94.

26. Thomas L. Wheelon and J. David Hunger, *Strategic Management and Business Policy*, 4th ed. (Reading, Mass.: Addison-Wesley, 1992).

27. Jaclyn Fierman, "How Gallo Crushes the Competition," *Fortune*, September 1, 1986, pp. 23–31.

28. John J. Curran, "Companies That Rob the Future," *Fortune*, July 4, 1988, pp. 84–89.

29. Curran, "Companies That Rob the Future."

30. Curran, "Companies That Rob the Future."

31. Hector, "Yes, You *Can* Manage Long Term."

32. Stephen J. Carroll and Henry L. Tosi, *Management by Objectives* (New York: Macmillan, 1973); A. P. Raia, *Managing by Objectives* (Glenview, Ill.: Scott, Foresman, 1974).

33. See Jack N. Kondrasuk, "Studies in MBO Effectiveness," *Academy of Management Review*, July 1981, pp. 419–430, for a review of the strengths and weaknesses of MBO.

Chapter 7

1. "Heinz's O'Reilly Drives Hard for Growth," *The Wall Street Journal*, February 7, 1991, p. A4; Gary Hoover, Alta Campbell, and Patrick J. Spain (eds.), *Hoover's Handbook—Profiles of Over 500 Major Corporations* (Austin, Tex.: The Reference Press, 1990), p. 283; "Heinz Ain't Broke, But It's Doing a Lot of Fixing," *Business Week*, December 11, 1989, pp. 84–88; "Tony O'Reilly: Turning Ketchup into Big Dough," *Business Week*, March 30, 1992, p. 58.

2. For a recent summary of the theory and practice of strategic management, see Cynthia A. Montgomery and Michael E. Porter (eds.), *Strategy* (Boston: Harvard Business School Press, 1991). For other discussions see Kenneth R. Andrews, *The Concept of Corporate Strategy*, rev. ed. (Homewood, Ill., 1980); H. Igor Ansoff, "The Emerging Paradign of Strategic Behavior," *Strategic Management Journal*, Vol. 8, 1987, pp. 501–515; James Brian Quinn, Henry Mintzberg, and Robert M. James, *The Strategy Process* (Englewood

Cliffs, N.J.: Prentice-Hall, 1988); and Henry Mintzberg, "Crafting Strategy," *Harvard Business Review,* July–August 1987, pp. 66–75.

3. Andrews, *The Concept of Corporate Strategy.*

4. Jeremy Main, "The Winning Organization," *Fortune,* September 26, 1988, pp. 50–60.

5. "Do You Believe in Magic?" *Time,* April 25, 1988, pp. 66–73.

6. Bill Saporito, "Uncovering Mars' Unknown Empire," *Fortune,* September 26, 1988, pp. 98–104.

7. See Andrews, *The Concept of Corporate Strategy.* See also Charles W. Hofer and Dan Schendel, *Strategy Formulation: Analytical Concepts* (St. Paul, Minn.: West, 1978); Gregory G. Dess, "Environment, Structure, and Consensus in Strategy Formulation: A Conceptual Integration," *Academy of Management Review,* April 1987, pp. 313–330; Gregory G. Dess, "Consensus on Strategy Formulation and Organizational Performance: Competitors in a Fragmented Industry," *Strategic Management Journal,* Vol. 8, 1987, pp. 259–277; and William D. Guth and Ian C. MacMillan, "Strategy Implementation Versus Middle Management Self-Interest," *Strategic Management Journal,* Vol. 7, 1986, pp. 313–327.

8. Warren Boeker, "Organizational Strategy: An Ecological Perspective," *Academy of Management Journal,* September 1991, pp. 613–635.

9. Brian Dumaine, "Corporate Spies Snoop to Conquer," *Fortune,* November 7, 1988, pp. 68–76.

10. Heinz Weihrich, "Europe 1992 and a Unified Germany: Opportunities and Threats for United States Firms," *The Academy of Management Executive,* February 1991, pp. 93–98.

11. R. T. Lenz, "Managing the Evolution of the Strategic Planning Process," *Business Horizons,* January–February 1987, pp. 34–39; R. Duane Ireland, Michael A. Hitt, Richard A. Bettis, and Deborah Auld De Porras, "Strategy Formulation Processes: Differences in Perceptions of Strength and Weaknesses Indicators and Environmental Uncertainty by Managerial Level," *Strategic Management Journal,* Vol. 8, 1987, pp. 469–485; Rohit Deshpande and A. Parasuraman, "Linking Corporate Culture to Strategic Planning," *Business Horizons,* May–June 1986, pp. 28–37.

12. Balaji S. Chakravarthy, "On Tailoring a Strategic Planning System to Its Context: Some Empirical Evidence," *Strategic Management Journal,* Vol. 8, 1987, pp. 517–534.

13. Walter Kiechel, III, "Corporate Strategy for the 1990s," *Fortune,* February 29, 1988, pp. 34–42.

14. See John A. Pearce, III, D. Keith Robbins, and Richard B. Robinson, Jr., "The Impact of Grand Strategy and Planning Formality on Financial Performance," *Strategic Management Journal,* Vol. 8, 1987, pp. 125–134.

15. For example, see Eugene T. Yon, "Corporate Strategy and the New Europe," *The Academy of Management Executive,* August 1990, pp. 61–66.

16. Anthony Di Primio, "When Turnaround Management Works," *The Journal of Business Strategy,* January–February 1988, pp. 61–64.

17. "Despite the Face-Lift, Avon is Sagging," *Business Week,* December 2, 1991, pp. 101–102.

18. "Mattel Again Is Heading the Toys Parade," *The Wall Street Journal,* June 5, 1990, p. A6.

19. For recent discussions of this approach, see Charles W. L. Hill and Gareth R. Jones, *Strategic Management: An Analytical Approach,* 2nd ed. (Boston: Houghton Mifflin, 1992); and Robert E. Hoskisson, "Multidivisional Structure and Performance: The Contingency of Diversification Strategy," *Academy of Management Journal,* December 1987, pp. 625–644.

20. Anil K. Gupta, "SBU Strategies, Corporate-SBU Relations, and SBU Effectiveness in Strategy Implementation," *Academy of Management Journal,* September 1987, pp. 477–500; Richard B. Robinson, Jr., and John A. Pearce II, "Planned Patterns of Strategic Behavior and Their Relationship to Business-Unit Performance," *Strategic Management Journal,* Vol. 9, 1988, pp. 43–60; Mark Kroll and Stephen Caples, "Managing Acquisitions of Strategic Business Units with the Aid of the Arbitrage Pricing Model," *Academy of Management Review,* October 1987, pp. 676–685.

21. See Hill and Jones, *Strategic Management,* 2nd ed., for a complete review.

22. Irene M. Duhaime and Inga S. Baird, "Divestment Decision-Making: The Role of Business Unit Size," *Journal of Management,* Vol. 13, 1987, pp. 483–498.

23. James H. Higgins and Julian W. Vincze, *Strategic Management and Organizational Policy,* 3rd ed. (Hinsdale, Ill.: Dryden Press, 1986).

24. Danny Miller, "The Structural and Environmental Correlates of Business Strategy," *Strategic Management Journal*, Vol. 8, 1987, pp. 55–76; James J. Chrisman, Charles W. Hofer, and William R. Boulton, "Toward a System for Classifying Business Strategies," *Academy of Management Review*, July 1988, pp. 413–428.

25. Raymond E. Miles and Charles C. Snow, *Organizational Strategy, Structure, and Process* (New York: McGraw-Hill, 1978).

26. John Clark, *Business Today: Success and Failures* (New York: Random House, 1979).

27. Michael Porter, *Competitive Strategy* (New York: Free Press, 1980). See also Vance H. Fried and Benjamin M. Oviatt, "Michael Porter's Missing Chapter: The Rise of Antitrust Violations," *The Academy of Management Executive*, February 1989, pp. 49–56.

28. For recent discussions of this approach, see Gareth R. Jones and John E. Butler, "Costs, Revenue, and Business-Level Strategy," *Academy of Management Review*, April 1988, pp. 202–213; Charles W. L. Hill, "Differentiation Versus Low Cost or Differentiation and Low Cost: A Contingency Framework," *Academy of Management Review*, July 1988, pp. 401–412; Alan I. Murray, "A Contingency View of Porter's 'Generic Strategies,'" *Academy of Management Review*, July 1988, pp. 390–400; and Theodore T. Herbert and Helen Deresky, "Generic Strategies: An Empirical Investigation of Typology Validity and Strategic Content," *Strategic Management Journal*, Vol. 8, 1987, pp. 135–147.

29. "Hispanic Supermarkets are Blossoming," *The Wall Street Journal*, January 23, 1989, p. B1.

30. Dave Ulrich and Dale Lake, "Organizational Capability: Creating Competitive Advantage," *The Academy of Management Executive*, February 1991, pp. 77–82.

31. Regis McKenna, "Marketing Is Everything," *Harvard Business Review*, January–February 1991, pp. 65–75.

32. Stuart Gannes, "America's Fastest-Growing Companies," *Fortune*, May 23, 1988, pp. 28–40; "The Health Craze Has Kellogg Feeling G-R-R-Reat," *Business Week*, March 30, 1987, pp. 52–53; "New Guard Brews Beer's New Image," *USA Today*, August 21, 1987, pp. B1, B2.

33. Douglas E. Castle, "Financing Options for the Corporate Strategist," *The Journal of Business Strategy*, January–February 1988, pp. 12–16.

34. Patricia L. Nemetz and Louis W. Fry, "Flexible Manufacturing Organizations: Implications for Strategy Formulation and Organization Design," *Academy of Management Review*, October 1988, pp. 627–638; Robert J. Mayer, "Winning Strategies for Manufacturers in Mature Industries," *The Journal of Business Strategy*, March–April 1987, pp. 23–30; Jack Meredith, "The Strategic Advantages of New Manufacturing Technologies for Small Firms," *Strategic Management Journal*, Vol. 8, 1987, pp. 249–258.

35. Jeffrey A. Sonnenfeld and Maury A. Peiperl, "Staffing Policy as a Strategic Response: A Typology of Career Systems," *Academy of Management Review*, October 1988, pp. 588–600; Cynthia A. Lengnick-Hall and Mark L. Lengnick-Hall, "Strategic Human Resources Management: A Review of the Literature and a Proposed Typology," *Academy of Management Review*, October 1988, pp. 454–470; Randall S. Schuler and Susan E. Jackson, "Linking Competitive Strategies with Human Resource Management Practices," *The Academy of Management Executive*, August 1987, pp. 207–219; Lloyd Baird and Ilan Meshoulam, "Managing Two Fits of Strategic Human Resource Management," *Academy of Management Review*, January 1988, pp. 116–128.

36. Jack R. Meredith, "Strategic Control of Factory Automation," *Long-Range Planning*, Vol. 20, 1987, pp. 106–112; Lex A. van Gunsteren, "Planning for Technology as a Corporate Resource: A Strategic Classification," *Long-Range Planning*, Vol. 20, 1987, pp. 51–60; Judith B. Kramm, "The Portfolio Approach to Divisional Innovation Strategy," *The Journal of Business Strategy*, January–February 1987, pp. 25–36; William K. Foster and Austin K. Pryor, "The Strategic Management of Innovation," *The Journal of Business Strategy*, January–February 1986, pp. 38–42.

37. Carol Davenport, "America's Most Admired Corporations," *Fortune*, January 30, 1989, pp. 68–94.

38. Hofer and Schendel, *Strategy Formulation*; Ari Ginsberg, "Operationalizing Organizational Strategy: Toward an Integrative Framework," *Academy of Management Review*, July 1984, pp. 548–557. See also Jay R. Galbraith and Robert K. Kazanjian, *Strategy Implementation: Structure, Systems and Process*, 2nd ed. (St. Paul, Minn.: West, 1986).

39. Danny Miller, "Strategy Making and Structure: Analysis and Implications for Performance," *Academy of Management Journal*, March 1987, pp. 7–32; Danny Miller, "Configurations of Strategy and Structure: Towards a Synthesis," *Strategic Management Journal*, Vol. 7, 1986, pp. 233–249; William G. Egelhoff, "Strategy and Structure in Multinational Corporations: A Revision of the Stopford and Wells Model," *Strategic Management Journal*, Vol. 9, 1988, pp. 1–14.

40. Jeremy Main, "The Winning Organization," *Fortune*, September 26, 1988, pp. 50–60.

41. Kenneth Labich, "The Seven Keys to Business Leadership," *Fortune*, October 24, 1988, pp. 58–66.

42. Peter Lorange, Michael F. Scott Morton, and Sumantra Ghoshal, *Strategic Control* (St. Paul, Minn.: West, 1986).

43. Labich, "The Seven Keys to Business Leadership," p. 59.

Chapter 8

1. Gary Hoover, Alta Campbell, and Patrick J. Spain (eds.), *Hoover's Handbook—Profiles of Over 500 Major Corporations* (Austin, Tex.: The Reference Press, 1990), p. 514; "Sun Microsystems Turns on the Afterburners," *Business Week*, July 18, 1988, pp. 114–118; Brian Dumaine, "The Bureaucracy Busters," *Fortune*, June 17, 1991, pp. 36–50.

2. For recent reviews of decision making, see E. Frank Harrison, *The Managerial Decision Making Process*, 3rd ed. (Boston: Houghton Mifflin, 1987); and David J. Hickson, Richard J. Butler, David Cray, Geoffrey R. Mallory, and David C. Wilson, *Top Decisions* (San Francisco: Jossey-Bass, 1986).

3. Charles R. Day, Jr., "Industry's Gutsiest Decisions of 1987," *Industry Week*, February 15, 1988, pp. 33–39; Stratford P. Sherman, "Inside the Mind of Jack Welch," *Fortune*, March 27, 1989, pp. 38–50.

4. George P. Huber, *Managerial Decision Making* (Glenview, Ill.: Scott, Foresman, 1980).

5. Huber, *Managerial Decision Making*. See also David W. Miller and Martin K. Starr, *The Structure of Human Decisions* (Englewood Cliffs, N.J.: Prentice-Hall, 1976); and Alvar Elbing, *Behavioral Decisions in Organizations*, 2nd ed. (Glenview, Ill: Scott, Foresman, 1978).

6. Huber, *Managerial Decision Making*.

7. See Avi Fiegenbaum and Howard Thomas, "Attitudes Toward Risk and the Risk-Return Paradox: Prospect Theory Explanations," *Academy of Management Journal*, March 1988, pp. 85–106; Jitendra V. Singh, "Performance, Slack, and Risk Taking in Organizational Decision Making," *Academy of Management Journal*, September 1986, pp. 562–585; and James G. March and Zur Shapira, "Managerial Perspectives on Risk and Risk Taking," *Management Science*, November 1987, pp. 1404–1418.

8. See Richard M. Cyert and Morris H. DeGroot, "The Maximization Process Under Uncertainty," in Patrick D. Larkey and Lee S. Sproull (eds.), *Information Processing in Organizations* (Greenwich, Conn.: JAI Press, 1984), pp. 47–61.

9. Glen Whyte, "Decision Failures: Why They Occur and How to Prevent Them," *The Academy of Management Executive*, August 1991, pp. 23–31.

10. See R. T. Lenz and Jack L. Engledow, "Environmental Analysis Units and Strategic Decision-Making: A Field Study of Selected 'Leading-Edge' Corporations," *Strategic Management Journal*, Vol. 7, 1986, pp. 69–89, for a recent analysis of how decision situations are recognized.

11. William Q. Judge and Alex Miller, "Antecedents and Outcomes of Decision Speed in Different Environmental Contexts," *Academy of Management Journal*, June 1991, pp. 449–463.

12. Day, "Industry's Gutsiest Decisions of 1987."

13. See Charles A. O'Reilly, III, "The Use of Information in Organizational Decision Making: A Model and Some Propositions," in Larry L. Cummings and Barry M. Staw (eds.), *Research in Organizational Behavior*, Vol. 5 (Greenwich, Conn.: JAI Press, 1983), pp. 103–139.

14. Carol Saunders and Jack William Jones, "Temporal Sequences in Information Acquisition for Decision Making: A Focus on Source and Medium," *Academy of Management Review*, January 1990, pp. 29–46.

15. Kenneth Labich, "Coups and Catastrophes," *Fortune*, December 23, 1985, p. 125.

16. "The Wisdom of Solomon," *Newsweek*, August 17, 1987, pp. 62–63.

17. Elbing, *Behavioral Decisions in Organizations*.

18. Herbert A. Simon, *Administrative Behavior* (New York: Free Press, 1945). Simon's ideas have been recently refined and updated in Herbert A. Simon, *Administrative Behavior*, 3rd ed. (New York: Free press, 1976), and Herbert A. Simon, "Making Management Decisions: The Role of Intuition and Emotion," *The Academy of Management Executive*, February 1987, pp. 57–63.

19. "Unisys: So Far, So Good—But the Real Test Is Yet to Come," *Business Week*, March 2, 1987, pp. 84–86; "So Far, Married Life Seems to Agree With Unisys," *Business Week*, October 3, 1988, pp. 122–126.

20. Stuart Gannes, "America's Fastest-Growing Companies," *Fortune*, May 23, 1988, pp. 28–40. See also "Can Ms. Fashion Bounce Back?" *Business Week*, January 16, 1989, pp. 64–70.

21. Barry M. Staw and Jerry Ross, "Good Money After Bad," *Psychology Today*, February 1988, pp. 30–33. See also Michael G. Bowen, "The Escalation Phenomenon Reconsidered: Decision Dilemmas or Decision Errors?" *Academy of Management Review*, January 1987, pp. 52–66; and Ed Bukszar and Terry Connolly, "Hindsight Bias and Strategic Choice: Some Problems in Learning from Experience," *Academy of Management Journal*, September 1988, pp. 628–641.

22. "How Wouk Epic Became a Sure Loser," *The Wall Street Journal*, November 11, 1988, p. B1.

23. Gannes, "America's Fastest-Growing Companies."

24. Kent D. Miller and Philip Bromley, "Strategic Risk and Corporate Performance: An Analysis of Alternative Risk Measures," *Academy of Management Journal*, December 1990, pp. 756–779; Philip Bromley, "Testing a Causal Model of Corporate Risk Taking and Performance," *Academy of Management Journal*, March 1991, pp. 37–59.

25. Thomas M. Jones, "Ethical Decision Making by Individuals in Organizations: An Issue-Contingent Model," *Academy of Management Review*, April 1988, pp. 366–395.

26. Marvin E. Shaw, *Group Dynamics—The Psychology of Small Group Behavior*, 3rd ed. (New York: McGraw-Hill, 1981); Edwin A. Locke, David M. Schweiger, and Gary P. Latham, "Participation in Decision Making: When Should It Be Used?" *Organizational Dynamics*, Winter 1986, pp. 65–79; Nicholas Baloff and Elizabeth M. Doherty, "Potential Pitfalls in Employee Participation," *Organizational Dynamics*, Winter 1989, pp. 51–62.

27. Andre L. Delbecq, Andrew H. Van de Ven, and David H. Gustafson, *Group Techniques for Program Planning* (Glenview, Ill.: Scott, Foresman, 1975); Michael J. Prietula and Herbert A. Simon, "The Experts in Your Midst," *Harvard Business Review*, January–February 1989, pp. 120–124.

28. Norman P. R. Maier, "Assets and Liabilities in Group Problem Solving: The Need for an Integrative Function," in J. Richard Hackman, Edward E. Lawler III, and Lyman W. Porter (eds.), *Perspectives on Business in Organizations*, 2nd ed. (New York: McGraw-Hill, 1983), pp. 385–392.

29. James H. Davis, *Group Performance* (Reading, Mass.: Addison-Wesley, 1969).

30. Richard A. Cosier and Charles R. Schwenk, "Agreement and Thinking Alike: Ingredients for Poor Decisions," *The Academy of Management Executive*, February 1990, pp. 69–78.

31. "American Cyanamid: An Overhaul That's More like a Tune-Up," *Business Week*, February 8, 1988, pp. 70–71.

32. Irving L. Janis, *Groupthink*, 2nd ed. (Boston: Houghton Mifflin, 1982).

33. Janis, *Groupthink*.

Chapter 9

1. Gary Hoover, Alta Campbell, and Patrick J. Spain (eds.), *Hoover's Handbook—Profiles of Over 500 Major Corporations* (Austin, Tex.: The Reference Press, 1990), p. 202; Bill Saporito, "Retailing's Winners and Losers," *Fortune*, December 18, 1989, pp. 69–80.

2. See Wayne W. Daniel, *Essentials of Business Statistics*, 2nd ed. (Boston: Houghton Mifflin, 1988), for an overview of basic forecasting methods.

3. See Robert Carbone and Wilpen Gorr, "Accuracy of Judgmental Forecasting of Time Series," *Decision Sciences*, Summer 1985, pp. 237–247.

4. R. Balachandra, "Technological Forecasting: Who Does It and How Useful Is It?" *Technological Forecasting and Social Change*, January 1980, pp. 75–85.

5. "Steve Jobs Comes Back," *Newsweek*, October 24, 1988, pp. 46–51.

6. Charles Ostrom, *Time-Series Analysis: Regression Techniques* (Beverly Hills, Calif.: Sage Publications, 1980).

7. See John C. Chambers, S. K. Mullick, and D. Smith, "How to Choose the Right Forecasting Technique," *Harvard Business Review,* July–August 1971, pp. 45–74, for a classic review.

8. Fred Kerlinger and Elazar Pedhazur, *Multiple Regression in Behavioral Research* (New York: Holt, 1973).

9. Chambers, Mullick, and Smith, "How to Choose the Right Forecasting Technique"; see also J. Scott Armstrong, *Long-Range Forecasting: From Crystal Ball to Computers* (New York: Wiley, 1978).

10. Edward Markowski and Carol Markowski, "Some Difficulties and Improvements in Applying Linear Programming Formulations to the Discriminant Problem," *Decision Sciences,* Summer 1985, pp. 237–247, provides a comprehensive explanation of the technique.

11. See Nicholas A. Glaskowsky, Jr., and Donald R. Hudson, *Business Logistics,* 3rd ed. (Fort Worth, Tex.: Harcourt Brace Jovanovich, 1992).

12. Glaskowsky and Hudson, *Business Logistics.*

13. Glaskowsky and Hudson, *Business Logistics.*

14. Edward Hannan, Linda Ryan, and Richard Van Orden, "A Cost-Benefit Analysis of Prior Approvals for Medicaid Services in New York State," *Socio-Economic Planning Sciences,* Vol. 18, 1984, pp. 1–14.

15. Glaskowsky and Hudson, *Business Logistics.*

16. Glaskowsky and Hudson, *Business Logistics.*

17. Everett Adam, Jr., and Ronald J. Ebert, *Production and Operations Management,* 5th ed. (Englewood Cliffs, N.J.: Prentice-Hall, 1992).

18. See Robert E. Markland, *Topics in Management Science,* 3rd ed. (New York: Wiley, 1989).

19. Markland, *Topics in Management Science.*

20. Adam and Ebert, *Production and Operations Management.*

21. Ramon L. Alonso and Cline W. Fraser, "JIT Hits Home: A Case Study in Reducing Management Delays," *Sloan Management Review,* Summer 1991, pp. 59–68.

22. Beau Sheil, "Thinking About Artificial Intelligence," *Harvard Business Review,* July–August 1987, pp. 91–97; Dorothy Leonard-Barton and John J. Sviokla, "Putting Expert Systems to Work," *Harvard Business Review,* March–April 1988, pp. 91–98.

Chapter 10

1. "Now in Hands of Delegator, Firm Hits Stride," *USA Today,* September 24, 1991, pp. B1, B2; Gary Hoover, Alta Campbell, and Patrick J. Spain (eds.), *Hoover's Handbook—Profiles of Over 500 Major Corporations* (Austin, Tex.: The Reference Press, 1990), p. 255.

2. Ricky W. Griffin, *Task Design—An Integrative Approach* (Glenview, Ill.: Scott, Foresman, 1982).

3. Adam Smith, *Wealth of Nations* (New York: Modern Library, 1937; originally published in 1776).

4. Griffin, *Task Design.*

5. Anne S. Miner, "Idiosyncratic Jobs in Formal Organizations," *Administrative Science Quarterly,* September 1987, pp. 327–351.

6. M. D. Kilbridge, "Reduced Costs Through Job Enlargement: A Case," *Journal of Business,* Vol. 33, 1960, pp. 357–362.

7. Griffin, *Task Design.*

8. Kilbridge, "Reduced Costs Through Job Enrichment: A Case."

9. Frederick Herzberg, *Work and the Nature of Man* (Cleveland: World Press, 1966).

10. Robert Ford, "Job Enrichment Lessons from AT&T," *Harvard Business Review,* January–February 1973, pp. 96–106.

11. J. Richard Hackman and Greg R. Oldham, *Work Redesign* (Reading, Mass.: Addison-Wesley, 1980).

12. For recent analyses of job design issues, see Ricky W. Griffin, "A Long-Term Investigation of the Effects of Work Redesign on Employee Perceptions, Attitudes, and Behaviors," *Academy of Management Journal,* June 1991, pp. 425–435; Michael A. Campion, "Interdisciplinary Approaches to Job Design: A Constructive Replication with Extensions," *Journal of Applied Psychology,* August 1988, pp. 467–481.

13. Richard L. Daft, *Organization Theory and Design,* 4th ed. (St. Paul, Minn.: West, 1992).

14. Daniel Twomey, Frederick C. Stherr, and Walter S. Hunt, "Configuration of a Functional Department: A Study of Contextual and Structural Variables," *Journal of Organizational Behavior,* Vol. 9, 1988, pp. 61–75.

15. A. V. Graicunas, "Relationships in Organizations," *Bulletin of the International Management Institute,* March 7, 1933, pp. 39–42.

16. Ralph C. Davis, *Fundamentals of Top Management* (New York: Harper & Row, 1951); Lyndall F. Urwick, *Scientific Principles and Organization* (New York: American Management Association, 1938), p. 8; Ian Hamilton, *The Soul and Body of an Army* (London: Edward Arnold, 1921), pp. 229–230.

17. David D. Van Fleet and Arthur G. Bedeian, "A History of the Span of Management," *Academy of Management Review,* 1977, pp. 356–372.

18. James C. Worthy, "Factors Influencing Employee Morale," *Harvard Business Review,* January 1950, pp. 61–73.

19. Dan R. Dalton, William D. Todor, Michael J. Spendolini, Gordon J. Fielding, and Lyman W. Porter, "Organization Structure and Performance: A Critical Review," *Academy of Management Review,* January 1980, pp. 49–64.

20. Brian Dumaine, "The Bureaucracy Busters," *Fortune,* June 17, 1991, pp. 36–50.

21. David Van Fleet, "Span of Management Research and Issues," *Academy of Management Journal,* September 1983, pp. 546–552.

22. See Edward E. Lawler, III, "Substitutes for Hierarchy," *Organizational Dynamics,* Summer 1988, pp. 4–15, for a recent analysis of these and other factors that can influence the appropriate span of management.

23. See Daft, *Organization Theory and Design.*

24. Carrie R. Leana, "Predictors and Consequences of Delegation," *Academy of Management Journal,* December 1986, pp. 754–774.

25. Daft, *Organization Theory and Design.* See also John Meyer, W. Richard Scott, and David Strang, "Centralization, Fragmentation, and School District Complexity," *Administrative Science Quarterly,* June 1987, pp. 186–201.

26. "IBM Unveils a Sweeping Restructuring in Bid to Decentralize Decision-Making," *The Wall Street Journal,* January 29, 1988, p. 3.

27. "Maverick Managers," *The Wall Street Journal,* November 14, 1988, p. R14.

28. James Thompson, *Organizations in Action* (New York: McGraw-Hill, 1967). For a recent discussion, see Bart Victor and Richard S. Blackburn, "Interdependence: An Alternative Conceptualization," *Academy of Management Review,* July 1987, pp. 486–498.

29. Jay R. Galbraith, *Designing Complex Organizations* (Reading, Mass.: Addison-Wesley, 1973); Jay R. Galbraith, *Organizational Design* (Reading, Mass.: Addison-Wesley, 1977).

30. Paul R. Lawrence and Jay W. Lorsch, "Differentiation and Integration in Complex Organizations," *Administrative Science Quarterly,* March 1967, pp. 1–47.

31. "Vaunted IBM Culture Yields to New Values: Openness, Efficiency," *The Wall Street Journal,* November 11, 1988, pp. A1, A4; Thomas Moore, "Goodbye, Corporate Staff," *Fortune,* December 21, 1987, pp. 65–76; and "CBS Frantically Woos Hollywood to Help It Win Back Viewers," *The Wall Street Journal,* February 9, 1989, pp. A1, A12.

Chapter 11

1. "Maybe the Limited Has Limits After All," *Business Week,* March 18, 1991, pp. 128–129; "Changing Clothing Limits Limited," *USA Today,* October 10, 1990, p. 3B; "Retailers Face Wild Ride to Recovery," *The Wall Street Journal,* April 9, 1991, pp. B1, B6.

2. See Richard L. Daft, *Organization Theory and Design,* 4th ed. (St. Paul, Minn.: West, 1992).

3. Fremont E. Kast and James E. Rosenzweig, *Contingency Views of Organization and Management* (Chicago: Science Research Associates, 1973).

4. Max Weber, *Theory of Social and Economic Organizations,* translated by T. Parsons (New York: Free Press, 1947).

5. "Postal Service Moves to Dispel Its Bureaucratic Image," *The Wall Street Journal,* May 27, 1988, p. 6.

6. For recent discussions of the strengths and weaknesses of the bureaucratic model, see James L. Perry and Hal G. Rainey, "The Public-Private Distinction in Organization Theory: A Critique and Research

Strategy," *Academy of Management Review,* April 1988, pp. 182–201; and Thomas A. Leitko and David Szczerbacki, "Why Traditional OD Strategies Fail in Professional Bureaucracies," *Organizational Dynamics,* Winter 1987, pp. 52–65.

7. Rensis Likert, *New Patterns in Management* (New York: McGraw-Hill, 1961); Rensis Likert, *The Human Organization* (New York: McGraw-Hill, 1967).

8. William F. Dowling, "At General Motors: System 4 Builds Performance and Profits," *Organizational Dynamics,* Winter 1975, pp. 23–28.

9. Daft, *Organization Theory and Design.*

10. For descriptions of situational factors, see Robert K. Kazanjian and Robert Drazin, "Implementing Internal Diversification: Contingency Factors for Organization Design Choices," *Academy of Management Review,* April 1987, pp. 342–354.

11. Joan Woodward, *Industrial Organization: Theory and Practice* (London: Oxford University Press, 1965).

12. Joan Woodward, *Management and Technology, Problems of Progress Industry,* No. 3 (London: Her Majesty's Stationery Office, 1958).

13. For recent discussions of the impact of technology on organization design, see Judith W. Alexander and W. Alan Randolph, "The Fit Between Technology and Structure as a Predictor of Performance in Nursing Sub-Units," *Academy of Management Journal,* December 1985, pp. 844–859; and Frank M. Hull and Paul D. Collins, "High-Technology Batch Production Systems: Woodward's Missing Type," *Academy of Management Journal,* December 1987, pp. 786–797.

14. Tom Burns and G. M. Stalker, *The Management of Innovation* (London: Tavistock, 1961).

15. Paul R. Lawrence and Jay W. Lorsch, *Organization and Environment* (Homewood, Ill.: Irwin, 1967).

16. For recent discussions of the environment-organization design relationship, see Masoud Yasai-Ardekani, "Structural Adaptations to Environments," *Academy of Management Review,* January 1986, pp. 9–21; Christine S. Koberg and Geraldo R. Ungson, "The Effects of Environmental Uncertainty and Dependence on Organizational Performance: A Comparative Study," *Journal of Management,* Winter 1987, pp. 725–737; and Barbara W. Keats and Michael A. Hitt, "A Causal Model of Linkages Among Environmental Dimensions, Macro Organizational Characteristics, and Performance," *Academy of Management Journal,* September 1988, pp. 570–598.

17. Derek S. Pugh and David J. Hickson, *Organization Structure in Its Context: The Aston Program I* (Lexington, Mass.: D. C. Heath, 1976).

18. Robert H. Miles and Associates, *The Organizational Life Cycle* (San Francisco: Jossey-Bass, 1980). See also "Is Your Company Too Big?" *Business Week,* March 27, 1989, pp. 84–94.

19. Alan Deutschman, "America's Fastest Risers," *Fortune,* October 7, 1991, pp. 46–68.

20. See Charles W. L. Hill and Gareth Jones, *Strategic Management: An Analytic Approach,* 2nd ed. (Boston: Houghton Mifflin, 1992).

21. Oliver E. Williamson, *Markets and Hierarchies* (New York: Free Press, 1975).

22. Williamson, *Markets and Hierarchies.*

23. Michael E. Porter, "From Competitive Advantage to Corporate Strategy," *Harvard Business Review,* May–June 1987, pp. 43–59.

24. Williamson, *Markets and Hierarchies.*

25. Jay B. Barney and William G. Ouchi, eds., *Organizational Economics* (San Francisco: Jossey-Bass, 1986); Robert E. Hoskisson, "Multidivisional Structure and Performance: The Contingency of Diversification Strategy," *Academy of Management Journal,* December 1987, pp. 625–644. See also Michael V. Russo, "The Multidivisional Structure as an Enabling Device: A Longitudinal Study of Discretionary Cash as a Strategic Resource," *Academy of Management Journal,* September 1991, pp. 718–733.

26. Stanley M. Davis and Paul R. Lawrence, *Matrix* (Reading, Mass.: Addison-Wesley, 1977).

27. Alex Taylor, III, "Why Fords Sell Like Big Macs," *Fortune,* November 21, 1988, pp. 122–125.

28. Davis and Lawrence, *Matrix.*

29. Harvey F. Koloday, "Managing in a Matrix," *Business Horizons,* March–April 1981, pp. 17–24.

30. Jeremy Main, "The Winning Organization," *Fortune,* September 26, 1988, pp. 50–60.

31. Jay Galbraith, *Designing Complex Organizations* (Reading, Mass.: Addison-Wesley, 1973); Jay Galbraith, *Organization Design* (Reading, Mass.: Addison-Wesley, 1977).

32. See William G. Egelhoff, "Strategy and Structure in Multinational Corporations: A Revision of the Stopford and Wells Model," *Strategic Management Journal,* Vol. 9, 1988, pp. 1–14, for a recent discussion of these issues.

33. Brian Dumaine, "The Bureaucracy Busters," *Fortune,* June 17, 1991, pp. 36–50.

Chapter 12

1. "The New IBM," *Business Week,* December 16, 1991, pp. 112–118; Carol J. Loomis, "Can John Akers Save IBM?" *Fortune,* July 15, 1991, pp. 40–56; Norm Alster, "IBM as Holding Company," *Forbes,* December 23, 1991, pp. 117–120.

2. For recent reviews of this area, see Richard W. Woodman, "Organization Change and Development: New Arenas for Inquiry and Action," *Journal of Management,* June 1989, pp. 205–228; and William Pasemore, "Organization Change and Development," *Journal of Management,* June 1992.

3. For additional insights into how technological change affects other parts of the organization, see Robert H. Hayes and Ramchandran Jaikumar, "Manufacturing's Crisis: New Technologies, Obsolete Organizations," *Harvard Business Review,* September–October 1988, pp. 77–85.

4. Allan D. Gilmour, "Changing Times in the Automotive Industry," *The Academy of Management Executive,* February 1988, pp. 23–28.

5. Kenneth Labich, "Was Breaking Up AT&T a Good Idea?" *Fortune,* January 2, 1989, pp. 82–87; and Zane E. Barnes, "Change in the Bell System," *The Academy of Management Executive,* February 1987, pp. 43–46.

6. John P. Kotter and Leonard A. Schlesinger, "Choosing Strategies for Change," *Harvard Business Review,* March–April 1979, p. 106.

7. See Gloria Barczak, Charles Smith, and David Wilemon, "Managing Large-Scale Organizational Change," *Organizational Dynamics,* Autumn 1987, pp. 22–35; Thomas H. Fitzgerald, "Can Change in Organizational Culture Really Be Managed?" *Organizational Dynamics,* Autumn 1988, pp. 4–15.

8. Kurt Lewin, "Frontiers in Group Dynamics: Concept, Method, and Reality in Social Science," *Human Relations,* June 1947, pp. 5–41.

9. See Connie J. G. Gersick, "Revolutionary Change Theories: A Multilevel Exploration of the Punctuated Equilibrium Paradigm," *Academy of Management Review,* January 1991, pp. 10–36.

10. "RJR Employees Fight Distraction Amid Buyout Talks," *The Wall Street Journal,* November 1, 1988, p. A8.

11. Patricia Sellers, "Why Bigger Is Badder at Sears," *Fortune,* December 5, 1988, pp. 79–84. See also "Sears Will Reorganize Its Bureaucracy as Part of Drive to Be More Competitive," *The Wall Street Journal,* March 30, 1989, p. B7.

12. "Is Eastern Frank Lorenzo's Vietnam?" *Business Week,* December 26, 1988, pp. 62–63.

13. "Steve Jobs Comes Back," *Newsweek,* October 24, 1988, pp. 46–51.

14. See Paul R. Lawrence, "How to Deal with Resistance to Change," *Harvard Business Review,* January–February 1969, pp. 4–12, 166–176, for a classic discussion.

15. Lester Coch and John R. P. French, Jr., "Overcoming Resistance to Change," *Human Relations,* August 1948, pp. 512–532.

16. Charles K. Day, Jr., "Management's Mindless Mistakes," *Industry Week,* May 29, 1987, p. 42. See also "Inspection from the Plant Floor," *Business Week,* April 10, 1989, pp. 60–61.

17. Harold J. Leavitt, "Applied Organization Change in Industry: Structural, Technical, and Human Approaches," in W. W. Cooper, H. J. Leavitt, and M. W. Shelly, II, eds., *New Perspectives in Organization Research* (New York: Wiley, 1964), pp. 55–71.

18. See Dawn Kelly and Terry L. Amburgey, "Organizational Inertia and Momentum: A Dynamic Model of Strategic Change," *Academy of Management Journal,* September 1991, pp. 591–612; Jerry Goodstein and Warren Boeker, "Turbulence at the Top: A New Perspective on Governance Structure Changes and Strategic Change," *Academy of Management Journal,* June 1991, pp. 306–330.

19. Brian Dumaine, "The Bureaucracy Busters," *Fortune,* June 17, 1991, pp. 36–50.

20. David A. Nadler, "The Effective Management of Organizational Change," in Jay W. Lorsch, ed., *Handbook of Organizational Behavior* (Englewood Cliffs, N.J.: Prentice-Hall, 1987), pp. 358–369.

21. Paul D. Collins, Jerald Hage, and Frank M. Hull, "Organizational and Technological Predictors of Change in Automaticity," *Academy of Management Journal,* September 1988, pp. 512–543.

22. Jeffrey A. Alexander, "Adaptive Change in Corporate Control Practices," *Academy of Management Journal,* March 1991, pp. 162–193.

23. For recent reviews, see Woodman, "Organization Change and Development: New Arenas for Inquiry and Action," and Pasemore, "Organization Change and Development."

24. Richard Beckhard, *Organization Development: Strategies and Models* (Reading, Mass.: Addison-Wesley, 1969), p. 9.

25. Wendell L. French and Cecil H. Bell, Jr., *Organization Development: Behavioral Science Interventions for Organization Improvement,* 2nd ed. (Englewood Cliffs, N.J.: Prentice-Hall, 1978). See also McLennan, *Managing Organizational Change* (Englewood Cliffs, N.J.: Prentice-Hall, 1989).

26. William G. Dyer, *Team Building Issues and Alternatives* (Reading, Mass.: Addison-Wesley, 1980).

27. Robert R. Blake and Jane Srygley Mouton. *The Managerial Grid III: The Key to Leadership Excellence,* 3rd ed. (Houston: Gulf Publishing Company, 1985).

28. Robert R. Blake and Anne Adams McCanse. *Leadership Dilemmas—Grid Solutions* (Houston: Gulf Publishing Company, 1991).

29. Roger J. Hower, Mark G. Mindell, and Donna L. Simmons, "Introducing Innovation Through OD," *Management Review,* February 1978, pp. 52–56.

30. "Is Organization Development Catching On? A Personnel Symposium," *Personnel,* November–December 1977, pp. 10–22.

31. For a recent discussion on the effectiveness of various OD techniques in different organizations, see John M. Nicholas, "The Comparative Impact of Organization Development Interventions on Hard Criteria Measures," *Academy of Management Review,* October 1982, pp. 531–542.

32. Michael Beer, "Revitalizing Organizations: Change Process and Emergent Model," *The Academy of Management Executive,* February 1987, pp. 51–55; and Willem Mastenbroek, "A Dynamic Concept of Revitalization," *Organizational Dynamics,* Spring 1988, pp. 51–61.

Chapter 13

1. Gary Hoover, Alta Campbell, and Patrick J. Spain (eds.), *Hoover's Handbook of American Business 1992* (Austin, Tex.: The Reference Press, 1991), p. 260; "Much More Than a Day's Work—For Just a Day's Pay?" *Business Week,* September 23, 1991, p. 40.

2. Patrick Wright and Gary McMahan, "Strategic Human Resources Management: A Review of the Literature," *Journal of Management,* June 1992.

3. For recent reviews, see Lloyd Baird and Ilan Meshoulam, "Managing Two Fits of Strategic Human Resource Management," *Academy of Management Review,* January 1988, pp. 116–128; and Cynthia A. Lengnick-Hall and Mark L. Lengnick-Hall, "Strategic Human Resources Management: A Review of the Literature and a Proposed Typology," *Academy of Management Review,* July 1988, pp. 454–470.

4. David P. Twomey, *A Concise Guide to Employment Law* (Dallas: Southwestern Publishing, 1986).

5. Equal Employment Opportunity Commission, "Uniform Guidelines on Employee Selection Procedures," *Federal Register,* August 25, 1978, pp. 38290–38315.

6. Robert Calvert, Jr., *Affirmative Action: A Comprehensive Recruitment Manual* (Garrett Park, Md.: Garrett Park Press, 1979). For recent perspectives on Affirmative Action, see "Affirmative Action Faces Likely Setback," *The Wall Street Journal,* November 30, 1988, p. B1.

7. "OSHA Awakens from Its Six-Year Slumber," *Business Week,* August 10, 1987, p. 27; "Workplace Injuries Proliferate as Concerns Push People to Produce," *The Wall Street Journal,* June 16, 1989, pp. A1, A8.

8. David Bowen, Gerald Ledford, Jr., and Barry Nathan, "Hiring for the Organization, Not the Job," *The Academy of Management Executive,* November 1991, pp. 35–45.

9. Thomas H. Stone and Jack Fiorito, "A Perceived Uncertainty Model of Human Resource Forecasting Technique Use," *Academy of Management Review,* July 1986, pp. 635–642.

10. "Shades of Geneen at Emerson Electric," *Fortune,* May 22, 1989, p. 39.

11. Leonard Greenhalgh, Anne T. Lawrence, and Robert I. Sutton, "Determinants of Work Force Reduction

Strategies in Declining Organizations," *Academy of Management Review*, April 1988, pp. 241–254.

12. Michael R. Carrell and Frank E. Kuzmits, *Personnel: Human Resource Management*, 3rd ed. (New York: Merrill, 1989).

13. Brian Dumaine, "The New Art of Hiring Smart," *Fortune*, August 17, 1987, pp. 78–81.

14. Mary K. Suszko and James A. Breaugh, "The Effects of Realistic Job Previews on Applicant Self-Selection and Employee Turnover, Satisfaction, and Coping Ability," *Journal of Management*, Fall 1986, pp. 513–523.

15. Frank L. Schmidt and John E. Hunter, "Employment Testing: Old Theories and New Research Findings," *American Psychologist*, October 1981, pp. 1128–1137; see also "New Test Quantifies the Way We Work," *The Wall Street Journal*, February 7, 1990, p. B1.

16. John F. Binning, Mel A. Goldstein, Mario F. Garcia, and Julie H. Scattaregia, "Effects of Preinterview Impressions on Questioning Strategies in Same- and Opposite-Sex Employment Interviews," *Journal of Applied Psychology*, February 1988, pp. 30–37.

17. Neal Schmitt, "Social and Situational Determinants of Interview Decisions: Implications for the Employment Interview," *Personnel Psychology*, Spring 1976, pp. 79–102. For an opposing view, see M. Ronald Buckley and Robert W. Eder, "B. M. Springbett and the Notion of the 'Snap Decision' in the Interview," *Journal of Management*, March 1988, pp. 59–67.

18. Tom Janz, Lowell Hellervik, and David C. Gilmore, *Behavior Description Interviewing* (Boston: Allyn & Bacon, 1986).

19. Dumaine, "The New Art of Hiring Smart."

20. Paul R. Sackett, "Assessment Centers and Content Validity: Some Neglected Issues," *Personnel Psychology*, Vol. 40, 1987, pp. 13–25.

21. Abby Brown, "To Test or Not to Test," *Personnel Administrator*, March 1987, pp. 67–70.

22. See Bernard Keys and Joseph Wolfe, "Management Education and Development: Current Issues and Emerging Trends," *Journal of Management*, June 1988, pp. 205–229, for a recent review.

23. Michael Brody, "Helping Workers to Work Smarter," *Fortune*, June 8, 1987, pp. 86–88.

24. "Videos Are Starring in More and More Training Programs," *Business Week*, September 7, 1987, pp. 108–110.

25. For recent discussions of why performance appraisal is important, see Walter Kiechel, III, "How to Appraise Performance," *Fortune*, October 12, 1987, pp. 239–240; and Donald J. Campbell and Cynthia Lee, "Self-Appraisal in Performance Evaluation: Development Versus Evaluation," *Academy of Management Review*, April 1988, pp. 302–314.

26. Jerry W. Hedge and Michael J. Kavanagh, "Improving the Accuracy of Performance Evaluations: Comparison of Three Methods of Performance Appraiser Training," *Journal of Applied Psychology*, February 1988, pp. 68–73; Gregory H. Dobbins, Robert L. Cardy, and Donald M. Truxillo, "The Effects and Purpose of Appraisal and Individual Differences in Stereotypes of Women on Sex Differences in Performance Ratings: A Laboratory and Field Study," *Journal of Applied Psychology*, August 1988, pp. 551–558; Clinton O. Longnecker, Dennis A. Gioia, and Henry P. Sims, Jr., "Behind the Mask: The Politics of Employee Appraisal," *The Academy of Management Executive*, August 1987, pp. 183–194.

27. Barry R. Nathan, Allan Mohrman, and John Milliman, "Interpersonal Relations as a Context for the Effects of Appraisal Interviews on Performance and Satisfaction: A Longitudinal Study," *Academy of Management Journal*, June 1991, pp. 352–369.

28. Edward E. Lawler, III, "The Design of Effective Reward Systems," in Jay W. Lorsch, ed., *Handbook of Organizational Behavior* (Englewood Cliffs, N.J.: Prentice-Hall, 1987), pp. 255–271; Robert J. Greene, "Effective Compensation: The How and Why," *Personnel Administrator*, February 1987, pp. 112–116.

29. Caroline L. Weber and Sara L. Rynes, "Effects of Compensation Strategy on Job Pay Decisions," *Academy of Management Journal*, March 1991, pp. 86–109.

30. Peter Cappelli and Wayne F. Cascio, "Why Some Jobs Command Wage Premiums: A Test of Career Tournament and Internal Labor Market Hypotheses," *Academy of Management Journal*, December 1991, pp. 848–868.

31. "To Each According to His Needs: Flexible Benefits Plans Gain Favor," *The Wall Street Journal*, September 16, 1986, p. 29.

32. "The Future Look of Employee Benefits," *The Wall Street Journal,* September 7, 1988, p. 21.

33. "Firms Forced to Cut Back on Benefits," *USA Today,* November 29, 1988, pp. 1B, 2B.

34. John A. Fossum, "Labor Relations: Research and Practice in Transition," *Journal of Management,* Summer 1987, pp. 281–300.

35. For recent research on collective bargaining, see Wallace N. Davidson, III, Dan L. Worrell, and Sharon H. Garrison, "Effect of Strike Activity on Firm Value," *Academy of Management Journal,* June 1988, pp. 387–394; John M. Magenau, James E. Martin, and Melanie M. Peterson, "Dual and Unilateral Commitment Among Stewards and Rank-and-File Union Members," *Academy of Management Journal,* June 1988, pp. 359–376; and Brian E. Becker, "Concession Bargaining: The Meaning of Union Gains," *Academy of Management Journal,* June 1988, pp. 377–387.

Chapter 14

1. "Workers: Risks and Rewards," *Time,* April 15, 1991, pp. 42–43; Nancy J. Perry, "Here Come Richer, Riskier Pay Plans," *Fortune,* December 19, 1988, pp. 50–58; "Paying Workers to Meet Goals Spreads, But Gauging Performance Proves Tough," *The Wall Street Journal,* September 10, 1991, pp. B1, B8.

2. Richard M. Steers and Lyman W. Porter, *Motivation and Work Behavior,* 5th ed. (New York: McGraw-Hill, 1991).

3. Jeremiah J. Sullivan, "Three Roles of Language in Motivation Theory," *Academy of Management Review,* January 1988, pp. 104–115.

4. Frederick W. Taylor, *Principles of Scientific Management* (New York: Harper and Brothers, 1911).

5. Elton Mayo, *The Social Problems of an Industrial Civilization* (Boston: Harvard University Press, 1945); Fritz J. Rothlisberger and W. J. Dickson, *Management and the Worker* (Boston: Harvard University Press, 1939).

6. Abraham H. Maslow, "A Theory of Human Motivation," *Psychological Review,* Vol. 50, 1943, pp. 370–396; Abraham H. Maslow, *Motivation and Personality* (New York: Harper & Row, 1954).

7. For a review, see Craig Pinder, *Work Motivation* (Glenview, Ill.: Scott, Foresman, 1984). See also Steers and Porter, *Motivation and Work Behavior.*

8. Clayton P. Alderfer, *Existence, Relatedness, and Growth* (New York: Free Press, 1972).

9. Clayton P. Alderfer, "An Empirical Test of a New Theory of Human Needs," *Organizational Behavior and Human Performance,* April 1969, pp. 142–175. See also Pinder, *Work Motivation.*

10. Frederick Herzberg, Bernard Mausner, and Barbara Snyderman, *The Motivation to Work* (New York: Wiley, 1959); Frederick Herzberg, "One More Time: How Do You Motivate Employees?" *Harvard Business Review,* January–February 1987, pp. 109–120.

11. Robert J. House and Lawrence A. Wigdor, "Herzberg's Dual-Factor Theory of Job Satisfaction and Motivation: A Review of the Evidence and a Criticism," *Personnel Psychology,* Winter 1967, pp. 369–389; Victor H. Vroom, *Work and Motivation* (New York: Wiley, 1964). See also Pinder, *Work Motivation.*

12. David C. McClelland, *The Achieving Society* (Princeton, N.J.: Van Nostrand, 1961); David C. McClelland, *Power: The Inner Experience* (New York: Irvington, 1975).

13. E. Cornelius and F. Lane, "The Power Motive and Managerial Success in a Professionally Oriented Service Company," *Journal of Applied Psychology,* January 1984, pp. 32–40.

14. David McClelland and David H. Burnham, "Power Is the Great Motivator," *Harvard Business Review,* March–April 1976, pp. 100–110.

15. Victor H. Vroom, *Work and Motivation* (New York: Wiley, 1964).

16. David A. Nadler and Edward E. Lawler, III, "Motivation: A Diagnostic Approach," in J. Richard Hackman, Edward E. Lawler, and Lyman W. Porter, eds., *Pespectives on Behavior in Organizations,* 2nd ed. (New York: McGraw-Hill, 1983), pp. 67–78.

17. Lyman W. Porter and Edward E. Lawler, III, *Managerial Attitudes and Performance* (Homewood, Ill.: Dorsey Press, 1968).

18. Nadler and Lawler, "Motivation: A Diagnostic Approach."

19. "How A&P Fattens Profits by Sharing Them," *Business Week,* December 22, 1986, p. 44.

20. Terrence Mitchell, "Expectancy Models of Job Satisfaction, Occupation Preference, and Effort: A Theoretical, Methodological, and Empirical Appraisal,"

Psychological Bulletin, December 1974, pp. 1053–1077; John P. Wanous, Thomas L. Keon, and Jania C. Latack, "Expectancy Theory and Occupational/Organizational Choices: A Review and Test," *Organizational Behavior and Human Performance,* August 1983, pp. 66–86. For recent findings, see also Lynn E. Miller and Joseph E. Grush, "Improving Predictions in Expectancy Theory Research: Effects of Personality, Expectancies, and Norms," *Academy of Management Journal,* March 1988, pp. 107–122.

21. J. Stacy Adams, "Towards an Understanding of Inequity," *Journal of Abnormal and Social Psychology,* November 1963, pp. 422–436; Richard T. Mowday, "Equity Theory Predictions of Behavior in Organizations," in Steers and Porter, *Motivation and Work Behavior,* pp. 91–113.

22. For a review, see Paul S. Goodman and Abraham Fiedman, "An Examination of Adam's Theory of Inequity," *Administrative Science Quarterly,* September 1971, pp. 271–288.

23. "Pay Problems: How Couples React When Wives Out-Earn Husbands," *The Wall Street Journal,* June 19, 1987, p. 19.

24. Richard A. Cosier and Dan R. Dalton, "Equity Theory and Time: A Reformulation," *Academy of Management Review,* April 1983, pp. 311–319; Richard C. Huseman, John D. Hatfield, and Edward W. Miles, "A New Perspective on Equity Theory: The Equity Sensitivity Construct," *Academy of Management Review,* April 1987, pp. 222–234.

25. B. F. Skinner, *Beyond Freedom and Dignity* (New York: Knopf, 1971).

26. Fred Luthans and Robert Kreitner, *Organizational Behavior Modification and Beyond: An Operant and Social Learning Approach* (Glenview, Ill.: Scott, Foresman, 1985).

27. Patricia Sellers, "How to Handle Customers' Gripes," *Fortune,* October 24, 1988, pp. 88–100.

28. Edwin Locke, "Toward a Theory of Task Performance and Incentives," *Organizational Behavior and Human Performance,* Vol. 3, 1968, pp. 157–189.

29. For recent developments, see Mark E. Tubbs and Steven E. Ekeberg, "The Role of Intentions in Work Motivation: Implications for Goal-Setting Theory and Research," *Academy of Management Review,* January 1991, pp. 180–199.

30. "When Are Employees Not Employees? When They're Associates, Stakeholders . . . ," *The Wall Street Journal,* November 9, 1988, p. B1.

31. Luthans and Kreitner, *Organizational Behavior Modification and Beyond;* W. Clay Hamner and Ellen P. Hamner, "Behavior Modification on the Bottom Line," *Organizational Dynamics,* Spring 1976, pp. 2–21.

32. "At Emery Air Freight: Positive Reinforcement Boosts Performance," *Organizational Dynamics,* Winter 1973, pp. 41–50.

33. Allan R. Cohen and Herman Gadon, *Alternative Work Schedules: Integrating Individual and Organizational Needs* (Reading, Mass.: Addision-Wesley, 1978).

34. Earl D. Weed, "Job Environment 'Cleans Up' at Texas Instruments," in J. R. Maher, ed., *New Perspectives in Job Enrichment* (New York: Van Nostrand, 1971), pp. 55–77.

35. Edward E. Lawler, III, *Pay and Organizational Development* (Reading, Mass.: Addison-Wesley, 1981). See also Edward E. Lawler, III, *Pay and Organizational Effectiveness: A Psychological View* (New York: McGraw-Hill, 1971).

36. Lawler, *Pay and Organizational Development.*

37. "Grading 'Merit Pay,' " *Newsweek,* November 14, 1988, pp. 45–46; Frederick S. Hills, K. Dow Scott, Steven E. Markham, and Michael J. Vest, "Merit Pay: Just or Unjust Desserts?" *Personnel Administrator,* September 1987, pp. 53–59.

38. Perry, "Here Come Richer, Riskier Pay Plans," pp. 50–58.

Chapter 15

1. Brian Dumaine, "The Bureaucracy Busters," *Fortune,* June 17, 1991, pp. 36–50; "The Bad Boy of Silicon Valley," *Business Week,* December 9, 1991, pp. 64–70.

2. Arthur G. Jago, "Leadership: Perspectives in Theory and Research," *Management Science,* March 1982, pp. 315–336.

3. Gary A. Yukl, *Leadership in Organizations,* 2nd ed. (Englewood Cliffs, N.J.: Prentice-Hall, 1989), p. 5.

4. See John P. Kotter, "What Leaders Really Do," *Harvard Business Review,* May–June 1990, pp. 103–111.

5. John R. P. French and Bertram Raven, "The Bases of Social Power," in Dorwin Cartwright, ed., *Studies in Social Power* (Ann Arbor, Mich.: University of Michigan Press, 1959), pp. 150–167.

6. Hugh D. Menzies, "The Ten Toughest Bosses," *Fortune,* April 21, 1980, pp. 62–73.

7. For more information on the bases and uses of power, see Philip M. Podsakoff and Chester A. Schriesheim, "Field Studies of French and Raven's Bases of Power: Critique, Reanalysis, and Suggestions for Future Research," *Psychological Bulletin,* Vol. 97, 1985, pp. 387–411; Robert C. Benfari, Harry E. Wilkinson, and Charles D. Orth, "The Effective Use of Power," *Business Horizons,* May–June 1986, pp. 12–16; and Yukl, *Leadership in Organizations.*

8. Bernard M. Bass, *Bass and Stogdill's Handbook of Leadership,* 3rd ed. (Riverside, N.J.: Free Press, 1990).

9. Shelley A. Kirkpatrick and Edwin A. Locke, "Leadership: Do Traits Matter?" *The Academy of Management Executive,* May 1991, pp. 48–60.

10. Robert G. Lord, Christy L. De Vader, and George M. Alliger, "A Meta-Analysis of the Relation Between Personality Traits and Leadership Perceptions: An Application of Validity Generalization Procedures," *Journal of Applied Psychology,* August 1986, pp. 402–410.

11. Rensis Likert, *New Patterns of Management* (New York: McGraw-Hill, 1961); Rensis Likert, *The Human Organization* (New York: McGraw-Hill, 1967).

12. The Ohio State studies stimulated many articles, monographs, and books. A good overall reference is Ralph M. Stogdill and A. E. Coons, eds., *Leader Behavior: Its Description and Measurement* (Columbus, Ohio: Bureau of Business Research, Ohio State University, 1957).

13. Edwin A. Fleishman, E. F. Harris, and H. E. Burt, *Leadership and Supervision in Industry* (Columbus, Ohio: Bureau of Business Research, Ohio State University, 1955).

14. Robert R. Blake and Jane S. Mouton, *The Managerial Grid* (Houston: Gulf Publishing, 1964); Robert R. Blake and Jane S. Mouton, *The Versatile Manager: A Grid Profile* (Homewood, Ill.: Dow Jones-Irwin, 1981).

15. See Jan P. Muczyk and Bernard C. Reimann, "The Case for Directive Leadership," *The Academy of Management Executive,* November 1987, pp. 301–309, for a recent update.

16. Robert Tannenbaum and Warren H. Schmidt, "How to Choose a Leadership Pattern," *Harvard Business Review,* March–April 1958, pp. 95–101.

17. Fred E. Fiedler, *A Theory of Leadership Effectiveness* (New York: McGraw-Hill, 1967).

18. Recent critiques include Ramadhar Singh, "Leadership Style and Reward Allocation: Does Least Preferred Co-Worker Scale Measure Task and Relation Orientation?" *Organizational Behavior and Human Performance,* October 1983, pp. 178–197; D. Hosking, "A Critical Evaluation of Fiedler's Contingency Hypothesis," *Progress in Applied Psychology,* Vol. 1, 1981, pp. 103–154; and Chester A. Schriesheim, B. D. Bannister, and W. H. Money, "Psychometric Properties of the LPC Scale: An Extension of Rice's Review," *Academy of Management Review,* April 1979, pp. 287–294.

19. Fiedler, *A Theory of Leadership Effectiveness;* Fred E. Fiedler and M. M. Chemers, *Leadership and Effective Management* (Glenview, Ill.: Scott, Foresman, 1974).

20. For recent reviews and updates, see Lawrence H. Peters, Darrell D. Hartke, and John T. Pohlmann, "Fiedler's Contingency Theory of Leadership: An Application of the Meta-Analysis Procedures of Schmidt and Hunter," *Psychological Bulletin,* Vol. 97, pp. 274–285; and Fred E. Fiedler, "When to Lead, When to Stand Back," *Psychology Today,* September 1987, pp. 26–27.

21. Martin G. Evans, "The Effects of Supervisory Behavior on the Path-Goal Relationship," *Organizational Behavior and Human Performance,* May 1970, pp. 277–298; Robert J. House and Terence R. Mitchell, "Path-Goal Theory of Leadership," *Journal of Contemporary Business,* Autumn 1974, pp. 81–98. See also Yukl, *Leadership in Organizations.*

22. For a thorough review, see Yukl, *Leadership in Organizations.*

23. Victor H. Vroom and Philip H. Yetton, *Leadership and Decision-Making* (Pittsburgh: University of Pittsburgh Press, 1973); Victor H. Vroom and Arthur G. Jago, *The New Leadership* (Englewood Cliffs, N.J.: Prentice-Hall, 1988).

24. Yukl, *Leadership in Organizations.*

25. Vroom and Jago, *The New Leadership*

26. Fred Dansereau, George Graen, and W. J. Haga, "A Vertical-Dyad Linkage Approach to Leadership Within Formal Organizations: A Longitudinal Investigation of the Role-Making Process," *Organizational Behavior and Human Performance*, Vol. 15, 1975, pp. 46–78; Richard M. Dienesch and Robert C. Liden, "Leader-Member Exchange Model of Leadership: A Critique and Further Development," *Academy of Management Review*, July 1986, pp. 618–634.

27. Paul Hersey and Kenneth H. Blanchard, *Management of Organizational Behavior*, 3rd ed. (Englewood Cliffs, N.J.: Prentice-Hall, 1977).

28. Yukl, *Leadership in Organizations*.

29. Steven Kerr and John M. Jermier, "Substitutes for Leadership: Their Meaning and Measurement," *Organizational Behavior and Human Performance*, December 1978, pp. 375–403.

30. See Charles C. Manz and Henry P. Sims, Jr., "Leading Workers to Lead Themselves: The External Leadership of Self-Managing Work Teams," *Administrative Science Quarterly*, March 1987, pp. 106–129.

31. James MacGregor Burns, *Leadership* (New York: Harper & Row, 1978). See also John J. Hater and Bernard M. Bass, "Superiors' Evaluations and Subordinates' Perceptions of Transformational and Transactional Leadership," *Journal of Applied Psychology*, November 1988, pp. 695–702; Karl W. Kuhnert and Philip Lewis, "Transactional and Transformational Leadership: A Constructive/Developmental Analysis," *Academy of Management Review*, October 1987, pp. 648–657.

32. Kenneth Labich, "The Seven Keys to Business Leadership," *Fortune*, October 24, 1988, pp. 58–66.

33. "Big Changes Are Galvanizing General Electric," *Business Week*, December 18, 1989, pp. 100–102.

34. Jeffrey Pfeffer, *Power in Organizations* (Marshfield, Mass.: Pitman Publishing, 1981), p. 7.

35. Victor Murray and Jeffrey Gandz, "Games Executives Play: Politics at Work," *Business Horizons*, December 1980, pp. 11–23; Jeffrey Gandz and Victor Murray, "The Experience of Workplace Politics," *Academy of Management Journal*, June 1980, pp. 237–251.

36. Don R. Beeman and Thomas W. Sharkey, "The Use and Abuse of Corporate Power," *Business Horizons*, March–April 1987, pp. 26–30.

37. Murray and Gandz, "Games Executives Play."

38. Beeman and Sharkey, "The Use and Abuse of Corporate Power."

39. Stefanie Ann Lenway and Kathleen Rehbein, "Leaders, Followers, and Free Riders," An Empirical Test of Variation in Corporate Political Involvement," *Academy of Management Journal*, December 1991, pp. 893–905.

Chapter 16

1. Brian Dumaine, "Who Needs a Boss?" *Fortune*, May 7, 1990, pp. 52–60; Gary Hoover, Alta Campbell, and Patrick J. Spain, eds., *Hoover's Handbook of American Business 1992* (Austin, Tex.: The Reference Press, 1991), p. 248.

2. See John J. Gabarro, "The Development of Working Relationships," in Jay W. Lorsch, ed., *Handbook of Organizational Behavior* (Englewood Cliffs, N.J.: Prentice-Hall, 1987), pp. 172–189.

3. See Marcelline R. Fisilier, Daniel C. Ganster, and Bronston T. Mayes, "Effects of Social Support, Role Stress, and Locus of Control on Health," *Journal of Management*, Fall 1987, pp. 517–528.

4. See Gregory Moorhead and Ricky W. Griffin, *Organizational Behavior*, 3rd ed. (Boston: Houghton Mifflin, 1992), for a review of definitions of groups.

5. Marilyn E. Gist, Edwin A. Locke, and M. Susan Taylor, "Organizational Behavior: Group Structure, Process, and Effectiveness," *Journal of Management*, Summer 1987, pp. 237–257.

6. Dorwin Cartwright and Alvin Zander, eds., *Group Dynamics: Research and Theory*, 3rd ed. (New York: Harper & Row, 1968).

7. See Gregory P. Shea and Richard A. Guzzo, "Group Effectiveness: What Really Matters?" *Sloan Management Review*, Spring 1987, pp. 25–31, for a discussion of performance in functional groups.

8. Robert Schrank, *Ten Thousand Working Days* (Cambridge, Mass.: MIT Press, 1978); Bill Watson, "Counter Planning on the Shop Floor," in Peter Frost, Vance Mitchell, and Walter Nord, eds., *Organizational Reality*, 2nd ed. (Glenview, Ill.: Scott, Foresman, 1982), pp. 286–294.

9. Marvin E. Shaw, *Group Dynamics—The Psychology of*

Small Group Behavior, 4th ed. (New York: McGraw-Hill, 1985).

10. Rupert Brown and Jennifer Williams, "Group Identification: The Same Thing to All People?" *Human Relations*, July 1984, pp. 547–560.

11. See Connie Gersick, "Marking Time: Predictable Transitions in Task Groups," *Academy of Management Journal*, June 1989, pp. 274–309.

12. Stuart Gannes, "America's Fastest-Growing Companies," *Fortune*, May 23, 1988, pp. 28–40.

13. David Katz and Robert L. Kahn, *The Social Psychology of Organizations*, 2nd ed. (New York: Wiley, 1978), pp. 187–221.

14. Robert L. Kahn, D. M. Wolfe, R. P. Quinn, J. D. Snoek, and R. A. Rosenthal, *Organizational Stress: Studies in Role Conflict and Role Ambiguity* (New York: Wiley, 1964).

15. See Donna M. Randall, "Multiple Roles and Organizational Commitment," *Journal of Organizational Behavior*, Vol. 9, 1988, pp. 309–317.

16. For recent research in this area, see Donna L. Wiley, "The Relationship Between Work/Nonwork Role Conflict and Job-Related Outcomes: Some Unanticipated Findings," *Journal of Management*, Winter 1987, pp. 467–472; and Arthur G. Bedeian, Beverly G. Burke, and Richard G. Moffett, "Outcomes of Work-Family Conflict Among Married Male and Female Professionals," *Journal of Management*, September 1988, pp. 475–485.

17. Daniel C. Feldman, "The Development and Enforcement of Group Norms," *Academy of Management Review*, January 1984, pp. 47–53. See also Monika Henderson and Michael Argyle, "The Informal Rules of Working Relationships," *Journal of Organizational Behavior*, Vol. 7, 1986, pp. 259–275.

18. "Companies Turn to Peer Pressure to Cut Injuries as Psychologists Join the Battle," *The Wall Street Journal*, March 29, 1991, pp. B1, B3.

19. Walter Kiechel, III, "Love, Don't Lose, the Newly Hired," *Fortune*, June 6, 1988, pp. 271–274.

20. For an example of how to increase cohesiveness, see Paul F. Buller and Cecil H. Bell, Jr., "Effects of Team Building and Goal Setting on Productivity: A Field Experiment," *Academy of Management Journal*, June 1986, pp. 305–328.

21. Dumaine, "Who Needs a Boss?"

22. "Team Builders Shine in Perilous Waters," *The Wall Street Journal*, October 29, 1990, p. B1.

23. "Teaching How to Cope with Workplace Conflicts," *Business Week*, February 18, 1980, pp. 136, 139.

24. Clayton P. Alderfer, "An Intergroup Perspective on Group Dynamics," in Lorsch, ed., *Handbook of Organizational Behavior*, pp. 190–222. See also Eugene Owens and E. Leroy Plumlee, "Intraorganizational Competition and Interorganizational Conflict: More Than a Matter of Semantics," *Business Review*, Winter 1988, pp. 28–32.

25. "Perot War with EDS Pits Former Friends in High-Stakes Affair," *The Wall Street Journal*, October 6, 1988, pp. A1, A12.

26. Danny Ertel, "How to Design a Conflict Management Procedure That Fits Your Dispute," *Sloan Management Review*, Summer 1991, pp. 29–39.

27. Joann S. Lublin, "Beecham's Chief Imports His American Ways," *The Wall Street Journal*, October 27, 1988, p. B9.

Chapter 17

1. Faye Rice, "Champions of Communication," *Fortune*, June 3, 1991, pp. 111–120; Brian Dumaine, "The Bureaucracy Busters," *Fortune*, June 17, 1991, pp. 36–50.

2. Henry Mintzberg, *The Nature of Managerial Work* (New York: Harper & Row, 1973).

3. See Karl E. Weick and Larry D. Browning, "Argument and Narration in Organizational Communication," *Journal of Management*, Summer 1986, pp. 243–259.

4. John Huey, "The New Power in Black & Decker," *Fortune*, January 2, 1989, pp. 89–94.

5. Mintzberg, *The Nature of Managerial Work*.

6. Mintzberg, *The Nature of Managerial Work*.

7. Walter Kiechel, III, "The Big Presentation," *Fortune*, July 26, 1982, pp. 98–100.

8. "Executives Who Dread Public Speaking Learn to Keep Their Cool in the Spotlight," *The Wall Street Journal*, May 4, 1990, pp. B1, B6.

9. Mintzberg, *The Nature of Managerial Work*.

10. Kiechel, "The Big Presentation."

11. Robert H. Lengel and Richard L. Daft, "The Selection of Communication Media as an Executive Skill," *The Academy of Management Executive,* August 1988, pp. 225–232.

12. Walter Kiechel, III, "Breaking Bad News to the Boss," *Fortune,* April 9, 1990, pp. 111–112.

13. Myron Magnet, "Is ITT Fighting Shadows—Or Raiders?" *Fortune,* November 11, 1985, pp. 25–28.

14. Brian Dumaine, "Corporate Spies Snoop to Conquer," *Fortune,* November 7, 1988, pp. 68–76.

15. A. Vavelas, "Communication Patterns in Task-Oriented Groups," *Journal of the Accoustical Society of America,* Vol. 22, 1950, pp. 725–730; Jerry Wofford, Edwin Gerloff, and Robert Cummins, *Organizational Communication* (New York: McGraw-Hill, 1977).

16. Keith Davis, "Management Communication and the Grapevine," *Harvard Business Review,* September–October 1953, pp. 43–49.

17. "Spread the Word: Gossip Is Good," *The Wall Street Journal,* October 4, 1988, p. B1.

18. See David M. Schweiger and Angelo S. DeNisi, "Communication with Employees Following a Merger: A Longitudinal Field Experiment," *Academy of Management Journal,* March 1991, pp. 110–135.

19. See Tom Peters and Nancy Austin, *A Passion for Excellence* (New York: Random House, 1985).

20. D. C. Dearborn and H. A. Simon, "Selective Perception: A Note on the Departmental Identification of Executives," *Sociometry,* Vol. 21, 1958, pp. 140–144.

21. Albert Mehrabian, *Non-verbal Communication* (Chicago: Aldine, 1972).

22. Michael B. McCaskey, "The Hidden Messages Managers Send," *Harvard Business Review,* November–December 1979, pp. 135–148.

23. Thomas Moore, "Make-or-Break Time for General Motors," *Fortune,* February 15, 1988, pp. 32–42; Brian O'Reilly, "How Jimmy Treybig Turned Tough," *Fortune,* May 25, 1987, pp. 102–104.

24. David Givens, "What Body Langauge Can Tell You that Words Cannot," *U.S. News & World Report,* November 19, 1984, p. 100.

25. Edward J. Hall, *The Hidden Dimension* (New York: Doubleday, 1966).

26. For a detailed discussion of improving communication effectiveness, see Courtland L. Bove and John V. Thill, *Business Communication Today,* 3rd ed. (New York: McGraw-Hill, 1992).

27. See Otis W. Baskin and Craig E. Aronoff, *Interpersonal Communication in Organizations* (Glenview, Ill.: Scott, Foresman, 1980).

28. Joseph Allen and Bennett P. Lientz, *Effective Business Communication* (Santa Monica, Calif.: Goodyear, 1979).

29. For a recent discussion of these and related issues, see Eric M. Eisenberg and Marsha G. Witten, "Reconsidering Openness in Organizational Communication," *Academy of Management Review,* July 1987, pp. 418–426.

30. Walter Kiechel, III, "Learn How to Listen," *Fortune,* August 17, 1987, pp. 107–108.

31. John J. Donovan, "Beyond Chief Information Officer to Network Manager," *Harvard Business Review,* September–October 1988, pp. 134–140.

32. Robert Johansen and Christine Bullen, "What to Expect from Teleconferencing," *Harvard Business Review,* March–April 1984, pp. 164–174. See also Richard C. Huseman and Edward W. Miles, "Organizational Communication in the Information Age: Implications of Computer-Based Systems," *Journal of Management,* June 1988, pp. 181–204.

33. "These Top Executives Work Where They Play," *Business Week,* October 27, 1986, pp. 132–134. See also "Escape from the Office," *Newsweek,* April 24, 1989, pp. 58–60.

34. Walter Kiechel, III, "Hold for the Communicaholic Manager," *Fortune,* January 2, 1989, pp. 107–108.

Chapter 18

1. "Queen Anne at the Mall," *Forbes,* June 24, 1991, pp. 78–80; "Retailers Face Wild Ride to Recovery," *The Wall Street Journal,* April 4, 1991, pp. B1, B6.

2. "Cash Squeeze," *Forbes,* September 30, 1991, pp. 70–72.

3. Charles W. L. Hill, "Differentiation Versus Low Cost or Differentiation and Low Cost: A Contingency Framework," *Academy of Management Review,* July 1988, pp. 401–412.

4. Peter F. Drucker, *Managing in Turbulent Times* (New York: Harper & Row, 1980).

5. Joel Dreyfuss, "Victories in the Quality Crusade," *Fortune,* October 10, 1988, pp. 80–88.

6. Dreyfuss, "Victories in the Quality Crusade."

7. "America's Leanest and Meanest," *Business Week,* October 5, 1987, pp. 78–84.

8. Ronald Henkoff, "Cost Cutting: How to Do It Right," *Fortune,* April 9, 1990, pp. 40–49.

9. Edward E. Lawler, III, and John G. Rhode, *Information and Control in Organizations* (Pacific Palisades, Calif.: Goodyear, 1976); Robert N. Anthony, *The Management Control Function* (Boston: Harvard Business School Press, 1988).

10. "The Sharper Image May Need to Refocus," *Business Week,* November 21, 1988, p. 84.

11. See Stephen G. Green and M. Ann Welsh, "Cybernetics and Dependence: Reframing the Control Concept," *Academy of Management Review,* April 1988, pp. 287–301.

12. Harold Koontz and Robert W. Bradspies, "Managing Through Feedforward Control," *Business Horizons,* June 1972, pp. 25–36.

13. Dreyfuss, "Victories in the Quality Crusade."

14. Anthony, *The Management Control Function.*

15. William G. Ouchi, "The Transmission of Control Through Organizational Hierarchy," *Academy of Management Journal,* June 1978, pp. 173–192; Richard E. Walton, "From Control to Commitment in the Workplace," *Harvard Business Review,* March–April 1985, pp. 76–84.

16. "As NBC News Cuts Costs Will It Clobber Quality?" *Business Week,* December 5, 1988, pp. 137–138.

17. "The Push for Quality," *Business Week,* June 8, 1987, pp. 130–135.

18. Peter Lorange, Michael F. Scott Morton, and Sumantra Ghoshal, *Strategic Control* (St. Paul, Minn.: West, 1986).

19. See Anil Gupta and Vijay Govindarajan, "Knowledge Flows and the Structure of Control Within Multinational Corporations," *Academy of Management Review,* October 1991, pp. 768–792, for a discussion of strategic control for international firms.

20. For other perspectives, see Georg Schreyogg and Horst Steinmann, "Strategic Control: A New Perspective," *Academy of Management Review,* January 1987, pp. 91–103.

21. Walter Guzzard, "Big Can Still Be Beautiful," *Fortune,* April 25, 1988, pp. 50–64.

22. "Champion Is Starting to Show a Little Spark," *Business Week,* March 21, 1988, p. 87; "Champion Spark Plug Agrees to Merge with Dana Corp. for $17.50 a Share," *The Wall Street Journal,* January 26, 1989, p. A4.

23. Charles G. Burck, "What Happens When Workers Manage Themselves," *Fortune,* July 27, 1981, pp. 62–69.

24. Cortlandt Cammann and David A. Nadler, "Fit Control Systems to Your Management Style," *Harvard Business Review,* January–February 1976, pp. 65–72.

Chapter 19

1. Brian Dumaine, "How Managers Can Succeed Through Speed," *Fortune,* February 13, 1989, pp. 54–59; Bro Uttal, "Speeding New Ideas to Market," *Fortune,* March 2, 1987, pp. 62–66; Brian Dumaine, "Earning More by Moving Faster," *Fortune,* October 7, 1991, pp. 89–94.

2. Robert E. Cole, "The Quality Revolution," *Production and Operations Management,* Winter 1992, pp. 118–120.

3. Ross Johnson and William O. Winchell, *Management and Quality* (Milwaukee: American Society for Quality Control, 1989).

4. W. Edwards Deming, *Out of the Crisis* (Cambridge, Mass.: MIT Press, 1986).

5. Joel Dreyfuss, "Victories in the Quality Crusade," *Fortune,* October 10, 1988, pp. 80–88.

6. "Workers Are the Key, Top Firms Find," *USA Today,* October 1, 1991, pp. 1B, 2B.

7. "How to Make It Right the First Time," *Business Week,* June 8, 1987, pp. 142–143.

8. "Quality Is Becoming Job One in the Office, Too," *Business Week,* April 29, 1991, pp. 52–56.

9. John W. Kendrick, *Understanding Productivity: An Introduction to the Dynamics of Productivity Change* (Baltimore: Johns Hopkins, 1977).

10. "Productivity Indicates Sluggish Economy," *The Wall Street Journal*, July 6, 1990, p. A2.

11. "Factories Get More Competitive," *USA Today*, August 3, 1987, pp. B1, B2.

12. "The Productivity Paradox," *Business Week*, June 6, 1988, pp. 100–113; "Productivity: Why It's the No. 1 Underachiever," *Business Week*, April 20, 1987, pp. 54–60.

13. "Bausch & Lomb Is Correcting Its Vision of Research," *Business Week*, March 30, 1987, p. 91.

14. Gene Bylinsky, "Turning R&D Into Real Products," *Fortune*, July 2, 1990, pp. 72–77.

15. Norm Alster, "What Flexible Workers Can Do," *Fortune*, February 13, 1989, pp. 62–66.

16. For a review, see Everett E. Adam, Jr., and Ronald J. Ebert, *Production and Operations Management*, 5th ed. (Englewood Cliffs, N.J.: Prentice-Hall, 1992).

17. Paul M. Swamidass, "Empirical Science: New Frontier in Operations Management Research," *Academy of Management Review*, October 1991, pp. 793–814.

18. Sylvia Nasar, "America's Competitive Revival," *Fortune*, January 4, 1988, pp. 44–52.

19. Richard B. Chase and Warren J. Erikson, "The Service Factory," *The Academy of Management Executive*, August 1988, pp. 191–196.

20. James Brian Quinn and Christopher E. Gagnon, "Will Service Follow Manufacturing into Decline?" *Harvard Business Review*, November–December 1986, pp. 95–103.

21. Dumaine, "How Managers Can Succeed Through Speed."

22. For a full discussion, see Everett Adam, "Towards a Typology of Production and Operations Management Systems," *Academy of Management Review*, July 1983, pp. 365–375. See also Byron J. Finch and James F. Cox, "Process-Oriented Production Planning and Control: Factors that Influence System Design," *Academy of Management Journal*, March 1988, pp. 123–153.

23. Adam and Ebert, *Production and Operations Management*.

24. Louis Kraar, "Japan's Gung-Ho U.S. Car Plants," *Fortune*, January 30, 1989, pp. 98–108.

25. See Chan K. Hahn, Daniel J. Bragg, and Dongwook Shin, "Impact of the Setup Variable on Capacity and Inventory Decisions," *Academy of Management Review*, January 1988, pp. 91–103.

26. Adam and Ebert, *Production and Operations Management*.

27. Adam and Ebert, *Production and Operations Management*.

Chapter 20

1. Brenton R. Schlender, "How Sony Keeps the Magic Going," *Fortune*, February 24, 1992, pp. 76–84; "Sony Hopes Next Year to Unveil Its Mini-Compact Disk Player," *The Wall Street Journal*, May 16, 1991, pp. B1, B5.

2. Joan Woodward, *Industrial Organization: Theory and Practice* (London: Oxford University Press, 1965).

3. Paul D. Collins, Jerald Hage, and Frank M. Hull, "Organizational and Technological Predictors of Change in Automaticity," *Academy of Management Journal*, September 1988, pp. 512–543.

4. "Computers Speed the Design of More Workaday Products," *The Wall Street Journal*, January 18, 1985, p. 25.

5. Robert Bonsack, "Executive Checklist: Are You Ready for CIM?" *CIM Review*, Summer 1987, pp. 35–38.

6. Sepehri, "IBM's Automated Lexington Factory Focuses on Quality and Cost Effectiveness," *Industrial Engineering*, February 1987, pp. 66–74.

7. "Computers Speed the Design of More Workaday Products."

8. "How Automation Could Save the Day," *Business Week*, March 3, 1986, pp. 72–74.

9. Otto Friedrich, "The Robot Revolution," *Time*, December 8, 1980, pp. 72–83.

10. "Boldly Going Where No Robot Has Gone Before," *Business Week*, December 22, 1986, p. 45.

11. Gene Bylinsky, "Invasion of the Service Robots," *Fortune*, September 14, 1987, pp. 81–88.

12. "Robots Head for the Farm," *Business Week*, September 8, 1986, pp. 66–67.

13. William C. Symonds, "Ramtron's Revolution: Cir-

cuits on Ceramics," *Business Week,* June 15, 1990, p. 64; Michael Bloom, "Advanced ICs: A Memory to Remember," *ESD,* October 1989, pp. 38–44; David Bondurant and Fred Gnadinger, "Ferroelectrics for Nonvolatile RAMs," *IEEE Spectrum,* July 1989, pp. 30–33; Joe Evans, "Ferroelectric Memories," *ESD,* August 1988, pp. 29–35.

14. See Richard Woodman, John Sawyer, and Ricky Griffin, "Organizational Creativity: A Proposal for Research on Creativity in Complex Social Systems," unpublished manuscript, Department of Management, Texas A&M University, 1992; and R. T. Brown, "Creativity: What Are We to Measure?" in J. A. Glover, R. R. Ronning, and C. R. Reynolds (eds.), *Handbook of Creativity* (New York: Plenum, 1989), pp. 3–32, for a discussion of these three categories.

15. The study of the impact of background characteristics on creativity has a long tradition, stemming from the work of F. Galton, *Hereditary Genius* (London: Macmillan, 1869). More recent work on background and creativity can be found in C. E. Schaefer and A. Anastasi, "A Biographical Inventory for Identifying Creativity in Adolescent Boys," *Journal of Applied Psychology,* 1968, pp. 42–48; D. K. Simonton, "Biographical Typicality, Eminence, and Achievement Styles," *Journal of Creative Behavior,* 1986, pp. 14–22; and B. Singh, "Role of Personality versus Biographical Factors in Creativity," *Psychological Studies,* 1986, pp. 90–92. This entire approach to understanding creativity has been criticized by F. B. Barron and D. M. Harrington, "Creativity, Intelligence, and Personality," *Annual Review of Psychology,* 1981, pp. 439–476.

16. See Barron and Harrington, "Creativity, Intelligence, and Personality," and Richard Woodman and Lyle Schoenfeldt, "An Interactionist Model of Creative Behavior," *Journal of Creative Behavior,* 1990, pp. 10–20, for summaries of this personality trait literature.

17. H. G. Gough, "Studying Creativity by Means of Word Association Tests," *Journal of Applied Psychology,* 1976, pp. 348–353; Barron and Harrington, "Creativity, Intelligence, and Personality."

18. M. Basadur, G. B. Graen, and S. G. Green, "Training in Creative Problem-Solving: Effects on Ideation and Problem Finding and Solving in an Industrial Research Organization," *Organizational Behavior and Human Performance,* 1982, pp. 41–70.

19. Lee Iacocca (with William Novak), *Iacocca: An Autobiography* (New York: Bantam, 1984).

20. See Thomas V. Busse and Richard S. Mansfield, "Theories of the Creative Process: A Review and a Perspective," *Journal of Creative Behavior,* 1980, pp. 91–103, for a discussion of this and other models of the creative process.

21. Kenneth Labich, "The Innovators," *Fortune,* June 6, 1988, pp. 50–64.

22. John A. Seeger, Jay W. Lorsch, and Cyrus F. Gibson, *First National City Bank Operating Group (A) and (B)* (Boston: Harvard Business School, 1975).

23. L. B. Mohr, "Determinants of Innovation in Organizations," *American Political Science Review,* 1969, pp. 111–126; G. A. Steiner, *The Creative Organization* (Chicago: University of Chicago Press, 1965); R. Duncan and A. Weiss, "Organizational Learning: Implications for Organizational Design," in B. M. Staw (ed.), *Research in Organizational Behavior,* Volume 1 (Greenwich, Conn.: JAI Press, 1979), pp. 75–123; J. E. Ettlie, "Adequacy of Stage Models for Decisions on Adoption of Innovation," *Psychological Reports,* 1980, pp. 991–995.

24. Beth Wolfensberger, "Trouble in Toyland," *New England Business,* September 1990, pp. 28–36.

25. See Alan Patz, "Managing Innovation in High Technology Industries," *New Management,* 1986, pp. 54–59.

26. An excellent guide to these kinds of management errors is Robert F. Hartley, *Management Mistakes and Successes,* 3rd ed. (New York: John Wiley, 1991).

27. See William G. Ouchi, *Theory Z* (Reading, Mass.: Addison-Wesley, 1980), for a discussion of quality circles at Oki Electric.

28. See Gifford Pinchot, III, *Intrapreneuring* (New York: Harper & Row, 1985).

29. See Steven P. Feldman, "How Organizational Culture Can Affect Innovation," *Organizational Dynamics,* Summer 1988, pp. 57–68.

Chapter 21

1. Gary Hoover, Alta Campbell, and Patrick J. Spain (eds.), *Hoover's Handbook of American Business 1992* (Austin, Tex.: The Reference Press, 1991), p. 566; "At Westinghouse, 'E-Mail' Makes the World Go

'Round," *Business Week*, October 10, 1988, p. 110; Thomas Stewart, "Westinghouse Gets Respect at Last," *Fortune*, July 3, 1989, pp. 92–98.

2. William B. Stevenson and Mary C. Gilly, "Information Processing and Problem Solving: The Migration of Problems Through Formal Positions and Networks of Ties," *Academy of Management Journal*, December 1991, pp. 918–928.

3. Lynda M. Applegate, James I. Cash, Jr., and D. Quinn Mills, "Information Technology and Tomorrow's Manager," *Harvard Business Review*, November–December 1988, pp. 128–136.

4. "At Today's Supermarket, the Computer Is Doing It All," *Business Week*, August 11, 1986, pp. 64–66.

5. Charles A. O'Reilly, "Variations in Decision Makers' Use of Information Sources: The Impact of Quality and Accessibility of Information," *Academy of Management Journal*, December 1982, pp. 756–771.

6. Carla Rapoport, "Great Japanese Mistakes," *Fortune*, February 13, 1989, pp. 108–111.

7. Brian Dumaine, "Corporate Spies Snoop to Conquer," *Fortune*, November 7, 1988, pp. 66–76.

8. John Huey, "Wal-Mart—Will It Take Over the World?" *Fortune*, January 30, 1989, pp. 52–61.

9. William J. Bruns, Jr., and F. Warren McFarlin, "Information Technology Puts Power in Control Systems," *Harvard Business Review*, September–October 1987, pp. 89–94.

10. See Jesse B. Tutor, Jr., "Management and Future Technological Trends," *Texas A&M Business Forum*, Fall 1988, pp. 2–5.

11. V. Thomas Dock and James C. Wetherbe, *Computer Information Systems for Business* (St. Paul, Minn.: West, 1988).

12. "An Electronic Pipeline That's Changing the Way America Does Business," *Business Week*, August 3, 1987, pp. 80–82.

13. Applegate, Cash, and Mills, "Information Technology and Tomorrow's Manager."

14. Jeremy Main, "At Last, Software CEOs Can Use," *Fortune*, March 13, 1989, pp. 77–83.

15. See George W. Reynolds, *Information Systems for Managers* (St. Paul, Minn.: West, 1988), for a detailed description of developing information systems.

16. "Computerizing Uncle Sam's Data: Oh, How the Public Is Paying," *Business Week*, December 15, 1986, pp. 102–103.

17. "How Do You Build an Information Highway?" *Business Week*, September 16, 1991, pp. 108–112.

18. "Linking All the Company Data: We're Not There Yet," *Business Week*, May 11, 1987, p. 151.

19. David Kirkpatrick, "Why Not Farm Out Your Computing?" *Fortune*, September 23, 1991, pp. 103–112.

20. "Office Automation: Making It Pay Off," *Business Week*, October 12, 1987, pp. 134–146.

21. "Office Automation: Making It Pay Off."

22. "Office Automation: Making It Pay Off."

23. John J. Donovan, "Beyond Chief Information Officer to Network Managers," *Harvard Business Review*, September–October 1988, pp. 134–140.

24. Jeremy Main, "The Winning Organization," *Fortune*, September 26, 1988, pp. 50–60.

25. See Reynolds, *Information Systems for Managers*.

26. "Computer Headaches," *Newsweek*, July 6, 1987, pp. 34–35.

27. Huey, "Wal-Mart—Will It Take Over the World?"

28. Dorothy Leonard-Barton and John J. Sviokla, "Putting Expert Systems to Work," *Harvard Business Review*, March–April 1988, pp. 91–98.

29. "Turning an Expert's Skills into Computer Software," *Business Week*, October 7, 1985, pp. 104–108.

Chapter 22

1. Gary Hoover, Alta Campbell, and Patrick J. Spain (eds.), *Hoover's Handbook of American Business 1992* (Austin, Tex.: The Reference Press, 1991), p. 126; "Firms Address Workers' Cultural Variety," *The Wall Street Journal*, February 10, 1989, p. B1.

2. Marlene G. Fine, Fern L. Johnson, and M. Sallyanne Ryan, "Cultural Diversity in the Workplace," *Public Personnel Management*, Fall 1990, pp. 305–319.

3. Badi G. Foster, Gerald Jackson, William E. Cross, Bailey Jackson, and Rita Hardiman, "Workforce Diversity and Business," *Training and Development Journal*, April 1988, pp. 38–42.

4. Sam Cole, "Cultural Diversity and Sustainable Futures," *Futures,* December 1990, pp. 1044–1058.

5. Walter Kiechel, III, "How to Manage Older Workers," *Fortune,* November 5, 1990, pp. 183–186.

6. Louis S. Richman, "The Coming World Labor Shortage," *Fortune,* April 9, 1990, pp. 70–77.

7. *Occupational Outlook Handbook* (Washington D.C.: U.S. Bureau of Labor Statistics, 1990–1991).

8. Jaclyn Fierman, "Do Women Manage Differently?" *Fortune,* December 17, 1990, pp. 115–118.

9. Jaclyn Fierman, "Why Women Still Don't Hit the Top," *Fortune,* July 30, 1990, pp. 40–62.

10. "Paternal, Managerial Roles Often Clash," *The Wall Street Journal,* September 12, 1991, pp. B1, B4.

11. *Occupational Outlook Handbook* (Washington D.C.: U.S. Bureau of Labor Statistics, 1990–1991).

12. Taylor H. Cox, Sharon A. Lobel, and Poppy Lauretta McLeod, "Effects of Ethnic Group Cultural Differences on Cooperative and Competitive Behavior on a Group Task," *Academy of Management Journal,* December 1991, pp. 827–847.

13. Michael Chisholm, "Cultural Diversity Breaks the Mold," *Geographical Magazine,* November 1990, pp. 12–16.

14. Based on Taylor H. Cox and Stacy Blake, "Managing Cultural Diversity: Implications for Organizational Competitiveness," *The Academy of Management Executive,* August 1991, pp. 45–56.

15. Cox and Blake, "Managing Cultural Diversity: Implications for Organizational Competitiveness."

16. For an example, see "Get to Know the Ethnic Market," *Marketing,* June 17, 1991, p. 32.

17. Patti Watts, "Bias Busting: Diversity Training in the Workforce," *Management Review,* December 1987, pp. 51–54.

18. See Stephenie Overman, "Managing the Diverse Work Force," *HRMagazine,* April 1991, pp. 32–36.

19. Lennie Copeland, "Making the Most of Cultural Differences at the Workplace," *Personnel,* June 1988, pp. 52–60.

20. "Firms Address Workers' Cultural Variety," *The Wall Street Journal,* February 10, 1989, p. B1.

21. "Learning to Accept Cultural Diversity," *The Wall Street Journal,* September 12, 1990, pp. B1, B9.

22. "Firms Address Workers' Cultural Variety."

23. "Firms Grapple With Language," *The Wall Street Journal,* November 7, 1989, p. B1.

24. Dinesh D'Souza, "Multiculturalism 101," *Policy Review,* Spring 1991, pp. 22–30.

25. This discussion derives heavily from Taylor H. Cox, "The Multicultural Organization," *The Academy of Management Executive,* May 1991, pp. 34–47.

Chapter 23

1. "Today's Mystery: Who Buys All Those Souvenir Spoons?" *The Wall Street Journal,* June 6, 1991, pp. A1, A11.

2. Nicholas C. Siropolis, *Small Business Management: A Guide to Entrepreneurship,* 4th ed. (Boston: Houghton Mifflin, 1990).

3. Alan Deutschman, "America's Fastest Risers," *Fortune,* October 7, 1991, pp. 46–68.

4. Murray B. Low and Ian C. MacMillan, "Entrepreneurship: Past Research and Future Challenges," *Journal of Management,* June 1988, pp. 139–159; Barbara Bird, "Implementing Entrepreneurial Ideas: The Case for Intention," *Academy of Management Review,* July 1988, pp. 442–453.

5. Siropolis, *Small Business Management.*

6. "Big vs. Small," *Time,* September 5, 1988, pp. 48–50.

7. "Small Business Hiring, A Locomotive For the Economy in the '80s, Is Slowing," *The Wall Street Journal,* March 16, 1990, pp. B1, B2.

8. "New Incorporations," *The Wall Street Journal,* November 19, 1984, p. 1.

9. "Small Companies Thrive by Taking Over Some Specialized Tasks for Big Concerns," *The Wall Street Journal,* September 11, 1991, pp. B1, B2.

10. Deutschman, "America's Fastest Risers."

11. "Japanese Bankroll Small U.S. Firms," *The Wall Street Journal,* November 2, 1989, pp. B1, B2.

12. "Think Small," *Business Week,* November 4, 1991, pp. 58–65.

13. Arnold C. Cooper and William C. Dunkelberg, "Entrepreneurship and Paths to Business Ownership," *Strategic Management Journal*, Vol. 7, 1986, pp. 53–68.

14. Jeremy Main, "Breaking Out of the Company," *Fortune*, May 25, 1987, pp. 82–88.

15. Siropolis, *Small Business Management*.

16. "Warning Flags Up," *The Wall Street Journal*, May 15, 1987, p. 10D–11D; and "Crisis Consultant," *The Wall Street Journal*, February 24, 1989, p. R32.

17. Siropolis, *Small Business Management*.

18. Siropolis, *Small Business Management*.

19. Faye Rice, "How to Succeed at Cloning a Small Business," *Fortune*, October 28, 1985, pp. 60–66; "Franchising Tries to *Divvy Up* Risk," *USA Today*, May 11, 1987, p. 5E.

20. Richard M. Hodgetts and Donald F. Kuratko, *Effective Small Business Management*, 3rd ed. (Chicago: Harcourt Brace Jovanovich, 1989).

21. "Persistence Pays in Search for Funds," *USA Today*, May 11, 1987, p. 3E; see also "Neighborhood Financing," *The Wall Street Journal*, February 24, 1989, pp. R13–R14.

22. Alan Deutschman, "A Case of Too Much Money," *Fortune*, November 7, 1988, pp. 95–104.

23. Siropolis, *Small Business Management*.

24. Siropolis, *Small Business Management*.

25. "Small Businesses Find Electronic Banking Can Be a Useful Tool in Managing Money," *The Wall Street Journal*, July 22, 1986, p. 31.

26. Siropolis, *Small Business Management*.

27. From a film produced by the U.S. Small Business Administration, *The Habit of Winning*, 1972.

28. Matthew Berke, "Elling Bros. Got Costs Under Control," *Inc.*, January 1982, pp. 45–50.

29. Howard H. Stevenson and José Carlos Jarrillo-Mossi, "Preserving Entrepreneurship as Companies Grow," *The Journal of Business Strategy*, Vol. 7, 1986, pp. 10–23. See also "Big vs. Small," *Time*, September 5, 1988, pp. 48–50; and "Money from the Boss," *The Wall Street Journal*, February 24, 1989, pp. R10–R11.

30. Gannes, "America's Fastest-Growing Companies."

Appendix 1

1. Monci Jo Williams, "Women Beat the Corporate Game," *Fortune*, September 12, 1988, pp. 128–138; Jaclyn Fierman, "Why Women Still Don't Hit the Top," *Fortune*, July 30, 1990, pp. 40–62.

2. For recent reviews of career literature, see Edgar H. Schein, "Individuals and Careers," in Jay W. Lorsch, ed., *Handbook of Organizational Behavior* (Englewood Cliffs, N.J.: Prentice-Hall, 1987), pp. 155–171; and Douglas T. Hall and Associates, *Career Development in Organizations* (San Francisco: Jossey-Bass, 1986).

3. Mary Pat McEnrue, "Length of Experience and the Performance of Managers in the Establishment Phase of Their Careers," *Academy of Management Journal*, March 1988, pp. 175–185.

4. Daniel C. Feldman and Barton A. Weitz, "Career Plateaus Reconsidered," *Journal of Management*, Winter 1988, pp. 69–80; and Walter Kiechel, III, "High Up and Nowhere to Go," *Fortune*, August 1, 1988, pp. 229–233.

5. Faye Rice, "Lessons from Late Bloomers," *Fortune*, August 31, 1987, pp. 87–91.

6. Kenneth Labich, "Take Control of Your Career," *Fortune*, November 18, 1991, pp. 87–96.

7. Glenn R. Carroll and Elaine Mosakowski, "The Career Dynamics of Self-Employment," *Administrative Science Quarterly*, December 1987, pp. 570–589.

8. Raymond A. Noe, "Women and Mentoring: A Review and Research Agenda," *Academy of Management Review*, January 1988, pp. 65–78; Charles D. Orth, Harry E. Wilkinson, and Robert C. Benfari, "The Manager's Role as Coach and Mentor," *Organizational Dynamics*, Spring 1987, pp. 66–74; Kathy E. Kram, *Mentoring at Work: Developmental Relationships in Organizational Life* (Glenview, Ill.: Scott, Foresman, 1985).

9. William Whitely, Thomas Dougherty, and George Dreher, "Relationship of Career Mentoring and Socioeconomic Origin to Managers' and Professionals' Early Career Progress," *Academy of Management Journal*, June 1991, pp. 331–351.

10. Dan Hurley, "The Mentor Mystique," *Psychology Today*, May 1988, pp. 38–43.

11. See Cherlyn Skromme Granrose and James D. Portwood, "Matching Individual Career Plans and Organizational Career Management," *Academy of Management Journal,* December 1987, pp. 699–720; and Douglas T. Hall, "Careers and Socialization," *Journal of Management,* Summer 1987, pp. 301–321.

12. "As Costs of Overseas Assignments Climb, Firms Select Expatriates More Carefully," *The Wall Street Journal,* January 9, 1992, pp. B1, B2.

13. "Corporate Women," *Business Week,* June 22, 1987, pp. 72–78.

14. Mariann Jelinek and Nancy J. Adler, "Women: World-Class Managers for Global Competition," *The Academy of Management Executive,* February 1988, pp. 11–19; Jan Grant, "Women as Managers: What They Can Offer to Organizations," *Organizational Dynamics,* Winter 1988, pp. 56–63.

15. "Many Hurdles, Old and New, Keep Black Managers Out of Top Jobs," *The Wall Street Journal,* July 10, 1986, p. 25.

16. "Beatrice Deal a Landmark for Black Business," *USA Today,* August 11, 1987, p. 2B.

17. "Paternal, Managerial Roles Often Clash," *The Wall Street Journal,* September 12, 1991, pp. B1, B4.

18. "Best Employers for Women and Parents," *The Wall Street Journal,* November 30, 1987, p. 21.

19. John Huey, "Where Managers Will Go," *Fortune,* January 27, 1992, pp. 50–60.

20. "The Do's and Don'ts of Outplacement," *Psychology Today,* May 1988, p. 26.

Appendix 2

1. See Belverd E. Needles, Jr., Henry R. Anderson, and James C. Caldwell, *Principles of Accounting,* 4th ed. (Boston: Houghton Mifflin, 1990).

2. Needles, Anderson, and Caldwell, *Principles of Accounting.*

3. Ford S. Worthy, "Accounting Bores You? Wake Up," *Fortune,* October 12, 1987, pp. 43–50; Robert S. Kaplan, "One Cost System Isn't Enough," *Harvard Business Review,* January–February 1988, pp. 61–66; Robin Cooper, "You Need a New Cost System When . . ." *Harvard Business Review,* January–February 1989, pp. 77–82.

4. Peter Pyhrr, "Zero-Base Budgeting," *Harvard Business Review,* November–December 1970, pp. 111–121.

5. "What It Means to Build a Budget from Zero," *Business Week,* April 18, 1977, p. 160.

6. Christopher K. Bart, "Budgeting Gamesmanship," *The Academy of Management Executive,* November 1988, pp. 285–294.

7. Needles, Anderson, and Caldwell, *Principles of Accounting.*

8. Needles, Anderson, and Caldwell, *Principles of Accounting.*

Photo Credits

Chapter 2

p. 31, © Mark Segal/Tony Stone Worldwide; p. 36, The Bettmann Archive; p. 42, Courtesy of AT&T Archives; p. 49, Logo reprinted with permission by Pep Boys; p. 52, Photo by Dana Duke. Courtesy of Echlin Inc.

Chapter 3

p. 64, Courtesy Ryder Systems, Inc./Saturn Corporation; p. 68, Business Week Magazine; p. 72, © Dan White 1992; p. 77, © Sarah Leen/Matrix; p. 80, Annie Wells/The Press Democrat.

Chapter 4

p. 94, Reprinted with permission of Anheuser-Busch; p. 100, © Wyman Meinzer; p. 104, Courtesy Du Pont Company; p. 108, Courtesy of Wendy's International; p. 109, Courtesy of Public Service Enterprise Group Inc./Photo: Lee Youngblood.

Chapter 5

p. 118, Courtesy Kellogg Company; p. 120, Photo courtesy of Commercial Metals Company; p. 127, Pascal LeSegretain/SYGMA; p. 129, © Len Sirman/Photoreporters; p. 137, © Torin Boyd.

Chapter 6

p. 153, Momatiuk/Eastcott/Woodfin Camp & Assoc.; p. 156, Copyright Barney Taxel, 1990.; p. 162, Courtesy Union Pacific Corporation; p. 166, Photo courtesy of Air Products and Chemicals, Inc.

Chapter 7

p. 177, Courtesy of The Tandy Corporation; p. 179, © D.E. Cox; p. 189, Courtesy Nabisco Foods Group; p. 191, © Steve Niedorf.

Chapter 8

p. 203, Bob Fila, Chicago Tribune; p. 209, David Strick/ONYX; p. 213, © Bill O'Connell; p. 216, © Jeff Zaruba.

Chapter 9

p. 230, Courtesy US West, Inc./John Blaustein Photography; p. 238, Courtesy Pitney-Bowes Inc./Scott Goodwin Photography; p. 245, Seville Universal Exposition.

Chapter 10

p. 260, © James Schnepf; p. 265, Courtesy W.R. Grace & Co.; p. 268, © Brian Smale; p. 274, Courtesy Coca-Cola Enterprises, Inc./Photo © Flip Chalfant.

Chapter 11

p. 285, © Katherine Lambert; p. 289, © Michael L. Abramson; p. 296, © 1992 Jonathan Love from Kay Reese & Assoc. Inc.; p. 302, Tom Craig/REA/SABA.

Chapter 12

p. 312, © 1992 Jonathan Levine, All Rights Reserved.; p. 316, © Doug Milner; p. 318, © Balthazar Korab Ltd.; p. 322, © Tom Wolff.

Chapter 13

p. 335, Northern States Power Company/Joe Michl/Jim Arndt Photography; p. 340, © 1992 Arthur Meyerson; p. 345, Courtesy W.W. Grainger, Inc.; p. 353, © Jacque Lowe; p. 354, Allard/REA/SABA.

Chapter 14

p. 373, © Mike Greenlar; p. 375, Photo courtesy of Nationwide Insurance, Columbus, OH; p. 381, Courtesy of First of America Bank Corp./John Gilroy Photography; p. 385, © Brian Smith.

Chapter 15

p. 392, Yunghi Kim/The Boston Globe; p. 397, Courtesy Browning-Ferris Industries, Inc.; p. 408, Courtesy BMW of North America, Inc.; p. 409, © Peter Poulides.

Chapter 16

p. 419, © Jim Caldwell; p. 423, © Alan Levenson; p. 430, John Swart/AP Wideworld Photos; p. 433, © Peter Vidor; p. 437, © John Harding.

Chapter 17

p. 446, John F. Johnson-Humana, Inc.; p. 449, © Kent Miles; p. 454, Courtesy Hyatt Corporation; p. 457, © 1991 Comstock; p. 462, © Jamie Tanaka.

Chapter 18

p. 475, Mathew McVay/SABA; p. 478, © Jeff Zaruba; p. 482, Peter Yates/SABA; p. 486, © Michael L. Abramson; p. 488, © Vic Huber.

Chapter 19

p. 502 (Deming) © Aldo Mauro, (Crosby) Ben Van Hook/Copyright 1992, (Juran) Blaine Harrington III; p. 503, General Systems Co. Inc.; p. 507, © Vittorio Sartor; p. 510, © 1991 Roger Ball; p. 514, Courtesy Boeing.

Chapter 20

p. 525, Courtesy TRW, Inc.; p. 529, © Alan Levenson; p. 530, © John Abbott; p. 538, © John Abbott; p. 540, Burk Uzzle/Lee Gross Associates, Inc.

Chapter 21

p. 548, Courtesy Pitney-Bowes Inc./Scott Goodwin Photography; p. 554, Courtesy U.S Healthcare, Inc./Photo: Steve Barth; p. 558, Reprinted with permission of Andersen Consulting; p. 562, Courtesy Sun Life Assurance Company of Canada; p. 565, Courtesy US West, Inc./John Blaustein Photography.

Chapter 22

p. 576, Courtesy The Dow Chemical Company; p. 579, © Mike Greenlar; p. 581, Karen Kasmauski/Woodfin Camp & Assoc.; p. 589, © Mark Katzman.

Chapter 23

p. 603, © Welton B. Doby III; p. 609, © James Schnepf; p. 615, © Brian Smale; p. 618, © John Abbott.

Name Index

Acar, William, 645n
Adam, Everett E., Jr., 645n, 655n, 668n
Adams, J. Stacy, 378, 662n
Adler, Nancy J., 673n
Agnelli, Giovanni, 331
Agnelli, Umberto, 331
Agnelli family, 331
Akers, John, 13
Alberthal, Les, 257, 258
Alderfer, Clayton P., 371, 384, 661n, 665n
Alexander, Jeffrey A., 659n
Alexander, Judith W., 657n
Alexander, Suzanne, 105
Alexander the Great, 34
Alfarabi, 34
Allen, Jim, 72
Allen, Joseph, 666n
Allen, Robert E., 13
Alley, William J., 13
Alliger, George M., 663n
Alonso, Ramon L., 655n
Alster, Norm, 541, 658n, 668n
Amburgey, Terry L., 658n
Amerman, John, 453, 454
Anastasi, A., 669n
Anderson, Henry R., 673n
Anderson, Janet, 335
Anderson, Jerry W., Jr., 647n, 648n
Andrews, Bruce H., 247
Andrews, Kenneth R., 650n, 651n
Ansoff, H. Igor, 650n
Anthony, Robert N., 667n
Applegate, Lynda M., 670n
Archibald, Nolan, 445
Argyle, Michael, 665n
Armstrong, J. Scott, 655n
Armstrong, Larry, 533
Arnault, Bernard, 183
Arnold, Robert, 478

Aronoff, Craig E., 666n
Ashmos, Donde P., 645n
Auerbach, Red, 4
Aupperle, Kenneth E., 645n, 648n
Austin, Nancy, 666n

Babbage, Charles, 35–36, 644n
Baird, Inga S., 651n
Baird, Lloyd, 652n, 659n
Balachandra, R., 654n
Baldo, Anthony, 544
Baloff, Nicholas, 654n
Bannister, B.D., 663n
Barczak, Gloria, 658n
Barlett, Steve, 11
Barlow, Frank, 297
Barnard, Chester, 38, 40, 644n
Barnes, Zane E., 658n
Barnett, Carole K., 330
Barney, Jay B., 645n, 646n, 657n
Barrett, Paul M., 87
Barron, F.B., 669n
Bart, Christopher K., 673n
Bartimo, Jim, 557
Basadur, M., 669n
Baskin, Otis W., 666n
Bass, Bernard M., 663n, 664n
Bass, R.E., 645n
Bates, Tom, 602
Baxter, Guy, 203
Becker, Brian E., 661n
Beckhard, Richard, 659n
Bedeian, Arthur G., 656n, 665n
Beeman, Don R., 664n
Beer, Michael, 659n
Bell, Cecil H., Jr., 659n, 665n
Benetton family, 497
Benfari, Robert C., 663n, 672n
Benzo, Miguel, 583
Berger, Michael, 421
Berke, Matthew, 672n
Berss, Marcia, 330

Bertalanffy, Ludwig von, 645n
Bettis, Richard A., 646n, 651n
Beutschman, Alan, 657n
Bhagat, Rabi S., 649n
Binning, John F., 660n
Bird, Barbara, 671n
Birkigt, Holger U., 118
Birnbaum, Phyllis, 421
Blackburn, Richard S., 656n
Blackett, P.M.S., 45
Blair, John D., 646n
Blake, Robert R., 324, 659n, 663n
Blake, Stacy, 671n
Blanchard, Kenneth H., 664n
Bloom, Anthony H., 648n
Bloom, Michael, 669n
Boccitto, Elio, 135
Boeker, Warren, 651n, 658n
Bond, Michael Harris, 35
Bondurant, David, 669n
Bonsack, Robert, 668n
Booth, David E., 645n
Booth, I. MacAllister, 538
Borucki, Chet, 330
Boulton, Willliam R., 652n
Bove, Courtland L., 666n
Bowen, David, 659n
Bowen, Michael G., 654n
Bowen, William, 645n
Bradspies, Robert W., 667n
Brady, Rose, 497
Bragg, Daniel J., 668n
Brannigan, Martha, 267
Bray, Nicholas, 57
Brecht, Bill, 209
Breckenfield, Gurney, 646n
Bristow, Nigel J., 644n
Brody, Michael, 660n
Broedling, Laurie, 643n
Bromley, Philip, 654n
Brown, Abby, 648n, 660n
Brown, R.T., 669n

Brown, Rupert, 665n
Browning, E.S., 327
Browning, Larry D., 665n
Bruns, William J., Jr., 670n
Brunstedt, Solveig, 548
Buckley, M. Ronald, 660n
Buell, Barbara, 69
Bukszar, Ed, 654n
Bullen, Christine, 666n
Buller, Paul F., 665n
Burck, Charles G., 667n
Burke, Beverly G., 665n
Burlingham, Bo, 113
Burnham, David H., 661n
Burnham, Duane L., 13
Burns, James MacGregor, 664n
Burns, Robin, 529–530
Burns, Tom, 288–289, 647n, 657n
Burrough, Bryan, 561
Burt, H.E., 663n
Bush, George, 4
Busse, Thomas V., 669n
Butler, John E., 652n
Butler, Richard J., 653n
Bylinsky, Gene, 521, 668n

Cadbury, Adrian, Sir, 647n
Cagliari, Gabriele, 487
Caldwell, James C., 673n
Callahan, Madelyn R., 17
Calvert, Robert, Jr., 659n
Cameron, Kim S., 647n
Caminiti, Susan, 568
Cammann, Cortlandt, 492, 493, 667n
Campbell, Alta, 173, 183, 187, 198, 207, 215, 222, 223, 297, 307, 467, 643n, 644n, 650n, 653n, 654n, 655n, 659n, 664n, 669n, 670n
Campbell, Donald J., 660n
Campbell, Eva, 419
Campbell, Norman, 419
Campion, Michael A., 655n
Caples, Stephen, 651n
Cappelli, Peter, 660n
Carbone, Robert, 654n
Cardy, Robert L., 660n
Carlzon, Jan, 393, 395
Carnegie, Andrew, 31, 97
Carrell, Michael R., 660n

Carroll, Archie B., 647n–648n, 648n
Carroll, Glenn R., 672n
Carroll, Stephen J., 644n, 650n
Carter, Jimmy, 636
Cartwright, Dorwin, 664n
Cascio, Wayne F., 660n
Cash, James I., Jr., 670n
Castle, Douglas E., 652n
Castro, Janice, 405
Caudron, Shari, 594
Cawthorn, Robert, 206–207, 208, 211
Chai, Alan, 173, 207, 297
Chakravarthy, Balaji S., 650n, 651n
Chambers, John C., 655n
Chase, Richard B., 668n
Chemers, M.M., 663n
Chisholm, Michael, 671n
Chrisman, James J., 652n
Churchill, Winston, 31, 463
Cimino, Aldo, 565–566
Claiborne, Liz, 214
Clark, John, 652n
Coch, Lester, 658n
Cochran, Philip L., 648n
Cochran, Thomas N., 135
Cohen, Allan R., 662n
Cohn, Bob, 383
Cole, Robert E., 667n
Cole, Sam, 671n
Coleman, W.C., 86
Collazos, Luis Carlos, 583
Collins, Guy, 331
Collins, Paul D., 657n, 659n, 668n
Confucius, 35
Connolly, Terry, 654n
Conway, William E., 35, 503
Cooke, Stephanie, 281
Coons, A.E., 663n
Cooper, Arnold C., 672n
Cooper, Robin, 673n
Copeland, Lennie, 671n
Cornelius, E., 661n
Cosier, Richard A., 654n, 662n
Cotting, James C., 13
Courtney, James F., Jr., 566
Cox, James F., 668n
Cox, Taylor H., 592, 671n
Crawford, Bob, 443

Crawford-Mason, Clare, 503
Cray, David, 653n
Crosby, Philip B., 502
Cross, Dawn M., 579
Cross, William E., 670n
Cullen, John B., 647n
Culler, Nelson, 104
Cummings, Larry L., 645n
Cummins, Robert, 666n
Curie, Marie, 529
Curie, Pierre, 529
Curran, John J., 646n, 650n
Cushman, Jonathon, 27
Cyert, Richard M., 653n

Daft, Richard L., 655n, 656n, 657n, 666n
Dalton, Dan R., 656n, 662n
Daniel, Wayne W., 654n
Daniels, John D., 649n
Dansereau, Fred, 664n
Dassler, Adi, 327
Davenport, Carol, 649n, 652n
David, Fred, 152, 649n
Davidson, Wallace, N., III, 661n
Davis, Bill, 397
Davis, James H., 654n
Davis, Keith, 453, 666n
Davis, Ralph C., 268, 656n
Davis, Stanley M., 657n
Day, Charles K., Jr., 658n
Day, Charles R., Jr., 653n
Deal, Terrence E., 646n
Dearborn, D.C., 666n
DeGeorge, Gail, 496
DeGroot, Morris H., 653n
Delbecq, Andre L., 654n
Dell, Michael, 69
Deming, W. Edwards, 35, 502, 667n
DeNisi, Angelo S., 666n
Depke, Deidre A., 69
DePorras, Deborah Auld, 651n
DePree, Max, 112
Deresky, Helen, 652n
Deshpande, Rohit, 651n
Dess, Gregory G., 651n
Deutschman, Alan, 671n, 672n
De Vader, Christy L., 663n
Dickson, W.J., 661n
Diehl, Stanford, 521

Dienesch, Richard M., 664n
Dillard, Alex, 568
Di Primio, Anthony, 651n
Disney, Walt, 259
Dittrich, John E., 649n
Dobbins, Gregory H., 660n
Dobyns, Lloyd, 503
Dock, V. Thomas, 670n
Dodge, John M., 485
Doherty, Elizabeth M., 654n
Donaldson, Lex, 644n
Donovan, John J., 666n, 670n
Dorrance, John, 198
Douglas, Frederick, 529–530
Dowling, William F., 657n
Dozier, Janelle Brinker, 648n
Drazin, Robert, 657n
Drexler, Mickey, 68
Dreyfuss, Joel, 667n
Drucker, Peter F., 667n
D'Souza, Dinesh, 671n
Duck, Thomas S., 625
Duhaime, Irene M., 651n
Dumaine, Brian, 86, 306, 511,
    651n, 653n, 656n, 658n, 660n,
    662n, 664n, 665n, 666n, 667n,
    668n, 670n
Dunbar, Edward, 17
Duncan, R., 669n
Dunkelberg, William C., 672n
Dupin, Charles, 36
Dutt, James, 394
Dyer, William G., 659n

Eames, Rick, 437
Eason, Henry, 389
Ebert, Ronald J., 645n, 655n, 668n
Eder, Robert W., 660n
Edison, Thomas, 529
Egelhoff, William G., 653n, 658n
Eisenberg, Eric M., 666n
Ekeberg, Steven E., 662n
Elbing, Alvar, 653n
Elliott, Stuart, 533
Emerson, Harrington, 36, 37, 40
Emshwiller, John R., 327
Engledow, Jack L., 653n
Epstein, Edwin M., 648n
Erikson, Warren J., 668n
Ertel, Danny, 665n
Ettlie, J.E., 669n

Evans, Joe, 669n
Evans, Martin G., 403, 663n
Ezoe, Hiromasa, 94

Faludi, Susan C., 307
Farnham, Alan, 648n
Fayol, Henri, 38, 39, 40, 644n
Feder, Barnaby J., 95
Feigenbaum, Armand V., 502, 503
Feldman, Amy, 513
Feldman, Daniel C., 665n, 672n
Feldman, Steven P., 669n
Ferguson, Mark, 4
Fernandez, Joe, 23
Ferraiolo, Diane, 26
Fiedler, Fred E., 400–403, 663n
Fiedman, Abraham, 662n
Fiegenbaum, Avi, 653n
Field, Nora E., 414
Fielding, Gordon J., 656n
Fields, Debbie, 4, 625
Fields, Randy, 449
Fierman, Jaclyn, 647n, 650n, 671n,
    672n
Finch, Byron J., 668n
Fine, Marlene G., 670n
Fins, Antonio N., 267
Fiorito, Jack, 659n
Fisher, Anne B., 647n
Fisher, Cynthia D., 645n
Fisilier, Marcelline R., 664n
Fitzgerald, Thomas H., 658n
Fleishman, Edwin A., 663n
Follett, Mary Parker, 41
Ford, Henry, 259, 598
Ford, Robert, 655n
Forest, Stephanie Anderson, 69,
    557
Forgione, Joe, 213
Forman, Craig, 57, 561
Forte, Samuel, 597, 598, 602
Fossum, John A., 661n
Foster, Badi G., 670n
Foster, Geoffrey, 281
Foster, William K., 652n
Frank, Allan Dodds, 297
Fraser, Cline W., 655n
Fraser, Margot, 80
French, John R.P., Jr., 658n, 663n
French, Wendell L., 659n
Fried, Vance H., 652n

Friedman, Milton, 101
Friedrich, Otto, 668n
Fry, Louis W., 652n
Fujita, Den, 223

Gabarro, John J., 664n
Gadon, Herman, 662n
Gagnon, Christopher E., 668n
Gaither, Norman, 645n
Galbraith, Jay R., 194, 652n, 656n,
    657n
Galen, Michele, 339
Galgay, Patricia J., 649n
Galton, F., 669n
Gandz, Jeffrey, 664n
Gannes, Stuart, 652n, 654n, 665n,
    672n
Ganster, Daniel C., 664n
Gantt, Henry, 36, 37, 40, 45
Garcia, Mario F., 660n
García, Oscar, 251
Garrett, Thomas M., 92, 647n
Garrison, Sharon H., 661n
Garvin, David A., 501
Garza, Christina Elnora, 33
Gates, Bill, 222, 540
Gault, Stanley, 149
Geneen, Harold, 450
George, Dev, 487
Georgopoules, B.S., 647n
Gerloff, Edwin, 666n
Gershkoff, Ira, 250
Gersick, Connie J.G., 658n, 665n
Ghoshal, Sumantra, 667n
Gibson, Cyrus F., 669n
Gibson, W. David, 467
Gifford, Kathie Lee, 61
Gilbreath, Robert D., 650n
Gilbreth, Frank, 36, 37, 40
Gilbreth, Lillian, 36, 37, 40
Gillen, Dennis J., 644n
Gilly, Mary C., 670n
Gilmore, David C., 660n
Gilmour, Allan D., 658n
Gioia, Dennis A., 660n
Gist, Marilyn E., 664n
Givens, David, 666n
Glasgall, William, 319
Glaskowsky, Nicholas A., Jr.,
    655n
Gnadinger, Fred, 669n

Goizueta, Roberto, 159
Goldstein, Mel A., 660n
Goodman, Paul S., 662n
Goodstein, Jerry, 658n
Goozner, Merrill, 513
Gorbachev, Mikhail, 27, 369
Gordon, Roddick, 113
Gorr, Wilpen, 654n
Gough, H.G., 669n
Govindarajan, Vijay, 667n
Graen, George B., 664n, 669n
Graham, Katharine, 14
Graicunas, A.V., 267–268, 656n
Granrose, Cherlyn Skromme, 673n
Grant, Jan, 673n
Graven, Kathryn, 561
Graves, Allene, 603
Green, Stephen G., 667n, 669n
Greene, Robert J., 660n
Greenhalgh, Leonard, 659n–660n
Griffin, Ricky W., 35, 645n, 655n, 664n, 669n
Grim, Don, 478
Grogan, Barbara, 268
Grove, Andrew, 31
Grush, Joseph E., 662n
Gubernick, Lisa, 617
Gupta, Anil K., 651n, 667n
Gupta, Udayan, 603
Gustafson, David H., 654n
Guth, William D., 651n
Guthrie, William, 602
Guzzard, Walter, 293, 667n
Guzzo, Richard A., 664n

Haber, Fritz, 467
Hackman, J. Richard, 262, 655n
Haga, W.J., 664n
Hage, Jerald, 659n, 668n
Hahn, Chan K., 668n
Hall, Douglas T., 624, 672n, 673n
Hall, Edward J., 666n
Hambrick, Donald C., 650n
Hamilton, Ian, 268, 656n
Hammond, Mike, 485
Hammonds, Keith H., 163, 222
Hamner, Ellen P., 662n
Hamner, W. Clay, 662n
Hampton, William J., 359
Hannan, Edward, 655n

Hanrahan, Keith, 335
Hardiman, Rita, 670n
Harper, Charles, 172
Harrington, D.M., 669n
Harris, Diane, 123
Harris, E.F., 663n
Harris, Hollis, 49
Harrison, E. Frank, 653n
Hart, David K., 643n
Hart, Jan, 11
Hartke, Darrell D., 663n
Hartley, Robert F., 669n
Hater, John J., 664n
Hatfield, John D., 648n, 662n
Hayes, Robert H., 646n, 658n
Healey, James R., 440
Hector, Gary, 388, 650n
Hedge, Jerry W., 660n
Hellerman, Myrna, 454
Hellervik, Lowell, 660n
Helper, Susan, 646n
Hempel, C.G., 645n
Henderson, Monika, 665n
Henkoff, Ronald, 594, 650n, 667n
Herbert, Theodore T., 652n
Hersey, Paul, 664n
Herzberg, Frederick, 371–373, 384, 655n, 661n
Hewlett, Bill, 19, 74
Hickson, David J., 653n, 657n
Higgins, James H., 651n
Hilder, David B., 319
Hill, Anita, 339
Hill, Charles W.L., 649n, 650n, 651n, 652n, 657n, 666n
Hill, Kenneth D., 643n
Hill, Steve, 620
Hills, Frederick S., 662n
Hilts, Philip J., 95
Hitt, Michael A., 645n, 646n–647n, 651n, 657n
Hodgetts, Richard M., 672n
Hofer, Charles W., 651n, 652n
Hoffman, David L., 462
Hoffman, Thomas, 569
Hofheinz, Paul, 27
Hofstede, Geert, 35
Holstein, William J., 603
Homer, 31
Hooper, Laurence, 306
Hoover, Gary, 163, 173, 187, 198,

207, 215, 222, 223, 297, 307, 467, 643n, 644n, 650n, 653n, 654n, 655n, 659n, 664n, 669n, 670n
Hopkins, H. Donald, 650n
Horton, Robert B., 462, 463
Hosking, D., 663n
Hoskisson, Robert E., 651n, 657n
Houghton, James, 14
House, Robert J., 403, 661n, 663n
Hower, Roger J., 659n
Huber, George P., 645n, 653n
Hudson, Donald R., 655n
Huey, John, 33, 405, 647n, 650n, 665n, 670n, 673n
Huizenga, H. Wayne, 496, 599
Hull, Frank M., 657n, 659n, 668n
Hunger, J. David, 650n
Hunt, J.B., 8, 9
Hunt, Walter S., 656n
Hunter, John E., 660n
Hurley, Dan, 672n
Huseman, Richard C., 662n, 666n
Hymowitz, Carol, 568

Iacocca, Lee, 51, 410, 529–530, 669n
Inamori, Kazuo, 521
Ireland, R. Duane, 645n, 651n
Itoh, Uichi, 541
Iverson, F. Kenneth, 486
Ivey, Mark, 172

Jackson, Bailey, 670n
Jackson, Gerald, 670n
Jackson, Susan E., 652n
Jacobs, Klaus, 513
Jacquard, Joseph Marie, 525
Jago, Arthur G., 404–407, 662n, 663n
Jaikumar, Ramchandran, 646n, 658n
James, Robert M., 650n–651n
Janis, Irving L., 654n
Janz, Tom, 660n
Jarrillo-Mossi, José Carlos, 672n
Jelinek, Mariann, 673n
Jermier, John M., 664n
Jobs, Steven, 194, 228, 315, 538, 599
Johansen, Robert, 666n

John Paul II, Pope, 4
Johnson, David, 198
Johnson, Fern L., 670n
Johnson, Maryfran, 569
Johnson, Ross, 667n
Jonas, H., 645n
Jones, David C., 26
Jones, Gareth R., 649n, 650n, 651n, 652n, 657n
Jones, Jack William, 653n
Jones, Steven D., 649n
Jones, Thomas M., 647n, 654n
Jordan, Michael, 163
Judge, William Q., 653n
Juran, Joseph M., 502–503

Kahn, Robert L., 665n
Kampf, Serge, 621
Kane, Louis, 385
Kanter, Rosabeth Moss, 643n
Kantrow, Alan M., 644n
Kaplan, Robert S., 673n
Kapor, Mitch, 222
Kast, Fremont E., 645n, 656n
Katayama, Hiroko, 83
Katcher, Allan, 17
Katz, David, 665n
Katz, Michael, 330
Katz, Robert L., 643n
Kavanagh, Michael J., 660n
Kazanjian, Robert K., 194, 652n, 657n
Keats, Barbara W., 646n–647n, 657n
Kedia, Ben L., 649n
Kee Jim, 457
Kelleher, Herbert, 3, 4, 7, 11, 12, 15–16, 21, 409
Kelly, Dawn, 658n
Kendrick, John W., 667n
Kennedy, Allan A., 646n
Keon, Thomas L., 662n
Kerlinger, Fred, 655n
Kerr, Jeffrey, 646n
Kerr, Steven, 643n, 664n
Kesner, Idalene F., 646n
Keys, Bernard, 660n
Kiechel, Walter, III, 339, 651n, 660n, 665n, 666n, 671n, 672n
Kiko, Princess, 83

Kilbridge, M.D., 655n
Kim Woo-Choong, 415
King, Resa W., 56
Kinnear, James, 4
Kinzel, Richard, 617
Kirkland, Richard I., Jr., 583, 646n, 650n
Kirkpatrick, David, 670n
Kirkpatrick, Shelley A., 663n
Klein, Janice A., 643n
Klonoski, Richard J., 92, 647n
Knight, Charles, 341
Knowlton, Christopher, 648n
Knowlton, Thomas A., 118
Koberg, Christine S., 657n
Koerner, Elaine M., 561
Kohler-Gray, Susan, 591
Koloday, Harvey F., 657n
Kondrasuk, Jack N., 650n
Koontz, Harold, 667n
Kotter, John P., 658n, 662n
Kraar, Louis, 649n, 668n
Kram, Kathy E., 672n
Kramm, Judith B., 652n
Kreitner, Robert, 662n
Kroger, Joseph, 213
Kroll, Mark, 651n
Kruse family, 620
Kuenheim, Eberhard von, 408
Kuhnert, Karl W., 664n
Kunz, Ruben, 104
Kupfer, Andrew, 17, 414, 485, 643n
Kuratko, Donald F., 672n
Kuzmits, Frank E., 660n
Kvint, Vladimir, 27, 369

Labate, John, 649n
Labich, Kenneth, 56, 395, 569, 643n, 653n, 658n, 664n, 669n, 672n
Lachman, Ran, 644n
Lake, Dale, 652n
Lane, F., 661n
Langbo, Arnold G., 118
Latack, Jania C., 662n
Latham, Gary P., 654n
Lawler, Edward E., III, 377, 656n, 660n, 661n, 662n, 667n
Lawrence, Anne T., 659n–660n

Lawrence, Paul R., 291, 306, 645n, 656n, 657n, 658n
Leana, Carrie R., 656n
Leavitt, Harold J., 658n
Ledford, Gerald, Jr., 659n
Lee, Andrea, 497
Lee, Cynthia, 660n
Lei, David, 650n
Leitko, Thomas A., 657n
Lengel, Robert H., 666n
Lengnick-Hall, Cynthia A., 652n, 659n
Lengnick-Hall, Mark L., 652n, 659n
Lenway, Stefanie Ann, 664n
Lenz, R.T., 651n, 653n
Leonard-Barton, Dorothy, 655n, 670n
Levering, Robert, 330
Lewin, Arie Y., 647n
Lewin, Kurt, 312–313, 658n
Lewis, Linda, 621
Lewis, Philip, 664n
Lewis, Reginald F., 628
Liden, Robert C., 664n
Lientz, Bennett P., 666n
Likert, Rensis, 286–288, 397–398, 657n, 663n
Litzinger, William D., 647n
Lloyd, Edward, 57
Lobel, Sharon A., 671n
Locke, Edwin A., 644n, 654n, 662n, 663n, 664n
Lombardi, Vince, 615
Longnecker, Clinton O., 660n
Loomis, Carol J., 26, 658n
Lorange, Peter, 650n, 653n, 667n
Lord, Robert G., 663n
Lorsch, Jay W., 291, 656n, 657n, 669n
Low, Murray B., 671n
Lublin, Joann S., 665n
Lubove, Seth, 135
Luthans, Fred, 643n, 662n

Ma, Michael, 529
McCallum, Daniel, 36
McCanse, Anne Adams, 324, 659n
McCarthy, Michael J., 215, 496
McCarver, Tim, 584

McCaskey, Michael B., 666n
McClelland, David C., 373, 661n
Maccoby, Michael, 395
McCormick, Cyrus, 330
McEnrue, Mary Pat, 672n
McFarlin, F. Warren, 670n
McGrath, Judy, 7
McGregor, Douglas, 42, 43, 44
McGuire, Jean B., 648n
Machalaba, Daniel, 9
Machiavelli, 31
Mack, Toni, 620
McKenna, Regis, 646n, 652n
McLain, Mike, 203
McLean, Vincent, 213
McLennan, 659n
McLeod, Poppy Lauretta, 671n
McMahan, Gary, 659n
McManus, Robert F., 457
MacMillan, Ian C., 646n, 647n, 651n, 671n
McNealy, Scott, 201, 202
McWilliams, Gary, 222, 591
Magenau, John M., 661n
Magnet, Myron, 666n
Maier, Norman P.R., 654n
Main, Jeremy, 141, 281, 646n, 648n, 651n, 653n, 657n, 670n, 672n
Maital, Shlomo, 545
Mallory, Geoffrey R., 653n
Mandell, Barbara, 591
Maney, Kevin, 369
Manley, Bruce R., 251
Mansfield, Richard S., 669n
Manz, Charles C., 664n
Manzi, Jim, 222
March, James G., 653n
Marcom, John, Jr., 155, 207, 395, 621
Markham, Steven E., 662n
Markland, Robert E., 655n
Markowski, Carol, 655n
Markowski, Edward, 655n
Marks, Michael, 207
Marks, Reuben, 626
Marram, Ellen, 623, 624
Marriott, Bill, Jr., 453
Marsh, Barbara, 603
Marsten, Roy E., 250

Martin, Harold, 179
Martin, James E., 661n
Martinez, Zaida, 648n–649n
Maslow, Abraham H., 42, 43, 44, 368–371, 384, 645n, 661n
Mason, Todd, 389
Mastenbroek, William, 659n
Maxwell, Robert, 135
Mayer, Robert J., 652n
Mayes, Bronston T., 664n
Maynard, Micheline, 271
Mayo, Elton, 41, 44, 49, 367, 644n, 661n
McGregor, Douglas, 645n
Mecherle, George, 26
Mehrabian, Albert, 666n
Melcher, Richard A., 27, 57
Menzies, Hugh D., 663n
Meredith, Jack R., 652n
Meshoulam, Ilan, 652n, 659n
Meyer, John, 656n
Miceli, Marcia P., 648n
Michaels, Susan, 609
Mikimoto, Kokichi, 83
Milbank, Dana, 33
Miles, Edward W., 662n, 666n
Miles, Raymond E., 652n
Miles, Robert H., 657n
Miller, Alex, 653n
Miller, Cyndee, 455
Miller, Danny, 647n, 652n, 653n
Miller, David W., 653n
Miller, Edwin L., 646n, 648n
Miller, Eric, 466
Miller, James P., 389
Miller, Karen Lowry, 441, 595
Miller, Kent D., 654n
Miller, Lynn E., 662n
Milligan, John W., 388
Milliman, John, 660n
Mills, D. Quinn, 670n
Minami, Kazumitsu, 389
Mindell, Mark G., 659n
Miner, Anne S., 655n
Minton, John W., 647n
Mintzberg, Henry, 16–19, 448, 643n, 649n, 650n–651n, 665n
Mita, Katsushige, 389
Mitchell, Jacqueline, 199

Mitchell, Terrence R., 661n–662n, 663n
Mitroff, Ian I., 78, 646n
Moffat, Susan, 87, 541, 545
Moffett, Richard G., 665n
Mohr, L.B., 669n
Mohrman, Allan, 660n
Montana, Joe, 432
Montgomery, Cynthia A., 650n
Moore, Thomas, 656n, 666n
Moorhead, Gregory, 645n, 664n
Morais, Richard C., 297
Morgan, J.P., 97
Morgenson, Gretchen, 568
Morohashi, Shinroku, 4
Morrison, Allen J., 649n
Morse, David, 531–532
Morton, Michael F. Scott, 653n, 667n
Mosakowski, Elaine, 672n
Moskowitz, Milton, 330
Mouton, Jane Srygley, 659n, 663n
Mowday, Richard T., 662n
Mozart, Wolfgang, 529
Muczyk, Jan P., 663n
Mullick, S.K., 655n
Munsterberg, Hugo, 41, 43, 644n
Murdoch, Rupert, 297
Murray, Alan I., 652n
Murray, Victor, 664n

Nader, Ralph, 70
Nadler, David A., 492, 493, 658n, 661n, 667n
Nakarmi, Laxmi, 415
Nasar, Sylvia, 668n
Nathan, Barry R., 659n, 660n
Near, James, 13
Near, Janet P., 648n
Needles, Belverd E., Jr., 673n
Neff, Robert, 223, 343
Nelson-Horchler, Joani, 112
Nemetz, Patricia L., 652n
Neubert, Ralph L., 648n
Neuborne, Ellen, 496
Newport, John Paul, Jr., 649n
Newstrom, John W., 453
Nicholas, John M., 659n
Nix, Timothy W., 646n
Noe, Raymond A., 672n

Norton, Bob, 20, 646n
Novak, William, 669n
Nulty, Peter, 222, 435, 463

Oakley, Annie, 617
O'Boyle, Thomas F., 568
Ohmae, Kenichi, 649n
Oldham, Greg R., 262, 655n
Oliver, Suzanne L., 544
Olivier, Maurice J., 27
O'Malley, Susan, 392
O'Neill, Bill, 343
O'Neill, Paul, 280
Ono, Yumiko, 421, 595
O'Reilly, Anthony F.J., 175, 176–177
O'Reilly, Brian, 666n
O'Reilly, Charles A., III, 653n, 670n
Orr, Julian, 33
Orth, Charles D., 663n, 672n
Osher, Herb, 213
Ostrom, Charles, 655n
Ouchi, William G., 51, 74, 645n, 646n, 657n, 667n, 669n
Overman, Stephenie, 671n
Oviatt, Benjamin M., 652n
Owen, Robert, 34–35
Owens, Eugene, 665n

Packard, David, 19, 74
Palmer, Alexa, 609
Paradice, David B., 566
Parasuraman, A., 651n
Parsons, Henry, 247
Pasemore, William, 658n, 659n
Patterson, Gregory A., 359, 520
Patz, Alan, 669n
Pearce, John A., II, 152, 649n
Pearce, John A., III, 651n
Pearl, Daniel, 56
Pearson, Samuel, 297
Pearson, Weetman, 297
Pedhazur, Elazar, 655n
Peiperl, Maury A., 652n
Penney, James Cash, 73
Pereira, Joseph, 87
Perot, H. Ross, 257, 258, 273, 437, 457
Perroni, Amedeo G., 644n

Perry, James L., 643n–644n, 656n–657n
Perry, Nancy J., 173, 648n, 649n, 661n, 662n
Peters, Lawrence H., 663n
Peters, Thomas J., 52, 74, 645n, 646n, 666n
Peters, Tom, 645n
Peterson, Donald, 623
Peterson, Melanie M., 661n
Pfeffer, Jeffrey, 644n, 664n
Phatak, Arvind, 649n
Phillips, Lawrence, 312
Pickens, T. Boone, 155
Pinchot, Gifford, III, 669n
Pinder, Craig, 661n
Plato, 31, 34
Plumlee, E. Leroy, 665n
Podsakoff, Philip M., 663n
Pohlmann, John T., 663n
Poole, Claire, 69
Poor, Henry, 36
Port, Otis, 389
Porter, Linda, 446–447
Porter, Lyman W., 377, 656n, 661n
Porter, Michael E., 76–77, 187–188, 296, 646n, 649n, 650n, 652n, 657n
Portwood, James D., 673n
Prietula, Michael J., 654n
Pritchard, Beth, 195
Pritchard, Robert D., 649n
Pryor, Austin K., 652n
Pugh, Derek S., 657n
Pulley, Brett, 187
Pyhrr, Peter, 673n

Quinn, James Brian, 650n–651n, 668n
Quinn, Phil, 247
Quinn, R.P., 665n

Racamier, Henry, 183
Radebaugh, Lee H., 649n
Raia, A.P., 650n
Rainey, Hal G., 643n–644n, 656n–657n
Ramanujam, Vasudevan, 650n
Randall, Donna M., 665n

Randolph, W. Alan, 657n
Rapoport, Carla, 155, 649n, 650n, 670n
Raven, Bertram, 663n
Reagan, Ronald, 339
Reed, John, 532
Regan, Julie, 449
Rehbein, Kathleen, 664n
Reier, Sharon, 297
Reimann, Bernard C., 663n
Resnick, Stewart, 269
Reynolds, George W., 670n
Rhode, John G., 667n
Rice, Faye, 83, 455, 463, 665n, 672n
Richards, Max D., 649n
Richman, Louis S., 671n
Ricks, David A., 648n–649n, 649n
Ritter, Cynthia, 203
Robbins, D. Keith, 651n
Robinson, David, 432
Robinson, Richard B., Jr., 651n
Rockefeller, John D., 31, 97, 617
Rockne, Knute, 617
Roddick, Anita, 113
Rodgers, Thurman John, 301, 302, 391, 392, 436
Roebuck, Alvah, 608
Rogers, Peter, 513
Roh Tae-Woo, 416
Roman, Monica, 544
Roosevelt, Franklin, 97
Rose, Frank, 33
Rosenberg, Richard, 388
Rosenfield, Ira, 9
Rosenthal, R.A., 665n
Rosenzweig, James E., 645n, 656n
Rosenzweig, Philip M., 646n, 649n
Ross, Ian M., 31
Ross, Jerry, 654n
Rossant, John, 331, 487
Roth, Kendall, 649n
Roth, Philip L., 649n
Roth, Terence, 327
Rothfeder, Jeffrey, 557
Rothlisberger, Fritz J., 661n
Rubin, Barry Louis, 583
Rubin, Jerrold, 250
Russo, Michael V., 657n
Rust, Ed, Jr., 26

Ryan, Linda, 655n
Ryan, M. Sallyanne, 670n
Ryan, Nolan, 432
Rynes, Sara L., 660n

Sackett, Paul R., 660n
Saddler, Jeanne, 603
Saito, Toshiaki, 441
Saporito, Bill, 123, 198, 293, 650n,
    651n, 654n
Saunders, Carol, 653n
Savage, Grant T., 646n
Sawyer, John, 669n
Scattaregia, Julie H., 660n
Schaefer, C.E., 669n
Schaefer, Thomas E., 647n
Scheier, Robert L., 485
Schein, Edgar H., 672n
Schendel, Dan, 651n
Scherr, Frederick C., 656n
Schine, Eric, 455
Schlender, Brenton R., 668n
Schlesinger, Leonard A., 643n,
    658n
Schmidt, Frank L., 660n
Schmidt, Warren H., 399–400,
    663n
Schmitt, Neal, 660n
Schneeweis, Thomas, 648n
Schneidawind, John, 222
Schoenfeldt, Lyle, 669n
Schrank, Robert, 664n
Schreyogg, Georg, 667n
Schriesheim, Chester A., 663n
Schroeder, Michael, 105, 280
Schuler, Randall S., 652n
Schultz, George, 307
Schwadel, Francine, 358
Schweiger, David M., 654n,
    666n
Schwenk, Charles R., 654n
Scott, K. Dow, 662n
Scott, W. Richard, 656n
Scott, William G., 643n, 644n
Sculley, John, 194, 315, 410
Sears, Richard, 608
Seashore, S., 647n
Sebouie, Mohamed, 478
Seeger, John A., 669n
Seitler, Harriet, 7

Sella, George, 218
Sellers, Patricia, 643n, 647n, 658n,
    662n
Selz, Michael, 86
Sepehri, 668n
Shaich, Ron, 385
Shapira, Zur, 653n
Sharkey, Thomas W., 664n
Shaw, Marvin E., 654n, 664n–
    665n
Shea, Gregory P., 664n
Sheil, Beau, 655n
Shepardson, Fred, 250
Sherman, Stratford P., 653n
Shewhart, Walter A., 35, 502
Shin, Dongwook, 668n
Shrivastava, Paul, 78, 646n
Simison, Robert L., 331
Simmons, Donna L., 659n
Simon, Herbert A., 212, 654n,
    666n
Simonton, D.K., 669n
Sims, Henry P., Jr., 660n, 664n
Sinetar, Marsha, 646n
Singh, B., 669n
Singh, Jitendra V., 646n, 649n,
    653n
Singh, Ramadhar, 663n
Siropolis, Nicholas C., 606, 612,
    671n, 672n
Skinner, B.F., 379, 662n
Slingo, Mabel de, 104
Smith, Adam, 259, 655n
Smith, Charles, 658n
Smith, D., 655n
Smith, Frederick, 167, 417
Smith, Page, 643n, 644n
Sneed, Mary Catherine, 353
Snoek, J.D., 665n
Snow, Charles C., 652n
Socrates, 34
Solomon, Barbara, 123
Sonnenfeld, Jeffrey A., 652n
Spain, Patrick J., 173, 183, 187,
    198, 207, 215, 222, 223, 297,
    307, 467, 643n, 644n, 650n,
    653n, 654n, 655n, 659n, 664n,
    669n, 670n
Spendolini, Michael J., 656n
Spinella, Arthur M., 229

Stalker, G.M., 288–289, 647n,
    657n
Starr, Martin K., 653n
Staw, Barry M., 645n, 654n
Steers, Richard M., 646n, 648n,
    661n
Stein, J. Dieter, 467
Steiner, George A., 649n, 669n
Steinmann, Horst, 667n
Steinway, Michael, 609
Stertz, Bradley A., 520
Stevenson, Howard H., 672n
Stevenson, William B., 670n
Stewart, Rosemary, 643n
Stewart, Thomas A., 140, 280,
    643n, 670n
Stiritz, William P., 13
Stogdill, Ralph M., 663n
Stoka, Ann Marie, 644n
Stone, Thomas H., 659n
Strang, David, 656n
Stroup, Margaret A., 648n
Sugiura, Hideo, 199
Sullivan, Jeremiah J., 645n, 661n
Sundgren, Alison, 648n
Suszko, Mary K., 660n
Sutton, Robert I., 659n–660n
Sviokla, John J., 655n, 670n
Swamidass, Paul M., 668n
Swartz, Laquita S., 381
Swisher, C. Kevin, 620
Symonds, William C., 668n–669n
Szczerbacki, David, 657n

Tannenbaum, A.S., 647n
Tannenbaum, Robert, 399–400,
    663n
Tapie, Bernard, 327
Taylor, Alex, III, 199, 271, 643n,
    657n
Taylor, Frederick W., 36–37, 40,
    45, 49, 367, 643n, 644n, 661n
Taylor, M. Susan, 664n
Teets, John W., 13
Teitelman, Robert, 544
Teresko, John, 435
Therrien, Lois, 172
Thill, John V., 666n
Thomas, Clarence, 338, 339
Thomas, Howard, 653n

Thompson, James D., 75, 646n, 656n
Thompson, Kirk, 9
Threadgill, John A., 251
Todor, William D., 656n
Tosi, Henry L., 650n
Toy, Stewart, 183
Toyne, Brian, 648n–649n
Toyoda, Kiichiro, 229
Toyoda, Shoichiro, 271
Trachtenberg, Jeffrey A., 123
Travolta, John, 535
Treece, James B., 441
Trevino, Linda Klebe, 647n
Treybig, Jim, 457
Truxillo, Donald M., 660n
Tubbs, Mark E., 662n
Turner, Ted, 215, 216
Tutor, Jesse B., Jr., 670n
Twomey, Daniel, 656n
Twomey, David P., 659n

Udwadia, Firdaus E., 78, 646n
Ueberroth, Peter, 327
Ulrich, Dave, 652n
Ungson, Geraldo R., 657n
Ure, Andrew, 36
Ursprung, Cecil, 615
Urwick, Lyndall F., 38, 40, 268, 656n
Uttal, Bro, 667n

Vanderbilt, Cornelius, 31, 32, 97
Van de Ven, Andrew H., 654n
Van Fleet, David D., 35, 656n
Van Gunsteren, Lex A., 652n
Van Orden, Richard, 655n
Vavelas, A., 666n
Venkatraman, N., 650n
Ventres, Romeo, 486
Vest, Michael J., 662n
Victor, Bart, 647n, 656n
Vincze, Julian W., 651n
Vogel, Todd, 56, 569
Vroom, Victor H., 374–375, 404–407, 661n, 663n
Vuitton, Louis, 183

Wada, Kazuo, 91
Wagner, Harold A., 166
Waitt, Ted, 485
Waldman, Peter, 215
Walker, Barbara A., 591
Walsh, Michael, 414
Walter, D. Bruce, 462
Walton, Richard E., 667n
Walton, Sam, 20, 405, 565
Wanous, John P., 662n
Warhol, Andy, 198
Wartick, Steven L., 648n
Waterman, Robert H., Jr., 52, 74, 645n, 646n
Watson, Bill, 664n
Watson, Margaret D., 649n
Watt, James, 524–525
Watts, Patti, 671n
Wayans, Keenan Ivory, 18
Weber, Caroline L., 660n
Weber, Max, 38, 40, 285–286, 644n, 656n
Weed, Earl D., 662n
Weick, Karl E., 665n
Weihrich, Heinz, 651n
Weinberger, Caspar, 307
Weis, Richard M., 644n
Weiss, A., 669n
Weitz, Barton A., 672n
Welch, Jack, 8, 9, 10, 21, 82, 202–203, 204, 410
Wellemeyer, Marilyn, 644n
Welsh, M. Ann, 667n
Welty, Gus, 9
Wetherbe, James C., 670n
Wheelon, Thomas L., 650n
Whenmouth, Edwin, 343
White, John, 316
White, Joseph B., 271
Whitehead, Carlton J., 646n
Whitely, William, 643n, 672n
Whitsett, David A., 644n
Whitwam, David R., 96
Whyte, Glen, 653n
Wigdor, Lawrence A., 661n
Wilemon, David, 658n
Wiley, Donna L., 665n
Wilkins, Alan L., 644n

Wilkinson, Harry E., 663n, 672n
Williams, Jennifer, 665n
Williams, Monci Jo, 645n, 672n
Williamson, Oliver E., 294, 657n
Wilson, David C., 4, 653n
Wilson, Doug, 533
Winchell, William O., 667n
Winger, Richard W., 497
Witten, Marsha G., 666n
Wofford, Jerry, 666n
Wolfe, D.M., 665n
Wolfe, Joseph, 660n
Wolfensberger, Beth, 669n
Woodman, Richard W., 658n, 659n, 669n
Woodruff, David, 112, 140, 440, 520
Woodward, Joan, 288–289, 524, 657n, 668n
Worrell, Dan L., 661n
Worthy, Ford S., 643n, 673n
Worthy, James C., 656n
Wozniak, Steve, 538
Wrege, Charles D., 644n
Wren, Daniel, 644n, 645n
Wright, Patrick, 659n
Wrigley, William, Jr., 187
Wriston, Walter, 625
Wszola, Stan, 521

Yamaguchi, Takahiro, 421
Yang, Dori Jones, 141
Yasai-Ardekani, Masoud, 657n
Yeltsin, Boris, 27
Yetton, Philip H., 404–407, 663n
Yoda, Junko, 581
Yoder, Stephen Kreider, 389
Yoffie, David B., 647n
Yon, Eugene T., 651n
Yorks, Lyle, 644n
Yuchtman, E., 647n
Yukl, Gary A., 662n, 663n, 664n

Zachary, G. Pascal, 307
Zahn, Paula, 584
Zakon, Alan, 497
Zander, Alvin, 664n
Zimmerman, Michael R., 485
Zinn, Laura, 113

Organization and Product Index

Abbott Laboratories, 13
ABC
  control at, 482
  decision making at, 214
Abercrombie & Fitch, 283
Adidas AG, 68, 163
  decision making at, 214
  revitalization at, 327
Aetna Life and Casualty Co., 386
Airborne Express, 417
Airbus Industrie, 141
Air Products, 166
Alcoa (Aluminum Company of
  America), 169
  incentive systems at, 386
  organization structure at, 280
  social responsibility at, 105
Allegheny International Inc.,
  98–99
Allen-Bradley, 508
Allied-Signal Inc., 353
Aluminum Company of America,
  see Alcoa
Amadeus Global Travel Distribu-
  tion, 583
AMAX, 152
American Airlines, Inc., 76, 116,
  245, 325
  information system at, 562
  operations management at, 509
  scheduling decisions at, 250
American Arbitration Association,
  354
American Brands, Inc., 13
American Cyanamid Co., 260, 299
  decision making at, 218
American Express Company, 48,
  116
  control at, 490
  goals of, 153

quality at, 504
  social responsibility at, 102
American Home Products Corp.,
  211
American Society for Quality Control, 500
American Telephone & Telegraph
  Co., see AT&T
Andersen Consulting, 558
Anheuser-Busch, Inc., 557
  alcohol awareness education
  and, 94
Answer Temps, The, (TAT), 603
A&P, 68
  expectancy theory at, 377
Apple Computer, Inc., 16, 69,
  201, 599
  conflict at, 437
  group activities at, 424
  innovation at, 535
  leadership at, 194, 410
  organization change at, 315
  organization design at, 303
  quality at, 501
ARCO, 382
Ashland Oil, Inc., 100
  environment and, 100
  social responsibility at, 103, 104
Associated Press, 482
Atari Corp., 74
Atlanta Braves, 430
Atlantic Richfield Co., 108
AT&T, 13, 30, 71, 80, 261, 311,
  611
  acquisition by, 210
  assessment center at, 344
  career-planning programs used
  by, 626
  human resources management
  at, 336

job enrichment at, 261
  mentor programs at, 626
  organization change at, 316
  technology at, 504
AT&T Bell Laboratories, 31
Au Bon Pain, 385
Avis, 510
Avon Products, Inc., 52, 83
  cultural diversity at, 575, 576,
  585, 588
  resistance to change at, 165–166
  strategy at, 182

Baker-Hughes, Incorporated, 265
Ball, 75
Bang and Olufsen, 120
BankAmerica Corp., 245
  career-planning programs at,
  626
  motivation at, 388
Bank of New England Corp., 45,
  319
Banquet, 172
BASF Corporation, 467
Bavarian Motor Works, see BMW
Bean, L.L., 245, 247
Beatrice Company, 628
  coercive power at, 394
Bechtel, 307
Beecham Group, The, 437
Beech-Nut
  ethics at, 93
  social responsibility at, 103, 104,
  109
Bell Atlantic, 40
Bell Laboratories
  mentor programs at, 626
  quality at, 502
Bendel, Henri, 283

Benetton Group SPA
  automation at, 526
  computer-aided design at, 526
  control at, 497
  distribution at, 511
Berlitz International, 135
Bethlehem Steel Corp., 36, 37, 260, 509
  quality at, 507
Bic, 188
Birkenstock Footprint Sandals, Inc., 80
Black & Decker Corp., 30, 161, 169
  communication at, 445, 455
  information system at, 560
Blockbuster Entertainment Corp., 599
  control at, 496
  initial paths taken by, 599
Blue Bell Creameries, 620
BMW, 408, 533
  decision making at, 209
  differentiation strategy at, 188
Body Shop International, 113
Boeing Co., The, 20, 22, 66, 76, 77, 116, 156, 169
  decision making at, 217
  ethics training programs at, 94
  layout at, 513–514
  product life cycle and, 189–190
  the 777 and international business, 141
Boise-Cascade, 518
Bombay Co., 473
  control at, 473, 474, 476, 477, 482
  planning at, 477
Bonfire of the Vanities, 534
Borden, Inc., 30
  control at, 486–487
  organizational size and, 293
Boston Consulting Group, 183
Boussac, 183
Brach, E.J., Corp., 513
Breakers hotel, 617
Breck shampoo, 181
Brenham Creamery Company, 620
Bristol-Myers, 544
British Museum, 4

British Petroleum Co. p.l.c., 22, 53
  communication at, 463
Brook Furniture Rental, 443, 444
Brooklyn Bottling, 466
Brooks Brothers, 207
  technology at, 289
Browning-Ferris Industries, 397
Broyhill, 509
BSN, 331
Burlington Industries, 461
Burlington Northern Inc., 278
Burroughs Wellcome Co., 213
Business Week, 70

Cable News Network, 215
Cadbury Schweppes, 160
Cadillac, 501, 520, 553
  control at, 488
Campbell Soup Company, 78, 172
  expert system at, 565–566
  focus strategy at, 188
  strategy at, 198
Canon, 538
Carnation Company, 71, 121, 134
Carnival Cruise Lines, Inc., 68, 81
  case on, 61, 62
Cartier, Inc., 83
Caterpillar Inc., 22, 116, 156, 169
  job design at, 258
  organization development at, 322
  productivity at, 508
  reactive change at, 311–312, 313, 316
CBS, 22, 215
  administrative intensity at, 278
  board of directors at, 156
  control at, 482
  cultural diversity at, 584
CBS Records, 173
Cedar Fair, 617
Celica, 529
Center for the Study of Responsive Law, 70
Central and South West Corp., 322
Century 21 Real Estate Corporation, 22
Cereal Partners Worldwide (CPW), 115, 120

Challenger, 219
Champion Spark Plug Company, 488, 489
Chap Stick, 210
Chase Manhattan Bank, N.A., The, 22, 299
Cheerios, 115
Chemical Bank, 93, 319
  organization change at, 319
Chevrolet, 116, 133, 191
  control at, 491
Chevron Corporation, 27, 101
Chips Ahoy, 189
Chiquita Bananas, 127
Chrysler Corp., 45, 48, 68, 353, 359, 517
  control at, 490
  creativity at, 530
  Japanese auto industry and, 212
  leadership at, 410
  organization change at, 318
  quality at, 501
  robots at, 527
  teams at, 440
CIGNA, 325
Cincinnati Milacron, 435
Citibank N.A., 245, 299, 625
  creativity at, 532
Citicorp, 22, 245, 319, 388
  international operations at, 118–119
  planning at, 167
  recruiting at, 343
Claiborne, Liz, Inc., 292
  decision making at, 214
  initial paths taken by, 599
  as success, 604
Clayton Environmental Consultants, 153
Clean Harbors, Inc., 601
Club Med Inc., 68
Coca-Cola Classic, 166, 211
Coca-Cola Company, The, 68, 69, 76
  decision making at, 211, 212
  goals and planning at, 159, 160, 166
  strategy at, 190–191
Coca-Cola Enterprises, Inc., 159
  decentralization at, 274
Coke (Coca-Cola), 163, 466

Coleman Co., Inc., 86
Colgate-Palmolive Co.
  innovation at, 542
  mentor programs at, 626
Colgate Venture Company, 542
Collin Street Bakery, 134
Columbia Pictures Entertainment
  Inc., 150, 173
Commonwealth Metals Company,
  120
Compaq Computer Corporation,
  22, 69, 291–292
  initial paths taken by, 599
Compaq Computer Corporation,
  602
Compucon Systems, 602
ConAgra, 172
Conoco Inc., 81, 181
Consolidated Edison Co. of New
  York, 22, 30
Consolidated Freightways, Inc.,
  22, 46
Consumers Union, 70
Contemporary Landscape, 4
Continental (Lincoln), 500
Continental Airlines, Inc., 49, 192
  organization change at, 315
Continental Can, 633
Contrarian Group, 327
Control Data, 152
Cooper Industries, 477
Coors Brothers Beer
  operations management at, 509
  strategy at, 191
Corn Flakes, 115
Corning Incorporated, 14, 69
  control at, 482
  creativity at, 531–532
  innovation at, 542
  mission statement of, 152
  motivation at, 373
  women employees at, 579
Corona beer, 466
Council of Better Business
  Bureaus, 70
Cox Enterprises, 496
CPC International Inc., 477
Creamette, 293
Crest, 186
Culinova Group, 542
Cummins Engine, 414

Cypress Semiconductor Corp.,
  169
  conflict at, 436
  information system at, 301
  leadership at, 391, 392
  organization design at, 302

Daewoo Corporation, 69
  leadership at, 415
Daily Press, 203
Daimler-Benz AG, 45, 116, 621
Dallas Police Department, 527
Data General, 213
Dayton-Hudson Corp.
  planning at, 225
  social responsibility at, 108
dBASE III, 552
Dean Witter, 288
Deere & Company, 116
  technology at, 195
Dell Computer Corp., 485, 602
  task environment and, 68, 69
Delta Air Lines, Inc., 22, 49, 52,
  71, 78
  communication at, 460
  informal groups at, 423
Detroit Edison Co., 45, 261
DHL Airways, 569
Dial Corporation, 181
  business screen and, 184
  strategy at, 181
Digital Equipment Corp., 52, 433,
  558, 625
  cultural diversity at, 577, 591
  expert system at, 246
  quality at, 501
Dillard's, 568
Dior, Christian, 183
Discovery Channel, 215
Disney Channel, 177
Disney Company, Walt, The, 52,
  68, 130–131
  financial strategy at, 192
  job specialization at, 259
  planning at, 160–161
  revitalization at, 326
  strategy at, 177
Disney World, 69, 617
Dodge, 440
Domino's Pizza, 381–382
Dom Perignon, 120

Dow Chemical Co., The, 14, 52
  cultural diversity at, 576
  internal audit and, 640
  mission statement of, 152
  technology at, 289
Dow Corning Corporation, 77, 78
  breast implants and, 95
Dreamaker Children's Book Seller,
  545
Dresser Industries, 640
Du Pont de Nemours, E.I., &
  Co., 12, 45, 52, 81, 169, 611
  production strategy at, 192
  social responsibility at, 104, 105
  strategy formulation at, 181

Eagle Snacks, 557
Eastern Air Lines, Inc., 315
Eastman Kodak Company, 51, 52,
  116, 226
  direct investments at, 121
  group norms at, 428
  innovation at, 541
  internal audit and, 640
  Keiretsu and, 155
  research and development
    strategy at, 193
  self-directed teams at, 618
  South African interests of, 100
  strategy formulation at, 180–181
Eaton, 67
EDS, 266, 273
Edsel, 534
Edwards, A.G., Inc., 325
Electrolux (AB), 140
Electronic Data Systems Inc.
  (EDS), 437, 621
  organization structure, 257, 258
  planning task force at, 156
Eli Lilly, 14
  decision making at, 217
Elle magazine, 530
Elling Brothers Mechanical Con-
  tractors, 616–617
Emerson Electric Co., 30
  human resources planning at,
    341
Emery Air Freight
  control at, 476, 480
  OB Mod at, 382
English Channel, 10

ENI, 487
Equicor-Equitable HCA Corp., 325
Escort, 441, 500
Esso S.A.F., 133
Euro Disney, 355
Excell, 552
Extra, 187
Exxon Corporation, 22, 32, 53, 66, 71, 77, 226, 245
  budgets at, 632
  group activities at, 424
  international operations at, 118
  planning at, 154
  production strategy at, 192
  social responsibility at, 103
  technology at, 289
  Valdez and, 100

FAA, 325
Fairfield Inn, 179, 550
Farmland Industries, Inc., 72
Federal Express Corp., 56, 80, 286, 462
  control at, 474
  decision making at, 218
  government influenced by, 107
  information system at, 569
  mentor programs at, 626
  political action committee of, 106, 107
  work teams at, 417, 418, 420, 421
  ZapMail, 167
Federal Paper Board Co., Inc., 75
Federal Reserve Bank, 265
Ferrari, 120
Fiat S.p.A., 22, 30, 487
  organization change at, 331
Fiesta Mart Inc., 188
Filament Fiber Technology, 603
Financial News Network, 215
Financial Times, The, 297
First of America Bank-Indianapolis, 381
Fleischman's margarine, 623
Florida State University, 4
Flow Control Group, 296
FMC Corporation, 477
Food Lion Inc., 333, 334

Ford Motor Co., 22, 48, 53, 66, 67, 71, 80, 116, 156, 226, 260, 311, 359, 382, 500, 532, 598, 623
  budgeting at, 636
  Fiat and, 331
  general environment at, 65
  incentive systems at, 386
  Japanese auto industry and, 212
  matrix design at, 298
  Mazda Motor Corporation and, 441
  motivation at, 368
  as multinational business, 117
  organization design at, 298, 300
  planning at, 167
  productivity at, 508
  quality at, 501
  strategic allies of, 71
  strategy at, 177
  task environment at, 67–68
  task force at, 422
  training methods at, 348
Fort Howard Corp., 188
Fort Jewelry, 597, 598
Fortune, 70
Fox Television, 18
Franklin Mint, The
  span of management at, 269
  strategy at, 193
Frito Lay, Inc., 556–557
Fruehauf, 477
Fuji, 141
Fuji Bank, Ltd., The, 22
Fujitsu, Ltd., 130
  international business and, 302

Gallo Vineyards, 162
Gap, Inc., The, 68, 283
  operations management at, 509
  pooled interdependence at, 275
Gateway 2000, 485
Genentech, 353
General Dynamics, 382
General Electric Co., 8, 9, 10, 21, 22, 41, 45, 82, 101, 140, 274, 482, 508, 560, 621
  BCG matrix and, 182–183
  Black & Decker and, 161
  budgets at, 632

business screen and, 184
  career-planning programs used by, 626
  computer-aided design at, 526
  control at, 480
  decision making at, 202, 203, 204, 205
  flat organization at, 269
  global management at, 135
  goals at, 149, 156
  information system at, 562
  leadership at, 410
  planning at, 156
  production strategy at, 192
  product-service mix at, 512
  purchasing management at, 515
  quality and productivity at, 499, 500, 503, 506
  reinforcement at, 379
  speed at, 510–511
  strategic business units at, 182
General Foods Corporation, 15, 68, 155, 182, 261
  career-planning programs used by, 626
  decision making at, 216
  incentive systems at, 386
  innovation at, 542
General Instrument Corp., 46
  licensing at, 120
General Mills, Inc., 15, 94, 120, 433, 554
  communication at, 461
  control at, 482
  in European market, 115
General Motors Corp., 22, 48, 64, 67, 71, 76, 133, 140, 156, 169, 293, 299, 311, 359, 437, 477, 501
  decision making at, 217
  dual-career couples and, 628
  EDS at, 257, 266
  human resources planning by, 341
  information system needs at, 553
  innovation at, 536
  Japanese auto industry and, 212
  marketing strategy at, 191
  organization change at, 317

General Motors Corp (*continued*)
  planning at, 154
  quality and productivity at, 501, 520
  small businesses and, 601
  as System 4 organization, 287–288
  uncertainty and, 76
Georgia-Pacific Corporation, 476
Gerber Products, 198
Getty Petroleum Corp., 32
Gillette Co.
  control at, 481
  innovation at, 535
Gioia, 293
Giorgio, 575
Girl Scouts of the United States of America, 23, 103
Glaxo Holdings, 544
Golden Grahams, 115
Golden West Financial Corp., 100
Goodrich Co., B.F., The
  incentive systems at, 386
  organization development at, 325
Goodyear Tire & Rubber Company, The, 67
  as manufacturer, 509
Gould Paper Company, Inc., 219
Grace, W.R., 265
Grainger Division, 345
Grand Affair, A, 609
Grant, W.T., 48
  strategy at, 187
Grau Limited, 52
Greyhound Dial, 13
  revitalization at, 326
GRiD Systems Corp., 462
Grinnel, 296
Groupe Bull, 302, 621
GTE Southwest Inc., 348
Gulf & Western, Inc., 227–228

Hallmark Cards Inc.
  culture of, 74
  work teams at, 260
Hartford Insurance, 186
Head and Shoulders, 186
Healthy Choice, 172
Hefty, 89

Heinz, H.J., Company, 175, 176–177, 179, 181
Hersey, 296
Hershey Foods Corp., 179, 181, 185–186
Hertz Corp., The, 67
Hewlett-Packard Co., 19, 51, 52, 95, 96, 521
  culture of, 73–74
  goals of, 147, 149, 150
  information system needs at, 553
  innovation at, 538–539
  motivation at, 368
Hewlett-Packard Spain, 583
Hitachi, Ltd., 72
  motivation at, 389
  social responsibility at, 105
Home Depot, Inc., The, 46
Honda Motor Co., Ltd., 30, 81, 83, 116, 134, 271, 500
  just-in-time at, 517
  purchasing management at, 516
  quotas of, 131
  speed at, 511
  strategy at, 199
Honda of America Motor Co., Ltd., 71
Hoover Universal, Inc., 152
Humana, 446
Hungarian Telecommunications Company, 228
Hunt, J.B., Transport Services, Inc., 9
Hyatt Corp., 100, 454
HyperDesk, Corp., 213
Hyundai Electronics Industries Company, 120

IBM, 13, 16, 17, 51, 52, 66, 69, 72, 82, 116, 165, 201, 205, 257, 261, 521, 558, 560, 568
  administrative intensity at, 278
  Boeing and, 141
  change at, 309, 310
  communication at, 460
  culture of, 73
  decentralization at, 274
  decision making at, 218
  dual-career couples and, 628

flat organization at, 269
flexible manufacturing systems at, 527
information system at, 553, 563
international business and, 302
layout at, 513
modified workweek at, 382
operations management at, 508–509
productivity at, 508
purchasing management at, 515
quality at, 501
revitalization at, 325, 326
social responsibility at, 102, 103, 105
South African interests of, 100
span of management at, 269
training and development programs at, 345
uncertainty and, 76
wage-level decisions at, 352
women at, 582
IKEA, 123
"I Know I Can" program, 375
Imperial Chemical Industries, 281
Infiniti, 533
Intel Corp., 31, 52
  uncertainty and, 76
Inter-Europe Student Exchange Program, 583
International Business Machines Corp., *see* IBM
International Harvester Co., 330, 398. *See also* Navistar
International Olympic Committee, 23
ITT Corp., 325, 502
  business screen and, 184
  communication at, 450
  strategy at, 186

Jalisco, 78
Jewel Food Stores, 626
John Hancock Mutual Life Insurance Co., 382
Johnson Controls Inc., 67
  just-in-time at, 517
Johnson & Johnson, 77, 78, 94
  innovation at, 542
  mentor programs at, 626

Johnson & Johnson (*continued*)
  mission statement of, 152
  social responsibility at, 108–109
Johnson, S.C., & Son, Inc.
  human resources at, 195
  innovation at, 542
JVC, 81

Kawasaki Heavy Industries, Ltd., 116
  Boeing and, 141
Kay, Mary, Cosmetics, 152
K-car, 530
Kellogg Co.
  in European market, 115
  global management at, 118
  strategy at, 191
Kelly Services, Inc., 22, 69
Kepner-Tregoe, 211
Kimberly-Clark Corporation, 30
  costs of, 633
Kinder-Care, Inc., 22
Kinko, 289
Kiwanis Club, 424
KLM, 76
K mart Corp., 22, 30, 68, 71, 86, 274, 405, 421
  coordination at, 276
  information system at, 562
  marketing strategy at, 191
  organization design at, 290
Kodak, *see* Eastman Kodak Company
Koito, 155
Kraft General Foods, 172, 267
  reaction planning at, 155, 156
Kroger Co., The, 68, 245
  information management at, 549, 550, 551
Kyocera Corporation, 521
Kyoto Ceramics, 521

Land's End, Inc.
  customer relations at, 99
  strategy at, 186
Lauder, Estée, 530
Lauren, Ralph, 188
League of Women Voters, 70
Lechmere department store, 508
Lee, 75

Lerner Stores Corp., 283, 298
Lever Bros. Co., 623
Levi Strauss & Co., 22, 96, 116
  control at, 484–485
  culture of, 73
  organization design at, 302
  social responsibility at, 99
  uncertainty at, 75–76
Lexus, 526
Life, 534
Limited Express, The, 283, 298
Limited, Inc., The
  organization design at, 283, 284, 291, 297–298
  strategy at, 177
Lincoln, 500
Lincoln Electric, 365, 366, 368, 377
Little, Arthur D., Inc., 45
Little League Baseball, 22, 103
Lloyd's of London, 30
  case on, 57
Lockheed, 518
Long Beach Memorial Hospital, 527–528
Lotus Development Corp., 201, 621
  decision making at, 222
Lotus 1-2-3, 552
LTV, 486
Lumina, 536
LVMH Moët Hennessy Louis Vuitton, 183

Maalox, 206
McCormick Harvesting Machine Company, 330
McDonald's Corp., 116, 274, 496
  as franchise, 607
  in Japan, 223
  materials requirements planning at, 518
  in Moscow, 369
  policy at, 162
  Ronald McDonald House program of, 103–104
  rules and regulations at, 163
  standard operating procedures at, 162
  standards at, 478
  strategy at, 190–191

McDonnell Douglas Corp., 65, 93–94
  computer-aided design at, 526
Machu Picchu, 31
Macintosh computer, 535
Macmillan, 135
Manufacturers Hanover Corp., 319
Marks & Spencer
  decision making at, 207
  Keiretsu and, 155
Marriot Corporation
  decision making at, 216
Marriott Corporation
  communication at, 453
  control at, 478
  information management at, 550, 551
  reciprocal interdependence at, 275
  strategy formulation at, 179, 180
Mars, Inc., 116
  strategy at, 177, 178
Martin Marietta, 502
Massachusetts Mutual Life Insurance Co., 348
Massey-Ferguson Inc., 22
MasterCard, 153
Matsushita, 545
Mattel Inc., 48
  communication at, 453, 454
  strategy at, 182
Maxwell House, 68, 550
Mayo Clinic, 421
Maytag Corporation, 52, 140
  job enlargement at, 261
  job specialization at, 259–260
Mazda Motor Corporation, 67–68, 71, 120, 155
  Ford Motor Co. and, 441
  human relations management at, 359
MCI Communications Corp., 102
Mead Corporation, The, 69
Memphis State University, 421
Mercedes-Benz, 120, 529, 533
Merck & Co., Inc., 14
  control at, 479
  dual-career couples and, 628
  innovation at, 542
  research and development strategy at, 193

Merrill Lynch & Co., Inc., 79–80, 510
  information system at, 561
Metalloy, 476
Metro-Goldwyn-Mayer/United Artists, 215
Metropolitan Edison, 78
Metropolitan Life Insurance Co., 22
  modified workweek at, 382
Miata, 441, 529
Microsoft Corp., 201, 222, 621
  innovation at, 535, 540
MicroSoft Word, 551
Midvale Steel Company, 36, 37
Mikimoto, 83
Miller, Herman, Inc., 112
Mini Chips Ahoy, 189
Minnesota Mining & Mfg. Co., see 3M
Minnesota Twins, 430
Minolta Camera Co., Ltd., 87
MIT, 541
Mitsubishi Corp., 4
  Boeing and, 141
  keiretsu of, 155
Mitsubishi Electric, 302
Mobil Corporation, 5, 12, 81, 116
  cultural diversity at, 589
  social responsibility at, 89, 90, 102
Molex Incorporated, 134
Momenta Corporation, 603
Monarch Marketing Systems, 548
Monopoly, 534
Monsanto Company, 14, 22, 66, 299
  cultural diversity at, 589, 594
  innovation at, 539, 542
  operations management at, 514
Montgomery Ward, 292, 488
Motel 6, 188
Mothers Against Drunk Drivers (MADD), 70–71
Motorola, Inc., 501
  communication at, 451
  cultural diversity at, 589
  organization design at, 291
  productivity at, 508
  recruiting at, 343
  speed at, 511
  women at, 582

Mrs. Fields Cookies, 625
  communication at, 449
Mrs. Fields Inc., 4, 625
MTV, 7
Mueller, 296

Nabisco Brands, Inc., 623
  strategy of, 189
Nabisco Cream of Wheat, 623
Nabisco, RJR, Inc., 314
NASA, 10–11, 14, 77, 78
  groupthink and, 219
National Bicycle Industrial Co. (NBI), 545
National Organization for Women (NOW), 70
National Rifle Association (NRA), 70
National Science Foundation, 23
Nationwide Insurance, 375
Navistar International Corp., 13, 30
  organization change at, 330
NBC Television, 484
NCR Corp., 80, 156, 299
  AT&T and, 210
Nerf ball, 534
Nestlé SA, 22, 30, 71, 115, 120, 130, 134
  career management at, 627
  direct investments at, 121
  as global business, 117
  organization design at, 302
Newcomers Club, 424
New Jersey Bell Telephone Co., 38
Newport News, 514
News Corp., 297
New York Times Company, The, 22
New Zealand Forest Service, 251
NeXT, Inc., 599
  technological forecasting at, 228
Nike, Inc., 68, 214, 327
  goals of, 153
  Reebok and, 163
Nikon, 538
9-Lives, 175
Nintendo, 87
Nippon Telegraph & Telephone, 156, 521

Nissan Design International (NDI), 533
Nissan Motor Co. Ltd., 48, 53, 71, 271, 500
  creativity at, 533
  production strategy at, 192
  sequential interdependence at, 275
NOK, 476
Nordstrom, Inc., 358
Northern Research & Engineering Corp., 238
Northern States Power Company, 335
Nucor Corp., 486
NutraSweet, 76
  cultural diversity at, 594

Ocean Spray Cranberry, 608
ODS Corporation, 421
Oki Electronics, 537
Oldsmobile, 520
Oneida Ltd., 526
Optima credit card, 153
Ore-Ida Food Co., Inc., 175
Ortho Pharmaceutical Corporation, 584
Owens-Corning Fiberglass Corp., 166

Pace Foods, 589
Pacific Gas & Electric Co., 22, 78
Pacific Intermountain Express, 301
Pacific Lumber, 340
Palm Top, 423
Panasonic Company, 87, 545
Parker Brothers, 533–534
Peace Corps, 66
Pearson PLC, 617
  organization design at, 295, 296, 297
  strategy at, 176
Pease Air Force Base, 307
Penn Central Railroad, 48
Penney, J.C., Company, Inc., 68, 73, 353
  conflict at, 435, 437
  decision making at, 208, 211
Penn State University, 5
Pennzoil, 33
Pentagon, 211

Pentops, 462
Pep Boys Automotive Supercenters, 49
Pepsi, 116, 163, 466
PepsiCo, Inc., 76, 166, 267, 557
  organization design at, 298
Personics Corporation, 545
Perulac, 130
Pfizer Inc., 477
  goals at, 165
  innovation at, 544
Philadelphia Electric Co., 307
Philip Morris Companies, Inc., 14, 96, 513
  planning at, 155–156
  social responsibility at, 103
Philips Electronics, 507
Philips Industries, 140, 299
Phillips Petroleum Co., 100
Phillips-Van Heusen, 312
Pitney Bowes, Data Documents Division of, 231
Pizza Hut Inc., 509
Playboy Enterprises, 636
Polaroid Corp., 30, 325
  innovation at, 534, 538
  inventory models of, 244
Premier Cruise Lines, Ltd., 61, 181
Previa, 529
Procardia, 544
Procter & Gamble Co., 15, 51, 52, 73, 325, 382, 433
  control at, 482
  costs and, 633
  environment and, 100
  innovation at, 542
  organization design at, 302
  product-service mix at, 511
  strategy at, 186
Profit International Business, 602
Prudential Insurance Co. of America, The, 14, 22, 81, 260, 299
  job characteristics approach at, 262
  organization change at, 316
Public Broadcasting System, 23
Pulsar NX, 533
Purolator Courier Corporation, 476

Quantum, 9

Ralston Purina Co., 82
Rand Corp., 217
Raytheon Co., 156
RCA, 172
Recruit Company, 94
Reebok International Ltd., 68, 153, 214, 292, 327
  Blacktop of, 163
  conflict at, 436
  groups at, 425, 426
  initial paths taken by, 599
  job creation at, 601
Reflexite Corp., 615
Regina Co., Inc., 93
Revlon, 584
Rice Krispies, 115
Risk, 534
Riunite, 120
Robins, A.H., Co., Inc., 210, 211
Robitussin, 210
Rockwell International Corp., 14
  decision making at, 216
Rolex Co.
  control at, 515
  differentiation strategy at, 188
Roman Catholic Church, 22
Rorer Group, Inc., 206–207, 208, 209, 211
Rotary Club, 424
Royal Dutch/Shell Group, 22
Rubbermaid Incorporated, 46
  goals of, 149, 150
Ryder System, 64
  departmentalization at, 266, 267

Safeway Stores, Inc., 22, 30, 68, 226
Salomon Brothers Inc., 93
Salvation Army, 64
Santa Fe Pacific Corporation, 9
Sanyo, 120
Sara Lee Corp., 69
Saturn, 64
Scandinavian Airlines System (SAS), 395
Schwinn Bicycle Co., 68
Scotchcast Plus, 191
Sears, Roebuck and Co., 22, 32, 80–81, 274, 405

budgets at, 631
career-planning programs used by, 626
flat organization at, 269
organization change at, 314–315
ownership of, 608
purchasing management at, 515
social responsibility at, 104
Seiko, 30, 53
Self-Healing Network Service, 565
Seminole Manufacturing Co., 556
Seoul Hilton International, 415
Seville, 488
SGS-Thomas Microelectronics, 302
Sharper Image Corp., 479
Sheraton Hotels, 186
Siemens, 302
Sierra Club, 70, 424
Simonds Rolling Machine Company, 36, 37
Singer, 477
Smucker, J.M., Co., 69
Sofu Industries, 521
Sogeti, 621
Sohio Pipe Line Co., 22
Sony Corp., 81, 83, 120, 421, 521
  goals of, 150
  innovation at, 523, 524, 534
  planning at, 173
  task group at, 423
Southwest Airlines Co., 3, 4, 7, 12, 13, 16, 21
  leadership at, 409
Southwestern Bell Corp., 311
Spellbound, 530
Sperry, 213
Standard Brands, 623
Stanford University, 541
Star-Kist Foods, Inc., 175
State Farm Insurance Company, 22
  case on, 26
Steelcase, Inc., 383
Stevens, J.P., 71
Studebaker, 48
Subaru, 289
Subway, 75
Suchard, 513
Summit Communications Group, 353

Sun Microsystems Inc., 602
  decision making in, 201, 202, 205, 216, 219
  initial paths taken by, 599
Suzuki, 116
Swartzkatz, 120

Taco Bell, 75
Tandem Computers Inc., 457
Tandy Brands, 473
Target, 188
  inventory models at, 244
  planning at, 225
  queuing models used by, 245
Tatanka, 529
Taurus, 298, 422, 500
Teamsters, 354
Tenneco Automotive, 155, 169
Tenneco Inc., 22, 80, 156, 414
Texaco Inc., 4, 32–33, 96
Texas A&M University, 72
Texas Instruments Incorporated, 20–21, 261, 292, 325, 433, 542
  budgeting at, 636
  communication at, 454
  culture of, 73
  decision making at, 216
  incentive systems at, 386
  information system at, 566
  innovation at, 542
  materials requirements planning at, 518
  motivation at, 368, 382
  socialization at, 429
Thomson SA, 203
3M, 19, 433
  goals of, 150
  innovation at, 540, 542
  minorities hired by, 100
  organization change at, 315
  strategy at, 191
Three Mile Island reactor, 307
Tiffany & Co., 83
Time, 80
Time Warner Inc., 71, 80
Timex Group Ltd., 53, 188
  control at, 515
  incentive systems at, 386
  marketing strategy at, 191
TLC Group, 628
Tobler, 513

Tone, 181
Toucan-Do, 449
Toyota Motor Corp., 6, 22, 48, 67, 76, 134, 500, 521
  computer-aided manufacturing at, 526
  creativity at, 529
  decision making at, 202, 203, 205
  just-in-time at, 229
  production strategy at, 192
  span of management at, 269, 271
Toys "R" Us
  entrepreneurial spirit at, 618
  in Japan, 137, 223
  strategy at, 191
Trammell Crow Real Estate Investors, 344
Travelers Corporation, 561
Tribune Company, 203
Trinova Corporation, 67
Tropical Fantasy, 466
TRW, 525
Tuffy's Pet Food, 175
Turner Broadcasting System, Inc., 215, 216
Tussaud, Madame, 297
Tyco, 296
Tylenol, 77, 78

Ugly Duckling Rent-a-Car, 625
U-Haul International, Inc., 267
Unilever, 22, 30
  organization design at, 302
Union Carbide Corp., 19, 78, 182, 227–228, 288
  conflict at, 434
Union Oil Co. of California, 340–341
Union Pacific, 414
  standard operating procedures at, 162
Unisys Corporation, 72, 461, 558
  communication at, 460
  formation of, 213
United Air Lines, Inc., 46, 76, 116
  Boeing and, 141
United Auto Workers, 68, 81, 330, 354, 437

Caterpillar and, 313, 316
  goals of, 424
United Food and Commercial Workers, 358
United Parcel Service, Inc. (UPS), 286, 417
  case on, 56
  information system at, 569
U.S. Army, 4
U.S. Chamber of Commerce, 81
U.S. Forest Service, 562–563
U.S. Healthcare, 554
U.S. Postal Service, 23
U.S. Steel, 509. See also USX Corporation
U.S. West Communications, 228
  information system at, 565
United Way of America, 4, 23
  goals of, 149–150
Universal Exposition, 243
University of Michigan, 482
University of South Carolina, 227
University of Texas, 72
Upjohn, 482
Urban Cowboy, 535
USX Corporation, 67, 486, 509
  incentive systems at, 386

Valdez, 78
Victoria's Secret, 283
Viper, 440
Visa, 153
Visa USA Inc., 528
Visions, 531
Vista, 435
Viviano Macaroni Co., 293
Volkswagen AG, 53, 67, 71, 120
  Fiat and, 331
Volvo AB, 116

Wall Street Journal, The, 70, 297
Wal-Mart Stores, Inc., 20, 86, 225, 556, 568
  ethics at, 92
  forecasting at, 232
  information management at, 550
  as international business, 117
  leadership at, 405
  marketing strategy at, 191
  strategy at, 181
  teleconferencing at, 565

Wang, 558, 560
War and Remembrance, 214
Warner, 80
Warner-Lambert Company, 382
Washington Bullets, 392
Washington Post Co., 14
Waste Management Corp., 496
Weight Watchers International
    Inc., 175, 181
Wells Fargo & Company, 22, 388
  history of, 29–30
Wendy's International Inc., 13
  organization design at, 290–291
  rumors and, 466
  social responsibility at, 108
Westcot Center, 160
Western Electric Company, Incor-
    porated, 41, 260
  human relations approach to
    motivation and, 367–368
  quality at, 502
Westinghouse Electric Corp., 140,
    169

budgeting at, 636
change at, 310
communication at, 451
decision making at, 218
information management at, 547
information system at, 562
Managerial grid for, 325
materials requirements planning
    at, 518
motivation at, 368
purchasing management at, 515
resistance to change at, 314
Weyerhaeuser, 475
Whirlpool Corporation
  code of ethical conduct at, 95,
    96
  in international business, 140
  technology at, 289
Whistler Corporation
  control at, 476, 477
  quality at, 503
Wickes Companies, Inc., 166
Windows software, 535

Winds of War, The, 214
Womenswear, Inc., 188
Woolworth Corporation, 298
WordPerfect, 551–552, 621
Word Star, 552
Wormald, 296
Wrangler, 75
Wrigley, Wm., Jr., Company,
    186, 187

Xenith, 306
Xerox Corp., 22, 93, 625
  anthropologists and, 33
  budgeting at, 636
  communication at, 446–447
  organization design at, 303, 306
  training methods at, 348

Yamaha Motor Co., Ltd., 68, 116,
    509

Subject Index

ABC analysis, 475

Acceptance sampling, as statistical quality control technique, 518

Acceptance stage, of small business, 610

Accountability, control and, 490

Accounting, for small business, 616–617

Accurate information, 549–550

Achievement need, motivation and, 373

Achievement-oriented leader behavior,inpath-goal theory, 403

Acquisitions, organizations responding to environment with, 80

Action plans, 155

Active Corps of Executives (ACE), 613, 614

Adaptation model, of business strategy, 185–187

Adaptive organizations, for organization design, 302–303

Administrative intensity, 278

Administrative management, 38, 39

Administrative managers, 12, 13–14

Administrative model, of decision making, 212–213

Adverse impact, equal employment opportunity and, 335

Affiliation need, motivation and, 373–374

Affirmative Action, 336–337

Age Discrimination in Employment Act, 336

Age distribution trends, cultural diversity and, 578–579

Aggregate productivity, 505

AIDS, 112
   legal aspects of, 338

AI, see Artificial intelligence

Alcoholism, legal aspects of, 338

Alliances, organizations responding to environment with, 80

Americans With Disabilities Act, 336

Analyzer strategy
   in adaptation model, 186
   organization design and, 293–294

Anthropologists, management theory and, 33

Antiquity, management in, 34, 35

Application, innovation and, 534

Application blanks, in selection process, 343

Areas of management, 12, 13–14

Artificial intelligence (AI), 246

Assembly lines, 30

Assessment centers, in selection process, 344

Aston studies, organizational size and, 291

Attitudes, effect of rewards on, 384

Attraction, groups and, 423, 430, 431

Audits, 640

Australia, cultural diversity in work force of, 582

Authority
   acceptance of, 38
   Fayol on, 39
   functional, 277
   line and staff, 277
   organization structure and, 271–272

Automation, 524–526

Automobile industry
   in Japan, 121, 155, 212, 500, 520
   in U.S., 212

Autonomous work groups, for motivation, 382. *See also* Teams

Avoidance, reinforcement and, 379, 380

Babylonians, management and, 34

Background experiences, creativity and, 529–530

Balance sheet, 637, 638

Balance sheet budget, 632

BARS, *see* Behaviorally Anchored Rating Scale

BCG matrix, 182–184

Behaviorally Anchored Rating Scale (BARS), 349, 351

Behavioral management theory, 30, 40–44, 49
   contributions and limitations of, 44
   Hawthorne studies and, 41–42, 49
   human relations movement and, 42–43
   organizational behavior and, 43

Behavioral model, of organization design, 286–288

Behavior modeling training, as training and development method, 347

Behaviors, effect of rewards on, 384

Beliefs, global management and, 132–133

Belongingness needs, organization satisfying, 369–370

Benefits, 352–353
   cultural diversity dealt with by, 588
   legal aspects of, 336, 337

Bill of materials (BOM), requirements planning, 517–518

Binding arbitration, in grievance procedures, 356

Birth, in organizational life cycle, 292

Blacks, *see* Cultural diversity

Board of directors
in internal environment, 72
planning by, 156

Body language, nonverbal communication and, 457

BOM, *see* Bill of materials

Boundary spanner, for information management, 79

Bounded rationality, in administrative model of decision making, 212, 213

Breakeven analysis, for planning, 235–238

Breakthrough stage, of small business, 610–611

Budgeting, 631. *See also* Budgets

Budgets, 631–637
balance sheet, 632
bottom-up approach to, 634–636
capital expenditures, 632
cash-flow, 631–632
developing, 634–636
effective use of, 641
expense, 632
financial, 631–632
fixed costs in, 633
nonmonetary, 632–633
operating, 632
profit, 632
revenue, 632
sales, 632
semivariable costs in, 633
strategy implementation and, 195
strengths and weaknesses of, 636–637
variable costs in, 633
zero-base, 636

Bureaucracy, 38
control and, 483–484
organization design as, 285–286

Business plan, for entrepreneur, 605–606

Business portfolio, in corporate strategy, 182–184

Business screen, 184

Business simulation, as training and development method, 347

Business strategy, 177–178
adaptation model for, 185–187
analyzer strategy in, 186, 293–294
competitive, 294
cost leadership strategy in, 189, 294
defender strategy in, 185–186, 187, 293
differentiation strategy in, 189, 294
focus strategy in, 189, 294
organization design and, 293–294
Porter's competitive strategies for, 187–189
product life cycle for, 189–190
prospector strategy in, 186, 293
reactor strategy in, 186–187, 294

Buyers, power of, 76

"Buy national" laws, international trade controlled by, 131

CAD/CAM, *see* Computer-integrated manufacturing

CAD, *see* Computer-aided design

Cafeteria benefits plans, 353

CAM, *see* Computer-aided manufacturing

Capacity, operations systems and, 512

Capital expenditures budget, 632

Capital structure, in finance policy, 192

Captains of Industry, social responsibility and, 97

Career planning
in human resources, 353
for organization change, 323
organizations having programs for, 626–627
see also Managerial careers

Careers, 623–625. *See also* Managerial careers

Career transitions, 628–629

Caribbean Common Market, 132

Case discussions, as training and development method, 346, 347, 348

Cash budget, *see* Cash-flow budget

Cash cow, in BCG matrix, 183, 184

Cash-flow budget, 631–632

Causal modeling, for forecasting, 230–231

Cellular telephones, 463, 464

Centralization
Fayol on, 39
in organization structure, 273–274

Certified public accountants (CPAs), external audits and, 640

Chain of command, 266

Challenger, 78

Change, *see* Organization change

Channel, in communication, 446

Charisma, referent power and, 394

Charismatic leadership, *see* Transformational leadership

Cheaper by the Dozen, 37

Checks and balances, for control, 491

Chief executive officer (CEO), 11, 12
planning by, 157
typical day of, 21

Chief information officer (CIO), 461–462

Civil Rights Act of 1964
human resources strategy and, 192
Title VII of, 335, 336, 339

Clan control, 484–485

Classical decision model, 106

Classical management theory, 36–40, 49
administrative management and, 38, 39
Babbage and, 35
contributions and limitations of, 38, 40
scientific management and, 30, 36–37

Cluster chain, 452, 453

Coaching, for organization change, 323

Coalitions, decision making and, 213

Codes of ethics, 95

Coercion
as political behavior, 411
power and, 394, 396

Coercive power, 394, 396
Cognitive abilities, creativity and, 530
Cohesiveness, in groups, 430–432
Collective bargaining, 355–356
Communication, 441–469
  barriers to, 458–459
  behavioral elements of, 454–457
  cases on, 466–467
  credibility for, 460
  cultural diversity dealt with by, 587
  definition of, 444–445
  downward, 449, 450
  effective, 444–445, 446
  electronic, 449, 462–464
  environment and, 458, 459
  feedback for, 459–460
  follow-up for, 461
  formal information systems for, 461–462
  grapevine and, 452–453, 464
  in group development, 425–426
  horizontal, 450, 451
  improving, 457–461
  informal, 453–454
  information flow regulation for, 461
  interpersonal, 447–449
  interpersonal dynamics and, 458, 459
  leader promoting, 194
  listening and, 459, 460
  management by wandering around and, 453, 454, 455
  managing, 461–464
  networks, 450, 451–452
  noise and, 459
  nonverbal, 456–457
  oral, 447–448, 449
  overload and, 459, 464
  perception in, 454–456
  perceptual organization and, 454, 456
  process, 445–447
  receiver and, 458, 459, 460–461
  selective perception and, 454, 455
  sender and, 458, 459–460, 461
  sensitivity for, 460
  telecommuting, 462–463
  two-way, 460

  upward, 450
  vertical, 449–451
  written, 448–449
Communication network, 450, 451–452
Company productivity, 505
Compensation, 351–352
  human resources strategy and, 192
  individual wage decisions in, 352
  job evaluation for, 352
  legal aspects of, 336, 337
  motivation and, 367
  reward systems and, 383–386
  wage-level decision in, 352
  wage-structure decision in, 352
  see also Benefits
Competition
  distinctive competence and, 177
  five competitive forces and, 76–77
  groups and, 430, 431
  organization change and, 311
  organization design and, 294
  quality and, 501
Competitive advantage
  cultural diversity and, 584–585
  strategies for, 187–188
Competitors
  companies affecting, 81
  ethical treatment of, 93
  in task environment, 68
Complete information, 550
Complete private ownership, global management and, 129
Complete public ownership, global management and, 129
Compressed workweek, 382
Computer-aided design (CAD), 526
Computer-aided manufacturing (CAM), 526
Computer-integrated manufacturing (CIM), 527
Computers
  change and, 320
  management science and, 45
  manufacturing and, 526–527
  see also Information systems
Conceptual skills of manager, 20
Concurrent control, see Screening control

Conferences, as training and development method, 347
Conflict
  causes of, 435–437
  confrontation approach for, 438
  coordination reducing, 437
  cultural diversity and, 585–586, 592
  encouraging, 437
  goals and, 436, 437–438
  interdependence and, 435–436
  interpersonal and intergroup, 434–438
  interpersonal dynamics and, 436–437
  intrarole, 427
  intrasender, 427
  managing, 437–538
  person-role, 427
  reducing, 437–438
  resolving, 438
  resource competition and, 436
  role, 427–428
Confrontation approach, for conflict resolution, 438
Confucianism, management and, 35
Conglomerate design, of organization, 295–296, 297
Consideration behavior, of leaders, 398
Consistency, of goals, 167
Consolidation, in revitalization, 326
Contacts, government influenced by, 106
Content perspectives, on motivation, 368–374
Content validation, in selection process, 342–343
Contingency planning, 157–158
Contingency theory, 48–49, 50
Continuous improvement, 359
Continuous-process technology, 289
Contraction, in revitalization, 326
Control, 5, 6, 7, 10–11, 38, 194, 472–497
  accountability and, 490
  accuracy and, 488
  areas of, 474–475
  bureaucratic, 483–484

Control (*continued*)
checks and balances for, 491
clan, 484–485
compounding of errors and, 476
controllers for, 477
costs minimized by, 476
deviation corrected for, 480–481
effective controls for, 490–491
employee involvement for, 477, 491
evaluation and action for, 480–481
flexibility and, 488
focus of, 490
in global economy, 138
goals and, 149–150
in groups, 426
importance of, 475–476
inefficiency and, 490
information management as, 550–551, *see also* Information systems
level of, 475
management by objectives for, 491
managing, 487–491
multiple control systems for, 483, 485
objectivity and, 489
operations, 475, 481–483, 485, *see also* Operations management; Quality control
organizational, 475, 483–485
organization change and, 476
organization structure and, 476
overcoming resistance to, 490–491
overcontrol and, 489–490
performance compared against standards for, 480
performance measured for, 479–480
planning and, 477, 488
postaction, 483
preliminary, 482
process, 477–481
purpose of, 474
resistance to, 489–491
resource focus of, 474–475
responsibilities for, 476–477
screening, 482–483
in small business, 616–617

small business failure and, 604–605
standards for, 478–479, 480, 481
status quo maintained for, 480
strategic, 475, 485–487
style of, 491–499
systems for, 488–490
timeliness and, 489
see also Financial control
Controllers, 477
Control systems, 488–490
change and, 320
in information systems, 551–552
Convergent thinking, creativity and, 530
Coordination
conflict reduction by, 437
in organization structure, 275–277
Copreneurs, 419
Core technology, organization design and, 288–289
Corporate social audit, social responsibility evaluated with, 109
Corporate strategy, 177
BCG matrix and, 182–184
business screen and, 184
grand strategy in, 181–182
growth strategy and, 181
internal growth, 292
organization design and, 292–293
portfolio approach, 292–293
related diversification and, 181, 292
retrenchment strategy and, 181–182, 292
stability strategy and, 182, 292
strategic business units and, 182, 183, 292–293
unrelated diversification and, 181, 292
Corporation, 608
Cost leadership strategy, 188
organization design and, 294
Costs
cultural diversity and, 584
fixed, 633
quality and, 501, 503
semivariable, 633
variable, 633

Counseling, for organization change, 323
Coverage ratios, 639
Creation of an obligation, as political behavior, 411
Creativity, 528–532
background experiences and, 529–530
cognitive abilities and, 530
creative process and, 530–532, 533
cultural diversity and, 585
incubation and, 531–532
insight and, 532
personality and, 530
preparation and, 530–531
verification and, 532
see also Innovation
Credibility, for communication, 460
Credit checks, in selection process, 344
Critical path, in PERT network, 241
Cross-training, productivity and, 508
Cultural diversity, 338, 574–595
age distributions and, 578–579
arguments for, 585
cases on, 594–595
communication for, 587
competitive advantage and, 584–585
conflict and, 585–586
as contemporary management challenge, 53–54
diversity training by, 589–590, 591
empathy for, 586–587
ethnicity and, 577, 580
in Europe, 581–582, 583
gender and, 577, 579, 580, 584
global management and, 581–583
in Japan, 581, 582
managing, 586–590
meaning of, 576
multicultural organization and, 590–592
organizational approaches to, 587–588
organizational culture and, 590

Cultural diversity (*continued*)
  organizational policies for, 588
  organizational practices for, 588
  reasons for increasing, 576–577
  social change and, 583–584
  tolerance for, 587
  understanding for, 586
  see also Equal employment opportunity
Cultural environment, of global management, 132–133, 135
Culture, *see* Cultural diversity; Organizational culture
Customer departmentalization, 264, 265
Customer evaluation technique, of sales forecasting, 232
Customers
  ethical treatment of, 93
  in task environment, 68
Cutbacks, as contemporary management challenge, 53

Data, information distinct from, 549
Debt policy, in finance policy, 192
Debt ratios, 639
Debt-to-equity ratio, 639
Decentralization, in organization structure, 273–274
Decisional roles of manager, 18, 19
Decision making, 5, 6, 7, 8, 200–223
  administrative model of, 212–213
  alternatives evaluated for, 208–209
  alternatives identified for, 207–208
  alternatives implemented for, 208, 210–211
  alternatives selected for, 208, 210
  behavioral aspects of, 211–216
  cases on, 222–223, 250–251
  under certainty, 204
  classical model of, 206
  coalitions in, 213
  conditions for, 204–205
  definition of, 202–203
  escalation of commitment in, 214

ethics and, 216
follow-up and evaluation for, 211
in group development, 425–426
intuition in, 214
nature of, 202–205
nonprogrammed decisions, 203–204
political forces in, 213
process, 202
programmed decisions, 203
rational perspectives on, 205–211
risk and, 204, 205, 215–216
situation recognized and defined for, 206–207, 208
steps in, 206–211
types of decisions, 203–204
under uncertainty, 204, 205
see also Decision-making tools; Group decision making; Planning
Decision-making tools, 241–246
  artificial intelligence, 246
  decision trees, 243–244
  distribution model, 245
  game theory, 245
  inventory models, 244–245
  payoff matrices, 241–243
  queuing models, 245, 247
Decision support system (DSS), 556–557
Decision tree, as decision-making tool, 243–244
Decline stage
  of career, 624–625
  innovation and, 535–536
Defender, organization design and, 293
Defender strategy, in adaptation model, 185–186, 187
Delegation, of authority, 272–273
Delphi procedure
  for forecasting, 232
  for group decision making, 217
Demand, small business success and, 602, 604
Deming Prize, 502
Demographics, cultural diversity in workplace and, 577
Departmentalization, 263–266, 267
  customer, 264, 265

functional, 264–265
  location, 264, 265
  matrix design and, 298
  product, 263–264
Depression era, social responsibility of, 97–98
Descriptive procedure, breakeven analysis as, 235
Developing economies, in global economy, 126–127
Development, 345
  in innovation process, 533–534
  see also Training programs
Diagnostic activities, for organization development, 321
Diagnostic and analytic skills of manager, 20–21
Differentiation strategy, 188
  organization design and, 291, 294
Direct investment, in international business, 121, 122
Directive leader behavior, inpathgoal theory, 403
Discipline, Fayol on, 39
Discrimination, in employment, 335–337
Disseminator, manager as, 17, 18
Distinctive competence, in strategy, 177
Distribution, as strategy, 511
Distribution channels, 191
Distribution model, as decision-making tool, 245
Disturbance handler, manager as, 18, 19
Divergent thinking, creativity and, 530
Diversification
  related, 181, 292
  unrelated, 181, 292
Diversity, *see* Cultural diversity
Diversity training, 589–590, 591
Dividend policy, in finance policy, 192
Divisional design, of organization, 296–298
Division of labor
  Fayol on, 39
  job specialization and, 259
Dog, in BCG matrix, 183, 184
Domestic business, 116–117

Downsizing, as contemporary management challenge, 53
Downward communication, 449, 450
Drug dependence, legal aspects of, 338
Drug tests, in selection process, 344
DSS, *see* Decision support system
Dual-career couples, 628
  equity theory and, 379
  human resources management and, 338

Econometric model, for forecasting, 231
Economic communities, global management and, 131–132
Economic dimension
  of general environment, 64
  of global management, 128–130
  management theory and, 32
Economic indicators, for forecasting, 231
Economic order quantity (EOQ), 518
Economic systems, global management and, 128–129
EC, *see* European Community
Education
  for management skills, 14–15
  for organization development, 322
Educational organizations, management of, 23
Effective communication, 444–445, 446. *See also* Communication
Effective management, principles for, 38, 39
Effectiveness
  global view of, 83
  meaning of, 6
  models of, 81–83, 84
Efficiency, 81
  meaning of, 6
Effort-to-performance expectancy, 384
  in expectancy theory, 376
Egyptians, management and, 34
EIS, *see* Executive information system

Electronic bulletin boards, 565
Electronic communication, 449, 462–464
Electronic databanks, 462
Electronic mail systems, 565
Employee-centered leader behavior, 398
Employee-employer relations, *see* Human resources management
Employee information system, human resources planning with, 341
Employee involvement
  for control, 477, 491
  productivity and, 508
  rewards and, 508
  total quality management and, 504
Employee motivation, *see* Motivation
Employee Retirement Income Security Act of 1974 (ERISA), 336, 337
Employees, in internal environment, 72–73. *See also under* Human resources; Labor relations; Organization development
Employee satisfaction, rewards and, 384
Employment at will, 338
Empowerment, for motivation, 383
Encoding process, in communication, 446
Entrepreneur, 597–599, 598
  business plan for, 605–606
  financing sources and, 608–609
  innovation and, 600
  intrapreneur and, 540–542, 617
  in large businesses, 617–618
  leading by, 613, 615–616
  manager as, 18, 19
  ownership of business and, 607–608
  paths taken by, 598–599, 599
  see also Small business
Entrepreneurial couples, 419
Entrepreneurial era, of social responsibility, 97
Entropy, 48

Environment, 60–87
  acquisitions and, 80
  alliances and, 80
  business and, 89, 90, 100, 112, 113
  cases on, 86–87
  change and complexity in, 75–76
  competitive forces and, 76–77
  direct influence of, 80–81
  environmental turbulence and, 77–78
  external, 62, 63, *see also* General environment; Task environment
  information management and, 79–80
  information system needs and, 553
  internal, 62–63, 72–74
  mergers and, 80
  organization change and, 310–311
  organization design and, 80, 289–291
  organizations effected by, 74–78
  organizations responding to, 79–81
  strategic response and, 80
  takeovers and, 80
Environmental analysis, for strategy formulation, 179, 180–181
Environmental Protection Agency (EPA), 23, 68, 70, 81, 105, 192
Environmental scanning, for information management, 79–80
Environmental turbulence, 77–78
EOQ, *see* Economic order quantity
Equal employment opportunity, 335–337. *See also* Cultural diversity
Equal Employment Opportunity Commission (EEOC), 70, 105, 335
  sexual harassment and, 339
Equal Pay Act of 1963, 336, 337
Equipment control, 475
Equity, Fayol on, 39
Equity theory, of motivation, 378–379

ERG theory, of motivation, 371

Escalation of commitment, in decision making, 214

Esprit de corps, Fayol on, 39

Establishment stage, of career, 624

Esteem needs, organization satisfying, 370

Ethical behavior, 90. *See also* Ethics

Ethical compliance, for social responsibility, 108

Ethics, 90–97
  codes of, 95, 96
  as contemporary management challenge, 53
  decision making and, 216
  definition of, 90
  individual, 90–91
  managerial, 92–93, 95
  managing, 94–97
  in organizational context, 93–94
  relationship of employees to firm and, 92–93
  relationship of firm to employees and, 92
  relationship of firm to other economic agents and, 92, 93, 95
  see also Social responsibility

Ethnicity, cultural diversity and, 577, 580

Europe, as market system, 126

European Community (EC), 126, 132, 331, 583

Evaluation
  in decision making, 211
  goals and, 149–150

Excellence movement, 52, 74

Executive committee, planning by, 157

Executive information system (EIS), 557

Executive MBA program, 15

Executive Order 11246, 336

Existence needs, organization satisfying, 371

Existing business, buying, 607

Expansion, in revitalization, 326

Expectancy theory
  of motivation, 374–378, 384
  path-goal theory and, 403

Expected value, in payoff matrix, 242–243

Expense budget, 632

Experience, for management skills, 14, 15–16

Expert power, 395

Expert system
  as artificial intelligence, 246
  in information systems, 565–566

Exploration stage, of career, 623–624

Exporting, in international business, 119–120, 122, 130, 131

Export restraint agreements, international trade controlled by, 131

External audits, 640

External environment, *see* Environment

External recruiting, 343

Extinction, reinforcement and, 380

Facilitation, for organization change, 316

Facilities, operations systems and, 512–514, 515

Facsimile machines, 463, 464

Fair Labor Standards Act, 336, 337

Family, individual's ethics and, 90–91

Family and Medical Leave Act, 107

Far East, management in, 35. *See also* Japan

Favors, government influenced by, 107

Federal Trade Commission, 23, 68, 105
  advertising and, 89
  Nintendo and, 87

Feedback
  communication and, 459–460
  in performance appraisal, 350–351
  survey, 322

Feedforward control, *see* Preliminary control

Figurehead, manager as, 16, 18

Financial audits, 640

Financial budget, 631–632

Financial control, 475, 637–640
  balance sheet, 637, 638
  coverage ratios, 639
  debt ratios, 639

effective use of, 641
  financial audits, 640
  financial statements, 637
  income statement, 637, 638
  liquidity ratios, 638–640
  operating ratios, 639
  profitability ratios, 639–640
  ratio analysis, 637–640
  return on assets, 639
  return on investment, 639
  see also Budgets

Financial managers, 12, 13

Financial statements, 637

Financial strategy, 190, 191–192
  organization design and, 294

Finished goods inventory, 516

First-line managers, 12–13

Five competitive forces, 76–77

Five Dragons, management in, 35

Fixed costs, in budgets, 633

Fixed-interval schedule, of reinforcement, 380

Fixed-position layout, of facilities, 513–514

Fixed-rate system, of rewards, 385

Fixed-ratio schedule, of reinforcement, 380, 381

Flat organizations, 268, 269, 270

Flexible manufacturing systems (FMS), 527

Flexible work schedule, 382

FMS, *see* Flexible manufacturing systems

Focus strategy, 188
  organization design and, 294

Follow-up
  for communication, 461
  in decision making, 211

Food and Drug Administration (FDA), 70, 105
  breast implants and, 78, 95

Force-field analysis, for organization change, 316–317

Forecasting, 226–232
  causal modeling for, 230–231
  econometric models for, 230
  economic indicators for, 230
  human resources demand and supply and, 340–341
  qualitative techniques for, 231–232

Forecasting (continued)
  quantitative techniques for, 228–231
  regression models for, 230–231
  revenue, 227
  sales, 226–227, 232
  techniques for, 228–232
  technological, 227–228, 232
  time-series analysis for, 228–230
Formal information systems, for communication, 461–462
Franchising, 607
Fringe benefits, see Benefits
Frustration-regression element, in ERG theory, 371
Functional authority, 277
Functional departmentalization, 264–265
Functional design, of organization, 294–295
Functional group, 421, 422
Functional strategy, 178
  financial strategy, 190, 191–192, 294
  human resources strategy, 190, 192–193, 294
  marketing strategy, 190–191, 192, 294
  organization design and, 294
  production strategy, 190, 192
  research and development strategy, 190, 192, 294
Functions of the Executive, The (Barnard), 38

Gain sharing, as incentive system, 386
Game theory, as decision-making tool, 245
Gantt chart, 37
Gender, cultural diversity and, 577, 579, 580, 585
General and Industrial Management (Fayol), 38, 39
General environment, 62, 63–67, 64–67
  economic dimension and, 64
  international dimension and, 66–67
  organization change and, 310–311
  political-legal dimension and, 66

sociocultural dimension and, 65–66
  technological dimension and, 64–65
General managers, see Administrative managers
General welfare, business and, 100
Glass ceiling, 579
Global business, 117, 121–122. See also International business
Global economy
  competing in, 133–138
  controlling in, 138
  developing economies in, 126–127
  leading in, 137–138
  management challenges in, 134–135, 137–138
  market systems in, 126
  mature market economies in, 124–126
  medium-size organizations in, 134
  multinational enterprises in, 133–134
  oil-exporting region in, 127–128
  organizing in, 135, 137
  planning in, 134–135
  small business and, 602, 603
  small organizations in, 134
  structure of, 123–128
  see also Global management; International business
Global management, 122–123
  business with former Soviet republics and, 27
  career planning and, 627
  cases on, 140–141
  cereal manufacturers and, 115
  challenges of, 53, 134–135, 137–138
  communication and, 467
  conglomerate design and, 295, 296, 297
  control and, 487, 497
  cultural diversity and, 581–583
  cultural environment of, 132–133, 135
  decision making and, 205–206, 207, 251
  economic communities and, 131–132

economic environment and, 128–130
  economic systems and, 128–129
  effectiveness and, 83
  electronic communication and, 462
  environmental analysis for, 179
  environmental challenges of, 128–133
  government stability and, 130
  human resources strategy and, 193
  IKEA and, 123
  information systems and, 561, 569
  infrastructure and, 130
  international dimension of general environment and, 66–67
  international trade and, 130–131
  language and, 133, 135
  leadership and, 395, 415
  marketing strategies and, 191
  motivation and, 369
  natural resources and, 129
  organization change and, 331
  organization structure and, 281
  planning and, 155
  political/legal environment and, 130–132
  product life cycle and, 189–190
  product-service mix and, 513
  research and development strategy and, 193
  revitalization and, 327
  small business and, 621
  social responsibility and, 105, 113
  span of management and, 271
  strategic business units and, 183
  Type Z model and, 51
  values, symbols, and beliefs and, 132–133, 135
  see also Global economy; International business; Japan
Global manager, skills for, 16, 17
Global sourcing, see Outsourcing
Goal approach, to effectiveness, 82
Goals, 4, 147, 149–153
  barriers setting, 164–166
  cases on, 172–173
  in changing environment, 165
  communication and participation for, 167

Goals (continued)
conflict and, 436, 437–438
consistency of, 167
for different areas, 150, 153
groups and, 424, 430, 431
guidelines for effective, 164, 166–167
improper reward system for, 165
inappropriate, 164–165
levels of, 150
management by objectives for, 167–169
mission and, 149, 150, 152, 153
multiple, 153
operational, 150, 153
optimizing and, 153
for organization change, 323
purposes of, 149–150, 166
reluctance to establishing, 165
resistance to change and, 165–166
responsibilities for setting, 153
revising and updating, 167
rewards for, 165, 167
strategic, 149, 150, 153, 179
tactical, 149, 150, 153
time frames and, 150, 151, 153
Goal-setting theory, of motivation, 381
Gossip chain, 452, 453
Government, 32–33
business and, 66
regulation by, 70, 81, 105–106
social responsibility of, 104–107
Government organizations, management of, 23
Government stability, global management and, 130
Grand strategy, in corporate strategy, 181–182
Grapevine, 452–453, 464
Graphic rating scales, for performance appraisal, 349, 350
Grievance procedures, 356
Group decision making, 216–219
advantages of, 217–218
Delphi groups for, 217
disadvantages of, 218–219
groupthink and, 218–219
interacting groups for, 216
managing, 219
nominal groups for, 217

Grouping of jobs, see Departmentalization
Groups, 420–441
attraction and, 423, 430, 431
cases on, 440–441
cohesiveness in, 430–432
communication and decision making in, 425–426
control and organization in, 426
definition, 420
functional, 421, 422
goals of, 424
group activities of, 424
informal, 70–71, 422–423
informal leadership in, 432–433
instrumental benefits of, 424
mature, 426–433
motivation and productivity in, 426
mutual acceptance in, 425
needs satisfied by, 424
norms in, 428–429, 431–432
performance of, 431–432
reasons for joining, 423–424
role ambiguity in, 427
role conflict in, 427–428
role overload in, 428
role structures in, 426–427
stages of development of, 424–426
task, 421–422, 423
see also Conflict; Group decision making; Organizations; Teams
Groupthink, 218–219
Growth, innovation and, 534
Growth needs, organization satisfying, 371
Growth strategy, 181

Halo error, in performance appraisal, 349–350
Hawthorne studies, 41–42, 49
Health and safety, legal aspects of, 336, 337–338
Healthcare facilities, management of, 24
H-form organization, see Conglomerate design
Hierarchy of needs, see Need hierarchy
Hiring, see Human resources man-

agement; Recruiting; Selection process
Hispanics, see Cultural diversity
Historical ratios, forecasting human resources needs with, 340
History
management and, 29, 30–33
management in antiquity and, 34, 35
management pioneers and, 34–36
see also Management theories
Hong Kong
cultural diversity in work force of, 582
management in, 35
Horizontal communication, 450, 451
Horizontal consistency, goals of, 167
HRM, see Human resources management
Human relations approach, to motivation, 367–368
Human relations movement, 42–43
Human resources, 5–6
attracting, see Human resources planning; Recruiting; Selection process
change and, 320
control of, 475
organization change in, 317, 320
Owen on, 34–35
strategy implementation through, 195
tactical planning and, 159–160
see also Human resources management; Organization development
Human resources approach, to motivation, 368
Human resources management (HRM), 332–359
AIDS and, 338
alcoholism and, 338
career planning and, 353
cases on, 358–359
drug dependence and, 338
equal employment opportunity in, 335–337

Human resources management
   (*continued*)
   health and safety and, 336, 337–338
   legal environment of, 335–338
   sexual harassment and, 338, 339
   social change and, 338, *see also* Cultural diversity
   strategic importance of, 334–335
   training and development programs for, 345–348
   see also Benefits; Compensation; Labor relations; Performance appraisal
Human resources managers, 12, 13
Human resources planning, 339–341
   employee information systems for, 341
   forecasting supply and demand of labor for, 339–341
   job analysis in, 339–340
   matching human resources supply and demand for, 341
   replacement chart for, 341
Human resources strategy, 190, 192–193
   organization design and, 294
Iliad (Homer), 31

Images, nonverbal communication and, 456
Importing, in international business, 119–120, 122, 130
Incentives, for international trade, 130–131
Incentive system, of rewards, 385–386
Income statement, 637, 638
Incremental innovations, 536
Individual productivity, 505
Individual wage decision, compensation and, 352
Inducement, as political behaviors, 410–411
Industrial productivity, 505
Industrial psychology, 41
Informal communication, 453–454
Informal group, 70–71, 422–423
Informal leader, of groups, 432–433

Information
   as accurate, 549–550
   characteristics of, 549–550
   as complete, 550
   definition of, 549
   as relevant, 550
   role of in manager's job, 548–549
   as timely, 550
   see also Information systems
Informational roles of manager, 17, 18, 19
Information distortion, power used by, 396
Information flow regulation, for communication, 461
Information management, organizational responding to environment with, 70–80
Information-processing requirements, organization design and, 301–302
Information resources, 5–6
Information systems
   area and, 553–554
   behavioral effects of, 563
   building blocks of, 551–552
   cases on, 568–569
   changes in, 320
   control system for, 551–552
   decision support systems, 556–557
   employee, 341
   environment and, 553
   establishing, 558–560
   executive information systems, 557
   expert systems and, 565–566
   formal, 461–462
   for information management, 80
   input medium in, 551
   integrating, 560–561
   level and, 554–555
   limitations of, 563–564
   management information systems, 555–556
   managerial determinants for, 553–555
   managing, 558–561
   networks and, 565
   organizational determinants for, 552–553

   organizational effects of, 563
   output medium in, 551
   performance effects of, 562–563
   processor in, 551
   size and, 553
   storage devices in, 551
   strategy implementation through, 194–195
   telecommunications and, 564–565
   transaction-processing systems, 555
   using, 560–561
Initiating-structure behavior, of leaders, 398
Initiative, Fayol on, 39
Innovation, 532–542
   application and, 534
   case on, 544
   cultural diversity and, 585
   decline and, 535–536
   development and, 533–534
   entrepreneurs and, 600
   failure of, 538, 540
   growth and, 534–535
   incremental, 536
   intrapreneurship promoting, 540–542
   inventor and, 540–541
   launch and, 534
   managerial, 536–537
   maturity and, 535
   opportunities not recognized and, 539
   organizational culture and, 542
   process of, 533–536, 537–538
   product, 537
   product champion and, 541
   promoting, 539–542
   radical, 536
   resistance to change and, 539
   resources lacking for, 538–539
   reward system promoting, 539–540
   small business and, 600
   sponsor and, 541
   technical, 536
   see also Creativity; Research and development; Technology
In-process sampling, as statistical quality control technique, 518

Input medium, in information systems, 551

Inside directors, 72

Inspirational appeal, power used by, 396

Inspirational leadership, *see* Transformational leadership

Instrumental compliance, power used by, 396

Integrating departments, for coordination, 276–277

Integration, organization design and, 291

Intelligence, creativity and, 530

Interacting groups, for group decision making, 216

Interactive videos, as training and development method, 347, 348

Interdependence, conflict caused by, 435–436

Interest group, *see* Informal group

Intergroup activities, for organization development, 322

Intermediate plans, 154–155

Internal audits, 640

Internal environment, 62–63, 72–74

Internal growth strategy, organization design and, 292

Internal processes approach, to effectiveness, 82

Internal recruiting, 341–342

International business
cultural diversity and, 576, 577–578
definition of, 117
domestic business and, 117
global business as, 117, 121–122
managing in, *see* Global management
meaning of, 116–117
multinational business as, 117, 121–122
nature of, 116–123
organization designs for, 302, 303
trends in, 117–119
see also Global economy; Global management

International dimension, of general environment, 66–67. *See also* Global management

Internationalization
direct investment and, 121, 122
exporting and, 119–120, 122
importing and, 119–120, 122
joint ventures/strategic alliances and, 120–121, 122
licensing and, 120, 122
process of, 119–122
see also International business

International management, 22. *See also* Global management

International trade
controls on, 131
exports, 119–120, 122, 130, 131
global management and, 130–131
imports, 119–120, 122, 130
incentives for, 130–131

Interpersonal communication, 447–449

Interpersonal dynamics
communication problems and, 459
in organizations, 418–420
see also Conflict; Groups

Interpersonal problem solving, for conflict resolution, 438

Interpersonal roles of manager, 16, 18

Interpersonal skills of manager, 20

Interrole conflict, 427

Interstate Commerce Commission, Emerson and, 37

Interviews, feedback, 350–351

In-transit inventory, 516–517

Intrapreneur, 540–542, 617. *See also* Entrepreneur

Intrarole conflict, 427

Intrasender conflict, 427

Intuition, in decision making, 214

Inventor, innovation and, 540–541

Inventory management, 46, 475, 516–517
just-in-time for, 228, 229, 245, 517

Inventory models, as decision-making tools, 244–245

Japan
automobile industry in, 121, 212, 500, 520, 533
bureaucracy in, 285
cultural differences and, 132
cultural diversity in, 581, 582
decentralization in, 274
global management in, 135, 137
groups in, 421
human resources management and, 359
information handling by, 549–550
innovation in, 523, 537, 541
international business and, 303
international trade and, 131
just-in-time in, 229, 517
keiretsu in, 155
McDonald's in, 223
management in, 35
managerial ethics in, 94
motivation in, 381–382, 383, 389
natural resources availability and, 129
outsourcing by, 121
planning in, 155
quality in, 521
recruiting in, 343
social responsibility and, 105
technology in, 545
Toys "R" Us in, 223
Type Z model and, 51
women in labor force of, 581, 582, 595

JIT, *see* Just-in-time

Job analysis, 339–340

Job-centered leader behavior, 398

Job characteristics approach, 261–263
for motivation, 382

Job descriptions, 339
for small business, 611

Job design, 258–263
job characteristics approach and, 261–263
job enlargement and, 261
job enrichment and, 261
job rotation and, 260
job specialization and, 259–260
see also Teams

Job enlargement, 261
for motivation, 382

Job enrichment, 261
for motivation, 382

Job evaluation, compensation and, 352

Job grouping, *see* Departmental-
ization
Job rotation, 260
for motivation, 382
Job satisfaction, 43
Job sharing, 382
Job specialization, 259–260
Job specification, 339–340
Joint ventures/strategic alliances,
in international business, 71–
72, 120–121, 122
Judgmental performance appraisal
methods, 349
Jury-of-expert-opinion approach,
for forecasting, 232
Just-in-time (JIT), for inventory
management, 228, 229, 245,
517

Kaisen, 359
Keiretsu, 155
Korea, management in, 35

Labor, 71. *See also under* Employee;
Labor relations
Labor-Management Relations Act,
336–337
Labor relations, 71, 353–356
binding arbitration in, 356
collective bargaining in, 355–356
grievance procedures in, 356
human resources strategy and,
192
legal aspects of, 336, 337
management and, 81
Mazda and, 359
organization change and, 311
strikes, 337
union-organizing process in,
354–355
Language, global management
and, 133, 135
Large-batch technology, 289
Large businesses, 22
Lateral relationships, information–
processing needs decreased
by, 301–302
Latin American Integration Association, 132
Launch, innovation and, 534
Layout, of facilities, 512–514, 515
Leader, manager as, 16, 18, 392

Leader-member relations, LPC
theory and, 401
Leadership, 5, 6, 7, 10, 38, 390–
415
behaviors, 397–399
cases on, 414–415
concern for people and, 399
concern for production and, 399
continuum, 399–400
definition of, 392
employee-centered leader behavior, 398
in global economy, 137–138
informal, 432–433
job-centered leader behavior,
398
Leadership Grid and, 399
life cycle model of, 408
LPC theory of, 400–403
management versus, 392–393,
395
Michigan studies of, 397–398
nature of, 392–396
Ohio State studies of, 398
path-goal theory of, 403–404,
405
political behavior in organizations and, 410–411
situational approaches to, 399–
408
in small business, 613, 615–616
social responsibility and, 108–
109
strategy implementation
through, 194
substitutes for, 408–409
traits, 396–397
transformational, 409–410
vertical-dyad linkage model of,
408
Vroom-Yetton-Jago model of,
404–407
see also Power
Leadership Grid®, 399
for organization change,
323–325
Least preferred co-worker (LPC)
measure, 400–403
Lectures, as training and development method, 346, 347
Legal compliance, for social responsibility, 108

Legitimate power, 393–394, 395
Legitimate request, power used
by, 395–396
Less-developed countries, international trade incentives and,
131
Levels of management, 11–13
Lewin model, of organization
change, 312–313
Liaison role
for coordination, 276
of manager, 16, 18
Licenses, research and development strategy and, 193
Licensing, in international business, 120, 122
Life cycle theory, of leadership,
408
Life experiences, individual's ethics
and, 91
Life planning, for organization
change, 323
Linear programming, 46
as planning tool, 232–235
Line positions
in organization structure,
277–278
planning by, 157
Liquidity ratios, 638–640
Listening, for communication,
459, 460
Lobbying, 81
government influenced by, 107
Location, of organization, 512
Location departmentalization,
264–265
Long-range plans, 154
LPC, *see* Least preferred co-
worker (LPC) measure
LPC theory, of leadership,
400–403
Lump-sum bonuses, as incentive
system, 386

Maintenance stage, of career, 624
Malcolm Baldrige Award,
500–501
Management
communication in, 445
contemporary challenges to, 52–
54
definitions of, 4–6

Management (*continued*)
  leadership versus, 392–393, 395
  nature of, 4–7
  scope of, 21–24
Management by objectives
  (MBO), 167–169
  for control, 491
Management by wandering
  around, as form of communication, 453, 454, 455
Management development
  as human resources strategy, 193
  programs for, 15
Management information system
  (MIS), 555–556
Management process, 7–11. *See
  also* Control; Leadership; Planning; Organizing
Management science, 30, 45
Management theories, 30–57
  cases on, 56–57
  contingency theory and, 48–49,
    50
  contributions to from outside
    discipline, 33
  economic forces and, 32
  excellence movement and, 52
  importance of, 30–31
  integrating framework for, 49–
    51
  management pioneers and,
    34–36
  political forces and, 32–33, *see
    also* Government
  popular, 51–52
  precursors to, 33–36
  social forces and, 32
  systems theory and, 47–48, 49, 50
  Type Z model, 51
  see also Behavioral management
    theory; Classical management
    theory; Quantitative manage-
    ment theory
Managerial approach, to formal
  information systems, 461
Managerial careers, 623–629
  career stages and, 623–629
  career transitions and, 628–629
  global management and, 627
  individual career planning and,
    625–626
  mentor relationships for, 626

organizational career planning
  and, 626–627
personal assessment for,
  625–626
see also Career planning; Cultural diversity;Dual-career
  couples; Equal employment
  opportunity; Women
Managerial ethics, 92–93, 95
Managerial Grid, 399
  for organization change,
    323–325
Managerial hierarchy, for coordination, 276
Managerial innovations, 536–537
Managerial roles, 16–19
  decisional, 18, 19
  informational, 17, 18, 19
  interpersonal, 16, 18
Managerial skills, 14–16
  conceptual, 20
  diagnostic and analytic, 20–21
  education and, 14–15
  experience and, 15–16
  interpersonal, 20
  technical, 19–20
Managers
  administrative, 12, 13–14
  by areas, 12, 13–14
  definition of, 6
  ethics and, 92–93, 95
  financial, 12, 13
  first-line, 12–13
  global, 16, 17
  human resource, 12, 13
  by levels, 11–13
  marketing, 12, 13
  middle, 12
  operations, 12, 13
  specialized, 14
  top, 11–12
  training programs for, 15–16
  work of, 21
Manufacturing, 509–510
  computers and, 526–527
  small businesses and, 602
  see also Operations management
Manufacturing technology,
  524–528. *See also* Technology
Maquiladoras, 121
Market economies, in global
  economy, 124–126, 128–129

Marketing, cultural diversity and,
  584–585
Marketing managers, 12, 13
Marketing strategy, 190–191
  organization design and, 294
  production strategy and, 192
Market position, 191
Market share, strategic plan and,
  159
Market systems, in global econ-
  omy, 126
Maslow's hierarchy of needs, moti-
  vation and, 368–371
Mass-production technology, 289
Master budget, *see* Balance sheet
  budget
Master limited partnerships, 608
Materials control, *see* Inventory
  management
Materials requirements planning
  (MRP), 517–518
Matrix design, of organization
  design, 298–300
Mature market economies, in
  global economy, 124–126
Maturity stage
  innovation and, 535
  in organizational life cycle, 292
  of small business, 612
MBA programs, in management,
  15
MBO, *see* Management by objec-
  tives
Mechanistic organization design,
  80, 290–291
Medium, in communication, 446
Medium-size organizations, in
  global economy, 134
Mentor relationships, for career
  planning, 626
Mergers, organizations responding
  to environment with, 80
Merit system, of rewards, 385
Mexico
  cultural diversity in work force
    of, 582
  maquiladoras and, 121
M-form organization, *see* Divi-
  sional design
Michigan studies, of leadership
  behavior, 397–398
Midcareer stage, of career, 624

Middle managers, 12
Midlife, in organizational life cycle, 292
Minorities, in managerial careers, 627–628. *See also* Cultural diversity
MIS, *see* Management information system
Mission, of organization, 149, 150, 152, 153
MNEs, *see* Multinational enterprises
Modified workweek, for motivation, 382
Monetary resources, 5–6
Monitor, manager as, 17, 18
Morals, individual's ethics and, 91
Motivation, 364–389
  behavior modification for, 382
  cases on, 388–389
  content perspectives on, 368–374
  definition, 366
  empowerment for, 383
  equity theory of, 378–379
  ERG theory of, 371
  expectancy theory of, 374–378, 384
  framework of, 366–367
  goals and, 149
  goal-setting theory of, 381
  in groups, 426
  historical perspectives on, 367–368, 369
  human relations approach to, 367–368
  human resources approach to, 368
  importance of in workplace, 366–367
  incentive pay system and, 367
  Japanese approach to, 381–382, 383
  leader promoting, 194
  Maslow's hierarchy of needs and, 368–371
  modified workweek for, 382
  nature of, 366–368
  need hierarchy approach to, 368–371
  participation for, 383
  Porter-Lawler extension of expectancy theory and, 377

process perspectives on, 374–379
reinforcement perspectives on, 379–381
reward systems for, 383–386
in small business, 615
traditional approach to, 367
two-factor theory of, 371–373
MRP, *see* Materials requirements planning
Multicultural organization, 590–592
Multinational enterprises (MNEs), 117, 121–122, 133–134
  organization design for, 302, 303
  world's largest, 135, 136
  see also International business
Multiple-command structure, in matrix design, 298, 299
Mutual acceptance, in group development, 425

National Emergency Strike provision, 337
Nationalization, global management and, 130
National Labor Relations Act of 1935, 71, 337
National Labor Relations Board (NLRB), 105, 337, 354
  Nordstrom and, 358
Natural resources, global management and, 129
Need hierarchy approach, to motivation, 42, 368–371
Needs, groups satisfying, 424. *See also* Motivation
Negotiator, manager as, 18, 19
Network, in information systems, 565. *See also* Communication network
New business
  small businesses and, 601
  starting, 607
  see also Entrepreneur; Small business
New Deal, social responsibility and, 97–98
New entrants, threat of, 76
New ventures, *see* Entrepreneur
NLRB, *see* National Labor Relations Board

Noise, in communication, 447, 459
Nominal group, for group decision making, 217
Nonmonetary budgets, 632–633
Nonprogrammed decisions, 203
Nontraditional settings, management in, 24
Nonverbal communication, 456–457
Normative procedure, linear programming as, 235
Norm conformity, in groups, 429
Norm generalization, in groups, 428
Norms
  cohesiveness and, 431–432
  in groups, 428–429, 431–432
Norm variation, in groups, 429
North America, as market system, 126
Not-for-profit organizations
  international dimension and, 66
  management in, 23–24

Objective performance appraisal measures, 348–349
Objectives, *see* Goals; Operational goals
Obligation creation, as political behavior, 411
OB Mod, 382
Occupational Safety and Health Act of 1970, 336, 337
Occupational Safety and Health Administration (OSHA), 70, 105, 192, 311, 335, 337–338
OD, *see* Organization development
Ohio State studies, of leadership, 398
Oil-exporting countries, in global economy, 127–128
On the Economy of Machinery and Manufactures (Babbage), 35
On-the-job training, as training and development method, 347, 348
Open systems, 47–48
Operating budgets, 632
Operating ratios, 639

Operational approach, to formal information systems, 461–462

Operational goals, 150, 153

Operational planning, 149, 160–164, 210
  operating procedures, 161, 162, 163–164
  policies, 161, 162
  programs, 161
  projects, 161, 163
  rules and regulations, 161, 163–164
  single-use plans, 160–161
  standing plans, 161–164

Operations control, 517–518 475, 481–483, 485. *See also* Operations management; Quality control

Operations management, 498, 508–511
  as control, 514–515
  importance of, 509
  manufacturing and production and, 509–510
  service organizations and, 510
  strategy and, 510–511
  see also Operations systems

Operations managers, 12, 13

Operations systems, 511–518
  capacity and, 512
  facilities and, 512–514, 515
  fixed-position layout and, 513–514
  inventory management and, 516–517
  layout and, 512–514, 515
  location of facilities and, 512
  operations control techniques and, 517–518
  operations management and, 514–515
  process layout and, 513
  product layout and, 512–513
  product-service mix and, 511–512, 513
  purchasing management and, 515–516
  using, 514–518
  see also Technology

Opportunity bias, objective performance measures and, 348

Optimization
  decision making considering, 210
  goals and, 153

Oral communication, 447–448, 449

Order, Fayol on, 39

Organic organization, 80, 290, 291

Organizational analysis, for strategy formulation, 179–181

Organizational behavior, 43

Organizational constituents, of social responsibility, 98–100

Organizational control, 475, 483–485

Organizational culture
  cultural diversity and, 590
  innovation and, 542
  in internal environment, 73–74

Organizational effectiveness, *see* Effectiveness

Organizational environment, *see* Environment

Organizational flexibility, cultural diversity and, 585

Organizational goals, *see* Goals

Organizational innovation, *see* Innovation

Organizational life cycle, organization design and, 291–292

Organizational planning, *see* Planning

Organizational simulation
  as planning tool, 238–239
  for training and development, 347

Organizational size
  information system needs and, 553
  organization design and, 291, 293

Organization change, 308–331
  areas of, 317–320
  cases on, 330–331
  communication for, 315–316
  comprehensive approach to, 313–314
  control and, 476
  definition, 310
  different perceptions of, 315
  education for, 315–316
  external forces for, 310–311

facilitation for, 316
  feelings of loss caused by, 315
  force-field analysis for, 316–317
  forces for, 310–311
  in human resources, 317, 320
  innovation and, 539
  internal forces for, 311
  Lewin model of, 312–313
  managing, 312–317
  in organization structure and design, 317, 318, 319
  overcoming resistance to, 315–317
  participation for, 315
  planned, 311, 312
  reactive, 311–312, 313
  resistance to, 314–315
  revitalization and, 325–327
  self-interests threatened by, 314–315
  in strategy, 317, 318
  teams as, 434
  in technology and operations, 317, 318–319
  uncertainty and, 314
  see also Organization development

Organization culture, social responsibility and, 108–109

Organization design, 282–307
  adapting organizations and, 302–303
  behavioral model of, 286–288
  bureaucratic model of, 285–286
  business strategy and, 293–294
  cases on, 306–307
  conglomerate, 295–296, 297
  corporate strategy and, 292–293
  definition, 284
  differentiation and, 291
  divisional, 296–298
  emerging issues in, 300–303
  environment and, 289–291
  functional, 294–295
  hybrid, 300
  information processing requirements and, 301–302
  information systems and, 563
  integration and, 291
  international business and, 302–303

Organization design (*continued*)
 international organizations and, 302, 303
 matrix, 298–300
 mechanistic, 80, 290–291
 organic, 80, 290, 291
 organizational life cycle and, 291–292
 organization change in, 317, 318, 319
 organization size and, 291, 293
 organizations responding to environment with, 80
 project-type teams for, 302–303
 situational influences on, 288–292
 strategy and, 292–294
 technology and, 288–289
 universal perspectives on, 284–288
Organization development (OD), 321–325
 assumptions of, 321
 coaching and counseling for, 323
 definition of, 321
 diagnostic activities in, 321
 education for, 322
 effectiveness of, 325
 intergroup activities for, 322
 Leadership Grid for, 323–325
 life and career planning for, 323
 organizational change and, 320
 planning and goal setting for, 323
 process consultation for, 323
 survey feedback for, 322
 team building in, 321–322
 techniques, 321–325
 technostructural activities for, 323
 third-party peacemaking for, 323
 see also Human resources; Organization change
Organization revitalization, *see* Revitalization
Organizations
 definition, 4
 interpersonal nature of, 418–420
 see also Groups
Organization structure, 256–281
 administrative intensity and, 278

authority and, 271–274
 cases on, 280–281
 centralization and, 273–274
 chain of command in, 266
 control and, 476
 coordination and, 275–277
 decentralization and, 273–274
 delegation and, 272–273
 information systems and, 563
 line positions in, 277–278
 organization change in, 317, 318, 319
 reporting relationships in, 266–271
 span of management in, 267–271
 staff positions in, 277–278
 strategy implementation through, 193
 tall versus flat organizations and, 268–269, 270
 see also Departmentalization; Job design
Organizing, 5, 6, 7, 8–10, 38
 definition, 258
 in global economy, 135, 137
 in small business, 611–613, 614
Outcomes, in expectancy theory, 376
Output medium, in information systems, 551
Outside directors, 72
Outsourcing, 121
Overcontrol, resistance to control and, 489–490
Overload, communication and, 459, 464
Owners, in task environment, 71
Ownership of business, 607–608
 as contemporary management challenge, 53

Pacific Rim, as market system, 126
PACs, *see* Political action committees
Partial productivity ratio, 505–506
Participation, for motivation, 383
Participative leader behavior, in path-goal theory, 403
Partnerships, 608
Patents, research and development strategy and, 193

Path-goal theory, of leadership, 403–404, 405
Pay for knowledge, as incentive system, 386
Payoff matrix, as decision-making tool, 241–243
Peers, individual's ethics and, 91
Pension funds, managers of, 71
People, *see* Human resources
Perception, in communication, 454–456
Perceptual organization, communication and, 454, 456
Performance appraisal, 348–351
 Behaviorally Anchored Rating Scale for, 349, 351
 for control, 479–480
 errors in, 349–350
 feedback in, 350–351
 human resources strategy and, 192
 judgment methods for, 349
 objective measures for, 348–349
 ranking for, 349
 rating for, 349, 350, 351
 special performance test for, 348–349
Performance-to-outcome expectancy, 384
 in expectancy theory, 376
Personal assessment, for career planning, 625–626
Personal identification, power used by, 396
Personality, creativity and, 530
Personnel, *see* Human resources management
Person-role conflict, 427–428
Persuasion, as political behavior, 411
PERT diagram
 for business plan, 606
 as planning tool, 239–241
Philanthropic giving, for social responsibility, 108
Philosophers, management theory and, 33
Physical exams, in selection process, 344
Physical resources, 5–6
Physiological needs, organization satisfying, 369, 370

Piecework pay system, 36, 37
Planned change, in organizations, 311, 312
Planning, 5, 6, 7, 8, 38
  action plans, 155
  automobile industry and, 155
  barriers to, 164–166
  board of directors for, 156
  business plan and, 605–606
  cases on, 172–173
  in changing environment, 165
  chief executive officer for, 157
  communication and participation for, 167
  contingency, 157–158
  control and, 477, 488
  executive committee for, 157
  in global economy, 134–135
  goal-setting practices and, 149
  guidelines for effective, 164, 166–167
  improper reward system for, 165
  intermediate plans, 154–155
  in Japan, 155
  line management for, 157
  long-range plans, 154
  management by objectives for, 167–169
  operational plans, 154
  for organization change, 323
  process, 148–149
  purposes of, 166
  reaction plans, 155–156
  resistance to change and, 165–166
  responsibilities for, 156–157
  revising and updating, 167
  rewards for, 165, 167
  short-range planning, 155–156
  in small business, 609–611
  staff for, 156
  tactical plans, 154, 158–160
  task force for, 156
  time frame for, 154–156
  see also Decision making; Goals; Operational planning; Human resources planning; Planning tools; Strategic plans
Planning staff, 156
Planning task force, 156
Planning tools
  breakeven analysis, 235–238

  linear programming, 232–235
  organizational simulation, 238–239
  PERT, 239–241
  strengths and weaknesses of, 246–247
  see also Forecasting
Policies, as standing plans, 161, 162
Political action committees (PACs), government influenced by, 106, 107
Political behavior, in organizations, 410–411
Political forces, management theory and, 32–33. See also Government
Political/legal dimension
  of general environment, 66
  of global management, 130–132
Polygraph tests, in selection process, 344
Pooled interdependence, coordination and, 275
Popular management theory, 51–52
Porter-Lawler extension, of expectancy theory, 377
Portfolio approach, organization design and, 292
Position power, LPC theory and, 401
Positive reinforcement, 379, 380
Postaction control, 483
Power, 393–396
  coercive, 394
  expert, 395
  legitimate, 393–394, 395
  need for and motivation, 374
  political behavior and, 410–411
  referent, 394
  reward, 394
  symbols of, 456–457
  using, 395–396
Predictive validation, in selection process, 342
Pregnancy Discrimination Act, 336
Preliminary control, 482
Preparation, in creative process, 530–531
Pricing, 191
Prince, The (Machiavelli), 31

Private ownership, global management and, 129
Probability, payoff matrix and, 241
Process consultation, for organization change, 323
Process innovations, 537–538
Process layouts, of facilities, 513
Processor, in information systems, 551
Process perspectives, to motivation, 374–379
Product champion, innovation and, 541
Product departmentalization, 263–264
Product development, research and development strategy and, 193
Product innovations, 537. See also Innovation
Production, 509–510. See also Operations management
Production management, 509. See also Operations management
Production planning, production strategy and, 192
Production strategy, 190, 192
  organization design and, 294
Productivity, 504–508
  cases on, 520–521
  as contemporary management challenge, 53
  cross-training for, 508
  employee involvement and, 508
  facilities refinements for, 508
  forms of, 505
  in groups, 426
  importance of, 506
  improving, 507–508
  levels of, 505
  meaning of, 505–506
  partial ratio, 505–506
  production strategy and, 192
  quality and, 501
  research and development and, 507
  service-sector, 507
  total factor, 505
  trends in, 506–507
  see also Operations management
Product layout, of facilities, 512–513

Product life cycle, 188–190

Product mix, marketing strategy and, 191

Product-service mix, operations systems and, 511–512, 513

Profit, challenged as basis of business, 33

Profitability ratios, 639–640

Profit budget, 632

Profit sharing, as incentive system, 386

Program Evaluation and Review Technique, *see* PERT diagram

Programmed decisions, 203

Programmed instruction, as training and development method, 346, 347

Programs, as single-use plans, 161

Project manager, in matrix design, 298, 299

Projects, as single-use plans, 161, 163

Project-type teams, for organization design, 302–303

Property ownership, global management and, 129

Prospecting organization, organization design and, 293

Prospector strategy, in adaptation model, 186

Psychology and Industrial Efficiency (Munsterberg), 41

Public ownership, global management and, 129

Public policy, 191

Punishment, reinforcement and, 380

Purchasing management, 515–516

Qualitative forecasting techniques, 231–232

Quality, 500–504
cases on, 520–521
competition and, 501
as contemporary management challenge, 53
costs and, 501, 503
definition, 500, 501
employee involvement and, 504
importance of, 500–503
pioneers in, 501, 502–503
productivity and, 501

quality circles and, 537
quality control and, 475, 503
statistical quality control and, 518
total quality management and, 503–504, 537
Zero Defects and, 502
see also Operations management

Quality circles, 537

Quality control, 475
Total Quality Control and, 503

Quality is Free (Crosby), 502

Quantitative management theory, 30, 45–47, 49
Babbage and, 35
contributions and limitations of, 46–47
management science and, 30, 45
operations management and, 45–46

Question mark, in BCG matrix, 183, 184

Queuing models, as decision-making tool, 245, 247

Quotas, international trade controlled by, 131

Race, *see* Ethnicity

Radical innovations, 536

Ranking, performance appraisal with, 349

Rating, performance appraisal with, 349, 350, 351

Ratio analysis, 637–640

Rational persuasion, power used by, 396

Raw materials inventory, 516

Reaction plans, 155–156

Reactive change, in organizations, 311–312, 313

Reactor strategy, in adaptation model, 186–187

Readings, as training and development method, 346, 347

Realistic job preview (RJP), 342

Receiver, in communication, 445–446

Reciprocal interdependence, coordination and, 275

Recruiting, 341–342
external, 342
internal, 341–342

in Japan, 343
realistic job preview for, 342
see also Selection process

Referent power, 394

Regression model, for forecasting, 230–231

Regulation
companies influencing, 81
by government, 105–106
human resources strategy and, 192
organization change and, 311
production strategy and, 192
in task environment, 70–71

Regulatory agencies, 70, 81

Reinforcement
avoidance and, 379, 380
extinction of, 380
fixed-interval schedule of, 380
fixed-ratio schedule of, 380, 381
motivation and, 379–381
positive, 379, 380
punishment and, 380
schedules for applying, 380–381
variable-interval schedule of, 380–381
variable-ratio schedule of, 380, 381

Related diversification, 181, 292
organization design and, 292

Relatedness needs, organization satisfying, 371

Relevant information, 550

Remuneration, Fayol on, 39. *See also* Compensation

Replacement chart, human resources planning with, 341

Republic (Plato), 31

Research and development strategy, 190, 192
organization design and, 294
productivity improvement and, 507
see also Innovation

Resource allocator, manager as, 18, 19

Resource competition, conflict and, 436

Resource deployment, in strategy, 176–177

Resources, *see* Human resources; Information resources; Nat-

Resources (*continued*)
    ural resources; Physical resources
Retail business, small businesses and, 601
Retirement, after career, 624–625
Retrenchment strategy, 181–182
    organization design and, 292
Return on assets (ROA), 639
Return on investment (ROI), 639
Revenue budget, 632
Revenue forecasting, 227
Revitalization, of organization, 325–327
Reward power, 394
Reward systems
    employee involvement and, 508
    for goals and plans, 165, 167
    innovation promoted by, 539–540
    for motivation, 383–386
Ripple effect, internal recruiting and, 342
Risk propensity, decision making and, 215–216
RJP, *see* Realistic job preview
ROA, *see* Return on assets
Robots and robotics, 527–528, 537
ROI, *see* Return on investment
Role overload, 428
Role playing, as training and development method; 346, 347
Roles, in groups, 426–427
Role structures, in groups, 426–427
Romans, management and, 34
Rules and procedures, for coordination, 276
Rules and regulations, as standing plans, 161, 163
Russia
    doing business with, 27
    motivation in, 369

Safety, *see* Health and safety
Salaries, *see* Compensation
Sales budget, 632
Sales-force-composition method, of sales forecasting, 232
Sales forecasting, 226–227, 232
    forecasting human resources needs with, 340

Sales promotion, 191
Satisfaction, *see* Job satisfaction
Satisficing, in administrative model of decision making, 212–213
SBA, *see* Small Business Administration
SBUs, *see* Strategic business units
Scalar chain, Fayol on, 39
Scalar principle, in chain of command, 266
Scientific management, 30, 36–37
Scope, of strategy, 176
S-corporations, 608
Screening control, 482–483
Second World War, The (Churchill), 31
Securities and Exchange Commission (SEC), 70, 106
    social responsibility and, 97–98
Security needs, organization satisfying, 369, 370
Selection process, 342–344
    application blanks in, 343
    assessment centers in, 344
    credit checks in, 344
    drug tests in, 344
    human resources strategy and, 192
    interviews in, 344
    physical exams in, 344
    polygraph tests in, 344
    tests in, 344
    validation in, 342–343
Selective perception, communication and, 454, 455
Self-actualization needs, organization satisfying, 370
Self-contained tasks, information-processing needs decreased by, 301
Semivariable costs, 633
Sender, in communication, 445–446
Sensitivity, for communication, 460
Sensitivity training, as training and development method, 347
Sequential interdependence, coordination and, 275
Service Corps of Retired Executives (SCORE), 613, 614

Service industries, 510
    productivity and, 507
    small businesses and, 601
    technology in, 528
Settings, nonverbal communication and, 456–457
Sexual harassment, 588
    cultural diversity and, 585
    legal aspects of, 338, 339
Short-range plans, 155–156
Simulation, *see* Organizational simulation
Singapore, management in, 35
Single-use plans, 160–161
Situational factors, individual's ethics and, 91
Situational models, of leadership, 399–408
Situational view, of organization design, 288–292
Size, *See* Organizational Size
Skills inventory, *see* Employee information system
Slack resources, information-processing needs decreased by, 301
Small-batch technology, 288–289
Small business, 599–605
    acceptance stage of, 610
    accounting for, 616–617
    in agriculture, 602
    big business contributions by, 601
    breakthrough stage of, 610–611
    cases on, 620–621
    control systems in, 604–605
    failures in, 604–605
    financial performance of, 599–600
    growth stages of, 610
    impact of, 599–601
    innovation and, 600
    job creation and, 600–601
    job descriptions for, 611
    managing the, 22, 609–617
    in manufacturing, 602
    maturity stage of, 611
    new-business formation and, 601
    organization charts for, 611–612
    ownership and, 607–608
    as retail business, 601

Small business (*continued*)
  as service organization, 601
  skill needs defined for, 611, 612, 613
  Small Business Administration and, 599, 600, 613, 614
  sources of assistance for, 612–613, 614
  successes in, 602–604
  undercapitalization and, 605
  in wholesaling, 601
  see also Entrepreneur
Small Business Administration (SBA), 599, 600, 603, 613, 614
Small Business Development Center (SBDC), 613, 614
Small Business Institute (SBI), 613, 614
Small organizations, in global economy, 134
Social change, human resources management and, 338. *See also* Cultural diversity
Social contribution, as social responsibility approach, 103–104, 105
Social era, of social responsibility, 98
Social forces, management theory and, 32
Socialization, norm conformity and, 429
Social obligation, as social responsibility approach, 103
Social obstruction, as social responsibility approach, 102–103
Social response approach, to social responsibility, 103
Social responsibility, 97–109
  areas of, 98–100
  arguments for and against, 101–102
  cases on, 112–113
  as contemporary management challenge, 53
  corporate social audit evaluating, 109
  depression era of, 97–98
  entrepreneurial era of, 97
  environment and, 89, 90, 100, 112, 113

ethical compliance for, 108
evaluating, 109
formal organizational dimensions for managing, 108
general social welfare and, 100
government and, 104–107
historical views of, 97–98
informal organizational dimensions for managing, 108–109
legal compliance for, 108
managing, 107–109
organizational approaches to, 102–104
organizational constituents of, 98–100
organization leadership and culture and, 108–109
philanthropic giving for, 108
social contribution approach to, 103–104, 105
social era of, 98
social obligation approach to, 103
social obstruction approach to, 102–103
social response approach to, 103
whistle blowing and, 109
see also Ethics
Sociocultural dimension, of general environment, 65–66
Socioemotional role, in groups, 426
Soldiering, 36
Sole proprietorship, 608
SOPs, *see* Standard operating procedures
South Korea, cultural diversity in work force of, 582
Soviet republics, doing business with the former, 27
Span of control, *see* Span of management
Span of management, 267–271
Special performance test, as objective performance measure, 348–349
Speed, as strategic issue, 510–511
Spokesperson, manager as, 18, 19
Sponsor, innovation and, 541
SQC, *see* Statistical quality control
Stability, Fayol on, 39

Stability strategy, 182
  organization design and, 292
Staff positions, in organization structure, 277–278
Standard operating procedures (SOPs), as standing plans, 161, 162, 163–164
Standards, for control, 478–479, 480, 481
Standing plans, 161–164
Star, in BCG matrix, 182, 184
Start-up businesses, management of, 22
State of certainty, for decision making, 204
State of risk, for decision making, 204, 205
State of uncertainty, for decision making, 204, 205
Statistical quality control (SQC), 518
Status quo, control maintaining, 480
Steering control, *see* Preliminary control
Steps in rational decision making, 206–211
Stereotyping, perceptual organization and, 456
Stockholders
  ethical treatment of, 93
  influence of, 71
Storage devices, in information systems, 551
Strategic alliances, in task environment, 71. *See also* Joint ventures/strategic alliances
Strategic business, organization design and, 292
Strategic business units (SBU), 182, 183
  BCG matrix for, 182–184
  see also Business strategy
Strategic constituencies approach, to effectiveness, 82
Strategic control, 475, 485–487
Strategic goals, 149, 150, 153, 179
Strategic management, 174–197
  cases on, 198–199
  components of strategy and, 176–177
  distinctive competence and, 177